MW00995255

PLANT
SYSTEMATICS

PLANT SYSTEMATICS

SECOND EDITION

Samuel B. Jones, Jr., Ph.D.
Professor of Botany
University of Georgia

Arlene E. Luchsinger, M.S., A.M.L.S.
University of Georgia Libraries

McGraw-Hill, Inc.
New York St. Louis San Francisco Auckland Bogotá
Caracas Lisbon London Madrid Mexico Milan
Montreal New Delhi Paris San Juan Singapore
Sydney Tokyo Toronto

This book was set in Times Roman by J. M. Post Graphics, Corp.
The editor was Mary Jane Martin;
the production supervisor was Charles Hess;
the cover was designed by Rafael Hernandez.
Project supervision was done by Publishing Synthesis, Ltd.

Printed and bound by Impresora Donneco Internacional
S.A. de C.V., a division of R. R. Donnelley & Sons Company.

Manufactured in Mexico

PLANT SYSTEMATICS

8 9 0   DOR/DOR   9 9 8 7 6 5 4 3

ISBN 0-07-032796-3

Library of Congress Cataloging in Publication Data

Jones, Samuel B.,
    Plant systematics.

    Includes bibliographies and indexes.
    1. Botany—Classification. I. Luchsinger, Arlene E.
II. Title.
QK95.J63   1986   581′.01′2   85-23048
ISBN 0-07-032796-3

CONTENTS

PREFACE

Unlike some fields of modern plant biology, plant systematics—or taxonomy—has a long history. It gave birth to other phases of botany but remains exciting, interesting, and important because it deals directly with the fascinating differences among the species of plants that inhabit the earth. Plant systematics serves as a major unifying force in biology because it uses data from a multitude of disciplines, such as molecular biology, biochemistry, comparative phytochemistry, and electron microscopy to develop a framework upon which classifications can be developed. Indeed, without the system of nomenclature provided by plant taxonomy, there could be no comparative reference to names of plants. The subject of systematics is one of the most attractive and useful of the plant sciences.

Recent developments in the field of plant systematics, coupled with new and exciting discoveries contributing to progress in the disciplines that provide information used in classification, have created the need for a second edition of *Plant Systematics*. The second edition is designed to present the current principles and practices of plant taxonomy and contemporary classifications, and to describe some of the important families and groups of vascular plants. The aim of this book is to provide a general overview of the field in the most effective and positive manner. The second edition of *Plant Systematics* is a broad, up-to-date synthesis of an active and fascinating field of botany. It includes new topics such as phenetics, cladistics, vicariance biogeography, and an enlarged treatment of biochemical systematics.

Plant Systematics is designed to meet the needs of undergraduate students in a one-semester (or one- to two-quarter) course in plant taxonomy. The chapters are largely independent so that the teacher may choose the desired sequence of topics. The level of presentation is based on the assumption that the students will have had an introductory biology or botany course. Also, it is hoped that this book will prove stimulating to serious amateurs, teachers, and professionals who specialize in other fields but utilize classifications and other taxonomic information about plants.

The bibliography has been arranged by chapter. The selected references at the end of each chapter provide direction for the person who desires further information on a topic. The references are not a complete bibliography for the subject matter of each chapter; rather, they are intended to provide an opportunity for the reader to obtain additional information on a particular subject, or to search out the original reference to a specific topic. Over two-thirds of the references provided are for relevant references published since 1970. All bibliographic citations have been verified and are given in a form that will facilitate their location in academic libraries.

The subject matter presented in the second edition of *Plant Systematics* is divided into fourteen chapters and four appendixes. As indicated earlier, the content of many of the chapters is largely independent and the sequence of their presentation can be varied by the instructor. Some teachers may not wish to cover all the chapters but may tailor their coverage to the needs of their students.

Chapters 1 through 3 place emphasis on the traditional aspects of plant systematics including history and nomenclature.

The principles and theoretical considerations, along with the sources of data used in classification are emphasized in chapters 4 and 5.

Chapter 6 provides a synthesis of the latest information on the origin of the angiosperms and compares the most recent systems of classification.

The methodology of biosystematics and a synopsis of evolutionary theory, as directly applicable to plant taxonomy, is given in Chapter 7.

Chapters 8 and 9 deal with curatorial routines and the practical procedures of collecting, preparing, and identifying plant specimens.

Reflecting the descriptive nature of taxonomy the essentials of terminology are covered and illustrated in Chapter 10.

Chapter 11 gives information about the bibliographic aids necessary for taxonomic research.

Chapters 12 and 13 provide descriptions and information for many of the pteridophytes and gymnosperms occurring in the United States and Canada. Technical terms unique to these plants are defined and some taxa are illustrated. Chapter 14 provides descriptions, information, and illustrations for over 100 families of flowering plants. These families were chosen because they are important elements of the flora of North America, are economically important, or illustrate examples of higher taxa of flowering plants.

Appendix 1 is a glossary of Greek and Latin terms as used in botany; Appendix 2 is a continuation of Chapter 11 providing annotated listings of over 250 references to aid in plant identification; Appendix 3 provides Cronquist's most recent classification of the flowering plants; Appendix 4 provides an outline of Thorne's classification system for those who wish to use it in their teaching. So that each family can be placed in a taxonomic scheme, and for the sake of conformity and clarity, the Cronquist system is adhered to throughout the book.

ACKNOWLEDGMENTS

In undertaking the task of preparing a textbook, it is necessary to use information from the publications of many writers. The authors are grateful to all these persons. In addition, the gratitude of the authors is expressed to those who have offered assistance, encouragement, and cooperation in the preparation of both the first and second editions of *Plant Systematics,* especially to Ted Barkley who critically read the entire manuscript of the first edition. John Beaman, Tom Cooperrider, and Duncan Porter provided valuable information at the time we began to revise *Plant Systematics,* and they later shared their expertise in the form of critical reviews. Many others provided encouragement, information, reprints, illustrations, and editorial assistance for the second edition including: John H. Beaman, Kare Bremer, Dennis Clark, Nancy Coile, Tom S. Cooperrider, Dan Crawford, Arthur Cronquist, Rolf Dahlgren, Melinda Denton, David Dilcher, Dan Evans, David Fairbrothers, Al Gentry, David Giannasi, Roland L. Hartman, Steven R. Hill, Chris Humphries, Judith Jernstedt, Almut Jones, Walter Judd, Gary Kochert, Merideth A. Lane, Thomas Morley, Frank Peterson, Duncan M. Porter, Gerald Smith, Douglas Soltis, K. R. Sporne, Todd Stuessy, Armen Takhtajan, and Robert Thorne. Anna Baker located numerous references and patiently made copies of the manuscript. Nancy Coile ably assisted with the proofreading of the revision. Valerie J. Hinesley prepared the illustrations. The authors were given every assistance by the University of Georgia Libraries and by the office staff of the Department of Botany. Gratitude is again extended to our spouses, Carleen A. Jones, and Dale Luchsinger for their continued patience in helping us to bring this revision to fruition.

Comments and suggestions regarding *Plant Systematics* would be welcomed from persons using the text.

Samuel B. Jones, Jr.
Arlene E. Luchsinger

CHAPTER 1

INTRODUCTION TO SYSTEMATIC BOTANY

Systematic botany, the science of identifying, naming, and classifying all plants is a challenging field of study. The potential economic uses of plants may not be immediately evident, but we must know which plants are related to one another in order to predict their properties. Wild relatives of our cultivated plants often have genes that can provide the desirable qualities, such as disease resistance, needed by plant breeders for crop improvement. Students are interested in learning about plants as part of a greater environmental awareness. Nonscientists can more readily understand evolution and variation by observing the relationships of form and function that are so conspicuous among flowers.

DEFINITIONS

Systematic botany is the broad field concerned with the study of the diversity of plants and their identification, naming, classification, and evolution. Since there is no agreement or etymological basis for the distinctions between *systematics* and *taxonomy* (Radford et al., 1974; Ross, 1974), these terms are used interchangeably in this text. However, it should be realized that some authors do differentiate between systematics and taxonomy, the former having the broad definition as just given, with taxonomy restricted to the study of classification.

Classification is the arrangement of plants into groups having common characteristics. These groups are then arranged into a system. Similar species of flowering plants are placed in a *genus* (plural, genera); similar genera are grouped into *families;* families with common features are arranged into *orders,* orders into *classes,* and classes into *divisions.* Classification results in the placing of plants into a hierarchy of ranks

1

or categories such as species, genera, families, and so on. In addition to expressing relationships based on common features, classification serves as a filing and information retrieval system and allows easier reference to the organisms comprising the filing system.

Identification or *determination* is the recognition of certain characters of flower, fruit, leaf, or stem and the application of a name of a plant with those particular characters. Recognition occurs when the specimen under consideration is similar to a previously known plant. If comparison of the specimen with all similar species reveals that it differs from them, it may be named as a new species. The term *classification* is often wrongly used in this sense and such use should be discouraged.

A *taxon* (plural, *taxa*) is a convenient and useful term applied to any taxonomic group at any rank: for example, species, genus, or family, or to a taxonomic group where rank is uncertain. As a general term, taxon can be used to indicate the rank of the group as well as its components. Taxa are separated from one another and are recognized by the features unique to each taxon in the same way we distinguish our friends from one another or differentiate among breeds of dogs or any other grouping of objects.

Nomenclature is the aspect of taxonomy concerned with the orderly application of names to taxa in accordance with the International Code of Botanical Nomenclature. This code provides procedures for selection of the correct name or formulation of a new name.

The *description* of a taxon is a listing of its features or morphological characteristics referred to as *taxonomic characters*. A shortened description consisting of only those taxonomic characters useful in separating a taxon from other related taxa is known as a *diagnosis*, and the characters used in the diagnosis are called *diagnostic characters*.

The term *flora* refers either to the plants growing in an area surrounded by a geographic or political boundary or to an inventory of the plants of a particular area or region. *Floristics* is the descriptive term used to refer to an investigation of the flora. A *manual* is a book that provides an inventory of the flora and the means of identifying the plants using descriptive keys.

Various approaches in systematics include *classical taxonomy,* which consists largely of museum research but often includes field work, and *biosystematics,* which involves ecological, cytological, and genetic investigations, and experimental studies of living populations in the field, experimental garden, laboratory, and greenhouse. *Numerical taxonomy* is the treatment of various types of taxonomic data by computerized methods. *Chemical taxonomy, chemotaxonomy,* or *chemosystematics* is the use of chemical features of plants in developing classifications.

SYSTEMATIC BOTANY

Primeval humans used food and medicinal plants that grew in their environment, recognizing hundreds of different plants. This early recognition of useful and harmful plants marked the beginning of systematic botany. The development of language made it possible for observations of plants to be accumulated, and this knowledge could be passed from one generation to the next.

Today the basic recognition and grouping of plants has developed into a highly complex science concerned with classifying plants into groups based on postulated evolutionary relationships. Systematic botany includes all activities that are part of the effort to organize and record the diversity of plants and acquaints us with the fascinating differences among the species of plants.

The activities of a plant taxonomist are basic to all other biological sciences, since systematics provides an inventory of plants, schemes for identification, plant names, and a system of classification of plants. Not only is systematics basic to other scientific fields, but also it depends on other disciplines for information and data useful in constructing classifications. A sound classification, bringing related plants together, may suggest problems worthy of study by ecologists, plant breeders, pharmacologists, horticulturists, and biochemists.

OBJECTIVES

Plant taxonomy has five objectives: (1) to inventory the world's flora; (2) to provide a method for identification and communication; (3) to produce a coherent and universal system of classification; (4) to demonstrate the evolutionary implications of plant diversity; and (5) to provide a single Latin "scientific" name for every group of plants in the world, both extant and fossil.

Although the inventory of the earth's flora is largely complete in the northern temperate zone, much remains to be done in the tropics. About 1 million of an estimated 1,500,000 species of all kinds of organisms have been described for the temperate regions, but in the tropics only about 500,000 of an estimated 3 million species of organisms have been described thus far. It has been estimated that there are about 15,000 species of flowering plants in South America that have not been named or made known to science (Prance, 1978). The primary tasks of systematic botany—that is, to explore, describe, and classify the flora of the world—is thus far from complete.

Once names and classification have been provided, there must be methods for persons to identify a taxon as being similar to another known entity. This is accomplished by producing descriptions, keys, catalogs, illustrations, manuals, or other publications that aid in the identification of specimens. Technology is presently available for the use of computers to aid in identification (Morse, 1971; Shetler, 1974). In the future, computer programs may be routinely used in plant identification. Nevertheless, training, practice and experience remain the best teachers in plant identification.

In the century since Darwin, biologists have been able to demonstrate that evolutionary lineages occur among taxa. The evolutionary development or lineage of a taxon is its *phylogeny*. Phylogenetic relationships exist that show that diverse species and the lineages they represent did not arise spontaneously, but may have had a common ancestral form. Modern classification attempts to use all available information about plants to develop a phylogeny. Since the fossil record is often fragmentary, especially for flowering plants, information must be gathered from a wide variety of sources to formulate a hypothesis about phylogeny.

Need for Names

A system of classification is necessary to allow us to identify plants and animals and to communicate scientifically with others. Indeed, classification is both an information storage and retrieval system without which scientific communication would be impossible. A plant's name is the key that unlocks the door to its total biology. Ecologists, biochemists, horticulturists, and others must have a reference system for the plants they use in their research. However, systematic botany is not meant only for scientists; it may be used by other people with varied interests and training who are interested in the natural history of plants. The scientific name of a plant communicates the species and genus, and from that the family may be easily determined. In addition, one can assume that there are other individual plants that share certain of the same features. For instance, when a forester identifies a white oak (*Quercus alba*), it can reasonably be assumed that there are other individual white oaks in nature that have similar morphological features, structure, and physiology. The knowledge that a plant is

FIGURE 1-1
Taxonomic Information Service

INPUT
DATA FROM VARIOUS SOURCES
SPECIMENS FROM FIELD WORK

PLANT SYSTEMATICS
Herbarium Collections
Description
Identification
Nomenclature
Bibliography
Classification

CONTRIBUTIONS
FLORAS
REVISIONS
MONOGRAPHS
FIELD GUIDES
EDUCATION
INFORMATION

USERS OF INFORMATION
Biologists
Ecologists
General Public
Agriculturists

Quercus alba automatically predicts that much information will be applicable to that plant.

As one of their roles, plant taxonomists work to provide an information service that is essential to all who deal with organisms. This might be termed a Taxonomic Information Service. It operates as shown in Figure 1-1.

PHASES OF PLANT SYSTEMATICS

Since one of the primary concerns of plant taxonomy is to provide an inventory of plants of the world, one phase is *exploration and discovery*. This is sometimes called *alpha taxonomy* and is an activity of even preliterate peoples. However, the most active recorded period began with the voyages of discovery by Western Europeans in the 1400s. The peak of botanical exploration, in terms of plants described, was the late 1800s, but exploration and discovery continue today, especially in the tropics. Plant material collected on these early expeditions to the far corners of the earth was sent to botanists in Europe for naming and description. In the late 1700s and early 1800s, botanists were overwhelmed with the amount of plant specimens collected for study. Collections of pressed and dried specimens called *herbaria* (singular, *herbarium*) were developed. Botanists frequently became interested in particular taxa and exchanged plant specimens with other botanists for extensive study. Some of these collections later formed the nuclei of world-renowned herbaria.

By the late 1800s, many botanical centers were established in Europe and North America. Their herbaria grew rapidly as access to remote regions of the earth increased. In this phase, many species were described, named, and classified into genera and families for the first time. The floras of given areas became known through herbarium specimens. Exploration and discovery continue today, especially in the tropics, although new collections from the temperate region are continually made.

After adequate herbarium material is accumulated for a given geographic or political region, the second phase called *synthesis* begins. Classification based on *morphology*, the form and structure of plants, is developed. This presents the means of identifying the plants of that area. Botanists who have the goal of developing improved classification investigate the distribution of characters in taxa. This synthesis phase reached its plateau in the late 1800s and continues with considerable study today.

The foundation of angiosperm classification was largely developed before the general acceptance of Darwin's evolutionary ideas of the late 1800s and was based on *typology*. The influence of this doctrine is evident in systematics today. The early adherents of typology reasoned that each natural taxon had an idealized pattern or "type." In its extreme form, such reasoning led to the denial of variability within taxa. Today, however, a loosely defined typology is a useful and necessary kind of thought in taxonomy. The endless array of plant groups encountered by taxonomists must be organized mentally. Thus, taxonomists seek repetitive patterns as aids in recognizing mosses, ferns, gymnosperms, dicots, grasses, sunflowers, oaks, and so on. Typology was most influential during the early years of the exploration and discovery phase. It also continues into the synthesis phase.

The third or *experimental* phase is the combining of data for interpretation in evolutionary or phylogenetic terms. The emphasis is on understanding the course of evolution and its cause at the specific or generic level. Studies are currently ongoing where workers are concerned with morphological and chemical variation and cytological features such as chromosome number, behavior, and morphology. Controlled experiments are conducted in genetics. Hybridization, common in plants, is studied. Such research has led to revised concepts of evolutionary theory. Most information obtained from experimental studies is used in improving our knowledge of species and genera and has therefore had an impact on the classification of higher plant families and orders. With experimental methods, variation within species has become well-documented, and the cause of variation among plants may often be deduced.

Critical Problems and Opportunities

The urge among many scientists to follow the newest approaches in the biological sciences in an attempt to exploit the greenest pastures of research has caused, in many universities, an imbalance in the biological sciences to the extent that systematics has been neglected (Hedberg, 1979). Fortunately, there seems to be a growing awareness among many biologists that systematics is a fundamental prerequisite for many biological investigations and that the lack of competent taxonomists is a limiting factor in certain areas of research, especially in ecology, plant exploration, and comparative biochemistry. There are many opportunities for students to make a contribution to society through plant systematics. Many floras and classifications were done over 100 years ago and are out of date. Classifications change as additional knowledge accumulates, so that some names as well as the arrangement of taxa used in older floras are now incorrect. Since the 1800s many new species have been named, but most have never been critically examined with reference to overall classifications.

Much field work remains to be done, especially in the tropics. In view of the rapid destruction of natural vegetation in tropical areas and because of agricultural practices and encroaching civilization, there is an urgent need to explore the flora of these regions. A striking example of the urgency in this respect can be examined in Ethiopia, where in 1954, forest covered about 16 percent of the countryside (Hedberg, 1979). By 1975, forest cover was only 4 percent and it is estimated that virtually all of the forest in Ethiopia will be destroyed by 1990.

The plants in most tropical rain forests have never been inventoried, yet the few that remain are rapidly being cleared (Figure 1-2). Many species that inhabit these areas may be lost forever. For example, a wet forest strip of coastal Ecuador was almost completely denuded of forest in the 1960s. A small area of less than 1 km² of forest preserve, recently investigated by taxonomists from the Missouri Botanical Garden, remains (Hedberg, 1979). This forest preserve is now completely surrounded by banana and oil palm plantations. Some 50 new species of flowering plants have been described from this 1 km² preserve. The major timber tree of this coastal region is *Persea theobromifolia*, which was not described until the 1970s. *Persea theobromifolia* is a relative of the cultivated avocado (*Persea americana*) and may possibly

FIGURE 1-2
Destruction of tropical forest near Manaus, Brazil. A. Newly constructed roadway in April 1974, undisturbed forest. B. Same location in November, 1974, forest clearing and settlement has rapidly followed construction of the road. (Photographs supplied by Al Gentry of the Missouri Botanical Garden.)

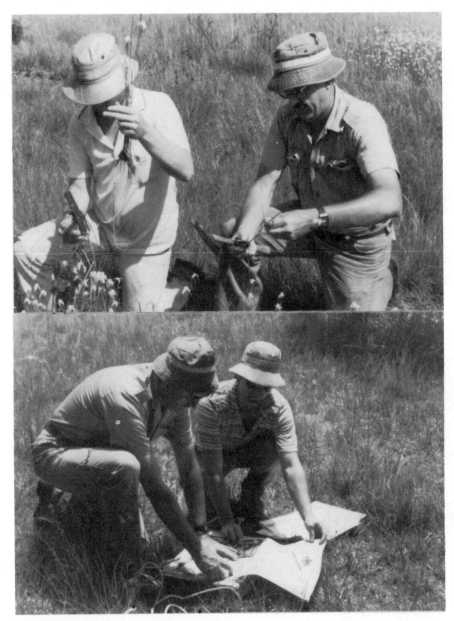

FIGURE 1-3
Sam Jones (right, top) and Mike Moore conducting field work in a grassy, long-leaf pine savannah on St. Catherine's Island, Georgia; top photograph collecting specimens, bottom photograph pressing specimens in the field. Worthwhile contributions to our knowledge of the flora of North America can be made by conducting floristic studies in areas (such as St. Catherine's Island) which have not been adequately botanized.

prove to be a desirable rootstock for it. Commercial avocado growers have been searching for an understock resistant to root-rot. Further, several species of pileas and gesnerias from the same region have recently been introduced into cultivation as ornamentals and are grown commercially by the tropical foliage plant industry.

It is of critical importance for plant taxonomists to examine the potential economic uses of plants. By way of example, the yeheb nut (*Cordeauxia edulis*), once abundant in Somalia where its pods were used as a staple food, was threatened by extinction in the early 1950s (Hedberg, 1979). Botanists became aware of its precarious situation and so secured the seeds, and it is now cultivated on a small scale in Somalia and Kenya. Because *C. edulis* thrives under extremely low precipitation, the shrub is an important potential food plant for arid regions where the human populations are frequently subjected to famine.

The continental United States is richly endowed with a marvelously diverse flora of approximately 20,000 species of vascular plants (Figure 1-3). Unfortunately, it is estimated that about 1,200 of these species are threatened, approximately 750 are in danger of extinction, and perhaps as many as 100 are already extinct (Prance and Elias, 1977). In the first half of the nineteenth century only about four species of plants are known to have become extinct in the United States, but in the first 50 years of the twentieth century, about 45 species of plants succumbed. To date, a few of the native plant species of North America have been studied in detail in terms of environmental requirements, ecological life histories, reproductive strategies, and seedling establishment. Indeed, such investigations may provide information about why a plant is rare and how populations of endangered species might be increased or preserved. Much remains to be learned about the details of species distribution in North America, including the precise locations of living stands of endangered species, and about the relative and sometimes changing frequencies of individual species. For these reasons there are active floristic research programs today in many individual American states and Canadian provinces.

SUMMARY

There is no doubt that we face crucial environmental decisions about the world in which we live. Clearly, systematics will play a vital role in the decision-making process. The natural environments of the earth are so complex as to defy the most talented scientists. Unfortunately, our knowledge of the living components of these environments is far from complete. For example, only recently have renewed efforts begun in cataloging the teeming diversity of plants and animals in the Amazon basin of South America. Knowledge of the species of plants in the rain forests of Latin America is very incomplete—a serious deficiency considering the potential economic importance and the vast numbers of species unknown to science. Information about the wild relatives of cultivated plants must be assembled if we are to meet the increasing demands for food and beverages. Systematists also have critical roles as scientists with major activities in biological research, the elucidation of evolutionary processes, conservation, and recently with the problem of endangered species.

Taxonomists have an opportunity as well as a responsibility to assist in the conservation of species, to establish natural preserves, and to locate and prevent the extinction of species that may provide germplasm resources or that may have medically useful chemical compounds. The tasks at hand are endless and urgent, but with the inevitable and rapid destruction of much of the world's vegetation, many taxa will be irretrievably lost in the next 10 to 20 years.

SELECTED REFERENCES

Constance, L.: "Systematic Botany—An Unending Synthesis," *Taxon,* **13:**257–273, 1964.

Davis, P. H., and V. H. Heywood: *Principles of Angiosperm Taxonomy,* Van Nostrand, Princeton, N.J., 1965.

Gómez-Pompa, A., C. Vázques-Yanes, and S. Guevara: "The Tropical Rain Forest: A Nonrenewable Resource," *Science (Wash., D.C.),* **177:**762–765, 1972.

Hagen, J. B.: "The Development of Experimental Methods in Plant Taxonomy, 1920–1950," *Taxon,* **32:**406–416, 1983.

Hedberg, I. (ed.): *Systematic Botany, Plant Utilization and Biosphere Conservation,* Almqvist & Wiksell, Stockholm, 1979.

Jeffrey, C.: *An Introduction to Plant Taxonomy,* 2nd ed., Cambridge University Press, New York, 1982.

Koopowitz, H. and H. Kaye: *Plant Extinction,* Stone Wall Press, Washington, D.C., 1983.

Lawrence, G.H.M.: *Taxonomy of Vascular Plants,* Macmillan, New York, 1951.

Lyte, C.: *The Plant Hunters,* Orbis Pub., London, 1983.

Mayr, E.: *The Growth of Biological Thought,* Belknap Press, Cambridge, Mass. 1982.

Morse, L. E.: "Specimen Identification and Key-Construction with Time-sharing Computers," *Taxon,* **20:**269–282, 1971.

National Research Council. Committee on Research Priorities in Tropical Biology.: *Research Priorities in Tropical Biology,* National Academy of Sciences, Washington, D.C., 1980.

Prance, G. T.: "Floristic Inventory of the Tropics: Where Do We Stand?," *Ann. Mo. Bot. Gard.,***64:**659–684, 1978.

Prance, G. T. and T. S. Elias (eds.): *Extinction Is Forever, Threatened and Endangered Plants in the Americas and their Significance in Ecosystems Today and the Future,* New York Botanical Garden, Bronx, 1977.

Radford, A. E., W. C. Dickison, J. R. Massey, and C. R. Bell: *Vascular Plant Systematics,* Harper & Row, New York, 1974.

Raven, P. H.: "Trends, Priorities, and Needs in Systematic and Evolutionary Biology." *Brittonia,* **26:**421–444, 1974.

Rollins, R. C.: "Taxonomy of Higher Plants." *Amer. J. Bot.,***44:**188–196, 1957.

Ross, H. H.: *Biological Systematics,* Addison-Wesley, Reading, Mass., 1974.

Shetler, S. G.: "Demythologizing Biological Data Banking," *Taxon,* **23:**71–100, 1974.

Simpson, G. G.: *The Principles of Animal Taxonomy,* Columbia, New York, 1961.

Sokal, R. R.: "Classification: Purposes, Principles, Progress, Prospects." *Science (Wash. D.C.),* **185:**1115–1123, 1974.

Stace, C. A.: *Plant Taxonomy and Biosystematics,* University Park Press, Baltimore, 1980.

CHAPTER 2

HISTORICAL BACKGROUND OF CLASSIFICATION

The history of classification is an exciting facet of plant systematics. Preliterate people arranged plants by their usefulness, whether edible, poisonous, or medicinal. As the purposes of classification expanded, the criteria for classification changed. The groupings of plants of the early hunter-gatherers eventually gave way to a classification reflecting plant affinities. Today we group plants by their presumed natural and phylogenetic relationships at the specific, generic, familial, and higher levels.

BEGINNINGS BY PRELITERATE HUMANS

The discoveries of the use of plants for food and later as medicine began at a very early stage in human evolution. Prehistoric people knew and used nearly all the important crop plants that we cultivate today. Food gatherers modified wild species by selecting plants with such features as tastiness in vegetables or higher yield in grains. Contemporary studies indicate that primitive peoples in remote areas today recognize and have precise names for large numbers of plants in their local environment. Some of these peoples regularly use plants for fish or arrow poisons, others for drugs to treat wounds or sickness, and still others for narcotic or hallucinatory purposes. Classification by preliterate people is at least partly based on the useful and harmful properties of plants. These groupings often parallel current classification concepts and have been referred to as *folk taxonomies;* that is, classifications that developed within the society through the need of the society and without scientific efforts (Berlin, Breedlove, and Raven, 1973).

EARLY WESTERN CIVILIZATIONS

Early Western civilizations developed in areas such as Babylonia and Egypt, where cultivation of crops was feasible. Since agriculture supported these civilizations, botanical lore was of great importance. But it was not until the development of writing and convenient writing materials such as papyrus, made from a Nile River sedge (*Cyperus papyrus*), that experience and knowledge of plants could be easily recorded.

Theophrastus (about 370–285 B.C.)

The Greek philosopher Theophrastus was a disciple of Aristotle and is often called the "father of botany." After Aristotle's death in 323 B.C., he inherited Aristotle's library and garden. Theophrastus is credited with several hundred manuscripts, but only two botanical discourses survive, *Enquiry into Plants* and *The Causes of Plants*. These are available in translation (Theophrastus, 1916, 1927). His writings summarize what was known of plants at the time and are similar to notes for lectures. Theophrastus classified plants into four major groups: herbs, undershrubs, shrubs, and trees. He described approximately 500 different species of plants. Theophrastus noted many differences in plants, such as corolla types, ovary positions, and inflorescences. He distinguished between flowering and nonflowering plants. He was aware of structural features, such as the pericarp of fruits, and the distinctions among plant tissues. The botanical information contained in the writings of Theophrastus was sound and sophisticated. The original contributions of his work were not improved upon until after the Middle Ages. Many names for plants today are derived from those used by Theophrastus.

Caius Plinius Secundus, "Pliny the Elder" (A.D. 23–79)

Pliny, a Roman naturalist and writer, held important military and governmental posts. He attempted to compile everything known in the world into an extensive 37-volume encyclopedia entitled *Historia naturalis* ("Natural History"). Nine of the volumes were devoted to medicinal plants. Although it contained many fables and was inadequate by today's standards, Pliny's account of plants remained for centuries as the only reflection of the achievements in Greek botany by Theophrastus.

Pedanios Dioscorides (first century A.D.)

The Roman military surgeon Dioscorides was the most important botanist after Theophrastus. Traveling extensively with the Roman armies, he had firsthand knowledge of plants used as remedies. Apparently interested in improving medical service in the Roman empire, Dioscorides prepared a truly outstanding book, *Materia medica,* which included descriptions of some 600 species of medicinal plants, 100 of which were not described by Theophrastus. Excellent illustrations were later added. For 1500 years this book was attentively studied. No drug was recognized as genuine unless named in *Materia Medica*. The most beautiful and famous copy was prepared about A.D. 500

for Emperor Flavius Olybrius Anicius as a gift to his daughter, Princess Juliana. It is available in facsimile, and the illustrations can be easily associated with familiar plants. The original manuscript is now in Vienna (Dioscorides, 1959). Many of the names used by Dioscorides appear today as familiar generic names. *Materia medica* was not a deliberate attempt at classification; however, some plants such as legumes, which today are regarded as closely related, were grouped together. *Materia medica* contained less botany than the works of Theophrastus, but its usefulness in medicine caused it to be considered the definitive work of plant knowledge until the end of the Middle Ages.

THE MIDDLE AGES

During the European Middle Ages, little progress was made in original scientific study of plants. Wars and the decay of the Roman Empire caused the destruction of much literature. Manuscripts were lost at a faster rate than they could be laboriously copied in the newly founded monasteries. Botanical knowledge was largely confined to the previously known works of Theophrastus, Pliny, and Dioscorides.

Islamic Botany

From around A.D. 610 to about A.D. 1100, some classical botanical works were preserved by the Moslem society because the Islamic scholars had a great admiration for Aristotle and other Greek scholars. Since their scientific interests were of a practical nature, pharmacy and medicine of the Islamic people were highly developed. Islamic botanists produced practical lists of drug plants but developed no original schemes of classification.

Albertus Magnus, "Doctor Universalis" (c. 1193–1280)

Albertus Magnus wrote on aspects of natural history and medicine during the Middle Ages. His botanical work *De vegetabilis* not only dealt with medicinal plants, as had the previous works by the Greeks and Romans, but it also provided descriptions of plants. These excellent descriptions were based on firsthand observations of the plants. Albertus Magnus attempted a classification of plants and is believed to have been the first to recognize, on the basis of stem structure, the differences between monocots and dicots. After Albertus Magnus more people looked at living plants in nature, and more significantly, they began to write and to print books about them.

HERBALISTS

With the coming of the Renaissance, there was a revival of scientific spirit, and interest in botany increased. The invention of printing with movable type in about 1440 allowed botanical books to be produced that were available to a wider audience than the former hand-copied manuscripts. Botanical books were produced with descriptions and illustrations made from woodblocks or metal plate engravings. They were intended to be used for identifying medicinal plants.

These books, or *herbals,* were in turn sought and used by the gatherers and diggers of medicinal plants, who were called *physicians* or *herbalists.* The herbals were written for utilitarian purposes; they were often cheaply done and of poor intellectual quality, sometimes containing independent observations but generally little that might be considered real scientific advancements. Often published locally, the herbals were entitled *Gart der Gesundheit* or *Hortus sanitatis.*

At this time botany was virtually synonymous with *herbalism,* the study of plants for their utilitarian values, especially in medicine. The herbalists forged an important link in the evolution of botany and taxonomy as well as in the development of *pharmacology* (the science of drugs). Recently, because of the resurgence of interest in natural foods and medicines, a number of the herbals have been reprinted and new modern herbals published (e.g., Grieve, 1967).

German Herbalists: Brunfels, Bock, Cordus, Fuchs

Germany in the sixteenth century was a center of botanical activity. The most outstanding contributions of this period were in the form of herbals by Otto Brunfels (1464–1534), Jerome Bock (1489–1554), Valerius Cordus (1515–1544), and Leonhard Fuchs (1501-1566). Brunfels, Bock, and Fuchs are sometimes called the "German Fathers of Botany."

Brunfels' *Herbarium vivae eicones* contains excellent illustrations. Brunfels was the earliest German Renaissance writer of note on botany. Bock's *Neu Kreuterbuck* contained excellent descriptions and some beginnings toward a system of classification. *Historia plantarum* was completed by Cordus in 1540 but was not published until 1561, some 17 years after his death. Cordus' herbal contains descriptions of 446 species in flower and fruit. He prepared botanical descriptions in an orderly format based on studies of living plants. Fuchs' *De historia stirpium,* elaborate with illustrations and descriptions, was better-documented and was the most noteworthy of the herbals of that period (Figure 2-1). Much knowledge of plants was summarized by the German herbalists, but no coherent classification scheme was produced perhaps because relatively few plants were discussed and there was no real need for an elaborate taxonomic scheme at this point in time.

The activities of the German herbalists signified a return to personal observations, descriptions based upon actual living plants, and attempts to enumerate the local flora. Indeed, hints of classifications or groupings began to appear; for example, Brunfels placed several species of plantain (*Plantago*) together; there were vague recognitions of kinds (species) and groups (genera).

Herbals of Other Countries or Civilizations

English botanical activity of the sixteenth century was represented by William Turner (1510–1568) and John Gerard (1542–1612). The Dutch were represented by Charles de L'Ecluse (Latinized as Carolus Clusius) (1526–1609), Rembert Dodoens (Dodonaeus) (1517–1585), and Mathias de l'Obel (Lobelius) (1538–1616). Pierandrea Mat-

POLYGONATVM
LATIFOLIVM

FIGURE 2-1
Solomon's Seal from Fuchs' *De historia stirpium* (1542) from A. Arber *Herbals Their Origin and Evolution,* used with permission of Cambridge University Press.

tiolia (Matthiolus) (1500–1577), an Italian botanist, published in numerous editions a popular annotated and illustrated work derived from the writings of Dioscorides. Botanical activity was flourishing throughout Europe.

Although we have focused on Western Europe, the botanical activity in other civilizations should not be overlooked. The Aztecs of Mexico developed botanical gardens, cultivated plants for both food and as ornamentals, and used medicinal herbs. The *Badianus Manuscript,* an Aztec herbal, was compiled in 1552 by two Aztecs (*Badianus Manuscript,* 1940).

Chinese civilization was older and much more advanced during the Middle Ages than civilization in Western Europe. The Chinese were printing on paper with movable block type before A.D. 1000. They were very interested in plants and introduced many species into cultivation. Botanical works were apparently produced in China around 3600 B.C.; however, the oldest manuscript still in existence dates back to about 200 B.C.

Agriculture was developed in India nearly 2000 B.C., and many different crops were cultivated. One interesting Indian botanical work, thought to have been written around the first century, indicates that methods of cultivation were well known. For an additional account of the early history of botany in various cultures the reader is referred to A. G. Morton's *History of Botanical Science* (1981).

THE ITALIAN RENNAISSANCE

Luca Ghini (1490–1556)

The development of botany in the first half of the sixteenth century owes much to the Italian, Luca Ghini. He is sometimes credited with the invention of the herbarium, which provided the technological advance needed for the rapid accumulation of knowledge on classification. Dried herbarium specimens could be studied at anytime, not just during the growing season, and could be used over a period of years, thus providing a "library" of pressed and dried plants. Herbaria were indispensable for the comparison and classification of plants. For example, most of Linnaeus' descriptions of non-Swedish plants were from herbarium specimens. Ghini was also instrumental in the establishment of botanical gardens at Pisa and Florence. Gardens provided living plants for study, and the plants grown in them were used to prepare realistic illustrations.

TRANSITION OF THE 1600s

The aggressive exploration of the New World in the 1600s was responsible for the discovery of many new plants. In Europe the herbalists studied these plants and added them to their herbals. Because of the large number of new species, botanists needed to develop a more precise system for naming and arranging plants.

For example in 1542, Fuchs was concerned with 500 species, Bauhin in 1623 with 6,000, and Ray listed 18,000 species in 1682. Coping with such an avalanche of plants required discrimination of species and clearly demonstrated a need to recognize and describe genera.

Andrea Cesalpino (1519–1603)

Cesalpino (Lat. Caesalpinus), an Italian botanist, followed Aristotelian reasoning and logic. Among the 1,500 plants of *De plantis libri,* which appeared in 1583, he sought a classification using a philosophical rather than a purely utilitarian approach by basing his classification on the features of plants. Cesalpino followed the methodology of downward classification by logical division, that is, starting with a number of easily recognized classes—for example, trees, shrubs, or herbs—then subdivide into subordinate sets of subclasses defined by single characters (Mayr, 1982). However, a study of his classification shows 32 groups of plants, recognized by him, that appear to be related. It is likely that Cesalpino started with these groups and then searched for characters that would permit him to arrange them in accordance with logical, downward division. Cesalpino profoundly influenced botanists of a later date including Tournefort, Linnaeus, and others who continued with the same methodology.

Caspar Bauhin (1560–1624)

In 1623, Bauhin, a Swiss botanist, published *Pinax theatri botanici,* a list of 6000 plants. *Pinax* provided a much-needed synonymy of plant names by listing for each plant all the names given to it by different botanists. This proved to be a valuable botanical catalogue of plant names. Bauhin used some binomial nomenclature (names consisting of only two words) and appeared to have an understanding of a concept of grouping species into genera. The genera were not described but were defined by the characters of the included species.

John Ray (1627–1705)

The English biologist Ray published numerous works (Figure 2-2). However, his two most significant botanical publications were *Methodus plantarum nova* (Ray, 1682) and *Historia plantarum* (Ray, 1686–1704), in three volumes. The last edition of *Methodus,* published in 1703, treated 18,000 species, many of which came from areas other than Europe.

FIGURE 2-2
John Ray: Line engraving by W. Elder after W. Faithorne. (Photograph provided by Hunt Institute for Botanical Documentation.)

However, some inflation in numbers of species occurred in these works because of Ray's narrow concept of species. Ray developed a system of classification based on form relationships by grouping together plants that resembled one another. Ray believed that an acceptable classification was one that joins together those plants that are similar in features and separates those that differ in their characteristics. He attempted to define species in the terms of morphology and reproduction. His classification was the greatest advance in theoretical botany of the seventeenth century. Ray's system later influenced the thinking of the de Jussieu and de Candolle families.

In Ray and Bauhin can be seen the beginnings of *natural classification,* that is, the grouping together of those plants that resemble one another. Today it is said that plants that resemble one another are usually closely related. However, it was not until the time of Darwin that the idea of lineages was firmly established.

Joseph Pitton de Tournefort (1656–1708)

The French botanist Tournefort is best known for his *Institutiones rei herbariae,* published in 1700. *Institutiones* was very popular because of the ease in identifying its 9000 species arranged into 700 genera. Compared with Ray's *Historia,* his system of classification was inferior because it was artificial. Its purpose was not to group closely related species but to aid in identification. Tournefort placed great emphasis on the genus. Although the roots of this concept are much older, dating to Aristotle, he is sometimes known as the "father of the genus concept." Tournefort used the concept of genus consistently and provided descriptions of the genera. From that point on, the concept of genus was well established in classification. There is evidence in his writing that he began to develop a system of groups at a higher level than that of the genus—that is, aggregates of genera.

CARL LINNAEUS (1707–1778) AND THE LINNAEAN PERIOD

Linnaeus, born in Råshult, Sweden, became the renowned botanist of the eighteenth century (Figure 2-3). He is sometimes called the "father of taxonomy." Today Linnaeus is best remembered for his consistent use of a referable system of nomenclature, that is, the binomial system of nomenclature.

Linnaeus entered the University of Lund in 1727 to study medicine. Dissatisfied with Lund, in 1729 he moved to the University of Uppsala, where he came under the influence of the Dean, Olaf Celsius, who introduced him to Professor Rudbeck, a professor of botany. On an expedition to Lapland in 1732, Linnaeus greatly increased his knowledge of natural history. In 1735 Linnaeus went to the Netherlands and quickly finished his medical degree at the University of Harderwijk. While in the Netherlands, he became the personal physician to the wealthy banker George Clifford, who had extensive botanical and horticultural interests. Clifford became the patron of Linnaeus. The three years spent in the Netherlands and traveling in Europe were important and creative years in Linnaeus' life. Before returning to Sweden in 1738, he published several books on natural history. He was also able to meet many of the prominent

FIGURE 2-3
Linnaeus (1707–1778). *(From Swingle, 1946: with permission.)*

naturalists of the time, including John Frederik Gronovius and Hermann Boerhaave from the Netherlands, Professor J. J. Dillen and Sir Hans Sloane in England, and the de Jussieu brothers in France. After establishing a medical practice on his return to Sweden, he became professor of medicine and botany at the University of Uppsala in 1741, a position he held until his death in 1778.

His three best-known works are the following: *Systema naturae,* 1735, et seq., presenting his system of classification in outline form; *Genera plantarum,* 1737, providing descriptions of many genera; and *Species plantarum,* 1753, a two-volume catalog used for plant identification. These have been reprinted many times and are available in most scientific libraries.

Linnaeus was hailed by many of his contemporaries as starting a new epoch in botany. We now view his work as the culmination of an attempt to create a workable system of identifying and classifying plants. Even though the system was useful for identifying plants, natural relationships were not stressed and unlike plants were often grouped together. Linnaeus divided plants into 24 classes based in large part on the number, union, and length of stamens. Plants with one stamen were placed in class Monandria, with two stamens class Diandria, and then Triandria, Tetrandria, Pentandria, and so on. Classes were divided into orders based on the number of styles in each flower. The strength of Linnaeus's artificial "sexual system" is its simplicity, since botanists could easily use it to apply names to plants.

Today we consider the greatest contribution of Linnaeus to be his consistent use of a precise and referable system of binomial nomenclature. "Referable" means that the name of the species immediately indicates the genus into which it is classified. In *Species plantarum,* each plant had a generic name, a polynomial descriptive phrase intended to serve as a definition of the species analogous to our dichotomous keys, and a trivial name (i.e., specific epithet) printed in the margin. This trivial name was used originally for purposes of indexing. Essentially, it was shorthand for the "real name," the polynomial. Only later was its usefulness recognized.

An example is shown below (see also Figure 2-4):

> glauca 8. SERRATULA *foliis ovato-oblongis accuminatis serratis, floribus corymbosis, calycibus subrotundis.*

The generic name is *Serratula;* the trivial name is *glauca,* and the polynomial descriptive phrase is *foliis ovato-oblongis accuminatis serratis, floribus corymbosis, calycibus subrotundis. Serratula glauca* forms the binomial. Information was also included about previous publications and illustrations, and about specimens in his herbarium and where the specimens were collected. The convenience of using the trivial name in combination with the generic name was immediately obvious, and the binomial system of nomenclature was widely accepted. Linnaeus was not the first to use two names for each species; Bauhin and others had done so, but not consistently. Linnaeus's nomenclatural scheme survives intact to this day.

Linnaeus recognized the limitations to be expected when only one set of characteristics is used (e.g., stamen number), but the convenience for identifying plants was great. This convenience may have even impeded botanical progress toward the development of a natural classification. His taxonomic scheme was purely artificial and was basically devoid of informational content. It was the influence of the nomenclature that caused the taxonomic system to impede the progress of botanical classification.

In any analysis of the work of Linnaeus, the conditions of the eighteenth century and the confused state of botanical nomenclature must be considered. Linnaeus made use of the works of Bauhin, Caesalpino, Ray, Tournefort, and others and put together a synthesis of their ideas. Linnaeus and his followers are best associated with a botanical era, that of the artificial sexual system of classification. Linnaeus brought order to the overwhelming array of literature, and consensus and simplicity back into taxonomy and nomenclature. He is remembered for his energetic enthusiasm, as a prodigious writer, and for his clear summaries. Linnaeus' *Genera Plantarum* listed and briefly described the plant genera, continuing the tradition of Bauhin and Tournefort. *Species Plantarum* provides much information on each species, but no generic descriptions (see Figure 2.4). Linnaeus' genera were often well-characterized groups of species; he obviously recognized such groups by visual inspection and elaborated logical division later on.

Linnaeus' teaching abilities resulted in his added importance as a naturalist. He attracted hundreds of enthusiastic students. Among his better-known students were Peter Kalm, Fredrick Hasselquist, Peter Forskål, Peter Thunberg, and Daniel Solander.

His collections were sold by his widow in 1783 to J. E. Smith, an English botanist and one of the founders of the Linnean Society of London. The herbarium of Linnaeus is now housed in London at the Linnean Society in Burlington House, Piccadilly. (The name of the society is the "Linnean." The term used to describe Linnaeus' methods is "Linnaean.") The herbarium sheets have been photographed and are available in microfiche in many research libraries. Much has been written on the life and works of Linnaeus, and more information may be found in references cited at the end of this

1146 SYNGENESIA : POLYGAMIA ÆQUALIS.

Cirſium inerme , caulibus adſcendentibus, foliis linearibus infra cinereis. *Gmel. ſib.* 2. *p.* 71. *t.* 28.*? ſed flo-
res majores.*
Habitat in Sibiria. *D. Gmelin.*
Caulis *angulatus, corymboſus , ramis itidem corymboſis,
ut terminetur denſiſſima ſylva florum, fere inſinitorum.*
Folia *ſaligna , ſubtus albo villo veſtita-* Calyces *cy-
lindrici Squamis glabris , acutis, purpuraſcentibus. Si-
milis præcedenti, ſed folia baſi parum decurrentia, ſubtus villoſa ,* & Calyces *copioſiores, argutiores, glabri
magis* & *lætius colorati.*

novebora-
cenſis.

6. SERRATULA foliis lanceolato-oblongis ſerratis pen-
dulis. *Hort. cliff.* 392. *Roy. lugdb.* 143.
Serratula noveboracenſis maxima, foliis longis ſerratis,
Dill. elth. 255. *t.* 263. *f.* 342.
Serratula noveboracenſis altiſſima, foliis doriæ molli-
bus ſubincanis. *Moriſ. hiſt.* 3. *p.* 133. *Raj. ſuppl.* 208.
Centaurium medium noveboracenſe luteum, ſolidagi-
nis folio integro tenuiter crenato. *Pluk. alm.* 93. *t.*
109. *f.* 3.
Habitat in Noveboraco , Virginia, Carolina, Canada,
Kamtſchatca. ♃

præalta

7. SERRATULA foliis lanceolato oblongis ſerratis pa-
tentibus ſubtus hirſutis. *Mill. dict. t.* 234.
Serratula virginiana , perſiæ folio ſubtus incano. *Dill.
elth.* 356. *t.* 264. *f.* 343.
Serratula præalta, anguſto plantaginis aut perſicæ folio.
Bocc. muſ. 2. *p.* 45. *t.* 32.
Eupatoria virginiana, ſerratulæ noveboracenſis latiori-
bus foliis. *Pluk. alm.* 141. *t* 280. *f.* 6.
Habitat in Carolina, Virginia, Penſylvania.
Receptaculum nudum, nec villoſum. Tozzet. app. 166.

glauca.

8. SERRATULA foliis ovato oblongis acuminatis ſer-
ratis , floribus corymboſis , calycibus ſubrotundis.
Gron. virg. 116.
Serratula marilandica , foliis glaucis cirſii inſtar denti-
culatis. *Dill. elth.* 354. *t.* 262. *f.* 341.
Centaurium medium marianum, folio integro cirſii no-
ſtratis more ſpinulis fimbriato. *Pluk. mant.* 40.
Habitat in Marilandia, Virginia, Carolina. ♃

ſquarroſa.

9. SERRATULA foliis linearibus , calycibus ſquarro-
ſis

FIGURE 2-4

Λ photograph of a page from C. Linnaeus, *Species plantarum*, 2 vols., Vienna, 1764, with the
trivial (i.e., specific) name printed in the margin. Number 8, *Serratula glauca*, was based upon a
specimen collected in Virginia by John Clayton and published in J. F. Gronovius, *Flora virginica*,
2 vols., Lugduni Batavorum, 1739–1743. The same plant had earlier been called *Centaurium
medium marianum* in L. Plukenet, *Almagesti botanici mantissa*, London, 1700, and named
Serratula marilandica in J. J. Dillenius, *Hortus elthamensis*, 2 vols., Lugduni Batavorum, 1732.
This species is now known as *Vernonia glauca* (L.) Willd. *(Photograph, University of Georgia
Libraries.)*

chapter (Blunt, 1971; Daniels et al., 1976; Frängsmyr, 1983; Fries, 1923; Stafleu, 1971; Stearn, 1957).

NATURAL SYSTEMS

By the end of the 1700s, most botanists realized that there were "natural affinities" among plants. Opposition developed to the artificial sexual classification scheme of Linnaeus because his system often placed unlike plants together (e.g., cacti and cherries). This opposition was especially strong in France, where the sexual system had never been fully accepted. There was gradual abandonment of (1) the use of single characters to classify plants, and (2) the selection of characters based on theory rather than experience or experimentation. The development of a classification system reflecting natural relationships—which could also be used to aid in identification—became a major focus of botanical activity.

A "natural system" of classification implies that plants presumed to be related are cataloged together. In its original context, the natural system was designed to reflect God's plan of creation and not one of lineages.

Michel Adanson (1727–1806)

The French naturalist Adanson traveled in tropical Africa, where the flora and fauna made him aware of the failings of one-character taxonomy. He questioned the validity of logical division and the sexual system and stated that the only natural method was to consider all parts of the plant. He advocated the use of as many characters as possible (Mayr, 1982). Adanson was the first botanist to attempt to determine how many characters should be used and whether there should be preference for certain characters. He realized that characters may vary in their taxonomic significance and proposed the weighting (placing emphasis) of characters *a posterori*.

The science of taxonomy has shown that some characters are in fact more valuable than others; yet, modern taxonomists try to use as many characters as possible. Adansonian methods have found advocates in recent years in numerical taxonomists who use computers to develop classifications from all the measurable features of plants.

Adanson described groupings similar to our modern orders and 58 families (a category suggested earlier by Ray) as set forth in *Familles des plantes* (1763).

J. B. P. de Lamarck (1744–1829)

The French biologist de Lamarck is generally best known for his unsuccessful attempts to provide an explanation for the idea of evolution, but he is also well known to taxonomists for his treatment of the plants of France. In *Flore française,* published in 1778, he set forth his procedures for determining which plant precedes another in a natural series, and he stated rules for the grouping of species and the treatment of orders and families.

Equally as important, de Lamarck developed an analytical method for identification similar to our modern keys found in various manuals.

de Jussieu Family

There were four botanists in the de Jussieu family: the brothers Antoine (1688–1758), director of the Jardin des Plantes in Paris; Joseph (1704–1779), explorer and collector in South America; and Bernard (1699–1777), founder of the royal Botanical Garden at Versailles; and their nephew Antoine-Laurent (1748–1836) (Figure 2-5), founder in 1793 of the Musée d'Histoire Naturelle de Paris.

Sometime before the French Revolution, a decision was made to arrange the plants in the garden at Versailles according to the Linnaean system. The garden was never arranged in this manner because Bernard de Jussieu felt that plants that "looked alike" (i.e., were presumed to be related) should be grouped together. This was not always true with Linnaeus' artificial sexual system, where unlike things were grouped together because they had the same number of stamens. It should, however, be remembered that the idea of evolution and lineages was not established until Darwin's time. In

FIGURE 2-5
Antoine Laurent de Jussieu: Line and stipple engraving by Ambroise Tardieu after an 1825 painting by Dumont. (Photograph provided by Hunt Institute for Botanical Documentation.)

1763 Antoine-Laurent de Jussieu joined his uncle and began to work on natural groupings of plants in the garden.

In 1789, during the French Revolution, Antoine-Laurent de Jussieu published *Genera plantarum secundum ordines naturales disposita,* a work resulting from his experiences in arranging the garden. The publication of *Genera plantarum* caused the idea of natural systems to be widely accepted. Antoine-Laurent de Jussieu recognized 100 carefully characterized groups of plants that are now called *families* (he called them *orders*). His system divided plants into three main groups—that is, the acotyledones (cryptogams and a few misplaced monocotyledons), monocotyledones (monocotyledons), and dicotyledones (dicotyledons and gymnosperms)—and it forms the immediate progenitor of our modern systems of classification. That this treatment was remarkable is indicated by the acceptance of most of the groupings today, along with the features by which they are recognized. The de Jussieu system was superior to the artificial sexual system of Linnaeus and was fundamental to further progress toward a natural system of classification. The philosophy of the natural system was firmly established in the scientific community by Antoine-Laurent de Jussieu. It would continue until the idea of organic evolution became firmly entrenched in the late 1800s.

de Candolle Family

The reputation of the Swiss-French de Candolle family was established by Augustin Pyramus de Candolle (1778–1841). Although born in Geneva, de Candolle (Figure 2-6) received his botanical training in Paris and was greatly influenced by the French botanists of that day. In 1813 he published *Théorie élémentaire de la botanique,* which set forth the principles of plant taxonomy. His classification scheme differed somewhat from the de Jussieu system, but it was a natural classification scheme dividing the

FIGURE 2-6
A. P. de Candolle (1778–1841). *(From Swingle, 1946, with permission; original from A. Gundersen, Brooklyn Botanic Garden.)*

plants into two major groups: the cellulares (nonvascular) and the vasculares (vascular plants).

A major effort of A. P. de Candolle from 1816 to his death in 1841 was the *Prodromus systematis naturalis regni vegetabilis,* an attempt to classify and describe every known species of vascular plant. Although never finished, it remains the only worldwide treatment of certain groups. The first seven volumes were written by A. P. de Candolle himself, while the next ten were written by specialists and were edited by his son, Alphonse (1806–1893).

Included in the *Prodromus* were all the dicotyledons (monocotyledons were not treated) accounting for 58,000 species in 161 families; de Candolle placed the gymnosperms among the catkin-bearing dicotyledons and began the dicotyledons with the family Ranunculaceae (buttercups and their relatives).

S. L. Endlicher (1805–1849)

Over 6800 genera of plants were classified in Endlicher's *Genera Plantarum.* This notable German botanist separated the Thallophyta (algae and fungi) from the higher plants (Cormophyta). He began the dicotyledon families with those having apetalous flowers.

A. T. Brongniart (1801–1876)

In 1843, Brongniart advocated the division of plants into Cryptogamae (nonseed-bearing) and Phanerogamae (the seed-bearing plants). Brongniart also suggested the need for the careful comparison of living and fossil forms of plants, a significant aspect of modern plant systematics.

George Bentham (1800–1884) and Sir Joseph Dalton Hooker (1817–1911)

Attention of many botanists during the first half of the nineteenth century was focused on the development and improvement of the natural systems of classification. This era was climaxed by the publication of Bentham and Hooker's *Genera plantarum* in 1862–1883. Bentham was a self-trained English botanist, and Hooker was director of the Royal Botanic Gardens at Kew, near London. *Genera plantarum* is a three-volume work in Latin, giving names and descriptions of all genera of seed plants. The classification system by which it is arranged is clearly derived from the systems of de Jussieu and de Candolle.

Bentham and Hooker divided the dicotyledons into: (1) Polypetalae (free petals), (2) Gamopetalae (fused petals), and (3) Monochlamydeae (apetalous). The dicotyledons were followed by the gymnosperms and monocotyledons. In all, 200 families and 7569 genera were treated.

Genera plantarum was one of the last great works in which the species concepts were based on the idea that species are fixed entities, unchanged through time and placed on earth by the Creator. Although it appeared after Darwin published his *The*

Origin of Species, it is pre-Darwinian in concept, despite the fact that Hooker and Bentham were both supporters of Darwin. Nevertheless, their delimitation of families and genera is based on natural relationships, reflecting the heritage of de Jussieu. The reason that *Genera plantarum* is so useful, even today, is that Bentham and Hooker prepared the generic descriptions from observations made of the plants themselves rather than by copying descriptions from the literature. Their generic descriptions are accurate, complete, and precise; the large genera are divided into sections and sub-sections; and the geographical range is given. Their system of classification was widely accepted and used in the British colonial floras and elsewhere. British herbaria, such as Kew and the British Museum, are still arranged according to it.

BOTANY IN THE NINETEENTH CENTURY

Many exciting and fascinating discoveries were made by botanists during the nineteenth century. The amazing Scotsman, Robert Brown, explored Australia and other exotic places, investigated floral morphology, recognized the naked ovule as the fundamental distinction between gymnosperms and angiosperms, and reported observations of the nuclei of cells. Wilhelm Hofmeister, the brilliant German botanist of the mid–1800s, determined the life cycles of cryptogams (plants that are not seed-bearing) and formulated the concept of alternation of generations. The epoch-making researches of Eduard Strasburger in the late 1800s demonstrated nuclear fusion in the ovules of gymnosperms and angiosperms and laid the foundation for plant cytology. He failed to notice, however, the extraordinary "triple fusion" of the polar nucleus with the second sperm nucleus of the pollen, a phenomenon peculiar to flowering plants, which was eventually discovered in 1898 by the Russian, S. G. Navashin. These important developments, and others brought about by technological improvements in microscopes, gave systematists a greater understanding of diversity and provided the information needed to adjust their classifications and to reflect biological entities.

THE INFLUENCE OF DARWIN'S THEORY OF EVOLUTION ON SYSTEMATICS

By the middle of the nineteenth century, the stage was set for the idea of evolution. The observations and collections of world travelers and the endless flow of specimens back into Europe made it impossible to ignore knowledge regarding the fossil record and variation in species of plants and animals. The history of the theory of evolution is as fascinating as that of the history of plant systematics; however, we shall consider only its impact on plant systematics.

Charles Darwin (1809–1882) and A. R. Wallace (1823–1913) wrote a paper entitled "On The Tendency of Species to Form Varieties and Species by Natural Means of Selection," which was read before the Linnean Society of London on July 1, 1858. On November 24, 1859, Darwin's *The Origin of Species* was published, and every copy of the first edition was sold that very day. Biology was irrevocably changed. By the twentieth century, the concept that species are not unchanging creations was widely accepted. Rather than endless generations of species created all alike, species are dynamic, variable population systems that change with time and form lineages of closely related organisms. This idea provided a conceptual framework that had great impact on systematics.

It should be pointed out that Darwin won his spurs as a taxonomist by eight years of study on the classification of barnacles. Darwin wrote that his work on the taxonomy of barnacles was of great value and provided insight to him when he had to discuss the principles of classification in Chapter 13 of *The Origin of Species*. In this chapter he recognized certain rules of classification, namely, that (1) organisms have lineages, (2) characters constant over large groups have value in developing classifications, (3) taxa should be based upon correlated complexes of characters, and (4) characters should be weighted based on *a posteriori* information.

TRANSITIONAL PHYLOGENETIC SYSTEMS

As the impact of evolutionary theory became apparent, taxonomists began to integrate evolutionary concepts into their classifications. There were no abrupt departures from previous systems, since the post–Darwinian systems were firmly based on plant morphology. Taxonomists consciously tried to arrange the natural groups of plants in an evolutionary sequence proceeding from the simplest to the most complex. Botanists struggled with the problem of structures, which seemed simple but in reality resulted from the reduction or fusion of more complex ancestral features. Attempts were made to develop classification systems that were evolutionary but that may seem naive to present-day taxonomists. Such systems are said to be *phylogenetic*. It was soon recognized that the development of phylogenetic classifications had several practical problems. In the flowering plants it is usually impossible to reconstruct past evolutionary pathways because of the absence of a clear-cut fossil record. Difficulty arises in assuming that each taxon is monophyletic; that is, the group has a common origin. Finally, there is the difficulty of arranging a branching system such as a flora within the confines of a linear sequence in a book, where the first taxa treated are the least specialized and the last are the most advanced and presumably derived.

August Wilhelm Eichler (1839–1887)

Germany was the leading center for the study of plant morphology during the second half of the nineteenth century. Classification at that time was exclusively morphological, and German plant morphologists began to consider their data in light of evolutionary theory. A number of workers made contributions. Among the most important was Eichler, who in 1883 developed what was to become a widely accepted classification of the plant kingdom. He divided the plant kingdom into the nonseed plants (the Cryptogamae) and the seed plants (the Phanerogamae), as previous botanists had already done. The former group contained algae, fungi, bryophytes, and seedless vascular plants, whereas the latter was divided into gymnosperms and angiosperms; angiosperms were further separated into monocotyledons and dicotyledons. The dicotyledons were subdivided into two groups, the Choripetalae (plants with flowers having free petals) and Sympetalae (those with fused petals); the old apetalae (flowers without petals) being distributed among the two groups. Eichler did not accept, or at least did not understand, the idea of secondary reduction (i.e., from complex back to simple flowers), which affected the placement of certain groups in his classification scheme.

Adolf Engler (1844–1930) and Karl Prantl (1849–1893)

Engler (Figure 2-7) was a professor of botany at the University of Berlin and director of the Berlin Botanical Garden from 1889 to 1921. He proposed a system of classification based on that of Eichler, differing only in detail. Along with his associate, Prantl, he published *Die natürlichen Pflanzenfamilien* in many volumes from 1887 to 1915. This monumental work includes keys and descriptions for all the plant families. *Die natürlichen Pflanzenfamilien* is abundantly illustrated, and the morphological, anatomical, and geographical literature are summarized. Engler and Prantl prepared many of the treatments, but a number were contributed by specialists. The size and scope of *Die natürlichen Pflanzenfamilien* gave it practical value far greater than its value as a classification device. Engler's taxonomic scheme was widely accepted because of the detail and elaborate form of its presentation. Most non-British herbaria and many floras still follow his sequence in arranging plants. Engler did not intend for the precise linear sequence of his system to be understood as evolutionary.

In the Englerian system, plants were grouped into a number of divisions, many of which were algal groups. In his scheme, the monocotyledons preceded the dicotyledons; the latter comprising two groups: the Archichlamydeae (Chloripetalae or Polypetalae), which preceded the Metachlamydeae (Sympetalae or Gamopetalae). The first group of dicotyledons began with the catkin-bearing plants and their relatives, called the Amentiferae. Engler believed that simple, unisexual flowers were primitive, and

FIGURE 2-7
Adolf Engler (1844–1930). *(From Swingle, 1946, with permission; original from A. Gundersen, Brooklyn Botanic Garden.)*

in his earlier work he rejected the idea of secondary reduction. His system of classification has undergone continual revision by his followers and has been published
many times in successive editions of *Syllabus der Pflanzenfamilien*. Volume 2 of the
twelfth and latest edition, edited by Melchior and treating the angiosperms, appeared
in 1964. Through the years the general outline has changed little, although some
families have been shifted within the classification. The present Englerian system is
generally regarded as obsolete since most botanists do not agree with its assumptions
about the primitive flower.

INTENTIONAL PHYLOGENETIC SYSTEMS

Taxonomic schemes that try to reflect evolution are said to be *phylogenetic*. By the
turn of the twentieth century, the impact of Darwinism and genetics was fully felt in
plant systematics, and systems of classification were proposed that were intentionally
phylogenetic. One of the advantages of phylogenetic systems is that they are rich in
informational content, since the identity of a plant implies kmowledge of its affinities
and evolutionary relationships. Actually, the natural systems and the phylogenetic
systems are similar in many respects, and the families and genera differ little in content.
The difference is in the placement of families and orders, as well as what is considered
to be the primitive flower.

The Englerian school considered simple, unisexual flowers to be primitive. Examples of an Englerian primitive flower would be something like the unisexual flowers
found in willow (*Salix*) or cottonwood (*Populus*). "Primitive = simple" in the Englerian context is a concept derived from reason, while in phylogenetic context,"primitive" means those things that were here first. However, without facts from
the fossil record some of the latter reasoning may well be circular (see Chapter 6).

Charles E. Bessey (1845–1915)

A professor of the University of Nebraska, Bessey (Figure 2-8) received part of his
training under Asa Gray, a noted botanist at Harvard. Bessey was the first American
to make a major contribution to the theory of plant classification. In 1894 Bessey,
greatly influenced by the evolutionary ideas of Darwin, published an intentionally
phylogenetic taxonomic system based upon the principles of organic evolution. He
considered the flowering plants to be monophyletic, that is, derived from one evolutionary line and representing a continuum of lineages. His system was based on a set
of *dicta* or concepts of primitive features found in ancient plants, versus the advanced
characters of more recently evolved plants. His system is basically a modified Bentham
and Hooker classification with emphasis on primitive ranalian dicotyledous stock giving
rise to the other dicotyledons and to the monocotyledons. His final classification was
published in outline form shortly after his death in 1915.

Among the lower plants, Bessey's system of classification was similar to Engler's
scheme; however, it was different in that the pteridophytes and gymnosperms were
subdivided into a number of divisions. Further, the dicotyledons were arranged in a
quite different classification and began with the Magnoliaceae-Ranunculaceae complex.

FIGURE 2-8.
Charles E. Bessey (1845–1915). *(With permission of the School of Life Sciences, University of Nebraska.)*

Hans Hallier (1868–1932)

In 1905 the German botanist Hans Hallier published a phylogenetic classification based on many of the same principles used by Bessey. Hallier began the flowering plants with the Ranunculaceae-Magnoliaceae complex and derived the monocotyledons from the dicotyledons. Since the time of Bessey and Hallier, most classifications of the flowering plants have used either a Bessey-Hallier system or a modified Englerian scheme. Changes were largely modifications at the level of family and order and in proposed lineages.

John Hutchinson (1884–1972)

The British botanist Hutchinson (Figure 2-9) was associated with the Royal Botanic Gardens at Kew. In his *Families of Flowering Plants* (1973) and *Genera of Flowering Plants* (1964–1967), he proposed a system of classification resembling Bessey's but differing in several fundamental points. Essentially, Hutchinson derived the flowering plants from hypothetical proangiosperms (i.e., the transitional plants from gymnosperms to angiosperms) and divided them into three lines: the Monocotyledones, Herbaceae Dicotyledones, and Lignosae Dicotyledones. The primitive monocotyledons were derived from the primitive herbaceous dicotyledons, their point of origin being in the Ranales. Hutchinson considered the woody versus herbaceous habit of fundamental importance among the dicotyledons. The woody line was derived from the woody Magnoliales and the herbaceous line from the herbaceous Ranales. Hutchinson's treatment of individual families and genera, and especially that of the monocotyledons,

FIGURE 2-9
John Hutchinson: Photograph
courtesy of R. A. Dyer, Pretoria,
South Africa, taken in the 1930s.
(Photograph provided by Hunt
Institute for Botanical
Documentation.)

is excellent. The division of the dicotyledons into woody and herbaceous lines is considered unfortunate and unnatural because it often places closely related families some distance apart. This has detracted from the overall value of his work.

CONTEMPORARY SYSTEMS OF CLASSIFICATION

At present, the classification of the plant kingdom continues to be modified as new information becomes available. In recent years, the classification of flowering plants has benefited from data from paleobotany, biochemical systematics, and ultrastructure using scanning and transmission electron microscopes. Used in conjunction with information derived from traditional sources such as comparative anatomy and gross morphology, these kinds of data further refine the classification.

The American plant taxonomist Robert Thorne (Figure 2-10) proposed a synopsis of his classification in 1968 and a somewhat more detailed exposition in 1976. Armen Takhtajan (1980) of the Soviet Union and Arthur Cronquist (1981) of the New York Botanical Garden presented detailed outlines of their classifications. The systems of Thorne, Takhtajan, and Cronquist are Besseyan in origin and tradition. G. L. Stebbins (1974) has developed a classification of the flowering plants in the Thorne-Takhtajan-Cronquist tradition but with some modifications.

FIGURE 2-10
Robert F. Thorne of the Rancho Santa Ana Botanic
Garden, Claremont, California.

These recent classifications continue to improve, and no doubt the future will see
more revisions as botanists attempt to develop phylogenetic classifications based on
evolutionary principles using newly available information.

Among such attempts is the work of the Danish botanist, Rolf Dahlgren (Figure
2-11) (1977, 1980, 1981), who bases his classification on the distribution of a large
number of characters drawn from many biological disciplines including embryology,
chemistry, and anatomy. Dahlgren follows the widely held modern view that none of

FIGURE 2-11
Rolf M. T. Dahlgren, Professor at the
Botanical Museum of the University of
Copenhagen, Denmark.

TABLE 2-1
HISTORICAL DEVELOPMENT OF CLASSIFICATION SYSTEMS

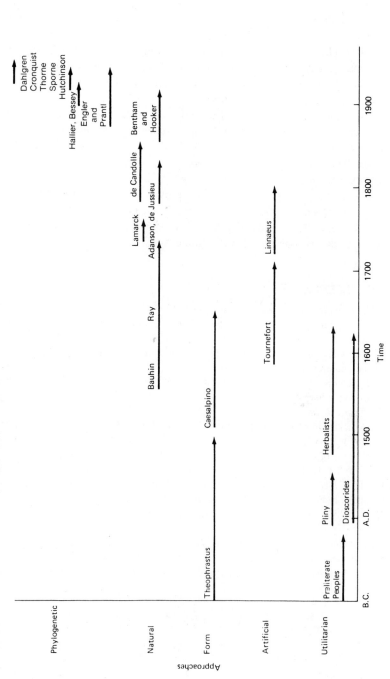

the extant groups of flowering plants is ancestral to any other present-day group. Thus, the Magnoliaceae-Ranunculaceae assemblage is not ancestral to the other flowering plants but has simply retained a large number of primitive features. In England, K. R. Sporne (1976) has focused his efforts on developing a classification using character correlation among angiosperms. Sporne presents his system in the form of a circular diagram with the derived groups radiating outward and the groups located near the center of the circle, regarded as primitive.

Table 2-1 summarizes the historical development of flowering plant classification. It should be emphasized that although the approaches to classification were separated by notable events, no one event really closed one era or started a new period of classification. The evolution of plant taxonomy has been one of gradual changes and improvements over the past.

Selected references to botanical history that provide a detailed yet readable synthesis are provided at the end of the chapter (Core, 1955; Gardner, 1972; Greene, 1909; Morton, 1981; Sachs, 1906; and Sirks and Zirkle, 1964). Stafleu (1967, 1976) provides an excellent selective guide to botanical publications.

SELECTED REFERENCES

Adanson, M.: *Familles des plantes,* 2 vols., Paris, 1763. (Facsimile edition, Lehre, 1966.)

Anderson, F. J.: *An Illustrated History of the Herbals,* Columbia University Press, New York, 1977.

Arber, A.: *Herbals, Their Origin and Evolution,* The University Press, Cambridge, England, 1938. (The classic reference on herbals.)

Badianus Manuscript (translated and edited by E. W. Emmart), Johns Hopkins, Baltimore, 1940. (An Aztec herbal.)

Bauhin, C.: *Pinax theatri botanici,* Basel, 1623.

Becker, K. M.: "Systems of Classification," in A. E. Radford et al. (eds.), *Vascular Plant Systematics,* Harper & Row, New York, 1974, pp. 583–644. (A detailed comparison of the various systems of classification.)

Bentham, G., and J. D. Hooker: *Genera planatarum,* 3 vols., London, 1862–1883.

Berlin, B., D. E. Breedlove, and P. H. Raven: "General Principles of Classification and Nomenclature in Folk Biology," *Amer. Anthrop.,* **75:**214–242, 1973.

Bessey, C. E.: "Phylogenetic Taxonomy of Flowering Plants," *Ann. Mo. Bot. Gard.,* **2:**109–164, 1915.

Blunt, W.: *The Complete Naturalist. A Life of Carl Linnaeus,* Collins, London, 1971.

Candolle, A. P. de: *Théorie élémentaire de la botanique,* Paris, 1813.

——— et al.: *Prodromus systematis naturalis regni vegetabilis,* 17 vols. and 4 index vols., Paris, 1824–1873.

Cesalpino, A.: *De plantis libri,* Florence, 1583.

Core, E. L.: *Plant Taxonomy,* Prentice-Hall, Englewood Cliffs, N.J., 1955, pp. 9–61. (An excellent history of plant taxonomy.)

Cronquist, A.: *The Evolution and Classification of Flowering Plants,* Houghton Mifflin, Boston, 1968.

———: *An Integrated System of Classification of Flowering Plants,* Columbia University Press, New York, 1981.

Dahlgren, R.: "A Commentary on a Diagrammatic Presentation of the Angiosperms in Relation to the Distribution of Character States," *Plant Syst. Evol., Suppl.* **1**:253–283, 1977.

———: "A Revised System of Classification of the Angiosperms," *Bot. J. Linn. Soc.*, **80**:91–124, 1980.

———, S. Rosendal-Jensen, and B. J. Nielsen: A Revised Classification of the Angiosperms with Comments on the Correlation Between Chemical and Other Characters, In D. A. Young and D. S. Seigler (eds.) *Phytochemistry and Angiosperm Phylogeny*, Praeger, New York, 1981, pp. 149–199.

Dahlgren, R., H. T. Clifford, and P. F. Yoe: *The Families of the Monocotyledons*, Springer-Verlag, Berlin, 1985

Daniels, G. S., et al.: "Linnaean Symposium at the Hunt Institute for Botanical Documentation," *Taxon*, **25**:3–74, 1976. (A series of eight special papers.)

Darwin, C.: *The Origin of Species*, London, 1859.

———: *The Origin of Species*, 6th ed., J. Murray, London, 1873. (The 6th edition is the edition most frequently cited.)

Dengler, R. E. See Theophrastus.

Dioscorides: *The Greek Herbal of Dioscorides*, R. T. Gunther (ed.), Hafner, New York, 1959.

Eichler, A. W.: *Blüthendiagramme construirt und erläutert*, 2 vols., Leipzig, 1875–1878. (Facsimile edition: Eppenhain, 1954.)

Emmart, E. W. See *Badianus Manuscript*.

Engler, A.: *Syllabus der Pflanzenfamilien*, 12th ed., 2 vols., H. Melchior and E. Werdermann (eds.), Gebrüder Borntraeger, Berlin, 1954–1964.

——— and K. Prantl: Die natürlichen Pflanzenfamilien, 23 vols., Leipzig, 1887–1915.

——— and ———: *Syllabus der Pflanzenfamilien*, 2d ed., Berlin, 1898. (In many editions, some of which were edited by other people, the 1st edition is cited as *Syllabus der Vorlesungen. . . , 1892.*)

——— and ———: *Die natürlichen Pflanzenfamilien*, 2d ed., W. Englemann, Leipzig, 1924–. (The 2d edition is not yet complete.)

Frängsmyr, T. (ed.): *Linnaeus, The Man and His Work*, University of California Press, Berkeley, 1983.

Fries, T. M.: *Linnaeus, the Story of His Life*, adapted by B. D. Jackson, Witherby, London, 1923.

Gardner, E. J.: *History of Biology*, 3d ed., Burgess, Minneapolis, 1972. (A good general reference on the history of biology.)

Garnsey, H. E. F. See Sachs, J.

Green, J. R.: *A History of Botany 1860–1900*, Clarendon, Oxford, 1909.

Greene, E. L.: "Landmarks of Botanical History," *Smithsonian Misc. Coll.*, **54**:1–329, 1909. (A basic reference on botanical history. Reprinted in 2 vols., Stanford University Press, 1983.)

Grieve, M.: *A Modern Herbal*, 2 vols., Hafner Publ. Co., New York, 1967.

Gunther, R. T. See Dioscorides.

Hallier, H.: "Provisional Scheme of the Natural (Phylogenetic) System of Flowering Plants," *New Phytologist*, **4**:151–162, 1905.

Hort, A. See Theophrastus.

Hull, D. L.: *Philosophy of Biological Science*, Prentice-Hall, Englewood Cliffs, N.J., 1974.

Hutchinson, J.: *The Genera of Flowering Plants*, 2 vols., Clarendon, Oxford, 1964–1967.

———: *Evolution and Phylogeny of Flowering Plants*, Academic Press, London, 1969.

———: *The Families of Flowering Plants*, 3d ed., Clarendon, Oxford, 1973.

Jackson, B. D. See Fries, T. M.

Jussieu, A. L. de: *General plantarum secundum ordines naturales disposita,* Paris, 1789.

Lamarck, J.: *Flore française,* 3 vols., Imprimerie Royale, Paris, 1778.

Linnaeus, C.: *Systema naturae,* Lugduni Batavorum, 1735. (Has been issued in many reprints and revisions.)

————: *Genera plantarum,* Lugduni Batavorum, 1737.

————: *Species plantarum,* 2 vols., Stockholm, 1753. (Facsimile edition: London, 1957–1959; there are numerous later editions of this work.)

Mayr, E.: "Biological Classification: Toward a Synthesis of Opposing Methodologies," *Science* (Wash. D.C.), **214:**510–516, 1981.

————: *The Growth of Biological Thought,* Belknap Press, Cambridge, Mass., 1982.

Melchior, H. See Engler, A.

Morton, A. G.: *History of Botanical Science,* Academic Press, New York, 1981.

Raven, P. H., B. Berlin, D. E. Breedlove: "The Origins of Taxonomy," *Science* (Wash. D.C.), **174:**1210–1213, 1971.

Ray, J.: *Methodus plantarum nova,* London, 1682. (Facsimile edition: Weinheim, 1962.)

————: *Historia plantarum,* 3 vols., London, 1686–1704.

Sachs, J.: *History of Botany (1530–1860),* translated by H. E. F. Garnsey and revised by I. B. Balfour, Clarendon, Oxford, 1906.

Sirks, M. J., and C. Zirkle: *The Evolution of Biology,* Ronald, New York, 1964. (Excellent literature citations.)

Sporne, K. R.: Character Correlations Among Angiosperms and the Importance of Fossil Evidence in Assessing Their Significance, in Beck, C. B. (ed.), *Origin and Early Evolution of Angiosperms,* Columbia University Press, New York, 1976, pp. 312–329.

Stafleu, F. A.: "Taxonomic Literature," *Regnum Veg.,* **52,** 1967. (A selective guide to botanical publications and authors.)

————: "Linnaeus and the Linnaeans," *Regnum Veg.,* **79,** 1971.

———— and R. Cowan: "Taxonomic Literature," 2d ed., *Regnum Veg.,* **94, 98, 105,** 1976– . (This will be a multivolume work when complete.)

Stearn, W. T.: "An Introduction to the *Species plantarum* and Cognate Botanical Works of Carl Linnaeus," in C. Linnaeus, *Species plantarum,* facsimile of the 1st ed., 1753, Ray Society, London, 1957.

————: Introduction to Facsimile Reprint of Ray, J., *Synopsis Methodica Stirpium Britannicarum Editio Tertia* 1724, Ray Society, London, 1973.

Stebbins, G. L.: *Flowering Plants,* Belknap Press, Cambridge, Mass., 1974.

Stevens, P. F.: "Metaphors and Typology in the Development of Botanical Systematics 1690–1960, or the Art of Putting New Wine in Old Bottles," *Taxon* **33:**169–211, 1984.

————: "Hauy and A.-P. Candolle: Crystallography, Botanical Systematics, and Comparative Morphology, 1780–1840," *J. Hist. Biol.,* **17:**49–82, 1984.

Swingle, D. B.: *A Textbook of Systematic Botany,* McGraw-Hill, New York, 1946.

Takhtajan, A.: *Flowering Plants–Origin and Dispersal,* Smithsonian Institution Press, Washington, 1969.

————: "Outline of the Classification of Flowering Plants (Magnoliophyta)," *Bot. Rev.,* **46:**225–359, 1980.

Theophrastus: *Enquiry into Plants,* 2 vols., translated by A. Hort, W. Heinemann, London, 1916.

————: *De causis plantarum,* translated by R. E. Dengler, Philadelphia, 1927.

Thorne, R. F.: "Synopsis of a Putatively Phylogenetic Classification of the Flowering Plants," *Aliso,* **6**(4)**:**57–66, 1968.

————: "A Phylogenetic Classification of the Angiospermae," *Evol. Biol.*, **9**:35–106, 1976.

————: Phytochemistry and Angiosperm Phylogeny: a Summary Statement, In D. A. Young and D. S. Seigler (eds.), *Phytochemistry and Angiosperm Phylogeny*, Praeger, New York, 1981, pp. 233–295.

Tournefort, J. P. de: *Institutiones rei herbariae*, 3 vols., Paris, 1700.

Walker, J. W.: "Comparative Pollen Morphology and Phylogeny of the Ranalean Complex," in C. B. Beck (ed.), *Origin and Early Evolution of Angiosperms*, Columbia, New York, 1976, pp. 241–299.

Wheeler, A. and J. H. Price (eds.): *History in the Service of Systematics*, Society for the Bibliography of Natural History, London, 1981.

Young, D. A. and D. S. Seigler, (eds.): *Phytochemistry and Angiosperm Phylogeny*, Praeger, New York, 1981, pp. 149–199.

CHAPTER 3

PLANT NOMENCLATURE

The assignment of names to plants is called *nomenclature.** It involves principles governed by rules developed and adopted by the International Botanical Congresses. The rules are formally listed in the International Code of Botanical Nomenclature (Voss, 1983) and are often referred to simply as the "Code." The ultimate goal of this precise system, as embodied in the Code, is to provide one correct name for each taxon. The rules of nomenclature are subdivided into *articles,* which must be adhered to, and *recommendations,* which are optional.

Although classification schemes may change with time, the scientific names of plants are relatively stable. The plant retains its name although the family or higher taxonomic categories are changed. Much effort has been devoted to establishing procedures for naming taxa and for changing names that were incorrectly assigned.

Nomenclature and classification are different but inseparable. The placement of a plant or group of plants in the classification scheme may be determined by knowing its name. When the generic name of a plant is known, it is possible with the proper bibliographic aids to determine the family to which that genus is usually assigned. Such a bibliographic tool is *A Dictionary of the Flowering Plants and Ferns* (Willis, 1973).

BASIS OF SCIENTIFIC NAMES

The present system of nomenclature is the result of a historic series of changes that gradually became formalized. The oldest plant names we now use are the common

---

Nomenclature is pronounced nō-́men-clā-́chur and its adjective form is *nomenclatural.* The word *nomenclatorial* is the adjective form of *nomenclator,* a person or book that deals with names.

names used in ancient Greece and Rome. Today all plant names have a Latinized spelling or are treated as Latin regardless of their origin. This custom originates from medieval scholarship and the use of Latin in most botanical publications until the middle of the nineteenth century. The assignment of names was relatively unstructured until the seventeenth century when the number of plants known to botanists began to increase greatly. This resulted in a need for a more precise naming system for plants. During several centuries before 1753, names were often composed of three or more words. These names are called *polynomials*. For example, in the herbal of Clusius (1583), the name *Salix pumila angustifolia altera* is used for a species of willow.

This complex name-description system was not workable because it was cumbersome and not readily expandable. In 1753, with Linnaeus's *Species plantarum*, the *binomial* format was substituted for the polynomial. This two-word format made naming more convenient and provided a readily expandable system. Our present formal nomenclature began with the publication of Linnaeus's *Species plantarum* (1753). Since 1753 nomenclatural procedures have become standardized through periodic legalistic revision so that plants are not named haphazardly.

Scientific Names versus Common Names

Latinized scientific names often appear formidable. There is a natural inclination to avoid words with unfamiliar and difficult pronunciations. Although scientific names may be difficult to pronounce, guides to pronunciation do exist (Johnson, 1971). To help in remembering names, Appendix 1 provides the meanings of some Latinized names.

Why do botanists use Latinized scientific names instead of common names? Common names present a number of problems. First, common or vernacular names are not universal and may be applied only in a single language. (Scientific names, on the other hand, are universal and are recognized throughout the world.) Second, common names usually do not provide information indicating the generic and family relationships. Third, if a plant is well known, it may have a dozen or more common names. For example, *Chrysanthemum leucanthemum* is called daisy, white daisy, ox-eye daisy, shasta daisy, or white weed; *Centaurea cyanus* is variously known as cornflower, bluebottle, bachelor's button, or ragged robin. Fourth, sometimes two or more plants may have the same common name. In Georgia, *Sida* in the family Malvaceae is called ironweed; but in the Midwest, *Vernonia* in the family Compositae is called ironweed. Fifth, many species, particularly rare ones, do not have common names.

Composition of Scientific Names

The genus name and specific epithet together form a binomial called the *species name*. The term *species name* is often erroneously used to refer to the specific epithet alone, but the species name consists of both the generic name and the specific epithet. A complete scientific name must be followed by the third element, the name of the person or persons who formally described the plant. For example, the complete scientific name for white oak is *Quercus alba* Linnaeus; the genus is *Quercus,* the specific epithet *alba,* and the author citation Linnaeus. The author element of a name is often abbreviated, and "L." is normally used for the authority in place of "Linnaeus." To be correct, the species name of white oak is not *"alba,"* but is *Quercus alba* L. Therefore, a complete scientific name of a species consists of three elements: (1) the genus (plural, genera), (2) the specific epithet, and (3) the author citation.

Generic Names   The generic name is a singular Latinized noun or a word treated as a noun. It is always written with an initial capital letter. After a generic name has been spelled out at least once, it may be abbreviated by using the initial capital letter; for example, *"Q."* for *Quercus.* Generic names may not consist of two words unless they are joined with a hyphen. Latin inflectional endings are used for both generic names and specific epithets. Section 3 of the International Code of Botanical Nomenclature deals with what makes a generic name. Stearn's *Botanical Latin* (1983) is an excellent reference for the mechanics and grammar of botanical Latin.

The name may be taken from any source, and it may commemorate some person of distinction. Genera such as *Linnaea* for Linnaeus or *Jeffersonia* for Thomas Jefferson are commemorative. Many ancient common names, such as *Asparagus* and *Narcissus,* were converted into generic names directly from Greek. Features of plants, such as the liverlike leaves of *Hepatica,* gave generic names to still others, the word *Hepatica* being derived from the Latin word for liver. Information about a plant is sometimes expressed in a generic name because it indicates in a general way the kind of plant under consideration. With familiar genera we can recognize the plants by their generic names, for example, *Rosa* as a rose and *Pinus* as a pine, both of which are ancient colloquial names.

Specific Epithets   Specific epithets may be derived from any source and may honor a person, or they may be derived from an old common name, a geographic location, or some characteristic of the plant, or they may even be composed arbitrarily (see Article 23 of the Code). The specific epithet is often an adjective illustrating a distinguishing feature of the species. Specific epithets consisting of two words must be hyphenated, as in the case of *Capsella bursa-pastoris* (L.) Medic.

The specific epithet usually agrees with the gender of the generic name if the specific epithet is an adjective. If the specific name is an adjective placed in a genus that has the masculine ending *-us,* a species might be spelled *albus,* but if it is a genus with a feminine spelling, it would be spelled *alba.* In spite of its *-us* ending, *Quercus* is feminine for the purposes of botanical Latin: thus, *Quercus alba.* It is customary to treat all trees in botanical Latin as feminine, as was usually the situation in classical Latin. A specific epithet may also be a noun in apposition carrying its own gender. When the noun is in apposition, it is normally in the nominative case—for example, *Pyrus malus* for the common apple. When a specific epithet is named after a person and ends in a vowel or *-er,* the letter *-i* is added (e.g., *glazioui*), but if it ends in a consonant, the letters *-ii* are added (e.g., *ramondii*) (Recommendation 73C of the Code). When named for a female, it ends in *-iae* or *-ae;* e.g., *luciliae.* Specific epithets derived from geographical names usually are terminated by *-ensis, -(a)nus, -inus,*

-ianus, or *-icus;* examples are *quebecensis, philadelphicus,* and *carolinianus* (Recommendation 73D).

The Code recommends that all specific epithets be written with a small initial letter, but capital letters may be used when epithets are derived from a person's name, from former generic names, or from common names. Both the generic name and the specific epithet are customarily underlined when written or typed; when printed, they are in italics or boldface. The author citation is never underlined.

Author   The name of the person or persons following the genus and specific epithet indicates the author. It is a source of historical information regarding the name of the plant (Clausen, 1938). By giving the author's name, one may discriminate among names. The author citation may be abbreviated; for example, "L." for Linnaeus or "Michx." for André Michaux. Frequently a name will have two authors, with the first in parentheses. For example, with *Vernonia acaulis* (Walter) Gleason, the positioning of these two authors shows that this species was first described by Walter, who supplied the specific epithet *acaulis.* Walter put it in a genus other than *Vernonia,* and at some later point Gleason transferred this species to *Vernonia.* When the rank of a taxon is changed or when a species is transferred from one genus to another, the name of the describing author is placed in parentheses and is followed by the name of the person who made the change. Transfers are sometimes necessary in taxonomic studies when new information suggests that taxonomic boundaries be realigned. Name changes should be made only after careful consideration of taxonomic relationships and must follow the requirements of the International Code of Botanical Nomenclature (Weatherby, 1946).

RULES OF NOMENCLATURE

The increased number of plants known to European botanists in the eighteenth century required the development of order and stability in plant nomenclature. The first elemental rules of naming plants were proposed by Linnaeus in 1737 and again in 1751. In the latter part of the eighteenth century, *priority,* or the use of the oldest name, was recognized as the cornerstone of nomenclature, ensuring that each plant had a unique name. Botanists who did not adhere to this principle created confusion in the naming of plants. A. P. de Candolle in his *Théorie élémentaire de la botanique* (1813), set forth a detailed set of rules on the process of assigning names. Later, the rules of A. P. and A. de Candolle evolved into our present International Code of Botanical Nomenclature. Numerous plants were inescapably named two or more times by accident, so in the years following Linnaeus a complex synonymy developed. Steudel in 1821 and 1840–1841 published an index of plant names, *Nomenclator botanicus,* which listed all names known to have been assigned to plants. This was useful for checking names and synonyms. It was the forerunner of *Index kewensis* (discussed in Chapter 11).

In 1867 the First International Botanical Congress was convened in Paris by Alphonse de Candolle, the son of A. P. de Candolle. Botanists from many countries met and adopted a set of rules for nomenclature. Most of the rules had been proposed by Alphonse de Candolle. The rules were an excellent beginning, but practical applications revealed some inherent deficiencies. The need to modify the rules became evident in the late 1800s when botanists at Kew Gardens in England, at the Botanical Gardens at Berlin, at the New York Botanical Garden, and elsewhere began to stray from the rules adopted in Paris.

Botanical Congresses were held in 1892, 1905, 1907, and 1910 in an attempt to resolve nomenclatural problems and establish internationally acceptable rules. Nomenclatural procedures were standardized on a worldwide basis with general agreement reached by the International Botanical Congress of 1930. Subsequent Congresses have been held on a regular basis and have offered only minor modifications in the rules. A detailed history of the development of the Code is discussed in Lawrence (1951) and Smith (1957). Many of the terms used in the Code are elaborated upon and easy to find in McVaugh, Ross, and Stafleu (1968).

Developments and changes in the Code are often discussed in the journal *Taxon*, published by the International Association for Plant Taxonomy.

Principles

Today botanists throughout the world use the International Code of Botanical Nomenclature, which is written in English, French, and German (Voss, 1983). A set of nomenclatural principles forms the philosophical basis of the Code:

1 "Botanical nomenclature is independent of zoological nomenclature. The Code applies equally to names of taxonomic groups treated as plants whether or not these groups were originally so treated." The first part of this is of practical concern; that is, the Code provides solely for the nomenclature of plants. The same name that has been assigned to a plant may also be used by zoologists for naming an animal. For example, *Cecropia* refers both to a moth and to a large genus of tropical trees in the family Moraceae.

2 "The application of names of taxonomic groups is determined by means of nomenclatural types." The "type" principle provides that each species name must be associated with a particular specimen, the nomenclatural type. The type for a genus is a species, for a family it is a genus, and so on.

3 "The nomenclature of a taxonomic group is based upon the priority of publication." This very important principle provides that the correct name is the earliest properly published name that conforms to the rules. Earliest published names take precedence over names of the same rank published later. Priority for plant nomenclature begins May 1, 1753 for vascular plants and some other groups, but not for all plants. This was the date of publication of the first edition of Linnaeus' *Species plantarum*.

4 "Each taxonomic group with a particular circumscription, position, and rank can bear only one correct name, the earliest that is in accordance with the rules, except in specified cases."

5 "Scientific names of taxonomic groups are treated as Latin regardless of their derivation." This rule requires that generic and specific epithets, as well as other names, be Latin or treated as if they were Latin. The Code must be consulted for details on selecting the proper grammatical endings for names of all taxa.

6 "The rules of nomenclature are retroactive unless expressly limited."

Rules adopted by the Congresses operate to affect nomenclatural matters carried out before the passing of the rules. Botanists should consult the latest International Code of Botanical Nomenclature when confronted with solving current nomenclatural problems.

Procedures

Detailed procedures based upon these principles are divided into *Rules* and *Recommendations*. The Code states, "The objective of the Rules is to put the nomenclature of the past into order and to provide for that of the future; names contrary to a rule cannot be maintained." The Recommendations dealing with minor points provide guidance and uniformity in naming plants. However, names that are contrary to the Recommendations cannot be rejected for that reason.

Ranks of Taxa

The formal taxonomic hierarchy is a system of categorical ranks with associated names (Scott, 1973). Generally, the species is the basic unit of classification (Article 2). Each species belongs to a series of taxa of consecutively higher rank. The International Code of Botanical Nomenclature provides the series of ranks with names that are the hierarchical categories (Articles 3 and 4). The ranks, in descending sequence, provided by the Code are shown in Table 3-1, along with an example of each.

The Code, in effect, defines the categories only by listing their sequence. It may not be necessary to use all the categories provided by the Code for a small order, family, or genus, but the sequence of categories must not change (Article 5). However, certain categories (i.e., species, genus, family) are essential if nomenclature is to function. The categories commonly used in the flowering plants are the class, subclass, order, family, genus, species, and sometimes either subspecies or variety or even sometimes both. Categories such as subfamily, tribe, subgenus, section, and so on may be used and are frequently necessary in large and complex groups. In actual practice, species are grouped into genera and genera into families and so on through the sequence of categories. Each rank in turn is more inclusive than the lower categories. This categorization gives order and accessibility to the classification of plants and provides a meaningful system of information input or retrieval.

The Code requires standardized grammatical endings for the categories from division down to subtribe. However, an exception is the use of certain family names which have been sanctioned by the Code because of old, traditional usage. These names do not end in the usual family ending of *-aceae* (Article 18). The names of these families, along with their alternative names, are Palmae (Arecaceae), Gramineae (Poaceae), Cruciferae (Brassicaceae), Leguminosae (Fabaceae), Guttiferae (Clusiaceae), Umbelliferae (Apiaceae), Labiatae (Lamiaceae), and Compositae (Asteraceae). Botanists are

TABLE 3-1
SERIES OF RANKS PROVIDED BY THE INTERNATIONAL CODE OF BOTANICAL NOMENCLATURE

Ranks of taxa	Example	Endings of ranks above genus
Division	Magnoliophyta	-phyta
Class	Magnoliopsida	-opsida
Subclass	Asteridae	-idae
Order	Asterales	-ales
Suborder		inales
Family	Asteraceae (or Compositae)	-aceae
Subfamily		-oideae
Tribe	Vernonieae	-eae
Subtribe	Vernonineae	-ineae
Genus	Vernonia	
Subgenus		
Section	Lepidoploa	
Subsection	Paniculatae	
Series	Verae	
Subseries		
Species	Vernonia angustifolia Michx.	
Subspecies	V. angustifolia ssp. angustifolia	
Variety		
Subvariety		
Form		
Subform		

44

authorized by the Code to use either of these alternatives. Some manuals use the older names and others use the -*aceae* names. Family names ending with -*aceae* are based on generic names; for example, *Brassica* is the base of Brassicaceae. To follow correct usage, family names are treated grammatically as plural nouns.

The Type Method

Names are established by reference to a nomenclatural type. Taxonomists use the type method as a legal device to provide the correct name for a taxon. The nomenclatural type of a species, a *type specimen,* is a single specimen or the plants on a single herbarium sheet. The type specimen for the species *Vernonia alamanii* DC. is located in the de Candolle Herbarium in Geneva, Switzerland. The type of genus is a species; for example, the type of the genus *Vernonia* is *V. noveboracensis* (L.) Michx. The type of family is a genus; for instance, the genus *Aster* is the type genus for the family Compositae (Asteraceae).

The nomenclatural type is not necessarily the most representative of a taxon; it is the specimen or specimens with which the name of that taxon is permanently associated, whether it is a correct name or a synonym. The type specimen in no way reflects the typological concept of an idealized specimen (as discussed in Chapter 1). The type specimen has nothing at all to do with variation but only indicates the attachment of a name to a particular specimen.

When a species new to science is collected, several things must be done: (1) it is given a name; (2) a Latin diagnosis or description is prepared; (3) a type is designated; and (4) the name and description are published. All these must be done in accordance with the Code. An example of a publication of the name and description of a new species is shown in Table 3-2. In this description, a type was designated and deposited in the New York Botanical Garden Herbarium and a Latin description was provided (see Article 7 and the Guide for the Determination of Types).

The Code designates several kinds of types (Article 7). The *holotype* for the name of a species is the one specimen used or designated by the author in the original publication as the nomenclatural type. If a holotype was designated by the author, it may not be rejected; and any type chosen after the original publication cannot be regarded as the holotype. Today it is essential that a holotype be designated for a newly described species and deposited in an established public herbarium.

An *isotype* is a duplicate specimen of a holotype collected at the same place and time as the holotype. A *lectotype* is a specimen chosen by a later worker from original material studied by the author of the species, when no holotype was designated or when the holotype has been lost or destroyed. A *syntype* is one of two or more specimens cited by an author of a species when no holotype was designated, or it is any one or two or more specimens originally designated as types. A *paratype* is cited in the original publication. It is a specimen other than the holotype or isotype. If the author cited two or more specimens as types, the remaining cited specimens are paratypes. A *neotype* is selected when all the original specimens and their duplicates have been lost or destroyed. If there is no holotype, a lectotype must be selected from among the isotypes or syntypes. If none are known to exist, a neotype may be selected. A

TABLE 3-2
DESCRIPTION OF A SPECIES NEW TO SCIENCE

Vernonia cronquistii S. B. Jones, sp. nov. TYPE: México: Guerrero: semi-open slopes in pine-oak forest in the mountains along the highway ca. 62 rd miles N of Acapulco, and 20 mi S of Chilpancingo, *Cronquist* 9705 (Holotype: NY! Isotypes: GH! MEX! MICH! MO! NY!).

Herba perennis, erecta, 1.5-metralis; caules purpurei necnon glabri. Folia caulina (6.5) 8–12 (15) cm longa, 1.9–4.5 cm lata (ratione longitudinis cum latitudine ca. 3–4), ad medium dilatata, ovato-lanceolata, supra scabridiuscula, infra glabrescentia, apicibus acuminatis, basibus anguste cuneatis, marginibus serratis; petioli 0.5–1.2 cm longi glabrescentes. Inflorescentiae paniculatae-umbellatae. Capitula 10–14(18)-flora, cum pedunculis 0.5–1.3 cm longis. Involucra anguste campanulata 5.5–8.5 mm longa, 3–7.5 mm lata; phyllaria ciliata, laxe imbricata, purpurea, eis interioribus lineari-lanceolatis, 4.2–7.5 mm longis, 0.9–1.5 mm latis, apicibus acutis vel cuspidatis, eis exterioribus lanceolatis, 1–2 mm longis, 0.6–0.9 mm latis. Pappi setae albae, eis interioribus 5–6.1 mm longis, eis exterioribus 0.6–1.1 mm longis. Corollae (7.3) 9–11 (12.6) mm longae, Vernoniapurpureae, glabrae. Antherae 2.7–3.3 mm longae. Achaenia 2.2–3.1 mm longa, piloso-hispida, ca. 9–11 nervata. Chromosome number $n = 17$. Flowering and fruiting occur from October to December. This species is distributed from Guerrero to Oaxaca along the Sierra Madre del Sur . . . It occurs on semi-open slopes in pine-oak or pine forests at elevations of 700–950 m. It is named in honor of Dr. Arthur Cronquist who made the type collection and has provided encouragement to me with my studies of *Vernonia*.

Additional specimens examined include: Mexico: Guerrero: Rincón de la Via, *Kruse* 739 ((ENCB); Plan de Carrizo, Galeana, *Hinton* 11035 (GH, K, MICH, NY, US); Oaxaca: 5–6 km NE Putla rd to Tlaxiaco, *McVaugh* 22273 (ENCB, MICH).*

---

*The specimens named in the last paragraph are paratypes. *Source: Rhodora,* **78:194,** 1973.

lectotype has precedence over a neotype because a lectotype was studied by the original author.

The early botanists did not designate types as is done today. To these early botanists, species were based upon all specimens, illustrations, and descriptions within the limits of the species. These elements or everything associated with the name at first publication are known collectively as the *protologue*. Recommendation 7B of the Code suggests that when the elements of the protologue are heterogeneous, the lectotype should be selected to preserve current usage.

Priority of Names

Priority is concerned with the precedence of the date of valid publication and determines the acceptance of one of two or more names that are otherwise acceptable. A name is said to be *legitimate* if it is in accordance with the rules and *illegitimate* if it is contrary to the rules (Article 6). The rule of priority states, "For any taxon from family to genus inclusive, the correct name is the earliest legitimate one with the same rank, except in cases of limitation of priority by conservation" (Article 11). The Code contains several limitations on the principle of priority. "The principle of priority does not apply to names of taxa above the rank of family" (Article 11).

To avoid disadvantageous changes caused by strict application of priority, some specific, generic, and family names are conserved by action of the International Botanical Congresses (Article 14). Conserved names are referred to as *nomina conservanda*. This means that some names, even though they are not the oldest legitimate names, are used in preference to the older names. Occasionally, family or generic names, perhaps published in obscure publications or otherwise not used, will have priority over well-known names despite not having been in regular use. Adoption of such generic names usually requires formally transferring specific epithets to the resurrected genus. To avoid the confusion this would cause, names are conserved by decisions of an International Botanical Congress. A list of the conserved family and generic names may be found in Appendixes 2 and 3 of the Code. Conservation of specific names is restricted to names of species of major economic importance (Greuter, 1981). The conservation of specific names was authorized only recently at the International Botanical Congress held at Sydney, Australia in 1981.

Priority of nomenclature for vascular plants (except fossils) begins with the publication of Linnaeus' *Species plantarum* on May 1, 1753 (Article 13).

Effective and Valid Publication of Names

To become a part of the legal botanical nomenclature, names of taxa must meet certain requirements when published. These requirements are explicitly stated by the Code. "Publication is effected, under this Code, only by distribution of printed matter (through sale, exchange, or gift) to the general public or at least to botanical institutions with libraries accessible to botanists generally. It is not effected by communication of new names at a public meeting, by the placing of names in collections or gardens open to the public, or by the issue of microfilm made from manuscripts, typescripts or other unpublished material. Offer for sale of printed matter that does not exist does not constitute publication" (Article 29).

Currently, publication of handwritten descriptions or descriptions printed in nursery catalogs or seed exchange lists is not considered to be effective publication (Article 29). A plant name is not effectively published if printed on a label attached to herbarium specimens even if the specimens are widely distributed (Article 31). Effective publication refers to the place and form of publication of the names of plants. The botanical community must communicate plant names in widely distributed scientific literature.

For valid publication, a name must be *effectively published* in the form specified by the Code. It must be accompanied by a description or a reference to a previously published description for that taxon (Article 32). Since 1935 all diagnoses of new taxa (algae and fossil plants are excepted) must be written in Latin to be validly published. The *diagnosis* is a statement by the author giving the distinguishing features of the taxon. The description itself need not be in Latin, although it is recommended. (See Table 3-2.)

Citation of Author's Name

To be accurate and complete, the name of a taxon should include a citation of the author or authors who originally described that taxon (Article 46): for example, *Vernonia arkansana* DC., for A. P. de Candolle; *Vernonia* Schreb., for J. D. C. von

Schreber; and the tribe Vernonieae Cass., for Henri Cassini. There are many sources of explanations of abbreviated names of authors, including the *Manual of the Vascular Plants of Texas* (Correll and Johnston, 1970), Gray's *Manual of Botany* (Gray, 1950) and the *Draft Index for Author Abbreviations* (1980) prepared at the Royal Botanic Gardens, Kew, England.

The author citation expedites locating the original plant description, which helps determine the type and date of publication for the taxon (Clausen, 1938). Sources providing references to original descriptions are *Index kewensis* on an international basis and the *Gray Herbarium Index* for New World plants. Either source provides references to the original descriptions. Another function of the author citation is to identify the name. Through unfortunate error an author may publish a name that is preoccupied; that is, the specific epithet may have been used for another taxon in the same genus. The author citation allows the distinction between the two names. Of course, only the earlier name is legitimate. Author citations can aid botanists in tracing the transference of species from one genus to another. For example, the author citation for *Vernonia noveboracensis* (L.) Michx. reveals that André Michaux transferred to the genus *Vernonia* a species originally described in another genus by Linnaeus. The original species name used by Linnaeus was *Serratula noveboracensis* L. Since *Serratula* L. was published in 1753 and *Vernonia* Schreb. in 1791, it appears as though *Vernonia* violates the rule of priority. Reference to Appendix 3 of the Code indicates that *Vernonia* Schreb., (1791) nom. cons., non L. 1753, has been conserved by international agreement over *Serratula* L. 1753, so Michaux's combination is legitimate.

When names are published by two authors, the author citations are linked by either *&* or *et* (Latin, "and")—for instance, *Opuntia pollardii* Britt. et Rose, for N. L. Britton and J. N. Rose. The author citation *Carex stipata* Muhl. ex Willd. indicates that the name was ascribed to G. H. E. Muhlenberg but was published by K. L. Willdenow, who attributed the name to Muhlenberg. When a name with a description supplied by one author is published in a work by another author, the word *in* should be used to connect the names of the two authors, for example *Viburnum ternatum* Rehder in Sargent.

Retention, Choice, and Rejection of Names

The Code has rules outlining the proper procedures for selecting the correct name when taxa are divided, transferred, or rejected. That is, a genus might be divided into two genera or a species transferred from one genus to another genus; or if a name is illegitimate, it is rejected. A brief synopsis of the major points of the most important rules concerning retention, choice, and rejection of names is presented here. Chapter 5 of the Code should be consulted for a complete account of the topic.

A change in the diagnostic limit separating the taxon from its nearest relatives is not justifiable cause for a change in the name of the taxon (Article 51). For example, change in the concept of diagnostic characters of a genus or species is not a reason to change a name. If a genus is divided into two or more genera, the original generic name is retained for the genus that includes the nomenclatural type species for the genus (Article 52). Likewise, when a species is divided into two or more species, the original specific epithet must be retained for the species that includes the type specimen (Article 53). This same rule applies to infraspecific taxa, that is, subspecies and varieties.

When a species is described in one genus and later transferred to another genus, the specific epithet, if legitimate, must be retained (Article 55). *Chrysocoma acaulis* Walt., 1788, is now treated as *Vernonia acaulis* (Walt.) Gleason, 1906. *Chrysocoma acaulis* Walt. is the *basionym* of *Vernonia acaulis* or the name-bringing synonym associated with Walter's type specimen, which is located in the Museum of National History in Paris. For many years this species was called *Vernonia oligophylla* Michx., 1803. In 1906 Gleason properly recognized that there was an older specific epithet and basionym for this taxon, *C. acaulis* Walt., 1788. If a taxonomist considers two previously distinct species to be the same species, the earlier epithet must be selected for the newly combined species. The latter name is then considered to be a taxonomic synonym. In such cases the identity of the basionym is important in determining the correct name for a species. When a subspecies or variety is transferred to another genus or species, it is no different than transferring specific epithets, for epithets hold their priority within rank (cf. Article 56 and Recommendation 60A). If it is transferred without change of rank, the original epithet must be retained, unless there is some nomenclatural barrier.

When two or more taxa of the same rank are united, the oldest legitimate name or epithet is selected (Article 57). For example, if the genera *Sloanea* L., 1753, *Echinocarpus* Blume, 1825, and *Phoenicosperma* Miq., 1865, are united, *Sloanea* L. is the oldest name and would be correct (Article 57). The other two names become taxonomic synonyms.

When identifying plants, one may notice that many manuals will cite one or more synonyms for certain species treated in that flora. This practice is helpful because familiar names may become synonyms. A fine example of this is Radford et al., *Manual of the Vascular Flora of the Carolinas* (1968). Following the description of *Solidago graminifolia* (L.) Salisbury, they cite as synonyms: *Euthamia graminifolia* (L.) Nutt. -S (for Small, 1933); *S. graminifolia* var. *nuttallii* (Greene) Fernald -F, G (for Fernald, 1950, and Gleason and Cronquist, 1963). From this information you can compare treatments of the taxa in different manuals.

During plant identification work, it may be necessary to refer to taxonomic revisions. In a revision, synonyms will be given in a complex and formal listing after the correct name. The following is an example:

Vernonia leiocarpa DC. Prodr. 5: 31. 1836. TYPE: MEXICO: *Karwinski* s.n. (HOLOTYPE: G-DC, as IDC microfiche G-DC!).

Cacalia leiocarpa (DC.) Kuntze, Rev. Gen. Pl. 2: 970. 1891.

Eremosis leiocarpa (DC.) Gleason, Bull. New York Bot. Gard. 4: 232. 1906.

Eremosis melanocarpa Gleason, Bull. New York Bot. Gard. 4: 232. 1906. TYPE: GUATEMALA: Santa Rosa: Chupadero, *Heyde & Lux 3416* (HOLOTYPE: NY!; ISOTYPES: F! GH! MO! US!).

Vernonia melanocarpa (Gleason) Blake, Contr. Gray Herb. 52: 18. 1917.

Vernonia leiocarpa, the correct name for the species, was published by A. P. de Candolle in *Prodromus,* Volume 5, page 34, in 1836. The type was collected in Mexico by Karwinski s.n. (Latin for *sine numero,* meaning "without [collection] number"). G-DC indicates that the type is located in the de Candolle Prodromus herbarium at the Conservatoire Botanique de Genéve, Switzerland. Each herbarium is assigned an abbreviation by the International Association for Plant Taxonomy. These abbreviations are found in Holmgren, Keuken, and Schofield (1981). The type specimen was viewed on IDC microfiche of the de Candolle Prodromus herbarium. The exclamation point (!) is an abbreviation for *vidi* (Latin, "I have seen it"), and it indicates that the author of the revision has seen the specimen cited.

Synonyms in a revision are listed in chronological order. For example, in 1891 Kuntze transferred the specific epithet to the genus *Cacalia,* making the combination *Cacalia leiocarpa* (DC.) Kuntze. In 1906 Gleason made the combination *Eremosis leiocarpa* (DC.) Gleason, by transferring *V. leiocarpa* DC. to *Eremosis.* Gleason also described *Eremosis melanocarpa* Gleason, based on the type collected in Guatemala by Heyde and Lux. *3416* is the collection number of the particular specimen of Heyde and Lux. This holotype is located in NY (New York Botanical Garden) and was examined by the author of the revision, as indicated by "!." Isotypes examined are located in F (Field Museum), GH (Gray Herbarium), MO (Missouri Botanical Garden), and US (United States National Museum). Blake did not recognize *Eremosis* and transferred the specific epithet *melanocarpa* to *Vernonia.* The result was the combination *Vernonia melanocarpa* (Gleason) Blake. The author of this taxonomic revision believed *V. melanocarpa* to be a taxonomic synonym of *V. leiocarpa.* A review of the formal taxonomic treatment provides a taxonomic history of the entity. There is a growing and useful practice to give all the names based on the same type specimen in one paragraph, thus using a paragraph for each basionym, its nomenclatural type, and its taxonomic synonyms. The *basionym* is the epithet with which the type is associated.

Another important rule of the Code is the following: "A legitimate name or epithet must not be rejected merely because it is inappropriate or disagreeable, or because another is preferable or better known, or because it has lost its original meaning" (Article 62). Therefore, the name *Scilla peruviana* cannot be rejected because it grows in the Mediterranean area rather than in Peru. *Vernonia crinita* Raf. is better known than the older *V. arkansana* DC., but *V. crinita* Raf. cannot be retained just because it is better known.

A name is a *later homonym* if it is spelled like a name previously and validly published for a taxon of the same rank based on a different type (Article 64). Different genera or different species within a genus cannot have the same name. If they do, the earlier name is legitimate and the later name is a later homonym. *Tapeinanthus* Boiss. ex Benth, 1848, is a later homonym of *Tapeinanthus* Herb., 1837. *Astragalus rhizanthus* Boiss., 1843, is illegitimate because it is a later homonym of *Astragalus rhizanthus* Royle, 1835.

The Code deals with other matters, including spelling of names and epithets (Nicolson, 1974; Nicolson and Brooks, 1974). The names of plants must be spelled as they were originally published unless there was a spelling or typographic error (Article 73).

A frequent source of confusion is the naming of infraspecific taxa (Clausen, 1941; Fosberg, 1942; Weatherby, 1942). If a subspecies or variety is described in a species not previously divided into infraspecific taxa, there is automatically a "type" subspecies or variety. This bears the same epithet as the species but is not followed by an author citation. This means that a species with infraspecific taxa must have at least two subspecies or varieties. For example, the two subspecies of *Vernonia obtusa* (Blake) Gleason are *Vernonia obtusa* subsp. *obtusa* and *Vernonia obtusa* (Blake) Gleason subsp. *parkeri* S. B. Jones (Subsp. *obtusa* is not followed by an author citation.) The Code requires that the epithet be repeated and the original type specimen be the type of subsp. *obtusa*. The logic for this is simple. Creation of a subspecies (or variety) automatically creates two subspecies: (1) the entity that the author has in mind when erecting the new subspecies, and (2) the remaining materials within the species. The former receives the new name (e.g., *Vernonia obtusa* subsp. *parkeri* S. B. Jones), while the latter is signified by repetition of the specific epithet (e.g., *Vernonia obtusa* subsp. *obtusa*). Names such as *Vernonia obtusa* subsp. *obtusa* are termed *autonyms* or automatically established names. For a discussion of some of the nomenclatural problems related to autonyms, the reader is referred to the paper by Reveal and Broome (1980).

Hybrids between different species in the same genus or between closely related genera are sometimes described and named. In order to be validly published, the names of hybrids follow the same rules as those that relate to names of nonhybrids (Article 40). Additional rules and recommendations needed for the naming of hybrids are found in the Code in Appendix 1, Names of Hybrids. Some of the more important points include the following: Hybrids between two species of the same genus are shown either by a formula—for instance, *Salix aurita* L. × *S. caprea* L.; or if desired, by a formal name—for example, *Quercus* × *beadlei* Trel., a hybrid of *Q. alba* L. × *Q. michauxii* Nutt. It is permissible under the Code to refer to them by formula or to give them a name (binomial). The opinions of plant taxonomists differ as to whether hybrids should or should not be named (Wagner, 1969, 1975).

Cultivated Plants

Article 28 of the Code deals with nomenclature for cultivated plants. Plants brought in from the wild and cultivated retain the names applied to the same taxa in their native habitat (Article 28). Horticultural plants that are produced in cultivation through hybridization, selection, or other processes and that are worthy of being named receive cultivar names. The term *cultivar* denotes an assemblage of cultivated plants that is clearly distinguished by any characters (morphological, physiological, cytological, chemical, or other), and that, following reproduction (sexual or asexual), retains its distinguishing characters (Brickwell, 1980). *Cultivar* is derived from the terms *cultivated variety*. It should be noted that the concept of the cultivar is not analogous to the botanical variety (*varietas*), the latter being a category below that of species and governed as such by the International Code of Botanical Nomenclature. Cultivar names are written with a capital initial letter. They are either preceded by the abbreviation cv. (meaning "cultivar") or placed in single inverted commas, for example, *Hosta* 'Decorata.' Cultivar names may be used after generic, specific, or common names. Examples of cultivars are *Camelia japonica* cv. Purple Dawn and *Citrullus* cv. Crimson Sweet (or watermelon cv. Crimson Sweet, or *Citrullus lanatus* cv. Crimson Sweet). The use of the term variety to refer to cultivars is improper, but the usage was traditional for a long time and is only now going out of style (Stuart, 1974).

Detailed information on specialized nomenclatural situations dealing with cultivated plants may be found in the International Code of Nomenclature for Cultivated Plants (Brickell, 1980). The nomenclature for cultivated plants must follow this Code. Some of the more important general rules governing cultivar names are the following:

1 New cultivar names must now be in modern languages and not be Latin names. For example, the Latin '*albo-marginata*' cannot be given to a new cultivar. The only exceptions to this are names of botanical taxa reduced to cultivar ranks.

2 If the botanical name of a species is changed, the cultivar name remains unchanged. For instance, if the scientific name of the tomato should be changed to conform with the Botanical Code, the cultivar names, such as 'Better Boy' or 'Ultra Girl,' remain unchanged.

3 Two or more cultivars in the same cultivar class are not permitted to bear the same name. A cultivar class is usually a genus but may also be a species, a crop type, or a group of cultivars. For example, since there is already a *Hosta* 'Decorata,' a second *H*. 'Decorata' could not be named.

4 Since January 1, 1959, new cultivar names must not be the same as a botanical or common name of a genus or a species. Thus, names such as *Hosta* cv. 'Rose' would not be permitted.

5 New cultivar names published after January 1, 1959, require a published or duplicated description that may be given in any language and dated at least to the year.

6 It is recommended that cultivar names be registered with a registration authority to prevent duplication or misuse of cultivar names. For example, the American Hosta Society acts as the registration authority for cultivars of the genus *Hosta*.

SUMMARY

The International Code of Botanical Nomenclature is a response to the fact that science requires a precise system of naming plants. The Code deals with the terms used to denote the ranks of taxa as well as with the scientific names applied to plants. There are valid reasons for the occasional but necessary changes of familiar plant names. Examples and problems for practice with the application of the Code may be found in St. John (1958) and Benson (1962). The use of the case method with these problems is an excellent way for a potential taxonomist to develop a working knowledge of the Code.

Davis and Heywood (1963) observe, "To most systematists, however, nomenclature is a time-consuming necessity that comes between them and the plant. Nevertheless, it is one of the tools of the taxonomists' trade and for that reason its principles must be mastered." It should be emphasized that for detailed knowledge of the rules of nomenclature, the Code itself must be consulted. Here we have considered only general principles and some of the more important points.

SELECTED REFERENCES

American Joint Committee on Horticultural Nomenclature: *Standardized Plant Names,* 2d ed., H. B. Kelsey and W. A. Dayton (eds.), J. Horace McFarland Co., Harrisburg, Pa., 1942.

Benson, L.: *Plant Taxonomy, Methods and Principles,* Ronald, New York, 1962.

Brickell, C. D. (ed.): "International Code of Nomenclature for Cultivated Plants—1980," *Regnum Veg.,* **104,** 1980.

Candolle, A. P. de: *Théorie élémentaire de la botanique,* Paris, 1813.

Clausen, R. T.: "On the Citation of Authorities for Botanical Names," *Science (Wash. D.C.),* **88:**299–300, 1938.

————: "On the Use of the Terms 'Subspecies' and 'Variety'," *Rhodora,* **43:**157–167, 1941.

Clusius, C. [l'Écluse, C. de]: *Rariorum aliquot stirpium,* 1583. (Facsimile, Akademische Druck-U. Verlagsanstalt, Graz, Austria, 1965.)

"Composite List of Weeds," *Weed Sci.,* **19:**437–476, 1971.

Correll, D. S., and M. C. Johnston: *Manual of the Vascular Plants of Texas,* Texas Research Foundation, Renner, Tex., 1970.

Davis, P. H., and V. H. Heywood: *Principles of Angiosperm Taxonomy,* Van Nostrand, Princeton, N.J., 1963.

Draft Index of Author Abbreviations, H. M. Stationary Office, London, 1980.

Fernald, M. L. See Gray, A.

Fosberg, F. R.: "Subspecies and Variety," *Rhodora,* **44:**153–157, 1942.

Gray, A.: *Manual of Botany,* 8th ed., M. L. Fernald (ed.), American Book, New York, 1950.

Greuter, W.: "XIII International Botanical Congress," *Taxon,* **30:**904–911, 1981.

Harvard University, Gray Herbarium: *Gray Herbarium Index,* 10 vols., G. K. Hall and Co., Boston, Mass., 1968.

Heller, J. C.: "The Early History of Binomial Nomenclature," *Huntia,* **1:**33–70, 1964.

Holmgren, P. K., W. Keuken, and E. K. Schofield: "Index Herbariorum," *Regnum Veg.,* **106,** 1981.

Index kewensis plantarum phanerogamarum, 2 vols., 15 suppl., Oxford, 1893–1970.

Jeffrey, C.: *Biological Nomenclature,* 2d ed., E. Arnold, London, 1977.

Johnson, A. T.: *Plant Names Simplified,* 2d ed., W. H. & L. Collingridge Ltd., London, 1971.

Kelsey, H. P. See American Joint Committee on Horticultural Nomenclature.

Lawrence, G. H. M.: *Taxonomy of Vascular Plants,* Macmillan, New York, 1951.

Linnaeus, C.: *Critica botanica,* Leyden, 1737.

————: *Philosophia botanica,* Stockholm, 1751. (Translated into English by H. Rose, 1775.)

————: *Species plantarum,* 2 vols., Stockholm, 1753. (Facsimile edition: London, 1957–1959.)

McVaugh, R., R. Ross, and F. A. Stafleu: "An Annotated Glossary of Botanical Nomenclature," *Regnum Veg.,* **56,** 1968.

National List of Scientific Plant Names, 2 vols., U.S. Dept. of Agriculture, Soil Conservation Service, Washington, D.C., 1982.

Nicolson, D. H.: "Orthography of Names and Epithets: Latinization of Personal Names," *Taxon,* **23:**549–561, 1974.

————— and R. A. Brooks: "Orthography of Names and Epithets: Stems and Compound Words,"
    Taxon, **23:**163–177, 1974.
Radford, A. E., H. E. Ahles, and C. R. Bell: *Manual of the Vascular Flora of the Carolinas,*
    The University of North Carolina Press, Chapel Hill, 1968.
Reveal, J. L. and C. R. Broome: "Autonyms and New Confusion in the International Code,"
    Taxon, **29:**495–498, 1980.
Rollins, R. C.: "The Need for Care in Choosing Lectotypes," *Taxon,* **21:**635–637, 1972.
St. John, H.: *Nomenclature of Plants,* Ronald, New York, 1958.
Scott, P. J.: "A Consideration of the Category in Classification," *Taxon,* **22:**405–406, 1973.
Smith, A. C.: "Fifty Years of Botanical Nomenclature," *Brittonia,* **9:**2–8, 1957.
Stafleu, F. A. (ed.): "International Code of Botanical Nomenclature," *Regnum Veg.,* **82,** 1972.
    (Appreciation is extended to Dr. Stafleu for permission to quote passages from the Code.)
Stearn, W. T.: *Botanical Latin,* 3rd ed., David & Charles, Newton Abbot, England, 1983.
Steudel, E. G.: *Nomenclator botanicus,* 2 vols., Stuttgart, 1821–1824.
—————: *Nomenclator botanicus,* 2d ed., 2 vols., Stuttgart, 1841.
Stuart, D. C.: "Some Problems at the Cultivar Level," *Taxon,* **23:**179–184, 1974.
Voss, E. G.: "Synopsis of Proposals on Botanical Nomenclature Sydney 1981," *Taxon,* **30:**95–293,
    1981.
—————: "International Code of Botanical Nomenclature," *Regnum Veg.,* **111,** 1983.
Wagner, W. H.: "The Role and Taxonomic Treatment of Hybrids," *BioScience,* **19:**785–789,
    1969.
—————: "The Spoken 'X' in Hybrid Binomials," *Taxon,* **24:**296, 1975.
Weatherby, C. A.: "Subspecies," *Rhodora,* **44:**157–167, 1942.
—————: "Changes in Botanical Names," *Amer. Midl. Nat.,* **35:**795–796, 1946.
Willis, J. C.: *A Dictionary of the Flowering Plants and Ferns,* 8th ed., revised by H. K. A.
    Shaw, Cambridge, London, 1973.

CHAPTER 4

PRINCIPLES OF PLANT TAXONOMY

Taxonomy is based on the similarities and dissimilarities among organisms. Historically, taxonomy has been a descriptive science based on the variation and form of morphological characters. The classification schemes of the taxonomists of the 1700s and 1800s placed similar-appearing organisms together in species, comparable species into genera, and genera with resemblances into families. Taxonomists sought the "ground plan" of the Creator.

With the advent of Darwinism in the late 1800s, the concepts of species relatedness and evolution were incorporated into classification. Darwin's evolutionary theory provided the concepts that species represent lineages and that species within a genus have evolutionary affinities with one another. Genera and families represent progressively older divergences in the lineages. Before Darwin, it was believed that each species was created individually by God and remained unchanged through time. This is the idea of *special creation,* a hypothesis now rejected by the scientific community.

Because similar appearance often reflects a close relationship, the Darwinian concept of lineages did not radically alter previous classifications. It did lead to the development of deliberate phylogenetic classification schemes. *Phylogenetic classifications* presume to express genetic relationships. In both theory and practice, genera, families, and so on should reflect the notion that the members of each group share a common origin. This concept had little effect on the species, genus, or family levels of classification, but the arrangement of families changed drastically from a linear sequence to a branching format designed to reflect evolutionary relationships.

Today most taxonomic treatments are implicitly phylogenetic. They attempt to recognize and bring together related groups of plants. New research methods have been developed, and taxonomists now use not only gross morphology but also chemistry, anatomy, ultrastructure, and a variety of sophisticated techniques to determine relationships that result in the classification of taxa. Changes in classification occur because of the discovery of new information and in the reinterpretation of existing information.

CATEGORIES

To communicate with others and to sort the vast numbers of plants, systematists name plants and arrange them into a hierarchy of categories. A *hierarchy* is an orderly array composed of a series of inclusive levels called *categories*. The categories are the ranks to which taxa are assigned; for example, species, genus, family, and so on. A diagram of a taxonomic hierarchy is shown in Figure 4-1. The higher categories, such as family or order, are more inclusive than the lower categories of genus or species. Table 3-1 lists the series of hierarchical categories provided by the International Code of Botanical Nomenclature. Although this contains many categories, normally only the order, family, genus, and species are used. The other categories are regularly used to reflect evolutionary relationships in very large and complex groups.

The categories are defined by the Code according to their position relative to other categories. The Code does not define or explain what is meant, in a biological sense, by a species, a genus, or a family. The classifications used in botany are based on the fundamental category of the species. Species are grouped into the higher category of genus, and then genera are grouped into families. Species can be subdivided into lesser categories such as subspecies or varieties.

Monophyletic Requirement of Categories

A *monophyletic* taxon is one derived from one ancestral population system, whereas a *polyphyletic* taxon has been derived from two or more ancestral population systems or taxa. It has become a common principle of systematics that taxa should be monophyletic. If assemblages of plants seem to be polyphyletic, they should be divided into monophyletic groups. Consequently, monophyletic categories at all ranks in the

FIGURE 4-1
A diagram of the common hierarchical categories indicating the increasing inclusive nature of the higher categories. *(Modified from Ross, 1974; with permission.)*

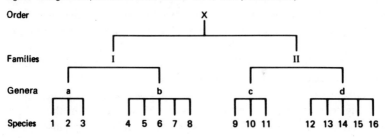

hierarchy express evolutionary lineages and relationships. Because of the sparse fossil record, it is often difficult to determine the origin of the higher ranks in the angiosperms, accounting for differences in contemporary classification systems (Chapter 6). In actual practice, determination of the monophyletic line represents a hypothesis inferred from the study of present-day members of the group.

Species

In taxonomic practice, a group of individual plants that is fundamentally alike is generally treated as a species. Ideally, a species should be separated by distinct mor-phological differences from other closely related species. This is necessary in order to have a practical classification that can be used by others. However, it is sometimes difficult to delimit a species precisely. If each minor variation in plant populations were to be made the basis of species distinction, there would be no end to the number of species. For systematic purposes, differences in features should not be allowed to obscure resemblances.

A species is a concept that cannot be defined in exact terms and is not absolute and inelastic. Rigorous definitions of species are not possible because the criteria may change with the characteristics of each group. Much of the disagreement about what is actually a species is vague or minor and tends to obscure the large amount of agreement on what constitutes a species.

In developing concepts of species, specimens should be regarded as samples of living, reproducing populations of genetically related individuals. Many different kinds of species have developed by diverse evolutionary and genetic mechanisms. Different species may have various strategies of reproductive isolation that reduce or prevent interbreeding. For example, many species are sexual, a few are asexual; some have arisen by polyploidy, changes in chromosome numbers, or other mechanisms. Since species represent lineages, systems of living populations may be found at various stages or levels of morphological divergence from one another in reproductive isolation. The importance of a concept of divergence was stressed by Fosberg (1942), who observed that many kinds of evolutionary processes produced numerous sorts of species at various stages of divergence from one another.

The *biological species concept* envisions the species as a distinct population system of central importance in nature and in evolutionary biology. According to this concept, biological species are kept separate from closely related species inhabiting the same general region by reproductive isolating mechanisms that prevent or greatly reduce gene exchange between them. Two such reproductively isolated species can coexist in the same general area and not lose their identity. In actual taxonomic practice, the biological species concept is difficult to apply to plant species. A diploid and a tetraploid cannot effectively exchange genes; but for practical purposes, different ploidy levels within a morphological species are sometimes regarded as representing the same spe-cies. When many plant species come into contact, they are in some cases able to exchange genes and may produce fertile hybrids. First-generation hybrids between plant species range in fertility from completely fertile to partially or completely sterile.

For this and other reasons, the ability or lack of ability to produce hybrids and exchange genes cannot be used as a general criterion for the erection of species boundaries in most plants.

Mishler and Donoghue (1982) suggest that a variety of species concepts is necessary to capture adequately the complexity of the variation patterns in nature. They urge systematists to develop a pluralistic approach to the criteria establishing species and urge specialists to develop species concepts for their particular taxonomic group reflecting the biology of the group. This is not to say that species are not meaningful groups, but simply the recognition that no one criterion can be used to delimit species in all groups of organisms.

Infraspecific Taxa   A species embraces the variation within its populations. To manage some of the recurring variation, three infraspecific categories are used by plant systematists to provide formal taxonomic recognition of variation within species. These are *subspecies, variety* (Latin, *varietas*), and *form* (Latin, *forma*).

The categories *subspecies* and *variety* are applied to populations of species in various stages of differentiation. A common process of evolution and speciation in many plants is the gradual divergence of a former homogeneous species or population system into two or more diverse population systems (Figure 4-2). Their divergence is usually related to adaptation to differing geographical areas or climates, or to local but sharply distinct ecological habitats. During the process of becoming adapted to different habitats, the local populations become genetically distinct. This genetic differentiation is reflected in both morphology and physiology. Often these differentiated populations, or *ecotypes,* occupy adjacent ranges where they interbreed and intergrade at the points of contact. Consequently, there can be gradual or sharp discontinuities in the variation

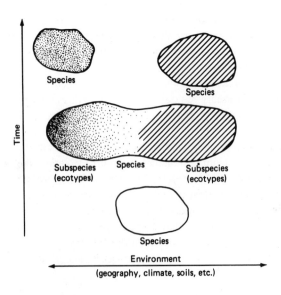

FIGURE 4-2
Differentiation of a single species in a relatively homogeneous environment into subspecies in differing environments, and eventually into two species following further differentiation of the populations.

patterns between the divergent populations, depending on the environmental gradient. These ecotypes most often form the basis of a subspecies or variety. Fosberg (1942) suggests that the stages of divergence can be indicated by the infraspecific category in which the populations are placed. This gives the taxonomist a great deal of flexibility by providing several infraspecific ranks that may be used to fit various evolutionary situations.

Variety was the first infraspecific category to be used for plants. To Linnaeus, it was primarily an environmentally induced variation. The term *subspecies* was introduced early in the 1800s by Persoon (1805–1807) and was considered a major variation in the species. Gray (1887) regarded the variety as a considerable change in the ordinary appearance of a species. In 1926 Hall argued that the term *variety* had so many uses and had been applied to so many different things, from races to cultivars, that its use should be discontinued. Others, such as Fernald, regarded the variety as a geographical subdivision of a species and the subspecies as parts of a species complex. The California school founded by Hall has used the term *subspecies* and the eastern school led by Fernald, Gleason, and Cronquist has favored use of *variety* for the major infraspecific rank.

In usual taxonomic practice, subspecies and varieties are recognizable morphological variations within species. Their populations have their own patterns of variation correlated with geographical distributions or ecological requirements. Whether the category "subspecies" or "variety" is employed often depends on the custom or philosophy of the systematist. Sometimes this is largely based on where or under whom the taxonomist was trained. Also, epithets have priority within rank, and historically some groups have numerous varieties and others, subspecies. If one category is used to the exclusion of the other, it would necessitate a swarm of nomenclatural transfers.

The category *form* is generally used to recognize and describe sporadic variations in a single morphological feature such as occasional white-flowered plants in a normally purple-flowered species. If these white flowers are not correlated with any other features of the plants, including geographical and ecological distributions, they might be described as a form. Little taxonomic significance is attached to the minor and random variation upon which forms are normally based. For this reason, few modern systematists use the rank of form. It is encountered most frequently in older taxonomic treatments or in treatments of horticultural interest.

Genera

Like species, the genus represents a concept. From a practical standpoint, the *genus* is an inclusive category whose species have more characteristics in common with each other than with species of other genera within the same family. Genera, therefore, are aggregates of closely related species (Lane and Turner, 1985). Lawrence (1951) writes that from an evolutionary viewpoint, the genus is an important concept because the sum of all characteristics is used to group closely related species, allowing the genus to be viewed as a unit. The function of the genus concept is to bring together species in a phylogenetic manner by placing the closest related species together within the generic classification (Rollins, 1953).

The genera in some families, for example, Magnoliaceae, show striking differences in features, whereas genera in other families, for instance, Compositae, are separated on less obvious characters. A possible reason for this difference is that extinction of species and genera has been greater in the older families (Magnoliaceae), resulting in well-marked distinctions in features among genera.

There is no size requirement for a genus. A genus consisting of but one species is said to be *monotypic*. *Leitneria* (Leitneriaceae), consisting of a single species, *L. floridana*, is monotypic (Cronquist, 1968). Some genera, such as *Senecio* of the Compositae family, contain 2000 to 3000 species.

Genera must be delimited following a worldwide study of their species. If the deciduous and the evergreen rhododendrons of North America are compared, they appear to be two distinct genera. Some taxonomists in the past have placed the deciduous species in the genus *Azalea*. With wider acquaintance of *Rhododendron* on a worldwide basis, the apparent discontinuities break down. As broadly and ordinarily interpreted, the genus *Rhododendron* includes both the deciduous azaleas and the evergreen rhododendrons of North America.

The collective group of species must be distinct from the other species groups to support two genera. If the species of two genera are not readily separable, most taxonomists would agree that it is more convenient to have larger units of classification. If necessary, the ranks of subgenus or section may be preferable to handle the classification and at the same time express relationships. When a genus is split into two or more genera, nomenclatural changes are required for certain of the species. Such changes may be avoided by the use of the infrageneric ranks because they do not cause changes in binomials. The present tendency in plant systematics is to have a broad, conservative view of generic concepts and limits. This is expressed in a relatively stable generic nomenclature. The category of genus is an old and useful concept that serves both the professional and the amateur botanist. Most colloquial or common names parallel generic concepts—for example, oak, pine, rose, buttercup, sunflower.

Families

Much of what has been said about the concept of the genus applies equally to the concept of the family. Ideally, families should be monophyletic and present both a biologically meaningful treatment and a practical taxonomy.

Both reproductive and vegetative features are used to characterize families (Cronquist, 1968). The parts of the flower and fruits of flowering plants are numerous and varied, and they are subject to little environmental modification. Consequently, they provide more characters for the definition of families than do vegetative features. The category of family is more inclusive than either the genus or the species, and there may be exceptions to certain characters. Families are often delimited by ovary position, kinds of pistils and stamens, carpel number, fruit type, symmetry of the flower, leaf arrangement, leaf morphology, and habit. The use of certain characters to delimit families does not preclude the use of that same character to delimit taxa at higher or lower ranks in the hierarchy. For example, the type of fruit is often used to separate families, but in the Rosaceae it delimits only subfamilies. Some families are recognized easily even by amateurs because of certain distinguishing features including the head (inflorescence) of Compositae, the schizocarp (fruit) and umbel (inflorescence) of Umbelliferae, and the winged schizocarps (fruit) of Aceraceae.

Some families are well defined and are relatively homogeneous, such as the Compositae, Cruciferae, Gramineae, Umbelliferae, and Sarraceniaceae. Leguminosae are a large family characterized by a unique type of fruit and seed, yet family members are not homogeneous. The diversity of the family Leguminosae is reflected by the differing classifications that have appeared from time to time. Some divide the legumes into three families, while others maintain one family with three subfamilies. Taxonomists agree on where the lines should be drawn, but they disagree on the rank to be assigned.

A great diversity of both reproductive and vegetative features may be found in families such as Ranunculaceae, Berberidaceae, and Rosaceae. Families, like genera, do not have a fixed size. The Compositae, one of the largest families of flowering plants, has around 22,000 species; the Leitneriaceae has but a single genus and one species. The size and diversity of plant families are the consequences of their evolutionary history, age, and radiation, coupled with our perception of the taxonomy of the group. Taxonomic schemes are by definition subjective; the whole point of taxonomy is to convey information through a derived scheme.

When distinctions are sharp among closely related families, there is no problem in defining the family. But as Cronquist (1968) wrote regarding whether *Phryma* should be placed in the Verbenaceae or in the Phrymaceae, "It is purely a matter of taste whether the evident relationship [with the Verbenaceae] or the obviously different gynoecium should be emphasized in determining the status of *Phryma,* but assignment of genera to poorly defined families is usually a matter requiring educated judgment." Thirteen years later Cronquist (1981) reversed his stand and included *Phryma* in the Verbenaceae noting, "The unusual gynoecium of *Phryma* is in pattern with other unusual types in the Verbenaceae. I see no value in keeping *Phryma* as a separate family if other peripheral groups are to be retained in the Verbenaceae."

Subjective classification is often criticized by biologists whose training does not include a knowledge of the principles of systematics or taxonomic methods. It may be defended, however, on the grounds of the *predictive value* of classifications developed using these principles. Predictive value suggests that because of their common ancestry the members of a monophyletic group will share some features not apparent at the time the classification was originally made. For example, if one wishes to look for new antitumor alkaloids similar to those found in certain species in the Rutaceae, the best place to look would be in other species of Rutaceae. Examples like this are common and have demonstrated the predictive value of classifications developed by systematists.

Most taxonomists favor broadly conceived family concepts that lend stability to classification. Although there is no clear discontinuity of features between the Labiatae and the Verbenaceae, the two are different, and custom maintains the two groups as separate families (Cronquist, 1968). In some instances, tradition is a taxonomic character. The Rosaceae may be broken into several families based on good logical evidence. However, the overall similarities within the family, rather than its intrafamily differences, has caused most taxonomists to treat the Rosaceae as a single family. Again, there is no set definition for a family; yet, there is relatively little disagreement on family classification. This suggests satisfaction among systematists with the delimitation of most families.

Orders

Orders include one or more families. The monophyletic requirement for establishing orders must be broadly interpreted and should not be too restrictive when developing a workable classification (Cronquist, 1968). Orders are much more difficult to define and delimit than families. The divergence in the lineages, as reflected in orders, occurred early in the evolutionary history of the flowering plants and left few fossil records. Orders and other higher categories are characterized by an aggregate of characters. Generally, there are greater numbers of exceptions at the level of order than at the lower ranks. Most taxonomists agree that orders should be monophyletic, but all do not agree as to their size or to the families included in each. Bessey (1915) used only a few orders with a large number of families. However, Hutchinson (1973) uses many orders that often contain only a few families. The classification used in this text (Cronquist, 1981) takes a somewhat broad approach by arranging the flowering plants into 83 orders. Kubitzki (1977) provides an excellent series of papers on the classification of higher categories.

Typological Concepts of Taxa

Systematists often remember the essential characteristics of a species, genus, or family and represent that taxon in their mind by an image embodying its salient features. This symbolism exemplifies what is meant by typological concepts of taxa. Taxonomists familiar with the flora of an area or traveling in new areas unconsciously use typological methods in recognizing the hundreds of species, genera, and families of the flora. For example, acorns, five-angled pith, and buds clustered at tips of twigs provide a recognition pattern for oaks (*Quercus*). Taxonomists also identify plant materials by comparison with previously identified specimens or by using keys, figures, and descriptions. Since these tools represent only a sample of the populations, a taxonomist builds up typological pictures of species, genera, and families from experience with the plants. As Davis and Heywood (1963) have observed, typology is a valid and necessary process in the identification and classification of plants when intelligently used. Only when its use obscures the natural variation in populations is it a liability to systematics.

CHARACTERS

The *characters* of an organism are all the features or attributes possessed by the organism that may be compared, measured, counted, described, or otherwise assessed. From this definition, it is clear that the differences, similarities, and discontinuities between plants or taxa are reflected in their characters. The characters of a taxon are determined by observing or analyzing samples of individuals and recording the observations, or by conducting controlled experiments. Herbaria contain millions of plant specimens providing a ready source of samples for descriptive plant systematics.

Plant taxonomy uses morphological and anatomical characters for the purposes of classification. Structures are observed with the eye, hand lens, or light microscope or by using scanning electron microscopy (SEM). Modern instrumentation allows comparative studies of physiological rates, such as photosynthesis, and analysis of chemical compounds produced by the plant. For classification purposes, there is increasing use of evidence from fields such as cytology, biogeography, paleobotany, palynology, phytochemistry, population biology, molecular biology, and ultrastructure. But as Cronquist (1975) noted, "For the present at least, comparative study of modern forms, from the eyeball to the SEM level, remains the mainstay of major taxonomic interpretation." He also concluded that because of the time and effort required to obtain molecular data ". . . morphology, in the broad sense, will continue to reign taxonomically supreme for some years to come." Turner (1977), however, disagrees and argues that Cronquist neglects the recent application of chemical data for purposes of classification.

Characters have many uses, including the following: providing information for the construction of taxonomic systems, supplying characters for construction of keys for identification, furnishing features useful in the description and delimitation of taxa, and enabling scientists to use the predictive value of classification.

Characters are such things as leaf width, stamen number, corolla length, locule number, and placentation. Some descriptive or numerical term must occur with the character to imply the *character state*. For example, a leaf width of 5 centimeters and basal placentation are character states. When used in description, delimitation, or identification, characters are said to be *diagnostic* or *key characters*. Characters of a constant nature, which are used to help define a group, are referred to as *synthetic characters*. *Quantitative characters* are those features that can be readily counted or measured, whereas *qualitative characters* are such things as flower color, odor, leaf shape, or pubescence. Quantitative characters are normally easier to obtain and communicate than qualitative characters. Successful observations of qualitative features provide a challenge to plant taxonomists. Another term often used by systematists is *good character*. This implies that the character is genetically determined, largely unaffected by the environment, and relatively constant throughout the populations of the taxa. The more constant a character, the greater is its reliability and resulting importance.

In order to provide character states, there must be differences in the features of flowering plants. Vegetative parts of angiosperms, such as leaves, stems, and roots, are relatively large and easy to observe, but they generally provide fewer characters for classification than reproductive structures, such as sepals, petals, stamens, pistils, and so on.

Clones of genetically identical flowering plants, when grown in diverse environments tend to be relatively uniform in characters of the flower and fruit but highly variable in overall size of the plants and leaves (Clausen, Keck, and Hiesey, 1940). Vegetative features of flowering plants, especially size and shape, tend to be more influenced by environmental factors than are reproductive features. As a result, certain vegetative characters are less reliable and less useful than reproductive characters in taxonomy.

A character that is diagnostic for separating two genera in one family may be a key character for families in another order. Some species are delimited by leaf arrangement, while leaf arrangement is a synthetic character of certain families. Characters become important after they are proved valuable by experience. The relative value and utility of characters are empirically determined, and there is no such thing (in a practical sense) as a "fundamental" character.

A rule of long taxonomic precedence requires that taxa at all ranks be established on the basis of a correlation of several characters, thus avoiding the incongruities of classification constructed on the basis of a single character. Ideally, classifications should be based on an understanding of all characters from every population of each species under consideration. But on a practical basis, this is not possible. Some geographic areas may be better sampled than others, and some characters have simply never been examined. There is not enough time to examine every possible character.

CLASSIFICATION

Although the theory of evolution had little immediate impact on the practice of taxonomic research at the level of species, genus, and family, it did impact on taxonomic theory. Systematists began to attempt to develop systems of classifications designed to reflect evolutionary lineages. It was reasoned that such classifications should reflect the course of evolution. Since the turn of the twentieth century, numerous workers in the field of flowering plant taxonomy have attempted to produce systems of classification reflecting the phylogeny of the flowering plants. This is a very difficult task, owing partly to the poorness of the fossil record and partly to the complexity and diversity of the plants themselves. The difficulty of developing a phylogenetic system is also complicated by the fact that some workers in this field have based their systems on characters that they believe to be primitive rather than on factual evidence. Speculative information does not lend itself to the development of phylogenetic systems having high predictive value.

By the 1980s most phylogenetic systems differ only in detail, and the authors of such systems attempt to avoid the pitfalls of earlier systems. In recent years, two schools of workers, the pheneticists and the cladists, have developed methodology in an attempt to bring about greater objectivity in the construction of classifications.

Numerical Phenetics

Phenetics involves the organizing of data on the basis of similarity for the purpose of obtaining a classification. *Pheneticists,* the workers in this field of taxonomy, emphasize the need for objectivity in classification. They attempt to develop schemes having high predictive values that allow the maximum number of generalizations to be made from the schemes. They stress the importance of using a large number of characters, at least 60 but preferably 80 to 100, that can be correlated on the basis of similarity.

Phenetic systems are based on data derived from the phenotypes of organisms—hence the designation phenetic systems.

The idea of phenetic systems of classification was proposed by Michel Adanson in the latter part of the eighteenth century. With the availability of computers in the 1950s, workers such as C. D. Michener, R. R. Sokal, P. H. A. Sneath, A. J. Cain, and G. A. Harrison began to propose computer-based methods for quantifying similarity and for the grouping of taxa using quantitative methods. One premise was that it should theoretically be possible to develop methodology that would quantitatively allow an experienced or inexperienced person to arrive at basically the same classification.

Sneath and Sokal summarized their philosophy in 1963 and in a revised edition in 1973. They believed in equal weighting of characters and made sweeping claims about the value of numerical phenetics. However, their refusal to weight characters and their tendency to ignore phyletic information had an initial negative impact on the validity and acceptance of their methods. Modifications of these extreme viewpoints by later pheneticists has brought about wider acceptance of the methodology.

In an attempt to be objective, pheneticists avoid referring to taxa by the species or generic names. Instead, they replace these groupings with *Operational Taxonomic Units* (OTU's), the term given to the lowest-ranking taxon studied in the investigation. However, the establishment of OTU's requires subjective judgments and considerable knowledge and experience. Another common problem is character definition and description; for instance, can leaf shape be defined as a single character or is it actually a summarization of several independent variables that determine the shape?

Simply stated, phenetic methodology requires that character states be determined for each OTU. A data matrix (OTU's versus character states) is prepared and the data are codified for computer processing. In cluster analysis, the computer sorts out (clusters) the OTU's according to their overall similarity, that is, according to the number of attributes or characters in common (Figure 4-3). The available computer programs produce a *phenogram* that is a dendrogram of phenetic relations in which less and less similar OTU's are successively linked together. Other numerical techniques may be *nonhierarchical* whereby the OTU's are linked with the contourlike lines encircling different numbers of OTU's or by linking OTU's with straight lines of varying lengths. These computer methods attempt to demonstrate a classification graphically that can be comprehended by the taxonomist (Figure 4-4). Some workers have attempted to delimit subjectively taxa by phenetic methods especially by equating different levels of similarity on the phenogram but, thus far, this has not been successful or practical. The overall purpose of phenetics is to lend objectively to what have previously been the somewhat subjective methods employed by traditional taxonomists.

While traditional taxonomists have not been enthusiastic about the methodology, the younger generation of numerical taxonomists seem to appreciate better the difference in information content of characters and is willing to weight characters based on *a posteriori* evidence. The basic philosophy of pheneticists has contributed to the development of logical and objective methodology and the formulation of better definition of characters in plant systematics.

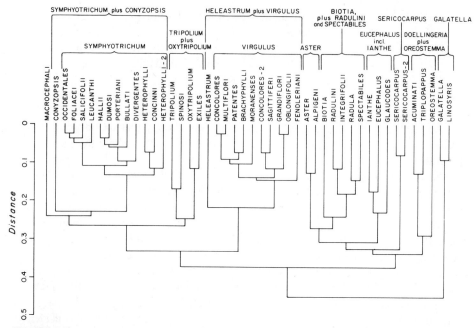

FIGURE 4-3
Phenogram obtained from cluster analysis of 46 groups of *Aster.* (Used with permission from A.
G. Jones and D. A. Young, *Syst. Bot.,* 8(1):71–84, 1983.)

Numerical methods appear to be useful in difficult groups where other methods
have not proved satisfactory. Most workers today agree that classifications developed
by numerical methods are probably no better or no worse than classifications produced
by the traditional taxonomist. One major advantage of the numerical approach is that
it forces the taxonomist to provide definitions of the characters, as well as data that
may be used by others in reassessing classification. Computer techniques allow the
taxonomist to incorporate many more character analyses than could be done by traditional "brain power."

Cladistics

Cladistic analysis attempts to summarize knowledge about the similarities among
organisms in terms of a branching diagram called a *cladogram*. The cladogram illustrates graphically the sequence of branching points in the phylogeny. Workers in this
school of classification are known as *cladists*. Cladistics has as its goal the production
of objective and repeatable branching diagrams depicting hypothetical evolutionary
histories, thus eliminating arbitrariness from classifications (Stuessy, 1980; Cracraft,
1983). The cladistic school of classification was founded by the German entomologist
Willi Henning around 1950. By the 1960s, Henning's methodology was being discussed by North America systematists, and a revised English version outlining his

FIGURE 4-4
First three dimensions of a principal components analysis of the genera of the tribe
Thelypodieae (Cruciferae). A nearest neighbor network, measured by Euclidean distance is
superimposed on the taxa; arrows point to nearest genus. Generic names are abbreviated:
CAU = *Caulanthus*, CHL = *Chlorocrambe*, MAC = *Macropodium*, ROM = *Romanschulzia*,
STY = *Stanleya*, STL = *Streptanthella*, STS = *Streptanthus*, THS = *Thelypodiopsis*,
THM = Thelypodium, WAR = *Warea*. (Used with permission from Hauser and Crovello, *Syst.
Bot.*, 7(3):249–268, 1982.)

methods of classification was published in 1966. Many systematic zoologists such as
J. Cracraft, J. S. Farris, G. Nelson, N. I. Platnick, E. O. Wiley, and many others
quickly adopted Henning's principles. Botanists are just beginning to realize the potential for applying the methods of cladistics to their problems.

   Henning was concerned with the branching of lineages and suggested that phylogeny
consists of a series of dichotomous events each representing the splitting of a parental
species into two daughter species. There are many viewpoints represented among
cladists; however, most will agree that natural monophyletic groups are recognized
by uniquely derived characters termed *synapomorphies,* and that only natural groups
defined by synapomorphies are to be included in classification schemes. A shared
primitive character-state is known as a *sympleisomorphy*. Cladists attempt to apportion
similarities on a branching diagram according to the hierarchical level at which the
similarities characterized groups, that is, the level at which they are postulated to be
a synapomorphy (Figure 4-5). Cladists reason that branching points are determined
by backward tracing of uniquely derived characters since derived characters are to be
found only among the descendants of the ancestor.

   In general, two comparative methods are used for evaluating characters—ontoge-

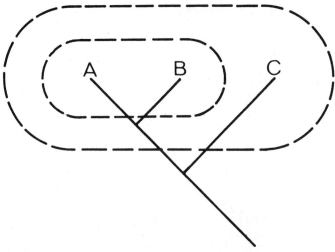

FIGURE 4-5
A directed or rooted cladogram illustrating hypotheses about synapormophic statements. Taxon
A is more closely related to taxon B than either are to taxon C; i.e., A and B share
synapomorphies nested within a larger synapomorphic pattern which includes C. A + B is a
sister group of C; A is a sister group of B.

netic criterion and outgroup criterion (Figure 4-6). Both methods attempt to establish
the partitioning of characters into ancestral or derived. A primitive or general character
is one that is more inclusive, whereas a derived character is less inclusive. An *ontogenetic criterion* uses data from comparative embryology to assess the direction of
character transformation. Although potentially useful, developmental information is
not usually available for plants. For this reason, most botanical cladists use *outgroup
comparison*. By this method, if a shared character within the group being studied is
also found outside the group in closely related taxa, it is reasoned that the character
is too general, or primitive, to define a subgroup. This requires that the systematist
know the relationship of one group to other related groups in order to analyze critically
the relationship within the group. Basically, cladists attempt to maximize the agreement
of characters while attempting to account for their distribution.

In theory, cladistic analysis has value as a method for delimiting monophyletic
groups. It forces the careful analysis of all characters; it introduces a new concept of
character weighting, that is, the possession of uniquely derived characters; and it helps
to clarify the relationship betwreen phylogeny and classification by permitting the
testing of phylogeny in the absence of a fossil record. Problems in communication
exist because of the excessively complicated terminology of the cladists. There are
further difficulties in determining primitive versus derived characters and the determination of the direction of evolutionary change. Some groups resist analysis because
of the absence of easily detectable synapomorphies. Continuous characters and variation within a taxon present difficulties when using cladistic methods. Also, OTU's
with a hybrid origin are usually omitted from cladistic analyses or require special

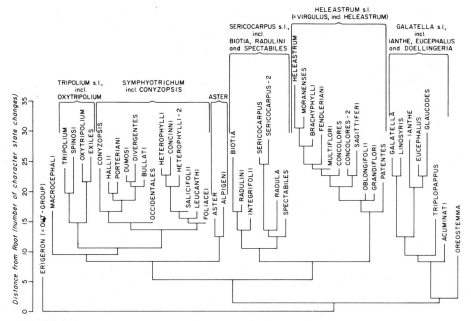

FIGURE 4-6
Cladogram resulting from the analysis of 46 groups of *Aster* using nine species of *Erigeron* as an outgroup. (Used with permission from A. G. Jones and D. A. Young, *Syst. Bot.*, 8(1):71–84, 1983.)

techniques because of their reticulate evolutionary history. Hybridization, while not of great importance in the origin of animal taxa, must be considered when examining plant taxa, as many appear to have been derived in this way.

At times there may be two cladistic hypotheses that are equally good at explaining character distributions. In such a case it is necessary for the systematist to judge the relative merits of the branching patterns and specify the hypothesis exhibiting the most agreement in the synapomorphy pattern. To this problem, cladists apply the principle of *parsimony* by selecting the hypothesis that can best be defended by the investigator as having the fewest character state changes.

One application of cladistic principles to flowering plant classification can be seen in the following example. Since (1) monophyletic groups are established by the use of unique, derived features inherited from the immediate ancestor of the group, and (2) species splitting has been mainly dichotomous, then the search for sister species or sister groups (subsets of a set defined by a synapomorphy) is the main procedure in the reconstruction hypothesis of the phylogeny. Using this criterion, Bremer and Wanntorp (1978) suggest that the division of the angiosperms into the dicotyledons and monocotyledons at equal rank is untenable. It is usually agreed that monocotyledons are derived from a group within the dicotyledons. If true, the monocotyledons cannot be a sister group of the dicotyledons and, therefore, the monocotyledons cannot have the same rank in classification as the dicotyledons. Using this reasoning, the mono-cotyledons should have the same rank as their sister group within the dicotyledons. From this and other examples in the literature, it is clear that the application of cladistics to botanical classification will have an impact on the practice of developing classifi-cations. For a bibliography of papers on cladistics see Funk and Wagner (1982).

BIOGEOGRAPHY

Classification depends on a hypothesis of the evolutionary development of the taxon, the present day relationships to the environment, and the analyses of the taxon's distribution pattern in relation to paleoclimatic and paleogeographic data. The study of the patterns of distribution of plants and animals is known as *biogeography*. The analysis of the distributional patterns of organisms is essential to the classification of all taxa at various ranks. Distribution patterns may be shown graphically by means of a single line enclosing the area of distribution or may be represented by dot distribution maps. The dots may represent the exact collection sites or may simply indicate the presence of the taxon in a political region such as a county (or parish), state, or province.

Taxa coexisting in the same general geographic region are said to be *sympatric*, while taxa whose ranges do not overlap are referred to as *allopatric*. Many taxa are partially sympatric. When the area occupied by a taxon includes sizable regions in which the taxon is not found, that taxon is said to have a *discontinuous* or *disjunctive* distribution and is described as a disjunct. Disjunctions are usually explained on the basis of disruptions of former wide distribution by paleoclimatic or paleographic changes, by present day environmental or topographic factors, or even by the possibility of random long-distance dispersal mechanisms.

Major discontinuities in distributional patterns may occur within a species, genus, or family when the range includes widely separated parts of a continent or location on separate continents. For example, taxa with disjunctions may be found among the floristic elements of the eastern Asia-eastern North America flora (Boufford and Spong-berg, 1983), and among the southern South America-Australasia-South African flora.

The geophysical theory that land masses of the earth have been steadily moving during the course of geological time has been called *continental drift,* or more properly, *plate tectonics* (McKenzie, 1972). The concept of plate tectonics provides a geophysical explanation for the isolation of land areas by sea floor spreading, the uplift of mountain ranges, the formation or disappearance of islands, and the shifting position of conti-nents. Latitudinal changes, rafting of floras, and environmental stresses due to plate tectonics surely played a major role in the evolution of the angiosperms (Raven and Axelrod, 1974; Schuster, 1976). For these reasons, *biogeographers,* who study the distribution of plants and animals, have recently reexamined distribution patterns, fossil records, and evolutionary history of the flowering plants in respect to plate tectonic theory.

The earliest known angiosperm pollen has been found in lower Cretaceous strata (Raven and Axelrod, 1974). During this geologic period, the northern groups of continents (North America and Eurasia), which geologists call *Laurasia,* had largely separated from the southern group of continents (South America, Africa, Australia, Antarctica, and the Indian subcontinent), called *Gondwanaland*. Figure 4-7 shows that the components of Gondwanaland and Laurasia were adjacent to each other or in close proximity when the angiosperms first appeared on the earth near the beginning of the Cretaceous period. The pollen record strongly suggests that much of the radiation of the angiosperms occurred when the continents of Gondwanaland were essentially close together, allowing direct interchange of floristic elements (Figure 4-8). Taxa have subsequently radiated in various directions, occupying suitable habitats and forming their present ranges.

Endemism refers to a distribution restricted to one region or area. An endemic is a taxon whose distribution is limited to a special habitat or very restricted geographic region. Certain habitats or geographic regions have a high proportion of endemics and are described as areas of endemism. For example, the granitic outcrops of the Piedmont of Georgia and the Carolinas have a number of endemic species. The bluffs of the Appalachicola River in Florida have many endemics such as the gymnosperms *Torreya taxifolia* and *Taxus floridana*. The native angiosperm flora of Hawaii is more than 90

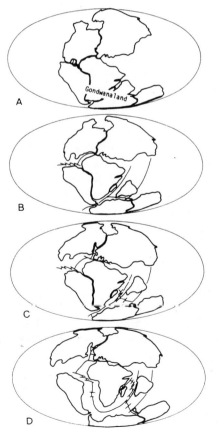

FIGURE 4-7
Continental drift. The maps show the relative position of the continents: (A) 200, (B) 180, (C) 135, and (D) 65 million years ago. (Reprinted from Bremer, *Svensk Bot. Tidskr.,* 77:33–40, 1983.)

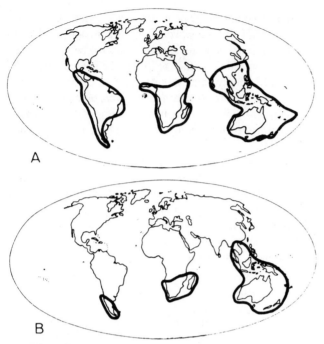

FIGURE 4-8
The distribution of the families Proteaceae (A) and Restionaceae (B). These and similar disjunct southern hemisphere distributions are presumed to be the result of the breakup of Gondwanaland. (Reprinted from Bremer, *Svensk Bot. Tidskr.*, 77:33–40, 1983.)

percent endemic. It is known from fossil evidence that *Ginkgo biloba* was once widespread but now occurs naturally only in a small area in China. The explanation of endemism is related to the past geographic and climatic history of the region and the subsequent isolation of the area involved as well as the present day environment of the area.

A given genus or family may show a marked concentration of related species or genera in one or more geographic regions. An area with such concentrations of related taxa is called the *center of genetic diversity* for that genus or family. For example, one center of genetic diversity for the genus *Vernonia* is south central Brazil. At one time, the center of genetic diversity was regarded also as the *center of origin* for the taxon. However, present evidence indicates that this is not necessarily true. The geographic and climatic histories of the area and their influence on the evolutionary history of the taxa may have shifted the center of genetic diversity away from the center of origin.

Vicariance Biogeography

In the past 25 years, a method of study has been formalized to analyze the relationships and histories of biotas by searching for common patterns of distributions of organisms.

These common distributional patterns are then coupled with hypotheses relating to the evolutionary histories found among the organisms inhabiting these biotas (Wiley, 1980). Once a number of distributional patterns reflecting some common pattern have been examined, it is possible to compare the distributions to events that might have influenced the evolution of the taxa. Since by definition each monophyletic taxon has a single center of origin, it may be possible to determine pathways of migration and evolution. The recurrence of replicated geographic patterns among unrelated taxa allows the taxonomist to sort out a series of distributional patterns that have a general explanation. This has led to the development of an approach called *vicariance biogeography*.

When one species is replaced by a similar, closely related species in separate geographic or ecological areas, the phenomenon is called *vicariance,* and the taxa involved are known as *vicariants*. The recurrence of replicated geographic patterns in unrelated taxa represent one or more vicariance events that fragmented a continuous ancestral biota. Such vicariance events include continental drift, mountain building, climatic change, disruption of drainage patterns by stream capture, etc. Vicariance biogeographers recognize that disjunctions may also result from dispersal of taxa from their center of origin, followed by evolution into new taxa.

As part of their methodology, vicariance biogeographers assess the frequency of agreement in the distribution of unrelated taxa. They attempt to relate these facts to the occurrence of common paleogeographic and paleoclimatic events that affected the evolution and distribution of two or more groups of organisms. Phylogenetic hypotheses

FIGURE 4-9
A combined area-cladogram for *Negria, Depanthus, Rhabobthammus, Corathera,* and *Fieldia* (Gesneriaceae). The geographic areas represented include New Guinea (NG), Borneo, Tasmania (Tas), New Zealand (NZ) and South America (SAm). Redrawn from C. J. Humphries in Funk and Brooks, 1981.

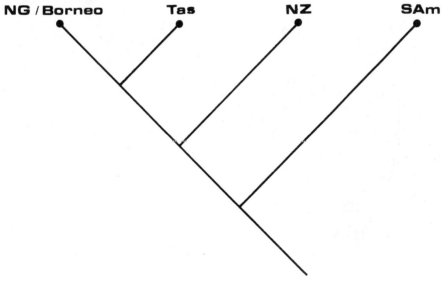

and coinciding geographic areas that the species inhabit can be depicted graphically
to form a branching *area cladogram* in which the species name is replaced by the area
in which the species occurs (see Figure 4-9). Vicariance events are reflected in the
branching pattern of the cladogram.

Vicariance biogeographers suggest that by developing a synthesis of distributional
patterns and evolutionary events, much new information can be provided as well as
uncovering questions for future study. Not all systematists, however, would agree
with the promises made by the proponents of vicariance biogeography. Briggs (1983)
and others argue that the concept of vicariance brings nothing new to evolutionary
biology, that it downplays long-distance dispersal, and that its application is limited
to groups, such as fishes, that have limited means of dispersal. Thus far, the concept
and techniques of vicariance have been applied largely to zoological systematists.
Certainly, it does seem that general patterns of relationships among certain areas of
endemism are best explained by vicariance of once widespread biota rather than solely
by independent, random dispersal events such as long-distance migration. Some areas
of endemism of flowering plants are interrelated among themselves, and it seems that
such relationships can be broken down also into species relationships.

Parallelism and Convergence

If two organisms of different lineage are alike in their features, the resemblance is
usually attributed to either parallelism or convergence. *Convergence* is the resemblance
between two or more distinct phyletic lines brought about through evolution by adaptation to similar environments or to similar reproductive biologies. Adaptation to
similar environments is most often apparent in the vegetative characters of plants, but
it may occur in reproductive parts. Convergence in vegetative features of unrelated

FIGURE 4-10
A desert Euphorbiaceae from Africa with a
cactus-like appearance.

FIGURE 4-11
A New World Cactaceae. Many desert species of Euphorbiaceae from Africa and Cactaceae from North and South America show convergent evolution in their vegetative features although they represent distinct phylogenetic lineages.

taxa occurring in the Mediterranean vegetation of California and Chile show the similarities in morphology caused by similar climates (Mooney, 1977). Many desert species of Euphorbiaceae from Africa and Cactaceae from North and South America demonstrate convergence with their "cactus-like" appearance, although their flowers immediately suggest the proper family (Figures 4-10 and 4-11). This convergence in vegetative features presumably reflects adaptive responses to aridity. Adaptation of reproductive biology in pollination or seed-dispersal mechanisms causes convergence in flowers, fruit, or seed. The weed *Camelina sativa* (Cruciferae) has an ecotype that infests flax fields. The flax field ecotype mimics the flax plants in size and weight of the seeds. This adaptation results when *Camelina* seeds resembling flax seeds are selected in the harvest and seed separation process. Another example of convergence, seemingly related to their pollination biology, is the development of pollinia in both the orchids and milkweeds.

With *parallelism,* the resemblance is due to a common ancestry and genetic background. Two phyletic lines may diverge up to some stage and cease to diverge and then run parallel. Parallel evolution is apparently a common feature of flowering plants but is difficult to document with certainty because of the poor fossil record. Parallel evolution may take place in related lineages at any stage in their separation, or at the level of infraspecific taxa, species, genera, families, or so on.

Parallelism and convergence are difficult concepts at best. If the angiosperms are monophyletic, the dividing line between parallelism and convergence is purely arbitrary. Given the sparse fossil record of the angiosperms, it may be impossible to distinguish between parallelism and convergence within closely related orders.

GUIDING PRINCIPLES OF ANGIOSPERM PHYLOGENY

The angiosperm phylogenist is faced with major problems of an inadequate fossil record, the prevalence of convergent evolution, and the extreme structural modifications of many flowering plants (Thorne, 1963, 1976). The relatively soft tissues of most angiosperm flowers and certain other plant parts provide nothing analogous to bones, exoskeletons, or shells for fossilization. Flowering plants do have resistant pollen, and some have hard woody tissue or waxy leaves suitable for fossilization. Even though the fossil record of flowering plants is meager, it is sufficient to indicate some general trends in the angiosperms. In addition, ancestral characteristics and the direction of trends of specialization can often be recognized in so called "living fossils." The classification of angiosperms is primarily based on the examination of contemporary flowering plants and establishing correlations of characters (Thorne, 1963).

The necessary use of contemporary plants to establish hypothetical lineages and inferred evolutionary relationships has inherent problems (Thorne, 1963). The prevalence of convergent evolution in flowering plants has made it difficult to develop monophyletic groups and the taxonomist is faced with the problem of deciding whether certain characters are due to common ancestry or to convergence. To overcome the problem of convergence, information from all possible sources regarding the plants must be assembled and evaluated. A voluminous literature of comprehensive comparative studies has been developed on groups thought to contain primitive characters (Bailey, 1957).

In 1915 Bessey presented a set of guiding principles of angiosperm phylogeny, or what he called "dicta," to facilitate piecing together data into a phylogenetic system of angiosperm classification (see Chapter 2.) The information reflected in these dicta has largely been determined from studies of comparative morphology and paleobotany. These "Besseyan principles" have been modified through the years by numerous phylogenists as new information appeared in the literature (Cronquist, 1968; Davis and Heywood, 1963; Gundersen, 1950; Hutchinson, 1973; Takhtajan, 1969; Thorne, 1963, 1976; and others). Although clearly Besseyan in origin, the present principles have been refined and restated, and most modern classifications conform to them. Given the diversity of the angiosperms, there are exceptions to these principles. They are not dogma and should be used only as guides. The modified "Besseyan principles" are listed below.

Possible Evolutionary Trends in Angiosperms

1 In most groups of flowering plants, woody plants usually have preceded the herbs, vines, and climbers. Perennials gave rise to biennials, and annuals have been derived from both. Terrestrial seed plants usually preceded closely related aquatics or epiphytes, saprophytes, and parasites.

2 Flowering plants with collateral vascular bundles arranged in a cylinder (dicotyledons) are more primitive than those with scattered vascular bundles (monocotyledons). Unstoried wood with scalariform endplates, scalariform side walls, and apotracheal wood parenchyma are regarded as primitive.

3 Alternate leaves with secretory cells and stipules are primitive; opposite or whorled leaves without secretory cells or stipules are regarded as advanced. In nearly all instances, simple, pinnately veined, evergreen leaves preceded compound leaves.

4 Bisexual flowers have traditionally been regarded as primitive, but evidence is accumulating that unisexual flowers may also represent a primitive condition. Most agree, however, that flowers borne separately in the axils of subtending leaflike bracts are primitive.

5 The many parted, spirally imbricate flower is primitive, while those with few parts, which are whorled or valvate, generally are more advanced. Regular (actinomorphic) flowers preceded irregular (zygomorphic) flowers.

6 Perianth parts that are separate and poorly differentiated into sepals and petals are more primitive than laterally fused perianth parts that are sharply differentiated. Usually, flowers with petals preceded apetalous ones.

7 Many separate stamens are more primitive than few or united stamens.

8 Hypogyny (superior ovary) is the primitive condition, and perigyny and epigyny (inferior ovary) are derived.

9 Generally, numerous, separate, carpels represent a more primitive condition than fewer fused carpels.

10 Pollen grains with one pore preceded those with 2 or more pores.

11 The primitive seed is arillate, has a small embryo, and contains abundant nuclear endosperm. Nonendospermic seeds are considered to be derived. Primitive families have ovules that are crassinucellate, while those in more advanced groups tend to have tenuinucellate ovules.

12 Axile placentation preceded free central placentation, and the latter is regarded as derived.

13 Single fruits preceded aggregate fruits formed from several ovaries. The capsule preceded the drupe or berry.

14 Those plants with leuco-anthocyanins and ellagitannins are regarded as primitive; recently these compounds have been referred to as pro-anthocyanins.

In summary, the trends in the evolution of the flower have come about by reduction in number, fusion, specialization of parts, and changes of symmetry. Simple structures are not necessarily primitive but have become simple as a result of reduction from more complex parts. The rate of evolution is not always the same for all structures of the plant. Some parts of a plant may become more specialized than others, and some taxa may have both advanced and primitive features.

SUMMARY

Following are some principles of taxonomy.

1 The goal of taxonomy is to develop a workable classification that reflects evolutionary relationships and provides for nomenclature and identification.

2 Species represent lineages produced by evolution, and branching genetic relationships exist among the taxa of each group.

3 Categories such as species, genera, families, and orders are not rigid but are flexible and individually delimited for each group. Their sequence in the hierarchy is established by the International Code of Botanical Nomenclature. Categories are subjective and are definable only with respect to their position in the hierarchy.

4 Taxa are based on the correlation of characters and discontinuities in the variation pattern. Characters may be selected from any attribute of the plant and do not have a fixed value at all ranks.

5 For delimiting taxa, characters should be constant and show little environmental variation.

6 Taxa should be monophyletic. On a practical basis, the monophyletic requirements for higher ranking taxa must be broadly interpreted.

7 Taxonomic treatments should be practical and consistent in their use of the various categories.

8 Taxa may resemble one another because of either convergence or parallelism.

9 Whenever possible in the development of classifications, taxa should be sampled throughout their range, and all taxa at lower ranks should be examined.

10 Ancestral features and trends of diversity may often be recognized in the structure of living angiosperms.

11 Careful consideration should be given to the facts regarding the early angiosperms as they are known from the fossil record.

12 Evolution may result in reduction or loss of parts. It can also proceed toward greater structural complexity.

13 Morphological indicators of phylogeny may provide guidance to primitive versus advanced features and aid in developing phylogenies. Thinking should remain flexible so that modifications in classification may be made as new evidence becomes available.

14 Phenetic taxonomy organizes and classifies taxa on the basis of similarities of the phenotypes of the organisms.

15 Cladistic taxonomy involves summarizing knowledge about the similarities among taxa in terms of a branching diagram called a cladogram depicting the hypothetical evolutionary histories of the organisms.

16 Biogeography analyzes the patterns of distribution of organisms and relates these to the systematics of the organisms.

17 Vicariance biogeography examines the relationships and histories of biotas by searching for common patterns of distributions among various organisms. These common distributional patterns are then coupled with hypotheses related to their evolutionary histories.

SELECTED REFERENCES

Abbott, L. A., F. A. Bisby, and D. J. Rogers.: *Taxonomic Analysis in Biology,* Columbia University Press, New York, 1985.

Allkin, R. and F. A. Bisby: *Databases in Systematics,* Academic Press, London, 1984.

Bailey, I. W.: "The Potentialities and Limitations of Wood Anatomy in the Study of the

Phylogeny and Classification of Angiosperms," *J. Arnold Arbor. Harv. Univ.*, **38**:243–254, 1957.

Bessey, C. E.: "Phylogenetic Taxonomy of Flowering Plants," Ann. Mo. Bot. Gard., **2**:109–164, 1915.

Boufford, D. E. and S. A. Spongberg: "Eastern Asian-Eastern North American Phytogeographical Relationships—A History from the Time of Linnaeus to the Twentieth Century," *Ann. Mo. Bot. Gard.*, **70**:423–439, 1983.

Bremer, K. and H. E. Wanntorp: "Phylogenetic Systematics in Botany," *Taxon*, **27**:317–329, 1978.

Briggs, J. C.: "Cladistics," *Amer. Sci.*, **71**:456, 1983. [Comments on the paper by J. Cracraft in *Amer. Sci.*, **71**:273–281, 1983.]

Bessey, C. E.: "Phylogenetic Taxonomy of Flowering Plants," *Ann. Mo. Bot. Gard.*, **2**:109–164, 1915.

Cain, A. J.: "The Post-Linnaean Development of Taxonomy," *Proc. Linn. Soc. Lond.*, **170**:234–244, 1959.

Camp, W. H. and C. L. Gilly: "The Structure and Origin of Species," *Brittonia*, **4**:323–385, 1943.

Clausen, J., D. D. Keck, and W. M. Hiesey: "Experimental Studies on the Nature of Species. I. Effect of Varied Environments on Western North America Plants," *Carnegie Inst. Washington Publ.*, No. 520, 1940.

Clifford, H. T. and W. Stephenson: *An Introduction to Numerical Classification*, Academic Press, N.Y., 1975.

Coney, P. J.: "Plate Tectonic Constraints on the Biogeography of Middle America and the Caribbean Region," *Ann. Mo. Bot. Gard.*, **69**:432–443, 1982.

Constance, L., et al.: "Amphitropical Relationships in the Herbaceous Flora of the Pacific Coast of North and South America: A Symposium," *Q. Rev. Biol.*, **38**:109–177, 1963.

Cracraft, J.: "Cladistic Analysis and Vicariance Biogeography," *Amer. Sci.*, **71**:273–281, 1983.

Cronquist, A.: *The Evolution and Classification of Flowering Plants*, Houghton Mifflin, Boston, 1968.

———: "Some Thoughts on Angiosperm Phylogeny and Taxonomy," *Ann. Mo. Bot. Gard.*, **62**:517–520, 1975.

———: *An Integrated System of Classification of Flowering Plants*, Columbia University Press, New York, 1981.

Davis, P. H., and V. H. Heywood: *Principles of Angiosperm Taxonomy*, Van Nostrand, Princeton, N.J., 1963.

Dunn, G. and B. S. Everitt: *An Introduction to Numerical Taxonomy*, Cambridge University Press, Cambridge, 1982.

Eldredge, N. and J. Cracraft: *Phylogenetic Patterns and the Evolutionary Process*, Columbia University Press, New York, 1980.

Fosberg, F. R.: "Subspecies and Variety," *Rhodora*, **44**:153–157, 1942.

Funk, V. A., and T. F. Stuessy: "Cladistics for the Practicing Plant Taxonomist," *Syst. Bot.*, **3**:159–178, 1978.

———, and D. R. Brooks: *Advances in Cladistics*, New York Botanical Garden, Bronx, NY, 1981.

———, and W. H. Wagner, Jr.: "A Bibliography of Botanical Cladistics: I. 1981," *Brittonia*, **34**:118–124, 1982.

Gilmartin, A. J., and M. J. Harvey: "Numerical Phenetics in Routine Taxonomic Work," *Syst. Bot.*, **1**:35–45, 1976.

Good, R. O.: *The Geography of the Flowering Plants,* 4th ed., Longman Group Ltd., London, 1974.

Graham, A. (ed.): *Floristics and Paleofloristics of Asia and Eastern North America,* Elsevier, Amsterdam, 1972.

Gray, A.: *The Elements of Botany for Beginners and for Schools,* American Book, New York, 1887. (Gray's Lessons in Botany reprinted by American Environmental Studies, 1970.)

Gundersen, A.: *Families of Dicotyledons,* Chronica Botanica, Waltham, Mass., 1950.

Hall, H.M.: "The Taxonomic Treatment of Units Smaller Than Species," *Proc. Int. Congr. Plant Sci.,* **2:**1461–1468, 1929.

Henning, W.: *Phylogenetic Systematics,* The University of Illinois Press, Urbana, 1966. (Translated by D. D. Davis and R. Zangerl. Reprinted 1979.)

Holt, P. C. (ed.): *The Distributional History of the Biota of the Southern Appalachians,* part II, *Flora,* Research Division Monograph 2. Virginia Polytechnic Institute and State University, Blacksburg, 1970.

Hopwood, A. T.: "The Development of Pre-Linnaean Taxonomy," *Proc. Linn. Soc. Lond.,* **170:**230–234, 1959.

Hull, D. L.: "Certainty and Circularity in Evolutionary Taxonomy," *Evolution,* **21:**174–189, 1967.

Hull, D. L.: "The Limits of Cladism," *Syst. Zool.,* **28:**415–440, 1979.

Humphries, C. J.: "Vicariance Biogeography in Mesoamerica," *Ann. Mo. Bot. Gard.,* **69:**444–463, 1982.

Hutchinson, J.: *The Families of Flowering Plants,* 3d ed., 2 vols., Clarendon, Oxford, 1973.

Kapadia, Z. J.: "Varietas and Subspecies: A Suggestion Towards Greater Uniformity," *Taxon,* **12:**257–259, 1963.

Kubitzki, K. (ed.): "Flowering Plants—Evolution and Classification of Higher Categories," *Plant Syst. Evol.,* Suppl. **1:**1–416, 1977. (A series of excellent papers on angiosperm classification.)

Lane, M. A. and B. L. Turner: "The Generic Concept in the Compositae: A Symposium," *Taxon,* **34:**5, 1985. [A series of 13 papers about the delimination of genera in the family].

Lawrence, G. H. M.: *Taxonomy of Vascular Plants,* Macmillan, New York, 1951.

McKenzie, D. P.: "Plate Tectonics and Sea-floor Spreading," *Amer. Sci.,* **60:**425–435, 1972.

——— and Sclater, J. G.: "The Evolution of the Indian Ocean," *Sci. Amer.,* **228**(5):63–72, 1973.

Mayr, E.: *"The Growth of Biological Thought,"* Belknap Press, Cambridge, 1982.

Mishler, B. D. and M. J. Donoghue: "Species Concepts: A Case for Pluralism," *Syst. Zool.,* **31:**491–503, 1982.

Mooney, H. A. (ed.): *Convergent Evolution in Chile and California: Mediterranean Climate Ecosystems,* Dowden, Hutchinson and Ross, Stroudsburg, Pa., 1977.

Nelson, G.: "Cladistic Analysis and Synthesis: Principles and Definitions with a Historical Note on Adanson's *Familles des Plantes* (1763–1764)," *Syst. Zool.,* **28:**1–21, 1979.

Nelson, G. J. and N. I. Platnick: *Systematics and Biogeography,* Columbia University Press, New York, 1981.

Patterson, C.: "Cladistics and Classification," *New Sci.,* **94:**303–306, 1982.

Persoon, C. H.: *Synopsis plantarum, seu Enchiridium botanicum* 2 vols., Paris, 1805–1807.

Raven, P. H., and D. I. Axelrod: "Angiosperm Biogeography and Past Continental Movements," *Ann. Mo. Bot. Gard.,* **61:**539–673, 1974.

Rollins, R. C.: "Cytogenetical Approaches to the Study of Genera," *Chron. Bot.,* **14:**133–139, 1953.

Ross, H.-H.: *Biological Systematics,* Addison-Wesley, Reading, Mass., 1974.

Schuster, R. M.: "Plate Tectonics and Its Bearing on the Geographic Origin and Dispersal of Angiosperms," in C. B. Beck (ed.), *Origin and Early Evolution of the Angiosperms,* Columbia, New York, 1976, pp. 48–138.

Slobodchikoff, C. N. (ed.): *Concepts of Species,* Dowden, Hutchinson, and Ross, Inc., Stroudsburg, Pa., 1976.

Sneath, P. H. A., and R. R. Sokal: *Numerical Taxonomy,* Freeman, San Francisco, 1973.

Sokal, R. R. and P. H. A. Sneath: *Principles of Numerical Taxonomy,* Freeman, San Francisco, 1963.

Sporne, K. R.: "Character Correlations Among Angiosperms and the Importance of Fossil Evidence in Assessing Their Significance," in C. B. Beck (ed.), *Origin and Early Evolution of Angiosperms,* Columbia University Press, New York, 1976.

Stott, P.: *Historical Plant Geography: An Introduction,* George Allen and Unwin, London, 1981.

Stuessy, T.: "Cladistics and Plant Systematics: Problems and Prospects. Introduction," *Syst. Bot.,* **5:**109–111, 1980. [An introduction to a series of five papers in this number.]

Takhtajan, A.: *Flowering Plants—Origin and Dispersal,* The Smithsonian Institution, Washington, 1969.

———: "Outline of the Classification of Flowering Plants (Magnoliophyta)," *Bot. Rev.,* **46:**225–359, 1980.

Thorne, R. F.: "Some Problems and Guiding Principles of Angiosperm Phylogeny," *Amer. Nat.,* **97:**287–305, 1963.

———: "A Phylogenetic Classification of the Angiospermae," *Evol. Biol.,* **9:**35–106, 1976.

Turner, B. L.: "Chemosystematics and Its Effects upon the Traditionalist," *Ann. Mo. Bot. Gard.,* **64:**235–242, 1977.

Valentine, D. H.: "The Taxonomic Treatment of Polymorphic Variation," *Watsonia,* **10:**385–390, 1975.

Wiley, E. O.: "Phylogenetic Systematics and Vicariance Biogeography," *Syst. Bot.,* **5:**194–220, 1980.

CHAPTER 5

SOURCES OF
TAXONOMIC EVIDENCE

Taxonomic evidence for the establishment of classifications and phylogenies is gathered from a variety of sources. Because all parts of a plant at all stages of its development can provide taxonomic characters, data must be assembled from many diverse disciplines. The use of information from studies on comparative anatomy, embryology, palynology, cytogenetics, chemistry, and so on has greatly improved the modern classification of plants.

MORPHOLOGY

The features of floral morphology are the most important characters in the classification of flowering plants. These features are easily observed, and they are practical for use in keys and descriptions. Morphology currently provides most of the characters used in constructing taxonomic systems. When considering the evolutionary lines of the flowering plants, each represented by perhaps thousands of species, it should not be expected that all morphological characters should occur uniformly among all species. The occasional absence of a synthetic or diagnostic character, or its rare occurrence in a group from which it is normally absent, may be expected.

Terms used in identification of angiosperms are morphological, and these are illustrated or defined in Chapter 10. *Morphology of the Angiosperms* (Eames, 1961) provides a comprehensive review for the flowering plants. Additional information may be found in Radford et al. (1974), Hickey and Wolfe (1975), Melville (1976), Corner (1976), and Cullen (1978).

Natural selection, associated with successful reproduction, maintains a basic similarity of the reproductive features of flowers, fruits, and seeds within the various species, genera, and families. This general constancy makes these structures ideal for characterizing taxonomic groups. In addition to being more constant than vegetative features, reproductive characters are generally more numerous and therefore provide more features to differentiate taxa. Floral features are often fundamental in defining natural groups. Variations in every conceivable part of the flower, fruit, and seed have proved to be useful in the classification of one or more groups of flowering plants.

Modifications in floral morphology usually can be related to the mode of pollination or specialized reproduction. Wind-pollinated taxa frequently have unisexual, reduced flowers that are individually inconspicuous. Insect-pollinated plants (which typically have large, colorful, bisexual flowers) are valuable to pollinators because of their nectar or pollen, and the showiness of the flowers helps attract pollinators. Corolla color, pollinator guides, and other modifications of the corolla are related to insect pollination.

Other modifications of flowers (in stamen number, anther position, ovary position, style length, stigma shape, number of carpels, number and fusion of perianth parts, inflorescence type, fruit and seed types) contribute to the reproductive success of the species. Although these characters play important functional roles in the plant's reproductive biology, the adaptive advantages are not always obvious. It is quite possible that some floral features have no adaptive advantage in themselves, but that either they had such advantages historically, or their elimination may require too much genetic manipulation, when the nonadaptive trait is linked to some essential feature.

When one becomes familiar with a number of families of flowering plants, it is possible to see that generalizations can be made about the use of certain reproductive features in the classification of one or more groups. For example, the mature fruits of the mustards (Cruciferae) and carrots and their relatives (Umbelliferae) are significant as diagnostic characters distinguishing the genera. For this reason, specimens of these families should include mature fruits to insure identification. Certainly, fruit and flower types are no less important in the classification of the Rosaceae. Likewise, the stamens and corollas of the figworts (Scrophulariaceae) and mints (Labiatae) are important floral features. Seed structure of taxa within the pink family (Caryophyllaceae) provides much information for classification at various taxonomic ranks within the family. The value of characters drawn from reproductive morphology varies from group to group within the angiosperms.

The growth habit (herbaceous or woody) of plants may be of primary usefulness in classification. The condition may be constant within a genus or family, or it may be variable. All members of the family Cruciferae are herbaceous. Some families, such as the Compositae, have both woody and herbaceous members. Genera or families that contain both tropical and temperate taxa are more likely to have both woody and herbaceous growth habits. Some semitropical or tropical herbaceous perennial species vary in their tendency to woodiness.

With some taxa, vegetative features are of little taxonomic value, but in other taxa they can be of major importance. For example, flowers and fruits are of little value in the elms (*Ulmus*), but leaf shape is an important taxonomic feature. Leaf characters are significant features also in the identification and classification of the oaks (*Quercus*) and birches (*Betula*). The diagnostically important basal rosette leaves of the Cruciferae may wither and die before flowering and are often lacking on fruiting specimens.

Stem types, buds, thorns, spines, and so forth on woody plants are often useful in identification. Leaf arrangement, type, form, duration, and venation are frequently used in both classification and identification. In trees with small reduced flowers of short duration, vegetative features often assume great importance in plant taxonomy and should be carefully observed. Vegetative underground structures such as rhizomes, corms, and bulbs may sometimes characterize a group.

COMPARATIVE PLANT ANATOMY

For over a century, taxonomy has used comparative plant anatomy to aid in classification, and several principles on the use of anatomical data have become established. These principles are the following: (1) anatomical features have the same inherent problems of other characters, that is, sampling, reliability, parallelism, and convergence (see Chapter 4); (2) anatomical characters must be used in combination with other features; and (3) anatomical characters tend to be most useful in classification of the higher categories and less useful below the rank of genus. Further information on comparative plant anatomy may be found by consulting the following sources: Esau (1965) for a general review of plant anatomy; Metcalfe and Chalk (1979–1983) and Metcalfe (1960, plus several additional books in this series) for anatomical information arranged by taxa; and Radford et al. (1974) for a list of pertinent citations and a summary of anatomical techniques for systematics. Other useful references include Metcalfe (1954, 1963), Robson, Cutler and Gregory (1970), and Fahn, (1982).

Since the 1930s the value of the evolutionary trends of specialization of the secondary xylem has been clearly established (Bailey, 1957). A progressive series from tracheids (commonly found in the gymnosperms) to specialized vessel elements occurs in the secondary xylem of angiosperms (Figure 5-1). All stages of specialization, from vesselless wood to highly specialized vessel elements, may be found in contemporary flowering plants. Those angiosperms with vesselless wood often have other features regarded as primitive. This evolutionary series of vessel elements has been used in combination with other morphological features to develop hypotheses about the phylogeny of the angiosperms.

Little information for classification has been obtained from anatomical studies of the phloem because of its lack of apparent variation (Dickison, 1975). However, types of sieve-element plastids have recently proved useful in classification (Behnke, 1977). Some comparative plant anatomists suggest that correlations of nodal anatomy with other features might provide significant information about angiosperm phylogeny (Dickison, 1975). Others find this of limited value because of convergence and reduction. Recently, nodal anatomy was used to help define the broad outline of dicot relationships among the primitive dicots.

It is often possible to interpret vestigial or modified parts of flowers by studying their vascularization (Eyde, 1975). This has been valuable in clarifying the relationships of some taxa.

FIGURE 5-1
Transverse sections of dicotyledonous woods. (*a*) *Trochodendron aralioides*, a primitive
vesselless angiosperm with the secondary xylem composed of tracheids. (*b*) *Schumacheria
castaneifolia*, with wood having solitary, annular vessels and mostly scanty axial parenchyma.
(*c*) *Dillenia pentagyna*, with wood having a comparatively primitive structure but the vessels are
more rounded in outline. (*d*) *Scytopetalum tieghemii*, with the vessels distributed as solitary and
pores and pore multiples (*e*) *Pittosporum tenuifolium*, having pores distributed in pore chains
and radial pore multiples (*f*) *Paulownia tomentosa*, a relatively advanced dicot: note the
vasicentric parenchyma. (*Used with the permission of Dr. W. C. Dickison and the* Ann. Mo. Bot.
Gard.)

Anatomical features of leaves frequently provide characters. For example, investigation of the anatomy of leaves, associated with C_4-photosynthetic pathways, has resulted in a revised classification for several genera in the grass family (Brown, 1975). C_4 species have prominent chlorenchymatous vascular bundle sheaths. Venation patterns of fossil leaves are beginning to yield significant information when examined with reference to the Cronquist-Takhtajan system of classification (Hickey, 1973; Doyle

FIGURE 5-2
Scanning electron micrographs of surface features of the shoot system of marijuana (*Cannabis sativa*). *1,* Lobe of a young leaflet. *2,* Adaxial surface of a young leaf. *3,* Mature region of a leaf tip. *4,* Surface of a petiole showing nonglandular hairs, capitate glands, and bulbous glands. *5,* Abaxial leaf surface. *6,* Adaxial leaf surface. *7,* Adaxial leaf surface showing a capitate gland, long and short systolith trichomes, and a ring of cells surrounding the long trichome. The SEMs were made from fresh specimens without any treatment. (*From P. Dayanandan and P. B. Kaufman,* Amer. J. Bot. **63:***578–591, 1971, with permission.*)

and Hickey, 1976). Petiolar vascularization has been helpful in classification of certain genera such as *Rhododendron* but has not proved applicable to classification problems of the higher categories.

Variation patterns of epidermal hairs or trichomes may provide characters for classification at species-genus-family levels (Figure 5-2). For example, trichomes are diagnostic characters for certain species of *Vernonia* (Faust and Jones, 1973). Emphasis is placed on the structure of the trichome; that is, the size, shape, and arrangement of cells making up the hair. The presence and structure of trichomes, as well as their distribution patterns among taxa, are taxonomically important. In the Compositae and several other families, trichomes are of value in analysis of suspected hybrids. A glossary of epidermal hair terminology can be found in Payne (1978).

Stomatal types, produced by characteristic arrangements of guard cells and subsidiary cells, can be of taxonomic use. Some 31 patterns of stomata and subsidiary cells are known to exist in the vascular plants (Pant, 1965; Stace, 1965; Van Cotthem, 1970; Fryns-Claessens and Van Cotthem, 1973). The patterns seem to be most valuable at the higher taxonomic levels. Perhaps one of the best examples is their use to characterize the subclasses of monocots (Cronquist, 1968).

Some workers regard anatomical features as conservative characters that are not easily modified by growing conditions. Closely related species or genera will often have the same anatomy, but there are exceptions. Leaves grown in sun may differ anatomically from those grown in shade. Anatomical features, like other characters, can be greatly influenced by selection. The stems of the hemp cultivar of marijuana (*Cannabis sativa*) have more fiber bundles than the stems from plants high in intoxicating resins. In most instances, variation such as this would not be expected in stem anatomy within a species. Anatomical features of vegetative structures have importance in separating gymnosperms from angiosperms and monocotyledons from dicotyledons. However, such features have proven of relatively minor value for the delimitation of subdivisions of these groups. Anatomical features tend to be most useful at the higher ranks or in determining relationships where there have been great structural modifications or reductions.

The concept of anatomical characters as conservative has been challenged by Carlquist (1969), who considers that anatomy is always related to adaptation and function. He stresses that the anatomy of floral structures should be viewed as part of a dynamic functioning system related to pollination biology and dispersal mechanisms.

EMBRYOLOGY

Embryology includes micro- and megasporogenesis, development of gametophytes, fertilization, and development of endosperm, embryo, and seed coats (Palser, 1975). For general, systematic, and comparative information on plant embryology, the following reference books may be consulted: Bhojwani and Bhatnagar (1979), Davis (1966), and Maheshwari (1950).

Although there are a few minor differences in embryology among the flowering plants, there is strong embryological unity throughout the angiosperms, as exemplified by double fertilization. The major embryological character separating the dicotyledons from the monocotyledons is the number of cotyledons. Cotyledon characters have been shown to be useful in developing classifications in the family Gesneriaceae. The embryological features most common to all flowering plants are (1) four microsporangia per anther; (2) two-celled pollen grains; (3) eight-nucleate embryo sac; and (4) nuclear endosperm (Palser, 1975). Dahlgren (1975) has compared the distribution of some embryological characters of the flowering plants within the framework of his system of classification. The number of nuclei in the pollen grains at the time of pollen dispersal is either two or three. It is generally regarded that binucleate pollen is primitive and the trinucleate pollen is derived.

Embryological features are ordinarily constant at the family level in the angiosperms. In those families where variation has been found, the features are usually constant at the generic level. Embryology has had systematic significance in the grass family, where with several other characters, it has been used to revise the family's classification. Embryological features tend to be less useful as taxonomic characters at the rank of order, subclass, or class. When used judiciously and in combination with other characters, they may be useful in determining relationships within families, genera, and species. The technical work and time required to obtain sufficient embryological information for comparative purposes has limited its overall value in taxonomy.

CYTOLOGY

Although cytology refers to the study of the cell, only information about the chromosomes—that is, chromosome number, shape, or pairing at meiosis—is used for classification purposes (Stebbins, 1971). *Cytotaxonomy* refers to the use of chromosome number and morphology as data for classification. *Cytogenetics* includes those studies dealing with observations of chromosome pairing or behavior at meiosis. For detailed discussions of cytotaxonomy and cytogenetics, consult Davis and Heywood (1965), Solbrig (1968), or Stebbins (1971).

The haploid number of chromosomes in angiosperms ranges from $n = 2$ in *Haplopappus gracilis* (Compositae) to around $n = 132$ in *Poa littoroa* (Gramineae). Most angiosperms have chromosome numbers ranging between $n = 7$ and $n = 12$. About 35 to 40 percent of the flowering plants are polyploids. *Polyploids* are organisms that have higher chromosome numbers because of multiplication of chromosome sets (i.e., genomes). In an extensive review article, Raven (1975b) suggests that the original basic chromosome number for most angiosperms was probably 7. Raven speculates that an initial burst of polyploidy occurred during the early evolution of flowering plants, since many of the families with primitive features have high chromosome numbers.

There are several kinds of polyploid number relationships in flowering plants. Some genera such as *Pinus* with $n = 12$ have no deviation among the species and the species are termed *homoploids*. In other genera, a polyploid series is present, for example, *Aster* (Compositae), with different species having $n = 9$, 18, or 27. There are still other genera with numbers that show no simple numerical relationship to one another (*aneuploids*)—i.e., *Brassica* (Cruciferae), with $n = 6$, 7, 8, 9, or 10. *Vernonia* in the Old World has n = 9 or 10, with polyploids of n = 18, 20, or 30, whereas in the New World it has n = 17, 34, 51, or 68.

As with many other characters, the value of cytotaxonomic data depends on the group or the category under consideration. A combination of information on chromosome number and chromosome morphology has proved useful for improving the classification of families, such as Agavaceae, or genera in the family Ranunculaceae. Base numbers and chromosome size have been very useful in understanding relationships in the grass family. In the family Onagraceae, information on chromosome number and morphology, in combination with experimental hybridizations and analysis of the chromosome set, provides clues for tracing evolution.

Because relatedness of taxa is often reflected in homology (similarity) of the chromosomes, determination of the amount of chromosome pairing at meiosis in hybrids of two species may aid in understanding relationships of closely related species. It is generally assumed that the more completely two chromosomes pair at meiosis, the more homologous they are. Or, if dealing with entire sets of chromosomes, the higher the percentage of pairing between the individual chromosomes of the two sets, the more closely the plants are presumed to be related. For additional information see Chapter 7.

ELECTRON MICROSCOPY

Unlike its application to the study of lower plants, electron microscopy is a relatively new approach to the study of flowering plants. Features observable only with the electron microscope are providing useful characters relevant to the phylogeny of the angiosperms (Cole and Behnke, 1975; Stuessy, 1979). *Ultrastructure* refers to those features observable with transmission electron microscopy (TEM), or with scanning electron microscopy (SEM).

SEM provides an image of unequaled depth of field, which is ideal for comparative studies of pollen grains and plant surfaces. An SEM micrograph of pollen grains is shown in Figure 5-3. SEM has a wide range of magnification and is relatively easy to use. Used to supplement light microscopy, SEM has been widely and readily adopted by plant systematists for pollen grains, small seeds, trichomes, and other surface features of plants.

Relatively few new characters have been uncovered by SEM, but the technique has enabled rapid and recordable, comparative study of numerous features (Barthlott, 1981; Heslop-Harrison, 1981). Recently, using SEM micrographs of starch grains, the laticifer cells of *Euphorbia* were demonstrated to be useful in the interpretation of evolution within the genus (Biesbor and Mahlberg, 1981).

Using TEM, Behnke (1972, 1977, 1981; Behnke and Dahlgren, 1976) demonstrated the taxonomic value of sieve-element plastids in flowering plant classification (Figures 5-4 and 5-5). Behnke found two distinct classes of plastids: the s-type which accumulates starch and the p-type that accumulates protein or protein and starch. This character was then successfully applied to taxonomic problems in the Caryophyllidae (Behnke, 1976) and the angiosperms (Behnke, 1977). TEM studies of thin sections of pollen grain walls can yield reliable taxonomic information of certain groups (Skvarla

FIGURE 5-3
SEM micrograph of a morning glory (*Ipomeoa*) pollen grain and a smaller unidentified
Compositae pollen grain. The sample was obtained from a fresh morning glory flower. Possibly
the Compositae grain was brought into the morning glory flower by a pollinator. The Compositae
grain is about 40 microns in diameter. Note the depth of field provided by the SEM.

and Turner, 1966). For example, some members of the family Compositae have
differing types of wall structure and these have proved useful as characters. Dilated
cisternae of endoplasmic reticulum are a characteristic feature of members of Cruciferae
and Capparaceae of the order Capparales (Behnke, 1977; Jørgensen, 1981). Membrane
bound protein bodies found in seeds may contain crystalloids that vary in size, shape,
and number (Lott, 1981). The cotyledon mesophyll cell bodies in the Cucurbitaceae
generally contain crystalloids, whereas those of the Composite and Cruciferae do not.
Although seed protein bodies of relatively few species have been studied with TEM,
there are indications that protein bodies could be a useful character for studies in plant
systematics.

In general, TEM has not been as successful as SEM in providing useful ultrastructural characters, for three reasons: (1) the general uniformity of cell organelles within
each type of tissue; (2) the small number of taxa and tissues sampled; and (3) the
greater difficulty and time required for specimen preparation. Ultrastructural characters

FIGURE 5-4
TEM micrograph of sieve-element plastids, s-type, with many starch grains from *Cocculus trilobus* (the plastids are about 2 microns in diameter). (*Micrograph courtesy of Dr. H.-D. Behnke.*)

FIGURE 5-5
TEM micrograph of sieve-element plastids, p-type, from *Dracaena hookeriana* (the plastids are about 1.5 microns in diameter). (*Micrograph courtesy of Dr. H.-D. Behnke.*)

may be found with TEM once tissues are compared and surveyed in groups that appear to have classification problems.

PALYNOLOGY

Palynology is the study of pollen and spores. As a result of the stimulus and availability of SEM, taxonomists no longer overlook pollen as a source of characters (Figure 5-3). The development and ready availability of SEM has revolutionized the study of the surface features of pollen grains by providing a depth of focus never possible with light microscopy. The availability of countless pollen samples from herbarium sheets and relatively rapid techniques for preparation allow a palynological survey of many taxa in a relatively short period of time. The taxonomic characters provided by pollen grains include pollen wall structure, polarity, symmetry, shape, and grain size. Pollen grains do not differ within most genera; however, pollen has been very useful in determining patterns of species relationships in *Vernonia* (Keeley and Jones, 1977). The order Caryophyllales is a large natural association of families diagnosed in part by a curved embryo surrounded by perisperm storage tissue. Two unique features found among certain families in the order, namely the betalain pigments and protein sieve-tube plastids, have brought the order under scrutiny. Using SEM, Nowicke and Skvarla (1979) have shown that pollen morphology reinforces the close relationships accorded the families and supports their distinctness from other nearby families.

Two basic kinds of pollen grains are found in the angiosperms: monosulcate and tricolpate. *Monosulcate pollen grains* (Figure 5-6) are boat-shaped and have one long germinal furrow and one germinal aperture (Walker, 1976). Pollen of the monosulcate type is characteristic of the primitive dicotyledons, the majority of the monocotyledons, the cycads, and the pteridosperms. Palynologists agree that the first flowering plants probably had monosulcate pollen grains (Raven and Axelrod, 1974; Beck, 1976). *Tricolpate grains* (Figure 5-7) are globosesymmetrical, typically have three germinal apertures, and are characteristic of the advanced dicotyledons. Walker and Doyle (1975) concluded that, with some exceptions, pollen morphology is consistent with the levels of advancement and the relationships shown in Takhtajan and Cronquist systems of classification.

For further information on palynology, consult Wodehouse (1935) for terms; Erdtman (1966) for techniques and terminology; Ferguson and Muller (1976) for a review of the evolutionary significance of the exine; and for additional references consult

FIGURE 5-6
SEM micrograph of a monosulcate pollen grain of *Magnolia fraseri*, 1300X. (*J. W. Walker.*)

FIGURE 5-7
SEM micrograph of a tricolpate pollen grain
of *Euptelea pleiosperma*, 3000X. (*J. W.
Walker.*)

Faegri and Iversen (1975), and Muller (1979). (See Chapter 6 of this text on fossil
pollen.)

PALEOBOTANY

Paleobotany uses microfossils, such as pollen, or macrofossils of leaves, stems and
other plant parts as sources of data. Paleobotanists attempt: (1) to elucidate the com-
position and the evolution of the floras of the past; (2) to trace these evolutionary
developments through stratigraphic sequences; (3) to integrate paleobotanical data with
comparative morphology; and (4) to determine past ecological conditions.

Students interested in additional readings should consult Taylor (1981) for a general
survey of the field, and Wolfe, Doyle, and Page (1975) and Beck (1976) for implications of paleobotany in studies of angiosperm phylogeny. The U.S. Geological
Survey has an extensive unpublished index to the fossil plant literature. It is housed
in the Smithsonian Institution in Washington and must be examined there.

Until recently, most systematists generally agreed that paleobotany could provide
little evidence on the origin and diversification of the flowering plants. However,
evidence is rapidly accumulating that paleobotany can provide significant information
about important aspects of the early history of angiosperms (Dilcher, 1979; Daghlian,
1981; Taylor, 1981). New techniques and approaches to the study of fossil flowering
plants are helping taxonomists discover exciting information (Taylor, 1981). The most
encouraging effect of the recent upsurge in research on angiosperm origins is the
recognition that the fossil record can furnish critical evidence for the origin and diversification of the flowering plants as it has for the vertebrates (Retallack and Dilcher,
1981). In recent years, the discovery by Dilcher (Figure 5-8) and his associates of
several angiosperm reproductive structures has greatly modified a number of early
ideas about primitive flower types. There have been many marvelous discoveries of
new fossils in recent years that have contributed a wealth of information about fossil

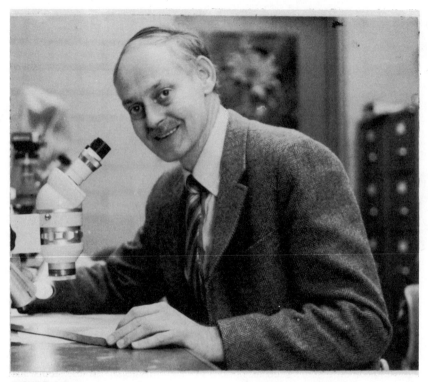

FIGURE 5-8
David Dilcher, Professor of Paleobotany at Indiana University. His special area of interest is the
fossil record of the flowering plants.

flowering plants (e.g., Crepet, Dilcher and Potter, 1974, 1975; Crepet and Daghlian, 1980). The application of the technique of SEM has provided a clearer picture of the complex micromorphology of fossil pollen grains, and the application of TEM is now providing information on the details of pollen ultrastructure. These new approaches have been especially rewarding.

Recent collections of well-preserved angiosperm flowers from Eocene sediments of the Southeastern United States and from Kansas include an interesting array of morphological types (Crepet, 1979). Diversified representatives of the present-day "Amentiferae-line" were common by Middle Eocene time. They were well adapted for wind pollination, and it appears from the fossil evidence that adaptation to wind pollination had, by that point, reached a high level. Flowers and inflorescences with structural features allowing pollination by beetles, flies, bees, and butterflies were also extant by the Middle Eocene. Fossil evidence recently uncovered by Crepet, Dilcher and others, coupled with observations of modern angiosperms, suggests that coevolution of flowers with insects was important in the radiation of the flowering plants. Their work clearly demonstrates that the Middle Eocene flora can help provide comprehensive information about the evolution of the flower.

An extraordinary data source has been provided by the organic chemical profiles of Miocene leaf specimens of five genera (*Acer, Celtis, Quercus, Ulmus* and *Zelkova*), which were compared with those of present-day counterparts (Giannasi and Niklas, 1977). A high degree of correlation between chemical compounds of the fossils and those of the modern species was found. This new information has allowed paleobotanists to formulate new concepts of early flowering plant evolution. These differ somewhat from the traditional view that was largely derived by circular reasoning from the morphology of so-called primitive groups. Data provided by paleobotany allow taxonomists to deal with the facts of the fossil record about angiosperms and their possible progenitors. Clearly, the best source of evidence is actual data from the fossil record.

CHEMOSYSTEMATICS

For centuries, chemosystematics (or biochemical systematics, or chemotaxonomy) has been practiced by human cultures as they recognized and classified plants by tastes, smell, color, and whether or not they were poisonous or of medicinal value. For example, the Greek philospher Socrates was forced to take his own life by drinking a broth of poison hemlock (*Conium maculatum*). By the first century after Christ, Dioscorides had recognized the aromatic mints and grouped them together. Later, the extensive explorations to the far corners of the world by European adventurers and merchants were fueled by the desires of Europeans for exotic spices and condiments. The value of the spices was for food preservation and masking odors and tastes of spoiling meat. Taxonomists of the nineteenth century often recognized chemical characters and used them in their work before the compounds were completely identified.

Plant *chemosystematics* is the application of chemical data to systematic problems. It is a rapidly expanding interdisciplinary field concerned with using chemical constitutents for explaining relationships between plants and inferring phylogeny. The development of several types of chromatography and various types of spectroscopic and instumentation techniques since the 1940s has simplified survey procedures and considerably eased compound identification. With the development of modern methods, information on natural plant products for phylogenetic comparisons is becoming increasingly available. Several books providing examples of the ways in which chemistry may be used in systematics are Bisby et al., 1980; Gibbs, 1974; Harborne, 1970, 1982; Hawkes, 1968; Swain, 1973; and Young and Seigler, 1981.

Plants produce many types of natural products, and quite often the biosynthetic pathways producing these compounds differ from one taxonomic group to another. In many instances, the distributions of these compounds and their biosynthetic pathways correspond well with existing taxonomic arrangements based on the traditional morphological features. In other cases, chemical data have contradicted existing classifications, thus requiring a reexamination of the classifications, or have provided decisive information where other forms of data were insufficient. Since many kinds of molecules are produced by plants, the discussion in this brief summary is necessarily selective.

Chemosystematists often divide the vast array of natural plant products into two major groups according to molecule size.[1] Compounds of relatively low molecular weight, that is, those compounds with a molecular weight of 1,000 or less—such as alkaloids, amino acids, glucosinolates (mustard oils), flavonoid pigments and other phenolic compounds, fatty acids, and terpenoids—are termed *micromolecules*. Compounds of high molecular weight (over 1,000), such as proteins, DNA, RNA, cytochrome *c*, ferredoxin, and complex polysaccharides, are referred to as *macromolecules*. The information-carrying proteins, such as DNA, RNA, and other proteinaceous materials are sometimes referred to as *semantides*.

Flavonoids

Among micromolecules, the flavonoids have been most widely and effectively used in chemosystematics. The reasons for this are several: their ubiquitous occurrence in nearly all plants; their ease of isolation and identification even from small amounts of plant material; their great structural variation (over 2,000 different flavonoids have been isolated from plants); the demonstrated genetic basis for this variation; their chemical stability, which allows analysis years after the material was collected; and the fact that they can be used at all taxonomic levels in most groups of plants (see Figures 5-9 and 5-10).

The simple but elegant use of the chromatographic patterns of flavonoids in the 1960s by R. E. Alston and B. L. Turner to document hybridization between species of *Baptisia* set the stage for the effective use of flavonoid data in plant systematics (Alston, 1967). Occasionally, when two species of *Baptisia* occur together, hybridization occurs. The hybrids resulting from this accidental crossing of two species often look different from either parent and sometimes confused plant taxonomists. Alston and Turner examined the flavonoid profiles of the two parents and found them to be mutually exclusive in all or at least in several compounds. They demonstrated that interspecific hybrids could be identified on the basis of *additive profiles;* that is, certain species-specific compounds from each parent were found together in the hybrids. Indeed the *Baptisia*-type work is so well documented that it is often assumed to be standard for flavonoid work. In the classical flavonoid situation, when chemically different parents are hybridized, the F_1 generation exhibits an additive profile of both parental types.

However, the early enthusiasm generated by the classical *Baptisia*-type studies has been tempered somewhat by later ones showing that hybrids do not always exhibit additive flavonoid profiles and that compounds not found in either parent may be found in the hybrids (Crawford and Giannasi, 1982). In a flavonoid survey of the deciduous Rhododendrons of Eastern North America, it was found that complementation did not occur in the classical sense. Instead, variable, nonadditive profiles were present in both natural and artificial hybrids. Giannasi and co-workers have shown both complementation and noncomplementation in hybrids between two species of *Solidago* often with the production of unique nonparental compounds. Additional, detailed

---

[1]The authors wish to thank Professors David Giannasi and Daniel Crawford for allowing us to quote freely from their published and unpublished work.

FIGURE 5-9
Composite representation of the chromatographic patterns of flavonoids in *Nerisyrenia* showing the complementation of the flavonoids. (*Courtesy of T. J. Mabry and John Bacon.*)

studies of flavonoid inheritance and expression in diploid and polyploid species are needed.

There has been a gradual shift in flavonoid work in the past 10 years from intensive studies of infraspecific variation in the manner of Alston and Turner toward comprehensive detailed flavonoid surveys from the interspecific to the subclass level. Some recent work based on Dahlgren's system of angiosperm classification showed that flavonoids can be useful in clarifying certain relationships. Also, these data suggest that there is a need for circumscribing a number of families using their overall flavonoid compounds.

The controversial placement of *Psilotum* as a living representative of the most primitive ferns has not been supported by recent flavonoid evidence. The possession of biflavonyls seems to place *Psilotum* closer to some lycopods and gymnosperms than to the leptosporangiate ferns as had been proposed.

Flavonoid data used in connection with information on betalain distribution have also been helpful in another problem area. In the subclass Caryophyllidae, the distribution of the betalain-producing families and those that produce only anthocyanins has led to reclassification of that subclass (Figure 5-11). The presence of betalains in the family Cactaceae is an example of chemical data aiding in determining relationships at higher taxonomic levels. Clearly, the Cactaceae (once placed elsewhere in classi-

FIGURE 5-10
Two-dimensional paper chromatogram of an extract from *Parinari parilis* (Chrysobalanaceae), a
Brazilian plant. The extract was spotted on the paper in the lower right-hand corner and
separated into the pattern by solvents flowing from right to left and bottom to top. Photography
by Ralph Rocklin under longwave ultraviolet light (*From D. E. Giannasi, in* McGraw Hill Yearbook
Science and Technology, *1980*).

fication schemes) should be placed in the Carophyllidae, the only subclass with betalains.

Further progress in flavonoid systematics may depend on work in comparative
enzymology and development of a better understanding of biosynthetic pathways. It
is likely that the results will provide a more biologically sophisticated and genetically
meaningful interpretation of flavonoid chemistry.

Terpenoids

Terpenoids have been used extensively in the chemosystematics of groups where they
are distributed; for example, mints, umbellifers, citrus plants, gymnosperms, and so
on. However, they have been used less than the flavonoids in systematics because of
their limited distribution among vascular plants and because of the complex instrumentation and experience needed for their analysis. The technology of gas chromatography used with terpenoids provides both a quantitative and qualitative measure of
chemical differences between plants. Terpenoids can be used for distinguishing specific
and subspecific entities, geographical races, and for documenting hybridization.

In the flowering plants, interesting studies have been carried out using rind and leaf
terpenoid patterns in *Citrus* in attempts to determine the origin of certain *Citrus*
cultivars. In the gymnosperms, terpenoids of the cortical oleoresins have been used

Red   Yellow

FIGURE 5-11
The structure and visible absorption maxima of typical (*a*) red and (*b*) yellow betalains and (*c*) red and (*d*) yellow anthocyanins. The betalains are found in several closely related families in Caryophyllidae. Anthocyanins occur in most other nonbetalain families of flowering plants. (*Courtesy of T. J. Mabry.*)

to distinguish geographic races of Douglas fir (*Pseudotsuga menziesii*). Extensive studies of the terpenoids of *Juniperus virginiana* and *J. ashei* refuted previous hypotheses about extensive hybridization and introgression between the two species.

A major contribution of terpenoid chemosystematics has been the use of sesquiterpene lactones, which for the most part are characteristic of the Compositae family (Seaman, 1982). Many of the tribes of the Compositae are characterized to a greater or lesser extent by the distinct types of sesquiterpene lactones they produce. Within the Compositae tribes, sesquiterpene lactone chemistry can be used effectively both phylogenetically and phytogeographically. Sesquiterpene lactones have been used in the tribe Vernonieae to show that the largest genus in the tribe, *Vernonia*, has two major centers of distribution, one in the Neotropics and the other in Africa.

Future studies of terpenoids will likely continue with surveys of taxa at higher and lower ranks and with investigations related to geographic factors and to hybridization. Additional work is needed to determine the genetic control of terpenoid expression.

Alkaloids

From ethnobotanical, medicinal, poisonous, chemical, and systematic viewpoints, alkaloids have elicited more intense interest than any other group of compounds. Relative to their value in plant systematics, alkaloids are a difficult and heterogenous group of compounds, both structurally and biosynthetically. Further, the published literature on alkaloids is overwhelming. Despite these difficulties, alkaloid distribution has been useful in taxonomic studies in *Veratrum* (Liliaceae) and related genera, in *Papaver* and *Argemone* (Papaveraceae), as well as *Lycopodium, Lupinus,* and taxa in the order Caryophyllales.

Glucosinolates

Glucosinolates (mustard oil glucosides) are useful in the classification of the order Capparales, including Cruciferae (mustards) and the Capparaceae (capers) (Crawford and Giannasi, 1982). At one time the Cruciferae, Capparaceae, Papaveraceae, and Fumariaceae were included in the single-order Rhoeadales, but chemical and other evidence supports the placement of the Cruciferae and Capparaceae in the order Capparales (which produce glucosinolates) and the Papaveraceae and Fumariaceae in the order Papaverales (which are alkaloid-containing). Two families of uncertain affinities, Bataceae and Gyrostemonaceae, were once placed in the Caryophyllales, but the presence of glucosinolates suggests that the two families be removed from this order. Detailed studies in the genus *Cakile* (Cruciferae) have shown that glucosinolates are also effective infrageneric characters and that glucosinolate patterns may be used to document hybridization.

Iridoids

Iridoids represent a class of compounds (mostly monoterpene lactones) that have increased in taxonomic significance. The iridoids have shown promise in clarifying interfamilial relationships in the orders Rubiales, Caprifoliales, Scrophulariales, and Cornales, and they bear on the debate over the probable ancestral progenitor of the Compositae. Several iridoid families have been suggested as the putative progenitor of the Compositae, including the Rubiaceae, Dipsacaceae, Calyceraceae, Caprifoliaceae, Scrophulariaceae, and Cornaceae, all of which produce iridoids, which are not found in the Composite. Only the Campanulaceae, Araliaceae, and Umbelliferae, which do not produce iridoids, remain as possible progenitor lines. The latter two families are also linked to the Compositae by sesquiterpene lactones and polyacetylenes, raising the possibility of an ancient relationship.

New Approaches in Micromolecular Chemosystematics

A new and intriguing approach in plant chemosystematics is comparative phytoalexin induction studies on legumes. This technique uses fungi such as *Helminthosporium* to induce chemical "antibiotic" interactions between tissues of different plant species and the fungus (Ingham and Harborne 1976). Also of interest is the fact that qualitative and quantitative differences in nectar amino acids have been found among the flowers of different plant species. This technique can be used to document hybridization between plant species and to study pollinator relationships. The biological and evolutionary significance of micromolecules as allelopaths, herbivore-feeding deterrents or attractants, visual or olfactory stimulants, phytoalexins, and phytotoxins point to the critical functions of micromolecules in the evolution and survival strategies of plants. Thus, the ecological role of micromolecules also plays a part in the phyletic distribution of micromolecules.

Macromolecules

Analysis of macromolecules (i.e. DNA, proteins) provides promise for helping to discover relationships among major groups of angiosperms, and more attention will be directed to their study in the future. Comparative protein analyses can be used as fundamental taxonomic characters, since proteins represent direct products of the DNA code. The genetic material (DNA) can also be analyzed and compared between plant taxa. Thus, certain direct questions of plant relationships can be addressed in systematic investigations of macromolecules that would not be possible with many micromolecules, which often involve complex biosynthetic pathways. There are, however, significant problems associated with the time-consuming techniques of macromolecular analysis requiring much technical laboratory expertise, as well as numerical problems associated with data handling and the proper interpretation of generated figures and graphs (Crawford and Giannasi, 1982; Cronquist, 1976; Fairbrothers, 1983). Because of the specialization in the field, it is likely that teamwork among researchers sharing their expertise will yield the most promising new insights into plant relationships. Macromolecular data will be considered under the following general headings: electrophoresis, amino acid sequencing, systematic serology, and nucleic acid sequencing.

Electrophoresis

Profiles produced by the electrophoretic separation and subsequent staining of seed and pollen proteins have been employed in a number of systematic studies (Gottleib, 1977). The technique is based on the assumption that proteins from different plants will migrate in a slab of agar gel under an electric current. Those proteins that migrate to the same place in the gels and yield similiar bands upon staining with a marker dye represent homologous proteins. This approach of using electrophoretic band patterns has been used in the investigation of the origin of polyploid taxa from diploids, for instance, *Solanum, Phlox, Brassica,* and so on. It has also been used at the interspecific level to determine whether differences exist among plants that are treated as distinct species. As with any technique, there are a number of technical and interpretive restrictions that require care in the use of protein profiles.

The electrophoresis of specific enzyme types has been widely used in animal systematics (less so in plants), allowing the products of individual genes to be studied (Gottlieb, 1977). In this method, the different alleles (variants) of a locus (gene) coding for molecular variants of a gene can also be made visible as colored bands in gels (see Figure 5-12). From a systematic standpoint the method is significant because a large number of different enzyme (gene) systems can be examined among a large number of plant species.

The data obtained are helpful at the level of the population, subspecies, species,

FIGURE 5-12
Photograph of illustrative gel of 16 individual oysters with genetic variation at the PGM (phosphoglucomutase) locus. Oysters 1 and 2 (at the left) have alleles 2 and 3; oyster 3 has alleles 1 and 2; and oyster 4 has alleles 2 and 4. The gel indicates the genotype of the oyster for the PGM locus. (*Photograph furnished by Wyatt Anderson.*)

or sometime genus (Avise, 1974; Hamrick and Allard, 1975). Minor variation in allozymes is compared between individuals within populations, or between populations, or among closely related taxa at low rank. Such data are not generally useful at higher ranks because of the wide distribution of similar allozymes in unrelated groups. They are ideally suited to detect interspecific gene flow and percentage of polyploids.

Amino Acid Sequencing

The phylogenies that have been generated from sequencing the amino acids making up a protein have produced data that require the use of complicated computer programs (Fairbrothers, 1983). Such computer-derived data and their systematic implications are sometimes more controversial than simpler types of distributional chemical information because of the uncertain acceptability of the numerical approaches themselves. The evaluation of these complex numerical data has not been easily comprehended, and thus, information from amino acid sequences has not been readily or universally accepted by the practicing plant systematist for solving systematic problems. Yet information from amino acid sequences will probably become more significant in helping to understand phylogenetic relationships among the flowering plants as the technology and understanding of the statistical techniques become more comprehensible to the nonspecialist.

Amino acid sequence data for cytochrome *c*, plastocyanin, and ferredoxin have been determined for about 30 species of vascular plants. With this approach, it is possible to compare amino acid sequences of the same protein among various plants (Figure 5-13). From the similarities and differences in the amino acid chain, it is also possible to infer the DNA nucleotide similarities for the same gene in various plants

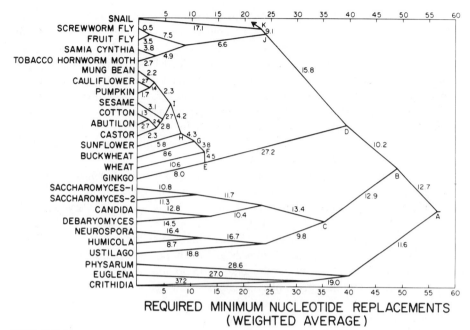

REQUIRED MINIMUM NUCLEOTIDE REPLACEMENTS
(WEIGHTED AVERAGE)

FIGURE 5-13
Probable phylogeny for some plants and animals computed through the study of mutations in the cytochrome c gene. (*Used with the permission of Dr. W. M. Fitch.*)

since specific units of DNA are coded for each amino acid of a protein. Thus, the amount of genetic (DNA) divergence may also be estimated. This has provided some phylogenetic information, but it is complicated by the likelihood that different classes of proteins (and hence their DNA) evolve at different rates (Fairbrothers, 1983). Some workers, however, have assumed that nucleotide substitutions occur at a generally constant rate for a given protein; that is, there is a molecular "clock." While this has been convincingly illustrated in animals, workers in plant evolution have questioned whether there is a "molecular evolutionary clock" and just how accurate is it since the clear evolutionary evidence seen in animals is not observed in amino acid sequences in plants. While the paucity of data and their interpretation have been questioned, amino acid sequence studies have produced excitement about the possibilities of such an approach, even though they have had as yet little actual impact on plant taxonomy.

Systematic Serology

Systematic serology had its origin in the early 1900s with the discovery of serological reactions and the development of the discipline of immunology. The technique was applied to comparative problems involving birds by J. Bordet, who noted that the immune reaction was relatively specific, and that the degree of cross-reactivity was proportional to the degree of relationships betwen organisms (Fairbrothers, 1977, 1983). The systematic implications of the immune reaction resides in the fact that the antigen-antibody responses are very specific. An animal will produce precise types of antibodies in response to the interaction with particular kinds of antigens. It is then possible to determine the degree of similarity between organisms (species, genera, families) by comparing the reactions of antigens from various plant taxa with antisera (antibodies) raised against the antigen of a particular taxon (Figure 5-14). Crude protein extracts from seed or pollen are commonly used for antigen production. However, recent developments of techniques in serology have led to the comparison of single proteins from different taxa.

Plant systematic serology has provided valuable data for the classification of flowering plants (Fairbrothers, 1983). Serological data have contributed to the classification of orders and the placement of families in the Apiales, Capparales, Caryophyllales, Cornales, Dilleniales, Dipsacales, Fagales, Juglandales, Magnoliales, Myricales, Nymphaeales, Papaverales, Primulales, Ranunculales, Restionales, Rubiales, Sapindales, Scrophulariales, Solanales, Typhales and many others (Fairbrothers, 1983). A definite and substantial rise in the use and incorporation of serological data in angiosperm classification has taken place in the past few years.

Nucleic Acids

The total number of plant taxa compared by using nucleic acid techniques has been few, largely because the necessary expertise and equipment are unavailable to most systematists. In addition, much of the methodology has been developed only recently, and there has been little time for the accumulation of data.

Basically, nucleic acid sequencing involves several techniques. Initially, the natural double-stranded DNA is separated into single strands. The single strands of DNA from one taxon are allowed to reassociate with similarly treated DNA from another taxon. Comparison is made with controls consisting of reassociation of strands from a single taxon. The percentage of reassociation of DNA between the two species (hybrid DNA) gives an indication of the degree of relatedness of the two species. Observable changes in sequences of DNA can provide information on speciation events that will aid in the reconstruction of phylogenies. Such techniques of DNA hybridization have also been used in studies of ribosomal RNA (rRNA)/DNA homologies among plants. Comparisons of plant organellar DNA (chloroplasts, mitochondria) also may offer some advantages in systematic studies. Plant organellar DNA represents a smaller amount of genetic code and thus allows sequencing of a less complicated molecule than that of nuclear DNA. Using the approach of digestion of organellar DNA with restriction endonucleases, the molecule can be broken up into smaller, more easily identifiable fragments whose specific gene function may also be identified. Comparison of precise DNA nucleotide sequences (and specific gene function) among species provides a powerful taxonomic tool. Indeed, recent studies comparing eight species of *Atriplex* (Chenopodiaceae) have provided estimates on time origins for the lineages as well as information useful in developing a new formal classification.

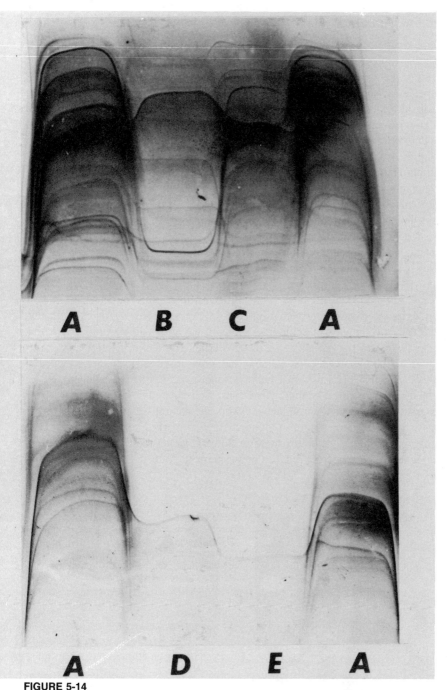

FIGURE 5-14
Line immunoelectrophoresis. The results of testing pollen protein extracts from five taxa: A. *Amphipterygium glaucum;* B. *Toxicodendron radicans;* C. *Rhus copallina;* D. *Myrica pensylvanica;* E. *Carya illinoensis;* reacted against a rabbit antiserum to *A. glaucum.* The results clearly show the serological relationships of the genus *Amphiterygium* to members of the family Anacardiaceae, i.e., *Toxicodendron* and *Rhus.* (*Photographs provided by Frank R. Peterson*).

ECOLOGICAL EVIDENCE

Information on the ecology of flowering plants is basic to systematics in providing an understanding of (1) the distribution of taxa, (2) the variation within taxa, and (3) the adaptations of plants. In delimiting taxa, it is necessary for taxonomists to comprehend developmental responses of plants as distinguished from genetically fixed characters. Ecological studies have demonstrated that the character states of many morphological features are correlated with environmental factors such as light, moisture, and soil fertility. Ecology contributes to systematic interpretations of the evolutionary process by seeking environmental explanations for discontinuities in the structure, function, and distribution of plants (Kruckeberg, 1969). Plant ecologists examine ecotypic variation, edaphic specializations, pollination mechanisms, the effect of habitat on hybridization, plant-herbivore interactions, seed-dispersal mechanisms, ecology of seedling establishment, function of plant structures, and reproductive isolating mechanisms (Figure 5-15). These features are important in the adaptation of populations to their environments and represent areas where ecologists make substantial contributions to systematics (Anderson, 1948; Clausen, 1951; Faegri and van der Pijl, 1979; Grant and Grant, 1965; Hadley and Levin, 1967; Harper et al., 1961; Jansen, 1966; Kruckeberg, 1969; Levin, 1971; Mooney, 1966; Muller, Muller, and Haines, 1964).

Much of the information derived from ecology has implications for classification below the level of genus. Yet ecological research has provided generalizations that may be applicable to the evolution of the flowering plants. For example, Stebbins (1974) presents the hypothesis that adaptive radiation of the angiosperms occurred in ecotones, or marginal or transitional habitats, under stresses of seasonal drought or cold, or in a mosaic of local edaphic conditions. Consequently, there may have been strong interactions between environmental factors and natural selection. He also favors a hypothesis of angiosperm origin in a climate having marked seasonal drought with a short season favorable for the formation of flowers. Under these conditions, natural selction might have favored the reduced angiosperm reproductive cycle.

FIGURE 5-15
Bumblebee (*Bombus*) queen pollinating flower of *Dodecatheon meadia* by vibrating pollen from the anther cone while stigma contacts residual pollen on the ventral side of the insect's thorax. (*Photograph furnished by Dr. L. W. Macior.*)

Although these hypotheses can be neither proved nor completely rejected, they do reflect the role that environmental factors play in the development of concepts about the origin of flowering plants. Furthermore, they express the idea that ecological data must be considered in the classification of plants.

PHYSIOLOGICAL EVIDENCE

Physiological and biochemical evidence is providing data of increasing importance to plant systematics. Of particular significance are data dealing with metabolic systems and biochemical pathways.

Recently, it has become apparent that a syndrome of anatomical and physiological features, related to a high-efficiency carbon fixation process, occurs in a large number of plants from tropical or warm temperate regions (Brown, 1975). This syndrome has been called the *Kranz syndrome,* C_4-photosynthesis, or the Hatch-Slack pathway. The most common pathway of carbon fixation is the *Calvin-Benson cycle,* or C_3-photosynthesis. In the algae, mosses, most ferns, gymnosperms, and many families of flowering plants, C_3-photosynthesis is the only known carbon fixation cycle. C_4-photosynthesis occurs in approximately 10 unrelated families of monocotyledons and dicotyledons (Downton, 1975). *Crassulacean acid metabolism* (CAM) has been found in both monocotyledon families and in dicotyledon families, and in ferns. CAM and C_4 both represent adaptations to arid climates. It was originally thought that the distribution of CAM would provide a useful taxonomic character; however, the random distribution of CAM has prevented it from being used in classification.

The Kranz syndrome has proved useful in characterizing *Panicum* and other taxa in the grass family (Brown, 1975). In the dicotyledon genus *Euphorbia* (Euphorbiaceae), C_3, C_4, and CAM species are known. Both C_3 and C_4 carboxylation occurs in *Zygophyllum* (Zygophyllaceae) and *Atriplex* (Chenopodiaceae).

Comparative studies of unique physiological processes of flowering plants might provide data of taxonomic significance. For example, the ability of halophytes to grow in highly saline soils seems to be restricted to relatively few families, but the phenomenon has not been well explained. There is much interest in the field of physiological plant ecology, but the major contributions to date have been in the physiology of ecotypes (Nobs, 1971). As more plants are examined with biochemical and physiological techniques, useful evidence will undoubtedly be found and applied to systematic problems.

SELECTED REFERENCES

Alston, R. E.: "Biochemical Systematics," in T. Dobzhansky *et al.,* (eds.), *Evolutionary Biology,* Vol. 1, Appleton-Century-Crofts, New York, 1967, pp. 197–305.
Anderson, E.: "Hybridization of the Habitat," *Evolution,* 2:1–9, 1948.
Andrews, H. N.: *Studies in Paleobotany,* Wiley, New York, 1961.
Avise, J. C.: "Systematic Value of Electrophoretic Data," *Syst. Zool.,* **23**:465–481, 1974.

Bailey, I. W.: "The Potentialities and Limitations of Wood Anatomy in the Study of the Phylogeny and Classification of Angiosperms," *J. Arnold Arbor, Harv. Univ.* **38**:243–254, 1957.

Baranova, M.: "On the Laterocytic Stomatotype in Angiosperms," *Brittonia,* **35**:93–102, 1983.

Barthlott, W.: "Epidermal and Seed Surface Characters of Plants: Systematic Applicability and Some Evolutionary Aspects," *Nord. J. Bot.,* **1**:345–355, 1981.

Beck, C. B. (ed.): *Origin and Early Evolution of Angiosperms,* Columbia, New York, 1976.

Behnke, H. D.: "Sieve Tube Plastids in Relation to Angiosperm Systematics, an Attempt Towards a Classification by Ultra Structural Analysis," *Bot. Rev.,* **38**:155–197, 1972.

———: "Ultrastructure of Sieve-Element Plastids in Caryophyllales (Centrospermae), Evidence for the Delimitation and Classification of the Order," *Plant Syst. Evol.,* **126**:31–54, 1976.

———: "Transmission Electron Microscopy and Systematics of Flowering Plants," *Plant Syst. Evol. Suppl.* **1**:155–178, 1977.

———, "Sieve-element Characters," *Nord. J. Bot.,* **1**:381–400, 1981.

——— and R. Dahlgren: "The Distribution of Characters Within an Angiosperm System. 2. Sieve-element Plastids," *Bot. Notiser,* **129**:287–295, 1976.

Bendz, G., and J. Santesson (eds.): *Chemistry in Botanical Classification,* Proceedings of the 25th Nobel Symposium, Academic, New York, 1973.

Bhojwani, S. S., and S. P. Bhatnagar: *The Embryology of Angiosperms,* 2nd ed., Vikas Publishing House, New Delhi, 1979.

Biesbor, D. D. and P. G. Mahlberg: "Laticifer Starch Grain Morphology and Laticifer Evolution in *Euphorbia* (Euphorbiaceae)," *Nord. J. Bot.,* **1**:447–457, 1981.

Bisby, F. A., J. G. Vaughn, and C. A. Wright (eds.): *Chemosystematics: Principles and Practices,* Academic, London, 1980.

Boulter, D.: "The Use of Comparative Amino Acid Sequence Data in Evolutionary Studies of Higher Plants," *Prog. Phytochem.,* **3**:199–229, 1972.

Brown, W. V.: "Variations in Anatomy, Associations, and Origins of Kranz Tissue," *Amer. J. Bot.,* **62**:395–402, 1975.

Cagnin, M. A. H. *et al.:* "Biochemical Systematics: Methods and Principles," *Plant Syst. Evol.,* Suppl. **1**:35–76, 1977.

Carlquist, S.: "Toward Acceptable Evolutionary Interpretations of Floral Anatomy," *Phytomorphology,* **19**:332–362, 1969.

Clausen, J.: *Stages in the Evolution of Plant Species,* Cornell, Ithaca, N.Y., 1951.

Cole, G. T., and H. D. Behnke: "Electron Microscopy and Plant Systematics," *Taxon,* **24**:3–15, 1975.

Constance, L., et al.: "Amphitropical Relationships in the Herbaceous Flora of the Pacific Coast of North and South America: A Symposium," *Q. Rev. Biol,* **38**:109–177, 1963.

Corner, E. J. H.: *The Seeds of Dicotyledons,* 2 vols., Cambridge, 1976.

Crawford, D. J.: "Flavonoid Chemistry and Angiosperm Evolution," *Bot. Rev.,* **44**:431–456, 1978.

——— and D. E. Giannasi: "Plant Chemosystematics," *BioScience,* **32**:114–118, 123–124, 1982.

Crepet, W. L.: "Some Aspects of the Pollination Biology of Middle Eocene Angiosperms," *Rev. Palaeobot. Palynol.,* **27**:213–238, 1979.

——— and C. P. Daghlian: Castaneoid Inflorescences from the Middle Eocene of Tennessee and the Diagnostic Value of Pollen (at the Subfamily Level) Within the Fagaceae," *Amer. J. Bot.,* **67**:739–757, 1980.

———, D. L. Dilcher, and F. W. Potter: "Eocene Angiosperm Flowers," *Science* (Washington, D.C.), **185**:781–782, 1974.

————, D. L. Dilcher, and F. W. Potter: "Investigations of Angiosperms from the Eocene of North America: A Catkin with Juglandaceous Affinities," *Amer. J. Bot.*, **62:**813–823, 1975.

Cronquist, A.: *The Evolution and Classification of Flowering Plants*, Houghton Mifflin, Boston, 1968.

————: "The Taxonomic Significance of the Structure of Plant Proteins: A Classical Taxonomist's View," *Brittonia*, **28:**1–27, 1976.

————: "On the Taxonomic Significance of Secondary Metabolites in Angiosperms," *Plant Syst. Evol.*, Suppl. **1:**179–189, 1977.

————: "Chemistry in Plant Taxonomy: An Assessment of Where We Stand," in Bisby, F. A. et al., *Chemosystematics: Principles and Practice*, Academic Press, London, 1980, pp. 1–27.

Cullen, J.: "A Preliminary Survey of Ptyxis (Vernation) in the Angiosperms," *Notes Roy. Bot. Gard. Edinb.*, **37:**161–214, 1978.

Czaja, A. T.: "Structure of Starch Grains and the Classification of Vascular Plant Families," *Taxon*, **27:**463–470, 1978.

Dahlgren, R.: "The Distribution of Characters Within an Angiosperm System, I. Some Embryological Characters," *Bot. Notiser*, **128:**181–197, 1975.

Daghlian, C. P.: "A Review of the Fossil Record of the Monocotyledons," *Bot. Rev.*, **47:**517–555, 1981.

Darrah, W. C.: *Principles of Paleobotany*, 2d ed., Ronald, New York, 1960.

Davis, G. L.: *Systematic Embryology of the Angiosperms*, Wiley, New York, 1966.

Davis, P. H., and V. H. Heywood: *Principles of Angiosperm Taxonomy*, Van Nostrand, Princeton, N.J., 1965.

Delevoryas, T.: "The Role of Paleobotany in Vascular Plant Classification," in V. H. Heywood and J. McNeil (eds.), *Phenetic and Phylogenetic Classification*, The Systematics Association, London, 1964, pp. 29–36.

————: "Paleobotany, Phylogeny, and a Natural System of Classification," *Taxon*, **18:**204–212, 1969.

Dickison, W. C.: "The Bases of Angiosperm Phylogeny: Vegetative Anatomy," *Ann. Mo. Bot. Gard.*, **62:**590–620, 1975.

Dietz, R. S., and J. C. Holden: "The Breakup of Pangaea," *Sci. Amer.*, **223**(4):30–41, 1968.

Dilcher, D. L.: "Approaches to the Identification of Angiosperm Leaf Remains," *Bot. Rev.*, **40:**1–157, 1974.

————: "Early Angiosperm Reproduction: An Introductory Report," *Rev. Palaeobot. Palynol.*, **27:**291–328, 1979.

Doyle, J. A., and L. J. Hickey: "Pollen and Leaves from the Mid-Cretaceous Potomac Group and Their Bearing on Early Angiosperm Evolution," in C. B. Beck (ed.), *Origin and Early Evolution of the Angiosperms*, Columbia, New York, 1976, pp. 139–206.

Downton, W. J. S.: "The Occurrence of C_4 Photosynthesis Among Plants," *Photosynthetica (Prague)*, **9:**96–105, 1975.

Eames, A.: *Morphology of the Angiosperms*, McGraw Hill, New York, 1961.

Erdtman, G.: *Pollen Morphology and Plant Taxonomy*, vol. 1, *Angiosperms* (corrected reprint of 1952 edition with a new addendum), Hafner, New York, 1966.

Esau, K.: *Plant Anatomy*, 2d ed., Wiley, New York, 1965.

Eyde, R. H.: "The Bases of Angiosperm Phylogeny: Floral Anatomy," *Ann. Mo. Bot. Gard.*, **62:**521–537, 1975.

Faegri, K., and L. van der Pijl: *The Principles of Pollination Ecology*, 3rd ed., Pergamon, New York, 1979.

———— and J. Iversen, *Textbook of Pollen Analysis*, 3rd ed., Blackwell, Oxford, 1975.

Fahn, A.: *Plant Anatomy,* 3rd ed., Pergamon Press, Oxford, 1982.

Fairbrothers, D. E.: "Perspectives in Plant Serotaxonomy," *Ann. Mo. Bot. Gard.,* **64:**147–160, 1977.

————: "Evidence from Nucleic Acid and Protein Chemistry, in Particular Serology, in Angiosperm Classification," *Nord J. Bot.,* **3:**35–41, 1983.

————, T. J. Mabry, R. L. Scogin, and B. L. Turner: "The Bases of Angiosperm Phylogeny: Chemotaxonomy," *Ann. Mo. Bot. Gard.,* **62:**765–800, 1975.

Faust, W. Z., and S. B. Jones: "The Systematic Value of Trichome Complements in a North American Group of *Vernonia* (Compositae)," *Rhodora,* **75:**517–528, 1973.

Ferguson, I. K., and J. Muller (eds.): *The Evolutionary Significance of the Exine,* Linnean Society Symposium Series, no. 1, Academic, London, 1976.

Fitch, W. M., and E. Margoliash: "The Usefulness of Amino Acid and Nucleotide Sequences in Evolutionary Studies," *Evol. Biol.* **4:**67–109, 1970.

Fryns-Claessens, E. and W. R. J. Van Cogghem: "A New Classification of the Ontogenetic Types of Stomata" *Bot. Rev.,* **39:**71–138, 1973.

Giannasi, D. E. and K. J. Niklas: "Flavonoid and Other Chemical Constituents of Fossil Miocene *Celtis* and *Ulmus* (Succor Creek Flora), *Science* (Washington, D.C.), **197:**765–767, 1977.

Gibbs, R. D.: *Chemotaxonomy of Flowering Plants,* 4 vols., McGill-Queens University Press, Montreal, 1974.

Gottlieb, L. D.: "Electrophoretic Evidence and Plant Systematics," *Ann. Mo. Bot. Gard.,* **64:**161–180, 1977.

Graham, A. (ed.): *Floristics and Paleofloristics of Asia and Eastern North America,* Elsevier, Amsterdam, 1972.

Grant, V., and K. A. Grant: *Flower Pollination in the Phlox Family,* Columbia, New York, 1965.

Grashoff, J., and B. L. Turner: " 'The New Synantherology'—A Case in Point for Points of View," *Taxon,* **19:**914–917, 1970. ("Must" reading for those who think taxonomy is a dull subject.)

Hadley, E. B., and D. A. Levin: "Habitat Differences of Three *Liatris* Species and Their Hybrid Derivatives in an Interbreeding Population," *Amer. J. Bot.,* **54:**550–559, 1967.

Hamrick, J. L., and R. W. Allard: "Correlations Between Quantitative Characters and Enzyme Genotypes in *Avena barbata,*" *Evolution,* **29:**438–442, 1975.

Harborne, J. B. (ed.): *Phytochemical Phylogeny, Academic, London, 1970.*

————: "Flavonoids and the Evolution of the Angiosperms," *Biochem. Syst. Ecol.,* **5:**7–22, 1977.

————: *"Introduction to Ecological Biochemistry,"* 2nd ed., Academic, London, 1982.

———— and B. L. Turner: *Plant Chemosystematics,* Academic Press, New York, 1984.

Harper, J. L., J. N. Clatworthy, I. H. McNaughton, and G. R. Sagar: "The Evolution and Ecology of Closely Related Species Living in the Same Area," *Evolution,* **15:**209–227, 1961.

Hawkes, J. G. (ed.): *Chemotaxonomy and Serotaxonomy,* Academic, London, 1968.

Heslop-Harrison, Y.: "Stigma Characteristics and Angiosperm Taxonomy," *Nord. J. Bot.,* **1:**401–420, 1981.

Hickey, L. F.: "Classification of the Architecture of Dicotyledonous Leaves," *Amer J. Bot.,* **60:**17–33, 1973.

———— and J. A. Wolfe: "The Bases of Angiosperms Phylogeny: Vegetative Morphology," *Ann. Mo. Bot. Gard.,* **62:**538–589, 1975.

Holt, P. C. (ed.): *The Distributional History of the Biota of the Southern Appalachians,* part

II, *Flora*, Research Division Monograph 2. Virginia Polytechnic Institute and State University, Blacksburg, 1970.

Ingham, J. L. and J. B. Harborne: "Phytoalexin Induction as a Dynamic Approach to the Study of Systematic Relationships Among Higher Plants," *Nature,* **260:**241–243, 1976.

Janzen, D. H.: "Coevolution of Mutualism Between Ants and Acacias in Central America," *Evolution,* **20:**249–275, 1966.

Jensen, U. and D. E. Fairbrothers (eds.): *Protein and Nucleic Acids in Plant Systematics,* Springer-Verlas, Berlin, 1983.

Jørgensen, L. B.: "Myrosin Cells and Dilated Cisternae of the Endoplasmic Reticulum in the Order Capparales," *Nord. J. Bot.,* **1:**433–445, 1981.

Jones, S. B.: "Cytogenetics and Affinities of *Vernonia* (Compositae) from the Mexican Highlands and Eastern North America," *Evolution,* **30:**455–462, 1976.

Keeley, S. C., and S. B. Jones: "Taxonomic Implications of External Pollen Morphology to *Vernonia (Compositae) in the West Indies,*" *Amer. J. Bot.,* **64:**576–584, 1977.

Kruckeberg, A. R.: "The Implications of Ecology for Plant Systematics," *Taxon,* **18:**92–120, 1969.

Leppik, E. E.: "Origin and Evolution of Bilateral Symmetry in Flowers," *Evol. Biol.,* **5:**49–58, 1972.

Levin, D. A.: "Plant Phenolics: An Ecological Perspective," *Amer. Nat.,* **105:**157–181, 1971.

Lott, J. N. A.: "Protein Bodies in Seeds," *Nord. J. Bot.* **1:**421–432, 1981.

Mabry, T. J.: "Pigment Dichotomy and DNA-RNA Hybridization Data for Centrospermous Families," *Plant Syst. Evol,* **126:**79–94, 1976.

Macior, L. W.: "Co-evolution of Plants and Animals—Systematic Insights from Plant-Insect Interactions," *Taxon,* **20:**17–28, 1971.

McKenzie, D. P.: "Plate Tectonics and Sea-floor Spreading," *Amer. Sci.,* **60:**425–435, 1972.

—— and Sclater, J. G.: "The Evolution of the Indian Ocean," *Sci. Amer.,* **228**(5):63–72, 1973.

Maheshwari, P.: *An Introduction to the Embryology of Angiosperms,* McGraw-Hill, New York, 1950.

Martin, A. C. and W. D. Barkley: *Seed Identification Manual,* University of California Press, Berkeley, 1961.

Melville, R.: "The Terminology of Leaf Architecture," *Taxon* **25:**549–561, 1976.

Metcalfe, C. R.: "An Anatomist's View on Angiosperm Classification," *Kew Bull.,* **9:**427–440, 1954.

——: *Anatomy of the Monocotyledons,* Vol. I., *Gramineae,* Clarendon, Oxford, 1960. (There are additional volumes in this series by Tomlinson, 1961, *Palmae;* Tomlinson, 1969, *Commelinales-Zingiberales;* Cutler, 1969, *Juncales:* Metcalfe, 1971, *Cyperaceae;* Ayensu, 1972, *Dioscoreales;* and Tomlinson, 1982, *Helobiae (Alismadidae).*

——: "Comparative Anatomy as a Modern Botanical Discipline, with Special Reference to Recent Advances in the Systematic Anatomy of Monocotyledons," *Adv. Bot. Res.,* **1:**101–147, 1963.

—— and L. Chalk: *Anatomy of the Dicotyledons,* 2nd ed., 2 vols., Clarendon Press, Oxford, 1979–83.

Millay, M. A. and T. N. Taylor: "Paleozoic Seed Fern Pollen Organs," *Bot. Rev.,* **45:**301–375, 1979.

Mooney, H. A.: "Influence of Soil Type on the Distribution of Two Closely Related Species of *Erigeron,*" *Ecology,* **47:**950–958, 1966.

Muller, J.: "Fossil Pollen Records of Extant Angiosperms," *Bot. Rev.,* **47:**1–146, 1981.

————: "Form and Function in Angiosperm Pollen," *Ann. Mo. Bot. Gard.,* **66:**593–632, 1979.

Muller, C. H., W. H. Muller, and B. L. Haines: "Volatile Growth Inhibitors Produced by Aromatic Shrubs," *Science, (Washington, D.C.)* **143:**471–473, 1964.

Nobs, M. A., et al.: "Physiological Ecology Investigations," *Carnegie Inst. Wash. Year Book,* **69:**624–662, 1971.

Nowicke, J. W. and J. J. Skvarla: "Pollen Morphology: The Potential Influence in Higher Order Systematics," *Ann. Mo. Bot. Gard.,* **66:**633–700, 1979.

Palser, B. F.: "The Bases of Angiosperm Phylogeny: Embryology," *Ann. Mo. Bot. Gard.,* **62:**621–646, 1975.

Pant, D. D.: "On the Ontogeny of Stomata and Other Homologous Structures," *Pl. Sci. Ser.,* **1:**1–24, 1965.

Payne, W. W.: "A Glossary of Plant Hair Terminology," *Brittonia,* **30:**239–255, 1978.

Radford, A. E., W. C. Dickison, J. R. Massey, and C. R. Bell: *Vascular Plant Systematics,* Harper & Row, New York, 1974.

Raven, P. H.: "Plant Species Disjunctions: A Summary," *Ann. Mo. Bot. Gard.,* **59:**234–246, 1972.

————: "Summary of the Biogeography Symposium," *Ann. Mo.Bot. Gard.,* **62:**380–385, 1975a.

————: "The Bases of Angiosperm Phylogeny: Cytology," *Ann. Mo. Bot. Gard.,* **62:**724–764, 1975b.

———— and D. I. Axelrod: "Angiosperm Biogeography and Past Continental Movements," *Ann. Mo. Bot. Gard.,* **61:**539–673, 1974.

Retallack, G. and D. L. Dilcher: "A Coastal Hypothesis for the Dispersal and Rise to Dominance of Flowering Plants," in K. J. Niklas (ed.) *Paleobotany, Paleoecology and Evolution,* Vol. 2, Praeger, New York, 1981,. pp. 27–77.

Robson, N. K. B., D. F. Cutler, and M. Gregory (eds.): *New Research in Plant Anatomy,* Academic, London, 1970.

Schuster, R. M.: "Plate Tectonics and Its Bearing on the Geographic Origin and Dispersal of Angiosperms," in C. B. Beck (ed.), *Origin and Early Evolution of the Angiosperms,* Columbia, New York, 1976, pp. 48–138.

Seaman, F. C.: "Sesquiterpene Lactones as Taxonomic Characters in the Asteraceae," *Bot. Rev.,* **48:**121–595, 1982.

Skvarla, J. J., and B. L. Turner: "Systematic Implications from Electron Microscope Studies of Compositae Pollen—A Review," *Ann. Mo. Bot. Gard.,* **53:**220–256, 1966.

Smith, P. M.: *"The Chemotaxonomy of Plants,"* Edward Arnold, London, 1976.

Solbrig, O. T.: "Fertility, Sterility and the Species Problem," in V. H. Heywood (ed.), *Modern Methods in Plant Taxonomy,* Academic, London, 1968, pp. 77–96.

Stace, C. A.: "Cuticular Studies as an Aid to Plant Taxonomy," *Bull. Br. Mus. (Nat. Hist.), Bot,* **4:**1–78, 1965.

Stebbins, G. L.: *Chromosomal Evolution in Higher Plants,* Addison-Wesley, Reading, Mass., 1971.

————: *Flowering Plants, Evolution Above the Species Level,* Belknap Press of Harvard University Press, Cambridge, 1974.

Stuessy, T. F.: "Ultrastructural Data for the Practicing Plant Systematist," *Amer. Zool.,* **19:**621–636, 1979.

Swain, T. (ed.): *Chemistry in Evolution and Systematics,* Butterworth, London, 1973.

Taylor, T. N.: *Paleobotany,* McGraw-Hill, New York, 1981.

Turner, B. L.: "Chemosystematics: Recent Developments," *Taxon,* **18:**134–151, 1969.

U.S. Geological Survey: *Compendium Index of Paleobotany,* Paleobotany Library, U.S. National Museum, Washington. (A literature index, unpublished, but may be consulted at the Smithsonian Institution in Washington.)

Van Cotthem, W. R. J.: "A Classification of Stomatal Types, *Bot. J. Linn. Soc.*, **63:**235–246, 1970.

Walker, J. W.: "Comparative Pollen Morphology and Phylogeny of the Ranalean Complex," in C. B. Beck (ed.), *Origin and Early Evolution of Angiosperms,* Columbia, New York, 1976, pp. 241–299.

———— and J. A. Doyle: "The Bases of Angiosperm Phylogeny: Palynology," *Ann. Mo. Bot. Gard.,* **62:**664–723, 1975.

Wodehouse, R. P.: *Pollen Grains,* McGraw-Hill, New York, 1935.

Wolfe, J. A., J. A. Doyle, and V. M. Page: "The Bases of Angiosperm Phylogeny: Paleobotany," *Ann. Mo. Bot. Gard.,* **62:**801–824, 1975.

Young, D. A. and D. S. Seigler (eds.): *"Phytochemistry and Angiosperm Phylogeny,"* Praeger, New York, 1981.

CHAPTER 6

THE ORIGIN AND CLASSIFICATION OF THE MAGNOLIOPHYTA (ANGIOSPERMS)

Among the plants inhabiting the earth, the angiosperms or flowering plants, have the greatest number of species and occupy more types of habitats than any other group. They include trees, shrubs, perennials, annuals, and lianas. They range in size from tiny duckweeds to giant trees. Adaptive radiation of angiosperms has produced parasites, saprophytes without chlorophyll, and epiphytes. Insectivorous species such as pitcher plants, Venus flytrap, and sundew represent unusual leaf adaptations. Diversity in flower structure is another remarkable feature of flowering plants. The term *flower* usually refers to a structure containing sepals, petals, stamens, and carpels. However, flowers may consist only of a single ovary or a single stamen.

Charles Darwin once called the origin of angiosperms an "abominable mystery" because little evidence was available to him to help trace the angiosperms back in time. The origin and evolution of angiosperms continues to present an intriguing challenge to those paleobotanists who specialize in the study of fossil angiosperms. The collections of fossils, the accumulated literature, and the experience available today provide a much better understanding of angiosperm origin. With the accessibility of increasing information from many sources, modern angiosperm systematics allows a synthesis of data never before, possible. Angiosperm classification research is in a new phase; basic and far-reaching results will produce the best classification possible.

CHARACTERISTICS OF FLOWERING PLANTS

The angiosperms and gymnosperms constitute the seed plants. Generally, the difference between them is the extent to which the ovules are exposed at the time of pollination. The characteristics of angiosperms are the following: (1) vessels in the xylem, (2) sieve elements and companion cells in the phloem, (3) an embryo sac of eight nuclei (one egg, two synergids, three antipodal, and two polar), (4) double fertilization, and (5) closed carpels. There are numerous exceptions to these characteristics.

Xylem vessels are not peculiar to angiosperms because they occur among some gymnosperms and there are certain angiosperms that have vesselless wood. Many exceptions are known to the eight-nucleate embryo sac. The gametophyte generation of flowering plants is generally more simplified and reduced than that found in the gymnosperms. The male and female gametophytes of flowering plants are small and function efficiently with relatively few cell divisions. Angiosperms have *double fertilization,* with one sperm fusing with the egg nucleus and the other sperm fusing with the two polar nuclei in the embryo sac. The latter results in initiation of *endosperm,* the nutritive tissue of the seed. In angiosperms, the embryo is formed directly from the zygote. Double fertilization is not known to occur in other groups of plants. In the angiosperms, the specialized megasporophylls (or carpels) that enclose the ovules are unique and provide the basis for the name *angiosperm,* "covered seed." The carpels cover the ovules and facilitate adaptations for seed dispersal. Pollen collects and germinates on a stigmatic surface, forming a pollen tube that carries the sperm nucleus to the egg nucleus located within the embryo sac of the ovule. However, in gymnosperms, the pollen grains must have direct access to the ovule. The germination of pollen on the stigmatic portion of the carpel, *not* directly on the ovule, is an important feature of angiosperms. Many of the unique reproductive characters of angiosperms, including an efficient and shortened life cycle, may have contributed to their success in the plant world.

The angiosperms share a number of common features. In bisexual flowers, the relative positions of the stamens and carpels do not vary. The carpels are always in the uppermost position of the floral axis. The types of appendages on the floral axis—that is, sepals, petals, stamens, and carpels—are uniform in the flowering plants. The structure of the angiospermous stamen is constant, with four sporangia in two pairs. The monosulcate pollen of certain dicotyledons and all the monocotyledons is analogous. Xylem vessels and phloem sieve tubes provide the angiosperms with a highly efficient conducting system resulting in their adaptability to arid regions. The leaves of many flowering plants have secondary and tertiary venation with isolated termination of veinlet endings. This is related to transpiration and permits the development of large, flat photosynthetic surfaces. Because of these and other adaptations, the angiosperms have been able to dominate successfully the terrestrial flora of the earth.

The angiosperms are a natural group, sharing characters that make them unique from all other vascular plants (Cronquist, 1968; Stebbins, 1974; Takhtajan, 1969). These common features suggest that the angiosperms be considered loosely monophyletic (see Faegri, 1980, for a philosophical discussion of the problem of mono- or polyphyletic origin of the angiosperms). Dahlgren (1983) suggests that the remarkably consistent character syndrome in present angiosperms evolved from one particular line of gymnosperms and thus they are monophyletic. Possibly the angiosperms are derived not necessarily from a common ancestral species but perhaps from a group of related organisms. Similar evolutionary changes may have taken place in several closely parallel lines to produce the features recognized today as angiospermous (Cronquist,

1965; Krassilov, 1977). For clues to a group that might have been ancestral to the angiosperms, it is necessary to examine the fossil record.

FOSSIL RECORD: TIME OF ORIGIN AND DIVERSIFICATION*

The rise of angiosperms to dominance was something remarkable in the earth's history. About 100 million years ago, during a period of only 10 million years, the flowering plants spread over the earth from the equator to the poles. This distribution was apparently undeterred by ocean barriers or competition from the established vegetation that was dominated by gymnosperms and ferns. How the angiosperms managed this remarkable dispersal has long been a puzzle, but the most encouraging effect of the recent upsurge in research on angiosperm origins is the recognition that the fossil record can furnish critical evidence for the origin and diversification of the flowering plants. In the past, paleobotanists, having been unsuccessful in illuminating the origin of the angiosperms, formulated three hypotheses to explain this failure (Hughes, 1976): (1) incompleteness of the fossil record and the lack of fossil flowers; (2) a long and slow evolutionary history of flowering plants; and (3) evolution of early angiosperms in upland areas away from the necessary basins where fossils could have been preserved.

These so-called "escape" hypotheses led some botanists to suggest that the angiosperms originated in the early Mesozoic or even the late Paleozoic and that they underwent extensive diversification by the Aptian-Albian stages of the lower Cretaceous (see Figure 6-1 for a geologic time scale). However, after reviewing the supporting evidence for this hypothesis, Wolfe, Doyle, and Page (1975) found ". . . no unequivocal evidence that indicates a pre-Cretaceous origin for the angiosperms." The best available evidence from the fossil record indicates that the angiosperms originated during the early Cretaceous about 130 to 135 million years ago.

Taylor (1981) suggests that pollen and megafossil data indicate the origin of the angiosperms during the very early Cretaceous or the latter stages of the Jurassic. It is likely that these early angiosperms were represented by a relatively small group of plants.

In the older Cretaceous sediments, the angiosperm fossil records are overshadowed by those of ferns and gymnosperms, and it is not until the late part of the Cretaceous that the angiosperms become dominant. The first monosulcate angiosperm pollen grains, characteristic of the primitive dicotyledons and the monocotyledons, appear in the Barremian stage of the lower Cretaceous. Tricolpate pollen grains, which are found in the more advanced dicotyledons, are first reported from slightly younger Aptian rocks. Pollen sequences have clearly shown a pattern of increasing diversity in the Cretaceous. The pollen of primitive angiosperms, however, is almost indistinguishable from gymnospermous pollen, creating uncertainty·about the identification of the older fossil pollen. At an early date the angiosperms split into the monocotyledons and

---

*See Table 6-1 and Figure 6-1 for a record of geologic events and a timetable.

10^6 years	Era	Period	Epoch		Stage	Approximate Age 10^6 years
		Quaternary	Holocene Pleistocene			
						2.5
		Tertiary	Neogene	Pliocene		12
				Miocene		
						25
	Cenozoic			Oligocene		38
			Paleogene	Eocene	Upper	46
					Middle	50
					Lower	
						54
				Paleocene		
65						
			Upper		Maestrichtian	70
					Campanian	80
					Santonian	85
					Coniacian	90
					Turonian	100
		Cretaceous			Cenomanian	
						110
	Mesozoic		Lower		Albian	
					Aptian	122
					Barremian	125
					Hauterivian	127
					Valanginian	130
					Ryazanian	132
135						135
		Jurassic				
180						
		Triassic				
225						
		Permian				
270						
		Carboniferous				
350						
		Devonian				
405	Paleozoic					
		Silurian				
440						
		Ordovician				
500						
		Cambrian				
600						

Note: The stages Albian through Ryazanian are bracketed as **Neocomian**.

Source: Modified and adapted from Tschudy and Scott (1969) and Raven and Axelrod (1974).

FIGURE 6-1
Geologic time scale.

TABLE 6-1
GEOLOGIC RECORD OF EVENTS

10^6 Years ago since start	Epoch or period	Geologic events, climatic trends, plant and animal development
2.5	Pleistocene	Cascades, Sierra and Coast Ranges rise, Rockies, Andes and Himalayas renewed; successive glaciations and warmings; development of modern floras, man evolves, large mammals develop and then die out.
12	Pliocene	Climate similar to present.
25	Miocene	Himalayas rise; cool at first, warming later.
38	Oligocene	Northern and southern continents widely separated, Alps rise, Rockies and Andes erode; warm early, cooler later; rapid approach to modern angiosperm families, Compositae pollen first appears.
54	Eocene	Temperature rise near end; angiosperm inflorescences and flowers well adapted to wind and insect pollination appear; modern lineages of vertebrates and insects appear; radiation of higher insects.
65	Paleocene	Lowland swamps decrease, Rockies and Andes complete major rise; climate cooler and more varied; groups of higher insects appear, primates arise; the Alismatidae appear.
110	Upper Cretaceous	Andes and Rockies arise, especially later; much of North America covered by seas; climate cooling at end; angiosperms become dominant; ca. 90–100 million years ago modern lineages of angiosperms appear, mammals and birds begin to diversify, dinosaurs become extinct at end; the Commelinidae, Liliidae, Arecidae, Dilleniidae, Caryophyllidae and Rosidae appear.

Continued

TABLE 6-1
GEOLOGIC RECORD OF EVENTS (CONTINUED)

10^6 Years ago since start	Epoch or period	Geologic events, climatic trends, plant and animal development
135	Lower Cretaceous	Climate warm and moist; oscillations of epicontinental seas; first documented angiosperms appear, monosulcate pollen ca. 125 million years ago, tricolpate pollen ca. 122 million years ago; the Hamamelidae and Magnoliidae appear.
180	Jurassic	Widespread seas in North America but with continental emergence toward end, Atlantic Ocean forming as continents drift; dinosaurs flourish, first birds, mammals and modern amphibian types; perhaps first angiosperms in a world dominated by gymnosperms and ferns.
225	Triassic	Continental drift, present continents form; climates varied; first dinosaurs; conifers highly diversified with most modern families present.
270	Permian	Appalachian Mountains arise; ginkgo-like plants appear, cycads appear.
325	Carboniferous (Pennsylvanian)	Climate warm, humid; coal deposited; major development of terrestrial vegetation, conifers appear, seed ferns abundant, bryophytes appear, lycopods dominant vegetation, equisetum-like plants reach maximum diversity.
350	Carboniferous (Mississippian)	Marine limestones deposited; marine evolution; ferns appear.
405	Devonian	Climate seasonal; fern-like plants appear, lycods appear early, equisetum-like plants appear, progymnosperms appear, terrestrial plants and animals arise, tree-like land plants appear, amphibians appear, seed-ferns appear.
440	Silurian	Vascular plants appear.
500	Ordovician	Radiation of marine animals, first fishes.
600	Cambrian	Seas expand; first abundant fossils.
4500	Pre-Cambrian	Earliest life arises.

dicotyledons and very slowly gained prominence in the terrestrial flora that was largely dominated by ferns and gymnosperms. The progression of pollen from primitive types in older strata to more derived types in younger sediments indicates to paleobotanists that angiosperms underwent much diversification during the Cretaceous (Raven and Axelrod, 1974; Wolfe, Doyle, and Page, 1975). By the Turonian and Coniacian stages, angiosperm pollen had become more abundant than fern spores and gymnosperm pollen.

Paleobotanists such as David Dilcher working with fossils of the middle Cretaceous have provided important new ideas about angiosperm evolution. Angiosperm reproductive structures found by Dilcher and colleagues indicate that some early angiosperms bore separate male and female flowers (Figure 6-2) and others were bisexual. They also suggest that some of the plants were wind pollinated or were generalists, that is, pollinated by both wind and insects. Also, the seeds lacked adaptations for animal dispersal, suggesting that these plants were generalists in seed dispersal as well. It also appears that early Cretaceous fossil pollen is predominantly "generalist" in size and structure.

Dilcher has found a fossil bisexual flower that is 95–93 million years old, the oldest bisexual flower thus far found. His work has shown that lineages of bisexual and unisexual flowers coexisted in the early history of the angiosperms. The fossil record indicates an extremely rapid radiation of types of angiosperm reproduction during the early Cretaceous. It appears possible that the extinct ancestors of today's major angiosperm groups may have been derived in the early phases of angiosperm evolution. By the Maestrichtian stage at the close of the Cretaceous, a number of modern orders are represented by fossil pollen and leaves. Members of such groups as the Magnoliales, Hammamelidales, Ranunculales, and Theales and some monocotyledons had appeared by this time. Evolution and diversification of the angiosperms continued into the Cenozoic. Fossil flowers are known from Eocene strata (Crepet, Dilcher, and Potter, 1974). Although there is some evidence that the group may be older, pollen of the Compositae (considered one of the most advanced families of dicotyledons) appears at the end of the Oligocene (Muller, 1970).

Only a few records are available of putative dicotyledonous woods of early Cretaceous age. They represent primitive types of xylem and lack the features of advanced angiosperms. Investigations of fossil leaves reveal a pattern of increasing diversity during the Cretaceous. These represent a transition from leaf types common to certain present-day Magnoliales to those morphologically similar to living Rosidae (Hickey and Doyle, 1977).

ANCESTORS OF THE FLOWERING PLANTS

At one time or another, almost every group of fossil vascular plants has been suggested as a possible progenitor of the angiosperms. With many of these suggestions discounted, the Mesozoic gymnosperms, especially the seed ferns, are believed to have been the progenitors of the angiosperms (Taylor, 1981). It should be remembered that the term *gymnosperm* describes a life habit and does not refer to a phyletically cohesive group. The major groupings of gymnosperms are shown in Table 6-2.

One order of gymnosperms that seems to have some angiosperm-like features is

FIGURE 6-2
Archaeanthus linnbergeri. Reconstruction of a leafy branch bearing a multifollicular axis from the mid-Cretaceous (uppermost Albian/mid-Cenomanian). Clusters of follicles were borne terminally on the axis; the scars at the base are interpreted as representing the places where stamens and perianth parts were attached. Drawing kindly furnished by Dr. David Dilcher.

the Caytoniales. This group of fossil seed ferns had ovules semi-enclosed in small pouches. Proponents of the Caytoniales as the ancestor of the angiosperms point to the almost sealed cupule as suggestive of the way a carpel might have evolved. The Caytoniales also exhibited leaves with a netlike pattern of venation, tubes leading to the micropyle of the ovule, and sporangia that superficially resemble anthers.

The seed fern order Glossopteridales has been considered to be a forerunner of the angiosperms (Figure 6-3). Well-preserved seeds borne on the surface of a partially enrolled megasporophyll that is identical to a typical leaf of the group support this

TABLE 6-2
CLASSIFICATION OF THE GYMNOSPERMS

Division Pinophyta (Gymnosperms)
    Subdivision Cycadophytina
        Class Lyginopteridopsida* (seed ferns)
            Order Lyginopteridales
            Order Medullosales
            Order Callistophytales
            Order Calamopityales
            Order Caytoniales
            Order Corystospermales
            Order Peltaspermales
            Order Glossopteridales
        Class Bennettitopsida* (Cycadeoids)
        Class Cycadopsida (Cycads)
    Subdivision Pinophytina
        Class Ginkgoöpsida (ginkgo)
        Class Cordaitopsida*
        Class Coniferopsida
            Order Voltziales* (transition conifers)
            Order Coniferales (conifers)
            Order Taxales (taxads)
    Subdivision Gnetophytina
            Order Ephedrales
            Order Welwitchiales
            Order Gnetales

*Known only from the fossil record

FIGURE 6-3
Ovuliferous structures in glossopterids (A–C). It is suggested that the "cupules" in the glossopterids correspond to the outer integument of an angiosperm ovule. (*From Dahlgren, Nord. J. Bot.,* **3:***119–149, 1983; used with permission.*)

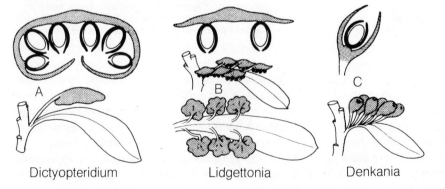

Dictyopteridium   Lidgettonia   Denkania

assumption. However, the pollen of the Glossopteridales is unlike that of early angiosperms.

The Czekanowskiales, an order of Jurassic seed plants belonging to the class Ginkgoöpsida, are regarded by some as early angiosperms. As in the Caytoniales, the ovule was surrounded by a cupule having a flange that somewhat resembled a stigmatic surface; however, the pollen apparently landed directly on the micropyle of the ovule.

The Bennettitopsida (cycadeoids) also have often been suggested as a progenitor of the angiosperms. This hypothesis is based largely on the nature and organization of the reproductive structures of the cycadeoids, which were superficially similar to a "flower." This structure consisted of a whorl of microsporophylls surrounding numerous stalked ovules. Among the ovules were scales that possibly fused to form a carpel-like structure.

The cycad line has also been proposed as a progenitor of the angiospermous condition. The recently described fossil family Dirhopalostachyaceae of the late Jurassic and early Cretaceous had paired capsules each with a flattened seed. Again, the suggestion is based largely on the ovule bearing unit.

The search for angiosperm features among fossils of the Jurassic and early Cretaceous focuses on the enclosure of the ovules to form a carpel-like structure. However, other unique features of angiosperms, such as double fertilization and endosperm, will not likely be detected in fossil specimens due to their microscopic aspect. Thus it is extremely difficult in pre-Cretaceous fossils to determine precisely what is and what is not an angiosperm. Taylor (1981) suggests that, "Perhaps a more realistic and rewarding avenue of investigation would be to view fossil angiosperms as representing a particular level of evolution, with the earliest forms not demonstrating the total complement of modern angiosperm characters."

Although some groups have been eliminated as likely ancestors of angiosperms, Darwin's "abominable mystery" is not completely solved. However, it appears likely that plants having some angiosperm features could have evolved from the seed fern line in the late Jurassic or very early Cretaceous. Certainly a vast gene pool was available at the time to give rise to the first angiosperms, which might be called the *proangiosperms*.

EARLY FLOWERING PLANTS

The early ideas of angiosperm evolution were based on analysis of modern, tropical plants. These models accounted for the paucity of fossils by hypothesizing that the first angiosperms were upland plants that diversified in arid or tropical regions in the Permian about 250 million years ago. The lack of fossils was explained by the fact that the plants from upland areas are not usually preserved as fossils. Migrations of the angiosperms to coastal and alluvial areas about 110 million years ago would have allowed deposition of plant remains and fossilization. One early popular idea suggested that the first angiosperms were tropical, mesophytic trees with pinnate leaves and clusters of large arillate follicles.

Another hypothesis based on living angiosperms suggested that the first angiosperms were *Magnolia*-like evergreen trees in tropical uplands and were pollinated by insects.

FIGURE 6-4
Magnolia campbelli (Magnoliaceae). (*a*) Section showing arrangement of stamens and carpels. (*b*) Stamen. (*c*) Seed. (*d*) Section of seed (Note tiny embryo). (*From J. Hutchinson,* The Families of Flowering Plants, *Oxford University Press, 1973; with permission.*)

This classical theory holds that the primitive angiosperm flower was solitary, terminal, bisexual, actinomorphic, with numerous sepals and petals (or tepals), stamens, and carpels all spirally arranged on an elongate axis (Takhtajan, 1969). The stamens were broad and leaflike. The carpels were large lacking both well-developed styles and distinctive terminal stigmas similar to those found in present-day Magnoliaceae (Figure 6-4). Flower structures with spirally arranged carpels similar to follicles (not unlike some of the Magnoliales) are common among fossil remains in the Lower Cretaceous (see Figure 6-2).

In some plants ancestral to the flowering plants, ovules were borne on the margins or scattered over the surface of open megasporophylls. The first angiosperms may have had megasporophylls resembling young leaves, and these were folded along their midrib with the ovules inside (Figure 6-5*c–f*). The megasporophylls upon reduction gave rise to a carpel. A *carpel* is a megasporophyll, that is, a modified leaflike structure bearing ovules (megasporangia). In the first angiosperms, the margins of the carpels may not have been fused at the time of pollination. Thus, the stigmatic surface, or the area where the pollen must land for germination, was along the entire marginal suture as it is in the living genus *Degeneria* (Figure 6-5).

The first flowering plants are believed to have had two integuments or tissue layers surrounding the embryo, which later form the seed coat. Ranalian families possessing primitive characters have an ovule with a large nucellus of many cells and an embryo sac (= megagametophyte) of eight nuclei. A large endosperm is found in many of the families today regarded as having primitive characters. Some botanists have reasoned that the first flowering plants had a minute embryo embedded in copious oily endosperm. This is similar to the embryo and endosperm of *Magnolia*. Double fer-

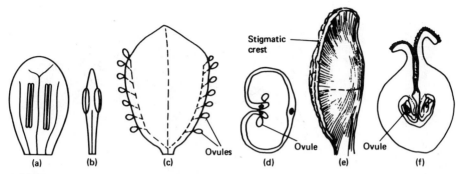

FIGURE 6-5
Stamens and carpels. (a) Leaf-like microsporophyll (stamen) believed by Takhtajan to be primitive. (b) Stamen from Winteraceae. (c) Hypothetical megasporophyll with ovules and three vascular strands. (d) Hypothetical megasporophyll (cross section) closed to form a carpel. (e) Primitive conduplicate carpel of *Drimys* (Winteraceae); note stigmatic crest along suture. (f) Cross section of a conduplicate carpel of *Degeneria* (Degeneriaceae); cross section cut in about the position of the dashed line shown in c. (e and f from Foster and Gifford, 1974; used with permission of W. H. Freeman Co.)

tilization is regarded as primitive because of its widespread distribution throughout the angiosperms.

Stebbins (1974) presented the opinion that the first angiosperms were small woody plants inhabiting pioneer habitats that were exposed to seasonal drought. They had small leaves and moderate sized flowers. Stebbins argues that the angiosperms arose under conditions of environmental stress that were favorable to the rapid development of flowers and seed.

More recently, Takhtajan (1980) suggested that the earliest angiosperms had the following characteristics: small woody plants; leaves simple, entire, pinnately veined; flowers solitary, both terminal and axillary, of moderate size, with an elongated receptacle, perianth of modified bracts; stamens leaflike; pollen monosulcate; and carpels unsealed, conduplicate with the stigmatic surface along the margin.

Alternative Views of the Primitive Angiosperm Flower

The prevailing ideas regarding the primitiveness of angiosperm flowers have changed in recent years (Carlquist, 1969; Gottsberger, 1974; Thorne, 1976). Morphologists and paleobotanists are questioning some of the concepts of the classical *"Magnolia* is primitive" school. They reject the idea that the long floral axis of *Magnolia,* with its many micro- and megasporophylls, is the prototype of flowers in the angiosperms. They object to the concept of leafy stamens and conduplicate (folded lengthwise) carpels as being primitive. However, Dilcher's fossils (Fig. 6-2) point out that flowers that are clearly Magnoliidae appear early in the history of the angiosperms.

As an alternative hypothesis, some morphologists suggest that the most primitive flowers were probably middle-sized and grouped together into lateral clusters or inflorescences much like those in family Winteraceae. The Winteraceae have small flowers in lateral clusters, with several stamens and one to several carpels. The flowers of *Drimys* (Winteraceae) are shown in Figure 6-6. The Winteraceae are regarded as

FIGURE 6-6
Drimys winteri (Winteraceae). (*a*) Vertical section of flower. (*b*) Flower with petals removed. (*c*) Stamen. (*d*) Cross section of carpels. (*e*) One carpel. (*f*) Carpel in vertical section. (*From J. Hutchinson,* The Families of Flowering Plants, *Oxford University Press, 1973; with permission.*)

primitive because they have: (1) great similarity between their micro- and megasporophylls; (2) unifacial (one-front surface) carpels and stamens; (3) high chromosome numbers suggesting a long evolutionary history; (4) morphology similar to the pteridosperms; and (5) vesselless wood similar to that of the gymnosperms (Ehrendorfer et al., 1968). Additionally, the beetle pollination of *Drimys* is of a less specialized type than that of *Magnolia*. The latter has many functional modifications for attracting beetles (Gottsberger, 1974).

The Fossil Record of Early Angiosperms

Paleobotanists such as Dilcher (1979), reason that the Magnoliales should no longer be thought to epitomize the only primeval angiosperm flower. Dilcher and his colleagues suggest that the floral structures of the Ranalian complex (the subclass Magnoliidae) may represent only one line of early angiosperm evolution and not necessarily the most primitive. They point out that the fossil record indicates that the very earliest angiosperms were probably woody, small-leaved plants occurring in the rift valley system adjoining Africa and South America. Retallack and Dilcher (1981) suggest that some of these angiosperms adapted to the disturbed coastal environments and became widespread during changing sea levels during the early Cretaceous. In North America angiosperms soon extended from the present Gulf of Mexico as far north as Alberta, Canada, around 110 million years ago. As they flourished, the angiosperms replaced the previous dominant plants of the coastal swamps, marshes, and levees along streams. However, in the uplands, the conifer-dominated vegetation was not yet affected.

Retallack and Dilcher further hypothesize that by the late Cretaceous these ancient angiosperms had become increasingly isolated because of both the continental drift and the retreat of the seas. The angiosperms may have migrated into a variety of disturbed and depositional environments and moved into the interior along the alluvial flood plains of streams. Migrations of these pioneering plants allowed further contact with insects and other animals and favored co-evolution with animals in relation to pollination and seed dispersal. Eventually, the angiosperms moved into the uplands and became dominant around 100 to 90 million years ago.

Dilcher (1979) argues that the first angiosperms were probably generalists, pollinated by both wind and a variety of insects. As their numbers increased, adaptive radiation soon produced species pollinated exclusively by wind or by insects as well as species whose pollination was that of a generalist. Fossils thus far studied suggest that the early angiosperms had unisexual and bisexual flowers with simple floral parts clustered on elongate axes or in catkinlike or headlike structures. This suggests that some of the features of the subclass Hamamelidae may be primitive rather than derived. The fossil record suggests that early angiosperm reproductive structures had few (3–10), free, floral parts, few to many carpels, radial symmetry, and small seeds dispersed by wind and water.

Some paleobotanists, such as D. I. Axelrod (Raven and Axelrod, 1974), suggest that the angiosperms evolved from some primitive gymnosperm, probably a shrub, in the Mesozoic and Paleozoic periods. This is earlier than can be documented from the fossil record. Axelrod suggests that early evolution of the angiosperms took place away from the lowland areas where fossils are normally found and that the first angiosperms had pollen that could not be distinguished from gymnosperm pollen. In this scenario, the angiosperms evolved into a variety of forms in the uplands of the tropics without the opportunity for their remains to have been made part of the fossil record. These tropical uplands had a climate with seasonal droughts, and under eco-logical stresses a number of adaptations developed that made angiosperms successful, for example, a shortened life cycle, small tough leaves, vessel elements, and a small seed that protects the embryo. This scenario by Axelrod differs primarily from that by Dilcher in the time and place of origin.

INTERRELATIONSHIPS OF ANGIOSPERMS AND ANIMALS

Biologists now realize that the flowering plants are closely interrelated with animals in the evolutionary processes. Noting the amazing correlation between host plants and certain animals (particularly insects), biologists have proposed that patterns of adap-tations are generated by a process of reciprocal interactions called co-evolution. Kras-silov (1977) believes angiosperm differentiation was directly related to mammalization and other processes in the development of Cenozoic flowering plants. One of the important areas of interaction and adaptation has been that of pollination and flower development.

Pollination

The early seed plants, various gymnosperms, were pollinated by wind. Ovules borne within cones on the edges of leaves exuded drops of sticky sap from their micropyles, trapping pollen grains as in present-day gymnosperms. It is likely that insects, probably beetles, very early were attracted by both the sticky droplets and pollen, and inad-vertently began to carry pollen from plant to plant.

According to Dilcher, the fossil record indicates that the first angiosperms were wind pollinated. In the case of the insect pollinated lines of angiosperms, the more attractive the plants were to beetles the more frequently they would be visited by the pollen-laden beetles and the more seeds they would produce. The activities of insects were encouraged by the evolutionary development of edible flower parts, protein rich pollen, and nectaries.

Beetles were plentiful when the angiosperms appeared and may have been the first animal pollinators. Today they assist with the pollination of *Magnolia, Drimys,* and numerous other flowering plants with primitive characters (Figure 6-7 and Figure 6-8). The accidental beetle pollination provided a more efficient method of pollination than chance pollination by wind. The insects—bees, butterflies, and so on—we usually think of as pollinators had not yet appeared when the first angiosperms evolved.

Pollen distribution was more effective, and therefore seed production increased when plants efficiently attracted insects. Through natural selection, the ancestral an-

FIGURE 6-7
First-day flower of *Magnolia grandiflora,* with beetles (*Trichiotinus piger*) chewing on stigmatic papillae. Note that the inner petals partially cover the gynoecium. Beetles enter the flower just as petals open. Later, as petals open completely, the stigmas turn brown and are not receptive to pollen (about 1X). In the process of eating pollen the insects become coated with pollen, and subsequent visits to receptive stigmas result in pollination. (*Photograph by L. B. Thein).*

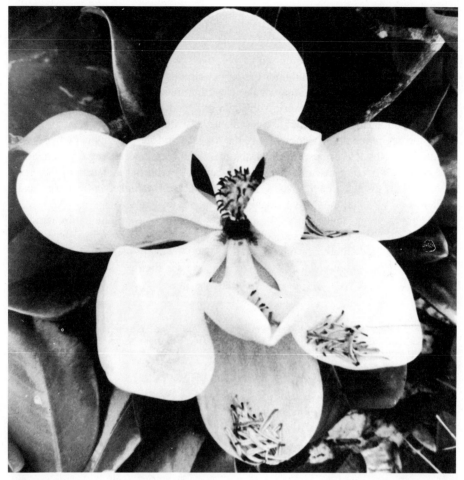

FIGURE 6-8
Late second-day flower of *Magnolia grandiflora*. The stigma have turned brown and the
dehisced stamens have fallen from the stalk of the gynoecium. When the stigmas are receptive
or the pollen dehisces from the stamens, the petals are partially or completely closed to
preserve food for beetles ($^3/_4$X). (*Photograph by L. B. Thein.*)

giosperms developed adaptations to encourage beetle pollination. The development of
a bisexual flower with adjacent carpels and stamens made beetle visits more efficient.
Plants that provided food in the form of nectar, pollen, sap, and succulent tidbits of
tissue attracted more beetles, giving these plants an advantage over plants that attracted
fewer insects. This successful attraction of insects created a problem. The ovules of
many early flowers were probably exposed on megasporophylls and required protection
to prevent them from being eaten. The hollow closed carpel functioned to protect the
ovules from insect predation. The protection afforded by the closed carpels allowed
the ovules to become smaller and capable of faster development. The development of

a shorter life cycle and reduced energy requirements was advantageous under conditions of stress and seasonal drought—conditions under which the angiosperms had an advantage over the gymnosperms and true ferns.

Before the evolution of the closed carpel, each ovule collected its own pollen by way of the micropyle droplet. After the carpel closed, the pollen-collecting function had to shift from each individual ovule to a centralized stigmatic area. Eventually, during the evolution of the flowering plants, a style and stigma developed that required the germination of pollen some distance from the ovule.

By the beginning of the Cenozoic era, the fossil record shows that the higher insects (including moths, butterflies, bees, wasps, and flies) were undergoing diversification. The rise of the higher insect orders was coincidental with the radiation of flowering plants, which provided energy sources for the insects. The higher insects profoundly influenced the evolutionary diversification of the angiosperms.

The angiosperms underwent a transition from promiscuous pollination by wind and unspecialized beetles to restricted pollination by insects and other animals specialized for flower pollination. By means of natural selection, many plant species developed floral features to accommodate their insect visitors (see Figure 6-9). The evolution of

FIGURE 6-9
Adaptive radiation for pollination by different pollen vectors in the *Phlox* family Polemoniaceae. (*From Stebbins, 1974; after Grant and Grant, 1965. Used with permission of Belknap Press of Harvard University Press and Dr. Verne Grant.*)

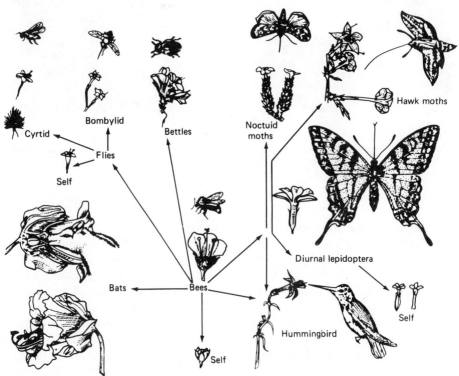

structural change in flowers permitted more effective pollination, resulting in the production of more of its kind. Diversification of the flowering plants also caused evolution in insects of features adapted for flower visitation. Thus, there was a mutual influence of plants on insects and insects on plants. Transfer of pollen by bees, wasps, moths, butterflies, flies, birds, and bats is generally considered advanced as compared with the primitive but effective pollination by beetles. Of course, there have been reversals in this trend. Secondary wind pollination has reappeared a number of different times in families, e.g., ragweed (*Ambrosia*) Compositae and the grasses (Gramineae).

Beetle Pollination   Plants pollinated by beetles typically have dull or white flowers, spicy, fermenting or fruity odors, edible petals or food bodies, and ovules heavily protected against the chewing mouthparts typical of beetles. In the members of the 16 families of beetles known to visit flowers, the sense of smell appears better developed than sight, thus explaining the strong odors and dull colors of beetle pollinated flowers.

Bee Pollination   Most of the 20,000 species of bees pollinate flowers and feed on nectar and pollen. Bees see in the ultraviolet part of the spectrum, thus shades of red appear black to a bee. Bee-pollinated flowers are typically brightly colored, usually blue or yellow (never pure red), often with a distinctive pattern or honey guides indicating the positions of the nectaries. Since the bee lands and enters the flower, a landing platform is typical for bee-pollinated species. Observations of bee behavior suggest that in some cases bees exhibit a high degree of constancy to particular species of flowers. This flower constant behavior is an important factor contributing to the evolutionary development of angiosperms.

Moth and Butterfly Pollination   Plants that have co-evolved with butterflies and with diurnal (day active) moths often have flowers similar to bee-pollinated flowers. However, there is some evidence that butterflies may be able to see red as well as blue and yellow. Most moths, however, are night active and pollinate white or yellow flowers that are open at night or those that stand out against a dark background. Many moth-pollinated flowers have heavy fragrances that assist the moths in locating them. Typical flowers have long slender corolla tubes or spurs with basal nectaries. These nectaries are accessible only to the long tongues of hovering moths and butterflies. Since moths and butterflies hover over the flower and do not land, moth- and butterfly-pollinated flowers do not have landing platforms typical of bee-pollinated flowers.

Bird Pollination   In the New World, hummingbirds visit numerous angiosperms, and in other parts of the world, specialized families of birds are adapted for flower visitation. Typical bird-pollinated flowers have large amounts of thin nectar, little fragrance, and bright red or yellow coloration. Birds have a poor ability to detect odors but a well-developed sense of visual acuity and often show flower constant behavior.

Bat Pollination   Flower-visiting bats occur in the tropical areas of both the Old and New World. Typical bat-pollinated flowers open at night and are dull in color. Flower visiting bats have long tongues, often with brushy tips, and feed at night, attracted by fermenting or fruity odors. Bats fly from tree to tree, lapping nectar, eating flower parts and protein rich pollen, and in the process, they carry pollen from plant to plant.

Seed Dispersal

According to the fossil record, the seeds of the early angiosperms were probably dispersed by water and by wind. At the time the angiosperms first appeared, reptiles were dominant, and there is little evidence of adaptations of seeds for animal dispersal. It is conceivable that angiosperm seed dispersal occurred as the abundant reptile populations moved about their habitats.

Then, in the late Mesozoic, birds and mammals replaced reptiles as the primary dispersers of seeds. Today flowering plants have many adaptations that promote seed dispersal.

Coevolution

Some groups of flowering plants have evolved various natural products such as alkaloids, tannins, flavonoids, terpenes, and even insect hormones. Many of these chemicals are regarded as defensive compounds that tend to protect the plants from selected herbivores. Still other herbivores may be found associated with these "protected" plants. Ehrlich and Raven (1964) coined the term *coevolution* to refer to any situation in which a pair of organisms act as selective agents for each other. According to their theory, plants and phytophagous insects have undergone adaptive radiation in a stepwise manner, with plant groups evolving new and highly effective chemical defenses against herbivores and the herbivores continually evolving means of overcoming these defenses. Probably part of the evolutionary success of angiosperms is linked to the chemical defenses they have erected. Ehrlich and Raven suggest that ". . . the plant-herbivore 'interface' may be the major zone of interaction responsible for generating organic diversity."

Mustard oils, characteristic of the family Cruciferae, are toxic to many animals (Feeny, 1977). Yet the volatile mustard oils attract other herbivores to plants of that family. The white adult of the imported cabbage worm (Lepidoptera), often seen flying around cabbage and broccoli, is guided to the cabbage by mustard oils. The larvae cause major damage to cultivated cabbages. The imported cabbage worm has exploited the chemical defenses of cabbage and uses the mustard oils to locate a host plant for laying its eggs. Present in the genus *Hypericum*, the chemical hypericin repels almost all herbivores. An exception is the beetle genus *Chrysolina*, which can detoxify hypericin and use it to locate the host plant (Whittaker and Feeny, 1971).

According to coevolutionary theory, not all herbivores will respond to a chemical defense in the same way. For example, laboratory feeding tests with five species of insects and two species of mammals demonstrated that a bitter sesquiterpene lactone from *Vernonia* is an effective deterrent to some *but not all* herbivores (Burnett et al., 1974). Defensive compounds act as filters, screening only a portion of potential herbivores (Burnett et al., 1974).

Some sex attractants in insects are derived from plants on which the insects feed.

The insects of one sex concentrate these substances and use them to attract the opposite sex.

Many complex systems involving plant-herbivore interactions occur in the tropics. In Mexico and Central America certain shrubby species of *Acacia* and the ants that inhabit them provide a remarkable example of this complexity (Figure 6-10). The Acacias occur in full sun in secondary shrubby thickets where competition with other plants is keen. The ants live in the swollen thorns of these Acacias and feed on nectaries located on the petioles of the leaves and Beltian bodies located at the tip of each leaflet. The ants defend the Acacias against other insect herbivores and girdle the shoots of competing vegetation. If the ants are removed from the Acacias, growth slows, and the Acacias often die.

This same type of interaction has been observed between a species of cactus (*Opuntia acanthocarpa*) and species of ants. The cactus possesses extrafloral nectaries embedded in the areoles of new reproductive and vegetative growth. The nectar secreted by these glands attracts ants and is a food source for them. Members of one attracted ant species

FIGURE 6-10
Swollen thorns of an *Acacia*,
Chiapas, México.

are aggressive and efficient defenders of the plants against other cactus-feeding insects (Pickett and Clark, 1979).

Some natural plant products ingested by insects aid in protecting the insects against predators or microbial pathogens. For example, the monarch butterfly ingests cardiac glucosides from milkweed plants (*Asclepias*). These poisons accumulate in the larval stages of the monarchs and are retained by the adults. The ingestion of monarch butterflies by blue jays causes the jays to become violently sick (Brower and Brower, 1964). Blue jays learn to recognize the toxic, brightly colored monarchs. Thus, the monarchs gain protection from predators using the cardiac glucosides of milkweed. (Consult Gilbert and Raven, 1980, for additional references concerning coevolution.)

CLASSIFICATION OF THE ANGIOSPERMS

Truly phylogenetic classifications are the ultimate aim of taxonomy. Such classifications are highly useful to systematists, other biologists, and lay people. Numerous systems have been developed, such as those of de Jussieu, de Candolle, Bentham and Hooker, Engler and Prantl, Bessey, Hallier, Hutchinson, and more recently Takhtajan, Sporne, Cronquist, Dahlgren, Stebbins, and Thorne.

Once widely accepted, and still widely used in published floras and herbaria, the Englerian system (Engler and Prantl, 1887–1915) has received considerable criticism from a phylogenetic viewpoint. This criticism is especially directed to the question of relative primitiveness of various groups and the linear sequence of families. One fault is the positioning of the monocotyledons before the dicotyledons, a placement reversed in the most recent edition of the *Syllabus der Pflanzenfamilien* (Engler, 1964). The major problem concerns the position of the Amentiferae, or catkin bearers, and other apetalous groups. The families making up the so-called "Amentiferae" (Betulaceae, Fagaceae, Juglandaceae, and so on) were perhaps regarded by Engler and his followers as the most primitive. The Amentiferae (which are now considered to be an advanced, heterogenous group and not a phylogenetic unit) were therefore placed before the petaliferous families such as Ranunculaceae and Magnoliaceae and were regarded as evolutionarily primitive. The flowers and inflorescences of the Amentiferae are now regarded as the products of phenomena similar to those associated with the miniaturization of flowers and inflorescences (Abbé, 1974). The critical weakness of the Englerian system is the failure to recognize the significance of reduction, and for this reason "simple" was equated with "primitive" (Cronquist, 1965).

Since all families were treated in the Englerian system, it became the standard way to arrange herbaria and manuals in the United States. The practice of using this outmoded linear sequence continues mainly because it is a convenient and well-known filing system.

Although largely original, the Besseyan system of classification (Bessey, 1915) is rooted in de Jussieu's work (1789), further expanded by de Candolle in 1813, and again later expanded by Bentham and Hooker (1862–1883). Bessey also drew information from the Engler and Prantl classification scheme. The Besseyan school regards the "ranalian complex" (those plants having flowers with many, free, equal, and spirally arranged parts) as primitive. Hence, the phylogenetic system developed by Bessey, often called the *ranalian concept of evolution,* is essentially the same as the "*Magnolia is primitive*" school. Diagramed, it took on the form of a cactus plant and came to be called "Bessey's cactus" (see Figure 6-11).

Bessey considered the angiosperms monophyletic and derived from a cycadeoid ancestor with bisexual strobili. Bessey began his scheme with the group considered the least modified from the ancestral prototype. Believing the primitive angiosperms were insect-pollinated, Bessey concluded that the wind-pollinated Amentiferae had resulted from reduction and much evolutionary change. He disagreed with Engler and Prantl, who regarded the Amentiferae as primitive. A comparison of Englerian and Besseyan concepts is presented in Table 6-3.

Bessey's major contribution was the first intentionally phylogenetic classification

FIGURE 6-11
Bessey's cactus. The chart shows the relationship of orders recognized by Bessey. (Ann. Mo. Bot. Gard., **2**:118, 1915. *Used by permission.*)

TABLE 6-3
COMPARISON OF THE ENGLERIAN AND BESSEYAN CONCEPTS

Features	Englerian school	Besseyan school
Primitive flower:	Apetalous; unisexual	Polypetalous, perianth of many, free, equal parts; bisexual
Primitive pollination mechanism:	Wind pollination	Insect pollination
Dicotyledons began with:	Amentiferae	Ranales
Monocotyledons derived from:	Gymnosperous stock	Primitive dicotyledons
Ancestors:	Coniferoid or gnetoid gymnosperms	Cycadicae gymnosperms, most likely, seed ferns
Philosophy:	Simple flowers are primitive	Many parted flowers are primitive

scheme; he attempted to create a taxonomy that would reflect evolution. In the process, Bessey proposed his "dicta" (see Chapter 4) to provide the scientific guideline for understanding the construction of his system. In Bessey's cactus the implication of direct descent of the orders from one another is open to criticism. Likewise, certain evolutionary lines proposed by Bessey are not accepted today. Regardless of these criticisms, the most recent taxonomic schemes of Cronquist, Takhtajan, and Thorne remain close to Bessey's system.

Hutchinson's classification was a modification of the Bentham and Hooker-Bessey tradition (Figures 6-12 and 6-13). Like Bessey, Hutchinson (1973) considered the flowering plants monophyletic, derived from a cycadeoid ancestor. Hutchinson, however, made the unfortunate error of separating the dicotyledons into two lines: one line primarily herbaceous and the second line primarily woody (see Figure 6-12). This unnatural division caused families with close affinities to be separated. For example, the family Labiatae was separated from the closely related Verbenaceae and the Araliaceae from the related family Umbelliferae. Evidence indicates that these pairs of families share many common features. Hutchinson also failed to provide evidence for his taxonomic decisions. However, he was extremely knowledgeable about flowering plant families on a worldwide basis, and his family treatments provide a major contribution to the understanding of angiosperms.

Takhtajan (Figure 6-14) is an adherent of the Besseyan philosophy and has been strongly influenced by some of the more progressive German workers (Takhtajan 1959, 1966, 1969, 1980). Published in Russian, the earlier versions of Takhtajan's work were not readily appreciated in the West. This disadvantage was largely overcome with the publication in 1969 of an English translation and summary prepared by Charles Jeffrey. A chart of the Takhtajan system is presented in Figure 6-15. Takhtajan has used much recent information and many diverse characters in the development of his classification scheme. One criticism of his work is that his taxa are too narrowly defined and that as a result unnecessary splitting of related groups has occurred.

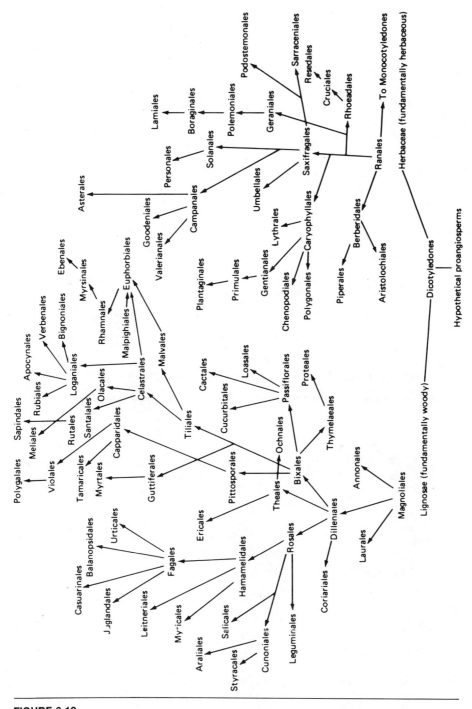

FIGURE 6-12
Hutchinson's diagram showing the probable phylogeny and relationships of the orders of dicotyledons. Note the division into largely woody and largely herbaceous lines. (*From J. Hutchinson*, The Families of Flowering Plants, *Oxford University Press, 1973; with permission.*)

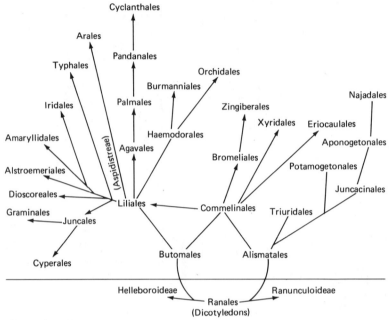

FIGURE 6-13
Hutchinson's diagram showing the probable phylogeny and relationships of the orders of monocotyledons. Note origin of the monocotyledons from dicotyledon lines. (*From J. Hutchinson, The Families of Flowering Plants. Oxford University Press, 1973; with permission.*)

FIGURE 6-14
Dr. Armen Takhtajan of the Botanical Institute, Academy of Sciences of the Soviet Union, Leningrad.

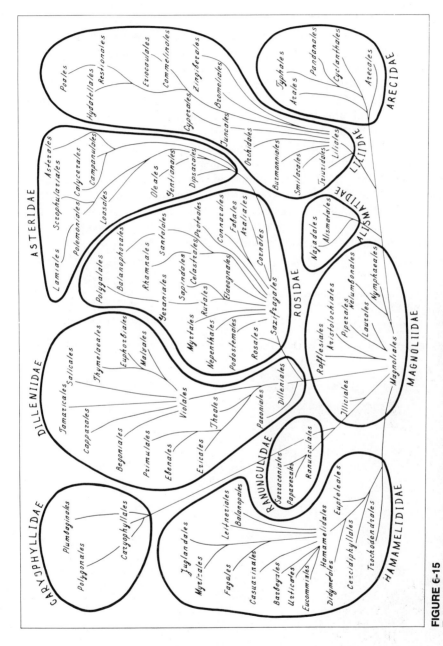

FIGURE 6-15

Takhtajan's (1980) classification of the angiosperms showing putative relationships among the classes, subclasses, and orders of flowering plants (*Used with permission.*)

Takhtajan (1980) classifies the angiosperms as Division Magnoliophyta and sub-divides them into the dicotyledons (Class Magnoliopsida) and monocotyledons (Class Liliopsida). The flowering plants are further divided into 10 subclasses, three of which are monocotyledons and the other seven dicotyledons. Takhtajan has used the rank of superorder (with a -anae ending) as a supplementary rank placed between subclass and order. The superordinal names, as well as all the other names of taxa above the rank of genus, are derived from generic names.

Cronquist (Figure 6-16) published a classification conceptually similar to Takhta-jan's system, but differing in detail (Cronquist, 1968, 1981). A modified diagram of Cronquists's classification is shown in Figure 6-17. Since it has been widely distributed in book format and offers detailed explanations, the system by Cronquist is widely used and referred to in the United States. A comparison of the placement of families in Takhtajan, Thorne, Engler, Hutchinson, and Bentham and Hooker in relation to the scheme of Cronquist 1968 is provided by Becker (1973). A brief survey of the arrangement of Cronquist is presented in what follows. Cronquist considers the an-giosperms to merit the rank of division (Magnoliophyta). (A list of angiosperm families according to Cronquist's system is provided in Appendix 3.)

FIGURE 6-16
Dr. Arthur Cronquist of the New York Botanical Garden. (*Photograph, New York Botanical Garden.*)

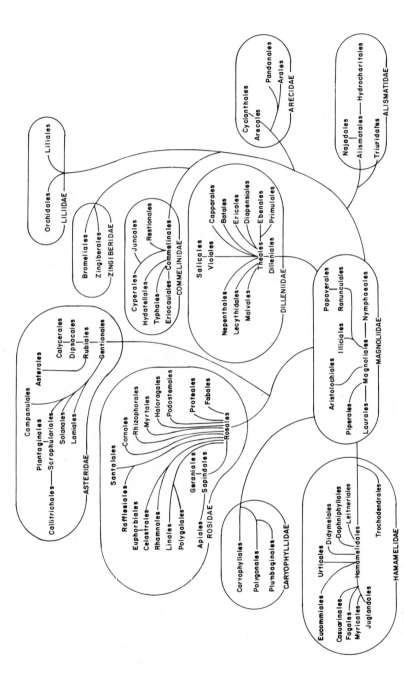

FIGURE 6-17

Diagram of Cronquist's 1981 classification of the angiosperms. The chart distance from the center bottom is in rough proportion to prevalence of advanced characters. (*Drawing prepared by Valerie Jones Hinesley*.)

In his 1981 treatment, Cronquist provides a synoptical arrangement of the flowering plant families within the orders and of the orders within the subclasses, etc., a classification similar to Takhtajan's. Cronquist classifies the angiosperms at divisional rank and treats the dicotyledons and monocotyledons as classes that in turn are broken into subclasses. Unlike Takhtajan, Thorne, and Dahlgren, Cronquist does not use the category of superorder. Cronquist's system has five subclasses of monocotyledons, versus three for Takhtajan, and six subclasses of dicotyledons as compared with the seven of Takhtajan. Cronquist includes Takhtajan's subclass Ranunculidae in the subclass Magnoliidae accounting for the discrepancy in number of dicotyledon subclasses. In the monocotyledons, Cronquist segregates the subclasses Commelinidae and Zingiberidae from Takhtajan's huge subclass Liliidae. Among the angiosperms, Cronquist recognizes 83 orders and 383 families versus Takhtajan's 92 orders and 410 families.

Robert Thorne (1968, 1976, 1983) has proposed a phylogenetic classification of the angiosperms. Thorne refers to the diagrammatic representation of the evolutionary interrelationships of the extant angiosperms as a "phyletic shrub" viewed from above (See Fig. 6-18). Following the Besseyan tradition, Thorne divides the angiosperms into the dicotyledons and monocotyledons at subclass rank. The two subclasses are further divided into superorders (with the ending of *-iflorae*), orders, and families. An outline of his classification is provided in Appendix 4.

K. R. Sporne (1976) has attempted by means of simple statistical tests to identify primitive and advanced characters among the angiosperms. Using the evidence available to him and especially by examining the fossil record, Sporne assembled 26 pairs of characters representing the primitive and advanced states for each character pair. With these data, Sporne constructed an advancement index for each family based upon the proportion of advanced characters possessed by the family. For example, among the dicotyledons, the order Magnoliales has the lowest advancement index and the subclass Asteridae has on the average the highest. Sporne has presented his conclusions in the form of a circular diagram. The degree of advancement is indicated by succeedingly larger concentric circles, with the distance of a taxon from the center of the diagram proportional to its degree of divergence. In Figure 6-19, Sporne has arranged the dicotyledon orders of Cronquist (1968) to reflect Cronquist's views of affinity and to show also the range of the advancement indexes of the families within each order. It can be seen that the orders belonging to the subclass Magnoliidae are grouped together within an area enclosed by a broken line and that the Magnoliales extend on the advancement index from 20 to 56. It should be noted that the three major subclasses (Magnoliidae, Dilleniidae, and Rosidae) all contain very primitive families and that some orders have a wide range of primitive to advanced characters. Sporne has constructed a similar advancement index for the monocotyledons; however, he feels less confident of this arrangement.

Following chiefly the system of Cronquist (1968), but with modifications according to the systems of Takhtajan, Thorne, and Hutchinson, and using many original concepts, Stebbins (1974) has presented a classification of the orders and families of angiosperms. It is presented diagramatically in a circular format suggestive of Sporne's advancement index (Figure 6-20). Stebbins favors this circular format to depict relative degrees of specialization of the orders of angiosperms rather than a conventional

FIGURE 6-18

Thorne Phylogenetic Shrub, October, 1982. Ballon size indicates the approximate number of accepted species though the very small taxa are enlarged to make them visible. The center of the diagram is left empty to indicate the extinct early angiosperms. The taxa nearest the center are regarded as the most primitive and nearest the periphery the most advanced. (*Courtesy of Robert Thorne.*)

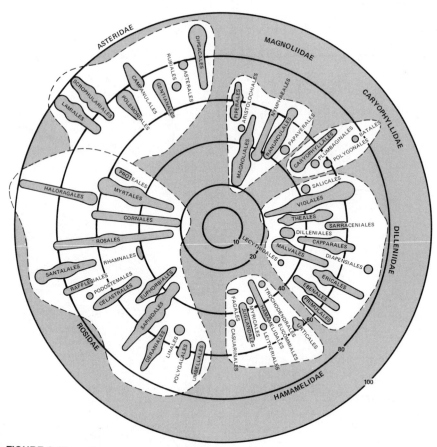

FIGURE 6-19
Sporne's diagram of the phylogenetic classification of the dicotyledons. The radial extent of each order corresponds to the range of advancement indices of its constituent families. (*From Sporne, 1976, used with permission.*)

phylogenetic tree. He reasons that the common ancestor of any two or more orders was probably so different from any of the extant orders that the common ancestor, if known, would be placed in a separate extinct order. Stebbins arranges the angiosperms into subclasses representing the monocotyledons and the dicotyledons, which are in turn broken down into superorders, for instance, Magnoliidae, and orders, for example, Magnoliales.

Rolf Dahlgren (1977, 1980, 1983) of the University of Copenhagen has developed an informative classification of the angiosperms based on the distribution of a wide range of phenetic characters (see Figure 6-21). Among plant taxonomists, Dahlgren's classification has an increasing following and many consider it the best yet developed. In his classification the angiosperms (class Magnoliopsida) are equivalent to the main groups of gymnosperms. The angiosperms are further divided into two subclasses, representing the dicotyledons and monocotyledons, the Magnoliideae and Liliidae

DICOTYLEDONS

1. Nympheales	11. Juglandales
2. Sarraceniales	12. Batales
3. Aristolochiales	13. Plumbaginales
4. Trochodendrales	14. Lecythidales
5. Cercidiphyllales	15. Salicales
6. Didymeleales	16. Diapensiales
7. Eupteleales	17. Podostemales
8. Eucommiales	18. Haloragales
9. Casuarinales	19. Cornales
10. Leitneriales	20. Rafflesiales
21. Rhamnales	

MONOCOTYLEDONS

22. Alismatales
23. Triuridales
24. Najadales
25. Hydrocharitales
26. Typhales
27. Cyclanthales

FIGURE 6-20
Diagram by Stebbins (1974) showing the relative degree of specialization of the orders of angiosperms (*Used with permission, copyright (c) 1974 by the President and Fellows of Harvard College.*)

FIGURE 6-21
Dahlgren's classification of the angiosperms based upon the distribution of a wide range of phenetic characters. (*Provided by Dr. Dahlgren.*)

respectively. Thus, Dahlgren's subclasses have a much broader circumscription than the subclasses used by Cronquist and Takhtajan. He notes that the division of the flowering plants into the dicotyledons and monocotyledons would not be allowed if one followed rigid cladistic approaches. However, Dahlgren believes the monocotyledons to be a unique group worthy of subclass rank.

Dahlgren further divides the subclasses into superorders similar to Thorne's. These bear the termination -*iflorae*. Dahlgren indicates that the use of superorders and orders allows increased flexibility in indicating affinities that might otherwise be restricted by the subclasses of Cronquist and Takhtajan. Further, he suggests that this approach allows better placement of superorders of unclear affinities.

The Two Classes of Magnoliophyta: Magnoliopsida (Dicotyledons) and Liliopsida (Monocotyledons)

Division Magnoliophyta includes all the angiosperms. This natural group consists of two major subgroups: the monocotyledons and dicotyledons. To conform to the International Code of Botanical Nomenclature, formal names with Latinized endings have been applied to each of the categories, Magnoliopsida for the dicotyledons and Liliopsida for the monocotyledons. The English names are useful and continue to be employed. The features by which the dicotyledons and monocotyledons differ are shown in Table 6-4.

In general, the dicotyledons are much more diverse in habit than monocotyledons. About 50 percent of the present-day species of dicotyledons are woody. Few of the monocotyledons are woody, and most of these are found in family Palmae. The Palmae

TABLE 6-4

A COMPARISON OF THE FEATURES OF DICOTYLEDONS AND MONOCOTYLEDONS

Characters	Dicotyledons (class Magnoliopsida)	Monocotyledons (class Liliopsida)
Cotyledons	2 (rarely 1, 3, or 4)	1 (embryo sometimes undifferentiated)
Leaves	Usually net-veined	Usually parallel-veined
Intrafascicular cambium	Usually present	Absent
Primary vascular bundles	In a ring	Scattered or in two or more rings
Pollen	Monosulcate in primitive families, but mostly tricolpate	Monosulcate
Floral parts (except carpels)	Sets of 5s or 4s	Sets of 3s, seldom 4s
Root system	Primary and adventitious	Adventitious
Habit	About 50% are woody	About 10% are woody, mostly in Palmae
Sieve-tube plastids	S-type (P-type in one family)	P-type

are regarded as relatively advanced in the monocotyledons. Most woody dicotyledons are highly branched, but the woody monocotyledons are generally unbranched.

Most systematists agree that monocotyledons were phyletically derived from the dicotyledons early in the evolutionary history of the angiosperms. Cronquist (1968) believes the monocotyledons arose from a primitive vesselless ancestor resembling present-day Nymphaeales. If this viewpoint is correct, the monocotyledons had an aquatic origin profoundly channelizing the evolutionary pathways available to them. If aquatic in origin, the first monocotyledons probably had apocarpous flowers with undifferentiated tepals and monosulcate pollen, and they lacked a functional cambium and xylem vessels. Cheadle (1953), using evidence from xylem vessels, rejected the idea of an aquatic origin. Instead, he suggested that monocotyledons arose from terrestrial woody dicotyledons that lacked xylem vessels. The characters (Table 6-4) separating the monocotyledons from the dicotyledons are usually regarded as second-arily derived with but one exception. The monosulcate type of pollen of monocoty-ledons is shared with certain living dicotyledons, as well as with their gymnospermous ancestors. This one exception really poses no problem, since a lineage of pollen types can be extended from the monocotyledons back through the primitive dicotyledons into gymnospermous stock. In addition to the morphological evidence, data from comparative biochemistry point to an origin of monocotyledons from dicotyledons (Harborne, 1977).

In recent years the classical circumscription of the monocotyledons has been chal-lenged, with some workers suggesting the placement of the Nymphaeales among the monocotyledons. The similarities in certain features between the dicotyledonous Pi-perales and some monocotyledons make the border line between the dicotyledons and monocotyledons appear less distinct than once believed. Other workers have noted the resemblance between the monocotyledonous Dioscoreales and certain orders of the Magnoliales. Dahlgren (1983), although noting the lack of sharp discontinuities, feels that the monocotyledons can be clearly circumscribed on the combination of (1) an embryo with a single cotyledon and (2) sieve-tube plastids with cuneate protein bodies. There are even unusual hypotheses, such as by Burger (1981), who argues that the ancestral angiosperms were monocotyledons. Whether the monocotyledons are mono-phyletic from one dicotyledonous ancestor or polyphyletic from two or more dicotyle-donous ancestors requires further study.

CHARACTERISTICS OF THE SUBCLASSES OF THE CRONQUIST SYSTEM OF CLASSIFICATION

Division: Magnoliophyta

Angiosperms or flowering plants (two classes, 11 subclasses, 83 orders, 383 families, and about 219,300 species).

   I   Class: Magnoliopsida   Dicotyledons (six subclasses, 64 orders, 318 families, and about 169,400 species). (See Table 6-5.)

TABLE 6-5
SOME OF THE GENERAL CHARACTERISTICS OF THE DICOTYLEDON SUBCLASSES

Subclass	Advancement	Carpels	Flowers	Stamens	Pollen
Magnoliiidae	Relatively primitive	Typically apocarpous	Well developed, with an evident perianth; polypetalous	Numerous; centripetal	Monosulcate, with one germ pore
Hamamelidae	Relatively advanced in one or more features	Mostly syncarpous, a few apocarpous	Reduced and often unisexual; perianth poorly developed; wind-pollinated	Often in staminate catkins	Mostly tricolpate, never with only one germ pore
Caryophyllidae	Relatively advanced in one or more features	Mostly syncarpous, a few apocarpous	Well developed; usually poly-petalous	When numerous, centrifugal	Mostly tricolpate, never with only one germ pore
Dilleniidae	Relatively advanced in one or more features	Mostly syncarpous, a few apocarpous	Well developed; usually polypetalous	When numerous, centrifugal	Mostly tricolpate, never with only one germ pore
Rosidae	Relatively advanced in one or more features	Mostly syncarpous, a few apocarpous	Well developed; polypetalous (rarely apetalous or sympetalous)	When numerous, centripetal	Mostly tricolpate, never with only one germ pore
Asteridae	Relatively advanced in one or more features	Syncarpous	Well developed; sympetalous	The same number or fewer than the number of corolla lobes and alternate with them	Mostly tricolpate, never with only one germ pore

1 Subclass: Magnoliidae   (Eight orders, 39 families, and about 11,000 species.) This subclass includes those dicotyledons that have retained one or, more often several primitive characters. The subclass originated about 122 million years ago in the Lower Cretaceous.

Magnoliidae generally have a many-parted, well-developed perianth of tepals, often differentiated into sepals or petals, but sometimes apetalous. The stamens are numerous and mature in a centripetal manner. The pollen typically is binucleate and monosulcate. The gynoecium is typically apocarpous with bitegmic and crassinucellate ovules. All families in the subclass have endosperm, with the exception of the Lauraceae. Magnoliales is the largest order. The Magnoliidae have their own set of chemical defenses, with a great many of the taxa producing isoquinoline alkaloids.

2 Subclass: Hamamelidae   (11 orders, 24 families, and about 3,400 species.) Hamamelidae is the smallest subclass of dicots. The subclass originated about 100 million years ago in the Lower Cretaceous as a group characterized by wind pollination and floral reduction. They were well established by 80 million years ago. With the exception of some taxa in the order Urticales, the families are typically woody and often contain relatively few species. The subclass is characterized by reduced, often unisexual flowers, which in the advanced groups are arranged in catkins. The perianth is either absent or poorly developed. The mature fruit contains a single ovule. At some stage in their evolution the Hamamelidae began to use tannins as their chemical defense against herbivores. Evidence is accumulating that this subclass, held together mainly by the bonds of reduced floral structure, probably should be regarded as only loosely monophyletic. Many familiar deciduous trees of eastern North America are members of subclass Hamamelidae.

3 Subclass: Caryophyllidae   (Three orders, 14 families, and about 11,000 species.) Several of the families in this mostly herbaceous subclass contain succulents or halophytes. The fossil record extends the Caryophyllidae back about 70 million years ago. The perianth of the group is morphologically complex and diverse. The primitive members have only a single perianth whorl, and from this, various modified perianths developed with apparent sepals and petals. The stamens are centrifugal in maturation sequence and produce trinucleate pollen. Placentation is free central to basal. The ovules are bitegmic and crassinucellate. They are either campylotropous or amphitropous, and when mature the embryos are often surrounded by perisperm. Betalains, a distinctive class of pigments, are found in many of the families in order Caryophyllales. Often called the Centrospermae, order Caryophyllales contains around 10,000 species representing the bulk of the subclass. The Caryophyllales have a unique P-type sieve tube plastid.

4 Subclass: Dilleniidae   (13 orders, 78 families, and about 25,000 species.) With the notable exception of the apocarpous order Dilleniales, subclass Dilleniidae is distinguished from typical members of subclass Magnoliidae by syncarpy. Members of subclass Dilleniidae have a centrifugal maturation of stamens and binucleate pollen, except for that of the family Cruciferae, which is trinucleate. Ovules are unitegmic or bitegmic and have crassinucellate to tenuinucellate endosperm. This subclass contains many woody species. Pollen that may represent the Dilleniidae has been found in the fossil record about 100 million years ago at the beginning of the Upper Cretaceous.

5 Subclass: Rosidae   (18 orders, 114 families, and about 58,000 species.) This is the largest subclass, in terms of numbers of families, but about the same size as the Asteridae in terms of the numbers of species. The flowers have numerous stamens that mature in centripetal sequence. The ovules are bitegmic or unitegmic and crassinucellate or tenuinucellate. The flowers have a polypetalous corolla, although a few apetalous and sympetalous flowers occur. The fossil record suggests that the Rosidae began to appear about 110 million years ago in the Lower Cretaceous.

6 Subclass: Asteridae   (11 orders, 49 families, and about 56,000 species.) Asteridae is the second largest subclass of dicotyledons. About one-third of the species belong to the family Compositae (Asteraceae), the largest family of dicotyledons. Flowers of this subclass are sympetalous and only rarely apetalous or polypetalous. The stamens are few and alternate with the petals. Members of subclass Asteridae usually have two carpels with unitegmic and tenuinucellate ovules. Of the dicotyledons, subclass Asteridae is probably the best defined. Present evidence strongly suggests that the Asteridae were likely derived from the evolutionary Rosidae line.

The Asteridae are the most advanced subclass of the dicotyledons and are the most recently evolved, appearing in the fossil record around 65 million years ago, but not becoming abundant until about 30 million years ago.

II Class: Liliopsida   Monocotyledons (five subclasses, 19 orders, 65 families, and about 49,900 species.) (See Table 6-6.)

1 Subclass: Alismatidae   (Four orders, 16 families, and about 500 species.) Alismatidae characteristically inhabit aquatic or wetland habitats and are herbaceous. Most are apocarpous and have trinucleate pollen. When mature, the seeds lack endosperm. Two subsidiary cells surround the stomates. Regarded as a relic side branch of the monocotyledons, subclass Alismatidae has retained a number of primitive characters. The fossil record extends the subclass back about 60 million years ago.

2 Subclass: Arecidae   (Four orders, five families, and about 5,600 species.) In habit, the members of subclass Arecidae vary from tiny macroscopic duckweeds to huge woody palms. About 50 percent of the species are arborescent. The flowers tend to be numerous, small, and often aggregated in a spadix subtended by a spathe (see Chapter 10). The stomatal subsidiary cells are mostly four but may be two or three. Many species have features that are atypical of monocotyledons, such as broad, petiolate, net-veined leaves. All but the order Arales contain vessels. Over half of the species belong to the order Arecales, which includes only the palm family (Arecaceae). The fossil record of the palms extends back to the Upper Cretaceous, about 80 million years ago.

3 Subclass: Commelinidae   (Six orders, 16 families, and about 16,200 species.) The vast majority of the species of subclass Commelinidae are herbaceous. They inhabit sites ranging from aquatic to terrestrial or even epiphytic. The flowers may have either well-defined sepals and petals or a perianth which is chaffy, bristly, or lacking. Primitive Commelinidae have showy insect-pollinated flowers, whereas advanced members with reduced perianths are wind-pollinated. Commelinidae pollen is either trinucleate or, less commonly, binucleate. About 50 percent of the species belong to the family Gramineae (Poaceae), and another 30 percent to the Cyperaceae. The

TABLE 6-6
SOME OF THE GENERAL CHARACTERISTICS OF THE MONOCOTYLEDON SUBCLASSES

Subclass	General information	Carpels	Flowers	Stomatal subsidiary cells
Alismatidae	Herbaceous, often aquatic; a relic side branch of the monocots	Mostly apocarpous	With many primitive features; stamens numerous	Two
Arecidae	Highly variable, ranging in habit from tiny duckweeds to woody palms	Mostly syncarpous	Small, aggregated into a spadix, subtended by a spathe	Mostly 4, but may have only 2
Commeliniidae	Mostly herbaceous; may be terrestrial, aquatic, or epiphytic, but generally terrestrial	Mostly syncarpous	Perianth highly variable, well developed to chaffy, bristly, or lacking; those lacking a perianth are usually wind-pollinated	Several
Zingiberidae	A largely tropical group; terrestrial or epiphytic, many xerophytic species	Mostly syncarpous	Regular to irregular, with septal nectaries	Several
Liliidae	Largely herbaceous; terrestrial or epiphytic	Mostly syncarpous	With petaloid sepals and petals; highly evolved for insect pollination	Usually absent, but sometimes two or more

subclass extends back in the fossil record about 85 million years, with the Gramineae (one of the more advanced families) appearing about 60 million years ago.

4 Subclass: Zingiberidae   (Two orders, nine families, and about 3,800 species.) The vast majority of the members of Zingiberidae are tropical and are either terrestrial or epiphytes with regular to irregular flowers, septal nectaries, and an inferior ovary. The two orders are distinctive, and although associated here, many other of their features appear to have developed independently. They differ from the many other monocotyledons in having retained the floral nectaries and in having achieved epigyny.

5 Subclass: Liliidae   (Two orders, 19 families, and about 25,000 species.) The members of the monocotyledonous subclass Liliidae are syncarpous, with petaloid sepals and petals. They are highly developed for insect pollination. The majority are terrestrial or epiphytic herbs. Leaves are linear and parallel-veined to broader with net venation. The ovary in subclass Liliidae is frequently inferior. Stomatal subsidiary cells are usually absent, but sometimes two or more are present. More than 80 percent of the species belong to the families Liliaceae and Orchidaceae. Pollen of the order Liliales appears in the fossil record at the close of the Upper Cretaceous, 70 million years before present.

SELECTED REFERENCES

Abbé, E. C.: "Flowers and Inflorescences of the 'Amentiferae'," *Bot. Rev.*, **40**:159–261, 1974.

Beck, C. B.: "On the Origin of Gymnosperms," *Taxon*, **15**:337–339, 1966.

Becker, K. M.: "A Comparison of Angiosperm Classification Systems," *Taxon*, **22**:19–50, 1973.

Bentham, G., and J. D. Hooker: *Genera plantarum*, 3 vols., London, 1862–1883.

Bessey, C. E.: "Phylogenetic Taxonomy of Flowering Plants," *Ann. Mo. Bot. Gard.*, **2**:109–164, 1915.

Brower, L. P., and J. V. Z. Brower: "Birds, Butterflies and Plant Poisons: A Study in Ecological Chemistry," *Zoologica* **49**:137–159, 1964.

Burger, W. C.: "Heresy Reviewed: The Monocot Theory of Angiosperm Origin," *Evol. Theory*, **5**: 189–225, 1981.

Burnett, W. C., S. B. Jones, and T. J. Mabry: "Evolutionary Implications of Sesquiterpene Lactones in *Vernonia* (Compositae) and Mammalian Herbivores," *Taxon*, **26**:203–207, 1977.

———, ———, ——— and W. G. Padolina: "Sesquiterpene Lactones—Insect Feeding Deterrents in *Vernonia*," *Biochem. Syst. Ecol.*, **2**:25–29, 1974.

Candolle, A. P. de: *Théorie élémentaire de la botanique*, Paris, 1813.

Carlquist, S.: "Toward Acceptable Evolutionary Interpretations of Floral Anatomy," *Phytomorphology*, **19**:332–362, 1969.

Cheadle, V. I.: "Independent Origin of Vessels in the Monocotyledons and Dicotyledons," *Phytomorphology*, **3**:23–44, 1953.

Constance, L.: "The Systematics of the Angiosperms," in *A Century of Progress in the Natural Sciences, 1853–1953*, California Academy of Science, San Francisco, 1955, pp. 405–483.

Crepet, W. L.: "Some Aspects of the Pollination Biology of Middle Eocene Angiosperms," *Rev. Paleobot. Palynol.*, **27**:213–238, 1979.

———, D. L. Dilcher, and F. W. Potter, "Eocene Angiosperm Flowers," *Science (Washington D.C.)*, **185**:781–782, 1974.

Cronquist, A.: "The Status of the General System of Classification of Flowering Plants," *Ann. Mo. Bot. Gard.*, **52**:281–303, 1965.

————: *The Evolution and Classification of Flowering Plants,* Houghton Mifflin, Boston, 1968.

————: "Broad Features of the System of Angiosperms," *Taxon,* **18**:188–193, 1969.

————: "On the Taxonomic Significance of Secondary Metabolites in Angiosperms," *Plant Syst. Evol.,* Suppl. **1**:179–189, 1977.

————: *An Integrated System of Classification of Flowering Plants,* Columbia University Press, New York, 1981.

————. "Some Realignments in the Dicotyledons," *Nordic J. Bot.,* **3**:75–83, 1983.

————, A. Takhtajan, and W. Zimmermann: "On the Higher Taxa of Embryobionta," *Taxon,* **15**:129–134, 1966.

Daghlian, C.P.: "A Review of the Fossil Record of Monocotyledons," *Bot. Rev.,* **47**:517–555, 1981.

Dahlgren, R.: "A Commentary on a Diagrammatic Presentation of the Angiosperms in Relation to the Distribution of Character States," *Plant Syst. Evol.,* Suppl. **1**:253–283, 1977.

————: "A Revised System of Classification of the Angiosperms," *Bot. J. Linn. Soc.,* **80**:91–124, 1980.

————: "General Aspects of Angiosperm Evolution and Macrosystematics," *Nordic J. Bot.,* **3**:119–149, 1983.

———— and H. T. Clifford: *The Monocotyledons: A Comparative Study,* Academic Press, London, 1982.

————, H. T. Clifford, and P. F. Yeo.: *The Families of the Monocotyledons,* Springer-Verlag, Berlin, 1985.

Dilcher, D. L.: "Early Angiosperm Reproduction: An Introductory Report," *Rev. Palaeobot. Palynol.,* **27**:291–328, 1979.

Doyle, J. A.: "Origin of Angiosperms," *Ann. Rev. Ecol. Syst.,* **9**:365–392, 1978.

Eames, A.: *Morphology of the Angiosperms,* McGraw-Hill, New York, 1961.

Ehrendorfer, F., F. Krendl, E. Habeler, and W. Sauer: "Chromosome Numbers and Evolution in Primitive Angiosperms," *Taxon,* **17**:337–353, 1968.

Ehrlich, P. R., and P. H. Raven: "Butterflies and Plants: A Study in Coevolution," *Evolution,* **18**:586–608, 1964.

Engler, A.: *Syllabus der Pflanzenfamilien,* 12th ed. vol. 2, H. Melchior and E. Werdermann (eds.), Gebrüder Borntraeger, Berlin, 1964.

————, and K. Prantl: *Die natürlichen Pflanzenfamilien,* 23 vols., Leipzig, 1887–1915.

Faegri, K.: "The Problem of Polyphyletic Origins with Special Reference to Angiosperms," *Taxon,* **29**:312–314, 1980.

Feeney, P.: "Defensive Ecology of the Cruciferae," *Ann. Mo. Bot. Gard.,* **64**:221–234, 1977.

Foster, A. S., and E. M. Gifford: *Comparative Morphology of Vascular Plants,* 2d ed., Freeman, San Francisco, 1974.

Friis, E. M. and A. Skarby: "Structurally Preserved Angiosperm Flowers from the Upper Cretaceous of Southern Sweden," *Nature,* **291**:485–486, 1981.

Gilbert, L. E., and P. H. Raven (eds): *Coevolution of Animals and Plants,* The University of Texas Press, Austin, 1975.

Gottsberger, G.: "The Structure and Function of the Primitive Angiosperm Flower—A Discussion," *Acta Bot. Neerl.,* **23**:461–471, 1974.

————: "Some Aspects of Beetle Pollination in the Evolution of Flowering Plants," *Plant Syst. Evol.,* Suppl. **1**:211–226, 1977.

Gottwald, H.: "The Anatomy of Secondary Xylem and the Classification of Ancient Dicotyledons," *Plant Syst. Evol.,* Suppl. **1**:111–121, 1977.

Grant, V., and K. A. Grant: *Flower Pollination in the Phlox Family,* Columbia, New York, 1965.

Harborne, J. B.: "Flavonoids and the Evolution of the Angiosperms," *Biochem. Syst. Ecol.,* **5:**7–22, 1977.

——— (ed.): *Biochemical Aspects of Plant and Animal Coevolution,* Academic Press, London, 1978.

Heywood, V. H.: "Principles and Concepts in the Classification of Higher Taxa," *Plant Syst. Evol.,* Suppl. **1:**1–12, 1977.

Hickey, L. J.: "Classification of the Architecture of Dicotyledonous Leaves," *Amer. J. Bot.,* **60:**17–33, 1973.

——— and J. A. Doyle: "Early Cretaceous Fossil Evidence for Angiosperm Evolution," *Bot. Rev.,* **43:**3–104, 1977.

Huber, H.: "The Treatment of the Monocotyledons in an Evolutionary System of Classification," *Plant Syst. Evol.,* Suppl. **1:**285–298, 1977.

Hughes, N. F.: *Paleobiology of Angiosperm Origins,* Cambridge, London, 1976.

Hutchinson, J.: *The Families of Flowering Plants,* 3d ed., 2 vols., Clarendon, Oxford, 1973.

Jussieu, A. L. de: *Genera plantarum secundum ordines naturales disposita,* Paris, 1789.

Krassilov, V. A.: "The Origin of Angiosperms," *Bot. Rev.,* **43:**143–176, 1977.

Kubitzki, K.: "Some Aspects of the Classification and Evolution of Higher Taxa," *Plant Syst. Evol.,* Suppl. **1:**21–31, 1977.

——— and O. R. Gottlieb: "Micromolecular Patterns and the Evolution and Major Classification of Angiosperms," *Taxon* **33:**375–391, 1984.

Lawrence, G. H. M.: *Taxonomy of Vascular Plants,* Macmillan, New York, 1951.

Leroy, J.-F.: "The Origin of Angiosperms: An Unrecognized Ancestral Dicotyledon, *Hedyosmum* (Chloranthales), with a Strobiloid Flower is Living Today," *Taxon,* **32:**169–175, 1983.

Melchior, H. See Engler, A.

Muller, J.: "Palynological Evidence on Early Differentiation of Angiosperms," *Biol. Rev. Cambridge Phil. Soc.,* **45:**417–450, 1970.

———: "Fossil Pollen Records of Extant Angiosperms," *Bot. Rev.,* **47:**1–142, 1981.

Nitecki, M. H. (ed.): *Coevolution,* University of Chicago Press, Chicago, 1983.

Philipson, W. R.: "Ovular Morphology and the Classification of Dicotyledons." *Plant Syst. Evol.,* Suppl. **1:**123–140, 1977.

Pickett, C. H. and W. D. Clark: "The Function of Extrafloral Nectaries in *Opuntia acanthocarpa* (Cactaceae)," *Amer. J. Bot.,* **66:**618–625, 1979.

Radford, A. E., W. C. Dickison, J. R. Massey, and C. R. Bell: *Vascular Plant Systematics,* Harper & Row, New York, 1974.

Raven, P. H., and D. I. Axelrod: "Angiosperm Biogeography and Past Continental Movements," *Ann. Mo. Bot. Gard.,* **61:**539–673, 1974.

Retallack, G. and D. L. Dilcher: "A Coastal Hypothesis for the Dispersal and Rise to Dominance of Flowering Plants," in K. J. Niklas (ed.), *Paleobotany, Paleoecology and Evolution,* Vol. 2, Praeger, New York, 1981, pp. 27–77.

Richards, A. J. (ed.): *The Pollination of Flowers by Insects,* Academic, London, 1978.

Rosenthal, G. A. and D. H. Janzen, (eds.): *Herbivores, Their Interaction with Secondary Plant Metabolites,* Academic, New York, 1979.

Sporne, K. R.: *The Morphology of Angiosperms,* St. Martin's, New York, 1975.

———: "Character Correlations Among Angiosperms and the Importance of Fossil Evidence in Assessing Their Significance," in C. B. Beck (ed.), *Origin and Early Evolution of Angiosperms,* Columbia University Press, New York, 1976, pp. 312–329.

Stebbins, G. L.: *Flowering Plants; Evolution Above the Species Level*, The Belknap Press, Harvard University Press, Cambridge, 1974.

Stewart, W. N.: *Paleobotany and the Evolution of Plants*, Cambridge University Press, Cambridge, 1983.

Takhtajan, A.: *Die Evolution der Angiospermen*, Gustav Fischer Verlag, Jena, 1959.

————: *Systema et Phylogenia Magnoliophytorum*, Soviet Publishing Institution, Nauka, 1966. (In Russian.)

———— *Flowering Plants—Origin and Dispersal*, Smithsonian Institution Press, Washington, 1969.

————: "Outline of the Classification of Flowering Plants (Magnoliophyta)," *Bot. Rev.,* **46:**255–359, 1980.

Taylor, T. N.: *Paleobotany: An Introduction to Fossil Plant Biology*, McGraw-Hill, New York, 1981.

Thein, L. B.: "Floral Biology of *Magnolia*," *Amer. J. Bot.,* **61:**1037–1045, 1974.

Thorne, R. F.: "Synopsis of a Putatively Phylogenetic Classification of the Flowering Plants," *Aliso,* **6**(4):57–66, 1968.

————: "A Phylogenetic Classification of the Angiospermae," *Evol. Bio.,* **9:**35–106, 1976.

————: "Proposed New Realignments in the Angiosperms," *Nordic J. Bot.,* **3:**85–117, 1983.

Whittaker, R. H., and P. P. Feeny: "Allelochemics: Chemical Interactions Between Species," *Science (Washington, D.C.)* **171:**757–770, 1971.

Wolfe, J. A., J. A. Doyle, and V. M. Page: "The Bases of Angiosperm Phylogeny: Paleobotany," *Ann. Mo. Bot. Gard.,* **62:**801–824, 1975.

CHAPTER 7

EVOLUTION, VARIATION, AND BIOSYSTEMATICS

By observing the diversity, structural complexity, and adaptative natures of plants, systematists have described taxa, developed classifications, and unraveled the processes of evolution. Biosystematics attempts to discover the mechanisms and processes in flowering plants that: (1) direct their evolution, (2) influence their variation patterns, and (3) cause speciation. Classical taxonomists emphasize the evolutionary end products and differences between taxa, often using biosystematic information sources in developing their classifications.

Organic evolution is the series of transformations of the genetic materials of populations through time. This is primarily caused by natural selection in response to changing environmental interactions (Dobzhansky et al., 1977). Evolution is not synonymous with speciation. Evolution is the gradual accumulation of small genetic changes through time which sometimes leads to speciation (Stebbins, 1950). *Speciation* describes the evolutionary divergence among similar populations.

The term *biosystematics* is derived from biosystematy and was introduced by Camp and Gilly (1943). As originally conceived, biosystematics was an attempt to produce a system of classification to express explicit relationships. Since the 1940s the term has come to mean the application of experimental, genetic, cytologic, and population approaches to systematic problems, especially at the levels of species and infraspecific taxa.

SOURCES OF VARIATION

The complexity and diversity of plant life is apparent among species and between individuals of the same species. This variation forms the basis of both evolution and classification. An understanding of the evolution of plants may be discovered by careful analysis of this variation. Systematists are confronted with variability in populations possessing three components: (1) developmental variation, (2) environmentally induced variation, and (3) genetic variation.

Developmental Variation

Adult plants are often strikingly different from the immature seedlings. This developmental variation that is genetically determined can cause confusion in the identification of flowering plants. For example, G. N. Jones (1968) found that specimens identified as *Tilia neglecta* were nearly always stump-sprout leaves of *T. americana*. Likewise, Crawford (1973) noted that the type specimen of *Chenopodium palmeri* was an immature plant and that key characters used to separate that species from *C. arizonicum* were based merely on differences in maturity. The adult leaves of gum tree (*Eucalyptus*) are alternate and usually pendulous, whereas those on young seedling shoots of many species are opposite and horizontal to the erect axis. The seedling leaves of ash (*Fraxinus*) are simple, but the mature leaves are pinnately compound. Because the seedling stage is the most critical in a plant's life, the characters present during this period surely have survival value. The needlelike seedling leaves of red cedar (*Juniperus*) and arborvitae (*Thuja*) may carry on more photosynthesis than the small scalelike leaves on the mature branches. The biosystematist studies these developmental differences in the garden and greenhouse, observing them at all stages of the life cycle. Developmental variation has been primarily of interest in understanding morphology and evolution.

Environmental Variation

Plants are quite variable, and some species may vary by altering their pattern of growth in response to environmental differences. *Phenoplasticity* (change in appearance) is caused by such variables as light, water, nutrients, temperature, and soil. A classic example of a type of water-controlled variation known as *heterophylly* may be found among some species of the aquatic plant arrowhead (*Sagittaria*). These plants have arrow-shaped leaves when emergent and long strap-shaped leaves when submerged. Similarly, the aquatic water buttercup (*Ranunculus aquatilis*) has dissected submerged leaves, but on the same stem will have lobed emergent leaves (Figure 7-1). Other environmental influences may produce variation in the sizes of many annuals. Chickweed (*Stellaria media*), for example, will reach only 3 centimeters in height in poor, dry soil but will exceed 20 centimeters in rich, moist soil.

Systematists must detect environmentally induced variation. This is usually done by growing cloned (genetically identical) plants under several different environmental conditions. When experimenting with wild plant material, the phenotype (the appearance of the plant) is usually rather plastic when grown in different environments (Clausen, Keck, and Hiesey, 1940). Characters that are easily modified are size of plant and individual organs, and number of branches, leaves, or flowers. Those characters that are less easily modified are lobing, serration, and pubescence of leaves, and the size, shape, and number of floral parts. Plasticity may have survival value

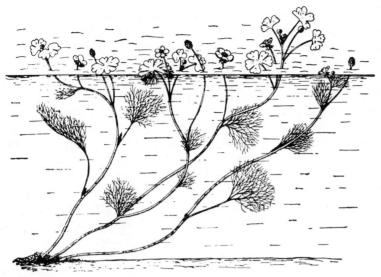

FIGURE 7-1
Habit sketch of a water buttercup (*Ranunculus aquatilis*) with submerged and emergent leaves. (*From Weaver and Clements, 1938; used with permission.*)

and contribute to the success of an organism because it allows the plant to adjust to its environment.

Genetic Variation

The third type of variation in plants is genetic variation (genotypic variation). Genotypic variation, which is heritable, has two sources: (1) mutation and (2) gene flow and recombination. *Mutation* is a transmissible change in the hereditary material. It is the ultimate source of variation in species and replenishes the supply of genetic variability. When broadly used, the term *mutation* includes both genic or point mutations (nucleotide substitutions) and chromosomal mutations (Stebbins, 1971a). By way of contrast, *gene flow* describes the exchange of existing genes among the populations within a species or, through interspecific hybridization, between populations of two distinct but related species. *Recombination* brings together via meiosis and fertilization the novel genes or alleles carried by different individuals and forms a new single genotype, thus multiplying the possible number of genotypes in a population. Although mutation is the ultimate source of genetic variation, gene flow and recombination provide an immediate source of variability in sexually reproducing plants.

   Gene Mutations   A gene mutation is an alteration in the sequence of nucleotides that brings about a change in the action of the gene (Grant, 1975). In higher plants, genic mutations are known to affect many features of plants, for example, the hairless peach or nectarine. The role of genic mutations in evolutionary change depends on several factors: (1) the amount of their effect upon the organism, (2) the adaptive advantage or disadvantage of the mutant individuals, and (3) the role of the mutant gene in population-environment interactions. The environment in which a mutation occurs will have a great effect on its incorporation into the local populations. Unless the environment is changing, mutations will most likely lower the level of adaptation of the species.

If a species is adjusted well to its environment, small mutations might possibly allow it to inhabit new or changing environments, but drastic changes are almost certain to make it function poorly. Analysis of hybrids between two distinct ecotypes of *Potentilla glandulosa* demonstrated that their features were controlled by a series of genes called *multiple genes* (Clausen, 1951). With multiple genes, the hereditary differences in quantitative characters are usually determined by two or more independent genes having similar and cumulative effects (Grant, 1975). Each of these local populations of *Potentilla* had become specialized or adapted for living under one particular set of conditions. Adaptedness in *Potentilla,* therefore, was achieved by the accumulation of many small changes through time rather than by large mutations (Grant, 1963).

Chromosomal Mutations   These include: (1) *polyploidy,* or multiplication of chromosome sets; (2) *aneuploidy,* or loss or gain of chromosomes from the set; and (3) gross structural changes in the chromosomes themselves. Structural changes may be any of the following: deficiencies or loss of segments from a chromosome; duplications of chromosome segments; translocations, or interchange of chromosome segments among nonhomologous chromosomes; or inversions of segments of chromosomes. Structural changes in chromosomes do not produce new genes but function in providing unique gene combinations, new gene arrangements, and different linkage groups (Stebbins, 1971b).

Gene Flow and Recombination   The movement and exchange of genes between breeding populations is described as *gene flow. Recombination* is the result of new combinations of previously existing genes. Gene flow and recombination involve genes already existing in nature. These processes are the main, immediate sources of variability in nature and are brought about by cross-fertilization between individuals, populations, and species. Recombination produces new gene arrangements by cross-fertilization and by the interchange (crossing over) of segments of homologous chromosomes followed by independent assortment of the chromosomes at meiosis. Many genotypic variations in a population may be due to recombination of genic differences that have existed in the population system for many generations. Of major importance is that the potential for this variability is already present in the populations (Grant, 1963). Biochemical polymorphisms have clearly demonstrated the existence of great stores of variability in natural populations of various organisms (Avise, 1974; Hamrich and Allard, 1975). However, as Raven (1980) has pointed out, recent conceptual and practical advances have suggested that severe limitations are imposed on gene flow as it actually occurs in nature. Work over the last several decades has fully established the fact that local populations of a species are highly adapted to local conditions and only rarely interbreed with other nearby populations. This suggests a limited short term evolutionary significance for gene flow, but the rare instances of interbreeding may have considerable evolutionary significance in the long run, particularly when the environment is changing.

Reproductive Systems The method or methods by which a plant reproduces itself are inseparably connected to the patterns of variability found in the species. Reproduction is an obvious necessity for the perpetuation of a plant through time, to provide the means for an increase in numbers, and for the colonization of new territories. The sexual process of cross-fertilization, involving meiosis and union of gametes, is recognized as a mechanism for promoting gene recombination. Recombination is, in turn, the chief source of hereditary variation in a sexually reproducing species and provides the raw material for response of the species to heterogeneous or changing environmental conditions. In contrast, it is generally recognized that self-fertilization and vegetative or other nonsexual means of reproduction are advantageous in a more or less constant local environment in which the populations of a species have become well adapted (Grant, 1981).

In natural populations of plant species, reproduction takes place by four common methods: (1) cross-fertilization or *allogamy,* predominantly between neighboring individuals that are presumably related; (2) self-fertilization or *autogamy,* resulting in highly inbred offspring; (3) vegetative propagation; and (4) production of seeds whose embryos develop from maternal tissue without fertilization, a process called *agamospermy* (Grant, 1981). The first two methods involve meiosis and fertilization and are thus sexual; in the last two, sexual reproduction is circumvented and reproduction is asexual.

Of the two systems of sexual reproduction, cross-fertilization promotes heterozygosity, resulting in a pattern of continuous variation with considerable diversity among individuals, similar to that in human populations. Self-fertilization on the other hand promotes homozygosity, yielding more uniform populations comprised of many similar individuals.

Vegetative reproduction may occur by fragmentation of individuals connected by stolons or rhizomes, by adventitious buds, by offshoots of corms or bulbs, or by the production of vegetative propagules arising within a flower or inflorescence. Widespread among perennials, vegetative propagation can produce clones of identical individuals that sometimes form large stands covering several acres, with all plants clonal in nature. Agamospermy has appeared among numerous, often unrelated, families of angiosperms. The effect of agamospermy on the variation pattern is to produce series of groups of identical individuals that differ from other such groups by rather minor characteristics. These asexual reproductive systems, collectively called *apomixis,* are considered in greater detail in the final section of this chapter.

It is generally agreed that the mode of reproduction of flowering plants influences the observable variation patterns of both local populations and the entire species. Among the flowering plants the spectrum of breeding systems ranges from obligate outcrossing at one extreme to almost complete autogamy at the other. Many species simultaneously employ two, three, or all of the four reproductive systems just described. It follows that species of flowering plants may be relatively uniform or highly variable and generalizations about species as a whole are difficult to make.

NATURAL SELECTION

In order for evolutionary change to occur, there must be a source of genetic variation that is, mutation or gene flow and recombination and a driving force. The prime force is called *natural selection,* and it is the most important of the evolutionary forces or processes. The consequence of natural selection is *adaptation,* or adjustment to the environment. Natural selection is the mechanism by which populations become modified in response to the environment (Grant, 1963).

Natural selection operates by differential reproduction of certain genotypes. The favored genotypes are those that have higher reproductive success and consequently contribute a disproportionate share of individuals to the succeeding generation. The adapations of plants that permit them to live successfully in given environments generally involve a combination and coordination of characters. Natural selection establishes and preserves favorable gene combinations ranging from flower color to changes involving the habit of the plant.

Evolutionists have described three kinds of selection (see Figure 7-2): (1) stabilizing,

FIGURE 7-2
The three kinds of selection: directional, stabilizing, and disruptive. Directional selection operates in a changing environment, stabilizing selection in a stable environment, and disruptive selection in a mosaic environment. *(From Grant 1977; used with permission.)*

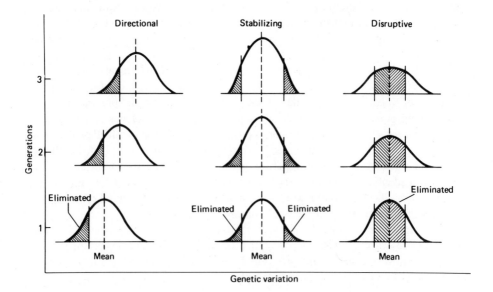

(2) directional, and (3) disruptive (Grant, 1977). These are determined by the organism's environment. Stabilizing selection favors "normal" individuals—that is, it eliminates variants, or deviations from the norm—and operates in a more or less constant environment. Directional selection operates in a unidirectional changing environment, that is, changes from a moist to dry climate following a modification of the weather pattern. Divergent selection pressures in a heterogeneous environment produce disruptive selection. This breaks up a uniform population. An example is the formation of ecotypes adapted to their own local environmental conditions.

RANDOM EVENTS

Theoretically, in the absence of natural selection, gene frequencies will remain relatively constant in natural populations (Dobzhansky, et al., 1977). However, gene frequencies may fluctuate because of the random sampling of genes transmitted in each generation. This effect is greatest in small, isolated populations. It may be verified by tossing coins; that is, a few tosses may give a disproportionate number of heads or tails, but in a large sample the number of heads and tails will be almost equal. Random change in gene frequencies resulting from sampling error between parents and their offspring is known as *genetic drift*. In small populations, genetic drift may play a role by permitting novel genotypes to become more frequent than selection would ordinarily permit. The overall importance of genetic drift in the evolution of flowering plants has long been debated, but it undoubtedly occurs in nature. It is difficult, if not impossible, to find good examples of drift in natural populations because of the interaction of drift with natural selections (Stebbins, 1971a). Some of the best examples are with human blood groups, but even here recent evidence indicates selection may be involved.

Minor racial variation can be found in a number of plant species that have a population system consisting of a series of small, colonial populations in environmentally diverse areas (Grant, 1981). Certain species of *Cupressus* in California, for example, exist in a series of small, isolated stands. Certain of these stands have plants that can be recognized as unique to the particular site.

The *founder principle* is a random event related to the chance distribution of individual seeds or propagules that colonize new areas. For example, a colonizing seed that arrives on an island or some other isolated area obviously cannot bring a complete sample of the genetic diversity of that species to the new area. Simply by chance, that seed could carry some genetic variant and establish a new population distinctly different from the original populations.

The gene frequencies of a population system may also be altered by a *genetic revolution* associated with a sudden reduction in the size of a population. By chance, the few survivors may possess systems of variability different from those found in the original population.

There has been an unresolved controversy regarding the adaptive nature of much biochemical or molecular variation (Ayala, 1974). One school of population genetics holds that gene frequency changes in biochemical traits have occurred solely through random processes. Classical evolution theory has demonstrated beyond any doubt that the basic mechanism for adaptive evolution is natural selection acting on variations produced by genetic changes. Our understanding has been greatly enriched by data from molecular biology, which has revealed many new and unexpected details about the genetic material of living organisms. The most surprising new information from molecular studies is that the great majority of nucleotide changes and hence of nucleotide variability in populations are selectively neutral or nearly so. Those who favor random processes, or the *neutrality theory* of protein evolution, generally agree that the evolution of most morphological and ecological traits is governed by natural selection, but they suggest that the evolution of most proteins, and the genes coding for them, is for the most part due to chance (Dobzhansky, et al., 1977). The neutrality theory of protein evolution assumes that a large proportion of all mutations is deleterious and that genes resulting from these harmful mutations are kept at low frequency by natural selection. On the other hand, a certain percentage of the naturally occurring mutations is adaptively equal, and the mutations do not affect the fitness of their carriers. Thus, the latter are not subjected to natural selection. According to the neutrality theory, evolution at the molecular level consists of a gradual replacement of one amino acid sequence with another sequence that is functionally equivalent to the first.

The neutrality theory also predicts that molecular evolution takes place over long time periods at relatively constant rates (similar to radioactive decay). Therefore, it follows that the degree of protein differentiation among species is indicative of their phylogenetic relatedness. For example, two species with similar cytochrome c amino acid sequences are more closely related to each other than they are to a third species with a very different cytochrome c amino acid sequence. When such data are related to the paleontological record, this so-called molecular clock can be used to measure the time of occurrence of events in a phylogeny and greatly increases knowledge of the evolutionary record.

Selectionists adhere to the theory that mutant substitutions in nucleotides must be adaptive and are caused by natural selection. They suggest that protein polymorphisms, as revealed by comparative studies of protein and DNA sequences, are adaptive and suggest further that the variation is maintained in species as some form of balancing selection acting as a buffer against the environment.

Catastrophic selection, whereby an entire population is suddenly eliminated by an environmental extreme such as drought, except for one or more exceptionally adapted individuals, may provide the conditions necessary for the establishment of a distinct population. Evidence for catastrophic selection has been reported by Lewis (1962) based on observations that ecologically marginal populations of *Clarkia* (Onagraceae) have become extinct during dry periods but in one population a rare genotype, marked by flower color, survived. By elimination of the parental population, catastrophic selection isolates the few survivors into small distinct eco-geographic areas. Raven (1964) suggested that since marginal populations are very likely to be growing on some soil type unusual for the species as a whole, catastrophic selection, caused by drought in arid regions, may be a potent force in the creation of new edaphically restricted endemics in arid regions such as the southwestern United States.

VARIABILITY IN POPULATIONS AND
RACIAL DIFFERENTIATION

Many years of experimental work have clearly demonstrated that local populations of species of flowering plants are highly variable. This variation is in morphological features and in cryptic differences such as allozymes, chromosomes, natural plant products, and so on. (Heslop-Harrison, 1964). Such local populations are often called ecotypes. For present purposes, an *ecotype* can be defined as a local population or a series of populations adapted to particular ecological conditions. Both *clinal variation* (gradual changes in particular characters) and mosaics of distinctive ecotypes may be recognized. The type of pattern depends on the geographical and ecological distributions of the species concerned. Forest trees, prairie grasses, and other plants found over large areas where environmental conditions change gradually tend to have clinal variation. However, plants occupying territories broken into mosaics of sharply distinct ecological conditions tend to have *mosaic variation*. Mosaic patterns are often related to soil and moisture conditions.

Experimental cultivation is a major technique for exploring phenotypic plasticity of species and for detecting differences between ecotypes (Langlet, 1971). In the early 1800s A. P. de Candolle advocated cultivation of critical forms side by side. In the middle 1800s the French botanist A. Jordan used comparative culture to study many species native to France. Finding much ecotypic variation, Jordan split many good Linnaean species. For example, he divided *Erophila verna* into 200 entities which are now refered to as "Jordanons." This was the ultimate in splitting.

In the 1920s G. Turesson pioneered the use of experimental cultivation to show the genetic differentiation of populations. Turesson coined the word *ecotype* for genetically adapted ecological races and proposed the term *genecology* for studies dealing with the ecology of ecotypes (Langlet, 1971). Turesson investigated several common species of plants from southern Sweden that grow in diverse habitats. When samples of these species were grown in a uniform garden, Turesson found they differed in a number of features, indicating genetic differentiation. He was able to demonstrate climatic and edaphic (soil) ecotypes in a number of herbaceous species. Shortly afterward at Edinburgh, J. W. Gregor, working with *Plantago,* was able to demonstrate an *ecocline*. This shows genetically based gradual changes in variation of a species, correlated with an observable gradient in environmental conditions.

The classic work in the United States was by a team of scientists: Jens Clausen, a cytologist; David Keck, a taxonomist; and William Hiesey, an ecologist. In the 1930s they established experimental plots at three locations in California which differed greatly in climate and altitude (Clausen, 1951). One experimental plot was at Stanford University at an elevation of 10 meters; another at Mather on the western side of the Sierra Nevadas, at 1400 meters; and the third at Timberline at an elevation of 3000 meters, near the summit of the Sierra Nevada. For their studies, they selected perennial plants that grew along the transect from sea level to alpine conditions. To facilitate their work, they selected plants that grow in clumps. These could be divided to produce genetically identical clones that were transplanted into each of the three gardens (see Figures 7-3 and 7-4). Thus, genetically identical plants were compared in the differing

FIGURE 7-3
Response of races of *Achillea* when grown in the garden at Stanford. Plants were taken from an east-west transect across central California. The arrows indicate the origin of the populations, frequency diagrams indicate variation in height, and the plant represents the mean. (*From Clausen, 1951; with permission.*)

FIGURE 7-4
The response of cloned individuals of *Achillea borealis* from the coastal region of California when transplanted to the gardens at Stanford (near sea level), Mather (4000 feet), and Timberline (10,000 feet.). (*From Clausen, 1951; with permission.*)

environments of each location. Their carefully documented work clearly demonstrated that local populations are distinctly adapted to their own environments. The experimental work of the California transplant experiments paved the way for much recent genecological work and had great influence on plant taxonomists.

Most species are subdivided by their distributions and breeding patterns into small local populations (Grant, 1963). This provides an ideal situation in which natural

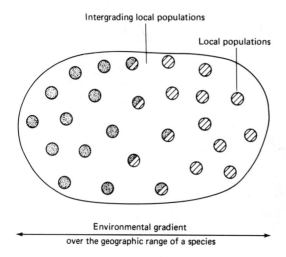

FIGURE 7-5
A diagrammatic drawing of the range (large circle) of a species and its local populations showing geographical differentiation in morphological and ecological features and intergrading local populations. A species is generally not continuous throughout its range but occurs in local populations in suitable habits.

selection may operate on the genetic variation without interference from gene flow from nearby populations. These local populations may differentiate physiologically, morphologically, ecologically, and geographically and eventually form genetically different ecotypes. Such ecotypes or races may be the basis of a taxonomic subspecies or variety. Pure races in the sense of homogeneous population systems do not exist in nature (Grant, 1963). Instead, geographical and ecological gradients are found in the variation pattern (Figure 7-5). Races normally intergrade if they continuously inhabit territory that provides intermediate ecological zones. If races are to be described and given names, they are usually delimited by sharp discontinuities in their variation pattern.

Where the habitats of ecotypes are not distinct but form an environmental continuum, ecologically adapted species exhibit a continuous range of variation termed a *cline*. Two types of clines have been recognized: (1) an *ecocline,* formed along an ecological gradient, such as from a seacoast beach to the adjacent inland area; and (2) a *topocline* situated along a geographic gradient such as a north/south transect through the Great Plains of the United States. When carefully studied in nature, it has generally been found that clinal variation is very complex and seldom forms clear-cut examples of either a pure ecocline or topocline.

ELECTROPHORETIC DATA IN BIOSYSTEMATICS

Electrophoretic separation and visualization of enzymes and seed proteins have been employed in a number of recent biosystematic studies. Electrophoresis is a rather simple but elegant and powerful tool for investigating a variety of questions in biosystematics (Gottlieb, 1977). Widely used in animal systematics, this technique is becoming increasingly important in plant systematics. Proteins and enzymes are extracted from plant parts. This extract is placed in a gel, which, along with the extract, is subjected to an electric current. Since each protein in the sample migrates in the electrical field of the gel at a rate depending on its molecular size and charge, it is possible to make its position visible by using stains that are specific for certain proteins or enzymes. It is assumed that seed proteins and enzymes from different plants that migrate to the same place in electrophoretic gels, and which after staining yield bands similar in appearance, represent homologous proteins.

Several types of biosystematic questions have been addressed by using seed protein profiles. One of the more common problems considered is determining the identity of the progenitors of taxa of hybrid origin. This approach is based on the assumption that certain proteins found in each of the supposed progenitors will also appear in the offspring. In a similar manner, seed protein profiles have also been used for testing hypotheses of phylogenetic relationships in a genus. At the interspecific level, seed protein profiles have been used to document differences among plants that have been traditionally treated as morphologically based species complexes and as a measure of genetic variation within species. Several factors may limit the utility of electrophoretic data of seed proteins in biosystematics. In most instances, the genetic bases of the seed proteins compared on the gels are not known. For this reason caution must be exercised in any interpretation of seed protein profiles. Technical problems and inter- pretation of the location and intensity of the bands may also cause difficulty in using this technique.

Enzyme data are significant because they allow the direct comparison of the products of individual genes. It has been well documented that different alleles at a single locus code for different molecular forms of an enzyme of different subunits in the more complex enzymes. These genetic variants can easily be made visible as colored bands in electrophoretic gels. These bands represent localized areas of an enzyme catalyzing a particular reaction. In many instances the genetic basis of the enzyme banding patterns may be determined by crossing plants with known enzyme banding patterns and examining the progeny by electrophoretic techniques.

From electrophoretic analysis of enzymes, allelic frequency data are obtained, and these data are employed to measure genetic similarities among species within a genus (congeneric populations), between populations within a species (conspecific popula- tions), or among subspecific taxa (subspecies or varieties). Such comparisons have indicated that conspecific populations are very similar in their enzymatic allelic fre- quencies. For the most part, allelic frequencies of different subspecific entities are comparable to the values obtained for conspecific populations of the same taxon. Cross-pollinating plants typically exhibit greater interpopulational variation of genes coding for enzymes than do self-pollinating species. Congeneric plant species exhibit lower similarities of enzymatic allelic frequencies than do conspecific or subspecific plants. However, this is not surprising since congeneric taxa are morphologically distinguishable, that is, divergent at genes determining morphological features and normally genetically isolated for a period of time.

Allelic frequency data are useful for examining populations within a species or genus or perhaps for comparing closely related genera. On the other hand, at higher taxonomic levels such as families, it is usually not possible to compare allelic frequency data for technical reasons related to homology of the enzymes. In biosystematics, one potential value of studies using allelic frequency data is to examine the cause or causes of problem species complexes in certain genera, that is, groups of species that are morphologically confusing. They may also be useful in investigating instances of hybrid speciation if the supposed parental taxa are extant and available for comparison.

Enzyme and seed protein electrophoresis has value for approaching a number of problems related to phylogenetic relationships in closely related species. In many modern studies in plant biosystematics, electrophoretic evidence is taken into account as part of a broad based reevaluation of evolutionary or systematic relationships in plant groups. Undoubtedly, its use will continue to increase in the future.

ISOLATION AND THE ORIGIN OF SPECIES

In his now classic *Variation and Evolution in Plants,* Stebbins (1950) noted that the most important principle derived from evolutionary studies was that evolution and the origin of species are not synonymous as implied by the title of Darwin's classic book. The present definitions of species stress the importance of genetic and morphological continuity within species and the discontinuity among closely related species. Yet systematists realize that an array of genetic variation may exist within the species. Infraspecific taxa are based on incomplete morphological separation as reinforced by ecological and geographical isolation. These two factors are the keys to recognizing genetically based distinctions. Therefore, taxa are maintained by limited gene exchange and adaptations to local environmental conditions.

Reproductive Isolation

Isolating mechanisms are phenomena that prevent interbreeding of closely related taxa. They are based on the following factors: (1) spatial distance, (2) environmental factors, and (3) reproductive biology. Isolating mechanisms are usually placed in one of two categories: *prezygotic* mechanisms, which prevent fertilization, or *postzygotic* mechanisms, which function after fertilization. A classification of reproductive isolating mechanisms is given in Table 7-1. In general, most instances of isolation in nature involve combinations of one or more mechanisms rather than a single mechanism.

Geographical isolation exists between two species whose respective geographical ranges are separated by gaps greater than the normal radius for dispersal of their pollen and seed. *Platanus occidentalis* and *P. orientalis* occur naturally in eastern North America and in the Mediterranean region. They are morphologically distinct and effectively isolated by spatial distance. Yet, when brought together in the garden, they form fully fertile hybrids.

When the ranges of two taxa do not overlap, as in the previous example, the species are said to be *allopatric.* When the ranges of two species coincide, the species are described as being *sympatric.*

Ecological isolation results from differentiation in habitat requirements. Although plants might live in the same region, interbreeding is prevented because they grow in different habitats. Two species of *Vernonia* occur in middle Georgia: *Vernonia noveboracensis* in sunny, moist roadsides and meadows; and *V. glauca* in shady, well-

TABLE 7-1
A CLASSIFICATION OF REPRODUCTIVE ISOLATING MECHANISMS

Prezygotic mechanisms

Geographical. Spatial distance prevents interbreeding because the taxa do not occur in the same area.
Ecological. The plants live in the same region but grow in distinctly different habitats.
Seasonal. The plants occur in the same region but flower at different times.
Ethological. The plants are isolated from one another by pollinator behavior patterns.
Mechanical. Pollination is prevented by structural differences in flower parts.

Postzygotic mechanisms

Hybrid Inviability. The hybrid zygote dies after fertilization or inviability occurs at some developmental stage before flowering.
Hybrid Sterility. First-generation hybrids are produced which flower, but the stamens abort or the gametes are infertile.
Hybrid Breakdown. First-generation hybrids are normal and produce fertile pollen, but second- or later-generation hybrids are weak and have reduced fertility.

Source: Grant, 1963; Stebbins, 1971a.

drained, mature hardwood forests. Where the two species are sympatric, hybrids are rarely found, although the cross may be easily made in the greenhouse.

Genetically controlled differences in reproductive features and habits may also block gene exchange. Sympatric species may be *seasonally isolated* and flower at different times. The ecological isolation between *V. noveboracensis* and *V. glauca* is reinforced by differences in flowering time. One species blooms in midsummer and the other in late summer.

Ethological isolation, or incompatible behavior patterns, is a very important isolating mechanism in animals. When interpreted to include plant reproduction, it involves the flower-visiting behavior of some insects and birds. Certain hummingbirds, bees, and hawkmoths as well as other insects and birds are species-specific. They have sensory perceptions enabling them to distinguish different flowers on the basis of odor, color, form, and so on (Grant, 1963). For example, hummingbirds are attracted to red flowers and hawkmoths to white flowers. Certain pollinators are flower-constant and have instincts that cause them to feed preferentially on one species during a succession of feeding visits. The advantage of flower-constant behavior to the insect is a matter of efficiency and energy (Heinrich and Raven, 1972). Once a colony of plants in flower is located and the floral mechanism learned, an insect can obtain more nectar and pollen in a shorter time by continuing to visit the same species.

The structural differences in flower parts may prevent cross-pollination. This *mechanical isolation* occurs in families with complex floral mechanisms, such as the Asclepiadaceae and Orchidaceae. In both of these families, pollen is released in pollen sacs or pollinia of various sizes and shapes. In the Asclepiadaceae, the proper pollinia must be inserted by the pollinator into slits in the gynoecium. Likewise, the location of the pollinium on the insect, whether on the head or thorax, may be very important for successful insertion of the pollinium (Pijl and Dodson, 1966) in the Orchidaceae.

Interspecific pollination does not necessarily lead to the formation of successful and fertile hybrids. Many developmental steps occur between pollination and production of mature fertile hybrids. Developmental blocks may occur in various stages in the production of sexually mature plants: for instance, the pollen tubes fail to reach the ovules, the sperm fails to unite with egg, or in *hybrid inviability* the hybrid zygote dies, the endosperm disintegrates causing death of the embryo, the fruit fails to set, the number of seeds is reduced, seeds fail to germinate, seedlings die, anthers abort, or gametes are sterile (Grant, 1963).

In *hybrid sterility*, first-generation hybrids are produced which flower, but they have aborted stamens, or more typically, infertile pollen. Hybrid sterility may be in part developmental, involving the development of reproductive structures. It may also result from abnormal segregation of chromosomes at meiosis. Doubling the chromosome number may partly overcome problems with meosis, but it has no effect on developmental sterility. Segregational sterility is caused by translocations, inversions, and other chromosomal rearrangements, as well as by cryptic structural differences in the chromosomes. Hybrids between two species may exhibit any degree of reduction in fertility. Some hybrids will be fully fertile, others semifertile, and still others completely sterile.

The final barrier to gene exchange between species, *hybrid breakdown*, occurs in second- or later-generation progeny. In some interspecific crosses in *Vernonia*, the first-generation hybrids are completely fertile, but the second-generation progeny exhibit continuous variation from fully fertile and vigorous to completely inviable. The causes of hybrid breakdown are not fully understood but are probably related to chromosome structure, gene content, and also to cryptic structural differences in the chromosomes. These cause developmental and segregational difficulties which interfere with the physiology and the formation of gametes.

Isolating mechanisms develop as a byproduct of evolutionary divergence. As parts of population systems differentiate ecologically, morphologically, and biochemically, barriers to gene exchange begin to develop. For example, the presence of a particular pollinator in large numbers in one part of the range of a species might, through natural selection, channelize the adaptation of floral structures toward those best-suited for that insect. The gradual accumulation of structural differences in the chromosomes in subpopulations will eventually lead to the origin of chromosomal barriers. The origin of isolating mechanisms is no different from any other type of evolutionary change.

Speciation

Speciation is the evolutionary divergence and differentiation of a formerly homogeneous population system into two or more separate species. Speciation requires genetic variations, which are universal in population systems, plus isolation. In the late 1860s the German zoologist Wagner (1889) and the Austrian botanist Kerner (1896–1897) formulated the idea that geographical and ecological radiation of populations is paralleled by morphological and physiological differentiation. Kerner also suggested that new races originate in areas marginal to the main population. The American zoologist

Mayr and other evolutionists have stressed the need for spatial distance as a prerequisite for speciation. This concept is designated the *geographical theory of speciation.*

Basic to this idea is the principle that before populations can differentiate, there must be divergent pressures of natural selection. These conditions generally must be met for any divergence, whether it is the formation of isolating mechanisms or that of races or species (Grant, 1963). Furthermore, the divergent element must be isolated enough so that the initial genetic divergence will not be overwhelmed by gene exchange with neighboring populations; for instance, on lead mine tailings there is selection for lead tolerance in grasses within 1 square meter, but speciation does not occur because of the proximity of nontolerant plants of the same species.

There are basically two modes of evolutionary change: phyletic evolution and divergent evolution (Figure 7-6). A change from one state to another state through time in which a species might evolve into something different from its ancestor is called *phyletic evolution.* In contrast, a single population system that differentiates into two evolutionary lines is called *divergent evolution.* As populations become genetically differentiated, isolating mechanisms also begin to develop (Figure 7-7). Partial reproductive isolation is commonly present between local populations of a species because of spatial distance, season of flowering, pollinating agents, ecological requirements, and so on. Differentiation of ecotypes in response to their environment reinforces the development of isolating mechanisms. As an ecotype becomes specialized for its environment, isolating mechanisms may build up, reducing gene exchange. As divergence increases, the elements of the populations become less and less able to exchange genes. Divergence leads to isolation, and isolation promotes speciation; that is, one event reinforces the other.

There has been unresolved debate about whether divergence without geographic isolation, or *sympatric speciation,* can occur. Sympatric speciation involves the dif-

FIGURE 7-6
The two modes of evolutionary change: (a) phyletic evolution and (b) evolutionary divergence. In phyletic evolution, the species moves in time from one state to another state, but in evolutionary divergence one species diverges through time into two species. *(From Grant, 1963; with permission.)*

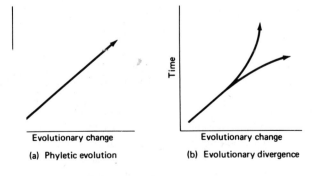

Evolutionary change

(a) Phyletic evolution

Evolutionary change

(b) Evolutionary divergence

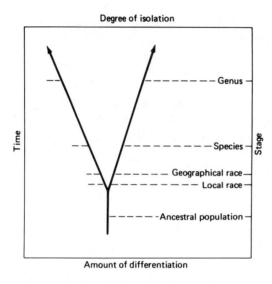

FIGURE 7-7
States of divergence. As the
divergence increases, the amount of
isolation increases. (*Modified from
Grant, 1977; used with permission.*)

ferentiation of closely related populations that coinhabit a geographical area—that is,
are sympatric. The answer to this is not yet clear. Theoretically, the possibility of
sympatric speciation seems more likely if the plants are self-fertilizing, because this
would tend to restrict gene flow. Although many evolutionists have minimized sympatric differentiation, it might happen under strongly divergent ecological differentiation, reduction of outbreeding, or structural changes in the chromosomes. In one
example, there was rapid (40 to 60 years) differentiation of populations of *Anthoxanthum odoratum,* an outbreeding grass, on small 20 by 35 meter plots in response
to pH (Snaydon, 1970). Variation in chromosomes not correlated with ecogeography
has been reported in *Lasthenia* in California (Ornduff, 1969).

Not all evolutionists accept the classical geographic theory of speciation. For example, Raven (1980), in a recent discussion of speciation in plants, argues that few
examples are available in which plants fit the classical model by the separation of
formerly continuous populations. Raven's assertions are based on many reports of
severe restrictions on gene flow and the high level of adaptation of local populations.
It has been observed in some plants, such as *Clarkia,* that morphological and physiological novelties constantly arise in a mosaic environment, providing raw material
for adaptation of local populations and for evolutionary novelties. Evolutionists who
support this view contend that reproductive isolation is not necessary for survival of
these unique features. Furthermore, it appears from the available evidence that chromosomal rearrangements (such as translocations) are not necessary for the survival of
evolutionary novelties.

Apparently, local populations acquire a set of distinctive features through a complex
variety of evolutionary mechanisms and then the adaptive novelties spread over certain
areas and replace less adaptive genotypes. The spread of novel features is undoubtedly
influenced by mode of reproduction, hybridization, or polyploidy, and by the environmental circumstances that confront the populations. Thus, it is impossible to fit a

rigid concept of the geographic theory of speciation to the differentiation of populations of plants. For these reasons, Raven (1980) suggests that the mechanisms of speciation in plants may be highly compatible with the theory of punctuated equilibria (Gould and Eldridge, 1977).

Darwinian Gradualism Versus Punctuated Equilibria   More than a century ago, Charles Darwin believed he had the answer to what has brought about the astounding diversity of plant and animal life. His answer was an eloquently simple one: Darwin suggested that if the fossil record were examined, it would show that today's plants and animals had emerged as survivors during a period of environmental change. The predecessors of the present-day flora and fauna were less able to cope with new or changing environments and produced fewer offspring; the unfit genotypes were eliminated or reduced by natural selection. Darwin believed that throughout the earth's history, the organisms living on its surface had found a constant struggle for survival. In each generation, those that were the fittest produced the greatest number of offspring and thus were evolutionarily successful. Examples of novel features that might have contributed to the success of certain plants could be leaves that allowed the plants to endure drought, or flowers and fruit that matured before the danger of frost. Darwin implied that these novel features accumulated gradually until a quite new plant or animal appeared as a form distinct from its ancestors many hundreds of thousands of generations before. According to Darwin, this series of gradual changes explained the origin of new species and accounted for the diversity of life as we know it.

Unable to demonstrate an unbroken series of fossils showing transitional forms, paleontologists such as Gould and Eldridge (1977) have attacked the concept of Darwinian gradualism and have attracted much attention in the popular press. They suggest that gradualism should be replaced by what they call *punctuated equilibria*. That is to say, the history of organic evolution is not one of gradual unfolding, but rather a story of homeostatic equilibria that are disturbed only rarely (relative to the length of geologic time) by rapid and episodic events of speciation brought about by catastrophic, worldwide events such as the rapidly expanding effects of a disrupted ecological food chain caused by droughts, flooding, temperature changes, meteorite impact, or increased ultraviolet radiation. The survivors of such catastrophes might have novel features that in the face of relaxed competition enabled new species to emerge and survive.

Where recent climatic changes have occurred, where mountain uplifts have taken place, where new oceanic islands have arisen, or where altered environments have occurred, rapid speciation of plants has been observed and documented. The association of rapid speciation of plants with such events appears compatible with the idea of punctuated equilibria.

HYBRIDIZATION

The role of hybridization in evolution has been a controversial topic in systematics (Grant, 1963). Linnaeus suggested a hybrid origin for several plant species. In the late 1800s and early 1900s, it was believed hybridization could be the starting point for new species. Until the early 1950s many floristic botanists were reluctant to recognize hybrids in nature. Today plant systematists regard interspecific hybrids to be common in many genera. Sunflowers (*Helianthus*) and oaks (*Quercus*) have species that are difficult to identify, because there has been interspecific hybridization blurring species lines.

Natural hybridization is more frequent in perennial plants than in annuals. The perennial nature ensures that occasional hybridization between species will not interfere with their existence, since the genotypes are preserved by the perennial habit. Therefore, there has not been strong selection against hybridization in perennials. Interspecific hybrids are more common in plants than in animals. There are several reasons for this: (1) ethological isolation is more effective with animals; (2) zoologists may have overlooked some hybridization because animals are not as easily collected as plants; and (3) because of the complex structure and sequence of development of animals in relation to plants, hybridization is more likely to cause problems in successful gene interaction and development in animals than it is in plants.

First-generation hybrids generally have characteristics that are intermediate between the parental species. Such hybrids represent crosses between normally well-adapted parents. First-generation hybrids are also frequently intermediate in their habitat requirements. They are usually at a competitive disadvantage unless the environment is changing or unless intermediate habitats are available. Two sympatric species may be ecologically isolated, with one species growing in a wet site and the other in a dry site. They may hybridize when intermediate habitats are located between adjacent populations of the two, such as along a wet to dry transect. An example of this occurs between *Vernonia fasciculata* and *V. baldwinii;* another between *Lysimachia quadrifolia* and *L. terrestris* (Cooperrider and Brockett, 1974).

Following natural hybridization, first-generation hybrids typically backcross to one of the parental species. There are several reasons for this. More plants with the parental genotype are present, increasing the changes of crosses with a member of the parental group. Fertility of the hybrids may be lower, so that they produce less-viable pollen than do the parents. Therefore, the most common effect of interspecific hybridization is successive backcrossing of hybrids with the parents. This results in the reversion of hybrid offspring toward the parental types. Backcross hybrids are usually more successful because they tend to approach the adaptive peaks of their parents. Backcrossing may result in the movement of genes from one species to another via the hybrids and backcrosses. This is referred to as *introgressive hybridization* (Anderson, 1949). Introgressive hybridization may lead to changes in the variation pattern because of gene flow.

The overall effect of hybridization depends largely on the environment where it takes place. In stable environments, it is likely to have no important effects. In unstable, new, or changing environments, hybrid segregates may be better-adapted than are the parental taxa. Because hybrids are often associated with disturbed habitats, Edgar Anderson (1949) coined the phrase *hybridized habitat*.

Because of hybridization, plant systematists must often deal with the phylogeny of reticulate networks rather than the dichotomously branched or phyletic tree that is the typical model commonly presented for various groups of animals (Grant, 1981). This, in itself, can make botanical classification more difficult than zoological classification. Additionally, the existence of numerous hybrids between many species of flowering plants can cause practical problems in identifying plants because the hybrids are not referable to any one species. Sometimes only an occasional hybrid between two species is found, but in many other instances hybridization between two, three, or more species has become so prevalent that the majority of the individuals in a population appear to be of hybrid origin.

Working especially with animal groups, naturalists and population biologists formulated some years ago what is called the *biological species* concept. That view suggested that individuals that can interbreed and form fertile hybrids constitute a single species, while those that cannot interbreed or that form sterile hybrids represent separate species. In zoology, the use of sterility of progeny as the basis for the biological species concept can be useful in delimiting species. The sterility of the mule, the offspring of a horse × donkey cross, is a well-known example.

With a long history of extensive practical knowledge about hybridization in plants, botanists have generally viewed with misgivings the efforts to apply the biological species concept to plants. Typical so-called biological species are found among flowering plants, but they represent only one type of population organization in angiosperms. Departure from typical, well-developed biological species is common among plants and should not be considered abnormal. In many genera, morphologically distinct species freely interbreed both in nature and in the garden. For this reason there is little adherence to a strict biological species concept as a definition of a species among higher plants. In recent years, botanists carrying out evolutionary studies have developed an increased appreciation of the role of hybridization in the adaptation and evolution of plant populations (Raven, 1980).

POLYPLOIDY

The multiplication of the chromosome set or genome, called *polyploidy,* is one of the most widespread and distinctive cytogenetic processes affecting the evolution of flowering plants (Stebbins, 1971a). Polyploidy refers to a numerical series based on multiple sets of chromosomes. In a diploid species, the basic haploid set of chromosomes, the genome, is $x = n$, but in the polyploid species, n is a multiple of x. For example, *Chrysanthemum* (Compositae) has closely related species that differ in chromosome number to form a *polyploid series,* with the basic set of chromosomes of $x = 9$ in the diploid $(2n = 2x = 18)$ species, but among the polyploid species there are tetraploids $(2n = 4x = 36)$, hexaploids $(2n = 6x = 54)$, and decaploids $(2n = 10x = 90)$.

Aneuploidy refers to instances where the chromosome number is not an exact multiple of the basic number. *Clarkia* (Onagraceae) has species with an aneuploid series of $n = 5$, $n = 6$, $n = 7$, $n = 8$, and $n = 9$ chromosomes. Such variation in chromosome numbers among plant taxa has provided an important source of information for biosystematics. For a more complete review of the subject, the reader is referred to Grant (1981) and Stebbins (1971b). Around 40 percent of the species of flowering plants and a higher percentage of the ferns are polyploids. The morphological and physiological effects of polyploidy may include an increase in cell size, a reduction in number of cell divisions, changes in shape and texture of plant parts, lowered fertility, and physiological imbalance.

Traditionally, polyploids derived from one species are known as *autopolyploids* and those from two parental species as *allopolyploids* or *amphiploids*. However, the situation in nature is much more complex than this, and natural polyploids often have various combinations of chromosomes. Unreduced gametes (2n), resulting from meiosis failure, may combine to yield a 4x polyploid (Harlan and de Wet, 1975). Polyploidy may also arise from mitosis failure during vegetative growth that later could develop a polyploid flower. (4x)

Like hybridization, polyploidy is often related to the growth habit. Annuals tend to have the lowest frequency of polyploidy, and herbaceous perennials have higher frequency than woody plants. Interspecific hybridization is often involved in groups having polyploidy, with crossing taking place between parental species and hybrid progeny at various ploidy levels, blurring distinctions between taxa.

APOMIXIS

The replacement of sexual by asexual reproduction is referred to as *apomixis* (Grant, 1971). Many groups of plants, especially those wholly or partially sterile because of complex patterns of polyploidy or aneuploidy, may survive primarily because of their ability to reproduce asexually by apomixis.

Apomixis is often associated with polyploidy, but it does appear in a few diploids such as *Citrus*. Many apomictic plants are adapted to microhabitats, as was clearly demonstrated by Solbrig and Simpson (1974) with dandelion. Some groups of facultative apomicts are capable of both sexual and asexual reproduction, for example, *Poa* and *Potentilla*. Some have geographical variation in sexual and asexual populations, for example, *Taraxacum* and *Bouteloua* (Grant, 1971). With apomixis, irregular meiosis and sexual sterility are no barrier to seed production, and triploids, pentaploids, and other odd-chromosome-numbered apomictic clones may be found (Figure 7-8).

The close association between agamospermy (embryo production without fertilization) and hybridization has been recognized for many years (Grant, 1981). Agamospermy is most commonly found among complex hybrid derivatives or species hybrids. Typical agamospermous groups contain large numbers of poorly demarcated populations often termed "microspecies." The numerous, slightly distinct, microspecies are so interrelated morphologically as to make taxonomic classifications virtually impossible. The variation pattern is similar to that observed in complex hybrid swarms and shows a continuum of variation between the two parental species. Since the population structure is based on hybridity, agamospermy permits continued reproduction of the successful genotypes of the presumably well-adapted "microspecies." Classic examples of such situations occur in two taxonomically difficult genera of the rose family, *Rubus* and *Crataegus*. In both these genera, it is difficult to organize satisfactorily the variation pattern into the taxonomic categories provided by the International Code of Botanical Nomenclature.

Vegetative propagation by buds, bulbs, rootstocks, and so on, is widespread among many perennials. Vegetative propagation in a hybridizing plant group permits multiplication of a well-adapted genotype that might disappear in the course of sexual

EVOLUTION AND BIOSYSTEMATICS

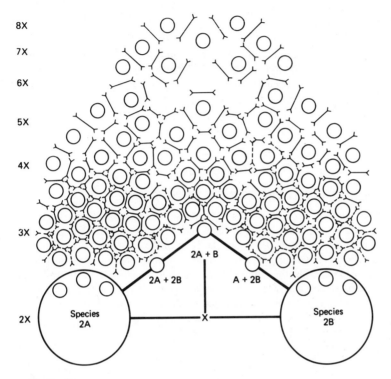

FIGURE 7-8
The structure of an agamospermic complex with both hybridization and
polyploidy (2X, 3X, and so on). The small circles represent morphologically
distinct, isolated, apomitic populations that provide a continuum of variation
between the two parental species. This causes much difficulty in establishing
a classification for the populations. (*Modified from Grant, 1977, with
permission.*)

reproduction. It has been found that many woody and herbaceous perennials can expand
through clonal growth. Hybrid, vegetatively reproducing clones are known in *Quercus,
Iris, Populus* and many other genera. It is generally agreed that clonal, vegetatively
reproduced complexes generally exhibit a simpler variation pattern than do agamospermous "microspecies."

SUMMARY

Since its beginnings in the 1920s, the field of biosystematics has provided conceptual
information on the nature, structure, and complexity of plant populations. Investigations of plant populations and a wealth of data from horticultural crosses have shown
that essentially theoretical concepts, such as that of the biological species, cannot be
applied to most flowering plants. Biosystematic studies have demonstrated the extreme
local nature of plant populations and the significance of restricted gene flow, and have
given an appreciation of the role of hybridization in the evolution of plant populations.

Recent studies have suggested that it may not be possible to apply the classical concept of geographic speciation to plants. Instead, differentiation of distinctive systems of populations into similar entities seems to be related to the ecological role of the population and to the selection of novelties with distinctive adaptive characters, and is perhaps best explained by the evolutionary theory of punctuated equilibria. Certainly, such events in plants are affected by hybridization, polyploidy, vegetative reproduction, agamospermy, and autogamy—particular patterns not common in higher animals. Only a relatively few plant taxa have been studied carefully by using detailed biosystematic approaches and many problems remain to be elucidated.

APPENDIX TO CHAPTER 7: Techniques

COUNTING CHROMOSOMES BY THE SQUASH TECHNIQUE*

Freshly collected flower buds are used for studies of chromosomes at meiosis. Many beginners tend to collect bud material that is too old. For most plants, an easy way to tell when bud material is past the appropriate stage is to examine the color of the anthers. If the anther sacs have already turned yellow, the pollen grains have been formed and the material is too old. When collecting bud material, collect an entire inflorescence, including buds just forming to those with anthers already turning yellow. The buds are dropped into a killing solution. Small, wide-mouth, screw-top vials are best for collecting buds in the field. *Voucher specimens must be made of the material collected.* Root tips for studying mitosis are usually collected from newly germinated seeds or from rapidly growing roots of pot-bound plants. A modified *Carnoy's solution* is used by many botanists as a killing and fixing solution:

For meiosis (4 : 3 : 1)—
   4 parts chloroform
   3 parts absolute alcohol
   1 part glacial acetic acid

Bud Squashing

The bud material in the 4 : 3 : 1 solution should be poured into a petri dish. The material need not be washed in water or other solutions. With tweezers or needles, select a promising bud and place it on a glass slide. If the buds are small, select several of approximately the same size. Add 1 or 2 drops of *acetocarmine* to stain the chromosomes. To make acetocarmine, boil 2 to 4 grams of carmine dye in 100 cubic centimeters (cc) of 45 percent acetic acid for several minutes, and then cool and filter. The resulting saturated solution is diluted with 45 percent acetic acid to obtain the required strength. For best results, use a 1 percent acetocarmine solution for meiotic material.

   Squash the buds with the smooth end of a glass rod. Observe the material under the low-power objective of a compound microscope, and make a rapid search. It is quite easy to see both tetrads and diads and even chromosomes in pollen mother cells (PMCs) under low power without a coverslip. If diads are observed, then some PMCs will be found to have metaphase divisions and perhaps a few cells at late prophase.

*Adapted from a handout of B. L. Turner; used by permission.

If, in superficial observation, the material is found to be either too young or too old, then the macerated material is wiped off immediately and a new bud is selected and placed in the acetocarmine, and the whole process is repeated. It is quite possible to look at 20 to 30 unpromising buds in a period of 15 or 20 minutes. If the bud material is adequate, the proper meiotic stages should be found soon.

If metaphase figures or diads are observed, remove the slide and macerate the tissue with a little more care. Using a pair of flattened needles, remove any remaining large floral tissues. Place a No. 1 coverslip over the squashed material. A blotter is placed over the top of the cover-slip (to absorb the extruded stain following pressure), and with the thumb, pressure is applied so that the cells are flattened. The degree of pressure that must be applied to the cover-slip varies and must be learned by experience.

Interpretation

Interpretation is the greatest difficulty in counting chromosomes from meiotic material. Beginners may feel frustrated when trying to make an accurate count from meoitic cells. The bivalents (paired chromosomes) are sometimes torn apart, and it is often difficult to determine the exact number present in any given cell. Another complication is that some species may be apomictic and show asynapsis with the chromosomes existing as univalents. If one chromosome is superimposed on another chromosome, it may appear as a single unit. Chromosomes that are superimposed will be about twice as dark as those in which the arms are separated and flattened in a single plane. Fine-adjustment manipulation can reveal the true nature of such chromosomes.

Some species will form chains or rings of four and six chromosomes at meiosis. These formations are best detected at diakinesis when their ring structure becomes apparent. At metaphase it is much more difficult to detect rings of four, since the extreme shortening will often make them appear as a single large bivalent. Chromosome fragments can usually be recognized by their very small size and their irregular pattern in the cell.

The best stage at which to count chromosomes in PMCs of nearly all species is that of diakinesis. While the chromosomes at diakinesis do not take such a dark stain as those at metaphase, they are widely separated and do not tend to stick, and their bivalent nature can be easily ascertained. However, in some species, particularly those with small chromosomes, metaphase is the best stage for chromosome counts.

Preparing Squashes of Plant Root Tips*

Seeds or rootstocks of plant material collected in the wild should be potted and placed in a lath-house or greenhouse until the plants become established in pots. Actively growing plants should be watered heavily in the late afternoon on the day before collecting the root tips. If the next day is bright and sunny, remove actively growing root tips around noon of the day after the heavy watering. The actively growing root tips should be white, and usually are translucent just back of the root cap. The time when the root tips are ready for removal will depend on the time of active mitosis and varies with plant material, the time of year, and probably on other factors as well.

The roots may be placed directly in fresh (3 parts 95 percent ethyl alcohol: 1 part 45 percent

*From a handout prepared by Dr. G. L. Smith, used with permission.

acetic acid) fixative and fixed overnight, or placed in a 0.1 percent to 0.5 percent (usually 0.2 percent) colchicine solution for a three- to five-hour pretreatment to shorten the chromosomes. After the pretreatment, the root tips are then fixed overnight in the 3 : 1 fixative.

One of the difficulties encountered in preparing root tip squashes is securing the satisfactory separation of cells, or of single layers of cells. Excessive numbers of cells or cells stacked on one another will often obscure the details of division. Various chemicals or enzymes have been used for maceration to secure separation of cells. One relatively simple technique is the use of hydrochloric acid (HCl) to soften the root tips. In this technique, the root tip is removed from the fixative, placed in concentrated HCl for three minutes and then washed several times in distilled water. Correct concentration, times, and procedures with the HCl will vary according to the nature of the plant material. Accordingly, dilute solutions of HCl, for comparatively brief periods, are advisable for some material.

Following the softening treatment, remove about 1 mm of the growing point of the root tip and place it on a slide in a drop of 1 percent aceto-orcein (prepared from Gurr's Orcein following the same method for preparing acetocarmine). Use a dissecting needle to tear up the growing point of the root tip thoroughly. This will take some time to insure that no sizable bits of tissue remain. If thin pieces of root epidermis resist tearing, remove them from the drop of aceto-orcein stain and discard. Apply a cover slip; sometimes additional 1 percent aceto-orcein stain may be needed under the cover slip. With the cover slip in place, heat the slide by passing it back and forth through the gentle flame of an alcohol lamp. It is important not to allow the acetic-orcein to boil, since this will ruin the cells; watch carefully for small bubbles, and stop heating at once. The heating of the cells (1) intensifies the staining of the chromosomes and (2) helps to clear the cytoplasm, giving maximum contrast of the chromosomes relative to the other cellular constituents.

Following the heating process a blotter is placed over the top of the cover slip (to absorb the extruded stain following pressure), and thumb pressure is applied to the cover slip so that the cells are flattened. The degree of pressure needed to keep from breaking the slide and ruining the preparation varies and must be learned by experience. After squashing, additional stain may be needed, but add sparingly or the cover slip will float off the preparation.

Examine the slide under the microscope and look for single cells, or for layers of tissue that are mostly one-cell thick. If chromosome divisions can be seen, the slide should be sealed with paraffin or clear nail-polish. The division figures may be examined at once, or after an hour or so. A root tip squash is often clearer after several hours. Observation of the chromosomes in root tips is usually made from metaphase figures.

Information can be obtained on both chromosome number and morphology by using the root tip squash method. An advantage of the root tip squash technique is that vegetative plant material can be used, while it is often difficult to obtain flower buds in the greenhouse, especially with tropical material or with perennials.

EXPERIMENTAL HYBRIDIZATIONS

Experimental crosses are used to help define and position taxa. Such experiments require time and greenhouse and garden space. Plants must be maintained daily. Six months to several years may be required to obtain flowering progeny. Some plants require environmental conditions that are difficult, if not impossible, to maintain in a greenhouse or garden. Other species flower for a brief period each year. The various species in a genus may be seasonally isolated, requiring timing on crosses. Synchronization of crossing may become critical in hybridization experiments.

These problems are mentioned to provide information for planning, not to discourage one from performing crossing experiments.

If collections of living plant material are not available, travel to the area where the plants grow may be required. Before the collecting trip, it must be determined where populations may be located and when they flower and produce seed. Growth habit—that is, annual, biennial, perennial, or woody—will influence the methods used to gather living material. This information may often be obtained from herbarium specimens. Annuals are best started with seed. Rootstocks of perennials and cuttings from woody plants are useful in propagation. Horticulturists who have worked with native plant material may give pointers for handling the plants.

Care must be taken with living material to ensure survival during movement from the field into the greenhouse and garden. Seeds should never be dried with heat. It is usually best to cut a large plant back to ground level. This keeps the root and shoot system in balance, since most roots are lost in digging. Rootstocks can be washed, tagged, and placed in heavy plastic bags. Never allow bags of living plant material to be directly exposed to the sun or to stay in a hot automobile.

Voucher specimens should be collected from all populations sampled. The plant material can be identified with a collection number. Seeds or plants obtained from other collectors may be given an accession number and recorded in a bound data book. One such system used is "85–33," for the thirty-third accession of 1985.

In many instances, collecting permits are needed and laws about endangered species must be considered. An import permit number must be obtained to import living material into the United States. The permit can be obtained from the Permit Section, Plant Protection and Quarantine Programs, Federal Building, Hyattsville, MD 20782.

The germination of seeds or establishment of rootstocks is most critical, and competent advice about these processes should be sought from horticulturists. Once the plants are established and flowering, the first step is to determine whether the taxa are self-incompatible, self-fertile, or apomictic. Individual plants should be isolated in a screened greenhouse or enclosed in insect-proof cages. Bagging of individual flowers or flower clusters to prevent pollination often causes problems with plant diseases because of high temperature and relative humidity. If seeds are not set in selfing tests, it is likely that the plants are self-incompatible, which can make crossing rather easy. If isolated plants set seed, they are either self-fertile or apomictic. This result should be followed with a progeny test. If the progeny are homogeneous, apomixis might be expected—especially if it has been reported in other studies of the genus. Apomixis can be verified by detailed embryo sac studies. Another approach might be to emasculate the flowers and to check for seed set. Self-fertile flowers pose difficulties in crossing experiments because they must be emasculated. The degree of difficulty depends on the size and morphology of the flower.

Experimental crosses should be carefully planned, and F_1s, F_2s, and backcrosses should be made, if time permits. The experiments should be designed with controls available for comparison with the experimental individuals. When fruit from the crosses is mature, estimates can be made of seed set percentages in the hybrids versus the controls. Seed set, however, does not in itself indicate if the seed will produce a viable hybrid.

Seeds from the hybrids should be planted and controls established to determine their viability. The squash technique may be used to estimate sterility by checking chromosome pairing at meiosis in pollen mother cells. Another estimation of fertility can be obtained by staining pollen grains. For this, the pollen grains are stained for 24 hours in a drop of 1 percent aniline blue in lactophenol on a microscope slide with a coverslip. Two hundred grains are counted and scored as either stained or not stained. The stained grains are used to estimate the frequency of fertile grains.

LOCAL POPULATION SAMPLES AND CHARACTER ANALYSIS

To study variation in plants, populations must be sampled and their characters analyzed. Considerations must be given to the objectives of the study, the proposed techniques, methods for obtaining the samples, the parts of the plants to be sampled, and the characters to be analyzed.

Collecting a local population sample involves pressing and drying a number of whole specimens or the critical parts of individual plants. Although not usually feasible, the best sample of a local population would be all the plants in the colony (Jones and Wilkins, 1971). Since this is not practical, a sample is taken that gives an estimation of the variation in the colony. *Local population samples* consisting of 25 to 75 plants will yield an estimate of the variation within and between populations and taxa. The number of plants sampled depends upon the variability and size of the population. With little other than normal variation, 25 individuals will be adequate; but if two species are hybridizing, 50 to 75 individuals are required. Care should be taken not to exterminate the colony. A sampling procedure should be used to ensure that the population sample is a random one representative of the local plants. This precaution is often difficult to implement in the field because the terrain or vegetation may restrict the mechanics of sampling.

Collect only the parts of the plants essential to the study, along with voucher specimens. This saves press and storage space and eases the drying problem. A voucher specimen is collected from each population. It is given a collection number, and data are recorded in the field book (see Chapter 8). Each local population sample receives a collection number.

There are several basic approaches used to analyze local population samples. First, an intensive study may be made of one or two characters, especially those that show geographical or ecological variation, using a large number of population samples. Second, an analysis of the interrelationships of 8 to 20 characters on fewer samples may be performed (Stebbins, 1950). The samples may be compared by means of diagrams, statistics, or numerical methods (Benson, 1962; Jones and Wilkins, 1971; Sneath and Sokal, 1973). Each approach has its own advantages and disadvantages. With few characters and large numbers of samples, they may be analyzed with ease, but great care is required in selecting characters. The use of many characters in the second approach helps with the critical problem of character selection. Interrelationships of characters can be shown, and it is sometimes possible to distinguish populations and taxa using a combination of characters.

Visual presentations of data are helpful when communicating with others. These include polygons, bar diagrams, scatter diagrams, ideographs, line drawings, graphs, dice grams, and so on. Benson (1962) and Davis and Heywood (1963) provide excellent examples. Frequently, population data are visually presented in relation to a background map or physiographic profile in order to convey not only the features of the populations but also their geographical relationships.

SELECTED REFERENCES

Anderson, E.: *Introgressive Hybridization,* Wiley, New York, 1949.

Avise, J. C.: "Systematic Value of Electrophoretic Data," *Syst. Zool.,* **23**:465–481, 1974.

Ayala, F. J.: "Biological Evolution: Natural Selection or Random Walk," *Amer. Sci.,* **62**:692–701, 1974.

Babbel, G. R., and R. K. Selander: "Genetic Variability in Edaphically Restricted and Widespread Plant Species," *Evolution,* **28**:619–630, 1974.

Baker, H. G., and G. L. Stebbins (eds.): *The Genetics of Colonizing Species,* Academic, New York, 1965.

Bartholomew, B., L. C. Eaton, and P. H. Raven: "*Clarkia rubicunda:* A Model of Plant Evolution in Semiarid Regions," *Evolution,* **27:**505–517, 1973.

Benson, L.: *Plant Taxonomy: Methods and Principles,* Ronald, New York, 1962.

Bradshaw, A. D.: "Evolutionary Significance of Phenotypic Plasticity in Plants," *Adv. Genet.,* **13:**115–155, 1965.

Brewer, G. J., and C. F. Sing: *An Introduction to Isozyme Techniques,* Academic, London, 1970. (Basic information on gel electrophoresis.)

Burger, W. C.: "Why Are There So Many Kinds of Flowering Plants," *Bioscience,* **31:**572–581, 1981.

Camp, W. H., and C. L. Gilly: "The Structure and Origin of Species," *Brittonia,* **4:**323–385, 1943.

Carson, H. L.: "The Genetics of Speciation at the Diploid Level," *Amer. Nat.,* **109:**83–92, 1975.

Chase V. C., and P. H. Raven: "Evolutionary and Ecological Relationships Between *Aquilegia formosa* and *A. pubescens* (Ranunculaceae), Two Perennial Plants," *Evolution,* **29:**474–486, 1975.

Clausen, J.: *Stages in the Evolution of Plant Species,* Cornell, Ithaca, N.Y., 1951.

———, D. D. Keck, and W. M. Hiesey: *Experimental Studies on the Nature of Species. I. Effect of Varied Environments on Western North American Plants,* Carnegie Institution of Washington Publication, no. 520, 1940.

Cooperrider, T. S., and B. L. Brockett: "The Nature and Status of *Lysimachia* x *producta* (Primulaceae)," *Brittonia,* **26:**119–128, 1974.

Crawford, D. J.: "Morphology, Flavonoid Chemistry, and Chromosome Number of the *Chenopodium neomexicanum* Complex," *Madrono,* **22:**185–195, 1973.

Davis, P. H., and V. H. Heywood: *Principles of Angiosperm Taxonomy,* Van Nostrand, Princeton, N.J., 1963.

de Wet, J. M. J., and H. T. Stalker: "Gametophytic Apomixis and Evolution in Plants," *Taxon,* **23:**689–697, 1974.

Dobzhansky, T., F. J. Ayala, G. L. Stebbins, and J. W. Valentine: *Evolution,* Freeman, San Francisco, 1977.

Ehrendorfer, F., et al.: "Biosystematics at the Cross-roads; Proceedings of a Symposium Held at the XI International Botanical Congress, Seattle, 1969," *Taxon,* **19:**137–214, 1970. (Papers by various authors.)

Fryxell, P. A.: "Mode of Reproduction in Higher Plants," *Bot. Rev.,* **23:**135–233, 1957.

Gadgil, M., and O. T. Solbrig: "The Concept of r- and K-selection: Evidence From Wild Flowers and Some Theoretical Considerations," *Amer. Nat.,* **106:**14–31, 1972.

Gottlieb, L. D.: "Biochemical Consequences of Speciation in Plants," in F. Ayala (ed.), *Molecular Evolution,* Sinauer Associates Inc. Publishers, Sunderland, Mass., 1976, pp. 123–159.

———: "Electrophoretic Evidence and Plant Systematics," *Ann. Mo. Bot. Gard.,* **64:**161–180, 1977.

Gould, S. J. and N. Eldridge: "Punctuated Equilibria: The Tempo and Mode of Evolution Reconsidered," *Paleobiology,* **3:**115–151, 1977.

Grant, K. A., and V. Grant: "Mechanical Isolation of *Salvia apiana* and *Salvia mellifera* (Labiatae)," *Evolution,* **18:**196–212, 1964.

Grant, V.: *The Origin of Adaptations,* Columbia, New York, 1963.

———: *Plant Speciation,* Columbia, New York, 1971.

———: *Genetics of Flowering Plants,* Columbia, New York, 1975.

———: *Organismic Evolution,* Freeman, San Francisco, 1977.

———: *Plant Speciation,* 2nd ed., Columbia, New York, 1981.

Grant, W. F. (ed.): *Plant Biosystematics,* Academic, New York, 1984.

Gregor, J. W., and P. J. Watson: "Ecotypic Differentiation: Observations and Reflections," *Evolution,* **15:**166–173, 1961.

Hadley, E. B., and D. A. Levin: "Habitat Differences of Three *Liatris* Species and Their Hybrid Derivatives in an Interbreeding Population," *Amer. J. Bot.,* **54:**550–559, 1967.

Hagen, J. B.: "The Development of Experimental Methods in Plant Taxonomy, 1920–1950," *Taxon,* **32:**406–416, 1983.

Hamrick, J. L., and R. W. Allard: "Correlations Between Quantitative Characters and Enzyme Genotypes in *Avena barbata,*" *Evolution,* **29:**438–442, 1975.

Harlan, J. R., and J. M. J. de Wet: "On Ö. Winge and a Prayer: The Origins of Polyploidy," *Bot. Rev.* **41:**361–390, 1975.

Heinrich, B., and P. H. Raven: "Energetics and Pollination Ecology," *Science (Wash. D.C.),* **176:**597–602, 1972.

Heiser, C. B.: "Introgression Re-examined," *Bot. Rev.* **39:**347–366, 1973.

Heslop-Harrison, J.: "Forty Years of Genecology," *Adv. Ecol. Res.,* **2:**159–247, 1964.

Hiesey, W. M., and M. A. Nobs: "Genetic and Transplant Studies on Contrasting Species and Ecological Races of the *Achillea millefolium* Complex," *Bot. Gaz.,* **131:**245–259, 1970.

Jones, D. A., and D. A. Wilkins: *Variation and Adaptation in Plant Species,* Heinemann, London, 1971.

Jones, G. N.: "Taxonomy of American Species of Linden (*Tilia*)," *Ill. Bio. Monog.,* **39:** 1968.

Jones, S. B.: "Cytogenetics and Affinities of *Vernonia* (Compositae) from the Mexican Highlands and Eastern North America," *Evolution,* **30:**455–462, 1976.

Kerner, A.: *The Natural History of Plants, 1831–1898,* 2 vols., Blackie, London, Glasgow, Edinburgh, and Dublin, 1896–1897. (Translation from the German by F. W. Oliver.)

Kimura, M.: *The Neutral Theory of Molecular Evolution,* Cambridge University Press, Cambridge, 1983.

Langlet, O.: "Two Hundred Years of Genecology," *Taxon,* **20:**653–721, 1971.

Lerner, I. M.: "The Concept of Natural Selection," *Proc. Amer. Philos. Soc.,* **103:**173–182, 1959.

Levin, D. A.: "Reinforcement of Reproductive Isolation: Plants Versus Animals," *Amer. Nat.* **104:**571–581, 1970.

————: "The Origin of Reproductive Isolating Mechanisms in Flowering Plants," *Taxon,* **20:**91–113, 1971.

————: and H. W. Kerster: "Natural Selection for Reproductive Isolation in *Phlox,*" *Evolution,* **21:**679–687, 1967.

Lewis, H.: "Catastrophic Selection as a Factor in Speciation," *Evolution,* **16:**257–271, 1962.

————: "Speciation in Flowering Plants," *Science (Wash. D.C.),* **152:**167–172, 1966.

Long, R. W.: "Artificial Interspecific Hybridization in Temperate and Tropical Species of *Ruellia* (Acanthaceae)," *Brittonia,* **27:**289–296, 1975.

Mayr, E.: "Isolation As an Evolutionary Factor," *Proc. Amer. Philos. Soc.,* **103:**221–230, 1959.

Ornduff, R.: "Reproductive Biology in Relation to Systematics," *Taxon,* **18:**121–133, 1969.

Pijl, L. van der, and C. H. Dodson: *Orchid Flowers: Their Pollination and Evolution,* University of Miami Press, Coral Gables, Fla., 1966.

Raven, P. H.: "Catastrophic Selection of Edaphic Endemism," *Evolution,* **18:**336–338, 1964.

————: "Hybridization and the Nature of Species in Higher Plants," *Canadian Bot. Assoc. Bull.,* **13:**Suppl. No. 1, pp 3–10, 1980.

Snaydon, R. W.: "Rapid Population Differentiation in a Mosaic Environment. I. The Response of *Anthoxanthum odoratum* Populations to Soils," *Evolution,* **24:**257–269, 1970.

Sneath, P. H. A., and R. R. Sokal: *Numerical Taxonomy,* Freeman, San Francisco, 1973.

Solbrig, O. T.: *Principles and Methods of Plant Biosystematics,* Macmillan, New York, 1970.

—— and B. B. Simpson: "Components of Regulation of a Population of Dandelions in Michigan," *J. Ecol.* **62:**473–486, 1974.

—— et al.: "IOPB Symposium on Biosystematics," *Taxon,* **16:**253–333, 1967. (Papers by various authors.)

Stebbins, G. L.: *Variation and Evolution in Plants,* Columbia, New York, 1950.

——: "The Inviability and Weakness of Interspecific Hybrids," *Adv. Genet.,* **9:**147–215, 1958.

——: "The Significance of Hybridization for Plant Taxonomy and Evolution," *Taxon,* **18:**26–35, 1969.

——: *Processes of Organic Evolution,* 2d ed., Prentice-Hall, Englewood Cliffs, N.J., 1971a.

——: *Chromosomal Evolution in Higher Plants,* Addison-Wesley, Reading, Mass., 1971b.

——: "Botany and the Synthetic Theory of Evolution," in, E. Mayr and W. B. Provine (eds.), *The Evolutionary Synthesis,* Harvard University Press, Cambridge, MA. 1980, pp. 139–152.

Straw, R. M.: "Isolation in *Penstemon*," *Amer. Nat.,* **90:**47–53, 1956.

Thompson, H. J.: "The Biosystematics of *Dodecatheon, Contrib.*" *Dudley Herb.,* **4:**73–154, 1953.

Wagner, M.: *Die Entstehung der Arten durch räumliche sonderung,* B. Schwabe, Basel, 1889.

Weaver, J. E., and F. E. Clements: *Plant Ecology,* 2d ed., McGraw-Hill, New York, 1938.

Wooten, J. W.: "Experimental Investigations of the *Sagittaria graminea* Complex: Transplant Studies and Genecology," *J. Ecol.,* **58:**223–242, 1970.

CHAPTER 8

SPECIMEN PREPARATION AND HERBARIUM MANAGEMENT

Collections of plant specimens are essential for taxonomic research. They circumscribe species and document their variability, they are the prime sources for floristic studies, and they are vouchers for experimental investigations. Plant materials must be carefully selected, prepared, and preserved, since herbarium specimens become a permanent record for later investigators to examine.

The taxonomist in the field observes plant locations and records habitat information. The variation within a single population or among populations of the same species in different environments may be measured. Observations may be made of patterns produced by hybridization or by changes in soil, moisture, slope, light, and so on. Features may be evident in living plants that are not easily observed in dried materials, for example, flower color or fragrance. Species response to environmental disturbances, such as fire, grazing, and clearing, may be noted. There is no substitute for firsthand knowledge of plants as living entities through field observations.

Student collections are fundamental to study and training in plant systematics. As a beginner's collection grows, methods change from those of a collector interested in natural history to those of a researcher interested in the taxonomic problems of a particular group.

Ideally, the best specimen for identification and research is an intact and complete plant. Attempts to identify a specimen from a single flower or leaf usually fail. Such specimens have little or no scientific value. It is possible to collect entire plants of small annual species and some herbaceous perennials. However, one would not attempt to press an entire tree. Underground parts of herbaceous perennials such as rhizomes, roots, and bulbs should be collected. Representative leaves and reproductive structures are essential. The flowers, fruits, and seed of flowering plants are especially important, since most keys for identification use reproductive characters. With large herbs, shrubs, and trees, the different kinds of foliage will be helpful. Individuals should be selected that are representative of all phases of the natural population. Insect-damaged plant material or monstrosities should be avoided. When pressed and dried, the specimen should yield the maximum amount of information concerning the living plant species and be representative of the population.

PRESSING AND DRYING PLANT SPECIMENS

The materials needed to press plants consist of five items: the press, straps or ropes, blotters, corrugate ventilators, and torn newspapers (Figure 8-1). The *press* may be purchased from a biological supply house or may be inexpensively constructed from

FIGURE 8-1
Field equipment: a plant press, pruning shears, digging tool, field book, plastic bag, and other items.

$^3/_8$-inch plywood cut into two 12 by 18 inch pieces to be used for either end of the press. *Straps or ropes* may be constructed from webbing with claw buckles or from window sash cord. The straps or ropes should be at least 5 feet long and are used to tighten the press. *Blotters* are heavy blotting papers that will absorb moisture from the plant specimen. They are 12 by 18 inches and may be purchased from paper companies or biological supply houses. The *corrugate ventilators* are sheets of corrugated 12 by 18 inch cardboard. They provide space for air passage through the press to remove water vapor. The corrugations must run the short distance rather than the long distance of the cardboard. This is because the press is usually dried with the 18-inch side down over the heat source, and the 12-inch corrugations act as vents. The *torn newspaper* receives and contains the specimen while in the press and until the time it is mounted. A double-page sheet of newspaper is torn or cut in half and then folded over. The newspaper should be just slightly smaller than the press.

TABLE 8-1
CHECKLIST OF FIELD EQUIPMENT AND SUPPLIES

I For both beginners and advanced students
 1 Bound field notebook (for collection data)
 2 Field press (complete)
 3 Drying press (complete)
 4 Digging tool (such as trowel, geological pick, bricklayer's hammer, dandelion digger)
 5 Pruning shears (avoid cheap shears; Wiss or Seymour Smith give years of service)
 6 Heavy-duty plastic bags (50-lb. fertilizer bags are excellent)
 7 Newspaper (for wrapping bundles of specimens and for pressing)
 8 Plastic milk jug with water (for moistening specimens)
 9 10X hand lens
10 Pocket knife
11 Soft lead pencils

II Additional items that may be needed for advanced students and professionals
 1 String tags
 2 Plastic pot labels (for making waterproof labels for living material)
 3 Collecting vials and jars
 4 FAA and Carnoy's killing and fixing solutions
 5 Seed envelopes
 6 Plastic bags for living material
 7 Highway, topographic, and geologic maps; county road maps; aerial photgraphs
 8 Camera and film
 9 Portable plant drier
10 Insect repellant
11 Pole pruner (for trees and large shrubs)
12 Semipermanent aluminum tag labels (for tagging plants in the field)
13 Plastic flagging (to relocate areas)
14 Altimeter
15 Compass
16 Entrenching tool (war surplus)
17 Folding pruning saw
18 Paper sacks

TABLE 8-2
ORGANIZATION OF THE FIELD PRESS AND THE
DRYING PRESS

Field press	Drying press
Plywood press	*Plywood press*
Corrugate	Corrugate
Blotter	Blotter
10 sheets of torn newspaper (each sheet will be used for one specimen)	Newspaper (with specimen)
	Blotter
	Corrugate
Blotter	Blotter
Corrugate	Newspaper (with specimen)
Blotter	Blotter
10 sheets of torn newspaper	Corrugate (Continue the sequence until the press reaches the maximum of 3 feet in height.)
Blotter	
Corrugate (Continue the sequence until 10 groups of 10 newspapers are present.)	*Plywood press*
Plywood press	

Useful tools include a heavy-duty trowel for digging roots, pruning shears for clipping tough plants, and pole pruners for collecting specimens from tall trees (see Table 8-1).

Plant specimens should be pressed as soon as possible after they are collected. The best preserved specimens are obtained by using a field press (see Table 8-2). This is arranged to hold 100 sheets of torn newspaper, allowing the pressing of 100 specimens. At the end of the day or by the next morning the specimens must be transferred (still in their own sheets of newspaper) to a drying press (see Table 8-2). By this time, the specimens will have relaxed and may be slightly rearranged to improve the quality of the specimens.

It is also possible to obtain suitable specimens by wrapping and rolling the freshly collected plants in newspaper while in the field. Be sure that the specimens are totally covered by the wrapping, or damage will result. The bundle should be tagged or labeled and tied with string. Water is poured through the open ends of the bundle and the excess drained away. Plastic milk jugs are excellent containers for taking water to the field. The ends of the bundle should be closed and the bundle placed upright in a large, heavy plastic bag. A second bag is placed over the end of the first bag to keep the plants moist. Specimens collected by this method will keep up to 20 hours. Specimens not pressed in the field are usually pressed directly in the drying press. Taxonomists formerly used a metal collecting can called a *vasculum* to collect plants, but these have largely been replaced by heavy-duty plastic bags such as a 50-pound fertilizer bag.

Plants pressed in the field will yield specimens of higher quality than those wrapped, bagged, and pressed later. The disadvantage of the field press is that fewer specimens may be collected in a day's time. Around 100 specimens may be collected in a day using the field press, but over 300 could be collected using the bagging technique.

The *placing and arrangement* of the specimens in the torn newspaper is a matter of great importance and requires careful attention to details. The final appearance of the specimen depends on how it is pressed and dried. Each specimen should be arranged to look more or less natural and show the essential botanical details. Unnecessary overlapping of leaves and other plant parts must be avoided, since this slows drying and lowers specimen quality. Whenever possible, at least one leaf (or parts of a compound leaf) should be arranged with the lower side uppermost. This will allow observation of the lower leaf surface even when the specimen is mounted. All soil and trash should be removed from underground parts of plants before pressing.

Maximum efficiency of the plant press is obtained when the surface of the newspaper is loosely covered with plant materials, but the plant specimen should never be over-crowded. Only one collection should be pressed in each newspaper to avoid the confusion of data. It is possible and desirable with small plants to have more than one plant of the same species per sheet if they are not overcrowded.

Slender plants may be folded in the shape of a V or W. Large plants require cutting into segments. Occasionally, two sheets for a single specimen may be required, but this should be avoided because of the problems of keeping the two parts together in the herbarium.

Bulky organs such as fruit may be reduced in thickness by slicing. Both cross and longitudinal sections of fruits are useful. Pads of folded newspaper or foam rubber may be placed on the leaves to keep them flat and to avoid crushing the bulky stems, fruits, or other materials. Cones may be tagged with the collection number on a stringed label and set aside. Cacti and succulents should be split and the inner parts removed before pressing. Some collectors salt the cut surface to aid drying. In humid tropical regions specimens are slow-drying, and decomposition of specimens may be a problem. This may be avoided by brushing or soaking the specimens with formaldehyde or alcohol to control decomposition. This treatment may, however, pose problems if fragments of the specimen are later removed for analysis of chemical constituents (Coradin and Giannasi, 1980).

Tall grasses, sedges, and rushes are difficult to press and will not stay bent during the pressing operation. A fold may be maintained in such material by slipping the bent end of the plant specimen through a 1-inch slit in a card. The card may later be removed and reused. Because of pressing and size considerations, specimens should never extend beyond the press.

Filamentous or filmy aquatic plants may be arranged by floating them in a pan of water over an $8^1/_2$ by 11-inch sheet of bond paper (Haynes, 1984). Slowly lift the paper out of the water with the specimen on it. The specimen will assume a fairly natural shape and will make an attractive specimen. The sheet of paper with the plant resting on it is then placed in the newspaper and the specimen is pressed and dried. The sheet of paper with the specimen adhering to it is often mounted on the herbarium paper.

Plants with mucilage or with delicate flowers that stick to newspapers may be pressed between waxed or tissue paper. Some plants with large flowers should have a few flowers split open and pressed. Actually, it is helpful to collect a few extra flowers and fruits and fill in vacant spaces to maximize the efficiency of the press and to increase the value of the specimen.

Once the plant specimens are arranged, the press must be tightly closed with ropes or straps to prevent wrinkling of the specimens. Place the press on the floor or ground and kneel on one end while tightening the ropes on that end. Repeat the process several times until the press is tight. The press is now ready for the drier.

For the best results, the specimens should be dried as rapidly as possible. When traveling in arid regions, the press may be placed on the luggage rack of a vehicle with the corrugations oriented to funnel the dry air through the press. In humid regions, a drier must be used. A wooden box 18 inches wide and 3 feet long made of 1 by 10-inch boards with five 60-watt light bulbs as a heat source will usually dry one press in 12 hours. Some small openings should be present in the bottom of the box to allow air to enter. The air will be heated and rise by convection through the corrugates. The press becomes loose when the plants are dry.

THE FIELD NOTEBOOK

A permanently bound field notebook with horizontal rulings is an indispensable item for the collector. Full data on each collected plant should be recorded in the field at the time the collection is made. The data should be so complete that the label may be prepared directly from the field notebook. An example of an entry from a field notebook is shown in Table 8-3.

Data recorded at the time of collection should include locality, elevation, habitat, information about the plants, date, and *collection number*. If the specimens were collected in the same location on a given day, the locality data may be recorded only once. Additional data for each species can be added down the page.

The collection number is a numerical series starting with number 1 and continuing throughout the collector's lifetime. Duplicate collections of one species that are taken on the same date at the same place are given the same collection number. Otherwise,

TABLE 8-3
AN EXAMPLE OF A TYPICAL FORMAT* FOR DATA ENTRY IN A FIELD NOTEBOOK

Union Co. Georgia   8 July 1977
Near summit of Brasstown Bald Mountain, ca. 8 miles ENE of Blairsville and ca. 5.5 miles SW of Hiawassee. Herb 1.5 m tall, corollas scarlet, locally abundant in openings in scarlet oak-black oak-*Rhododendron-Kalmia* forest. Elevation ca. 4000 ft.

23155† *Monarda fistulosa* L.

---

*This format can be modified if more than one species is collected so as to have only one location heading and individual notes on each plant continued down the page.
†23155 is the collection number.

the numbers are not duplicated. Taxonomists routinely collect duplicate specimens in sets of 5 or 10 or 20 for exchange to other herbaria. At the time the collection is pressed, the collection number should be recorded on the long margin of the newspaper opposite the fold. Later, when the specimen is identified, its complete scientific name (genus, specific epithet, author) is written in the long margin of the newspaper and added to the field notes. Additional notes about the specimen are sometimes written on the margin. The specimen will stay in this same newspaper until it is mounted, so the collection number serves as an identification number associating the specimen with data in the field book.

If not pressed in the field, the specimens must be tagged or labeled so that errors of associating specimens with incorrect collecting localities will not be made. Pocket-size tape recorders are sometimes useful in the field. The tapes are then used to edit the field notes later that day. Never delay recording data in the field notebook or editing the field notes.

COLLECTING, CONSERVATION, AND THE LAW

Increasing human population and changing land-use patterns in North America during the past century have reduced or destroyed some habitats. This has had serious impact on the size of the population system of species that have specific habitat requirements. Those critical habitats that remain are often under constant threat from development, forestry practices, agriculture, actions of governmental agencies, and pressures from the increasing population. Many plant species that were once common are now rare. It is essential that collectors be thoughtful conservationists and use good judgment when collecting, and not collect rare or uncommon plants. The wise collector will not dig the only plant of a species at a locality. Some species have become extinct at particular sites because of thoughtless collecting. Some conservationists advocate a ban on all collecting, which would severely limit specimen collection.

There are many laws that protect native plant species. The Federal Endangered Species Act of 1973 protects plants determined to be threatened or endangered, and federal and state agencies have obligations under this act. Collectors should be aware of laws that apply to the areas where they are gathering specimens. Collecting is generally prohibited in city, county, state, and national parks. States may have laws giving further protection to specific endangered plants. Obtain the necessary permissions, including collecting permits in advance, if at all possible. For some foreign countries, this may require six months to a year and probably the assistance of a local contact. Consult the local district ranger before collecting in national forests or on lands managed by the Bureau of Land Management. Whenever possible, it is advisable to obtain permission in writing before collecting on private lands.

IDENTIFICATION

Professionals usually identify their specimens after they have been pressed and dried. Beginners should attempt to identify their collections by using fresh material. If it is necessary to make dissections, herbarium material may be softened by boiling or by using a wetting agent. One such wetting agent is prepared by the following formula: aerosol O T (dicotyl sodium sulfosuccinate), 1 percent; distilled water, 74 percent; methanol, 25 percent (vol/vol). Specimens are identified by the techniques discussed in Chapter 9. Once identified, the names are typed on the labels and the specimens are mounted.

HERBARIA

A collection of pressed and dried plants arranged in some order and available for reference or study is known as a *herbarium* (plural, *herbaria*). Many large research and educational institutions serving as basic resources for systematic botany had their beginning as gardens which included herbaria. A herbarium may contain a few hundred specimens collected locally or millions of gradually accumulated specimens which document the flora of one of more continents. The overall goal of herbarium management is to collect and preserve plant specimens with adequate label notes and to collect the literature of taxonomy in the herbarium library. *Herbarium News,* a valuable monthly newsletter published by the Missouri Botanical Garden, communicates current events in the herbarium community.

Herbaria began early in the sixteenth century in Italy as collections of dried plants sewn on paper. Luca Ghini probably initiated the first collection and may have passed the concept along to his students and associates. Its value was appreciated by those interested in plants, and the technique quickly spread over Europe. By the mid–1500s the Englishmen John Falconer and William Turner are reported to have had collections. Up to the early part of the nineteenth century, plants were sewn or pasted on plain pages and bound into volumes. Linnaeus apparently popularized the current practice of mounting specimens on single sheets of paper and storing them horizontally. From such simple beginnings, herbaria have developed into facilities housing millions of specimens, usually in steel cases. A list of the herbaria of the world and their standard abbreviations can be found in Holmgren, Keuken, and Schofield (1981). The sizes of the larger herbaria in North America and elsewhere are shown in Table 8-4. The larger herbaria tend to be national institutions supported by governmental funds. University herbaria generally are smaller because of limited resources.

FUNCTIONS OF HERBARIA

Herbaria are permanent repositories of plant specimens and are sources of information about plants and vegetation. Practically all taxonomic research involves the use of preserved specimens that yield vast amounts of data when properly prepared. For practical purposes, only in a herbarium can all the related species of a genus or family be gathered together for study. The classification of the world's flora is primarily based on herbarium material and the literature associated with it (which, in turn, was derived from herbarium materials).

A recent outgrowth of the environmental movement in North America has been the use of herbarium specimens to compile lists of endangered species. Many states and provinces now have published lists of their endangered plant species. These lists help

TABLE 8-4
SOME OF THE MAJOR HERBARIA OF THE WORLD AND THE NUMBER OF
THEIR SPECIMEN HOLDINGS

Outside of North America	
Museum of Natural History, Paris	6.5 million
Royal Botanic Gardens, Kew	over 5 million
Komarov Botanical Institute, Leningrad	over 5 million
Conservatory and Botanical Garden, Geneva	5 million
British Museum of Natural History, London	4 million
University of Lyon, Lyon	3.8 million
Natural History Museum, Vienna	3.5 million
University of Uppsala, Uppsala	2.2 million
Botanical Garden and Botanical Museum, Berlin	
(Largely destroyed in World War II.)	2 million
National Botanical Garden of Belgium, Brussels	over 2 million
Royal Botanic Garden, Edinburgh	1.7 million
National Herbarium of Victoria, Melbourne	1 million
Botanical Survey of India, Calcutta	1.3 million
North America	
Combined Herbaria, Harvard University, Cambridge	4.5 million
New York Botanical Garden, Bronx	4.3 million
U.S. National Herbarium (Smithsonian), Washington, D.C.	4.1 million
Field Museum of Natural History, Chicago	2.4 million
Missouri Botanical Garden, Saint Louis	2.9 million
Academy of Natural Sciences, Philadelphia	2 million
University of California, Berkeley	1.5 million
University of Michigan, Ann Arbor	1.4 million
University of Texas, Austin	900 thousand
Vascular Plant Herbarium, Ottawa	675 thousand
University of Montreal, Montreal	630 thousand
University of North Carolina, Chapel Hill	561 thousand

Source: From Holmgren, Keuken and Schofield, 1981

in educating both professionals and the public on the species not to be disturbed. More importantly, these lists also serve private conservation groups such as *The Nature Conservancy* and governmental agencies, guiding them in decisions on which critical habitats are most in need of conservation.

Herbaria supplement the limited individual field studies by using the results of travel and collecting by many botanists. Monographers of genera and families study not only the specimens of their own herbaria but also those in other herbaria. This is accomplished through loans of specimens or by visits to other institutions.

No longer are taxonomists content to study a single or a limited number of specimens of each species. The importance of studying a multitude of specimens has become evident as the complexity of species has become better-understood. Ideally, specimens studied from several herbaria will include most of the range of the geographic and ecological variations of the species and will reveal the trends (constancy or instability) of characters. Many distinct populations are represented since herbaria usually contain a series of specimens collected in different places at different times by many individuals.

Herbaria are *the* repository of "original documents"—that is, specimens upon which all our knowledge of the taxonomy, evolution, distribution, and so on of the flora rests. All manuals, monographs, and wild flower books eventually stem from herbarium resources. Questions about the nature of species, classification, identification, and nomenclature ultimately lead to the herbarium. The activities of herbaria are categorized as follows:

1 Providing a standard reference collection for verifying the identification of newly collected plants. This is a major function of many small herbaria.

2 Serving as a reference collection for plant taxonomy and other botany courses.

3 Training graduate and undergraduate students in herbarium practices.

4 Documenting the presence of a species at particular locations and providing data on its geographic range. It is often possible to go back to the exact spot where a plant was originally collected and to find again the plant material.

5 Providing samples of the flora of an area. For example, it is possible for an ecologist to go to the herbarium and put together a series of specimens that represent the major vegetational components of a region. By studying these specimens, much time may be saved while in the field. Also, a taxonomist writing the flora of a region would go through the herbarium to ascertain which species are represented in the flora.

6 Pointing out the existence of classification problems. A preliminary examination of herbarium specimens may indicate that a species contains plants that do not combine the characters normally listed in manuals, therefore suggesting the need for additional studies.

7 Providing plant material and data for analysis. Data are available in the form of vegetative and reproductive morphology; pollen samples; leaf samples for chemical analysis; anatomical samples; data for distribution maps; and ecological, economic, and ethnobotanical data from the labels.

8 Preserving type specimens and serving as a repository of chromosome, chemosystematic, and experimental vouchers. Examination of type material allows a researcher to determine which plant was described by the original author and to find the exact specimen associated with the name. Modern taxonomic literature is documented by reference to individual plant specimens according to herbarium, collector, and collection number. If a mistake is made in the identification of a plant used for chromosome counts, the mistake may later be corrected if a voucher was prepared and deposited in a herbarium. It is now impossible to publish chromosome counts or chemosystematic data without reference to a deposited voucher.

LABELS

Herbarium labels are an important and essential part of permanent plant specimens (see Figure 8-2). The label provides pertinent collection data that cannot be determined by examination of the specimen itself. Ideally, a herbarium label should be a miniature essay on the plant and its habitat. It is essential that labels be legible, neat, and

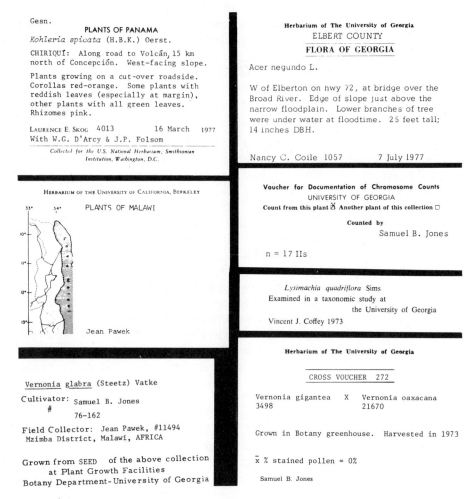

FIGURE 8-2
A series of various types of herbarium labels.

permanent. The paper should be of high rag content, preferably 100 percent rag. Unless done by offset printing, labels should be typewritten. Xeroxed labels are acceptable only if reproduced on high-rag-content paper. Labels should be approximately $2^3/_4$ by $4^1/_4$ inches, which is adequate to accommodate the necessary data. Larger labels take up space needed for mounting the specimen. They should never be folded. Although often used by governmental agencies, printed labels that designate the data to be provided are cluttered and are seldom satisfactory.

Each herbarium label should contain the following information:

1 *Heading.* State or province; county or parish; country (if necessary); name of the institution (or person) with which the specimen originated.

2 *Scientific name.*   Genus, specific epithet, author or authors. When the complete scientific name (including the author) is known, the reference to the original publication may be found in *Index Kewensis.*

3 *Locality.*   Be specific with localities. Refer to some town, latitude and longitude, or a permanent geographic feature. Indicate the place of collection in terms of distance in a particular direction from the nearest permanent and readily located point of reference. Some labels have a map with a spot or arrow indicating the location. Ideally, someone else should be able to read your label and by following your directions go back to the same locality.

4 *Habitat*   Describe the kind of place where the plant was growing—vegetation type, moisture, parent material, soil, elevation (if critical), direction of slope, side of mountain range (because of differences in moisture due to rain shadow), physiographic region, and so forth.

5 *Date of collection.*

6 *Name of collector.*   The full name of the collector should be used. If several people are on the field trip, place their names on the label.

7 *Collection number.*   The literature of plant systematics identifies and refers to the specimen by the collector's name and collection number.

The following additional information may be placed on labels when appropriate: (1) associated plants, (2) flower color, (3) pollinators, (4) bark, (5) abundance, (6) height or diameter at breast height (DBH), (7) life form, (8) economic uses, (9) folklore, and so on.

Labels are glued by one edge to the lower right corner of the specimen sheets. In addition to the collection label, other labels may be found on herbarium sheets. *Annotation labels* are added when an expert examines the sheet and checks its identification. They are usually 2 by 11 centimeters in size. The annotation label will carry the full name of the person who examined the specimen along with the date examined. Other labels may indicate that pollen has been removed from the specimen or that it is a cytological or phytochemical voucher.

MOUNTING

Mounting is the process by which a specimen is attached to a sheet of mounting paper and a label affixed at the lower right corner. Most herbaria in North America use a standard-size herbarium or mounting sheet of $11^1/_2$ by $16^1/_2$ inches. Various paper companies and biological supply houses can supply suitable mounting sheets. The quality of the paper used will vary according to the needs of the herbarium. For research herbaria, paper approaching 100 percent rag content is used for durability. Teaching collections use less expensive paper with lower rag content. The paper should be relatively stiff to prevent damage to the specimens when the sheets are handled.

A number of methods are used for attaching specimens to the mounting sheets (see Figure 8-3). A good quality paste or glue such as Swifts Z-5032, Elmer's Glue-All, Nicobon B, or Wilhold 128 is adequate. "Yes" brand paste is used by some to affix

FIGURE 8-3
A plant specimen and genus folder. Note the fruit sections and the use of straps.

labels to sheets. Glue is applied to the back of the specimens, and then the specimens are pressed onto the mounting sheets. Bulky parts may be sewn or fastened down with strips of linen tape. Archer's (1950) plastic formula is sometimes used for strapping bulky materials. Resyn 35-6262 is useful for specimens with leaves of hard textures since it retains elasticity. Weights of scrap iron, heavy washers, large nails, and so on are used to hold down the specimen until the glue has set. Valuable loose parts, such as seeds, fruits, or flowers, are placed in fragment folders glued to the mounting paper or placed in a small folded packet, which is glued to the sheet. After the specimen has been mounted the name of the herbarium is stamped or embossed on the mounting sheet, and an accession number is added.

FILING

Plant specimens are filed in herbaria by some preselected arrangement. In small teaching herbaria, the filing system may be entirely alphabetical by family, genus, and species. In research herbaria, the specimens are arranged by family or genus according to one of the well-known systems of classification. When filed by families or genera, the folders are numbered, and an index is displayed in the herbarium. Many herbaria use family and genus numbers from Dalla Torre and Harms (1900–1907), in which each family and genus has a place in a numbered sequence based on the Engler system of classification.

Specimens are filed in manila genus folders $16^5/_8$ by 12 inches in size when folded. Names of the included plant material are placed on the lower edge of the folder. Folders are often segregated geographically, and various color schemes are employed to indicate political and physiographic areas. Such segregation prevents unnecessary handling of specimens and facilitates locating the specimens. Species within a genus are filed alphabetically or by sections to show relatedness.

Special arrangements are required for filing bulky material such as palm leaves and flowers or gymnosperm cones. These are often tagged and placed in boxes designed to be stored in the pigeonholes of herbarium cases. Standard herbarium cases are insect- and dust-proof filing cases made of welded steel construction with two tiers of pigeonholes, each 19 inches deep, 13 inches wide, and 8 inches high.

Dummy sheets and folders may be used to refer the user to other folders when familiar names are changed in the course of taxonomic revisions or to specimens filed elsewhere in the herbarium. Most herbaria will have a folder at the end of each genus for specimens not determined to species.

INSECT CONTROL

Precautions must be taken to safeguard herbarium collections from damage by insects. All the compounds used as repellants or fumigants are hazardous to some degree. Mandatory heating, freezing, or fumigation upon entry of the specimens, containment and occasional use of fumigants in the collection, and a herbarium climate inhospitable to insects must be the cornerstones of any workable and safe (to humans) policy. (Edwards, Bell, and King, 1981).

Particularly troublesome insect pests of dried material are the cigarette beetle, the drugstore beetle, and the black carpet beetle, often collectively called *dermestid beetles*. The most destructive pest is the cigarette beetle, which can complete its life cycle in 45 to 50 days with three to six generations per year. Any of these pests may ravage specimens during periods of unattended storage. Recommendations for control and precautionary measures vary, but they may be summarized and grouped under one of the three following categories: (1) heating or freezing, (2) repellents, and (3) fumigants.

Incoming specimens may be treated by *heating* in a specially constructed cabinet at 60°C for a period of six hours. This temperature will effectively kill eggs, larvae, pupae, and adults of the dermestids. If the herbarium is kept clean, at below 21°C, and with a relative humidity of 30 to 40 percent and if all incoming specimens are heated, chances of infestation may be greatly reduced.

Recently, some herbaria have used microwave ovens to treat incoming specimens (Hall, 1981), but it is not always effective and microwave treatment may also cause damage to the specimens (Hill, 1983). Ultracold freezers set at $-60°C$ have proven successful for some herbaria in controlling dermestids on plant specimens.

Repellents are substances that keep insects away from the herbarium specimens because of their offensive odor or taste. Paradichlorobenzene (PDB) and naphthalene have been widely used as repellents in herbaria. A 2- to 3-ounce cloth bag refilled once a year is sufficient for a standard herbarium case. Contact with either repellent should be kept to a minimum. For people working in the herbarium eight hours a day, five days a week, air exposure should not exceed 75 parts per million (ppm) for PDB and 10 ppm for naphthalene. PDB is currently under review by the Environmental Protection Agency (EPA) for carcinogenic effects (Edwards, Bell and King, 1981).

Fumigants are chemicals used in the form of a gas and applied in an enclosure to kill insects. Fumigation of herbaria has been a necessary and common procedure for many years. Recent information indicates that many of the chemicals routinely used for this purpose may be extremely dangerous to humans, and in many instances, the traditional methods of application of these chemicals are also hazardous. The Federal Insecticide, Fungicide, and Rodenticide Act prohibits the sale of fumigants except for precisely those uses for which they are labeled. Herbaria are required to comply with the Occupational Safety and Health Act.

Dowfume-75 has been cleared by the Environmental Protection Agency as a fumigant for control of dermestid beetles and other pests in herbaria. Fumigation of the herbarium with Dowfume-75 should be conducted only by a trained fumigator wearing a full-face gas mask. Large herbaria use hospital-type sterilizers for fumigation chambers. All incoming specimens are fumigated with either ethylene dioxide, methyl bromide, or ethylene dibromide at a temperature of 38°C for three to four hours. All such equipment must be carefully designed and operated.

Under controlled conditions, vapona resin strips (Raid® Strips) are suitable for use as a fumigant in herbarium cases (Lellinger, 1972). One-third of a resin strip should be applied in each case for seven to ten days twice a year. The cases must not be opened during fumigation. Work with the resin strips should only be assigned for short periods, perhaps around 30 to 60 minutes for cutting and placing and 15 minutes for removing each day. The work location should be well ventilated and excessive exposure to vapona avoided. Disposable plastic gloves should be used while handling the material. Workers must be trained to wash carefully after handling vapona or any toxic chemicals. If exposures are to be excessive, a full-face gas mask should be worn. Some herbaria have reported vapona resistance in dermestid beetles.

Three parts of ethylene dichloride (1,2 dichloroethane) mixed with one part of carbon tetrachloride (CCl_4) was once used for the fumigation of herbarium cases. The mixture was applied at the rate of 6 ounces in a beaker placed on the top shelf of each case. The case remained sealed for four or five days. Ethylene dichloride is explosive without CCl_4 and has the property of causing injury to the human liver and kidney from either excessive single or repeated exposures (Monro, 1969). Carbon tetrachloride is extremely toxic to humans, causing liver damage (Monro, 1969). These two chemicals should be considered extremely dangerous to the persons conducting the fumigation.

TYPE SPECIMENS

Type specimens (or *types*, as they are usually called) are specimens on which the name of a taxon is based (see Chapter 3). Type specimens are often housed separately from the general collection because of their inherent value. Every precaution should be taken to reduce unnecessary handling and to prevent damage or loss of type specimens. Some herbaria include types in the general collection, but they are filed separately in specially colored and marked genus folders. Photographs of type specimens from some collections and herbaria are available on microfiche. In many instances, these photographs rather than the specimens themselves can be used to solve nomenclatural problems.

LOANS

Revisionary studies require the examination of as much relevant material as possible. This may necessitate obtaining material on loan. Travel to other herbaria to study their holdings often is too costly or not practical; for this reason, specimens may be borrowed for serious taxonomic studies. This service by herbaria to research workers in taxonomy also benefits the lending institution since the individual requesting the loan has the responsibility of annotating the specimens and revising identifications. Herbaria lend to other institutions and only rarely to individuals. Loans are requested by the curator of the herbarium for study by a specific researcher.

Specimens arriving from lending institutions should be carefully checked for transit damage and the packing list verified. Many institutions number and code the sheets lightly with pencil in the lower left corner on borrowed specimens. Consecutive numbers and the herbarium abbreviation facilitate later return of the loan. Borrowers must be meticulously careful to adhere to all provisions of the loan. Specimens are studied only on the institutional premises and are housed in standard metal herbarium cases when not in use. Dissections are made with care and all fragments placed in fragment folders. Special permission may be required to remove pollen or other samples. The borrower must annotate the specimens before returning the loan. Annotations for revisionary studies are made not directly on the collection labels or on the sheets, but on annotation labels glued above the herbarium label. Each annotation label should have the complete scientific name of the plant (genus, specific epithet, and author), full name of the person making the annotation, and the year in which the annotation was made. A convenient way to agree with an identification is by using an exclamation point (!), meaning "I have seen it and agree with the identification."

Since specimens are irreplaceable, details of packing for return shipment are highly important. Ideally, the original boxes and packing materials are saved and used for the return shipment.

EXCHANGES

Exchanges of duplicate specimens among herbaria and collectors are a means of augmenting a collection at minimal cost. Exchanges are generally made on a one-for-one basis. Specimens for exchange are normally unmounted and loose in the pressing paper and include adequate labels. Arrangements for an exchange should be made before shipping the specimens. Poor-quality specimens made for class purposes are not normally acceptable by most curators as exchange material.

HERBARIUM ETHICS

Herbaria should provide visitors with policy statements including such information as: (1) hours, (2) filing arrangements, (3) reshelving, (4) loan procedures, (5) annotation labels, (6) use of library collections, (7) microscopes, and so on. Visitors have an obligation to adhere to the policy statements and to act accordingly.

Specimens are dry and fragile. They are mounted on paper that is flexible and should not be bent. The sheets should be kept flat. Folders should not be leafed through by turning sheets like pages in a book. Instead, they should be lifted one at a time and put aside. When carrying specimens, support the stack on a sheet of cardboard (e.g., a press ventilator). One should never attempt to force an extra-large stack of specimens into a herbarium case pigeonhole. Heavy objects, elbows, books, coffee cups, and so forth must not be placed on the specimens. Specimens should be studied only with a long-armed microscope to avoid bending the sheets. Loose material clearly identifiable with a particular specimen should be placed in fragment folders. Damaged specimens should be put aside for repair and called to the attention of curators. Flowers and fruits from herbarium specimens should be dissected sparingly. First soften by boiling or with a wetting agent; then examine the specimen; and then return the specimen to the fragment folder. Notes from the dissection may be recorded on the fragment folder. Reshelve specimens only with permission and always with extreme care.

Visits to other herbaria are often profitable in terms of examining critical specimens and collections, searching the undetermined folders, and exchanging ideas with other systematists. A note in advance will help the curator to prepare for your visit and to provide a place to work and a microscope. Many herbaria are closed in the evenings or on weekends. The privilege of visiting after normal hours may be offered but should not be requested.

CHALLENGES FACING HERBARIA

Systematic collections of plants in herbaria provide a permanent record of the earth's flora and its diversity. They are vital for a wide range of basic activities and play irreplaceable roles in sustaining society. The collections provide information for identification services, conservation and land-use planning, education, national defense, medicine and public health, business and industry, and agriculture and forestry.

Herbaria have an educational role in the training of undergraduates. At the graduate level, the student in systematics is an apprentice scientist engaged in original research. Many herbaria maintain programs of education in natural history for the general public and attempt to create an understanding of and appreciation for the living environment.

Faced with both increasing costs and demands for services, herbarium managers have a constant challenge to maintain financial security. Thus, it is essential for herbaria to develop and use modern management techniques. Continued development of computer software for data-processing, data-base management, word-processing, bibliographic aids, and management aids will result in the development and increased use of cost-effective computer methodology in collection management (Morris and Glen, 1978; Morris and Manders, 1981; Sarasan and Neuner, 1983).

SELECTED REFERENCES

American Society of Plant Taxonomists, Advisory Committee for Systematic Resources in Botany: *Systematic Botany Resources in America. Part II. The Cost of Services,* New York Botanical Garden, Cary Arboretum, Millbrook, New York, 1979.

Archer, W. A.: *Collecting Data and Specimens for Study of Economic Plants,* U.S. Department of Agriculture Miscellaneous Publications, no. 568, 1945.

————: "New Plastic Aid in Mounting Herbarium Sheets," *Rhodora,* **52:**298–299, 1950.

Beaman, J. M.: "The Present Status and Operational Aspects of University Herbaria," *Taxon,* **14:**127–133, 1965.

Coradin, L. and D. E. Giannasi: "The Effects of Chemical Preservations on Plant Collections to be Used in Chemotaxonomic Surveys," *Taxon,* **29:**33–40, 1980.

Croat, T. B.: "Survey of Herbarium Problems," *Taxon,* **27:**203–218, 1978. [Reports on mounting procedures and control of pests at 70 large herbaria.]

Dalla Torre, C. G. de, and H. Harms: *Genera Siphonogamarum ad Systema Englerianum Conscripta,* W. Englemann, Leipzig, 1900–1907.

Davis P. H.: "Hints for Hard Pressed Collectors," *Watsonia,* **4:**283–289, 1961.

Edwards, S. R., B. M. Bell, and M. E. King (eds.): *Pest Control in Museums: A Status Report,* Association of Systematics Collections, Lawrence, Kansas, 1981.

Fosberg, F. R., and M. H. Sachet: "Manual for Tropical Herbaria," *Regnum Veg.,* **39,** 1965.

Franks, J. W.: *A Guide to Herbarium Practice,* Handbook for Museum Curators, part E, sec. 3, Museums Association, London, 1965.

"Fumigants . . . Procedures, Precautions and Institutional Responsibility for Their Safe Use," *ASC Newsletter,* **4**(1):5–6, 1976.

Hall, D. W.: "Microwave: A Method to Control Herbarium Insects," *Taxon,* **30:**818–819, 1981.

Haynes, R. R.: "Techniques for Collecting Aquatic and Marsh Plants," *Ann. Mo. Bot. Gard.,* **71:**229–231, 1984.

Hicks, A. J. and P. M. Hicks: "A Selected Bibliography of Plant Collection and Herbarium Curation," *Taxon,* **27:**63–99, 1978.

Hill, S. R.: "Microwave and the Herbarium Specimen: Potential Dangers," *Taxon,* **32:**614–615, 1983.

Holmgren, P. K., W. Keuken, and E. K. Schofield: "Index Herbariorum. Part I. The Herbaria of the World," 7th ed., *Regnum Veg.,* **106,** 1981.

Irwin, H. S., W. W. Payne, D. M. Bates, and P. S. Humphrey: *America's Systematic Collections: A National Plan,* Association of Systematics Collections, 1973.

Kobuski, C. E., C. V. Morton, M. Ownbey, and R. M. Tryon: "Report on the Committee for Recommendations on Desirable Procedures in Herbarium Practice and Ethics," *Brittonia,* **10:**93–95, 1958.

Lee, W. L., B. M. Bell, and J. F. Sutton (eds.): *Guidelines for Acquisition and Management of Biological Specimens,* Association of Systematics Collections, Lawrence, Kansas, 1982.

[Provides valuable information on voucher specimens used to document data in archival reports.]

Lellinger, D. B.: "Dichlorvos and Lindane as Herbarium Insecticides," *Taxon*, **21**:91–95, 1972.

McNeill, J.: "Regional and Local Herbaria," in V. H. Heywood (ed.), *Modern Methods in Plant Taxonomy*, Linnean Society, Academic, London, 1968, pp. 33–44.

Monro, H. A. U.: *Manual of Fumigation for Insect Control*, 2d ed., FAO Agricultural Studies, no. 79, 1969.

Mori, S. A. and L. B. Holm-Nielsen: "Recommendations for Botanists Visiting Neotropical Countries," *Taxon*, **30**:87–89, 1981.

Morris, J. W. and H. F. Glen: "Precis, the National Herbarium of South Africa (PRE) Computerized Information System," *Taxon*, **27**:449–462, 1978.

——— and R. Manders: "Information Available with the PRECIS Data Bank of the National Herbarium, Pretoria, With Examples of Uses to Which It May Be Put," *Bothalia*, **13**:473–486, 1981.

Sarasan, L. and A. M. Neuner (Compilers): *Museum Collections and Computers: Report of an ASC Survey*, Association of Systematics Collections, Lawrence, Kansas, 1983.

Savile, D. B. O.: *Collection and Care of Botanical Specimens*, Canada Department of Agriculture Publication, no. 1113, 1962.

Shetler, S. G.: "The Herbarium: Past, Present, Future," *Proc. Biol. Soc. Wash.* **82**:687–758, 1969.

Smith, C. E.: *Preparing Herbarium Specimens of Vascular Plants*, Agricultural Information Bulletin, no. 348, A.R.S., U.S.D.A., 1971.

Stern, W. L., et al.: "Lindane and Dichlorvos for Protection of Herbarium Specimens Against Insects," *Taxon*, **17**:629–632, 1968.

Stuessy, T. F. and K. S. Thomson (eds.): *Trends, Priorities and Needs in Systematic Biology*, Association of Systematics Collections, Lawrence, Kansas, 1981.

Womersley, J. S.: "Plant Collecting and Herbarium Development," *FAO Plant Production and Protection Paper*, 33, FAO, 1981.

CHAPTER 9

METHODS OF IDENTIFYING VASCULAR PLANTS

Identification is an integral part of all taxonomic work. Plants may be identified by comparing them with named plant specimens. This process, combined with the determination of the correct name applicable to that plant, is sometimes referred to as *specimen determination*. Aids to identification have been developed so that with some training and practice, one may readily identify most groups of plants in North America with no major problem. In order to make identifications, it is necessary to possess: (1) knowledge of taxonomic methods, characters and terms; (2) knowledge of manuals and other resources, such as herbaria; and (3) experience in the identification of plants.

Identification assumes that a classification scheme exists that has distinguished groups of plants and has applied names to them. Once specimens are identified and scientific names applied, the information stored in the classification system becomes available. The names of plants permit retrieval of information, such as chromosome numbers, natural products, distribution maps, and so on, from the system. Accurate identifications are a prerequisite to using classifications as information-retrieval mechanisms, and are fundamental to such research fields as biogeography, biochemistry, ecology, genetics, and physiology—that is, the whole realm of science involving plants, including agricultural and biomedical disciplines. Names are a vital part of our language and are ultimately important to everyone. They help us to communicate facts about the world around us.

Most systematists spend at least some part of their time doing identification work for others or themselves. They use several methods to achieve correct identifications. Persons familiar with the flora of an area can usually recognize thousands of species and can apply a name at some rank to specimens. It may be necessary to aid and improve identification by comparing the specimen with previously identified plants in the herbarium.

Unknown specimens are often identified by means of *keys*. A key is a device for easily identifying an unknown plant by a sequence of choices between two (or more) statements. If a herbarium is available, direct comparison is used after an identification has been made by keying. If the identification cannot be checked locally, some collections may be sent to a person who has become an expert in the identification of that particular group of plants.

OBSERVING THE PLANT BEFORE IDENTIFICATION

Examining a specimen carefully before beginning identification is a good habit to develop. The beginner should select a freshly collected plant with roots (on herbs), stems, leaves, flowers, fruits, and seeds. A specimen with all these parts will facilitate identification. For practice, make sure the plant selected has large flowers on which the parts can be easily seen. It is frustrating for a beginner to attempt to identify plants with small complex flowers. To observe the plant properly, you will need a good hand lens of 10X magnification, a pair of sharp-pointed forceps, a straight dissecting needle, and some single-edged razor blades.

Steps in observing the plant include the following (refer to Chapter 10 for diagrams and definitions of morphological terms):

1 Determine whether it is woody or herbaceous. If herbaceous, is it annual or perennial?

2 Observe the flower and name its parts.

3 Count the numbers of sepals and petals.

4 Determine whether the sepals and petals are fused or separate.

5 Count the number of stamens. Observe where they are attached. Note any fusion of the filaments or anthers. Observe the disposition of the anthers.

6 Count the numbers of pistils, styles, and stigmas of the gynoecium.

7 Remove the perianth and stamens. Make a cross section of the ovary with the razor blade. Count the number of locules. Observe the number of ovules and the type of placentation.

8 Select another flower and make a longitudinal section of the entire flower through its center. Note the ovary position and any fusion of the perianth.

9 Note the leaf type, arrangement, and venation.

10 Note the distribution and kinds of surface coverings.

When these characteristics are determined in advance, the process of identification will be much easier and you will be confident of step-by-step decisions. After the plant has been carefully examined, the next step in identification is keying.

IDENTIFICATION WITH KEYS

It is far more efficient to identify a specimen by the use of keys than to shuffle through a stack of previously named herbarium specimens until a likely comparison is found.

In North America, unknown plants can usually be identified by means of keys. A key is fundamentally similar to an outline where the topics are arranged in order of descending importance. The use of a key provides the correct identity of a specimen by a process of elimination. Keys have long been used to identify plants, and most manuals contain them.

Plants were the subject of description and illustration in classical and medieval writing, especially in those works where accurate identification was a matter of practical importance. This eventually led to the development of bracketed diagrams in the seventeenth century which functioned both as a classification device or *conspectus* and as an identification tool. According to Voss (1952), the Latin *clavis,* or "key," was apparently not used in connection with such diagrams until Linnaeus used it in 1736 (and then with reference to a diagram in which he was classifying botanists, not plants). The use of modern keys for identification is usually credited to Lamarck (1778).

Keys are constructed using contrasting characteristics to divide the possible names in the key into smaller and smaller groups. Each time a choice is made, one or more taxa are eliminated. Statements in the keys are based on the characters of the plants. For example, a key might separate taxa using the following choices: (1) herbaceous versus woody; if herbaceous, the woody plants are eliminated; (2) the next choice, zygomorphic flowers versus actinomorphic; if zygomorphic, the plants with actinomorphic flowers are eliminated; and so forth. Each time a choice is made, the number of taxa that remain is reduced by the use of contrasting characters. If sufficient numbers of characters are contrasted, the number of possibilities is eventually reduced to one.

The use of a key is analogous to traveling a highway that forks repeatedly, each fork having roadside directions. If the traveler follows the proper directions, the destination will be reached. If the traveler lacks information or if the road signs are faulty, the destination may not be reached except by trial and error.

In most manuals, the first step in identification of an unknown plant involves the use of keys to determine the family. Next, a key to genera will provide the generic name. After the genus is determined, the keying process is repeated within the genus for a determination of the species.

Descriptions are normally available in manuals for families, genera, and species. By consulting descriptions, the likelihood of errors due to mistakes in observations or "keying" will be reduced. A few manuals use keys with many characters in each choice and do not use descriptions. In this case, additional references with illustrations or descriptions are useful.

Suggestions for the Use of Keys

1 Obtain as much information as possible about the characters of the unknown plant before starting to key. Attempts to use the key are likely to fail if a specimen consists of a single leaf or just a flower.

2 Select keys appropriate for the plant material and for the geographic area where the plant was obtained.

3 Read the introduction to the keys for abbreviations and other details.

4 Always read both choices carefully, observing punctuation.

5 Be sure you understand all the terms found in each choice. Use a glossary.

6 If the specimen doesn't seem to fit the key and all choices are unlikely, you probably made a mistake. Retrace your steps.

7 If both choices seem possible, try going both ways.

8 Confirm your choices by reading descriptions.

9 Verify your results by comparing the specimen with an illustration or with a herbarium specimen.

Types of Keys

Keys used in floras are usually diagnostic, that is, identifying an unknown plant by stating only the conspicuous features by which the various taxa can be recognized. The *diagnostic characters* used in such a key should be conspicuous and clear cut. Diagnostic characters are sometimes referred to as *key characters*. Diagnostic keys are generally artificial in that the sequence of taxa within the key does not necessarily reflect their phylogeny. Most keys used today are *dichotomous*. A dichotomous key presents two contrasting choices at each step. Each pair of choices is called a *couplet*. The key is designed so that one part of the couplet will be accepted and the other rejected. The first contrasting characters in each couplet are referred to as the primary key characters. These are usually the best contrasting characters. Characters following the lead are *secondary key characters*.

A few keys may not be dichotomous and may provide three or four choices, but pairs of choices are preferred.

Several different formats for arranging the couplets are used for plant identification. The *indented* or *yoked* key is the one most widely used in manuals for the identification of vascular plants. In the indented key, each of the couplets is indented a fixed distance from the left margin of the page. An example of the indented key is shown below (Jones, 1976):

1 Plants usually floating on the water of swamps and ponds; stems
  hollow and inflated.   **1** *Hottonia*
1 Plants terrestrial, not floating; stems solid, not enlarged.
  2 Leaves all basal.   **3** *Dodecatheon*
  2 Leaves cauline as well as basal.
    3 Leaves alternate.
      4 Plant usually less than 1 decimeter in height; flowers and
        fruits sessile; mature fruit circumscissile.   **6** *Centunculus*
      4 Plant usually more than 1 decimeter in height; flowers and
        fruits on stalks 1 to 2 centimeters long; mature fruit five-
        valved.   **2** *Samolus*
    3 Leaves opposite.
      5 Flowers yellow; perennial; mature fruit valved.   **4** *Lysimachia*
      5 Flowers scarlet, salmon, blue or white; annual; mature
        fruit circumscissile.   **5** *Anagallis*

In the second type, the *bracket* or *parallel* key, the two couplets are always next to each other in consecutive lines on the page. At the end of each line there is either a name or a number referring to a couplet later in the key.

1 Plants usually floating on the water of swamps and ponds; stems
  hollow and inflated.   **1** *Hottonia*
1 Plants terrestrial, not floating; stems solid, not enlarged.   **2**
  2 Leaves all basal.   **3** *Dodecatheon*
  2 Leaves cauline.   **3**
3 Leaves alternate.   **4**
3 Leaves opposite.   **5**
  4 Plant usually less than 1 decimeter in height; flowers and fruit
    sessile; mature fruit circumscissile.   **6** *Centunculus*
  4 Plant usually more than 1 decimeter in height; flowers and fruits
    on stalks 1 to 2 centimeters long; mature fruit five-valved.   **2** *Samolus*
5 Flowers yellow; perennial; mature fruit valved.   **4** *Lysimachia*
5 Flowers scarlet, salmon, blue, or white; annual; mature fruit
  circumscissile.   **5** *Anagallis*

Both the indented and bracket keys have advantages and disadvantages. When an indented key is used, the lines become more indented for each couplet. This can be uneconomical, since additional pages are required. In contrast, the bracket keys make good use of page space. Indented keys may have the second part of the couplet on a page much later than the first part of the couplet. This may cause confusion when one tries to find the second part of the couplet. In bracket keys, both parts of the couplet are adjacent.

The indented key groups similar elements so that their morphology can be grasped visually, often making identification easier. In the example of the indented key, *Centunculus* and *Samolus* are grouped under leaves alternate. *Lysimachia* and *Anagallis* are grouped under leaves opposite. In the example of the bracket key, this grouping is not immediately apparent.

Modern dichotomous keys are conventionally published in either the indented or bracketed style. Although various other styles have been proposed, these traditional formats serve their purpose well and have gained general acceptance. The major considerations in key construction are ease, quickness, and accuracy.

When preparing a key, several techniques should be followed:

1 The key should be dichotomous.

2 The first word of each lead of the couplet should be identical. For example, if the first lead of a couplet begins with the word *stamens*, the second lead of the same couplet must begin with the word *stamens*.

3 The two parts of the couplet should be made up of contradictory statements so that one part will apply and the other part will not.

4 Avoid the use of overlapping ranges or vague generalities in the couplets, that is, 4 to 8 millimeters versus 6 to 10 millimeters long, or large versus small, or southern versus northern.

5 The couplets should be written to make positive statements. An example to avoid is "leaves narrow versus leaves not narrow."

6 Use readily observable features. Avoid using geographical location as a sole separation character.

7 The leads of consecutive couplets should not begin with the same word, since this may cause confusion when one looks away to observe the plant specimen.

8 It may be necessary to provide two sets of keys in some groups; flowering versus fruiting material, vegetative versus flowering, or staminate versus pistillate for dioecious plants.

9 Couplets of a key may be numbered or lettered, or may use some combinations of lettering and numbering, or may be left blank in the case of indented keys.

How to Locate Keys and Manuals

Appendix 2 (page 459) contains references to manuals for the identification of vascular plants found in North America north of Mexico. In addition, lists of books are provided for identification of special groups such as grasses, ferns, legumes, and others. For most references, the title alone provides the geographic area. If not, annotations are provided at the end of the reference.

Floras are constantly being written or updated, and new books for plant identification can be found in libraries and bookstores. Inquiries can also be made of herbarium curators or botany professors who teach plant taxonomy for suggestions of books to aid in plant identification.

Two excellent books are available to aid in the identification of flowering plants down to the family level on a worldwide basis. They are *Thonner's Analytical Key to the Families of Flowering Plants* (Geesink et al., 1981) and *The Identification of Flowering Plant Families* (Davis and Cullen, 1979).

UNCONVENTIONAL IDENTIFICATION METHODS

Keys are the traditional method of identification in systematic botany. If keys are well written, if adequate specimens are in hand, and if the person doing the keying is careful, then the specimen can be successfully identified. Keys, however, have several major disadvantages. The use of certain characters is required even if the character is not evident in the unknown specimen. Entry is usually possible only at one point in the key.

Thus, the standard dichotomous key with one entry point is known as a *single-access* or *sequential* key. Attempts to improve on the traditional identification process by using keys have resorted to either polyclaves or computer techniques. These methods provide *multientry* (or *multiaccess*) opportunities for the user; that is, the place of entry is not fixed by the format of the key.

Polyclave Identification

A *polyclave* is a multientry, order-free key implemented in one of several different formats. One form is a diagnostic key that uses cards placed on top of one another to eliminate taxa that disagree with the specimen to be identified. Another form is a computer-stored multientry key. Still another polyclave is a printed table or matrix giving the status of various taxa and characters useful for separating the taxa.

Polyclaves have a tremendous advantage over dichotomous keys, since the user of the key rather than the author of the key selects the characters to be used. The user is free to select appropriate characters for each unknown specimen. The route taken to a particular taxon may differ considerably from one specimen to another. The logic of identification with a polyclave is the same as that in a key, but the user is free to choose any character, in any sequence, thus avoiding the rigid format of traditional keys. This freedom of choice is particularly valuable in attempts to identify fragmentary material.

A number of *field key polyclaves* are in existence: (1) cards with holes, commonly referred to as "peek-a-boo" or "window" cards; (2) edge-punched or "key sort" cards; (3) semitransparent overlays; and (4) standard computer cards.

The peek-a-boo or window card key to world angiosperm families uses a card for each character (Hansen and Rahn, 1969). Round holes are punched beside a family number for the families that have that character. The plant to be identified is examined and its characters noted. With a good specimen, it is possible to find 20 to 25 characters. One selects those cards corresponding to the characters found on the plant. The cards are then put on top of one another in a stack. Families having all the observed characters will be indicated by the holes, or "windows," which are easily seen when the cards are held in front of a light. The logic is simple. Each time a card is added, families not perforated in this new card are excluded. With 20 to 25 cards, it is likely that the family may be determined or the search narrowed to several families. Until recently, field key polyclaves had to be manufactured specially, but now they may be punched by computer on standard computer cards (Pankhurst, 1974).

Two general kinds of *computer-based polyclaves* have been developed. One kind, developed for qualitative taxon-character data, employs elimination. The other, developed for use of taxon-character frequency tables, employs likelihood ratios or other probabilistic techniques. In the latter case, the computer, on the basis of the characters supplied, can indicate the taxa that have been eliminated as well as the taxa that remain. The computer may also prompt the user by suggesting additional characters that might be observed, for instance, locule number. If locule number is unavailable, the user could input other characters available from the specimen.

Computerized Identification

A computer functions by commands derived from a computer program. The computer program is a machine-independent procedure or *algorithm,* which is a set of rules selected from some group of commonly understood rules or actions. An algorithm is evaluated by carrying out the action of a computer program in the specified order.

This produces some described result, no less and no more. The result is produced in the last step of the evaluation of the algorithm.

A traditional taxonomic key is actually an example of an algorithm. The basic format of a taxonomic key includes directions for continuing the sequence of evaluation on the basis of directed observations of a specimen. The result, the identification of a specimen, is given at the end point of the path taken through the key.

Computers are machines intended only for the evaluation of data. The computer can be programmed to identify or to construct a key only if an initial algorithm has been successfully prepared by a taxonomist.

The major research efforts in computerized identification may be grouped into four major approaches: (1) computer-stored dichotomous keys, (2) computer-constructed keys, (3) simultaneous character-set methods or matching coefficients, and (4) automated pattern recognition.

Computer-stored keys may be programmed to provide a dialog between the user and the computer. The computer asks a question, awaits an answer, then asks another question appropriate to that response. In general, computer-stored keys offer no advantage over printed keys and have the disadvantage of requiring access to a computer for each identification. Until computers are cheaper and easier to use than books, this approach will attract little interest.

The second major approach, *computer-constructed keys,* shows promise as a technique. Traditional dichotomous keys may be constructed by computer from machine-readable files of taxonomic data. The challenging aspect of this topic lies more in the realm of data collecting and coding than in the computer algorithm itself. Character definition and coding are particularly troublesome in handling all taxonomic information. If these problems are overcome, computer aids to constructing keys and diagnostic descriptions could be helpful.

Simultaneous character-set methods are those in which values or states of a predefined set of characters are recorded for the unknown plant and then submitted to a computer program. The computer program suggests one or more possible identifications or concludes that the specimen differs from those considered as possibilities. Because of the time and expense involved, it is likely that character-set methods will prove useful only in very difficult situations when traditional identification methods are not adequate, for example, hybrid or apomictic swarms, or with cultivated plants.

Automated pattern-recognition systems providing fully automated specimen identification may be possible for at least certain organisms. This technique combines automated character observation by optical scanning and pattern-recognition procedures. Such programs and techniques have been developed for analysis of chemical spectra and photomicrographs of chromosomes, recognition of abnormal cells in cytological samples, pattern recognition of remote-sensing imagery in vegetation and agricultural surveys, and so on. Its successful use in plant identification will most likely combine analysis of the chemical constituents with pattern recognition.

Computer programs are available to aid in the identification of plants and handle related aspects of plant taxonomy. These programs include routines for specimen identification, key construction, and description preparation. Also included are programs for comparing taxa, inverting data files, and producing punched-card field keys.

The routine application of computer-stored data matrices to specimen identification presents problems: (1) terminals must be located in herbaria; and (2) a network of accessible taxonomic data matrix files must be prepared and be available. Until a critical mass of such data files are accessible via a network of computer terminals, there will be insufficient use to justify the cost.

Identification aided by the computer is possible with present technology. In the future, libraries of computer programs and taxonomic data matrices may play a role in information processing and data retrieval in taxonomy. In the immediate future, identifications will be done with traditional keys and manuals.

SELECTED REFERENCES

Bossert, W.: "Computer Techniques in Systematics," in *Systematic Biology,* National Academy of Science Publication, 1692, Washington, D.C., pp. 595–614, 1969.

Davis, P. H. and J. Cullen: *The Identification of Flowering Plant Families,* 2nd ed., New York, Cambridge, 1979.

Duke, J. A.: "On Tropical Tree Seedlings. I. Seeds, Seedlings, Systems, and Systematics," *Ann. Mo. Bot. Gard.,* **56:**125–161, 1969.

Furlow, J. J., and J. H. Beaman: "Sample Taxonomic Data Matrices for Vascular Plants Prepared by Students at Michigan State University," in John J. Furlow and John H. Beaman (comps.), *Flora North America Report No. 56:1–118,* FNA Secretariat, Smithsonian Institution, Washington, D.C., 1971.

Geesink, R., A. J. M. Leeuwenberg, C. E. Ridsdale, J. F. Veldkamp (eds.): *Thonner's Analytical Key to the Families of Flowering Plants,* Leiden University Press, The Hague, 1981.

Hansen, B., and K. Rahn: "Determination of Angiosperm Families by Means of a Punched-card System," *Dan. Bot. Ark.,* **26:**1–46, plus 172 punched cards, 1969.

Jones, S. B.: "Mississippi Flora. VI. Miscellaneous Families," *Castanea,* **41:**189–212, 1976.

Lamarck, J. B. P.: *Flore Française,* Imprimerie Royale, Paris, 1778.

Morse, L. E.: "Specimen Identification and Key Construction with Time-sharing Computer," *Taxon,* **20:**269–282, 1971.

———: *Computer Programs for Specimen Identification, Key Construction and Description Printing Using Taxonomic Data Matrices,* Publications of the Museum of Michigan State University Biological Series, East Lansing, 1974a.

———: "Computer-assisted Storage and Retrieval of the Data of Taxonomy and Systematics," *Taxon,* **23:**29–43, 1974b.

———, J. H. Beaman, and S. G. Shetler: "A Computer System for Editing Diagnostic Keys for Flora North America," *Taxon,* **17:**479–483, 1968.

Osborne, D. V.: "Some Aspects of the Theory of Dichotomous Keys," *New Phytol.,* **62:**144–160, 1963.

Pankhurst, R. J.: "A Computer Program for Generating Diagnostic Keys," *Computer J.,* **13:**145–151, 1970.

———: "Botanical Keys Generated by Computer," *Watsonia,* **8:**357–368, 1971.

———: "Automated Identification in Systematics," *Taxon,* **23:**45–51, 1974.

——— (ed.): *Biological Identification with Computers,* Academic, London, 1975. (Articles are generally free of computer jargon.)

Shetler, S. G.: "Demythologizing Biological Data Banking," *Taxon,* **23:**71–100, 1974.

Voss, E. G.: "The History of Keys and Phylogenetic Trees in Systematic Biology," *J. Sci. Lab. Denison Univ.,* **43:**1–25, 1952. (An excellent paper with many references.)

CHAPTER 10

TERMINOLOGY OF FLOWERING PLANTS

Because the identification and classification of plants is based chiefly on the details of their external features, a knowledge of the terminology of plant morphology is essential. The description of plant structures is called *phytography*, and it includes the descriptive terminology of whole plants and their component parts.

The major components of a plant are referred to as *organs*. The *vegetative organs* are the roots, stems, and leaves. The *reproductive organs* are the flower, fruit, and seed. Adjectives referring to each of these organs are used to designate their various states or forms. The commonly encountered terminology for descriptive plant taxonomy is illustrated and defined in this chapter and is arranged under broad headings for each organ. Mastery of these selected terms will allow one to use most manuals. The best way to learn the terms is to study them concurrently with selected plant material. The learning experience is much more pleasant and rewarding if critical features are seen in actual plant material.

VEGETATIVE MORPHOLOGY
Duration

Duration is the length of time an individual plant exists. Note the following definitions having to do with duration:

Annual. A plant that lives for one growing season and then dies. A *winter annual* germinates in the fall, overwinters, produces seeds in the spring, and then dies.

Biennial. A plant that requires two growing seasons to complete the life cycle of two years' duration.

Herbaceous perennial. A nonwoody plant that lives for several years; the shoot system dies back each winter.

Woody perennial. A tree or shrub. The shoot system remains above ground during winter; the stems and the roots become woody and live for a number of years. Some woody perennials are *monocarpic*, living for several years then flowering and dying—for example, *Agave*, the century plant.

Roots

Unlike stems, roots (Figure 10-1) do not have regularly spaced buds and leaves. They branch irregularly and may produce adventitious buds. In general, roots provide relatively few features for identification and classification; however, they are often essential to determine whether the plant is an annual or a perennial. In some families, such as grasses, it is essential that roots be collected if the specimens are to be correctly identified. Terminology essential to the description of roots includes:

Adventitious. Developing from something other than the hypocotyl or another root.

Aerial. Growing in the air.

Fibrous. Threadlike and usually tough.

Fleshy. Relatively thick and soft, with storage tissue.

Haustorial. Specialized, penetrating other plants and absorbing nutrients from them.

Primary. Developing from the radicle of the embryo; the root that first appears from the seed.

Secondary. Developing from the primary root; branch roots.

Tap. A main primary root that more or less enlarges and grows downward.

Tuberous. Term applied to a relatively thick and soft root: enlarged and with storage tissue.

FIGURE 10-1
Forms of roots.

Fibrous   Tuberous   Tap

Stems

Stems (Figure 10-2) are the main axes of plants. As opposed to roots, they have nodes and internodes and usually have leaves with a bud in the leaf axil. Stems may bear flowers. Many stems are highly specialized, particularly those underground stems which function as storage or overwintering mechanisms. Variation in stems is of importance in classification, and stems provide many useful taxonomic characters.

FIGURE 10-2
Specialized stems.

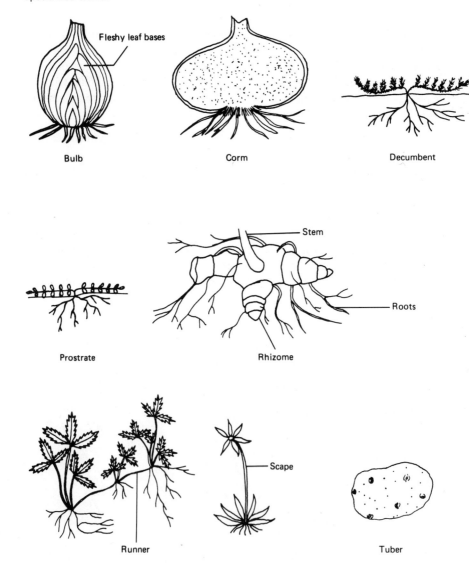

Many genera of native trees may be easily recognized in their winter condition by examination of their stem features. Essential stem terminology includes the following:

Acaulescent. Stemless, or with the stem inconspicuous.

Arborescent. Becoming treelike and woody, usually with a single main trunk.

Bud. An immature stem tip; an embryonic shoot (see also page 221).

Bulb. A short, basal, underground stem surrounded by thick fleshy leaves,, e.g., an onion. *Bulbils* or *bulblets* are small bulbs.

Caespitose. Term applied to stems growing in a mat, tuft, or clump.

Caudex. The hard, overwintering base of a herbaceous perennial.

Caulescent. With a distinct stem.

Cladophyll. A flattened, leaflike, green stem.

Climbing. Clinging to other objects, e.g., English ivy.

Corm. A short, upright, hard or fleshy bulblike stem, usually covered with papery, thin, dry leaves, e.g., *Gladiolus.*

Decumbent. Term applied to stems lying flat on the ground but turning up at the ends.

Erect. Growing upright.

Fruticose. Shrublike and woody.

Herbaceous. Not woody; dying to the ground at the end of the growing season.

Internode. The part of the stem between two successive nodes.

Lenticels. Lens-shaped or wartlike patches of parenchymatous tissue on the surface of a stem.

Node. The area of a stem where a leaf and bud are borne.

Pith (Figure 10-3). The spongy tissue in the center of a stem. The pith may be (1) *continuous,* or solid throughout; (2) *diaphragmed,* or continuous, but with firmer cross plates at intervals; or (3) *chambered,* in which the tissue between plates has disappeared.

Prickle. A sharp pointed extension of the cortex and epidermis.

FIGURE 10-3
Types of pith.

Continuous   Diaphragmed   Chambered

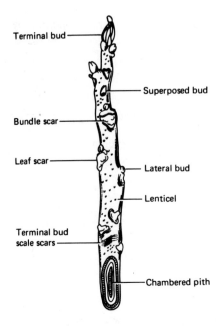

Terminal bud

Superposed bud

Bundle scar

Leaf scar

Lateral bud

Lenticel

Terminal bud
scale scars

Chambered pith

FIGURE 10-4
A stem tip in the winter condition. The terminal bud scale scars indicate the location of last year's terminal bud scales.

Prostrate. Growing flat on the ground.

Rhizome. A horizontal, prostrate, or underground stem with reduced scalelike leaves, as in German iris.

Rootstock. The underground portion of a plant; often referring to a caudex or a rhizome.

Runner. A horizontal aboveground stem, usually rooting and producing plants at the nodes, e.g., strawberry. See *Stolon*.

Scandent. Climbing.

Scape. Leafless flowering stem, arising from the ground, sometimes with small, scale-like leaves.

Scapose. Having a scape.

Scars (Figure 10-4). The remains of a point of attachment. These include: (1) *leaf scars*, where a leaf was attached; (2) *stipule scars*, where stipules were attached (in some taxa, e.g., Magnoliaceae, they form a ring around the stem called a *stipular ring*); and (3) *scale scars*, where the bud scales are sloughed off. In the temperate zone, the age of twigs may be determined by counting each set of *terminal bud scale scars*.

Shrub. Plant having several main stems, more or less woody throughout, and usually less than 4 to 5 meters in height.

Spine. A stiff pointed outgrowth.

Stolon. Horizontal stem rooting at the nodes; a runner.

Suffrutescent. Tending to be woody, especially at the base.

Tendril. A small, twisting appendage that attaches a scandent plant to other plants or objects.

Thorn. A reduced, sharp, pointed stem. See *Prickle*.

Tree. A woody plant, usually with one main trunk and normally 4 to 5 meters or more in height.

Tuber. An enlarged fleshy tip of an underground stem; e.g., Irish potato.

Woody. Hard in texture and containing secondary xylem.

Buds

Buds are short, embryonic stem tips bearing leaves or flowers or both (see Figure 10-5). They may be quite useful in the identification of woody plants in the winter condition. Some of the common descriptive terms for buds include the following:

Accessory. An extra bud produced to either side of an axillary bud.

Adventitious. Term applied to a bud developing from some place other than a node of a stem.

Axillary. Term applied to a bud located in the axil of a leaf.

Collateral. Bud(s) lateral to the axillary bud.

FIGURE 10-5
Bud types.

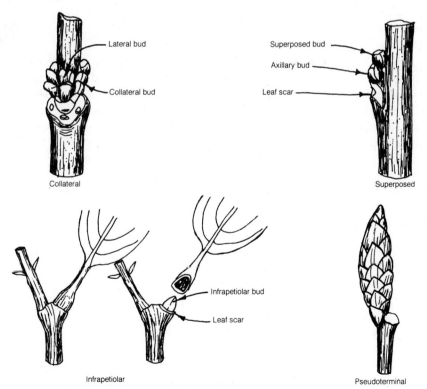

Dormant. Inactive; may be due to dry weather or winter condition.

Flower bud. A stem tip containing or producing embryonic flowers.

Infrapetiolar. An axillary bud surrounded by base of petiole, e.g., sycamore.

Lateral. Produced on the side of a stem, as opposed to *terminal.*

Leaf bud. A stem tip containing leaves.

Mixed. Term applied to a bud containing both embryonic leaves and flowers.

Naked. Not covered by bud scales.

Pseudoterminal. Term applied to a lateral bud which takes over the function of the terminal bud, e.g., persimmon.

Reproductive. Containing embryonic flowers.

Scaly. Covered by bud scales; a scaly bud is sometimes called a *covered* bud.

Superposed. Bud(s) located immediately above the axillary bud.

Terminal. Located at the stem tip.

Vegetative. Containing embryonic leaves.

Leaves

Leaves are generally broad, flattened, and photosynthetic and are borne at the nodes of a stem. Just above the point of attachment of the leaf base or petiole, there is an axillary bud. Leaves are of considerable value in identification and classification. Some flowering plants have a particular form of leaf and may be recognized by their leaves alone. Some angiosperms are leafless and a few have leaves which are variable in form.

Leaf Parts   A complete leaf (see Figure 10-6) is composed of a blade, petiole, and stipules, any one of which may be lacking or highly modified. The expanded, flattened part of the leaf is the *blade* (or *lamina*). The supporting stalk is called the *petiole*. The base of the petiole is variously shaped, or it may be rather enlarged and termed a *pulvinus*. In some taxa, the petiole is lacking and the leaf is said to be *sessile*. *Stipules* are a pair of appendages which, when present, either are located at the base of the petiole or are attached to the stem at the node on either side of the petiole. Stipules are usually green and leaflike or scalelike, but they may be modified into tendrils (e.g., *Smilax*) or prickles (e.g., *Robinia*), or they may form a papery sheath around the stem called an *ocrea* (e.g., *Polygonum* and *Rumex*) (Figure 10-7). A plant lacking stipules is said to be *exstipulate*. In some plants, such as the grasses and the sedges, the basal part of the leaf surrounds the stem and is called the *sheath*. In grasses, there often is a *ligule,* which is a small portion of the sheath extending beyond the junction of the sheath and the blade (Figure 10-7).

Venation   The positioning of the veins (vascular bundles) in the leaf blade is called *venation* (Figure 10-8). Some leaves, especially those of monocots, have *parallel* venation, that is, the primary veins occur side by side without intersecting. In contrast, most dicots have *net* or *reticulate* venation, with primary veins that branch and intersect. There are two main patterns of net venation: (1) *palmate,* with the main veins radiating from the point where they join the petiole; and (2) *pinnate,* with one central vein or

Blade

Parts of a simple leaf

Axillary bud

Petiole

Stipule

Leaflet

Rachis

Petiolule

Petiole

Axillary bud

Pulvinus

Parts of a compound leaf

Alternate

Opposite

Whorled

Once pinnately compound

Palmately compound

Bipinnate

Tripinnate

Odd-pinnate

Even-pinnate

Pinnately trifoliate (ternate)

FIGURE 10-6
Leaf types and parts.

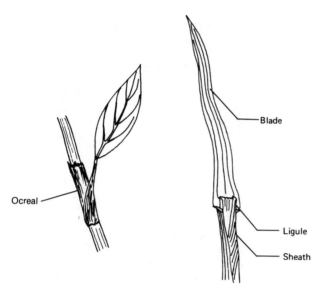

FIGURE 10-7
Specialized parts of leaves. *Left:* An ocrea of *Polygonum. Right:* A
grass leaf with a ligule and sheath.

midrib that has lateral veins arising along its length and at angles from it. In *dichotomous* venation, the veins fork into equal-sized branch veins. This is a common pattern in ferns and is the venation pattern of the leaves of *Ginkgo*.

Leaf Arrangement, or Phyllotaxy   Stem, or *cauline,* leaves are generally arranged in one of three rather definite ways: (1) *alternate,* having one leaf at each node, usually arranged in spirals around the stem; (2) *opposite,* having leaves paired at each node on opposite sides of the stem; and (3) *verticillate,* or *whorled,* having three or more leaves at each node. See Figure 10-6.

The spiral patterns associated with the alternate arrangement are usually definite for a given genus. They may be determined by observing the number of nodes required to make a complete turn around the stem. When alternate leaves appear on just two sides of the stem, they are called *two-ranked* or *decussate.*

Leaf arrangement is generally a reliable character for identification, but some genera (e.g., *Helianthus*) may have opposite leaves below and alternate leaves near the inflorescence. In a few instances, opposite or whorled may intergrade as a result of either extremely fast or slow growth. With woody plants, leaf arrangement should be determined by examining normal, terminal, long shoots rather than by observing lateral, dwarf, or spur shoots; accurate determination of the leaf arrangement may be difficult because of the very short internodes on spur shoots.

In *acaulescent* species (without conspicuous leafy stems), the leaves often form a cluster at ground level and are said to be *basal* or *radicle* (Figure 10-9). An acaulescent plant, such as dandelion, has a stem, but the internodes are extremely short, thereby

Parallel

Pinnately netted

Palmately netted

Dichotomous

FIGURE 10-8
Venation of leaves. Palmate and pinnate are also netted.

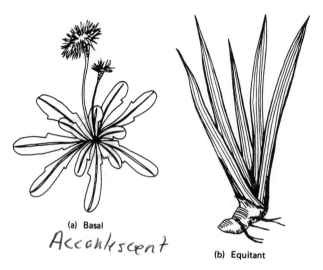

(a) Basal

Acconlescent

(b) Equitant

FIGURE 10-9
Leaves with specialized disposition: (a) basal and (b) equitant.

producing a stacked spiral of leaves that forms a *bouquette* rosette on the ground. *Iris* has two-ranked leaves with overlapping leaf bases and the leaves folded together lengthwise; this arrangement is called *equitant* (Figure 10-9).

Leaf Type   See Figure 10-6. A leaf with the blade in a single part, although it may be variously divided, is a *simple* leaf, while one with the blade divided into smaller, bladelike parts is termed *compound*. The individual bladelike parts of a compound leaf are called *leaflets* or *pinnae*. The main axis of the leaf to which the leaflets are attached is called the *rachis*. The leaflets may be sessile or attached to the rachis by stalks called *petiolules*. To determine whether a leaf is simple or compound, follow it to the stem until an axillary bud is reached. Buds occur only in the axils of a complete leaf, not in the axils of the leaflets. In some plants, especially if immature, it may be difficult to find the axillary bud. It may be necessary to determine whether a leaf is a variously divided simple leaf or if it is a compound leaf. Generally, if the leaflets are well-developed and separate from the rachis, the leaf is regarded as compound.

If the leaflets are attached to both sides of one central rachis, the leaf is *once-pinnately compound*. If they diverge from a common point at the end of the petiole, much like fingers from the palm of the hand, the leaf is *palmately compound*. Pinnately compound leaves may have the leaflets divided. This type of leaf is said to be *twice-pinnately compound* or *bipinnate*. If the leaflets are divided twice, the leaf is *thrice-pinnately compound* or *tripinnate*. A once-pinnately compound leaf with paired leaflets and one leaflet at the tip is *odd-pinnate*, because it has an odd number of leaflets. If it does not have a leaflet at the tip, it is *even-pinnate*. A leaf with three leaflets is called *trifoliolate* or *ternate*.

Duration of Leaves Leaves are often temporary organs, and *duration* the length of time they function. In the temperate zone, duration is usually 1 the onset of lower temperatures, but in regions with seasonal rainfall, it may be regulated by drought. The following definitions are important:

Deciduous. Falling at the end of the growing season; not evergreen; referring to leaves falling in the autumn.

Evergreen. Persistent, not deciduous; often used to describe the plant.

Fugacious. Falling shortly after development; soon falling.

Marcescent. Withering, but not falling off.

Persistent. Evergreen, not deciduous; functioning over two or more growing seasons; often used to describe the leaves.

Shape of Blade Although the overall size of the leaf blade may be environmentally influenced, the shape of a leaf or leaflet (Figure 10-10) is often characteristic for the species. Some common leaf shapes are listed below:

Cordate. Heart-shaped, with a basal notch.

Cuneate. Wedge-shaped, tapering toward point of attachment.

Deltoid. Triangular.

Elliptical. Having the shape of a flattened circle, usually more than twice as long as broad.

Hastate. Arrowhead-shaped.

Lanceolate. Lance-shaped, tapering from a broad base to the apex; much longer than wide.

Linear. Long and narrow with nearly parallel sides.

Oblanceolate. Lanceolate, but with the broadest part near the apex.

Obovate. Ovate, but with the broadest part near the apex.

Ovate. Egg-shaped, with the broadest part toward the base.

Peltate. With the petiole attached to the lower surface of the blade rather than on the margin; shield-shaped.

Perfoliate. Term used to describe opposite leaves having their bases united around the stem and the stem apparently passing through the leaves.

Reniform. Kidney-shaped.

Subulate. Tapering from a broad base to a sharp point, awl shaped.

Apex of Leaf Blade The tip of a leaf farthest removed from the petiole is termed the *apex* (Figure 10-10). Some common types are listed below:

Acuminate. Tapering gradually to a prolonged point.

Acute. Ending in a point that is less than a right angle, but one that is not acuminate; distinct and sharp, but not drawn out.

Aristate. With a bristle at the tip.

Cuspidate. Tipped with a sharp and rigid point.

Emarginate. Shallowly notched and indented at the apex.

Mucronate. Abruptly tipped with a small point, projecting from the midrib.

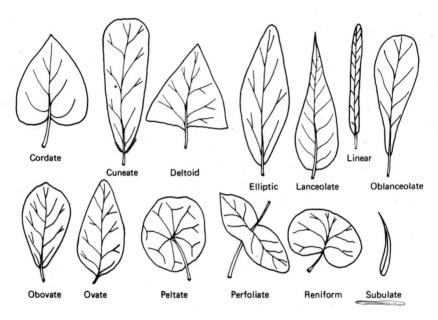

Cordate   Cuneate   Deltoid   Elliptic   Lanceolate   Linear   Oblanceolate

Obovate   Ovate   Peltate   Perfoliate   Reniform   Subulate

(a) Shape of blade

Acuminate   Acute   Aristate   Cuspidate   Emarginate   Mucronate   Obtuse   Rounded   Truncate

(b) Apex of blade

Auriculate   Cordate   Cuneate   Hastate   Oblique   Rounded   Sagittate   Truncate

(c) Base of blade

FIGURE 10-10
Leaf blades, (a) Shape of blade; (b) shape of apex; (c) shape of base.

Obtuse. With a blunt or rounded tip.

Rounded. With a broad arch at the apex.

Truncate. Cut squarely across at the apex.

Base of Leaf Blades   The part of the leaf blade where the petiole is attached is the *base* (Figure 10-10). Note the following definitions:

Auriculate. With earlike appendages at the base.

Cordate. Heart-shaped, with a notch at the base.

Cuneate. Wedge-shaped, gradually narrowed toward point of attachment.

Oblique. Asymmetrical, having one side of the blade lower on the petiole than the other; inequilateral.

Rounded. With a broad arch at the base.

Sagittate. Term describing basal lobes drawn into points on either side of the petiole, like the base of an arrowhead.

Truncate. Cut squarely across at the base.

Margins of Leaf Blades   The edge of a leaf blade is referred to as the *margin* (Figure 10-11). Margins fall into these categories:

Crenate. With low rounded or blunt teeth.

Dentate. Having sharp, marginal teeth pointing outward.

Dissected. Cut into more or less fine divisions.

FIGURE 10-11
Leaf margins.

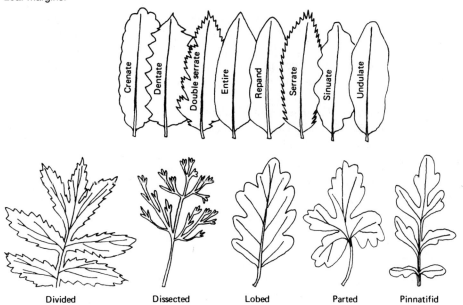

Crenate · Dentate · Double serrate · Entire · Repand · Serrate · Sinuate · Undulate

Divided · Dissected · Lobed · Parted · Pinnatifid

Divided. Cut into distinct sections, extending to the midrib or base.

Doubly serrate. With small serrations on larger serrations.

Entire. Smooth; devoid of any indentations, lobes, or teeth.

Lobed. Divided into parts separated by rounded sinuses extending one-third to one-half the distance between the margin and the midrib.

Parted. Cut or dissected almost to the midrib.

Pinnatifid. A pinnately parted leaf, divided almost to the midrib.

Repand. Slightly wavy.

Revolute. With the margin rolled inward toward the underside of the leaf.

Serrate. Having marginal teeth pointing toward the apex.

Sinuate. Having a deeply wavy margin.

Undulate. Having a slightly wavy margin.

Modifications of Leaves   Many plants produce leaves that are quite different from the customary foliage leaves. Some of these are not easily recognizable as leaves. Among the modifications are the following:

Bract. A greatly reduced or highly modified leaf often found in the inflorescence or subtending a flower; e.g., lemma and palea of grasses, or the brightly colored bracts of poinsettias.

Bud scale. A small scale surrounding the bud.

Bulb scales. Fleshy, succulent storage leaves; e.g., the bulb of an onion.

Chaff. A bract at the base of the achene in the family Compositae; i.e., a pale.

Glume. A bract, usually found in pairs at the base of the grass spikelet.

Involucral bract. Subtending the head of the family Compositae; i.e., a phyllary.

Lemma. The outer of the two bracts subtending the grass floret (see *Palea*).

Pale. See *Chaff*.

Palea. The inner bract subtending the grass floret. See *Lemma*.

Phyllary. A bract subtending the head in the Compositae family, sometimes called an involucral bract.

Pitcher. A tubular, insectivorous leaf able to hold water; e.g., *Sarracenia*.

Spathe. An enlarged bract enclosing an inflorescence; e.g., *Calla* and *Anthurium*.

Surfaces, Surface Covering, and Texture   The surface features (Figure 10-12) of angiosperms provide many valuable taxonomic characters. The terminology tends to be somewhat subjective and in practice is difficult to apply:

Arachnoid. With entangled hairs, giving a cobwebby appearance.

Bloom. The waxy coating on the parts of certain plants.

Canescent. Gray pubescent.

Ciliate. With a marginal fringe of hairs.

Coriaceous. A tough and leathery texture.

Fimbriate. Finely cut into fringes.

Floccose. With irregular tufts of loosely tangled hairs; having a woolly appearance.

Glabrate. Nearly glabrous, or becoming glabrous with age.

Glabrous. Without pubescence of any kind; smooth.

Pilose

Villous

Hispid

Tomentose

Hirsute

Strigose

Glandular

Stellate

Arachnoid

Puberulent

FIGURE 10-12
The more common types of pubescence or surface coverings

231

Glandular. Having glands or small secretory structures.

Glandular-pubescent. Surface having both glandular and pubescent trichomes.

Glandular-punctate. Dotted across the surface with glands.

Glaucous. Having a waxy appearance due to a bloom or powdery coating of wax, i.e., a waxy bloom.

Hirsute. With long, shaggy hairs, often stiff or bristly to the touch.

Hispid. With stiff, rough hairs.

Lanate. Woolly, with long, intertwined, coiled hairs.

Pilose. With scattered, long, slender, soft hairs.

Puberulent. Somewhat or minutely pubescent.

Pubescent. Covered with short, soft hairs.

Rugose. Wrinkled.

Scabrous. Rough to the touch.

Scarious. Thin and membranous, usually dry.

Scurfy. Covered with scales.

Sericeous. With soft, silky hairs, usually all pointing in one direction.

Stellate. With star-shaped hairs.

Stinging hairs. Hairs which cause a stinging or burning sensation when they come into contact with the skin.

Strigose. Stiff hairs often appressed (i.e., pressed next to the stem) and pointing in one direction.

Tomentose. With densely matted soft hairs; woolly in appearance.

Velutinous. Velvety.

Villous. Covered with long, fine, soft hairs.

REPRODUCTIVE MORPHOLOGY

Much of the classification of flowering plants is based on reproductive structures, and a knowledge of the terminology of flowers, fruits, and seeds is essential to identify plants and to understand classifications.

A *flower* is a highly modified shoot with specialized appendages. Flowers may arise in the axil of a leaf or, more often, in the axil of a reduced leaf called a *bract*. Ripened ovaries in the flower develop into the *fruit*. Fruits may have other floral structures associated with them and normally contain *seeds,* which are ripened ovules. The seed germinates and produces a new plant.

Parts of a Generalized Flower

The major components of the unmodified flower (Figure 10-13) are the *perianth,* the *androecium,* and the *gynoecium*. These structures are attached to the *floral axis* or receptacle. A *hypanthium* may be present and is sometimes wholly or partly receptacular in nature; at other times it is composed wholly or partly of perianth and androecial tissue. The *perianth,* or *floral envelope,* is subdivided into the *calyx* (composed of the sepals) and the *corolla* (made up of the petals). A group of *stamens,* where the pollen is produced, is called the *androecium*. The *gynoecium* consists of

FIGURE 10-13
The parts of a generalized flower.

one or more carpels, when two or more, they may be either separate (simple pistils) or united (compound pistils). Some terms associated with the generalized flower are defined below:

Androecium. The male part of the flower; a collective name for the stamens of a flower and the parts derived from stamens. The androecium occupies a position inward from the perianth.

Anther. That part of the stamen where the pollen is produced.

Calyx. The collective name for the sepals. The calyx occupies the outermost position in the flower. Together with the corolla, the calyx makes up the perianth. The calyx is usually green but is sometimes colored; e.g., *Fuchsia*. Sometimes the calyx intergrades into the corolla; e.g., water lily.

Carpel. A simple pistil; one part of a compound pistil. The carpel is the innermost part of the flower, bearing one or more ovules. It is thought to have evolved from an ovule-bearing leaf, i.e., megasporophyll. (See Chapter 6.)

Corolla. The inner part of the perianth, composed of the petals. The corolla is usually larger than the calyx and is often brightly colored. The petals may be fused or separate.

Filament. The stalklike part of the stamen that supports the anthers and which is attached to the receptacle. It may be fused to the petal(s) for part of its length.

Fruit. Mature ovary or ovaries containing seed.

Gynoecium. The female part of the flower; the collective term for the carpels or pistils. It is the innermost part of a flower and is composed of one or more carpels, which may or may not be united into a compound pistil.

Hypanthium. A floral cup or tube formed either from the receptacle or from fusion of the bases of the sepals, petals, and stamens or both. The hypanthium appears to bear sepals, petals, and stamens on the rim of its cup or tube.

Ovary. The usually enlarged, basal portion of the pistil where the ovules are borne. The ovary, sometimes with associated floral structures, develops into the fruit.

Ovule. The structure in the ovary which develops into the seed.

Pedicel. The stalk of each individual flower.

Peduncle. The stalk bearing the entire inflorescence or a solitary flower.

Perianth. The collective term for the floral envelope, i.e., calyx and corolla.

Petals. The individual parts of the corolla occupying a position between the sepals and stamens.

Pistil. A structure composed of one or more carpels and usually having a stigma, style, and ovary. The carpels in a flower are collectively termed the *gynoecium.* A *simple pistil* is composed of a single carpel; a *compound pistil* is composed of two or more united carpels.

Rachis. The central axis of an inflorescence, e.g., grasses.

Receptacle. The portion of the stem which bears flower parts. It consists of several short nodes and internodes.

Seed. A matured ovule consisting of a seed coat (integument), an enclosed nucellus, embryo, and the remains of the megagametophyte.

Sepals. The individual components of the calyx; the outermost whorl of the flower. The sepals are usually green, but may be petaloid and colored.

Stamens. The pollen-producing part of the flower, located just inside the corolla. Stamens usually have an anther and a filament. The stamens in a flower are collectively known as the *androecium.*

Staminode. A sterile stamen.

Stigma. The portion of the style that is receptive to germination of pollen.

Style. The elongated stalk connecting the stigma and ovary.

Inflorescences

The term *inflorescence* refers to the arrangement of the flowers on the plant (Figure 10-14). Some inflorescences are simple and readily distinguishable, but others are complicated aggregations that are difficult to characterize.

Several terms are associated with inflorescences and are essential to their understanding. *Determinate* inflorescences are those where the flowering sequence begins with the terminal flower at the tip of the stem or at the center of the flower cluster. In contrast, *indeterminate* inflorescences have a flowering sequence which starts at or near the base of the inflorescence, or the outside of the cluster, and proceeds upward or toward the center.

The following are some common types of inflorescences:

Ament. A deciduous, erect or lax, spikelike inflorescence, with scaly bracts and unisexual, apetalous flowers.

Capitulum. See *Head.*

Catkin. A soft spike or raceme of small unisexual flowers, the inflorescence usually falling as a unit. See *Ament.*

Compound. Composed of two or more simple inflorescences aggregated together, e.g., a panicle.

Corymb. A broad inflorescence in which the lower pedicels are successively elongate, giving the inflorescence a flat-topped appearance; indeterminate.

Cyme. A broad, more or less flat-topped inflorescence with the main axis terminating in a single flower that opens before the lateral flowers; determinate.

FIGURE 10-14
The major types of inflorescences.

Head

Compound corymb

Simple corymb

Compound cyme

Scorpioid cyme

Helicoid cyme

Compound umbel

Simple umbel

Spike

Raceme

Panicle

Verticil

Thyrse

Spadix

Spathe

Catkin

235

Head. A dense cluster of stalkless flowers; a capitulum.

Helicoid. Curved or spiral inflorescence.

Panicle. A compound inflorescence in which the main axis is branched one or more times and may support spikes, racemes, or corymbs.

Raceme. An inflorescence with a single axis and the flowers arranged along the main axis on pedicels; indeterminate.

Scorpioid cyme. A cyme that appears to coil, like a scorpion's tail.

Solitary. With a single flower.

Spadix. A thick or fleshy spikelike inflorescence with very small flowers which are massed together and usually enclosed in a spathe, e.g. Araceae.

Spike. An inflorescence with a single axis and flowers without pedicels.

Thyrse. A compound, compact panicle with an indeterminate main axis and laterally determinate axes.

Umbel. An inflorescence of few to many flowers on pedicels of approximately equal length arising from the top of a peduncle; indeterminate; common in the Umbelliferae and Liliaceae.

Verticil. An inflorescence with the flowers arranged in whorls at the nodes.

Numerical Plan

Most families of dicotyledons have a numerical plan of 4 or 5, or multiples of 4 or 5. Monocotyledons typically have 3-merous flowers or with parts in multiples of 3. For example, the family Liliaceae has three sepals, three petals, six stamens, and a three-locular ovary. The ending *-merous* is used with a numerical prefix indicating the number of each of the parts. For example, a "5-merous calyx" implies that the calyx is made up of five sepals.

Symmetry

The perianth in some flowers is so arranged that any line bisecting the flower through the central axis will produce symmetrical halves. Flowers having this radial symmetry (Figure 10-15) are called *regular* or *actinomorphic*, e.g., rose or petunia. Other plants have flowers that may be divided into symmetrical halves only on one line. These flowers have bilateral symmetry and are described as *irregular* or *zygomorphic*; e.g., snapdragon.

Insertion of Floral Structures

The attachment and arrangement of floral parts is called *insertion*. The term *inserted* implies that one part is attached to or growing out of another part—e.g., stamens inserted on the petals. The parts of a flower may be fused together but eventually are attached to the receptacle. The petals normally alternate with the sepals in point of attachment, and the stamens alternate with the petals.

The *insertion of the ovary* relative to the position of the other floral parts is a widely used taxonomic character. If the ovary is attached to the receptacle above the attachment

(a) Regular — actinomorphic   (b) Irregular — zygomorphic

FIGURE 10-15
The symmetry of flowers: (a) regular; (b) irregular.

of the other floral parts, it is *superior*. The ovary is called *inferior* when it lies below the attachment of the perianth and androecium and is embedded in receptacle tissue.

Flowers may be classified into one of three groups: *hypogynous, perigynous,* or *epigynous,* depending upon the ovary, perianth, and androecium positions (Figure 10-16).

In a *hypogynous* flower, the perianth and androecium are inserted around the base of the gynoecium. In some hypogynous flowers, the stamens may be adnate to the base of the petals, but the bases of the perianth are not fused together to form a floral cup. In addition, no floral structures are fused to the ovary. Hypogynous flowers have superior ovaries.

The *perigynous* flower has the perianth and stamens united by their bases to form a cuplike *hypanthium,* or else has a hypanthium developed from receptacle tissue. The hypanthium is free from the pistil, although it surrounds the ovary. The upper part of the sepals, petals, and stamens are inserted upon the rim of the hypanthium and appear to grow from it. The ovary is superior in a perigynous flower.

FIGURE 10-16
Ovary position and insertion of flower parts. Superior and inferior describe the ovary; hypogynous, perigynous, and epigynous describe the flower.

Superior — hypogynous   Superior — perigynous   Inferior — epigynous

An *epigynous* flower has a hypanthium fused to the ovary, and therefore the sepals, petals, and stamens appear to arise from the top of the ovary. The ovary is obviously inferior in an epigynous flower, since it occurs below the point of attachment of the perianth and androecium. In some instances, the ovary is sunken in the receptacle. In some groups, the hypanthium extends only partially up the ovary, and the ovary is termed *half-inferior*. The hypanthium may extend beyond the top of the ovary, forming a cup or tube around the style.

Many intergradations exist among the idealized flower types and ovary positions. To determine whether the flower is hypogynous, perigynous, or epigynous, view the flower after making a longitudinal cut.

Union of Floral Parts   Manuals use a number of terms to describe the connection (fusion or lack of fusion) among floral parts. Some of the more frequently encountered terminology include the following:

Adhesion. Union of unlike parts.

Adnate. United to a part of a different kind; e.g., stamens united to petals.

Apo-. A prefix meaning free, separate; e.g., apocarpous, which refers to separate carpels.

Coalescence. Union of similar parts; e.g., the sepals.

Coherent. Having like parts united, such as all the petals united.

Cohesion. Fused together.

Connate. United to similar parts; coalescence, e.g., petals united to petals.

Connivent. Coming together but not fused.

Distinct. Separate; not united.

Free. Not attached to a member of the same whorl nor to a member of another whorl of floral parts; not fused to another part.

Gamo-. A prefix meaning "unitied" or "fused"; e.g., *gamopetalous,* referring to united petals.

Imbricate. Overlapping like the shingles on a roof.

Poly-. A prefix indicating "many"; used in descriptions to imply many separate petals or sepals; e.g., *polypetalous* and *polysepalous.*

Syn-. A prefix meaning "united" or "fused"; e.g., *syncarpous,* "having fused carpels." The prefix becomes *sym-* before the letters b, m, and p, as in *sympetalous,* "having united petals."

Valvate. With margins of adjacent structures touching only at their edges.

Presence or Absence of Floral Parts, and Sexuality   The following are the essential terms in describing the sexuality and the presence or absence of floral parts:

Apetalous. Without petals, or with only a single perianth whorl.

Bisexual. Having both stamens and pistils in the same flower.

Complete. Having calyx, corolla, stamens, and pistils.

Dioecious. Having staminate and pistillate flowers on different plants; e.g., American holly or willow.

Imperfect. Refers to a flower having either stamens or pistils but not both; i.e., one sex but not both.

Incomplete. Used to describe a flower that lacks one of the four whorls of a typical flower, but usually with reference to the absence of petals or sepals or both.

Monoecious. Having stamens and pistils in different flowers on the same plant; e.g., corn.

Naked. Lacking a perianth or enclosing bracts.

Obsolete. Rudimentary; or not evident.

Perfect. Having both stamens and pistils in the same flower.

Pistillate. Term applied to plants or flowers with pistils, but no functional stamens.

Polygamous. Having perfect, pistillate, and staminate flowers all on the same plant. *Polygamo-dioecious:* polygamous, but mostly dioecious, *Polygamo-monoecious:* polygamous, but mostly monoecious.

Staminate: Term applied to plants or flowers with stamens, but no functional pistils.

Unisexual. Having only stamens or pistils, but not both, i.e., imperfect.

Perianth

See Figure 10-17. A calyx or a corolla of many separate sepals or petals is classified as *polysepalous* or *polypetalous*. If the sepals or petals are united, they are described as either *synsepalous* or *gamosepalous* and either *sympetalous* or *gamopetalous*. The corolla and sometimes the calyx may be formed into a basal cylindrical structure called the *tube*. The inside opening of the tube is referred to as the *throat*. The spreading part of of a sympetalous corolla is the lobe or *limb*. The calyx often has prominent veins called *nerves*. The narrowed, petiolelike base of some petals or sepals is the *claw*. The *spur* is a hollow protrusion of the corolla or calyx; e.g., the corolla spur of *Linaria*. Several terms are used to refer to the shape of sympetalous corollas (Figure 10-18).

FIGURE 10-17
Corolla. Claw, limb, and tube.

Petals

Bilabiate   Campanulate   Funnelform   Rotate

Salverform   Tubular   Urceolate

FIGURE 10-18
Corolla shapes.

Bilabiate. Two-lipped, with two unequal divisions.
Campanulate. Bell-shaped.
Funnelform. Having the shape of an elongate funnel.
Rotate. Radiately spreading in one plane, with a short tube.
Salverform. A term used to describe a corolla with a cylindrical elongate tube and spreading rotate limbs that are abruptly flared.
Tubular. Cylindrical and hollow; having an elongated tube and short limb.
Urceolate. A term used to describe a corolla with united petals forming a tube that is expanded below the middle and narrow at the top, urn-shaped.

Androecium

The collection of stamens in the flower is termed the *androecium* (Figure 10-19). Stamens are composed of the pollen-producing part, the *anther,* and the *filament.* Some taxonomic characters that are derived from the androecium include: number, fusion, and insertion. Terms used to describe the androecium include:

Versatile   Basifixed

Diadelphous

FIGURE 10-19
Anther types and diadelphous stamens.

Basifixed. A term to describe an anther attached by its base to the filament.

Centrifugal. Developing first at the center and then gradually toward the outside, used to describe the sequence of stamen maturation in a single flower with many stamens.

Centripetal. Developing first at the outside and then gradually toward the center, used to describe the sequence of stamen maturation in a single flower with many stamens.

Connective. Term describing the tissue between the two locules of an anther.

Diadelphous. The term applied to stamens which form two groups by the union of their filaments.

Didynamous. A term used to describe flowers with two long and two short stamens; common in the Labiatae.

Epipetalous. Having stamens inserted on the petals.

Exserted. Having stamens extending beyond the corolla.

Extrorse. Facing outward from the axis; e.g., anther sacs opening away from the center of the flower.

Gynostemium. The column resulting from the fusion of stamens and pistil; e.g., orchids.

Included. A term used to describe stamens not protruding from corolla; not exserted.

Introrse. Facing inward toward the axis; e.g., anther sacs opening toward the center of the flower.

Monadelphous. Having the stamens united by their filaments into a single structure; e.g., Malvaceae.

Poricidal. Opening by means of pores; e.g., the anther sacs opening through a pore at the apex, as in some Solanaceae and Ericaceae.

Staminode. A sterile stamen; a rudimentary or showy structure arising from the stamen whorl; e.g., *Penstemon*.

Synantherous. Term applied to stamens fused together by their anthers; e.g., the Compositae family.

Tetradynamous. Having four long and two short stamens, as in most members of the family Cruciferae.

Versatile. Attached at the middle; describing an anther attached at its midpoint to the apex of the filament; e.g. lily.

Gynoecium

The collection of carpels in the flower is the *gynoecium* (see Figure 6-4). The *carpel* is generally considered to have been derived from an enrolled leaflike structure bearing ovules. A gynoecium of one or more separate or individual carpels is described as *apocarpus,* and the individual carpel is a *simple pistil.* If the gynoecium is composed of two or more united carpels, it is *syncarpous* and is a *compound pistil.*

A typical gynoecium is composed of a pollen-receptive area at the apex called the *stigma,* a stalklike *style,* and an enlarged basal portion bearing ovules called the *ovary.* A simple or *unicarpellate* ovary has one chamber within it where the ovules are borne. The chamber is called either a *"cell,"* or more properly, the *locule.* A *multicarpellate* ovary may have one or more locules. If an ovary has two or more locules, the interior wall separating the locules is the *septum* (plural, *septa*) (see Figures 10-20 and 10-21).

The stalk that attaches the ovule to the ovary wall is called the *funiculus.* The *placenta* is the point of attachment of an ovule to the ovary wall. It is sometimes difficult to determine the number of carpels in a gynoecium, but in many instances each group of placentae represents the location of a separate carpel. The arrangement of the placentae, or *placentation,* describes the way in which the ovules are arranged in the ovary.

The five main kinds of placentation are marginal, axile, parietal, free-central, and basal (see Figure 10-20). In simple (unicarpellate) pistils, the placentation is marginal. The four other basic types of placentation are found in compound pistils. When there are separate locules for each carpel, with placentae at the center, the placentation is *axile.* If the septa between the carpels are absent, resulting in a one-chambered ovary with placentae on the walls, the placentation is *parietal.* A simple ovary of one carpel and several ovules usually has parietal placentation. A syncarpellate ovary in which the septa are absent and the placentae are on a central stalk arising from the base of the ovary is said to be *free central.* If the central stalk is absent and the placentation is directly on the floor of the locule, the placentation is *basal.*

FIGURE 10-20
Placentation. The ovary with axile placentation has three locules; the others each have one locule.

Marginal   Axile   Parietal   Free central   Basal

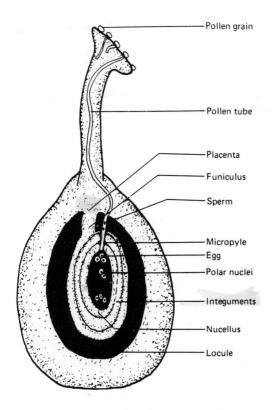

Pollen grain

Pollen tube

Placenta

Funiculus

Sperm

Micropyle
Egg
Polar nuclei

Integuments

Nucellus

Locule

FIGURE 10-21
Pollen germination and fertilization in angiosperms.

Pollination

The movement of pollen from the anther to the stigma is known as *pollination*. Some of the terms frequently related to the agents of pollination of flowers include:

Anemophilous. Wind-pollinated.
Cantharophilous. Beetle-pollinated.
Chiropterophilous. Bat-pollinated.
Entomophilous. Insect-pollinated.
Hydrophilous. Pollinated by water.
Malacophilous. Pollinated by snails and slugs.
Ornithophilous. Bird-pollinated.

The following are several additional, frequently encountered technical terms also relating to the pollination of plants:

Allogamy. Cross-pollination.
Autogamy. Self-pollination.
Cleistogamous. Characterized by self-pollination due to the flower buds' remaining closed.

Dichogamy. Term used of a plant which is unable to pollinate itself because stamens and carpels mature at different times.

Protandrous. Term applied when the pollen of a flower matures and is shed before the stigma becomes receptive.

Protogynous. Term applied when the stigma becomes receptive before the stamens mature in the same flower.

Pollen, Fertilization, and Embryo Development

See Figure 10-21. *Microsporogenesis* (production of microspores by meiosis) occurs in the anther, eventually giving rise to pollen grains or male gametophytes. Pollen is shed either in the *binucleate* (with two nuclei) or less often in the *trinucleate* (with three nuclei) stage. The pollen grain of an angiosperm consists of two cells: the *tube cell* and the *generative cell.* When a pollen grain lands on a receptive stigma, the tube cell grows rapidly and forms a tube; then by digesting its way through the stigma and style and into the locule, the pollen grain enters the ovule through the micropyle. The generative cell produces two male gametes or sperms that follow the tube nucleus into the tube.

Pollen grains are variously shaped (see Figures 5-6 and 5-7). *Monosulcate* pollen grains have a single, long furrow that develops on one side of the grain and are characteristic of gymnosperms, monocotyledons, and certain families of dicotyledons. *Tricolpate* pollen grains have three meridionally placed furrows, and are characteristic of most of the dicotyledons.

The outer wall of an angiosperm ovule is composed of one or two integuments. The *micropyle* is a minute opening through the integuments. The integuments later form the seed coat. The ovule contains a megasporangium called the *nucellus.* Megasporogenesis (production of megaspores by meiosis) occurs inside the nucellus, eventually giving rise to the *embryo sac* or female gametophyte. The embryo sac, which is embedded in the nucellus, has a group of eight nuclei. The three most important nuclei in the embryo sac are the *egg nucleus,* or female gamete, and the two *polar nuclei.*

When the pollen tube enters the embryo sac, the sperms are discharged into the embryo sac. One sperm fuses with the egg nucleus to form a *zygote.* The zygote rapidly develops into the *embryo* within the ovule. The second sperm unites with the polar nuclei to form a primary endosperm nucleus that develops into a tissue called *endosperm.* The endosperm becomes a nutritive source for the embryo during embryo development and often during germination of the seed. Endosperm may or may not be present when the seed matures.

Seed

A *seed* is a matured ovule containing an embryo and sometimes endosperm; it is surrounded by a seed coat. At maturation of the ovule and before germination of the seed, the embryo consists of an *epicotyl* (which will develop into the shoot), a *radicle*

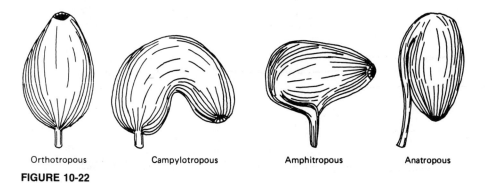

| Orthotropous | Campylotropous | Amphitropous | Anatropous |

FIGURE 10-22
Types of ovules

(which forms the primary root), a *hypocotyl* (which connects the epicotyl and radicle), and one or two *cotyledons,* or seed leaves. The seed coat, or *testa,* develops from the integuments and often has variations in its surface features. Among these are markings or patterns, wings, or tufts of hairs. Some seeds, e.g., litchi and nutmeg, have an *aril,* which is an outgrowth or covering of the seed developed generally from the *funiculus,* or seed stalk. The direction that the ovule or seed points, in relation to the funiculus that supports it, is sometimes an important taxonomic character (see Figure 10-22). The scar on the seed at the point where the funiculus was attached is the *hilum.* Some seeds, such as castor beans, have a *caruncle,* or appendage, near the hilum.

The following terms are important in the classification of angiosperms:

Bitegmic ovule. An ovule with two integuments, considered to be the primitive condition.

Crassinucellate ovule. An ovule with a massive nucellus in which the megaspore mother cell is deeply embedded.

Perisperm. A term applied to nutritive tissue in seeds derived from the integuments or nucellus or from both these tissues; prominent in the families Caryophyllaceae, Polygonaceae, Chenopodiaceae, and Phytolaccaceae.

Tenuinucellate ovule. An ovule in which there is a small amount of nucellus with the megaspore mother cell located subepidermally.

Unitegmic ovule. An ovule with a single integument; considered advanced relative to the bitegmic ovule.

Fruits

A *fruit* (Figure 10-23) is a matured ovary, including its contents. It may have other floral parts fused to it, including the receptacle, involucre, calyx, hypanthium, and so forth. Fruits may be diagnostic at the family level or used to delimit taxa within families. There are numerous kinds of fruits, some easy to classify, and others more difficult.

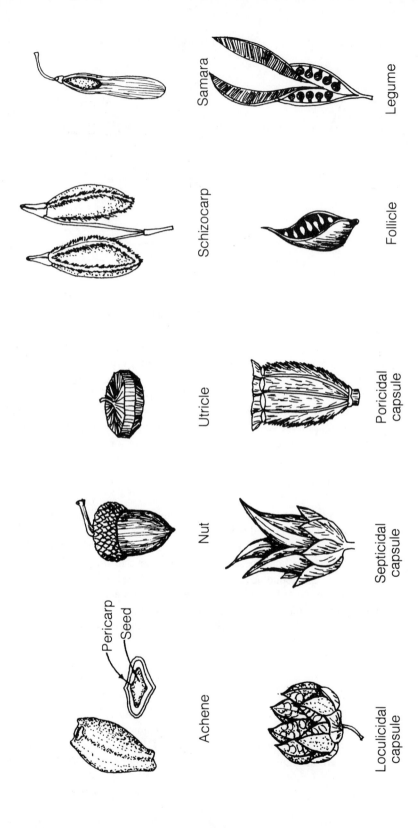

Samara

Legume

Schizocarp

Follicle

Utricle

Poricidal
capsule

Nut

Septicidal
capsule

Pericarp

Seed

Achene

Loculicidal
capsule

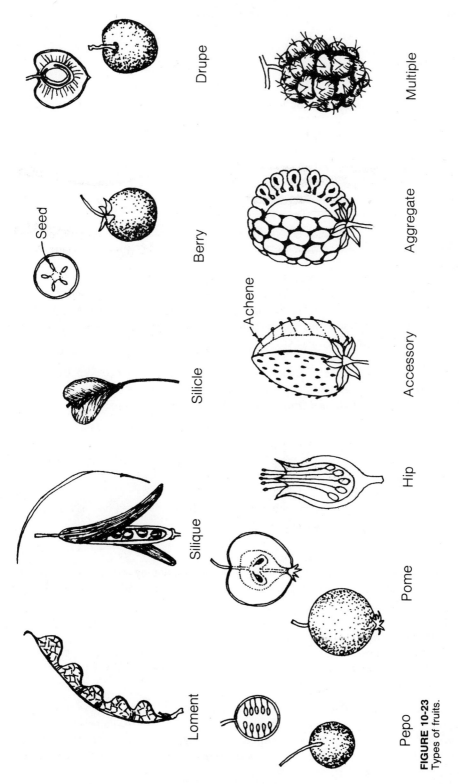

FIGURE 10-23
Types of fruits.

Drupe

Multiple

Seed

Berry

Aggregate

Silicle

Achene

Accessory

Silique

Hip

Loment

Pome

Pepo

247

Definitions   The following terms should be noted:

Accessory structures. Parts of fruits derived from nonovarian tissues.

Beak. Persistent style or style-base; the slender elongated ending of a fruit; e.g., *Brassica*.

Circumscissile. Dehiscent horizontally at or above the middle, the top part falling away as a lid.

Dehiscent. Opening and shedding contents in a regular and often distinctive manner.

Endocarp. The inner part of the pericarp, including the wall of the seed chamber.

Exocarp. The outer part of the pericarp.

Fleshy. Soft and juicy.

Indehiscent. Without a specialized structure for opening; remaining closed and not shedding contents until opened by weathering, fire, or other external agents or by decay.

Mesocarp. The middle, often fleshy, layer of the pericarp.

Pericarp. The entire wall of the fruit, from the skin to the lining of the seed chamber.

Suture. The line along which the fruit opens, or some other seam along the fruit. A suture usually represents the marginal fusions of the carpel or carpels.

Valve. A segment of a capsule.

Fruit Types   For ease of understanding, fruits may be divided into five major groups. Within each category, the various types of fruits are listed and described.

1   Dry, Indehiscent, and One-Seeded   This group contains the following types:

Achene. A dry, one-seeded fruit with a firm, close-fitting wall, but with the pericarp free from seed; examples include sunflower "seeds."

Caryopsis. A fruit in which the pericarp is fused with the seed; a grain; e.g., the fruit of the grasses.

Grain. See *Caryopsis*.

Nut. A fruit developed from a pistil with more than one carpel and having a hard woody coat; e.g., hickory, pecan, or oak.

Nutlet. A small nut.

Samara. An achene with a wing; e.g., ash.

Schizocarp. A single, compound ovary that splits simulating separate fruits derived from the ovaries of a simple pistil, e.g., the dry seedlike fruits derived from an inferior ovary, as in the Umbelliferae.

Utricle. A one-seeded fruit with a thin, bladdery, persistent, sometimes inflated wall; found in some amaranths.

Winged Schizocarp. Splitting samaras that are winged and dry, e.g. maple.

2   Dry, Dehiscent, and Having Several to Many Seeds   In this group are the following types:

Capsule. A fruit originating from two or more carpels. There are several types of capsules: *loculicidal*, dehiscent lengthwise down the middle of the carpels (e.g., *Iris*); *poricidal*, dehiscent by pores at the top (e.g., poppy); *pyxis*, dehiscent in a circumscissile manner (e.g., *Plantago*); *septicidal*, dehiscent lengthwise at the junction of the carpels (e.g., *Yucca*).

Follicle. A fruit developing from a single pistil and dehiscing along one margin; e.g., *Delphinium*.

Legume. A one-locular fruit dehiscent on two sutures; e.g., beans and peas.

Loment. A flat modified legume that is constricted between seeds and falling apart into one-seeded joints; e.g., *Desmodium*.

Silicle. A short, two-locular fruit, composed of two valves which separate from the central partition, e.g., *Capsella* and other short-fruited members of the Cruciferae.

Silique. An elongated, two-locular fruit with two parietal placentae, and usually with two valves that separate from the partition on dehiscence; e.g., *Brassica* and other long-fruited members of the Cruciferae.

3 Fleshy, Derived From a Syncarpous Gynoecium of a Single Flower This group has the following types:

Berry. A fruit with a soft and fleshy pericarp; e.g., tomato, grape.

Drupe. A fruit with a fleshy mesocarp and a stony endocarp which forms a hard covering around the seed; e.g., peach, plum.

Hesperidium. A berry with a tough, leathery rind; e.g., a citrus fruit.

Pepo. A one-locular fruit developed from an inferior ovary with parietal placentae, having a hard outer covering; e.g., a gourd.

4 Derived From a Single or Compound Ovary and Nonovarian Tissue Such as the Receptacle or Hypanthium; Accessory Fruit This group contains two types:

Hip. An aggregation of achenes surrounded by a cup-like receptacle and hypanthium; e.g., rose fruit.

Pome. A fruit developed from a compound inferior ovary with the seeds encased within a cartilaginous wall, as in an apple. The fleshy part of the pome is largely developed from the hypanthium.

5 Resulting From the Union of Many Separate Carpels of a Single Flower, or the Fusion of Several Fruits of Separate Flowers A fruit in this category can be aggregate or multiple:

Aggregate. A cluster of fruits clearly traceable to separate pistils of the same flower and inserted on a common receptacle; e.g., *Rubus* and *Ranunculus*.

Multiple. Term describing fruits on a common axis that are usually fused and derived from the ovaries of several flowers; e.g., mulberry. The *syconium* of the fig, which is a collection of achenes borne on the inside of a hollowed-out receptacle or peduncle, is a multiple fruit. The fruit of the pineapple results from a fusion of rachis, bracts, and ovaries.

DESCRIPTIVE METHODS

Floral Formulas

The floral formula method (Table 10-1) has been used for many years to describe graphically the floral morphology of the angiosperms. Although the formulas used by different authors may differ in a few details, they are all designed to compare graphically floral structure. Morphological features, such as the calyx (CA), corolla (CO),

TABLE 10-1
FLORAL SYMBOLS, FORMULAS, AND EXAMPLES

CA	Calyx, sepals	CO^X	Petals variable in number
CAZ	Calyx zygomorphic	CO^0	Apetalous
CO	Corolla, petals	A^6	Stamens 6
COZ	Corolla zygomorphic	A^{4+2}	Stamens 6, 4 in one set, 2 in another
CO(Z)	Corolla sometimes zygomorphic	A^{4-5}	Stamens either 4 or 5
A	Androecium	$A^{4(5)}$	Stamens 4 rarely 5
G	Gynoecium	$G^{③}$	Gynoecium of 3 fused carpels
$\underline{G}$	Ovary superior	$A^{⑩}$	Androecium of 10 stamens fused by their filaments
$\overline{G}$	Ovary inferior		
$\overline{\underline{G}}$	Ovary either superior or inferior	$\overparen{CO\ A}$	Corolla and androecium united
X	Variable	$\underparen{A\ G}$	Androecium and gynoecium united
∞	Many	$CA^3CO^3A^6\underline{G}^{③}$	Sepals 3, petals 3, stamens 6, gynoecium of 3 united carpels, ovary superior
$4+2$	4 in one set, 2 in another		
$2-3$	2 or 3	$CA^{⑤}CO^0A^5\underline{G}^{⑤}$	Calyx of 5 united sepals, corolla absent, stamens 5, gynoecium of 5 united carpels, ovary superior
0	None		
( )	Exceptional		
○	Fused		
⌢	United above		
⌣	United below		

androecium (A), and the gynoecium (G), are represented by letters. The number of parts of each whorl is shown by numerals. CA^3 and A^6 convey the message that the plant has a calyx of three sepals and an androecium of six stamens. Symbols and other distinguishing marks, relatively few in number, are used to describe further the flowers; e.g., $CA^{⑤}$, a calyx of five fused sepals, or $\overline{G}$, an inferior ovary, versus $\underline{G}$, a superior ovary.

Most descriptives methods have advantages and disadvantages, and floral formulas are no exception. One problem is that there has been no attempt to standardize the symbols and systems. Formulas, when broadly generalized, may not convey to the user all the variation present within a family. Families may contain genera which are somewhat atypical of the majority of the genera. A floral formula of A^{3-6} conveys the fact that the group has some plants with three stamens and others with six stamens, but it does not convey the relative frequency of each. Actually, six stamens may be very common and three is very rare. That could be shown by $A^{6(3)}$. On the other hand, if the formula system is made increasingly complicated by handling all special cases, the purpose of the system is defeated. When allowances are made for its weakness,

FIGURE 10-24
Representative floral diagrams. *1, 2, 5,* and *6* are terminal flowers; *3* and *4* are axillary—the stem is represented by the black dot above, and the leaf in the axil of which the flower is borne is shown below. *1, Ranunculus. 2, Geranium. 3, Penstemon* (irregular). *4, Lilium. 5, Sanguinaria. 6, Taraxacum,* with calyx a pappus represented by dots (co, corolla; s, stamen; o w, ovary wall; ov, ovule; r, receptacle). (*Swingle, 1946; with permission*).

the floral formula may be a valuable tool. Floral formulas are provided for each of the families treated in Chapter 14, Angiosperm Families.

Floral Diagrams

Floral diagrams (Figure 10-24) visually depict the essential features of a flower in cross section. The floral parts are represented by semidiagrammatic symbols or ideographs. This illustrates both the number of whorls and floral parts and other features, such as fusion of structures and flower symmetry. Although ovary position must be shown in a second drawing using a longitudinal section, this drawback does not diminish the overall value of such diagrams.

SELECTED REFERENCES

Featherly, H. I.: *Taxonomic Terminology of the Higher Plants,* Iowa State College Press, Ames, 1954.

Gray, A.: *The Elements of Botany for Beginners and for Schools,* American Book, New York, 1887. (Reprinted by American Environmental Studies, 1970.)

Jackson, B. D.: *A Glossary of Botanic Terms, with Their Derivation and Accent,* 4th ed., Duckworth, London, 1928. (Reprinted by Hafner, 1971.)

Lawrence, G. H. M.: *Taxonomy of Vascular Plants,* Macmillan, New York, 1951.

Lindley, J.: *Excerpt From Illustrated Dictionary of Botanical Terms,* Stanford, Stanford, Calif., 1964. (This is a reprint of an excerpt from Lindley's *Illustrated Dictionary of Botanical Terms,* 1848.)

Radford, A. E., W. C. Dickison, J. R. Massey, and C. R. Bell: *Vascular Plant Systematics,* Harper & Row, New York, 1974.

Stearn, W. T.: *Botanical Latin,* 3rd ed., David and Charles, Newton Abbot, England, 1983.

Swingle, D. B.: *A Textbook of Systematic Botany,* McGraw-Hill, New York, 1946.

Systematics Association Committee for Descriptive Biological Terminology: "I. Preliminary List of Works Relevant to Descriptive Biological Terminology," *Taxon,* **9:**245–257, 1960.

———: "II. Terminology of Simple Symmetrical Plane Shapes (Chart 1)," *Taxon,* **11:**145–156, 1962.

CHAPTER 11

SELECTED LITERATURE
OF SYSTEMATIC BOTANY

The literature of plant systematics is one of the oldest and most complicated literatures of the sciences. Plants have been named and described in innumerable books and periodicals in many languages. Taxonomists must have a thorough knowledge of the literature and bibliographic aids, because these tools are an essential part of identification, nomenclature, and revisionary studies.

Indexes to plant names and illustrations provide references to the original publication of names and the placement of a particular plant in a classification scheme. These indexes form the basis of a taxonomic library and are essential for nomenclatorial research. Taxonomists must not overlook the important *bibliographies, indexes, and guides* for location of the literature. There is no one book or series of volumes that treats all species of vascular plants known. There are, however, several important *comprehensive works* that present classifications of families, genera, or species. Stafleu (1967) and Stafleu and Cowan (1976) are excellent sources of information, especially for dates of publication of works published over a long period of time.

The following annotated lists are not exhaustive, but are intended to summarize commonly used bibliographic resources.

INDEXES TO PLANT NAMES AND ILLUSTRATIONS

Christensen, C. F. A.: *Index filicum*, 12 parts, 4 supplements, Hagerup, Hafniae, 1906–1965. (Supplement *Regnum Veg.*, **37,** and Bence *et al.* Clarendon Press. This index provides the source of original publication of generic and specific names of ferns.)

Dalla Torre, C. G. de, and H. Harms: *Genera siphonogamarum ad systema Englerianum conscripta,* W. Engelmann, Leipzig, 1900–1907. (*Genera siphonogamarum* provides a numbered list of families and genera of seed plants arranged according to the Engler system. In addition, names are given for subfamilies, tribes, and so on, together with the names of genera assigned to them. Included is an extensive index. Many herbaria use the Dalla Torre-Harms numbers for filing and indexing their collections. *Genera siphonogamarum* has been updated with the issue of the *Register [Register zu de Dalla Torre et Harms,* J. Cramer, Weinheim, West Germany, 1958]).

Farr, E. R., J. A. Leussink and F. A. Stafleu: "Index Nominum Genericorum (Plantarum)," *Regnum Veg.,* **100–102,** 1979. (An index to names of genera.)

Gray Herbarium Index: Gray Herbarium, Harvard University, Cambridge, Mass., 1896–. (This card index is issued quarterly to subscribers and lists all new names and new combinations of names for vascular plants from the New World. Included are the names of genera, species, and infraspecific taxa. All Latin names published for Western Hemisphere plants since 1885 have been included and are arranged alphabetically by genus. In some ways it duplicates *Index kewensis* but is invaluable as a source of names for infraspecific taxa in the New World. The index for 1896–1967 was reprinted in 1968 by G. K. Hall, Boston, in 10 volumes. A 2-volume supplement covering the literature from 1967–1977 was published by G. K. Hall in 1978.)

Index kewensis plantarum phanerogamarum: 2 volumes, 16 supplements. Oxford, 1893–. (Compiled at the Royal Botanic Gardens at Kew, *Index kewensis* is an alphabetical index to the generic names and binomials of seed plants. It is used to determine the source of the original publication of a generic name or binomial. It has worldwide coverage for names published since 1753. The basic volumes include names from 1753 to 1885, and supplements have been regularly published since that time. All known specific epithets published for a particular genus are in alphabetical order under each generic name. Also included are authors of the names, brief literature citations, and the geographical origin of the plants. Names considered to be synonyms appear in italics in the older volumes. Names of infraspecific taxa are excluded. In recent supplements, indication of synonymy has been discontinued but references to illustrations have been added. The original volumes were compiled by B. D. Jackson under the direction of J. D. Hooker.)

Index Londinensis to Illustrations of Flowering Plants, Ferns and Fern Allies: 6 volumes, with one 2-volume supplement, 1929–1931; supplement, 1941. (Compiled at Kew by O. Stapf, *Index Londinensis* is an index to the illustrations of vascular plants from 1753 to 1935. It is arranged alphabetically by genus and species. The names used in *Index Londinensis* are those accompanying the illustrations and may be obsolete. To locate illustrations of vascular plants published from 1753 to 1935, *Index Londinensis* should be used; after 1935, *Index kewensis* has this information.)

National List of Scientific Plant Names, 2 vols., U.S. Department of Agriculture, Soil Conservation Service, Washington, D.C., 1982. (A list of families, genera, species, subspecies and varieties; includes authors of the names, source manuals, habit, and distribution; coverage is of Canada, continental United States, Hawaii, and the Caribbean region.)

Pichi-Sermolli, R. E. G. See Christensen, C. F. A.

Rouleau, Ernest: *Guide to the Generic Names Appearing in the Index Kewensis and Its Fifteen Supplements,* Chatelain, Lac de Brome, 1981. (An index to the genera published in *Index Kewensis* and supplements; includes the volume in which these names appear.)

Willis, J. C.: *A Dictionary of the Flowering Plants and Ferns,* 8th ed., revised by H. K. A. Shaw, Cambridge, London, 1973. (Willis's, *Dictionary* provides an alphabetical list of all generic names published since 1753 and all family names published since 1789. It provides concise information on the authors, synonyms, family, number of species, and distribution of genera. Descriptions are given for the families. This is a handy reference for checking spellings, synonyms, and number of species in a genus.)

BIBLIOGRAPHIES, INDEXES, AND GUIDES TO THE LITERATURE OF SYSTEMATIC BOTANY

Biological Abstracts and *Biological Abstracts/RRM*: BioSciences Information Service, Philadelphia. [Biological Abstracts (BA), 1929–, is a bi-weekly publication listing abstracts of papers appearing in periodicals. Biological Abstracts/RRM(BA/RRM), 1965–, is a biweekly publication indexing research reports from symposia, meetings, and so on, which may or may not appear in periodicals. Each issue of both BA and BA/RRM contains author, biosystematic, and cross-subject indexes, as well as a biosystematic index arranged by division, class, and family. Both publications are available on computer tape, and it is possible to obtain printouts of literature citations for various taxonomic groups, i.e., genera, tribes, or families.]

Blake, S. F., and A. C. Atwood: "Geographical Guide to Floras of the World," U.S.D.A. Misc. Pub. No. 401 and 797, 1942–1961. (An index to older floras and floristics studies.)

Chaudhri, M. M. See Lanjouw, J. *Draft Index of Author Abbreviations,* H. M. Stationary Office, London, 1980. (An alphabetic list of authors for plant names and their approved abbreviations.)

Federov, A. A. (ed.): *Chromosome Numbers of Flowering Plants,* Academy of Sciences of the USSR, V. L. Komarov Botanical Institute, 1969. (An index to chromosome numbers published for plants through 1966. Literature citations are provided. See Moore, 1973, and Goldblatt, 1981 for chromosome numbers published since 1967.)

Goldblatt, P. (ed.): "Index to Plant Chromosome Numbers," *Monog. Syst. Bot.,* **5, 8,** 1981, 1984. (A continuation of the Index previously published in *Regnum Vegetabile.* Coverage is for 1975–78 and 1979–81.)

Henderson, D. M. (Comp.): *International Directory of Botanical Gardens,* 4th ed., Koeltz Scientific Books, Koenigstein, 1983.

Holmgren, P. K., W. Keuken and E. K. Schofield: "Index Herbariorum. Part I. The Herbaria of the World," 7th ed., *Regnum Veg.,* **106,** 1981. (This guide to the herbaria of the world is arranged by the cities in which they are located. It provides addresses and general information for each herbarium and also has a list of standard acronyms for herbaria abbreviations.)

Hunt Botanical Library: *Botanico-Periodicum-Huntianum,* G. H. M. Lawrence, et. al. (eds.), Hunt Botanical Library, Pittsburgh, 1968. (B-P-H is a list of over 12,000 botanical or botanically related periodicals. It is often used to identify obscure journal citations and to provide standard abbreviations for literature citations. It is especially helpful in locating references cited in *Index kewensis.*)

Index to American Botanical Literature: Bull. Torrey Bot. Club, 1886–. (This index appears in each issue of the *Bulletin* and is later issued on cards. The listings are arranged alphabetically by author under subject groupings in the journal. The card file is alphabetical by author. The index for 1886–1966 was reprinted in 1969 by G. K. Hall, Boston, in 4 volumes, and a one-volume supplement for 1967–1976 was issued in 1977. The index permits a review of all the papers written by an author.)

Index Herbariorum. See Lanjouw, J.; Holmgren, P. K.

Jackson, B. D.: *Guide to the Literature of Botany,* Longmans, Green, London, 1881. (A guide to older botanical literature including about 6000 titles not listed in Pritzel's *Thesaurus.* Jackson and Pritzel should be used together. Facsimile reprint Otto Koeltz Science Publishers, Koenigstein, 1974.)

Kew Record of Taxonomic Literature Relating to Vascular Plants: Kew Royal Botanic Gardens, Kew, 1971–. (An annual publication listing all taxonomic literature published in periodicals, books, and papers. Coverage is worldwide. Entries are arranged in systematic groups.)

Lanjouw, J., and F. A. Stafleu: "Index Herbariorum, Part 2. Index to Collectors," (1) A–D; (2) E–H; (3) I–L; (4) M; (5) N–R; *Regnum Veg.,* **2, 9, 86,** and **93, 109,** 1954, 1957, 1972,

1976, 1983. (This alphabetical list of collectors cites where their collections are deposited and is useful in locating types. M. M. Chaudhri, I. H. Vegter, and C. del Wall compiled I–L; I. H. Vegter compiled M, N–R.)

Lawrence, G. H. M. See Hunt Botanical Library.

Moore, R. J. (ed.): "Index to Plant Chromosome Numbers 1967–1971," *Regnum Veg.,* **90,** 1973 (See Federov, 1969, for an index to chromosome numbers published before 1967. Literature citations are provided. Indexes have also been published for 1972, 1973–1974, *Regnum Veg.,* **91** and **96,** 1974 and 1977.)

Pritzel, G. A.: *Thesaurus literaturae botanicae,* rev. ed., 1872–1877. (This is a basic reference and guide to the botanical literature up to 1851 and should be used with Jackson. Pritzel is extremely valuable for verifying old original descriptions and those not listed in Stafleu. Facsimile reprint, Otto Koeltz Antiquariat, Koenigstein, 1972.)

Solbrig, O. T., and T. W. J. Gadella: "Biosystematic Literature; Contributions to a Biosystematic Literature Index (1945–1964)," *Regnum Veg.,* **69,** 1970. (A handy source of selected references to literature dealing with biosystematics.)

Stafleu, F. A.: "Taxonomic Literature," *Regnum Veg.,* **52,** 1967. (A selective guide to older botanical publications. It provides dates of publication which are important in matters of priority. Included are concise bibliographies on the lives and works of important taxonomists.)

——— and R. S. Cowan: "Taxonomic Literature," 2d ed., *Regnum Veg.,* **94, 98, 105, 110** 1976–.(An enlarged version of the 1967 edition.)

Tralau, H. (ed.): *Index Holmensis, a World Phytogeographic Index,* vol. 1., *Equisetales— Gymnospermae;* vols. 2–3, *Monocotyledoneae;* vols. 4–, *Dicotyledonae,* Scientific Publishers, Ltd., Zurich, 1969–. (An alphabetical index to plant distribution maps.)

Vegter, I. H. See Lanjouw, J.

COMPREHENSIVE WORKS OF A BROAD SCOPE

Baillon, H.: *Histoire des plantes,* 13 volumes. Hachette, Paris, 1867–1895. (*The Natural History of Plants,* a translation of the first 8 volumes, was published 1871–1888. *Histoire des plantes* treats families and genera of vascular plants, is well illustrated, and has an extensive bibliography.)

Bentham, G., and J. D. Hooker: *Genera plantarum,* 3 volumes. Reeve, London, 1862–1883. (*Genera plantarum* provides generic descriptions for seed plants and was prepared from the plants themselves rather than from the literature. Written in Latin, it is a valuable reference for classifications between the sectional and family levels.)

Candolle, A. P. de, et al.: *Prodromus systematis naturalis regni vegetabilis,* 17 volumes and 4 index volumes, Paris, 1824–1873. (Intended to treat all species of seed plants, but only covers the dicots. The first seven volumes were prepared by A. P. de Candolle, the others by contributors, and edited by his son Alphonse. The title *Prodromus* indicates that de Candolle considered it only a preliminary treatment, but it remains the only comprehensive revision of some genera.)

Copeland, E. B.: "Genera Filicum, the Genera of Ferns," in *Annales cryptogamici et phytopatholgici,* vol. 5, Chronica Botanica, Waltham, Mass., 1947. (A treatment of the ferns arranged in a phylogenetic sequence. Descriptions, keys, and references to the literature are given.)

Cronquist, A.: *The Evolution and Classification of Flowering Plants,* Houghton Mifflin, Boston, 1968. (Provides a comprehensive system of classification for the angiosperms.)

———: *An Integrated System of Classification of Flowering Plants,* Columbia, New York, 1981.

Engler, A.: *Das Pflanzenreich*, Nos. 1–107, Berlin, 1900–1968. (*Das Pflanzenreich* is an incomplete series of monographs on the plant kingdom. An index to the series is provided in Stafleu, 1967, pp. 133–145.)

————: *Syllabus der Pflanzenfamilien*, 12th ed., 2 volumes (edited by H. Melchior and E. Werdermann), Gebrüder Borntraeger, Berlin, 1954–1964. (Provides the most recent synopsis of the Engler system of classification. Volume 1 treats the bacteria through the gymnosperms. Volume 2 treats the flowering plants and contains descriptions of the higher categories and has an extensive bibliography.)

———— and K. Prantl: *Die natürlichen Pflanzenfamilien*, 23 volumes, W. Engelmann, Leipzig, 1887–1915. (This monumental work contains keys and descriptions for all families and genera of plants from algae to Compositae. Written in German, it is well illustrated and contains extensive literature citations. The plants are arranged according to the Engler system of classification.)

———— and ————: *Die Natürlichen Pflanzenfamilien*, 2d ed., W. Engelmann, Leipzig, 1924–. (The 2d edition is not yet complete. Twenty-one volumes have thus far been published.)

———— and ————: *Syllabus der Pflanzenfamilien*, 2d ed., Berlin, 1898. (This treatise has been published in many editions; the first edition is cited as *Syllabus der Vorlesungen . . .* 1892.)

Hutchinson, J.: *Genera of Flowering Plants*, 2 volumes, Clarendon, Oxford, 1964–1967. (This is an attempt to update Bentham and Hooker's *Genera plantarum*. Hutchinson provides family and generic descriptions, as well as a classification scheme.)

————: *Key to the Families of Flowering Plants of the World*, Clarendon, Oxford, 1967. (This is perhaps the best key to families on a worldwide basis.)

————: *The Families of Flowering Plants*, vol. I, *Dicotyledons*, vol. II, *Monoctyledons*, 3d ed., Clarendon, Oxford, 1973. (Provides a synopsis of Hutchinson's scheme of classification. Treatments of families are accompanied by descriptions and illustrations.)

Melchior, H. See Engler, A., 1954–1964.

Rendle, A. B.: *The Classification of Flowering Plants*, vol. 1, *Gymnosperms and Monocotyledons;* vol. 2, *Dicotyledons*, 2d ed., University Press, Cambridge, 1925–1930. (A classification in the Englerian sense with excellent descriptions of families.)

Takhtajan, A.: *Die Evolution der Angiospermen*, Gustav Fischer Verlang, Jena, 1959.

————: *System et Phylogenia Magnoliophytorum*, Soviet Publishing Institution, Nauka, Moscow, and Leningrad, 1966. (In Russian.)

————: *Flowering Plants—Origin and Dispersal*, Smithsonian Institution Press, Washington, 1969. (This translation, by Charles Jeffrey, is quite readable and is recommended to the student.)

Wettstein, R.: *Handbuch der Systematischen Botanik*, 2 volumes, 4th ed., Franz Deuticke, Leipzig, 1933–1935. (Presents an improved Englerian classification.)

MONOGRAPHS AND REVISIONS

A *monograph* of a group of plants (usually a genus or family) is a comprehensive taxonomic treatise that synthesizes all information known about the group and presents a classification based on this information. Inherent in a monograph is an exhaustive literature review, as well as a thorough report on the author's original research. Normally treating a family or genus on a worldwide basis, a monograph accounts for all elements (included taxa) of the group under study. Further, such a scholarly work will provide an introductory literature review; several detailed reports on field and garden studies, as well as herbarium work; data on the plants regarding their cytology, anatomy, morphology, chemistry, paleobotany, ecology, and phytogeography; all nomenclatural information including designated type specimens; exhaustive descriptions; keys to all taxa; full synonymies; citations of specimens examined; distribution maps; habitat descriptions; a taxonomic treatment, which constitutes the author's classification of all taxa in this group; and a discussion of possible phylogenetic relationships. Classic examples of monographs include: Mirov's (1967) *The Genus Pinus,* Goodspeed's (1955) *The Genus Nicotiana* and *The Genus Datura* by Blakeslee *et al.* (1959).

Revisions differ from monographs primarily in their degree of scope and completeness. Like monographs, the obligatory and most important element is the taxonomic treatment presenting the author's classification scheme. However, revisions are less detailed providing a minimum of introductory material and a synoptic literature review. Revisions may treat an entire family or genus, or may account for only a section of a genus or that part of a genus restricted to a particular geographic or political area. Normally, it is desirable to prepare a revision treating all of the natural elements of a group (section, genus or family) on a worldwide basis rather than just those elements appearing in a limited area. Revisions typically provide complete synonymies, keys to identify the taxa within the group, descriptions, distribution maps, a classification, and a brief discussion of supporting data.

The scientific value of both monographs and revisions depends largely on the amount of original research that they contain. Authors of such works attempt to evaluate critically the citation of each name and each synonym and to examine each type specimen relating to the group. Nothing is accepted by the author, including distribution records, that cannot be personally confirmed. These safeguards are designed to insure against the continued repetition of errors.

Groups of plants in need of revision are selected largely based on inconsistencies of the characters within the taxon's geographic range or by noting difficulties with the identification of elements within the taxon. Most professional taxonomists have encountered such problems and can suggest groups that appear to be in need of revision. For one considering a revisionary project, it is essential that the choice of a project be made, certainly in the light of advice and wisdom of others, but by the person who is to prepare the revision. Successful original research depends largely on the personal curiosity and excitement of the investigator. For those interested in the how-to-do details of revisionary work, see Lawrence (1951) *Taxonomy of Vascular Plants,* Davis and Heywood (1963), *Principles of Angiosperm Classification,* and Benson (1962), *Plant Taxonomy, Methods and Principles.* These three references provide excellent suggestions on the essentials of taxonomic research. In addition, there are hundreds of excellent examples of revisions in taxonomic journals such as *Brittonia, Rhodora,* and *Systematic Botany.*

Taxonomic revisions based on original research form the central core of systematic botany. There is a special need and an opportunity for young persons interested in taxonomy to undertake revisionary studies of groups that are largely found in the neotropics. Major contributions can be made in this geographic area.

FLORISTIC TREATMENTS

For the convenience of those who wish to identify vascular plants and become familiar with the plants of a particular area, many floras and manuals treating the local flora have been prepared. A *manual* is a book that provides keys and descriptions to aid in identifying plants. A *flora* is an inventory of the plants that live in a particular area or region; the term *flora* may also refer to the plants of an area. Floristic treatments cover a wide range of formats from the most comprehensive, almost monographic approach, to the barest of species checklists. Of the hundreds of floras and manuals that have been prepared, varying degrees of exhaustiveness and authoritativeness may be found. A typical manual will normally contain information on the area of coverage and keys and descriptions to the families, genera, and species. Much additional information is usually provided for each species, including the accepted scientific name followed by the author (or authors) for that name; major synonyms; information on infraspecific taxa, if any; ecological and distributional data; common names; and some manuals may provide illustrations and distribution maps. Many manuals have been revised and reprinted numerous times; for example, Gray's (1950) *Manual of Botany* is now in its eighth edition. Such manuals often become the standard reference for the flora of a particular area of coverage.

Appendix 2 provides a selected list of manuals and floras for North America north of Mexico.

Professional and amateur taxonomists can make significant contributions through floristic studies. For information on the accepted procedures and techniques for floristic research, the reader is again referred to the books by Lawrence, Benson, and Davis and Heywood listed in the previous section.

Floristic studies, by today's standards, require much attention to detail and documentation of the taxa by means of herbarium specimens deposited in recognized herbaria. Sight-records of taxa, unsupported by herbarium specimens are regarded as inadequate. In addition, the modern floristic researcher directs much attention to typification, nomenclature, distribution and ecology in addition to the basic comparative morphology. As pointed out in Chapter 1, a critical need exists for basic floristic studies in the Neotropics. For those willing to undertake such work, a marvelous opportunity presents itself to make major contributions.

NONTECHNICAL FLORAS

The phase of botany that appeals to the layperson is the recognition and naming of the pteridophytes and flowering plants native to his or her area. Increasing numbers of amateurs enjoy learning the names of at least the most conspicuous elements of the local flora. Many amateurs become remarkably proficient and delight in identifying all but the most difficult groups. To aid them in their attempts to identify and to learn the names of the native plants, a considerable number of illustrated books have been prepared. A selected list of these popular books is presented in Appendix 2.

With the lowering of color printing costs, an amazing number of popular wild flower books with color photographs has become available. The illustrations in these books are invaluable; however, they do have some weaknesses. As color printing is still somewhat expensive, only a small percentage of the local flora can be illustrated. Additionally, since many species are much alike in general appearance, a given photograph might apply equally well to several of them. Furthermore, much time must be spent rambling through such books searching for the correct illustrations. Of course, this confirms the value of taking time and effort to learn how to use keys as an aid to identification. To simplify identification, nontechnical floras are often restricted to conspicuous species or to certain groups of plants, for instance, wildflowers, native shrubs, native trees, pteridophytes, and so on, or to restricted geographic or political areas, thereby reducing the number of species, for example, Southeastern United States, or the Northeastern United States.

SELECTED REFERENCES

Benson, L.: *Plant Taxonomy,* Ronald Press, New York, 1962.

Blakeslee, A. F., A. G. Avery, S. Satina, and J. Rietsama: *The Genus Datura,* Ronald Press, New York, 1959.

Davis, P. H. and V. H. Heywood: *Principles of Angiosperm Taxonomy,* D. Van Nostrand, New York, 1963.

Goodspeed, T. H.: *The Genus Nicotiana,* Chronica Botanica Company, Waltham, Mass., 1955.

Gray, A.: *Manual of Botany,* 8th ed., M. L. Fernald (ed.), American Book Company, New York, 1950.

Lawrence, G. H. M.: *Taxonomy of Vascular Plants,* Macmillan, New York, 1951.

Mirov, N. T.: *The Genus Pinus,* Ronald Press, New York, 1967.

CHAPTER 12

PTERIDOPHYTES

The pteridophytes are represented today by over 13,000 living species: the wisk ferns (3), club mosses (about 300), spike mosses (about 700), quillworts (about 65), horsetails (about 25) and ferns (about 12,000). In North America, north of Mexico, there are about 400 species. In past geologic periods they were more numerous, and individual plants were much larger than most are at present. The pteridophytes are few in number, and it is possible to gain some familiarity with the common ferns and fern allies of a region in a relatively short period of time. Many professional and amateur botanists find that the location and observation of the various species can be a challenging and rewarding avocation.

The ferns and fern allies are described and discussed in many excellent regional and state manuals and field guides. The best single reference for identification of North American pteridophytes and for other pertinent information is John Mickel's (1979) *How to Know the Ferns and Fern Allies*. Other recommended manuals and guides for identification of the ferns and fern allies are listed in Appendix 2.

The ferns and fern allies reproduce by spores, whereas the gymnosperms and angiosperms reproduce by seeds. The spores of pteridophytes are single-cell structures at time of dispersal. The spores are produced in sporangia that at first glance may be easily overlooked. In the case of ferns, the sporangia are usually clustered together into small groups called sori and located on the undersides of the leaves. However, in other species entire leaves or parts of leaves may be modified in some species to produce spores. Other leaves may be immature or sterile and have no sporangia at all. In many instances, fertile leaves must be present to identify ferns.

The pteridophytes, sometimes called the "lower" vascular plants have vascular tissues (xylem and phloem) arranged into bundles that conduct water, food and minerals. In addition to reproducing by spores, the ferns are technically vascular plants with *megaphylls*. Found also in the gymnosperms and angiosperms, megaphylls (literally large leaves) are complex leaves with a branching vein system. When the vascular system of a megaphyll branches from the stem, it interrupts the stem's vascular system at the node leaving a *nodal leaf gap*. Most other lower vascular plants, such as the club mosses, horsetails, quillworts, and spike mosses have *microphylls*. The vascular system of microphylls (small leaves) is much less complex, with a single, unbranched vein that does not modify the vascular pattern of the stem of the node, and therefore does not leave a nodal leaf gap.

Most pteridophytes have roots, stems, and leaves, although in many temperate

FIGURE 12-1
Diagram of a frond of the lady fern. *A*, pinna; *B*, pinnule; *C*, rachis, *D*, stipe: *E*, rootstock; and *F*, sorus with a curved or straight indusium. (*From McVaugh and Pyron, 1951; with permission.*)

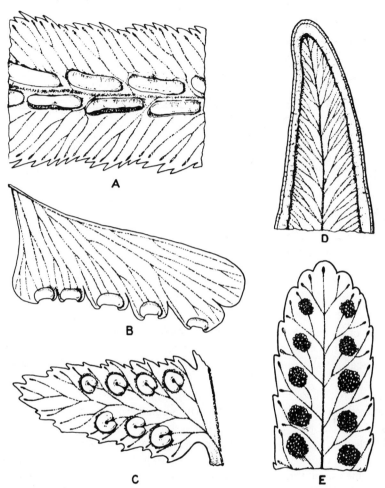

FIGURE 12-2
Portion of the leaflets of five common ferns, illustrating differences in sori and indusia, 4x (a) *Woodwardia;* (b) *Adiantum;* (c) *Dryopteris;* (d) *Pteridium;* (e) *Polypodium.* In a the indusium is elongate. In b and d a false indusium is seen, while in e there is no indusium. In c the indusium is reniform. (*From Haupt, 1953; with permission.*)

species of ferns, the stems consist of creeping rhizomes bearing adventitious roots (Figures 12-1 and 12-2). The leaves, or *fronds,* of ferns are quite distinctive and often variously dissected. The fronds usually show a characteristic unrolling during their development called *circinate vernation,* which produces fern fiddleheads or crosiers.

The life cycle of pteridophytes alternates between two distinct generations, represented by separate and unlike plants. For example, the familiar leafy fern plant represents the *sporophyte* phase of growth. It produces spores on the back of its leaves in small hollow cases called *sporangia.* These sporangia are borne on the underside

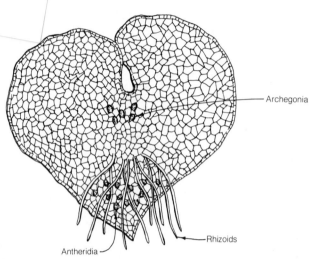

Archegonia

Rhizoids

Antheridia

FIGURE 12-3
Fern prothallus, drawing by Valerie Jones Hinesley.

of ordinary leaves or on very specialized fertile fronds or segments of a fertile frond. Sporangia usually occur in clusters called *sori*. After being shed, the spore germinates to form the independent alternate generation known as the sexual or *gametophytic* plant.

The fern gametophyte is a small, haploid, green, heart-shaped *prothallus* rarely more than 1 centimeter in diameter (Figure 12-3). The prothallus bears sexual structures on its underside. Near its base are the male *antheridia,* which produce swimming sperms. When bathed in water from dew or rain, the sperms swim toward the female *archegonia* (containing eggs) located near the indented apex of the prothallus. The zygote formed by the union of the haploid male and female gametes gives rise to the sporophyte (Figure 12-4). The sporophyte is diploid. Later the cells in the sporangium undergo meiosis to form the haploid spores.

A few living pteridophytes are *heterosporous,* producing large *megaspores* and small *microspores* in separate sporangia, but most are *homosporous,* with all spores being alike. In heterosporous pteridophytes, the gametophytes are sexually differentiated and reduced in structure. The megaspores develop into megagametophytes that form archegonia, and the microspores develop into microgametophytes that produce antheridia.

PTERIDOPHYTE CLASSIFICATION

The ferns and fern allies represent, more or less, the same evolutionary level, but they are not closely allied to each other (Mickel, 1979). It is not clear whether or not they are monophyletic, as their origins extend back some four hundred million years. Since

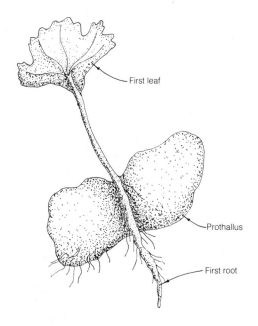

First leaf

Prothallus

First root

FIGURE 12-4
Prothallus with a young fern sprophyte,
drawing by Valerie Jones Hinesley.

the living pteridophytes represent such old lineages, their classification is often ex-
ceedingly difficult. Few groups of plants, especially the ferns, have undergone so
many changes in taxonomy and nomenclature (Pichi-Sermolli, 1973). There is difficulty
in understanding the interrelationships between the main groups of pteridophytes, as
well as in delimiting and arranging the taxa at lower ranks (Pichi-Sermolli, 1973).
Many classifications of the pteridophytes exist, derived in part from the different
philosophies of the various pteridologists and complicated by the peculiarities of the
pteridophytes.

The main groups of pteridophytes were extant by the Devonian Period. Today they
consist of a complex of heterogeneous groups reflecting their antiquity and diverse
evolutionary pathways. The fern families in particular are not always easily characterized and classified. Differences within and between the fern families are usually
based on a series of small characters rather than on one or two sharp distinctions.

At the rank of division, Cronquist, Takhtajan, and Zimmermann (1966) recognize
four groups of pteridophytes (see Figure 12-5): Psilotophyta (whisk ferns), Lycopodiophyta (club mosses, spike mosses, and quillworts), Equisetophyta (horsetails), and
Polypodiophyta (ferns and water ferns). These groups represent distinct evolutionary
lines; they are lumped together for convenience, not in an attempt to reflect relationships. The distinctions between the first three divisions are generally clear; however,
the classification problem is not yet fully resolved for the ferns to the satisfaction of
all pteridologists.

Crabbe, Jermy, and Mickel (1975) presented a useful generic sequence for arranging
pteridophytes in the herbarium, along with a valuable working list of generic synonyms.

(a)

(b)

Strobilus

(c)

Sterile

Fertile

(d)

EXPLANATION OF SOME SPECIAL TERMS ASSOCIATED WITH
THE PTERIDOPHYTES

Annulus. A thick-walled ring of cells surrounding the sporangium which at maturity breaks the sporangium, releasing the spores.

Antheridium (plural, *antheridia*). The sperm-producing structure on the prothallus or gametophyte.

Archegonium (plural, *archegonia*). The egg-producing structure on the prothallus or gametophyte.

Areole. The small spaces in a leaf surrounded by veins.

Auricle. The basal lobe of a pinna.

Circinate vernation. The coiled arrangement of a young fern frond, a fiddlehead.

Compound. Made up of multiple parts.

Dimorphic. In ferns, fronds or parts of fronds differentiated into fertile and sterile portions.

Fertile frond. A frond or part of frond that bears sporangia.

Free venation. A term used to describe veins that do not form a network but pass directly to the margin of the leaf.

Frond. The entire leaf of a fern, including the petiole (Figure 12-1).

Gametophyte. A gamete-producing plant.

Heterosporous. Having two different kinds of spores, microspores and megaspores.

Homosporous. Having spores of only one kind.

Indusium (plural, *indusia*). The tissue covering a fern sorus. A false indusium is present in some with the leaf margin folded over the sori.

Megaspore. The larger of the two kinds of spores produced by heterosporous pteridophytes, developing into gametophytes which produce eggs.

Microspore. The smaller of the spores produced by heterosporous pteridophytes, developing into gametophytes that produce sperm.

Midrib. The central vein of a frond or the central vein of a division of a frond.

Paraphyses. Hairlike structures associated with the sori.

Pinna (plural, *pinnae*). A blade division spaced on rachis, as in a feather; the openings between pinnae extend to the midrib.

Pinnate. Divided into pinnae; pinnately compound.

Pinnule (plural, *pinnules*). The division of a pinna.

Prothallus (plural, *prothalli*). The gametophyte stage of a fern, developing from a spore (Figure 12-3).

Rachis. The main axis (or midrib) of a compound fern frond extending from the base of the blade upward.

FIGURE 12-5
Opposite page: Psilotum, Selaginella, Equisetum, and *Lycopodium,* (a) Upper portion of a shoot of *Psilotum nudum* with sporangia (*from Haupt, 1953; with permission*). (b) *Selaginella,* branch with leaves and strobili (*from Haupt, 1953; with permission*). (c) Sterile and fertile shoots of *Equisetum (from McVaugh and Pyron, 1953; with permission.* (d) *Lycopodium* with strobili (*from Smith, 1955; with permission*).

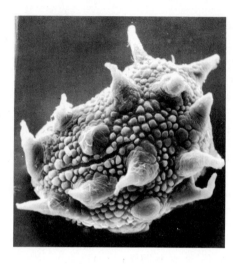

FIGURE 12-6
SEM of a fern spore. *Pteyopsis piloselloides,*
1500X. *(Courtesy of Dr. W. H. Wagner, Jr.).*

Rhizoids. Hairlike structures on the gametophytes that absorb moisture; found also on the rhizomes of whisk ferns.

Rhizome. An underground stem, usually horizontal.

Rootstock. The entire rhizome-root system.

Scale. In ferns, the thick, dry, straw-colored chaff on the rootstocks and stipes.

Sorus (plural, *sori*). A cluster of sporangia in ferns (see Figure 12-2).

Spike. In pteridophytes, an elongated cluster of sporophylls and sporangia; a strobilus; a special reproductive structure of the Ophioglossaceae.

Sporophyte. A spore-producing plant.

Sporangiophore. A special stalk bearing sporangia; e.g., *Equisetum.*

Sporangium (plural, *sporangia*). A spore-producing structure, site of meiosis.

Spore. A one-celled microscopic structure produced in sporangia, which germinates to form the gametophyte (Figures 12-6 and 12-7).

Sporocarp. A bean-shaped structure containing sporangia and spores found in some ferns.

Sterile. In ferns, a frond lacking sporangia.

Stipe. The petiole or stalk of a fern frond.

Strobilus (plural, *strobili*). The conelike cluster of sporophylls found in *Equisetum, Lycopodium* and *Selaginella.*

MAJOR FAMILIES OF PTERIDOPHYTES
NATIVE TO NORTH AMERICA

The families follow the sequence of Crabbe, Jermy, and Mickel (1975). The Gleicheniaceae, with one species found only sporadically along certain Gulf of Mexico coastal islands, is excluded, along with the Grammitidaceae, which is known from one locality in North Carolina where it exists only as a gametophyte.

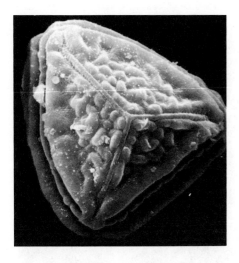

FIGURE 12-7
SEM of a fern spore. *Gymnogramma chrysophylla*, 2000X. (*Courtesy of Dr. W. H. Wagner, Jr.*)

Listed below are the family names, common names, a brief diagnosis, plus generalized distribution and habitat data.

Eusporangiate Pteridophytes

These pteridophytes have large sporangia called *eusporangia,* with numerous spores (several hundred to thousands in each sporangium). The sporangium develops from several initial cells on the shoot.

1 Division Psilotophyta *Psilotaceae: Whisk Ferns* Epiphytic or terrestrial; perennials; stem dichotomously branching appearing rather like a bundle of green forking sticks; rhizome with rhizoids, rootless; leaves or enations small or minute, one-veined; sporangia fused into groups of two or three; homosporous; gametophytes subterranean; distribution largely tropical or subtropical (Figure 12-5). *Psilotum* is grown as a greenhouse plant and is found naturally in the warmer parts of the Southeastern states (Figure 12-8). *Tmesipteris* is the other genus in the family and it occurs in Australia, New Zealand, the Philippines, and some islands of Polynesia.

2 Division Lycopodiophyta *Lycopodiaceae: Club Mosses, Ground Pine* Epiphytic or terrestrial; perennials; stems dichotomously branching; leaves simple with a single vein; minute, more like needles or scales; sporangia in the axils of leaves, very commonly the leaves with the sporangia are slightly modified and aggregated together into a strobilus; homosporous; gametophytes green when on the soil surface or nongreen when subterranean; distribution tropical and temperate (Figure 12-5). *Lycopodium* is common in some parts of North America. Certain species were once gathered in large quantities for making Christmas wreaths, and the dry spores were once used as flash powder and condom lubricants. The lycopods were literally the forests of the Carboniferous Period, which formed the present-day coal deposits so

FIGURE 12-8
Photograph of *Psilotum*.

critical to our energy needs. In addition, they have the longest continuous fossil record of any group of vascular plants.

Selaginellaceae: Spike Mosses   Terrestrial or epiphytic; perennials; stems dichotomously branching; leaves small with a single vein; heterosporous; gametophytes form within the spore walls; largely tropical but also temperate in distribution (Figure 12-5). Several species of *Selanginella* are cultivated in greenhouses as ornamentals. In nature, some inhabit xeric places, others mesophytic to moist habitats; most species live in the wetter tropics. Superficially, spike mosses resemble club mosses; however, spike mosses have terminal strobili which are usually four-sided.

Isoetaceae: Quillworts   Terrestrial; perennials; stems short, erect, cormlike, having secondary growth; leaves long, quill-like, with a single vein; sporangia axillary, large, sunken in base of leaves; heterosporous; gametophyte forming within spore walls; distribution is tropical and temperate. *Isoetes* is an emergent plant of shallow ponds or vernal pools and is easily overlooked because of its grasslike appearance. The fleshy stem of quillworts resembles a corm and the sporangia are embedded in the enlarged leaf bases (Figure 12-9).

As just noted, both the spike mosses and quillworts are heterosporous, producing two kinds of sporangia, megasporangia (female) and microsporangia (male). Megasporangia produce a few large megaspores and the microsporangia produce relatively large numbers of small microspores. After cracking open, the megaspore grows producing several archegonia; the microspore divides producing several sperms. When the sperm are released they swim to the archegonia, fertilizing the egg. The resulting

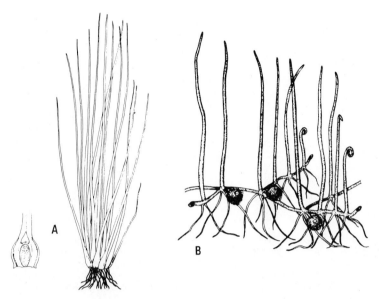

FIGURE 12-9
Quillwort (*Isoetes*) and pillwort (*Pilularia*); A. *Isoetes engelmannii*, insert
showing leaf base and sporangium; B. *Pilularia americana*, sporangia borne in
round sporocarps formed at the base of leaf stalks, reprinted from *Ferns of
Georgia* by permission of the University of Georgia Press © 1951 by The
University of Georgia Press.

zygote develops into a new sporophyte. Heterospory is evolutionarily significant as it
is the first step in the evolution of seed producing plants.

3   Division   Equisetophyta   *Equisetaceae: Horsetails,   Scouring   Rushes*
Terrestrial; annuals or perennials; stems conspicuously jointed, ribbed, unbranched,
or with whorls of branches easily mistaken for leaves; leaves greatly reduced to a
whorl of scales forming a sheath at the nodes; strobili terminal; sporangia attached to
special holders or sporangiophores; spores green with four long, twisting arms, or
elaters, which coil and uncoil in response to charges in humidity; homosporous; gametophytes green and found on the soil surface; distribution both tropical and temperate
(Figure 12-5). One genus only, *Equisetum:* several species are native to North America.
The rough silica-containing stems were supposedly used by the early settlers to scour
pots and pans, leading to the common name of scouring rush. Some species of *Equisetum* cause poisoning of livestock.

**4   Division   Polypodiophyta   *Ophioglossaceae: Adder's   Tongue   and   Grape
Ferns***   Terrestrial (two species epiphytic); perennials; leaves simple or much divided,
differentiated into a sterile and a fertile portion; sporangia aggregated into an upright
fertile region or spike; homosporous; gametophytes subterranean; distribution both

FIGURE 12-10
Adder's-tongue fern, *Ophioglossum engelmannii,* the sporangia
are large and borne on a fertile spike arising from the stipe,
reprinted from *Ferns of Georgia* by permission of the University of
Georgia Press © 1951 by the University of Georgia Press.

tropical and temperate. *Ophioglossum* (adder's tongue) and *Botrychium* (grape fern)
are both represented in North America. Some species of this family are rather small
and easily overlooked (Figure 12-10).

Leptosporangiate Pteridophytes

These pteridophytes have small sporangia called *leptosporangia,* which produce a
relatively small number of spores, usually 128 spores or fewer in each sporangium.
The sporangium develops from one cell or a small group of cells.

   Osmundaceae: Royal, Cinnamon, and Interrupted Ferns   Terrestrial; perennials;
plants various, large rosette ferns (ours) or small "filmy" ferns; leaves pinnately compound with the fertile pinnae differentiated from the sterile; sporangia large with many
spores, the family is intermediate between the typical eusporangiate and typical leptosporangiate condition; gametophytes occur on the surface of the soil and are green;
distribution is both tropical and temperate. The Osmundaceae have a long fossil record.
Osmunda is common in parts of North America: *O. regalis* (royal fern), *O. cinnamomea*
(cinnamon fern), and *O. claytoniana* (interrupted fern).

   Schizaeaceae: Curly Grass Fern, Climbing Fern   Terrestrial; perennials; morphology diverse, including grasslike tufted plants and vines; sporangia have an apical
annulus, a common feature of the family; gametophytes occur either on the surface
or below ground; distribution is both tropical and temperate. *Lygodium palmatum*
(climbing fern) is widespread in the Eastern United States. One introduced species,
L. japonicum, has escaped cultivation and is weedy in the warmer parts of the South.
Schizaea is the curly grass fern. *Anemia* is native to the extreme Southern United
States.

Parkeriaceae: Water Fern Family   Aquatic or semiaquatic on mud; leaves large, fleshy, divided; distribution tropical to warm temperate. Contains only the genus *Ceratopteris,* which occurs as a weed and is used in aquaria as an ornamental.

Adiantaceae: Maidenhair, Cloak, and Lip Ferns   Terrestrial or epiphytic; perennials; small plants often of specialized habitats, such as basic rocks, or xerophytic habits, also in rich woods; pinnae dichotomously veined; sori along veins, in grooves, or along reflexed margins of pinnae; distribution tropical and temperate. *Adiantum pedatum* (northern maidenhair) is a beautiful fern which ranges over much of the Eastern United States. Largely tropical, southern maidenhair (*A. capillus-veneris*) grows on limestone rock in the Southern states. Some of the genera include: *Cheilanthes* (lip fern), *Pellaea* (cliffbrake fern), *Vittaria* (shoestring fern), *Pteris* (wall fern), *Acrostichum,* and *Notholaena.*

Hymenophyllaceae: Filmy Fern   Terrestrial or epiphytic; perennials; occurring on moist rocks, trees, stream banks; leaves very thin, only one cell thick (except at the midvein); sori marginal, indusium tubular or bivalved; distribution mostly tropical, a few temperate. *Trichomanes* (bristle fern) and *Hymenophyllum* (tunbridge fern) are found in the Southeastern states.

Polypodiaceae: Polypody, Rockcap, Resurrection Ferns   Typically epiphytic; perennials; rhizomes creeping and covered with scales; leaves often simple though usually lobed; sporangia forming a moundlike rounded sorus, indusia absent; distribution chiefly tropical, a few temperate. Some species of *Polypodium* are often cultivated in greenhouses as ornamentals. The staghorn fern (*Platycerium*) is commonly cultivated. The resurrection fern (*P. polypodioides*) is a common epiphytic fern in the Eastern states.

Dennstaedtiaceae: Hayscented Fern, Bracken   Terrestrial or rarely climbing; perennials; rhizome creeping; leaves large and divided; sori along leaf margin or on back of leaf, indusium cuplike, two-lipped, or lateral along the margin; distribution mostly tropical, but with a few temperate species. *Pteridium aquilinum* (bracken fern), ranging over much of the world, is one of the most widespread species of vascular plant. The common name of *Dennstaedtia punctilobula* (hayscented fern) is well-suited because of the strong fragrance of the dried leaves, which have an odor resembling alfalfa.

Thelpteridaceae: Beech, Marsh, New York Ferns   Terrestrial; perennials; rhizomes short and erect to creeping; petioles with two vascular strands; sori usually round, indusium kidney-shaped; spores bilateral (as opposed to tetrahedral), perispore or membranous spore covering present; distribution mostly tropical. *Thelypteris* is common in parts of North America.

Aspleniaceae: Wood Ferns, Spleenworts, Sensitive Fern, Cliff Fern   Primarily terrestrial, often growing on rocks; perennials; sori round or elongate, indusia kidney-shaped or linear; spores bilateral (as opposed to tetrahedral), surrounded by a perispore or membranous covering; distribution both temperate and tropical, one of the most abundant groups of ferns. Important genera in North America include *Asplenium* (spleenwort), *Onoclea* (sensitive fern), *Athyrium* (lady fern), *Woodsia* (cliff fern), *Cystopteris* (brittle fern), *Polystichum* (Christmas fern), and *Dryopteris* (wood fern). Walking fern (*Asplenium rhizophyllus*) is unusual because of its habit of "walking"

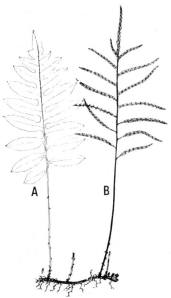

A   B

FIGURE 12-11
Netted chain fern, *Woodwardia areolata* (= *Lorinseria areolata),* A. sterile frond, B. fertile frond (fronds diamorphic), reprinted from *Ferns of Georgia* by permission of the University of Georgia Press © 1951 by The University of Georgia Press.

across rocks vegetatively by plantlets produced by adventitious buds at the tip of the leaves. *Matteuccia* (ostrich fern) is a well-known edible species.

Davalliaceae: Boston and Rabbit's Foot Fern   Mostly epiphytes; perennials; indusia kidney-shaped or somewhat tubular; spores bilateral with a perispore; distribution largely tropical, but also warm temperate. A popular house fern, *Nephrolepis exaltata* (Bostern fern) is the source of numerous vegetatively propagated cultivars. *Davallia fejeensis* (rabbit's foot fern), with handsome rhizomes and divided leaves, is often used to form hanging fern balls.

Blechnaceae: Chain Fern   Mostly terrestrial; perennials; indusia linear, opening toward midvein; spores bilateral, covered with a perispore; distribution mostly tropical, but with a few temperate species. Genera include *Blechnum* and *Woodwardia* (chain fern) (Figure 12-11).

Water Ferns

All these ferns are heterosporous with megaspores and microspores. The water ferns are definitely not fernlike in appearance. Two of the families are floating aquatics, and the third is emergent or rooted in mud. Crabbe, Jermy, and Mickel (1975) state that they place the water ferns here, ". . . not because we feel they are related to each other, but out of convenience. They are quite distinct and there are no firm data to justify placing them elsewhere."

Marsileaceae: Water Clovers, Pillwort   Emergent aquatic or rooted on mud; leaves resemble a small bunch of grass or clover with four or two leaflets. Reproductive structures are hard, modified basal leaflets called *sporocarps*; distribution tropical and temperate. *Marsilea* has cloverlike leaves, whereas *Pilularia* is similar but lacks the

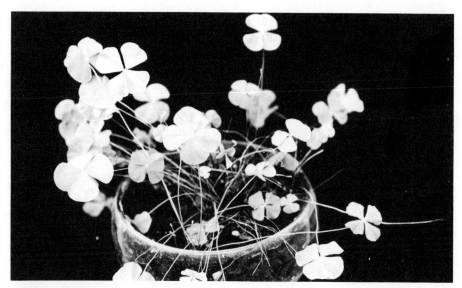

FIGURE 12-12
Photograph of *Marsilea.*

leaflets leaving only the stipes, thus is grasslike in appearance (Figure 12-9). *Marsilea* is amphibious, growing in shallow water, and it is also able to survive on mud when the water level falls (Figure 12-12).

   Salviniaceae: Water Spangles   Floating aquatics; plants small; leaves in whorls of three, two floating and simple, and one very divided and dangling resembling a root; reproductive structures (sporocarps) occur among root-like leaves; distribution tropical and temperate. Salviniaceae has one genus, *Salvinia,* frequently used as an aquarium ornamental. Most species of *Salvinia* are native to Africa, but one species occurs in the United States (Figure 12-13).

FIGURE 12-13
Water fern or water spangles, *Salvinia minima* (= *S. rotundifolia),* reprinted from *Ferns of Georgia* by permission of the University of Georgia Press © 1951 by the University of Georgia Press.

Azollaceae: Mosquito Fern   Floating aquatic; plants very small; leaves in two rows, scalelike and overlapping, harboring blue-green algae; distribution tropical and temperate. Azollaceae has one genus, *Azolla,* often grown as an ornamental in aquaria. Two species of *Azolla* occur in the United States, often coloring the water of swamps red when the plants are in full sun.

SELECTED REFERENCES

Banks, H. P.: "The Early History of Land Plants," in E. T. Drake (ed.), *Evolution and Environment,* Yale, New Haven, 1968, pp. 73–107.

———: "Early Vascular Land Plants: Proof and Conjecture," *BioScience,* **25:**730–737, 1975.

Bierhorst, D. W.: "The Systematic Position of *Psilotum* and *Tmesipteris,*" *Brittonia,* **29:**3–13, 1977.

Bower, F. O.: *The Ferns (Filicales),* 3 vols., Cambridge, London, 1923–1928.

Bruce, J. G.: "Gametophytes and Subgeneric Concepts in *Lycopodium,*" *Amer. J. Bot.,* **63:**919–924, 1976.

Crabbe, J. A., A. C. Jermy, and J. T. Mickel: "A New Generic Sequence for the Pteridophyte Herbarium," *Fern Gaz.,* **11:**141–162, 1975.

Cronquist, A., A. Takhtajan, and W. Zimmermann: "On the Higher Taxa of Embryobionta," *Taxon,* **15:**129–134, 1966.

Evans, A. M.: "A Review of Systematic Studies of the Pteridophytes of the Southern Appalachians," in P. C. Holt (ed.), *The Distributional History of the Biota of the Southern Appalachians,* part II. *Flora,* Research Division Monograph 2, Virginia Polytechnic Institute and State University, Blacksburg, 1970, pp. 117–146.

Gensel, P. G.: "Morphologic and Taxonomic Relationships of the Psilotaceae Relative to Evolutionary Lines in Early Land Vascular Plants," *Brittonia,* **29:**14–29, 1977.

Haupt, A. W.: *Plant Morphology,* McGraw-Hill, New York, 1953.

Holttum, R. E.: "The Family Names of Ferns," *Taxon,* **20:**527–531, 1971.

———: "Posing the Problems," in A. C. Jermy et al. (eds.), "The Phylogeny and Classification of the Ferns," *Bot. J. Linn. Soc.,* **67**(Suppl. 1):1–10, 1973.

Klekowski, E. J.: "Genetical Features of Ferns as Contrasted to Seed Plants," *Ann. Mo. Bot. Gard.,* **59:**138–151, 1972.

McVaugh, R., and J. H. Pyron: *Ferns of Georgia,* University of Georgia Press, Athens, 1951.

May, L. W.: "The Economic Uses and Associated Folklore of Ferns and Fern Allies," *Bot. Rev.* **44:**491–528, 1978.

Mickel, J. T.: "Phyletic Lines in the Modern Ferns," *Ann. Mo. Bot. Gard.,* **61:**474–482, 1974.

———: *How to Know the Ferns and Fern Allies,* Wm. C. Brown Co. Pub., Dubuque, Iowa, 1979.

———: *The Home Gardener's Book of Ferns,* Ridge Press: Holt, Rinehart and Winston, New York, 1979.

Pichi-Sermolli, R. E. G.: "Historical Review of the Higher Classification of the Filicopsida," in A. C. Jermy et al. (eds.), "The Phylogeny and Classification of the Ferns," *Bot. J. Linn. Soc.,* **67**(Suppl. 1):11–40, 1973.

Smith, G. M.: *Cryptogamic Botany,* vol. II, *Bryophytes and Pteridophytes,* 2d ed., McGraw-Hill, New York, 1955.

Sporne, K. R.: *The Morphology of Pteridophytes: the Structure of Ferns and Allied Plants,* 4th ed., Hutchinson, London, 1975.

Taylor, T. N., and J. T. Mickel (eds.): "Evolution of Systematic Characters in the Ferns," *Ann. Mo. Bot. Gard.,* **61:**307–482, 1974. (Papers presented at the 1973 Amherst Symposium.)

Wagner, W. H.: "Some Future Challenges of Fern Systematics and Phylogeny," in A. C. Jermy et al. (eds.), "The Phylogeny and Classification of the Ferns," *Bot. J. Linn. Soc.,* **67**(Suppl. 1):245–256, 1973.

———: "Systematic Implications of the Psilotaceae," *Brittonia,* **29:**54–63, 1977.

CHAPTER 13

GYMNOSPERMS

The term *gymnosperm* refers to the mode of seed production. As a group, the gymnosperms include several unrelated evolutionary lines with divergent forms. The major distinguishing feature of the gymnosperms is their so-called naked seeds, which are borne more or less exposed to the air on the surface of cone scales or on stalks among the leaves. In comparison, the seeds of angiosperms are borne within fruit tissue that develops from the ovary or some other floral structure. Pollen grains of gymnosperms germinate on the exposed ovules and pollen tubes grow from each pollen grain to penetrate the ovular tissues. In contrast, the pollen grains of angiosperms do not come in contact with the ovules but instead are borne by various means to the stigmatic portion of the carpel where they germinate. The pollen tubes of angiosperms may grow through considerable tissue before they finally penetrate ovular tissues.

Additional features distinguishing gymnosperms from angiosperms are: (1) the lack of double fertilization, which is unique to the angiosperms (the nutritive tissue of gymnosperms is haploid gametophytic tissue formed before fertilization); (2) the absence of xylem vessels except in the gnetophytes (an unusual group of gymnosperms); (3) the lack of companion cells in the phloem; (4) the presence of a many-celled or many-nucleated female gametophyte; and (5) the presence of archegonia in the female gametophytes, with the exceptions of *Gnetum* and *Welwitschia*. Further, all gymnosperms are considered to be woody; whereas, many angiosperms are herbaceous.

Although they consist of only 500 or more species, ca. 61 genera and 9 to 11 families, the gymnosperms rank among the most economically important, biologically interesting, and familiar of all plants. They are the major constituents of the vegetation in many parts of the world and include such well-known groups of plants as pines, cedars, firs, hemlocks, spruces, junipers, and araucarias. The major groups of living gymnosperms are the coniferophytes, including ginkgo, conifers and taxads; the cycadophytes, the cycads; and the gnetophytes including the joint firs (*Ephedra*), gnetums (*Gnetum*), and *Welwitschia*.

In North America, the conifers are most common. They include the families Pinaceae, Taxodiaceae, Cupressaceae, and Taxaceae. Some other gymnosperms found in North America are *Zamia* (Cycadaceae), with one species native to Florida, and *Ephedra* (Ephedraceae), a genus of bushy shrubs found in Southwestern deserts.

Gymnosperms are more important than indicated by the numerical size of the group. Many species of gymnosperms are significant as timber trees, as ornamental plants, as food and medicinal plants, and as sources of essential oils and other products. They are important in erosion control, protection of watersheds, enhancement of recreational uses of forests, and are often the first trees to appear in secondary succession. Gymnosperms have interested biologists because of their diversity of form and structure, their past and present distributions, and their well documented and relatively complete fossil record.

CLASSIFICATION

Many of the modern species and genera have a markedly disjunct geographic distribution, and there are many species with a limited distribution. Such a distribution pattern reflects their great antiquity. The geological record of the gymnosperms extends from the late Devonian (see Table 6-1). Each of the families of conifers has a fossil record extending from the Mesozoic Era. Their fossil evidence shows a much wider geographic distribution than that of the living conifers. Leaves identical with *Ginkgo biloba* occurred as far back as the Permian. The group of gymnosperms represented today only by *Ginkgo biloba* was once almost worldwide in distribution but is restricted now to a small and relatively inaccessible area in South China.

The gymnosperms have had various taxonomic interpretations. Traditionally they have been classified together in one large group equal in rank to the angiosperms, with the rank of division, subdivision, or subclass, depending on the classification scheme used. In these traditional classifications, great weight was placed on one feature of the gymnosperms, that is, their naked seeds. In contrast, some classification schemes separate the gymnosperms into four independent divisions (the Cycadophyta, Ginkgophyta, Coniferophyta, and Gnetophyta), thus placing greater weight on many basic differences among the groups and deemphasizing the importance of the naked seeds. The latter argument is based on the opinion that the divergences among such extant genera as *Zamia, Cycas, Ginkgo, Pinus, Ephedra,* and so on overshadow their common gymnospermous features. Also, the paleobotanical evidence suggests several long-distinct evolutionary lines and that the seed-producing habit (that is, their gymnospermous features) arose several times during the history of land plants. Other interpretations suggest that the differences observed in the living gymnospermous genera should not be allowed to obscure their similarities.

The classification presented following is no more correct than any of several others but is a sound one. The definitive classification of such an ancient, large, and diverse group as the gymnosperms will perhaps never be achieved, mainly because each scheme presented depends on individual interpretation and weighting of data.

Division Progymnospermophyta
Ancestors of the gymnosperms. Possessed gymnospermous anatomy but reproduced by spores. Extended form the Devonian into the lower Carboniferous.
Division Pinophyta (gymnosperms)
Woody plants, wood without vessels, except in the Gnetophytina; phloem without companion cells; low shrubs to tall trees. Ovules naked, not enclosed in an ovary; female gametophyte with 500 or more cells (or nuclei) and, except in *Gnetum* and *Welwitschia,* producing definite archegonia.
Subdivision Cycadophytina
Palmlike to fernlike plants; leaves mostly compound; wood soft and loose, without vessels; microstrobili, when present, simple. Ovules with one integument.
Class Lyginopteridopsida (seed ferns)
Treelike with large fernlike fronds, some lianalike. Pollen-producing organs and seeds borne on leaves; microsporangia aggregated into clusters; seeds solitary or grouped into protective structures called cupules. Eight orders, all extinct, are recognized (Taylor, 1981).
Order Lyginopteridales: Mississippian and Pennsylvanian
Order Medullosales: Mississippian to Permian
Order Callistophytales: Pennsylvanian
Order Calamonpityales: Upper Devonian to Lower Mississippian
Order Caytoniales: Triassic to Cretaceous
Order Corystospermales: Triassic
Order Peltaspermales: Triassic
Order Glossopteridales: Permian to Triassic
Class Bennettitopsida (cycadeiods)
Extinct cycadlike plants from the Triassic to the Cretaceous. Leaves typically once-pinnate; the strobilus was bisporangiate, with ovules borne on simple megasporophylls and with pinnately compound microsporophylls at the base of the strobilus. Syndetocheilic stomatal ontogeny (the two guard cells and subsidiary cells all had their origin from the division of a single cell).
Class Cycadopsida (cycads)
Palmlike or fernlike plants from the Triassic to the present. Leaves pinnately compound; forming a crown at the tip of the stem; stems with massive pith and cortex containing resin canals; dioecious; living species with motile sperms; seeds borne on megasporophylls aggregated into strobili, except in *Cycas* where the megasporphylls are borne in same spiral as leaves; microsporophylls simple, in strobili. Haplocheilic stomatal ontogeny (guard cells have their origin from a common cell while adjacent subsidiary cells are derived from other epidermal cells).
Subdivision Pinophytina
Plants with simple leaves; wood without vessels, relatively dense; microstrobili simple; ovules with one integument.

Class Ginkgoöpsida (ginkgo)

Trees from the Permian to the present. Leaves strap-shaped or fan-shaped, with dichotomous venation; dioecious; ovules 2–10, terminal on branched or almost unbranched axes; microstrobili catkinlike; sperm motile. Many fossil representatives; one living species, *Ginkgo biloba.*

Class Cordaitopsida (cordaites)

Extinct trees from the Devonian to the Permian. Trunk bases with stiltlike roots; leaves strap-shaped; pollen and seed producing organs complex and borne on tips of leaf-bearing branches.

Class Coniferopsida (conifers)

Mostly trees, some shrubs; from the Pennsylvanian to the present. Usually evergreen, leaves typically scalelike or needlelike; pollen cones contain sporangia on the abaxial surface of the microsporophylls; seed cones contain flattened ovules attached to the upper surface of an ovuliferous scale subtended by a bract.

Order Voltziales (transition conifers)

Woody trees from the Pennsylvanian into the Mesozoic. Leaves small, spirally arranged; reproductive organs morphologically intermediate between those of the class Cordaitopsida and the cones of modern conifers.

Order Coniferales (conifers)

Trees or shrubs from the Carboniferous to the present. Leaves needlelike to scalelike to linear or broad; microstrobili simple, conelike; megastrobili compound, often conelike. Six modern families (Pinaceae, Taxodiaceae, Cupressaceae, Podocarpaceae, Cephalotaxaceae, and Araucariaceae) and the extinct family Palissyaceae.

Order Taxales (taxads)

Trees or shrubs from the Triassic to the present. Extant members are evergreen with spirally arranged leaves. Leaves linear, needlelike; microstrobili conelike; ovules solitary and terminal on a modified shoot; in *Taxus,* the ovule is partially surrounded by a fleshy aril. Most authorities recognize 5 extant genera and about 20 species in 1 family, the Taxaceae.

Subdivision Gnetophytina (gnetophytes)

Problematic gymnospermous plants of interesting morphology, and often, unusual structure. Compound male and compound female strobili. Embryos with 2 cotyledons.

Order Ephedrales (joint firs)

Profusely branched shrubs of desert regions. Leaves decussate to whorled, scalelike to needlelike; some with jointed stems; xylem vessels present; re productive organs dioecious. One family, Ephedraceae, with a single genus, *Ephedra.*

Order Welwitschiales

Plant unusual, with only two strap-shaped leaves that arise from the rim of a conelike structure; and with a long tap root; xylem vessels present, strobili conelike. One family, Welwitschiaceae with a single species, *Welwitschia mirabilis,* of Namibia (Southwest Africa).

Order Gnetales (gnetums)

Woody vines, or occasionally, shrubs or trees. Leaves opposite, with a pinnate, reticulate venation pattern, which resembles many dicotyledons; vessels present in wood; strobili not conelike. One family, Gnetaceae, with a single genus *Gnetum,* inhabiting the tropical rain forests in Asia, South America, and Africa.

Not included in the preceding outline are two orders, Vojnovskyales and Pentoxylales, extinct gymnosperms of uncertain affinities (see Taylor, 1981).

Since the living gymnosperms belong to clearly distinct groups, the problem of classification is not one of intergradation, but an evaluation of their relationships and a determination of the rank to be accorded to each group. Some morphologists regard gymnosperms as a particular level of evolution rather than a taxonomic group. If true, this should be reflected in their classification. The fossil record suggests that the major groups of gymnosperms were derived from several ancestral groups.

Cycads (class Cycadopsida) appeared in the upper Triassic. They exhibit a number of primitive features, such as pinnately compound leaves, sparingly branched low habit, circinate vernation, and motile sperm. The cycads probably evolved from the pteridosperms or seed ferns (class Lyginopteridopsida), which were still abundant in the Triassic.

The group of gymnosperms represented today only by *Ginkgo biloba* (Class Ginkgoöpsida) probably originated in the Permian Period of the late Paleozoic Era and became widespread and moderately abundant during mid-Mesozoic times. The ancestor of the ginkgo lineage is not known. Ginkgoöpsida has some characters of both the conifers (freely branching stems) and the cycads (motile sperm). However, its relations are probably closer to the conifer line (Sporne, 1974).

When compared with other gymnosperms, the conifers (class Coniferopsida) are relatively advanced in some features, but primitive in others. Traces of early conifers have been identified from the late Carboniferous. The earliest conifers may have been similar to *Araucaria heterophylla* (Norfolk Island pine). The entire group is fertilized by nonmotile sperm conveyed to the egg by a pollen tube.

The Pinaceae are essentially a family of the Northern Hemisphere and are the largest family of conifers (see Table 13-1). Half of the Cupressaceae occur in the Northern Hemisphere and the other half in the Southern Hemisphere. The Taxodiaceae had an important place in the paleoforests of the Northern Hemisphere, but today they show only a relict distribution. Some workers separate the Taxaceae from the conifer group because of the uniform presence of a single ovule covered or partially covered by a fleshy structure called an *aril*. The Taxaceae, however, share many vegetative features with the conifers. They are largely confined to the Northern Hemisphere. The most important family of conifers in the Southern Hemisphere is the Podocarpaceae. They have a wide range of morphological characters. In some species, the ovules are borne in cones; in others, there is a single terminal fleshy receptacle. Cephalotaxaceae are represented today by one genus. *Cephalotaxus,* restricted to eastern Asia, although in past geological history there were representatives in Europe and western North America. The fossil record of the Araucariaceae extends back to the Triassic and includes both hemispheres. Today it is found only in the Southern Hemisphere.

TABLE 13-1
CONIFER FAMILIES IN NORTH AMERICA

Families	Ovule, bract, and scale	Cones and seeds	Leaves
Pinaceae	Bract and scale distinct, ovules two on each scale	Woody cone; seeds terminally winged or wingless	Persistent or deciduous; needlelike or linear
Taxodiaceae	Bract and scale partially fused, ovules two to nine per scale	Woody cone; seeds laterally winged	Persistent or deciduous; linear or ovate
Cupressaceae	Bract and scale fused, ovules two to many on each scale	Woody, leathery, or fleshy cone; seeds laterally winged or wingless	Persistent; scalelike, or awl-shaped
Taxaceae	Ovulate structure comprising a single erect ovule	Aril or drupe-like; seed single, enclosed or partially enclosed by fleshy tissue	Persistent; linear

Source: Adapted from Harlow and Harrar, 1968, with permission.

Subdivision Gnetophytina (*Ephedra, Gnetum,* and *Welwitschia*) is an unusual group with practically no fossil record. Its noteworthy features are the following: (1) the presence of xylem vessels (unique among gymnosperms), (2) compound stroboli, (3) a perianthlike structure in the male flowers, (4) several envelopes around the ovary, and (5) a micropyle of a long, bristlelike tube. *Ephedra* pollen has been found in the Eocene. *Welwitschia*-like pollen has been found in the Permian, and possible *Gnetum* pollen is known from the Tertiary. Some have suggested that this group was the forerunner of the angiosperms; however, the prevalent view is that the group is a strange variation of the gymnosperms.

Information on fossil groups may be obtained from several of the selected references listed at the end of the chapter.

MORPHOLOGY ESSENTIAL TO IDENTIFICATION OF GYMNOSPERMS

Pinus is used as a primary example, since it is the most familiar and widespread genus of gymnosperms in North America (see Figure 13-1).

Vegetative Morphology

Shoots   The *spur shoots* of *Pinus* are lateral branches of determinate growth which abscise. The *long shoots* are lateral or terminal branches of indeterminate growth. Indeterminate short shoots forming a spur branch are found in several genera including *Larix, Ginkgo,* and *Cedrus,* giving an unusual branching pattern.

FIGURE 13-1
Pinus virginiana; s.l., scale leaf; n.l., needle leaf; l.s., long shoot; s.s., spur shoot;
me-1, megastrobilus first year; me-2; megastrobilus second year; and me-3,
megastrobilus three years old. (*From Bold, 1973; with permission.*)

Needle Leaves   In *Pinus*, the needle leaves are produced on short branches (or *spur shoots*) in clusters (or *fascicles*) of one to eight needle leaves depending on the species (Figure 13-2). A *sheath* of scale leaves surrounds the base of the fascicle.

Scale Leaves   In addition to the needle leaves, inconspicuous scale leaves are produced in *Pinus* on the main branches or *long shoots* and at the bases of the spur shoots. The scale leaves are brownish, small, and triangular. With the exception of *Pinus*, most conifers have needle leaves or scalelike leaves arranged directly on the long shoots without basal sheaths.

Reproductive Morphology

Cones   The microsporangia and megasporangia of *Pinus* occur in separate cones, or *strobili* (singular, *strobilus*). In *Pinus*, both types of strobili occur on the same individual; therefore, *Pinus* is *monoecious*. This contrasts with the *dioecious* condition in which a single plant bears either microsporangia or megasporangia (e.g., *Juniperus*).

Polliniferous Cones or Microstrobili   In *Pinus*, the microstrobili develop in clusters around the base of the terminal buds. When mature, these pollen-producing cones range in size from 1 to 4 centimeters long. A microstrobilus consists of a central axis

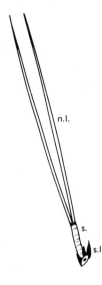

FIGURE 13-2
Spur shoot and fasicicle of *Pinus;* n.l., needle leaf; s.l., scale leaf; s., sheath.

bearing spirally arranged microsporophylls. Each microsporophyll bears on its lower side two elongate pollen sacs, or microsporangia. Each pollen mother cell gives rise to four characteristic winged pollen grains. Pines are wind-pollinated and produce large quantities of pollen.

Ovuliferous Cones or Megastrobili   The megastrobili are borne on spur shoots near the tip of some of the long shoots of the current season's growth (see Figure 13-3). They are small and inconspicuous at the time of pollination. The ovules develop on *ovuliferous scales* or *cone scales* which in turn are borne in the axils of *bracts* spirally arranged on the strobilus axis. The ovuliferous scales each bear two ovules. In *Pinus,* the bract is short, but in *Pseudotsuga menziesii* (Douglas fir), the three-pronged bracts are exserted beyond the scales. In some conifers, such as the Taxodiaceae and Cupressaceae, the bract is partially or entirely fused with the scale.

Additional details of vegetative and reproductive morphology of the various groups of gymnosperms can be obtained by consulting Foster and Gifford (1974), Bold (1973), or Bierhorst (1971).

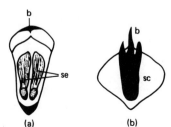

(a)   (b)

FIGURE 13-3
Ovuliferous scales. (*a*) Ovuliferous scale of *Pinus:* se, winged seed (on upper side of scale); b, bract extending from lower side of scale. (*b*) *Pseudotsuga* ovuliferous scale: lower side with three-pronged bract exserted beyond the scale: sc, scale; b, bract.

ADDITIONAL TERMINOLOGY FOR IDENTIFICATION OF GYMNOSPERMS

Vegetative Features

Acicular leaf. Needlelike.

Awl-shaped leaf. Narrow and sharp-pointed, gradually tapering from base to stiff point, relatively short, as in some leaves of *Juniperus.*

Fascicled. In clusters or bundles, as in needle leaves in *Pinus.*

Linear leaf. Long and narrow with parallel sides, as in *Picea, Taxus.*

Persistent leaves. Evergreen.

Scale leaf. Small, flat, appressed leaves, as in *Cupressus.*

Sterigma. Small, woody, peglike outgrowth of the twig bearing leaves or needles, as in *Picea.*

Subulate. Awl-shaped.

Reproductive Features

Apophysis. The part of the cone scale that is exposed when the cone is closed.

Aril. Tissue that forms a fleshy covering of the seed, as in *Taxus, Torreya;* or rudimentary at the base of the fleshy seed, as in *Cephalotaxus.*

Cone. Aggregation of sporangia-bearing structures of either sporophylls and scales, or just of sporophylls forming a *strobilus.* The female cone (or megasporangiate strobilus) bears ovules and later seed. The male cone (or microsporangiate strobilus) produces pollen in microsporangia.

Megasporophyll. Modified leaf that bears ovules, as in *Cycas, Zamia* (and in conifers too).

Microsporophyll. Modified leaf that bears microsporangia.

Serotinous. Cones that remain closed long after the seeds are mature.

FAMILIES OF GYMNOSPERMS NATIVE TO NORTH AMERICA

Cycadaceae: Cycad Family

Field Recognition   *Stems palmlike, sparingly branched; leaves compound and fern-like; plants dioecious.*

Description   *Habit*   Stems palmlike in appearance, tuberous, usually armored, sparingly branched.

Leaves   Spirally inserted, pinnately compound, terminating the stem; young pinnae circinate, leaf bases remaining after the leaves drop.

Reproduction   Plants dioecious. Microsporangia and megasporangia produced on strobili (except in *Cycas,* which has loosely grouped megasporophylls with ovules borne on petiole margins of sporophyll); cones variable in size. Seed usually drupelike and often brightly colored.

Systematics The Cycadaceae are sometimes treated as three families: Cycadaceae (*Cycas*), Stangeriaceae (*Stangeria*), and Zamiaceae (*Zamia*). The division is based largely on leaf characters.

Size, Distribution, and General Information A family of about 10 genera and 100 species confined to tropical and subtropical regions, especially in Mexico, the West Indies, South America, Australia, and South Africa. One genus, *Zamia,* occurs in North America north of Mexico.

Some of the genera are *Cycas* (20);* *Zamia* (30–40) (coonties, Florida arrowroot); *Dioon* (3–5); *Ceratozamia* (4); *Microcycas* (1); and *Encephalartos* (30).

Cycas ranges from Africa and Madagascar to Southeast Asia and Australia. Often grown as an ornamental in the warmer parts of the United States, *C. revoluta* occurs in tropical China and Japan. Sago starch is obtained from the pith of *C. circinalis* of Indonesia and the Philippines.

Zamia was known to the Seminole Indians as "conti hateka," which means "white root" or "white bread plant." The starchy underground stem of *Z. floridana* was used by the Seminoles and later by the early settlers as a source of flour.

Indigenous to Mexico, *Dioon edule* has starchy seeds that are ground into a meal used for food.

Economic Importance The Cycadaceae are of limited economic value. Some are grown as ornamentals in warmer regions. Several species have starchy stems or seeds which can be used as food. Leaves of several Cycadaceae are used in the florist trade. Some are poisonous.

Pinaceae: Pine Family

Field Recognition *Cone scales flattened and distinct from the subtending bract; bract usually shorter than the scale* (except in *Pseudotsuga*).

Description *Habit* Trees, rarely prostrate or creeping shrubs; branches whorled or opposite.

Leaves Mostly evergreen (deciduous in a few genera), needlelike or linear, arranged in spirals or in fascicles.

Reproduction Plants monoecious; microsporangia in small herbaceous strobili; each microsporophyll bearing two to six sporangia on the lower side. Ovulate strobili with scales in spirals, with two ovules borne on the upper surface; the scale subtended by bracts, closed until seeds are ripe; cones woody. Seeds winged or wingless.

Size, Distribution, and General Information A family of about 10 genera and 250 species of the Northern Hemisphere, south to Sumatra, Java, Mexico, Central

---

*The number in parentheses is the estimated number of species in the genus.

America, and the West Indies. Pinaceae are the largest and most important family of the gymnosperms.

The chief genera are *Pinus* (70–100) (pine); *Abies* (50) (fir); *Pseudotsuga* (7) (Douglas fir); *Tsuga* (15) (hemlock); *Picea* (50) (spruce); *Larix* (10–12) (larch, tamarack); *Pseudolarix* (2) (larch, golden larch); and *Cedrus* (4) (true cedar).

Pinus, the largest genus in the family, is characterized by the needles that are borne in fascicles on short shoots. The cones vary in length from around 2 or 3 centimeters to over 45 centimeters. Some important species in North America are *P. strobus* (white pine), *P. monticola* (Western white pine), *P. lambertiana* (sugar pine), *P. edulis* (piñon pine), *P. monophylla* (singleleaf piñon), *P. palustris* (longleaf pine), *P. taeda* (loblolly pine), *P. echinata* (shortleaf pine), *P. elliottii* (slash pine), *P. ponderosa* (ponderosa pine), *P. coulteri* (Coulter pine), and *P. radiata* (Monterey pine).

The firs (*Abies*) are evergreen trees. *Abies balsamea* (balsam fir) is an important tree of the boreal forest formation of Canada. Other species of North America are *A. fraseri* (balsam fir) of the southern Appalachians; and in western North America, *A. concolor* (white fir), *A. lasiocarpa* (subalpine fir), *A. grandis* (grand fir), and *A. nobilis* (noble fir). *Pseudotsuga menziesii* (Douglas fir) is a valuable timber tree of western North America. *Tsuga* (hemlock) has flat needles with two white lines beneath. *Tsuga canadensis* is a large tree of eastern North America, and its western counterpart is *T. heterophylla.*

The spruces (*Picea*) are important timber, pulp, and ornamental trees. Some important species are *P. glauca* (white spruce) and *P. mariana* (black spruce), both important elements of the Canadian boreal forest; *P. abies* (Norway spruce), *P. rubens* (red spruce), *P. sitchensis* (Sitka spruce), and *P. engelmannii* (Engelmann spruce) of subalpine forests; and *P. pungens* (Colorado blue spruce), a widely planted ornamental.

The larches (*Larix*) are deciduous, differing from most other conifers which are evergreen. *Larix laricina* (tamarack) is characteristic of the boreal forest of Canada; *L. occidentalis* (western larch) is a large tree of the northern Rockies. Venetian turpentine is obtained from the European larch (*L. decidua*).

The true cedar (*Cedrus*) ranges from the Mediterranean to the Himalayas. *Cedrus libani* (cedar of Lebanon) is the cedar mentioned in the Bible, and it appears on the Lebanon flag. *Cedrus deodara* and *C. atlantica* are often grown as ornamentals.

Economic Importance   The Pinaceae are of considerable direct economic importance for lumber, pulpwood, chemicals (turpentine, rosin, essential oils, and so on), and ornamentals.

Cupressaceae: Cypress Family

Field Recognition   *Leaves small and scalelike, opposite or whorled; cones generally smaller than other families of gymnosperms, cone scales opposite or whorled.*

Description   *Habit*   Trees or shrubs.
Leaves   Evergreen, opposite or whorled, small and scalelike, often closely appressed to branches.

Reproduction Plants monoecious or dioecious. Male strobili small, terminal or axillary. Ovulate strobili terminal or lateral, on short branches; the mature cones small, dry and woody, or fleshy and berrylike at maturity. Seeds often winged.

Size, Distribution, and General Information A family of about 19 genera and 130 species of worldwide distribution.

The chief genera are *Cupressus* (15–20) (true cypress); *Juniperus* (60) (red cedar, juniper); *Chamaecyparis* (7) (Port Orford cedar, white cedar); *Thuja* (5) (arborvitae); and *Callitris* (16) (cypress pine).

Thuja occurs in North America and eastern Asia. *Thuja plicata* (western red cedar) is a valuable timber species which yields a rot-resistant wood. It occurs along the northwestern coast of North America, and it reaches a height of about 75 meters. *Thuja orientalis* of China and Korea is often grown as an ornamental. *Thuja occidentalis* is found in eastern North America.

The cones of *Juniperus* become fleshy at maturity and are known as "juniper berries." A volatile oil extracted from the cones of *J. communis* is used in flavoring gin. A number of species and cultivars of juniper are used as ornamentals. The aromatic wood of *J. virginiana* (red cedar) is used in making cedar chests. It is the alternate host for the cedar-apple rust and should not be permitted to grow near apple orchards.

Chamaecyparis occurs in North America and eastern Asia. White cedar (*C. thyoides*) occurs along the east coast of North America; *C. lawsoniana* (Port Orford cedar), in Oregon and California; and *C. nutkatenis* (Alaska yellow cedar), from Alaska to Oregon.

Cupressus, the true cypress, has several species often grown as ornamentals. The Monterey cypress is *C. macrocarpa. Cupressus sempervirens* (Mediterranean cypress) occurs along the Mediterranean.

Economic Importance Several of the genera yield valuable wood; others are cultivated as ornamentals. Crushed ovulate cones of Juniper are used for flavoring gin, and oil of cedar is obtained from *Thuja occidentalis*.

Taxodiaceae: Taxodium or Bald Cypress Family

Field Recognition *Trees; twigs and leaves deciduous or persistent; leaves scalelike or needlelike, sometimes dimorphic; cone scales flat or peltate, lacking distinct bracts, each scale producing two to nine seeds.*

Description *Habit* Trees, lateral branches deciduous or persistent.

Leaves Scalelike to needlelike, sometimes dimorphic, persistent or deciduous.

Reproduction Plants monoecious. Staminate strobili small, catkinlike clusters. Ovulate strobili woody, globose, terminal; sporophylls with two to nine ovules; the bracts and scales partially or completely fused; cone scales flat or peltate.

Size, Distribution, and General Information   A family of about 10 genera and 16 species from eastern Asia, Tasmania, and North America. Three genera are native to North America north of Mexico.

Some of the genera are *Taxodium* (3) (bald cypress, pond cypress); *Sequoia* (1) (coast redwood, redwood); *Sequoiadendron* (1) (big tree); *Metasequoia* (1) (dawn redwood); *Cryptomeria* (1) (Japanese cedar); *Cunninghamia* (3) (China fir); and *Sciadopitys* (1) (parasol pine, umbrella fir).

Taxodium distichum (bald cypress) is an important timber tree of river swamps of the Southeastern United States. Like the redwood, its wood is resistant to termites and wood-decaying fungi. The "knees" are unique features projecting upwards out of the soil or water. *Taxodium mucronatum,* the big cypress tree of Tule in the state of Oaxaca, Mexico, is about 12 meters in diameter and is estimated to be from 2000 to 4000 years old. It may have resulted from natural grafting of several trees planted close together.

Sequoia sempervirens (redwood) reaches about 110 meters in height and *Sequoiadendron giganteum* (big tree or giant sequoia) about 96 meters. Giant sequoia does not attain the height of the redwood but greatly surpasses it in diameter. The redwood is valued for its decay-resistant timber.

Metasequoia glyptostroboides (dawn redwood), from central China, is often called a living fossil since it was found living after it was named and described originally from fossil material.

Cryptomeria, Sciadopitys, and *Cunninghamia* are often grown as ornamentals in parts of North America.

Eckenwalder (1976) has proposed the inclusion of Taxodiaceae in the family Cupressaceae on basis of the pattern of similarities that the genera display.

Economic Importance   The family is of considerable importance as a source of decay-resistant lumber. Several species are used as ornamental trees.

Taxaceae: Yew or Taxus Family

Field Recognition   *Microsporophylls peltate; ovules solitary and terminal; seed surrounded by a fleshy aril.*

Description   *Habit*   Much-branched trees or shrubs.

Leaves   Evergreen, alternate, often two-ranked, with three light-green and two dark-green bands beneath.

Reproduction   Plants dioecious. Microsporophylls shield-shaped with six to eight microsporangia, occurring in strobili. Ovulate structure a solitary, terminal ovule with a fleshy aril at the base. Seed dry, nutlike, surrounded or enveloped by a fleshy, often brightly colored aril.

Size, Distribution, and General Information   A family of about 5 genera and 20 species of the Northern Hemisphere, south to Mexico, the Celebes, and New Caledonia.

The two genera occurring in North America are *Taxus* (10) (yew, taxus, Florida yew) and *Torreya* (6) (California nutmeg, stinking cedar, torreya).

Taxus is the largest genus in the family. Among its better-known species are *T. baccata* (common or English yew) of Europe, *T. canadensis* (Canada yew), and *T. brevifolia* (Pacific yew). *Taxus floridana* is endemic along the Apalachicola River in Florida. The wood of the yew is valuable. During the Middle Ages, *T. baccata* was the chief wood used in making bows. The leaves of *Taxus* are poisonous, but the aril is harmless.

Torreya has two species in North America: *T. californica* (California nutmeg) and *T. taxifolia* (stinking cedar) from Florida. The wood of stinking cedar is durable. This species is now rare, since many plants were destroyed for making fence posts.

Economic Importance   Several species and cultivars of *Taxus* are grown as ornamentals, and the wood is used in cabinet making. The family is of relatively little economic importance.

Ephedraceae: Ephedra Family

Field Recognition   *Stems jointed and photosynthetic; horsetail-like; with shrubby habit; leaves reduced to scales; cones small, deciduous, borne in stem axils.*

Description   *Habit*   Shrubs, much-branched; stem photosynthetic.
Leaves   Opposite, united, reduced to scales.

Reproduction   Plants usually dioecious. Staminate strobili compact, subglobose to oblong, compound, usually axillary, opposite or in whorls of three or four at nodes. Ovulate strobili elongated, opposite or in whorls of three to four at nodes, with several pairs of bracts along the axis; a single terminal ovule with two integuments, the outer of four bracts, the inner of two bracts which elongate at time of pollination. Seed has leathery covering, globose to cylindric, membranous or winged or forming a berrylike red structure.

Size, Distribution, and General Information   A family of one genus, *Ephedra*, and about 40 species of America and Eurasia. In the southwestern United States, *Ephedra* is called "joint fir" or "Mormon tea" from its use in making a beverage by Mormon pioneers. The Asiatic species, *E. sinica* and *E. equisetina*, are the source of the drug ephedrine.

Economic Importance   The family is important as the source of ephedrine and for species grown as ornamentals in desert areas.

SELECTED REFERENCES

Arnold, C. A.: "Classification of the Gymnosperms from the Viewpoint of Paleobotany," *Bot. Gaz.*, **110:**2–12, 1948.
————: "Origin and Relationship of the Cycads," *Phytomorphology*, **3:**51–65, 1953.

Bailey, L. H.: *The Cultivated Conifers in North America,* Macmillan, New York, 1933.

Bierhorst, D. W.: *Morphology of Vascular Plants,* Macmillan, New York, 1971.

Bold, H. C.: *Morphology of Plants,* 3d ed., Harper & Row, New York, 1973.

Chamberlain, C. J.: *Gymnosperms: Structure and Evolution,* The University of Chicago Press, Chicago, 1935. (Reprinted by Dover, New York, 1966.)

Coulter, J. M., and C. J. Chamberlain: *Morphology of Gymnosperms,* The University of Chicago Press, Chicago, 1917.

Cronquist, A., A. Takhtajan, and W. Zimmermann: "On the Higher Taxa of Embryobionta," *Taxon,* **15:**129–134, 1966.

Dallimore, W., and A. B. Jackson: *A Handbook of Coniferae and Ginkgoaceae,* 4th ed., S. G. Harrison (ed.), St. Martin's, New York, 1967. (A standard reference work on the world's conifers, illustrated.)

Eckenwalder, J. E.: "Re-evaluation of Cupressaceae and Taxodiaceae: A Proposed Merger," *Madroño,* **23:**237–256, 1976.

————: "Comments on A New Classification of the Conifers," *Taxon,* **25:**337–339, 1976.

————: "Taxonomy of the West Indian Cycads," *J. Arnold Arboretum,* **61:**701–722, 1980.

Ferguson, D. K.: "Some Current Research on Fossil and Recent Taxads," *Rev. Paleobot. Palyno.,* **26:**213–226, 1978.

Foster, A. S., and E. M. Gifford: *Comparative Morphology of Vascular Plants,* 2d ed., Freeman, San Francisco, 1974.

Hardin, J. W.: "Studies on the Southeastern United States Flora. II. The Gymnosperms," *J. Elisha Mitchell Soc.,* **87:**43–50, 1971.

Harlow, W. M., and E. S. Harrar: *Textbook of Dendrology,* 5th ed., McGraw-Hill, New York, 1968.

Hutchinson, J.: "Contributions Towards a Phylogenetic Classification of Flowering Plants. III. The Genera of Gymnosperms." *Kew Bull.,* 49–66, 1924.

Meyen, S. V.: "Basic Features of Gymnosperm Systematics and Phylogeny as Evidenced by the Fossil Record," *Bot. Rev.,* **50:**1–111, 1984.

Miller, C. N., Jr.: "Mesozoic Conifers," *Bot. Rev.,* **43:**217–280, 1977.

Ouden, P. den, and B. K. Boom: *Manual of Cultivated Conifers Hardy in the Cold- and Warm-temperate Zone,* Martinus Nijhoff, The Hague, Netherlands, 1965. (Illustrated, useful for ornamentals.)

Rehder, A.: *Manual of Cultivated Trees and Shrubs,* 2d ed., Macmillan, New York, 1940. (Comprehensive, useful for ornamentals.)

Sporne, K. R.: *The Morphology of Gymnosperms,* 2nd ed. Hutchinson University Library, London, 1974.

Stewart, W. N.: *Paleobotany and the Evolution of Plants,* Cambridge University Press, Cambridge, 1983.

Taylor, T. N.: *Paleobotany: An Introduction to Fossil Plant Biology,* McGraw-Hill, New York, 1981.

CHAPTER 14

ANGIOSPERM FAMILIES

In addition to nomenclature, history, and theoretical considerations of systematics, students of taxonomy are expected to become familiar with the more important families of flowering plants. It is beyond the scope of this book to deal with all the families of angiosperms. Those that have been selected for discussion were chosen because of their large number of species, economic importance, or unusual features. The arrangement of categories follows that of Cronquist (1981).

Treatments of the families have been made as uniform as the individual situations permit. The characters of each family have been compiled from the literature, including Heywood (1978), Hutchinson (1973), Lawrence (1951), and Willis (1973). The floral formulas follow the method outlined in Chapter 10. Variation in number of floral parts is indicated in the following manner: "sepals (3)5(10)" indicates "normally 5 but sometimes 3 or 10 sepals;" ∞ means "variably numerous."

The number of taxa in the families was obtained from Willis (1973) or more recent sources such as Cronquist (1981). Scientific names generally follow Hutchinson (1973) and Willis (1973). The number of species in a genus is indicated in parentheses, for example, *Magnolia* (80). The distribution of each family is generalized and serves to indicate the region of natural occurrence. Illustrations of selected representative taxa have been provided to portray the more significant structural features. Many of the illustrations have been redrawn from Baillon (1867–1895). Several families that are likely to be confused are compared in Table 14-1.

TABLE 14-1
A COMPARISON OF SOME FAMILIES THAT ARE LIKELY TO BE CONFUSED*

A. Families	Leaves	Stems	Perianth	Bracts†	Fruit
Juncaceae	Basal, forming tufts, sheaths closed	Round, solid	6-parted	Several	Capsule
Gramineae	Ligulate, sheaths open (mostly), 2-ranked	Round, hollow at internodes	Lodicule(s)	2 (palea, lemma)	Grain or caryopsis (achene, berry)
Cyperaceae	Sheaths closed, 3-ranked	3-sided, solid	Bristles, hairs, scales	1	Achene, nutlet

B. Families	Leaves	Leaf bases	Gynoecium	Fruit
Alismataceae	Basal, simple	Sheathing	Many separate carpels	Achene
Ranunculaceae	Compound, alternate (opposite)	Mostly sheathing	3-many separate carpels	Follicle, achene, berry, capsule
Rosaceae	Compound (simple), alternate	Stipulate	Highly variable, ovary free or adnate to hypanthium	Achene, aggregate, drupe, pome, follicle
Saxifragaceae	Alternate, simple	Exstipulate	2 (−5) united carpels	Capsule
Crassulaceae	Simple, alternate or opposite, usually succulent	Exstipulate	3 (+) separate carpels subtended by glandular scale	Follicle

C. Families	Leaves	Symmetry	Stamens	Gynoecium	Fruit	Inflorescences	Other
Scrophulariaceae	Alternate (opposite)	Zygomorphic	(2) 4 (+ staminode)	2 carpellate	Capsule, berry	Various	Some parasitic
Boraginaceae	Alternate	Actinomorphic	5, epipetalous	4-lobed ovary (bicarpellary)	4 nutlets	Coiled cymes	Rough texture
Verbenaceae	Opposite or whorled	Zygomorphic-salverform	(2) 4 (5) didynamous	Single, terminal style	Drupe or nutlet	Cymes	Often woody in tropics
Lamiaceae	Opposite or whorled	Zygomorphic-bilabiate	(2) 4 didynamous	Gynobasic style, 4-lobed ovary (bicarpellary)	4 nutlets	In whorls or axillary	Glandular, volatile oils
Solanaceae	Alternate	Actinomorphicrotate to tubular (zygomorphic)	5 (2, 2 + 2, 4)	2 carpels	Berry	Cymose	enlarged calyx in fruit (some), rank smell

*Note that *not* all features are present in all members of the family and that there are *few* families distinguished by a single, uniform feature.
†Bracts subtending the inflorescence are not considered.

CLASS MAGNOLIOPSIDA: Dicotyledons

SUBCLASS I, MAGNOLIIDAE: ORDER 1, MAGNOLIALES

Winteraceae: Winter's Bark Family

Field Recognition   Trees and shrubs; leaves alternate, simple, conspicuously glaucous beneath; $CA^{2-6} CO^{4-\infty\ 15-\infty} A^{15-\infty} \underline{G}^{1-\infty\ or\ \boxed{1-\infty}}$.

Description *Habit* Trees or shrubs.
Leaves Alternate, leathery, entire, simple, without stipules.
Inflorescences Mostly in fascicles or cymes.
Flowers Usually bisexual, actinomorphic, parts spirally inserted. Calyx of 2–6 sepals. Corolla of 4 to many petals, calyx and corolla not well differentiated. Androecium of 15 to many short, broad stamens. Gynoecium of 1 to several stalked, free to fused carpels, ovules few to many, placentation marginal, ovary superior, with an elongate, decurrent stigma. See Figure 14-1.
Fruit Berrylike, of follicular origin.
Seed Endosperm abundant, embryo rudimentary.

FIGURE 14-1
Drimys winteri (Winteraceae). (a) Flowering branch and (b) vertical section of flower.

(a)

(b)

Winteraceae

Size, Distribution, and General Information   A family of around 9 genera and about 100 species found in montane to cool temperate forests of continents bordering the South Pacific and on islands in the South Pacific. The family is of morphological interest because of its primitive vessel-less wood, largely undifferentiated stamens, and style-less, unsealed carpels with their long stigmatic surface. The best known genus is *Drimys* with 4 species from Mexico to the southern tip of South America. *Drimys winteri* is often grown in botanical gardens.

Economic Importance   Some species have horticultural and/or medicinal value. Winter's bark, from *D. winteri,* was once used to prevent scurvy.

SUBCLASS I, MAGNOLIIDAE; ORDER 1, MAGNOLIALES
Magnoliaceae: Magnolia Family

Field Recognition   Trees or shrubs; leaves simple, alternate; stipules deciduous and leaving a stipular ring at each node; flowers conspicuous, actinomorphic; stamens and carpels numerous; perianth$^{6-18}$ A$^\infty$ $\underline{G}^\infty$.

Description   *Habit*   Shrubs or trees.
Leaves   Alternate, simple, pinnately veined, petioled; stipules present and enclosing the bud, early deciduous and leaving a stipular scar or ring at each node.
Inflorescences   Usually solitary.
Flowers   Bisexual, rarely unisexual, actinomorphic. Perianth spiral to cyclic in 3 or more series of 6 to 18 parts. Androecium of numerous stamens, spirally arranged on the basal part of the floral axis. Gynoecium of numerous (rarely few), separate, simple pistils, each with a unilocular carpel, spirally arranged on the upper part of the elongated floral axis, placentation marginal, ovary superior. See Figure 14-2.
Fruit   A follicle, a samara, or (rarely) a berry, sometimes aggregated into a woody conelike structure.
Seed   Often suspended within the follicle by a threadlike funiculus.
Embryo   Minute, in a large endosperm.

Systematics   Present-day members of the Magnoliaceae are relatively specialized in certain vegetative, floral, and cytological features. The family is characterized by oil passages in its parenchyma tissue. Magnoliaceae is divided into two tribes. Magnolieae and Liriodendreae. *Liriodendron* is the only genus in the Liriodendreae.

Size, Distribution, and General Information   A family of about 12 genera and 230 species occurring primarily in the warm temperate regions of the Northern Hemisphere, with aggregates of species in eastern North America and eastern Asia. It ranges southward into Malaysia, the West Indies, and Brazil. The majority of the species are Asiatic.

Magnoliaceae

FIGURE 14-2
Magnolia (Magnoliaceae). (a) Flower showing numerous stamens
and carpels on an elongate receptacle and (b) dehisced fruits with
seed attached by thread-like funiculus (latter redrawn from
Heywood, 1978).

Some of the important genera are *Magnolia* (80) (bullbay, cucumber tree); *Liriodendron* (2) (tulip tree, yellow poplar); and *Michelia* (50) (banana shrub).

The evergreen *Magnolia grandiflora,* with its large shining leaves and handsome cream-white flowers, has become a symbol of the Deep South of the United States. When its petals open wide, they form a soft cup 20 centimeters across. The tulip tree or yellow poplar (*Liriodendron tulipifera*) of the eastern United States often grows rapidly to the height of 30 meters or more, and its diameter at breast height (DBH) may be nearly 2 meters. Its flowers appear tuliplike, with three recurved sepals and six stiff petals. As the carpels ripen into samaras, the winged fruits break off and are carried away by the wind.

Economic Importance   The Magnoliaceae are important as ornamentals and as a source of wood. *Magnolia soulangiana, M. stellata,* and other cultivars of Asiatic origin are widely grown as ornamentals in North America; *M. grandiflora* is a well-known ornamental tree. *Liriodendron tulipfera* is an important timber species in the southern Appalachians. *Michelia fuscata* is planted as an ornamental shrub in the warmer parts of the United States.

SUBCLASS I, MAGNOLIDAE; ORDER 1, MAGNOLIALES
Annonaceae: Custard Apple Family

Field Recognition   Trees and shrubs; leaves two-ranked, without stipules, with a glaucous or metallic sheen; perianth^{3+3+3} A$^{\infty}$ (rarely few) $\underline{G}^{\infty}$.

Description   *Habit*   Trees and shrubs (with one exception), sometimes lianalike.
Leaves   Alternate, two-ranked, entire; without stiples.
Inflorescences   Flowers solitary or inflorescences of various types.
Flowers   Bisexual (rarely unisexual). Perianth usually in three whorls of three, one or two of the outer whorls sepaloid. Androecium of numerous, spirally arranged stamens (rarely few). Gynoecium of few-numerous, usually separate carpels, placentation marginal or basal, ovary superior. See Figure 14-3.
Fruit   Berrylike. (In *Annona,* the berries coalesce with the fleshy receptacle).
Seed   Seeds with endosperm, of complicated and variable construction.

Size, Distribution, and General Information   The largest family in the Magnoliales with about 130 genera and 2300 species, largely pantropical but centered in the Old World Tropics. Some noteworthy genera are: *Annona* (120), *Asimina* (8), *Xylopia* (100–150), and *Monodora* (20).

Economic Importance   The family is cultivated in the tropics for fruits and flavorings.

The genus *Annona* was named after *anon,* the Haitian name for custard apple that is the tasty fruit of *Annona reticulata,* now widely cultivated in the tropics. Combining the flavors of strawberries, pineapples, and cinnamon, another West Indian species, *A. muricata,* is termed sour sop; while *A. squamosa* produces sweet sop and *A.*

FIGURE 14-3
Asimina triloba (Annonaceae). (a) Flowering shoot (redrawn from Heywood, 1978) and (b) vertical view of flower; note the numerous stamens located below the several pistils.

(b)

(a)   Annonaceae

cherimola, the cherimoya, is said to be the tastiest of the four. *Asimina* is one of the few temperate-zone members of the family although most of its species are not found much further north than Florida. *Asimina triloba* is a large shrub common in mesic woodlands as far north as New York. The source of Guinea pepper is *Xylopia aethiopica,* a shrub from tropical West Africa. The seeds of *Monodora myristica,* an African species, contain an oil used as a nutmeg substitute. Brought to the West Indies by slaves, it became known as Jamaican nutmeg.

SUBCLASS I, MAGNOLIIDAE; ORDER 2, LAURALES
Calycanthaceae: Strawberry-shrub Family

Field Recognition   Shrubs; leaves opposite, simple, without stipules; perianth$^\infty$ A$^{5-30}$ $\underline{G}^\infty$.

Description   *Habit*   Shrubs, deciduous or evergreen.
Leaves   Opposite, simple, entire; without stipules.
Inflorescences   Flowers axillary and solitary.
Flowers   Bisexual, actinomorphic, and fragrant. Perianth spirally arranged, in several overlapping series with a gradual transition from sepals to petals. Androecium of numerous stamens, inserted on rim of a thick cuplike receptacle, the inner stamens sterile. Gynoecium of up to 20 separate carpels, attached to hollowed axis of receptacle, each carpel one locular, with 1 or 2 ovules in each locule, placentation marginal, ovary superior. See Figure 14-4.
Fruit   One-seeded achenes enclosed by the enlarged receptacle.
Seeds   Embryo large, with relatively little endosperm.

Size, Distribution, and General Information   A small family of 2 (sometimes 3) genera with 5 species in North America and eastern Asia. *Calycanthus* (3) occurs in the southwest and eastern United States; and *Chimonanthus* (4) is found in eastern Asia.

Calycanthaceae

FIGURE 14-4
Calycanthus floridus (Calycanthaceae). Vertical section of flower.

Economic Importance   The family is of minor importance for several ornamental shrubs. *Calycanthus floridus* (sweet shrub or Carolina all-spice) and *C. occidentalis* are prized for their scented, spring blooming flowers; *Chimonanthus fragrans* (wintersweet) is cultivated for its fragrant winter flowers. The seeds of *Calycanthus* are poisonous.

SUBCLASS I, MAGNOLIIDAE; ORDER 2, LAURALES
Lauraceae: Laurel Family

Field Recognition   Aromatic trees or shrubs; leaves usually alternate; perianth small and undifferentiated; stamens 3-merous in several whorls, anthers with valvate dehiscence; fruit a single seeded drupe or berry; $CA^{3\ +\ 3}\ CO^0\ A^{3+3+3+3}\ \underline{G}^1$.

Description   *Habit*   Aromatic trees or shrubs; one genus is a parasitic vine.

Leaves   Alternate, rarely opposite, simple, pinnately veined, usually entire, deciduous in temperate regions, evergreen in tropics; without stipules.

Inflorescences   Usually axillary, panicles, spikes, racemes, or umbels.

Flowers   Usually bisexual, sometimes unisexual, actinomorphic. Calyx of 6 sepals, in 2 series united into a tube at the base. Corolla lacking. Androecium of 4 whorls of 3 stamens each, or 1 or more whorls reduced to staminodes or absent, adnate to perianth tube. Gynoecium a simple pistil with 1 carpel, 1 locule, and 1 ovule, placentation marginal, ovary superior, style 1, stigma 1. See Figure 14-5.

FIGURE 14-5
Sassafras albidum (Lauraceae). (a) Leafy branch, (b) staminate flower, and (c) pistillate flower.

(a)   (b)   (c)

Lauraceae

Fruit   A drupe or berry often surrounded at the base by a cupule derived from the persistent calyx tube.

Embryo   Large, straight; endosperm absent.

Systematics   The family is divided into two subfamilies: Lauroideae, which is arborescent; and Cassythoideae, with the parasitic twiner *Cassytha*. Lauroideae is classified into five tribes: (1) Perseeae (*Persea*); (2) Cinnamomeae (*Cinnamomum*); (3) Laureae (*Lindera*); (4) Cryptocaryeae (*Cryptocarya*); and (5) Hypodaphnideae (*Hypodaphnis*).

Size, Distribution, and General Information   A family of 30 or more genera and 2000 to 2500 species distributed in tropical and subtropical regions of both hemispheres, with the greatest diversity in Southeast Asia. *Umbellularia californica* (myrtle, bay tree, or pepperwood) occurs along the Pacific Coast in the western United States. The family is common in the southeastern United States. *Sassafras albidum* and *Lindera* (spicebush) extend into Canada.

Some of the important genera are *Cinnamomum* (250); *Persea* (150); *Sassafras* (3); *Lindera* (100) (spicebush); *Nectandra* (100); *Cassytha* (20); and *Laurus* (2) (laurel).

According to Greek legend, the large evergreen shrub *Laurus nobilis* (laurel) was sacred to Apollo, and branches were woven into crowns for victors in the ancient Olympic games. Later, laurel became the symbol of triumph in Rome. Today the shrub is cultivated in the warmer parts of the United States, and laurel wreaths are still used ceremonially in some parts of the world.

Economic Importance   Economically, the family is of importance for its aromatic oils. *Cinnamomum camphora* of China and Japan yields camphor; *C. zeylanicum* is cultivated for cinnamon in Sri Lanka and elsewhere. The avocado is *Persea americana*. *Sassafras albidum* yields oil of sassafras, and the bark from the roots is boiled for tea. The leaves of *Sassafras* are used in Creole cooking along with those of *Persea borbonia*. The woods of some species are used in cabinetmaking or marine shipbuilding. *Ocotea bullata* (black stinkwood) from southeastern Africa is used in making heavy, handsome furniture.

SUBCLASS I, MAGNOLIIDAE; ORDER 3, PIPERALES
Piperaceae: Pepper Family

Field Recognition   Leaves alternate, simple, petioles winged; stem jointed; flowers small, bisexual or unisexual in racemes or spikes that are leaf-opposed, appearing terminal; CA^0 CO^0 A^{1-10} $\underline{G}\overline{(2-4)}$.

Description *Habit*   Herbs, woody climbers, shrubs or small trees.

Leaves   Alternate, simple, entire, petiole base winged; stipulate.

Inflorescences   Racemose or spicate; usually leaf-opposed.

Piperaceae

FIGURE 14-6
Piperaceae. (a) *Piper nigrum* fruiting branch; (b) *Piperomia* fruiting branch and (c) flower.

Flowers Bisexual or unisexual. Perianth absent. Androecium of 1–10 stamens. Gynoecium of 2–4 united carpels, 1-locular, 1-seeded, placentation basal, ovary superior, stigmas short, 1–5. See Figure 14-6.
Fruit A small drupe.
Seed With mealy perisperm.

Size, Distribution, and General Information A pan-tropical family of about 10 genera and a large but highly uncertain number of species variously estimated to be from about 1400 to over 2000. The bulk of the species belong to only two genera, *Piper* and *Peperomia*. The Piperaceae are unusual for dicotyledons in their vascular anatomy by having scattered vascular bundles.

Economic Importance Cultivars of *Piper nigrum* are the source of black pepper. The fresh leaves of *Piper betle* (betel pepper) are chewed as a masticatory in tropical Asia and also in Africa. Many species of *Peperomia* are grown as house plants and are important in the tropical foliage plant industry because of their lovely leaves.

SUBCLASS I, MAGNOLIIDAE; ORDER 4, ARISTOLOCHIALES
Aristolochiaceae: Birthwort Family

Field Recognition   Herbs or shrubs (mainly lianas); leaves alternate, often cordate and palmately veined; $CA^{3(4)} CO^{0(3)} A^{6-36} \overline{G} \overline{(4-6)}$ or $\overline{A^{6-36}} \overline{G(4-6)}$.

Description   *Habit*   Herbs or shrubs, the latter mostly twining lianas.

Leaves   Alternate, often cordate, usually simple, often palmately veined; without stipules.

Inflorescences   Flowers axillary, solitary or arranged in racemes or cymes.

Flowers   Bisexual, actinomorphic or zygomorphic. Calyx 3 or 4 lobed (or irregularly 1–3 lobed). Corolla usually absent, rarely with 3 vestigial petals. Androecium of 6–36 stamens, free or partially fused, forming a staminal column (gynostemium). Gynoecium a compound pistil of 4–6 carpels, ovules numerous, placentation axile or parietal, ovary inferior, with 3–6 stigmas. See Figure 14-7.

Fruit   A many seeded capsule.

Seed   Seeds small with much endosperm.

Size, Distribution, and General Information   A family of some 8 to 10 genera and about 600 species distributed in tropical and temperate America, Asia, Africa, and Europe but absent in Australia. Two of the larger genera are *Aristolochia* (500), and *Asarum* (70).

FIGURE 14-7
Aristolochiaceae. (a) *Asarum (Hexastylis) virginicum,* flowering shoot, (b) *Aristolochia* vertical section of flower, and (c) intact flower.

Aristolochiaceae

Economic Importance   Many species of *Asarum* and *Aristolochia* are cultivated as ornamentals. Because of its bent perianth tube and brownish flowers, *Aristolochia macrophylla* is called Dutchman's pipe and is often grown as an ornamental vine. *Aristolochia serpentaria* (Virginia snakeroot) has been used medically.

SUBCLASS I, MAGNOLIIDAE; ORDER 6, NYMPHAEALES
Nymphaeaceae: Water Lily Family

Field Recognition   Perennial aquatic herbs; leaves long-petioled, peltate; flowers large, long-peduncled, floral parts often numerous; $CA^{3-\infty} CO^{3-\infty} A^{\infty} \underline{G}^{\infty}$.

Description   *Habit*   Perennial aquatic herbs with large rhizomes.
Leaves   Alternate; floating, submerged, or emersed; pinnately veined, petiolate, peltate.
Inflorescences   Axillary and solitary.
Flowers   Bisexual, actinomorphic. Calyx of 3 to many sepals. Corolla of numerous petals frequently grading into the stamens. Androecium of numerous stamens. See Figure 14-8. Gynoecium of numerous simple pistils each having 1 carpel, with 1 locule, ovules numerous, placentation marginal, ovary superior to inferior.
Fruit   A spongy berry.
Seed   With endosperm and perisperm and sometimes arillate.

FIGURE 14-8
Nymphaea (Nymphaeaceae). Vertical section of flower with part of the perianth removed.

Nymphaeaceae

Size, Distribution, and General Information   A family of 5 genera and 80 species of cosmopolitan distribution. The five genera are *Nymphaea* (50) (water lily); *Nuphar* (25) (cow lily, spadderdock, yellow pond lily); *Ondinea* (1). *Euryale* (1); and *Victoria* (3) (royal water lily).

Members of the water lily family are favorite plants for garden pools. The variously colored flowers of *Nymphaea* open just above the surface of the water. The golden-yellow flowers of *Nuphar advena* extend up and out of the water. *Nymphaea lotus* is considered to have been the original sacred lotus of Egypt. (*Nelumbo* [Nelumbonaceae], often called *sacred lotus,* was not introduced into Egypt until about 500 B.C.) The South American *Victoria amazonica* is often grown in conservatories.

Economic Importance   Horticultural hybrids of *Nymphaea* are numerous. *Nymphaea* sometimes becomes weedy in lakes and ponds.

SUBCLASS I, MAGNOLIIDAE; ORDER 7, RANUNCULALES
Ranunculaceae: Buttercup, Crowfoot Family

Field Recognition   Mostly herbs; leaves with sheathing leaf bases, blades often divided; flowers mostly bisexual with spirally arranged, numerous stamens and carpels, $CA^{3-\infty}\ CO^{5-\infty}\ A^{\infty}\ \underline{G}^{3-\infty(1-3)}$.

Description   *Habit*   Annual or perennial herbs, sometimes shrubs or vines.

Leaves   Mostly alternate, often palmately divided, petioles sheathing at base; lacking stipules.

Inflorescences   Solitary to paniculate, or in racemes or cymes.

Flowers   Typically bisexual, actinomorphic or zygomorphic, parts spirally arranged. Calyx of 3 to many sepals. Corolla of 5 to many petals, rarely absent; nectariferous glands often present. Calyx and corolla often not differentiated. Androecium of 5 to many stamens, free, spirally arranged. Gynoecium of 3 to many simple pistils having 1 carpel, with 1 locule, ovules 1 to many, placentation marginal, ovary superior, style 1, and stigma 1. See Figure 14-9.

Fruit   A follicle, achene, or berry, or rarely a capsule.

Seed   With minute embryo and oily endosperm.

Ranunculaceae

FIGURE 14-9
Vertical section of a generalized flower of *Ranunculus* (Ranunculaceae).

Systematics The perianth varies greatly and is of importance in delimiting genera. Generic concepts have varied widely over the past 70 years in North America, as illustrated by the different treatments in various floras.

Size, Distribution, and General Information A family of about 50 genera and 1900 species found primarily in the temperate regions of the Northern Hemisphere, with concentrations in eastern Asia and eastern North America.

Some of the important genera are *Ranunculus* (400) (buttercup); *Clematis* (250) (Virgin's bower); *Thalictrum* (150); *Aquilegia* (100) (columbine); *Delphinium* (250) (larkspur); *Anemone* (150) (windflower); *Helleborus* (20) (Christmas rose, Lenten rose); and *Aconitum* (300) (monkshood).

Many people recognize the widespread, often weedy genus *Ranunculus*. *Hepatica* (liverleaf) grows across Eurasia and in North America, and its three-lobed leaves resembling the liver were formerly used to treat liver ailments. Cattle raisers in some parts of the West refer to *Delphinium* as "locoweed" because cattle that eat *Delphinium* may develop a staggering walk and other symptoms.

Economic Importance The Ranunculaceae are important as ornamental, drug, and poisonous plants. They are best known for their flowers, e.g., columbine, larkspur, buttercup, windflower, Lenten rose, and Christmas rose. Alkaloids are obtained from *Aconitum; A. ferox* of Nepal is the source of bikh poison. Wolfbane of Europe, *A. napellus,* yields aconite. Roots of the golden seal (*Hydrastis*), used to treat stomach ailments, are sold in the crude drug trade.

SUBCLASS I, MAGNOLIIDAE; ORDER 7, RANUNCULALES
Berberidaceae: Barberry Family

Field Recognition Herbs or shrubs; stamens biseriate, the outer opposite the petals, anthers dehiscing by flaps; $CA^{3+3} CO^{3+3} A^6 \underline{G}^1$.

Description *Habit* Perennial herbs and shrubs.

Leaves Alternate or basal, simple or compound, deciduous or evergreen, often spiny; stipules absent.

Inflorescences Solitary, cymes, or racemes.

Flowers Bisexual, actinomorphic. Calyx of 3 to 6 sepals, free and distinct. Corolla of 3 to 6 petals, free and distinct; petal-like nectaries sometimes present. Androecium of 6 stamens, distinct, anthers opening by flaps. Gynoecium of a simple pistil having 1 carpel with 1 locule, ovules few and basal, placentation marginal, ovary superior. Figure 14-10.

Fruit A berry or follicle.

Seed With copious endosperm.

Embryo Small (elongate in *Berberis*).

Berberidaceae

FIGURE 14-10
Berberis (Berberidaceae). (a) Flowering branch and (b) flower.

Size, Distribution and General Information   A family of about 13 genera and 650 species widely distributed throughout much of the Northern Hemisphere and South America.

Some important genera are *Berberis* (450) (barberry); *Mahonia* (70) (Oregon grape); *Nandina* (1) (heavenly bamboo); and *Podophyllum* (11) (mayapple).

The Berberidaceae have several genera with disjunct eastern North American—eastern Asian ranges. *Podophyllum* has one species in eastern North America, others in eastern Asia. *Diphylleia* has one species in the southeastern United States and one in Japan. *Jeffersonia* has one species in eastern United States and one in Manchuria. *Caulophyllum* has one species in eastern United States and another in eastern Asia.

Economic Importance   The family is of economic importance as a source of many beautiful garden shrubs: *Berberis thunbergii* (Japanese barberry); *Mahonia aquifolium* (Oregon grape); and *Nandina domestica* (heavenly bamboo). The common barberry (*B. vulgaris*) is the host for the sexual phase of the wheat stem rust. A drug prepared from the rhizome of *Podophyllum peltatum* (mayapple) promotes the discharge of bile from the liver.

SUBCLASS I, MAGNOLIIDAE; ORDER 8, PAPAVERALES

Papaveraceae: Poppy Family

Field Recognition   Herbs; flowers bisexual; sepals deciduous; petals crumpled in the bud; stamens numerous in several whorls; ovary unilocular; fruit usually a capsule; sap usually milky or colored; $CA^{2-3} CO^{4-\infty} A^{\infty} \underline{G}^{2-\infty}$.

Description   *Habit*   Annual to perennial herbs, rarely woody, usually with milky or colored sap.

Leaves   Alternate, basal or cauline, often much divided.

Inflorescences   Solitary showy flowers.

Flowers   Bisexual, actinomorphic. Calyx of 2 to 3 distinct, early deciduous sepals. Corolla of 4 to 6 or more petals, in two series, often crumpled in the bud. Androecium of numerous stamens, free. Gynoecium a compound pistil of 2 or more united carpels, with 1 locule, placentation of 2 to many parietal placentas, ovary superior. See Figure 14-11.

FIGURE 14-11
Papaver somniferum
(Papaveraceae). (a) Flowering
shoot and (b) fruit.

(a)　　　　　　(b)

Papaveraceae

Fruit   A capsule opening by valves or pores.
Seed   Numerous and small.
Embryo   Minute, in copious fleshy or oily endosperm.

Size, Distribution, and General Information   A family of about 25 genera and 200 species mostly of Northern Hemisphere distribution.

Some important genera are *Papaver* (100) (true poppy); *Eschscholzia* (10) (California poppy); *Sanguinaria* (1) (bloodroot); *Argemone* (10) (prickly poppy); and *Chelidonium* (1) (celandine).

The true poppies (*Papaver*) have a milky white juice, and the capsule resembles a pepper shaker opening by a series of small holes around the rim of the flat top. Here the seeds are protected from the rain and can only escape when the capsule is shaken. *Papaver somniferum* is the opium poppy. The drug is obtained by cutting notches in the half-ripened capsules, from which the latex exudes. The seeds of this species are used to add a slight tang to breads and cookies. When pressed, the seeds yield a cooking oil.

One of the first spring wild flowers in eastern North America is *Sanguinaria canadensis,* or bloodroot. It is named for its bright orange-red juice that oozes quickly from its freshly cut rhizome. Its rhizome yields an alkaloid used in medicine.

Economic Importance   The family is of little economic importance except for opium and its narcotic alkaloids. It is illegal to grow the opium poppy in the United States. Several other species of *Papaver* are grown as ornamentals, including *P. orientale* (oriental poppy) and the Iceland poppy (*P. nudicaule*). The bright red flowers of the European field poppy are associated with some of the battlefields of World War I. The California poppy (*Eschscholzia california*), which has brilliant golden-orange flowers, is common in parts of the southwestern United States.

SUBCLASS I, MAGNOLIIDAE; ORDER 8, PAPAVERALES
Fumariaceae: Fumitory or Dutchman's Breeches Family

Field Recognition   Herbs with watery juice, the perennials in the family have swollen cormlike root-stocks; leaves usually variously divided; CA^2 CO^{2+2} A^6 $\underline{G}^{②}$.

Description   *Habit*   Annual and perennial herbs.
Leaves   Leaves alternate, variously divided (rarely simple), sometimes with tendril-like leaf axes.
Inflorescences   Usually racemose.
Flowers   Bisexual, zygomorphic, of complex and unusual structure. Calyx of 2 sepals, deciduous. Corolla of 2 series of 2 petals each, one or both outer petals more or less spurred at base, the apexes of the inner 2 petals often fused around the anthers.

(a)   (b)

Fumariaceae

FIGURE 14-12
Corydalis sempervirens (Fumariaceae).
(a) Flowering shoot, (b) flower.

Androecium of 2 bundles, positioned opposite the inner petals, each bundle divided
into 3 parts at the apex, the central division bearing a complete anther, the 2 lateral
parts of each bundle bearing half an anther. Gynoecium a compound pistil of 2 united
carpels, 1-locular, with 1 to many seeds, placentation parietal, ovary superior. See
Figure 14-12.

Fruit   A one-seeded nutlet or slender capsule.

Seed   Black and shiny, often with an aril or caruncle.

Size, Distribution, and General Information   A family of about 19 genera and
400 or more species, occurring mainly in temperate North America, Europe, Asia,
and Africa. The best known genera are: *Fumaria* (50), *Corydalis* (300), and *Dicentra*
(20).

Economic Importance   Of little economic importance; however, species of *Dicentra* (Dutchman's breeches, bleeding heart) are grown as garden perennials. Some
species of *Fumaria* are weeds.

SUBCLASS II, HAMAMELIDAE; ORDER 2, HAMAMELIDALES
Platanaceae: Plane-Tree or Sycamore Family

Field Recognition   Deciduous trees; leaves alternate, simple, usually palmately lobed and veined, swollen petiole base covering axillary bud; spherical heads of unisexual flowers; $CA^{3-8}\ CO^{3-8}\ A^{3-8}\ \underline{G}^{6-9(3)}$ [the floral formula has various interpretations by specialists in the group].

Description   *Habit*   Large trees with scaling bark.
Leaves   Deciduous, alternate, simple, palmately lobed or veined (rarely elliptic-oblong and pinnately veined); petiole base covering the axillary bud; stipules large, embracing the stem, deciduous.
Inflorescences   Unisexual flowers in spherical heads on long, separate peduncles.
Flowers   Unisexual, borne on same tree. Calyx of 3–8 small, free, hairy sepals. Corolla of 3–8 large spathulate petals [some authorities recognize a basic 4-merous pattern, others reject the presence of a perianth]. Male flowers with 3–8 stamens; female flowers often with 3–4 staminodes. Gynoecium with 6–9(3) free carpels, ovules 1 or 2 per carpel, ovary superior, styles tapering, stigmatic portion on inner surface. See Figure 14-13.
Fruit   A globose head of achenes or caryopses with persistent styles, each individual fruit surrounded by a ring of long bristly hairs.
Seed   Each fruit with one seed, little endosperm, and wind-dispersed.

Size, Distribution, and General Information   A small family of 1 genus (*Platanus*) and 6 or 7 species in the north temperate zone; 2 species are Old World species and the remainder occur in North America.

Economic Importance   Plane tree or sycamores are often grown as street trees.

SUBCLASS II, HAMAMELIDAE; ORDER 2, HAMAMELIDALES
Hamamelidaceae: Witch Hazel or Sweet Gum Family

Field Recognition   Trees and shrubs; leaves usually alternate, simple or palmately lobed; $CA^{\overline{4-5}}\ CO^{4-5(0)}\ A^{4-5(10)}\ \overline{\underline{G}}^{②}$.

Description   *Habit*   Trees and shrubs.
Leaves   Usually alternate, simple or palmately lobed; stipules present.
Inflorescences   Racemose, often a spike or head; sometimes with an involucre of colored bracts.
Flowers   Bisexual or unisexual, monoecious or dioecious. Calyx of 4 to 5 united sepals. Corolla of 4 to 5 separate petals or sometimes absent. Androecium of 4–5(10) stamens. Gynoecium of 2 united carpels, with 2 locules and 2 styles, ovules 1 or more in each locule, ovary superior to inferior. See Figure 14-14.
Fruit   Capsule with woody exocarp.
Seed   Embryo straight, containing endosperm.

Platanaceae

FIGURE 14-13
Platanus (Platanaceae). Fruiting branch.

Size, Distribution, and General Information   A family of about 26 genera (13 of them monotypic) and 100 species, with a discontinuous subtropical and temperate distribution. The family appears loosely knit with many apparent relict genera. Some of the genera include *Hamamelis* (6), *Liquidambar* (6), *Fothergilla* (4), *Corylopsis* (20), *Loropetalum* (3).

Economic Importance   The family is the source of many ornamental trees and shrubs such as *Fothergilla, Loropetalum, Hamamelis* and *Corylopsis*. The witch hazel of pharmacy is *Hamamelis virginiana*. A fragrant gum is obtained from sweet gum

FIGURE 14-14
Hamamelis (Hamamelidaceae). Flowering branch (redrawn from Heywood, 1978).

Hamamelidaceae

(*Liquidambar styraciflua* and *L. orientalis*), the former yielding a low quality timber that is difficult to split for firewood.

SUBCLASS II, HAMAMELIDAE; ORDER 6, URTICALES
Ulmaceae: Elm Family

Field Recognition   Trees or shrubs with watery sap; leaf bases oblique; fruit an evenly winged samara or drupe; $CA^{\overline{(4-8)}}CO^0 A^{4-8} \underline{G}^{\circledS}$.

Description   *Habit*   Trees or shrubs.
Leaves   Alternate, simple, deciduous, blades often oblique at base; stipules paired.
Inflorescences   Solitary, cymose, or fasciculate.
Flowers   Bisexual or unisexual, reduced. Calyx of 4 to 8 united sepals. Corolla lacking. Androecium of 4 to 8 stamens, inserted at bottom of calyx. Gynoecium a compound pistil of 2 carpels, with 1(2) locules, ovules solitary in each locule, ovary superior, pistil 1, styles 2. See Figure 14-15.
Fruit   A samara or drupe.
Seed   Without endosperm.

Systematics   The family is classified into two well-marked subfamilies: Ulmoideae and Celtidoideae.

FIGURE 14-15
Ulmus (Ulmaceae). (a) Branch with leaves, note the unequal leaf bases, and (b) bisexual flower.

(a)   (b)

Ulmaceae

Size, Distribution, and General Information   A family of about 18 genera and 150 or more species mostly of the north temperate zone.

Some important genera are *Ulmus* (20) (elm); *Zelkova* (6 to 7); *Planera* (1) (water elm); and *Celtis* (70) (sugarberry, hackberry).

Elms, such as *Ulmus americana* (American elm) and *U. laevis* (European white elm), were once important street trees in Western Europe and in eastern North America, but Dutch elm disease is gradually destroying these magnificent shade trees. Horticulturists are planting *Zelkova* as a possible replacement.

Economic Importance   The family is of importance for timber and for shade trees. Elms and hackberry trees, especially the latter, are of prime importance as horticultural plants throughout the western half of the United States and Canada. *Ulmus pumila* is widely planted, as are other Oriental elms. Hackberry trees are the standard avenue tree in the Rocky Mountain and Great Basin states.

SUBCLASS II, HAMAMELIDAE; ORDER 6, URTICALES
Cannabaceae: Hemp Family

Field Recognition   Erect (*Cannabis*) or climbing (*Humulus*), aromatic herbs; leaves opposite, palmately compound (in former), simple (in latter); flowers unisexual, plants dioecious, gynoecium unilocular; fruit an achene, partially hidden by persistent calyx; $(CA^5 CO^0 A^5 G^0)$ and $(CA^5 CO^0 A^0 \underline{G}^1)$. See Figure 14-16.

Size, Distribution, and General Information   A small family of 2 genera and 3 species; native to the north temperate zone. The Cannabaceae are sometimes placed in the Moraceae; however, the Cannabaceae differ notably from the Moraceae by having five floral parts instead of four.

Economic Importance   The highly variable species *Cannabis sativa* is the source of psychotropic drugs (marijuana and hashish) and hemp fiber. *Humulus lupulus* (hops) is cultivated and used in brewing beer; *H. japonica* (Japanese hops) is sometimes used as an ornamental vine.

SUBCLASS II, HAMAMELIDAE; ORDER 6, URTICALES
Moraceae: Mulberry Family

Field Recognition   Trees and shrubs, rarely herbs, with milky sap; flowers unisexual; stigmas usually 2; $(CA^4 CO^0 A^4 G^0)(CA^4 CO^0 A^0 \underline{G}^2)$.

Description   *Habit*   Trees, shrubs, or rarely herbs, with milky sap.
Leaves   Alternate, simple, pinnately or palmately veined, evergreen or deciduous, often lobed; stipules 2.
Inflorescences   Plants monoecious or dioecious; flowers in racemes, spikes, umbels, or heads or on the inside of a hollow receptacle.

(a)   (b)

Cannabaceae

FIGURE 14-16
Cannabaceae. (a) Pistillate branch of *Cannabis sativa* and (b) leaf and
cluster of pistillate flowers of *Humulus lupulus*.

Flowers   Unisexual, much reduced. Calyx of 4 sepals, free or united, sometimes
absent. Apetalous. Androecium of 4 stamens, opposite the sepals. Gynoecium a compound pistil of 2 united carpels, with 1 locule, ovary superior to inferior, pistil 1,
styles usually 2. See Figure 14-17.

Fruit   Basically drupes, often aggregated or united into a multiple fruit, or achenes
within or upon a fleshy receptacle.

Seed   With or without endosperm, embryo usually curved.

Size, Distribution, and General Information   A family of about 40 genera and
1000 species mostly of tropical and subtropical distribution; a few are temperate.

Some important genera are *Morus* (10) (mulberry); *Maclura* (12) (hedge apple,
osage orange); *Broussonetia* (7 to 8) (paper mulberry); *Ficus* (500) (fig, rubber plant,
Indian rubber tree); and *Artocarpus* (47) (breadfruit, jackfruit).

The leaves of *Morus alba* (white mulberry) are used to feed silkworms. Mulberry
fruits are edible, and *M. nigra* (black mulberry) is sometimes cultivated for its large
and juicy fruits.

Breadfruit (*Artocarpus altilis*) became the center of historical adventure associated
with the voyage of Captain William Bligh and his ship *Bounty* from Tahiti. Captain
Bligh collected breadfruit plants for introduction to the West Indies, after which

(a)   (b)   (c)

Moraceae

FIGURE 14-17
Morus alba (Moraceae). (a) Fruit and leaf, (b) staminate flower, and (c)
cluster of pistillate flowers.

Fletcher Christian (one of his officers) and many of the crew mutinied. Bligh was
placed adrift in a small boat, but he managed to survive and later introduced breadfruit
into Jamaica.

Ficus elastica (Indian rubber tree or rubber plant) is grown as a houseplant. Rubber
was made from its sap before the use of latex from Brazilian rubber trees of the family
Euphorbiaceae. The commercial fig is *F. carica*. Some species of *Ficus* are known
as strangler figs. They germinate high on the trunk of a tree and send roots down
around the trunk of the supporting plant. The roots interlace, and they appear to be
strangling the tree, which they often eventually succeed in doing.

Economic Importance   The Moraceae are perhaps most important as the source
of several food plants—e.g., fig and breadfruit—and a few ornamentals such as the
rubber plant and the osage orange.

SUBCLASS II, HAMAMELIDAE; ORDER 6, URTICALES

Urticaceae: Nettle Family

Field Recognition   Mostly herbs, many with stinging hairs; inflorescences cymose
on short axillary shoots; ovary unilocular, style 1; (CA$^{4-5}$ CO^0 A$^{4-5}$ G^0)(CA$^{4-5}$ CO^0
A^0 $\underline{G}^1$).

Description   *Habit*   Fibrous herbs, or rarely subshrubs or small, soft-wooded
trees.

Leaves   Alternate or opposite, simple, sometimes with stinging hairs; stipulate.

Inflorescences   Plants monoecious or dioecious; flowers are in cymes or heads,
or reduced to a solitary flower.

Flowers   Unisexual, actinomorphic, greatly reduced. Calyx of 4 to 5 sepals, free
or united, or calyx absent. Apetalous. Androecium of mostly 4 stamens, exploding
when ripe. Gynoecium a simple pistil of 1 carpel, with 1 locule, ovary superior. See
Figure 14-18.

Urticaceae

FIGURE 14-18
Urtica (Urticaceae). (a) Inflorescence, (b) staminate flower, and
(c) pistillate flower.

Fruit   An achene or fleshy drupe.
Seed   Mostly with endosperm.

Size, Distribution, and General Information   A family of about 45 genera and
700 species of tropical and temperate distribution.
Some important genera are *Urtica* (50) (nettle); *Laportea* (23) (wood nettle); *Pilea*
(400) (clear weed); *Boehmeria* (100) (ramie); and *Parietaria* (30) (pellitory).
Urtica (stinging nettle) has sharp, stiff, stinging hairs. When people or animals
brush against the plants, the hairs penetrate the skin. A material is released which
causes a sharp burning pain or stinging rash that may last a few minutes or several
hours.

Economic Importance   The family is of little economic importance. Species of
Pilea are grown as houseplants. *Boehmeria nivea* is cultivated in China for the fiber,
China grass or rhea, obtained from the inner bark; it is perhaps the longest and most
silky of all vegetable fibers. In the tropics, *B. nivea* var. *tenacissima* yields the fiber
ramie. The young tops of *Urtica* (stinging nettle) may be cooked and eaten like spinach.

SUBCLASS II, HAMAMELIDAE; ORDER 7, LEITNERIALES
Leitneriaceae: Corkwood Family

Field Recognition   Deciduous shrubs; leaves alternate, simple, entire, somewhat
leathery, long-petioled; inflorescences of unisexual cymules in erect, catkinlike spikes;
flowers unisexual, borne on separate plants, each flower subtended by a bract; (CA^0
CO^0 A^{12} G^0) (Perianth$^{2-6}$ A^0 $\underline{G}^1$). See Figure 14-19.

(a)   (b)   (c)   (d)

Leitneriaceae

FIGURE 14-19
Leitneria floridana (Leitneriaceae). (a)
Branch with pistillate catkins, (b) branch with
staminate catkins, (c) bract with stamens,
and (d) pistil.

Size, Distribution, and General Information   A monotypic order with one species *Leitneria floridana* of limited distribution from Missouri to Texas and Florida.
An unimportant family, interesting because of its obscure affinities with other families;
it is possibly related to the Myricaceae.

SUBCLASS II, HAMAMELIDAE; ORDER 8, JUGLANDALES
Juglandaceae: Walnut Family

Field Recognition   Deciduous trees; leaves pinnately compound, alternate, aromatic; flowers unisexual with staminate flowers usually in catkins; $(CA^{3-6} CO^0 A^{3-\infty}$
$G^0)(CA^4 CO^0 A^0 \overline{G} \underline{(2-3)})$.

Description   *Habit*   Deciduous trees.
Leaves   Alternate, pinnately compound, aromatic; without stipules.
Inflorescences   Plants monoecious; staminate flowers in catkins.
Flowers   Apetalous, unisexual. Staminate flowers with a variable number of bracts
and a calyx of 3 to 6 sepals; androecium of 3 to 100 stamens. Pistillate flowers with
a number of bracts and a calyx of 4 sepals. Gynoecium a compound pistil of 2 to 3
united carpels, with 1 locule, ovule 1, ovary inferior, stigmas 2, often plumose. See
Figure 14-20.
Fruit   A drupelike nut with a dehiscent or indehiscent leathery or fibrous husk,
or sometimes a winged nutlet.
Seed   With 2 to 4 lobes, solitary.
Embryo   Very large, cotyledons often much contorted.

Size, Distribution, and General Information   A family of about 7 genera and
60 species occurring in the north temperate zone and subtropics south to India and
Indochina and in the New World into the Andes of South America.
Some important genera are *Juglans* (15) (walnut) and *Carya* (25) (hickory, pecan).

FIGURE 14-20
Juglans regia (Juglandaceae). (a) Pistillate flower, (b) leaf, and (c) cluster of staminate flowers.

Economic Importance   The Juglandaceae are valuable for the wood used in furniture making and for walnuts, pecans, and hickory nuts. *Juglans regia* is the English walnut; *J. nigra* is the black walnut of eastern North America. Black walnut trees bring the highest price of any timber tree in eastern North America. *Carya illinoensis* (pecan) is extensively cultivated in the southeastern United States. Some cultivars of pecan contain up to 70 percent vegetable oil in their seeds.

SUBCLASS II, HAMAMELIDAE; ORDER 9, MYRICALES
Myricaceae: Wax-myrtle or Bay-berry Family

Field Recognition   Aromatic trees or shrubs; leaves alternate, simple or pinnatifid; flowers unisexual, borne on axillary catkinlike spikes, male flowers with 2-4 bracteoles and a disk at the base of the stamens, female flowers with 2–4 bracteoles, ovary superior and 1 locular composed of two fused carpels; fruit a small waxy-warted drupe with a hard endocarp; $(CA^0 \; CO^0 \; A^{4(2-16)} \; G^0) \; (CA^0 \; CO^0 \; A^0 \underline{G}^{②})$. See Figure 14-21.

FIGURE 14-21
Myrica pensylvanica
(Myricaceae). (a) Fruiting
branch, (b) staminate flower,
and (c) pistillate flower.

Myricaceae

Size, Distribution, and General Information   A small family of 3 genera (*Myrica* (48), *Comptonia* (1) and *Canacomyrica* (1)) of almost cosmopolitan distribution.

Economic Importance   The fruits of some species are boiled to produce a wax which is used in making bay-berry candles. Several species are utilized as ornamental shrubs. *Myrica cerifera* is a common understory shrub in the southeastern pine forests, contributing significantly to the fire hazard in these forests.

SUBCLASS II, HAMAMELIDAE; ORDER 10, FAGALES
Fagaceae: Beech or Oak Family

Field Recognition   Trees or shrubs; leaves alternate (in oak, leaves and buds clustered at the ends of the branches, pith 5-angled); fruit a nut, at least partially covered by a cupule of hardened bracts; $(CA^{4-7} \ CO^0 \ A^{4-40} \ G^0) \ (CA^{4-6} \ CO^0 \ A^0 \ \overline{G}^{(3-6)})$.

Description   *Habit*   Deciduous or evergreen trees and shrubs.
Leaves   Alternate, simple, pinnately veined; with stipules.
Inflorescences   Plants usually monoecious; staminate flowers solitary, in catkinlike racemes or in heads; pistillate flowers solitary or few in a cluster.

Fagaceae

FIGURE 14-22
Fagaceae. Fruiting branches of (a) *Castanea pumila* and (b) *Quercus alba.*

Flowers   Unisexual. Corolla lacking. Staminate flowers with 4 to 7 calyx lobes and 4 to 40 stamens. Pistillate flowers solitary or in 2 to 3 flowered cymules; calyx lobes 4 to 6; gynoecium a compound pistil of 3 to 6 carpels, with 3 to 6 locules, placentation axile, ovary inferior. See Figure 14-22.

Fruit   A 1-seeded nut.

Seed   Solitary by abortion.

Systematics   The family is classified in three subfamilies: (1) Fagoideae (*Fagus* and *Nothofagus*); (2) Castaneoideae (*Lithocarpus, Castanopsis, Castanea,* and *Chrysolepis*); and (3) Quercoideae, (*Quercus* and *Trigonobalanus*).

The important genus *Quercus* is divided in our area into two subgenera: Leucobalanus (white oak) and Erythrobalanus (red oak). The red oaks have sharp points on each lobe around the margin of the leaf, and the white oaks have rounded lobes. The white oaks have small, thin-walled summer wood pores, whereas the red oaks have large, thick-walled summer wood pores.

Size, Distribution, and General Information   A family of about 8 genera and 900 species of cosmopolitan distribution but absent from tropical Africa southwards.

Some important genera are *Quercus* (450) (oak); *Fagus* (10) (beech); and *Castanea* (12) (chestnut, chinquapin).

Castanea dentata (American chestnut) was one of the dominant species of the forests of the Appalachian Mountains, but almost none remain today. It supplied nutritious nuts and a decay-resistant wood. The chestnut was doomed by a devastating fungus that was introduced into New York in 1904. The few American chestnuts remaining are generally sprouts that arise from the roots of a former tree. They are short-lived since they are infected by fungus spores carried on the feet of birds. Most chestnuts used for food today come from the European chestnut (*C. sativa*). The fruit of the Oriental chestnut (*C. mollissima*), widely planted in the southeastern states, is undesirable.

Oaks provide a hard, heavy, durable lumber used in construction, in hardwood floors, and for other purposes. White oak (*Q. alba*) is used in making watertight barrels that are charred and used to age bourbon whiskey.

Economic Importance   The family is of considerable economic importance for the lumber produced by its members. The bark and wood of *Castanea* is used in tanning. Cork is obtained from the bark of *Quercus suber*. Many species of oak and beech are cultivated as shade or ornamental trees.

SUBCLASS II, HAMAMELIDAE; ORDER 10, FAGALES
Betulaceae: Birch Family

Field Recognition   Deciduous trees or shrubs; leaves simple, serrate; staminate flowers in catkins; (CA$^{0\ or\ 4}$ CO^0 A$^{2-4}$ G^0) (CA^0 CO^0 A^0 $\overline{\text{G}}^{②}$).

Description   *Habit*   Deciduous trees and shrubs.
Leaves   Alternate, simple, pinnately veined; with stipules.
Inflorescences   Plants monoecious, both staminate and pistillate flowers in catkins.
Flowers   Unisexual, in condensed cymules. Perianth minute, lacking in pistillate flowers. Staminate flowers in catkins, naked or minutely 4-parted, stamens 2 to 4 in each flower (2 to 20 per cymule). Pistillate flowers 2 or 3 in each cymule subtended by a 3-lobed bract; gynoecium a compound pistil of 2 united carpels, ovary inferior. See Figure 14-23.
Fruit   A small, 1-seeded samara or nut.

Systematics   The family is sometimes divided and treated as two families, the Betulaceae and Corylaceae.

Size, Distribution, and General Information   A family of about 6 genera and around 120 species. Betulaceae occur particularly in the north temperate zone, but in the New World extend into tropical mountains and along the Andes to Argentina.

(a)   (b)

Betulaceae

FIGURE 14-23
Alnus (Betulaceae). (a) Branch with woody pistillate catkins and (b) staminate catkins (redrawn from Heywood, 1978).

Some of the genera are *Alnus* (35) (alder); *Betula* (60) (birch); *Carpinus* (35) (hornbeam, ironwood); *Corylus* (15) (hazelnut, filbert); and *Ostrya* (10) (hop hornbeam).

American Indians once used the bark of paper birch (*Betula papyrifera*) for covering the frames of canoes. Many alders grow in bogs or swamps and add nitrogen to the soil from large nodules containing nitrogen-fixing bacteria on their roots.

Economic Importance   The family is of some importance as a source of ornamental trees; hardwood timber is obtained from *Betula* (birches); hazelnuts and filberts are produced from *Corylus;* and a wintergreenlike oil is extracted from the twigs of *Betula*. Some birch is used for veneer, and *Alnus rubra* (red alder) of western North America provides a wood that is a good imitation of mahogany.

SUBCLASS III, CARYOPHYLLIDAE; ORDER 1, CARYOPHYLLALES
Aizoaceae: Carpetweed or Mesembryanthemum Family

Field Recognition   Fleshy herbs or low shrubs; leaves usually succulent; stamens numerous; petals numerous and of staminodial origin; fruit typically a dry capsule; seed with a large curved embryo surrounded by a mealy endosperm; $CA^{5(4-8)}$ CO° A^{∞} $G^{2-5-\infty}$. See Figure 14-24.

Aizoaceae

FIGURE 14-24
Mesembryanthemum (Aizoaceae). Flowering branch.

Size, Distribution, and General Information   A family of about 143 genera
(some authors recognize fewer genera) and 2300 species chiefly of South Africa but
also pantropical. Some of the genera include *Mesembryanthemum* (1000) (ice plant);
Tetragonia (50–60) (*T. expansa* is New Zealand spinach); *Sesuvium* (8) (sea purslane);
Lampranthus (100); *Lithops* (50) (living rocks); *Faucaria* (36) (tiger jaws); and *Mollugo*
(20) (carpet-weed).

The Aizoaceae include the Linnaean genus *Mesembryanthemum* that today has been
split by some authors into over 100 genera. Many of these related taxa grow in arid
zones of southern Africa and represent extreme cases of adaptation to these habitats
and are mostly leaf-succulents. *Lithops* so successfully resembles small stones that it
is exceeding difficult to distinguish it from the stony soil. The flowers of these plants
resemble daisies in shape and often carpet barren stretches of southern Africa with
flowers.

Economic Importance   Because of their unusual appearances, many species are
grown as greenhouse and garden ornamentals.

SUBCLASS III, CARYOPHYLLIDAE; ORDER 1, CARYOPHYLLALES

Cactaceae: Cactus Family

Field Recognition   Succulent, fleshy habit, usually spiny herbs, with the spines arranged in areoles; flowers solitary and showy with numerous perianth parts; stamens numerous; ovary inferior; $CA^X \, CO^\infty \, A^\infty \, \overline{G}^{(2-\infty)}$.

Description   *Habit*   Fleshy, herbaceous or woody, sometimes branched or tree-like, with spines or bristles or both at areoles.

Leaves   Usually scalelike, or flat and fleshy, much reduced.

Inflorescences   Flowers solitary and usually showy.

Flowers   Bisexual, actinomorphic or nearly zygomorphic. Perianth parts numerous, showing a gradual transition from sepals to petals. Calyx often petaloid. Petals epigynous in several series. Androecium of numerous stamens, epipetalous or inserted at base of petals. Gynoecium a compound pistil of 4 united carpels, with 1 locule, ovules numerous, placentation parietal, ovary inferior. See Figure 14-25.

Fruit   A berry, often spiny or bristly.

Seed   Little or no endosperm.

Systematics   Over the years, the family affinities have been somewhat uncertain; but discovery of the presence of the betalain pigments rather than anthocyanins has finalized the placement of Cactaceae in subclass Caryophyllidae. This supports evidence obtained from embryology, floral morphology, and anatomy. The genera are not well defined.

Size, Distribution, and General Information   A family of about 30 to 200 genera depending on the author and 2000 species chiefly localized in the drier regions of tropical America, but extending from British Columbia to Patagonia, and reaching altitudes of over 3600 meters in the Andes. Several are epiphytes. The only Cactacteae

FIGURE 14-25
Opuntia (Cactaceae). (a) Flowering branch and (b) vertical section through a flower.

(a)

(b)

Cactaceae

perhaps native to the Old World are species of *Rhipsalis,* perhaps introduced, in Africa, Madagascar, Mauritius, Seychelles, and Sri Lanka. Several species of *Opuntia* have become naturalized and are often troublesome weeds in South Africa, India, and Australia. In general, the Cactaceae are New World stem-succulents, protected from grazing animals by spines.

Some genera are *Opuntia* (250) (prickly pear, beaver tail, cholla); *Cereus* (50) (hedge cactus); *Echinocactus* (10) (barrel cactus); *Mammillaria* (200 to 300) (pincushion cactus); and *Lemaireocereus* (25) (organ pipe cactus).

The symbol of the deserts of the American Southwest is the giant saguaro cactus (*Carnegiea gigantea*). It may reach 15 meters in height with a diameter of 50 centimeters. Saguaro seedlings grow very slowly, and because of human activity, the saguaros may be doomed to extinction.

The short days and long nights of December bring the colorful Christmas cactus (*Zygocactus truncatus*) of Brazil into flower. In Mexico, cacti are set in rows to form living fences. The jumping chollas (*Opuntia*) of the American Southwest obtained their name from the ease by which their terminal segments became hooked on animals passing the plant. The cholla segment, once fallen or removed from the animal, will usually take root.

Economic Importance   The Cactaceae are important as ornamentals. The fruits of the prickly pear are edible, and the stems of some are used as emergency fodder. *Lophophora williamsii* (peyote), which contains an alkaloid called *mescaline,* is hallucinogenic and is eaten by certain groups of American Indians for religious purposes. The dried bodies of mealybugs that live on *Opuntia* yield the red dye cochineal used in cosmetics.

SUBCLASS III, CARYOPHYLLIDAE; ORDER 1, CARYOPHYLLALES
Chenopodiaceae: Goosefoot Family

Field Recognition   Herbs or shrubs, often succulent; flowers small and greenish, scarious bracts absent; $CA^{\widehat{2-5}} CO^0 A^{2-5} \overline{G}^{\widehat{2-3}}$.

Description   *Habit*   Often xerophytic or halophytic annual or perennial herbs, or sometimes shrubs; sometimes succulent with nearly leafless stems, sometimes jointed.

Leaves   Usually alternate and simple; sometimes fleshy or reduced to scales; stipules absent.

Inflorescences   Cymose, often bracteate, plants dioecious.

Flowers   Bisexual or unisexual, actinomorphic. Calyx of 2 to 5 sepals, small, united, persistent in fruit. Corolla absent. Androecium of 2 to 5 stamens, opposite the calyx lobes. Gynoecium a compound pistil of 2 to 3 carpels, with 1 locule, ovule solitary, ovary superior or inferior, styles 1 to 3. See Figure 14-26.

Fruit   A nutlet, indehiscent.

Seed   Embryo usually surrounding the endosperm.

Chenopodiaceae

FIGURE 14-26
Chenopodium (Chenopodiaceae) flower.

Size, Distribution, and General Information   A family of about 102 genera and 1400 species of worldwide distribution, but centered in xeric and saline habitats.

Some of the important genera are *Chenopodium* (100 to 150) (lamb's quarter, goosefoot); *Beta* (6) (beet, Swiss chard); *Atriplex* (200) (saltbush); *Salicornia* (35) (glasswort); and *Salsola* (150) (glasswort, Russian thistle).

The common weed lamb's quarter (*Chenopodium album*) has plagued farmers in many agricultural regions but is avidly sought as a pot herb. Russian thistle (*Salsola kali*) is a noxious prickly weed which has become established across North America. The stubby glassworts (*Salicornia*), which grow in salt marshes, lack leaves. Their stem will noisily break, hence the name *glasswort*.

Economic Importance   The family is important as a source of beet sugar, the garden vegetable beet, and Swiss chard, all from *Beta vulgaris*. Spinach is *Spinacia oleracea*. *Chenopodium ambrosioides* is the source of wormseed or Mexican tea, used as a vermifuge, and *C. quinoa* is a food plant in South America. Its seeds, boiled like rice, were a staple food in the Inca Empire.

SUBCLASS III, CARYOPHYLLIDAE; ORDER 1, CARYOPHYLLALES

Amaranthaceae: Pigweed Family

Field Recognition   Herbs, rarely woody; inflorescence dense or congested; flowers minute, green, subtended by dry, scarious, papery bracts; stamens united by their filaments; CA^{3-5} CO^0 $A^{\textcircled{5}}$ $\underline{G}\,\overline{\textcircled{2-3}}$.

Description   *Habit*   Annual or perennial herbs, rarely undershrubs or climbers.
Leaves   Alternate or opposite, simple, usually entire or nearly so; without stipules.
Inflorescences   Spikes, heads, or racemes; dense and congested; plants dioecious or polygamodioecious; often spiny because of the firm bristle tips on the inflorescence bracts.
Flowers   Bisexual or unisexual, actinomorphic, with scarious bracts. Calyx of 3 to 5 sepals, free or united, more or less dry and membranous. Corolla lacking. Androecium usually of 5 stamens, opposite the sepals, filaments united at the base into

(a)   (b)   (c)

Amaranthaceae

FIGURE 14-27
Amaranthus (Amaranthaceae). (a) Vertical view of staminate flower, (b)
vertical section through pistillate flower, and (c) fruit, a circumscissile
utricle.

a short tube. Gynoecium a compound pistil of 2 to 3 carpels, with 1 locule, ovules
solitary or rarely several, ovary superior, styles 1 to 3. See Figure 14-27.

Fruit   A circumscissile capsule or a utricle or nutlet, dehiscing by a lid or indehiscent.

Seed   Globose, embryo annular, surrounding the copious endosperm.

Size, Distribution, and General Information   A family of about 65 genera and
900 species, mostly of tropical America and Africa but extending into the temperate
zones.

Some important genera are *Celosia* (60) (celosia, cockscomb); *Amaranthus* (60)
(pigweed, careless weed); *Iresine* (80) (gizzard plant, blood leaf); *Alternanthera* (200)
(alligator weed); and *Gomphrena* (100) (globe amaranth).

Best known of the tumble weeds of western North America is *Amaranthus grae-
cizans*. It grows in disturbed soil or waste places. It drys into a ball, breaking loose
from the soil and spreading seeds as the wind rolls it around.

Economic Importance   The family is of little economic importance except for
several widespread weeds in *Amaranthus, Iresine,* and *Acnida,* as well as ornamentals
from *Amaranthus, Celosia, Gomphrena,* and *Iresine.* Some species of *Amaranthus*
are cultivated for their edible seeds.

SUBCLASS III, CARYOPHYLLIDAE; ORDER 1, CARYOPHYLLALES

Portulacaceae: Purslane Family

Field Recognition   Annual or perennial herbs, leaves usually fleshy; sepals 2;
placentation basal; pistil with 2 to 5 styles and a unilocular ovary; CA^2 CO^{4-6}
A^{8-10} $\overline{G}\underline{(2-3)}$.

(a)

(b)

Portulacaceae

FIGURE 14-28
Portulaca oleracea (Portulacaceae). (a) Habit of plant and (b) vertical section
of flower.

Description   *Habit*   Annual or perennial herbs or undershrubs.

Leaves   Alternate or opposite, often fleshy, simple; usually with scarious or setose stipules.

Inflorescences   Flowers solitary, or cymose or racemose.

Flowers   Bisexual, actinomorphic, showy. Calyx of 2 sepals, free or united at base. Corolla of 4 to 6 petals, imbricate, free or united at base, soon falling. Androecium of 4 to many, free stamens. Gynoecium a compound pistil of 2 to 3 carpels, with 1 locule, placentation basal, ovules 1 to many, ovary superior or half inferior, styles 2 to 5. See Figure 14-28.

Fruit   A capsule dehiscing by valves or circumscissile; rarely a nut and indehiscent.

Seed   Embryo curved around the perisperm.

Systematics   Recent anatomical evidence suggests that the 2 sepals are bracts and the "petals" are actually the sepals.

Size, Distribution and General Information   A family of about 20 genera and 500 species, cosmopolitan in distribution but occurring particularly in western North America and southern South America.

Some important genera are *Portulaca* (200) (purslane, moss rose); *Talinum* (50); *Claytonia* (35) (spring beauty); and *Calandrinia* (150) (red maids).

The flowers of many Portulacaceae remain closed in wet weather and open only when the sun is shining. This can be observed in the showy *Portulaca grandiflora* from Argentina. *Claytonia* (spring beauty) signals the departure of winter and the arrival of spring in parts of North America.

Economic Importance   The family is of little economic importance except for several ornamentals, notably *Portulaca grandiflora* and several species of *Calandrinia*, *Lewisia*, and *Talinum*. The weedy *P. oleracea* is sometimes used as a pot herb and in salads.

SUBCLASS III, CARYOPHYLLIDAE; ORDER 1, CARYOPHYLLALES

Caryophyllaceae: Pink Family

Field Recognition   Herbs with swollen nodes; leaves opposite, connected at the base with a transverse line; pistil with free central placentation; fruit a many-seeded capsule opening by teeth or valves; $CA^5 \ CO^{5(0)} \ A^{5-10} \ \underline{G} \boxed{2-5}$.

FIGURE 14-29
Silene (Caryophyllaceae). (a) Flowering shoot (redrawn from Heywood, 1978) and (b) flower, note the notched or "pinked" petals which are characteristic of many of the species in the Carophyllaceae.

(a)

(b)

Caryophyllaceae

Description   *Habit*   Annual or perennial herbs with swollen nodes.

Leaves   Opposite, simple, connected at the base by a transverse line, entire; stipules absent or scarious if present.

Inflorescences   Cymose or with solitary flowers.

Flowers   Bisexual, actinomorphic. Calyx of 5 sepals, free or united into a tube. Corolla of 5 petals, sometimes small or none, often notched at tip. Androecium of 5 or 10 stamens. Gynoecium a compound pistil of 2 to 5 united carpels, with 1 locule, ovules numerous, placentation free central, ovary superior, styles 2 to 5. See Figure 14-29.

Fruit   A dry capsule usually opening by valves or teeth.

Seed   Embryo usually curved around the perisperm.

Size, Distribution, and General Information   A family of about 75 genera and 2000 species, mainly of north temperate or warm temperate distribution but cosmopolitan.

Some of the genera are *Stellaria* (100) (chickweed); *Cerastium* (100) (mouse-ear chickweed); *Arenaria* (250) (sandwort); *Silene* (400) (catchfly, campion); *Lychnis* (12) (campion); *Gypsophila* (125) (baby's breath); *Dianthus* (300) (carnation, pink, sweet william); and *Paronychia* (50) (whitlow wort).

Economic Importance   The family includes several ornamentals; pinks, sweet william, carnation (*Dianthus*), and baby's breath (*Gypsophila*). Several troublesome weeds occur in the family, including chickweed (*Stellaria media*) and mouse-ear chickweed (*Cerastium*).

SUBCLASS III, CARYOPHYLLIDAE; ORDER 2, POLYGONALES
Polygonaceae: Buckwheat, Smartweed, or Knotweed Family

Field Recognition   Mostly herbs with swollen nodes; leaves with nodal ocrea, or in their absence, flowers in involucrate heads; calyx petaloid often in two series; CA^{3+3} CO^0 A^{3+3} $\underline{G}^{③}$ or CA^5 CO^0 A^{5-8} $\underline{G}^{③}$.

Description   *Habit*   Herbs, shrubs, vines, or rarely trees, usually with swollen nodes.

Leaves   Alternate, simple, usually with an ocrea (modified stipule) sheathing the stem at the base of the petiole.

Inflorescences   Racemose, paniculate, spicate, or capitate.

Flowers   Usually bisexual, small, actinomorphic. Calyx of 3 to 6 sepals, imbricate, often enlarged and becoming membranous in fruit. Corolla lacking. Androecium of 3 to 8 stamens, free or united at the base. Gynoecium a compound pistil of 3 united carpels, with 1 locule, ovule solitary, placentation basal, ovary superior, stigmas 2 to 4. See Figure 14-30.

Fruit   A lens-shaped or triangular achene.

Seed   With a curved or straight embryo and abundant endosperm.

Flower   Sepals and stamens   Pistil

Polygonaceae

FIGURE 14-30
Floral structures of family Polygonaceae: flower, sepals with stamens, and pistil.

Size, Distribution, and General Information   A family of about 30 genera and 1000 species chiefly of north temperate distribution, with a few located in the tropics, the arctic, and the Southern Hemisphere.

Some of the larger genera are *Rumex* (200) (dock); *Rheum* (50) (rhubarb); *Polygonum* (200) (smartweed, knotweed); *Fagopyrum* (15) (buckwheat); *Coccoloba* (125) (sea grape); and *Eriogonum* (250) (false buckwheat).

Buckwheat produces grain-like seed and was once grown extensively in the northeastern United States. The bees visiting the flowers of buckwheat produce a dark, uniquely flavored honey. The petioles of rhubarb are used in salads, stewed as a dessert, or used to fill pies. The leaf blades of rhubarb contain oxalic acid and are poisonous, often causing loss of livestock. The sea grape (*Coccoloba uvifera*) grows on sandy beaches in subtropical Florida, the West Indies, and South and Central America. It is often cultivated as an ornamental, and the fruits are used to make jelly.

Economic Importance   The family is of little economic importance except for buckwheat (*Fagopyrum esculentum*) and rhubarb (*Rheum rhaponticum*). Some species of *Polygonum* and *Rumex* are weeds. The Eurasian *P. orientale*, which is known as *kiss-me-over-the-garden-gate,* is one of the few ornamentals from this family.

SUBCLASS IV, DILLENIIDAE; ORDER 2, THEALES
Theaceae: Tea or Camellia Family

Field Recognition   Shrubs or small trees; leaves simple, alternate, leathery; flowers showy, bisexual, axillary, solitary; stamens numerous, united to petals; gynoecium of 5 united carpels; fruit a woody capsule; $CA^{4-7} CO^{4-\infty} A^{4-\infty \text{ or } (4-\infty)} \overline{G}^{3-5(2-10)}$. See Figure 14-31.

Size, Distribution, and General Information   A family of about 40 genera and 600 species; tropical, subtropical, and warm-temperate in distribution.

Theaceae

FIGURE 14-31
Stewartia malacondendron (Theaceae).
Flowering shoot.

Economic Importance   The most important species is tea, *Camellia sinensis,* an Asian shrub or small tree. *Camellia japonica* has been cultivated for centuries in Japan and was introduced to the western world in 1739. Other ornamental shrubs include *Cleyera, Eurya, Franklinia, Stewartia* and *Gordonia. Franklinia altamaha* once grew near the coast of Georgia but is no longer extant in the wild. It is now widely cultivated in eastern North America and in Europe.

SUBCLASS IV, DILLENIIDAE: ORDER 2, THEALES
Guttiferae or Clusiaceae: Hypericum or Mangosteen Family

Field Recognition   Herbs, shrubs, or trees; leaves opposite, often glandular dotted; flowers usually yellow; stamens numerous; $CA^{4-5}\ CO^{4-5}\ A^\infty\ \underline{G^{(3\ or\ 5)}}$.

Description   *Habit*   Trees, shrubs, herbs.
Leaves   Opposite, simple, entire, often glandular-dotted; without stipules.
Inflorescences   Cymose or subumbellate.
Flowers   Bisexual or unisexual, actinomorphic. Calyx of 4 to 5 free sepals. Corolla of 4 to 5 free petals. Androecium of numerous stamens, fascicled. Gynoecium a compound pistil of 3 to 5 united carpels, with (1) 3 to 5 locules, ovules numerous, placentation axile, ovary superior. See Figure 14-32.
Fruit   A capsule or berry, rarely a drupe.

Systematics   Classified into two subfamilies: Clusioideae, with mostly unisexual flowers; and Hypericoideae, with mostly bisexual flowers.

Size, Distribution, and General Information   A family of about 50 genera and 1000 species distributed mainly in temperate and tropical regions.

(b)

(a)

Guttiferae

FIGURE 14-32
Hypericum (Guttiferae or
Clusiaceae). (a) flowering
shoot and (b) flower.

Some of the genera are *Hypericum* (350) (St. John's wort); *Garcinia* (200) (mangosteen); and *Clusia* (200) (autograph tree).

Economic Importance   The family is of no significant importance, although the fruits of many species of *Garcinia* are edibile, especially that of *G. mangostana* (mangosteen). Several species of *Hypericum* are grown as ornamentals. In the western United States, *Hypericum perforatum* (Klamath weed) once caused poisoning of livestock. But Klamath weed was brought under biological control by the introduction of two species of beetles which feed upon it.

SUBCLASS IV, DILLENIIDAE; ORDER 3, MALVALES
Malvaceae: Mallow Family

Field Recognition   Herbs and shrubs; with stellate pubescence; leaves palmately veined;   stamens united by their filaments;   pistil of many carpels: $CA^{3-5}CO^5A^{\infty}$ $G^{(1-\infty)}$.

Description   *Habit*   Herbs, shrubs, or rarely small trees.
Leaves   Alternate, simple, palmately veined; with stipules.
Inflorescences   Flowers solitary or cymose.
Flowers   Bisexual, actinomorphic. Calyx of 3 to 5 sepals, more or less united, often subtended by an involucre of bracteoles. Corolla of 5 petals, free, often fused at base to staminal column. Androecium of numerous stamens, filaments united into a tube or column. Gynoecium a compound pistil of 1 to many (often 5) carpels, with

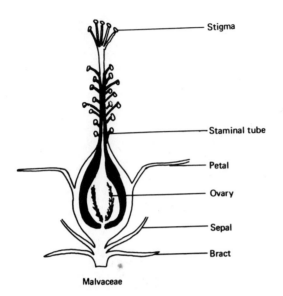

Malvaceae

FIGURE 14-33
Diagrammatic vertical view of a flower
of the family Malvaceae.

2 to 5 or more locules, ovules numerous, placentation axile, ovary superior, style
often branched above. See Figure 14-33.

Fruit A capsule, schizocarp or rarely a berry.

Seed Embryo curved, usually without endosperm.

Size, Distribution, and General Information   A family of about 75 genera and
1000 species of tropical and temperate distribution.

Some of the genera are *Althaea* (12) (hollyhock, marshmallow); *Malva* (40) (mallow); *Sida* (200); *Abutilon* (100) (velvet leaf, flowering maple, Indian mallow); *Hibiscus* (300) (okra, rose mallow, flower-of-an-hour); *Gossypium* (20) (cotton).

Hibiscus rosa-sinensis (rose of China or hibiscus) has hundreds of cultivars and is
enjoyed for its brilliant large flowers. The shrubby rose of Sharon (*H. syriacus*) is
hardier than rose of China and is used in colder climates as an ornamental. The roots
of *Althaea officinalis* were once an ingredient in marshmallow confections. *Althaea
rosea* is the perennial garden favorite, hollyhock. Cotton, the symbol of the Old South,
is grown in favorable climates in many different countries and in numerous varieties.
Its cultivated history extends back as far as 3000 B.C. in India, Egypt, and South
America.

Economic Importance   The family is of considerable importance for cotton fibers,
cottonseed meal, and cottonseed oil. The cultivated forms of cotton arose from *Gossypium barbadense* and *G. hirsutum*, both of the New World, and *G. arboreum* and
G. herbaceum from the Old World. People in the southeastern United States enjoy
okra (*Hibiscus esculentus*), a vegetable largely unappreciated by Yankees who consider

it to be slimy, stringy, and disagreeable. Several species of *Sida* are weeds. Many Malvaceae are valued as ornamentals. *Abutilon avicennae,* cultivated in China, is the source of a fiber called *China jute*.

SUBCLASS IV, DILLENIIDAE; ORDER 5, NEPENTHALES
Sarraceniaceae: Pitcher Plant Family

Field Recognition   Plants insectivorous, herbaceous perennials, leaves tubular or vaselike, usually filled with water and dead insects; flowers bisexual, actinomorphic; style simple and forming an umbrellalike structure; fruit a capsule; CA^{4-5} CO^5 A^∞ $\underline{G}^{\boxed{3(5)}}$. See Figure 14-34.

Size, Distribution, and General Information   A small family of 3 genera of bog plants, *Sarracenia* (8), *Darlingtonia* (1), and *Heliamphora* (6). *Sarracenia* occurs in eastern North America, largely on the Atlantic and Gulf Coastal Plains, *Darlingtonia* in California and *Heliamphora* is restricted to Venezuela and Guyana.

Economic Importance   Occasionally cultivated as ornamental or botanical curiosities.

FIGURE 14-34
Sarracenia purpurea (Sarraceniaceae). Habit of plant in flower.

Sarraceniaceae

SUBCLASS IV, DILLENIIDAE; ORDER 6, VIOLALES
Violaceae: Violet Family

Field Recognition   Herbs (ours); flowers zygomorphic, 5-merous; petals 5, the anterior ones spurred; stamens 5, frequently 1 is spurred at the base; CA^5 COZ^5 A^5 $\underline{G^{③}}$.

Description   *Habit*   Annual or usually perennial herbs, or shrubs.

Leaves   Alternate or rarely opposite, simple; stipules often leafy or small.

Inflorescences   Flowers solitary, to paniculate; some species have cleistogamous flowers.

Flowers   Bisexual, zygomorphic or actinomorphic. Calyx of 5 sepals, persistent. Corolla of 5, mostly unequal petals, anterior petal larger and spurred. Androecium of 5 stamens, abaxial stamen often spurred at base. Gynoecium a compound pistil of 3 united carpels, with 1 locule, ovules numerous, placentation parietal, ovary superior, style simple. See Figure 14-35.

Fruit   A capsule.

Seed   With endosperm.

Size, Distribution, and General Information   A family of about 16 or more genera and 900 species of tropical and temperate distribution.

Two of the larger genera are *Viola* (400) (violet) and *Hybanthus* (150) (green violet). The woody pantropical genus *Rinorea* has nearly 300 species.

During the summer months, several species of violets produce an inconspicuous set of flowers without petals. In some species, these cleistogamous flowers are hidden

FIGURE 14-35
Viola (Violaceae). Habit of plant in flower.

Violaceae

underground. They never open, but pollinate themselves. In many places in eastern North America, annual violets, called *Johnny-jump-ups,* herald the arrival of spring with a sea of blue flowers.

Economic Importance   The family is of little economic importance except for the garden favorites; violets, violas, and pansies.

SUBCLASS IV, DILLENIIDAE; ORDER 6, VIOLALES
Cucurbitaceae: Cucurbit or Gourd Family

Field Recognition   Coarse, tendril-bearing vines; flowers usually yellow, unisexual; ovary inferior; fruit a berry or pepo; $(CA^{\circledS}\ CO^{\circledS}\ A^{\widehat{5}}\ G^{0})\ (CA^{\circledS}\ CO^{\circledS}\ A^{0}\ \overline{G}^{\circledS})$.

Description   *Habit*   Climbing with spirally coiled tendrils, or prostrate annual herbs.
Leaves   Alternate, entire or lobed.
Inflorescences   Of various types, often axillary, plants monoecious or dioecious.
Flowers   Unisexual, rarely bisexual, actinomorphic. Calyx of 5 sepals, tubular, fused to ovary wall. Corolla of 5 petals. Androecium of 1 to 5 stamens (often 5 stamens, with 2 groups of 2 fused together, giving 2 compound stamens, plus 1 simple stamen, the total appearing as 3 stamens). Gynoecium a compound pistil of 1 to 10 (usually 3) fused carpels, ovules numerous, placentation parietal or free central, ovary inferior, style simple or 3-parted. See Figure 14-36.
Fruit   A fleshy, berrylike pepo.
Seed   Often flattened.

Size, Distribution, and General Information   A family of about 90 genera and 700 species mainly of tropical and subtropical distribution.
Some genera are *Citrullus* (3) *(watermelon, citron melon); Lagenaria* (6) (bottle gourd); *Luffa* (6) (vegetable sponge, loofah); *Sicyos* (15) (nimble kate, bur cucumber); *Curcurbita* (15) (pumpkin, squash, gourd, vegetable marrow); *Cayaponia* (45); *Melothria* (10) (creeping cucumbers); *Cucumis* (25) (cucumber, canteloupe, muskmelon, gherkin); and *Echinocystis* (15) (wild cucumber).
The merits of the various Cucurbitaceae were early recognized by primitive agriculturists. Muskmelons were mentioned in Egyptian records from 2400 B.C. Watermelons have been cultivated for so long in Africa that they are unknown in the wild. Hard shelled gourds serve as scoops, ladles, and buoyant floats for fish nets. In North America, gourds are sometimes used as birdhouses. American Indians cultivated pumpkins and squashes for food. The fibers from the fruit of the vegetable sponge or loofah are used for fuel filters, air filters, and packing material.

Economic Importance   The Cucurbitaceae are important as a source of food: pumpkin, squash, cucumber, gherkin, muskmelon, and watermelon. A few species are grown as ornamentals. Some are weedy.

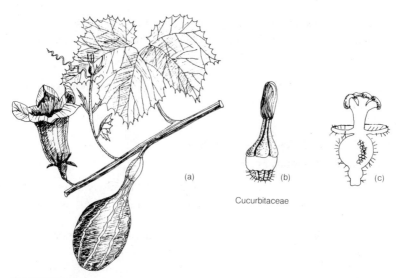

Cucurbitaceae

FIGURE 14-36
Cucurbita (Cucurbitaceae). (a) Flowering and fruiting stem, (b) vertical view of
staminate flower with the perianth removed, and (c) vertical section of pistillate
flower with the perianth removed.

FIGURE 14-37
Passiflora caerulea (Passifloraceae). Flower with
conspicuous filamentous corona.

Passifloraceae

SUBCLASS IV, DILLENIIDAE; ORDER 6, VIOLALES
Passifloraceae: Passion Flower Family

Field Recognition Trees, shrubs, herbs, often climbers with axillary coiled tendrils; leaves alternate, entire or lobed; flowers usually bisexual, actinomorphic, on a jointed, bracteate peduncle; corona present, of 1 or more series of threadlike filaments; ovary 1-locular, ovules numerous; styles free or united, stigmas capitate or discoid, fruit a berry or capsule; $CA^{5 \text{ or } \cup} CO^{5 \text{ or } \cup (0)} A^5 \underline{G}^{(3-5)}$. See Figure 14-37.

Size, Distribution, and General Information A medium-size family of 16 genera and about 650 species. The largest genus is *Passiflora* with around 400 species. The family is native to the tropics and warm temperate regions.

Economic Importance Several species of *Passiflora* are cultivated for their edible fruits: *P. quandrangularis* (giant granadilla), *P. edulis* var. *flaviocarpa* (yellow passion fruit), *P. edulis* var. *edulis* (purple granadilla), and *P. maliformis* (sweet calabash). In addition, numerous species of *Passiflora* are cultivated for their attractive and interesting flowers. Many members of the family produce cyanide so care must be taken in eating the fruit of unidentified species.

SUBCLASS IV, DILLENIIDAE; ORDER 7, SALICALES
Salicaceae: Willow Family

Field Recognition Deciduous trees and shrubs; plants dioecious; catkin bearing; flowers seemingly subtended by bracts with a cup-like disc or a gland; seeds with tufts of hairs; $(CA^0 \ CO^0 \ A^{2-X} \ G^0) \ (CA^0 \ CO^0 \ A^0 \ \underline{G}^{②})$.

Description *Habit* Trees or shrubs.
Leaves Deciduous, simple, alternate; stipules small or sometimes foliaceous and persistent.
Inflorescences Plants dioecious; flowers dense in erect or pendulous catkins.
Flowers Unisexual, naked. Staminate flowers with 1 to 2 nectariferous glands and 2 to 30 stamens. Pistillate flowers with 1 to 2 nectariferous glands (in *Populus* nectaries are absent). Gynoecium a compound pistil of 2 carpels, with 1 locule, ovules numerous, placentation parietal or basal, ovary superior, styles 2 to 4. See Figure 14-38
Fruit A capsule with numerous hairy seeds (the hair is restricted to a coma and not scattered over the seed).

Size, Distribution, and General Information A family of 2 genera and about 340 species, chiefly of north temperate climates but of wide distribution. The genera are *Salix* (300) and *Populus* (40).

Salicaceae

FIGURE 14-38
Salix (Salicaceae). (a) Branch with staminate catkins, (b) pistillate flower,
and (c) staminate flower.

Stems of pussy willow (*Salix discolor*) are used in floral arrangements. They are gathered in late winter and brought inside where the yellow, fluffy, staminate catkins soon appear. Weeping willow is *S. babylonica*. Quaking aspen (*Populus tremuloides*) produces a striking appearance when its leaves flutter in the breeze. *Populus deltoides* (cottonwood) of eastern and central North America and *P. trichocarpa* (black cotton-wood) of western North America are large native trees.

Economic Importance   The Salicaceae are important for several species grown as ornamentals and for use in basket making or for pulpwood. It is interesting to note that salicylic acid, the root compound for aspirin, is named for *Salix*. In ancient times, the soft inner bark of *Salix* was widely esteemed as a headache cure. Its chemical derivative (aspirin) still is. Convention has it that willow wood was the traditional material from which polo balls and cricket bats were made.

SUBCLASS IV, DILLENIIDAE; ORDER 8, CAPPARALES
Cruciferae or Brassicaceae: Mustard Family

Field Recognition   Herbs with an odorous, watery juice; flowers of 4 sepals, 4 petals, and 6 stamens; fruit a silique or silicle; $CA^4\ CO^4\ A^{4+2}\ \underline{G}^{\circledtwo}$.

Description   *Habit*   Annual, biennial, or perennial herbs with a pungent, watery juice.

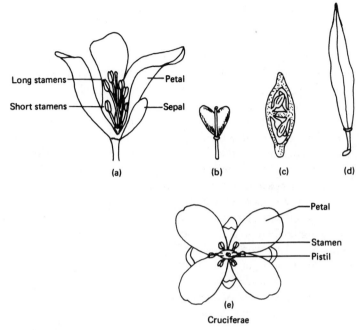

FIGURE 14-39
Flower and fruits of Cruciferae family. (a) Vertical section of flower; note the two short and the four long stamens. (b) Silicle. (c) Cross section of a silicle. (d) Silique. (e) Flower (top view).

Leaves   Alternate, simple, often dissected, pubescence of simple to stellate hairs; stipules absent.

Inflorescences   Usually racemose, rarely bracteate.

Flowers   Bisexual, actinomorphic. Calyx of 4 sepals. Corolla of 4 petals (rarely none) arranged in a cross—hence cruciform; petals often long-clawed. Androecium of 6 stamens, with 4 long and 2 short. Gynoecium a compound pistil of 2 carpels, with 2 locules, ovules many, placentation parietal, ovary superior, stigmas 2. See Figure 14-39.

Fruit   A silique (long fruit) or silicle (short fruit), variable, important in classification.

Size, Distribution, and General Information   A cosmopolitan family of about 350 genera and 3000 species, occurring mainly in the north temperate zone, particularly in the Mediterranean region.

Some of the genera are *Brassica* (50) (Brussel sprouts, broccoli, mustard, cabbage, cauliflower, and so on); *Barbarea* (20) (winter cress); *Arabis* (120) (rock cress); *Cardamine* (150) (bitter cress); *Alyssum* (100) (madwort); *Draba* (300) (whitlow grass); *Sisymbrium* (90) (tumble mustard); *Capsella* (5) (shepherd's purse); *Lepidium* (130) (peppergrass); *Cakile* (7) (sea rocket); *Raphanus* (8) (radish); *Dentaria* (20) (toothwort); and *Iberis* (30) (candytuft).

Economic Importance　The family is of considerable economic importance for food crops, ornamentals, and weeds. *Brassica nigra* is black mustard, and *B. oleracea* gave rise to cabbage, cauliflower, broccoli, Brussels sprouts, kohlrabi, and kale. Turnip is *B. campestris,* and *B. napus* is rape. Horseradish is *Armoracia rusticana,* and radishes are *Raphanus sativus.* Cruciferae produce an abundance of vitamin C. The sulfur compounds of the family help to give them their pungent odor. Black mustard seeds are ground to make the condiment called *mustard* to which horseradish may be added to make a hotter blend. Cruciferous vegetables such as broccoli and cauliflower have recently gained attention as possible anticancer food items.

A blue dyestuff called *woad* was once obtained from *Isatis tinctoria,* whose dried leaves were fermented—a malodorous process requiring several weeks. Woad was replaced by the blue dye indigo. There is a semantic theory that the word *weed* is a permutation of the Anglo-Saxon root word *woad.*

Among the ornamentals are honesty or moneywort (*Lunaria*), stocks (*Matthiola*), candytuft (*Iberis*), and sweet alyssum (*Lobularia*). Troublesome weeds include the weedy mustards (*Brassica, Barbarea,* and *Sisymbrium*), shepherd's purse (*Capsella bursa-pastoris*), and peppergrass (*Lepidium virginicum*).

SUBCLASS IV, DILLENIIDAE; ORDER 10, ERICALES

Ericaceae-Pyrolaceae-Monotropaceae

Many manuals traditionally treat this group of three families as one family, the Ericaceae, but most taxonomists now separate the group into three families as treated here.

Ericaceae: Heath Family

Field Recognition　Woody, often shrubby; leaves alternate, evergreen or deciduous; flowers urceolate or campanulate; stamens distinct, often twice as many as the petals, anthers opening by terminal pores; $CA^{(4-5)} CO^{(4-5)(4-5)} A^{8-10} \overline{G}^{(4-5)}$.

Description　*Habit*　Shrubs or rarely small trees.

Leaves　Mostly alternate, simple, often evergreen; stipules absent.

Inflorescences　Solitary or racemose.

Flowers　Bisexual, actinomorphic or slightly zygomorphic. Calyx of 4 to 5 united sepals. Corolla of 4 to 5 united or sometimes free petals, often urceolate or campanulate. Androecium of stamens mostly double the number of corolla lobes, free or fused at base; anthers usually opening by apical pores. Gynoecium a compound pistil of (2)4 to 5(10) united carpels, with 4 to 5 locules, ovules numerous, placentation axile, ovary superior or inferior. See Figure 14-40.

Fruit　A capsule, berry, or drupe.

Seed　Embryo cylindrical, in endosperm.

(a) (b) (c)

ERICACEAE

FIGURE 14-40
Vertical sections of representative flowers of the Ericaceae family. (a) *Rhododendron,* (b) *Kalmia,* and (c) *Vacinium.*

Size, Distribution, and General Information   A family of about 125 genera and 3500 species of cosmopolitan distribution except in deserts; confined to high elevations in the tropics. The taxa grow in acid soils on peat, moors, swamps, and woodlands; associated with endotrophic mycorrhiza.

Some of the chief genera are *Erica* (600) (heath); *Kalmia* (8) (mountain laurel, laurel, ivy); *Rhododendron* (850) (rhododendron, azalea); *Arctostaphylos* (70) (manzanita); *Vaccinium* (450) (blueberry, huckleberry, cranberry); *Gaylussacia* (49) (huckleberry); and *Bejaria* (30) (Andes rose).

Horticulturalists have produced many handsome cultivars by crossing the various species of *Rhododendron*. Some rhododendrons are deciduous, others are evergreen.

The anthers of *Kalmia* are held in pockets of the corolla, and the filaments are bent like bows when the flower is open. An insect visiting the flower releases the anthers, which strike the insect, loading it with pollen. When grazing is in short supply, livestock are sometimes forced to eat the leaves of *Kalmia,* which may cause poisoning.

Sourwood (*Oxydendrum arboreum*) is a small tree that is a favorite of honeybees in the southern Appalachians. The Scottish Highlands have a conspicuous covering of heather, *Calluna vulgaris.*

Arbutus and *Gaultheria* are strikingly abundant along the Pacific Coast. The former is called *Madrono* or *Madrone*. *Gaultheria* is known as *sallal,* except for a few miles on the Oregon Coast where it is known as *shallal;* both are Indian words.

Epigaea repens is the trailing arbutus, a well-loved wild flower.

Economic Importance   Economically, the family is important for its ornamentals and for blueberries and cranberries. The commercial cranberry is *Vaccinium macrocarpon,* and blueberries are obtained from several species and cultivars. Briar pipes are made from the burls of *Erica scoparia* of southern France. Ornamental shrubs are obtained from *Kalmia, Rhododendron, Erica, Pieris, Leucothoe,* and others.

Pyrolaceae: Pyrola Family

Field Recognition   Herbaceous; leaves evergreen; flowers 4- or 5-merous; petals separate; stamens 10, anthers opening by terminal pores; CA^{4-5} CO^{4-5} A^{8-10} $\underline{G}\,\boxed{4-5}$.

Description   *Habit*   Perennial herbs.
Leaves   Usually alternate, sometimes somewhat whorled, evergreen, entire or toothed; stipules absent.
Inflorescences   Flowers in racemes, umbels, or sometimes corymbs, or scapose and solitary.
Flowers   Bisexual, actinomorphic, nodding. Calyx of 4 to 5 sepals, persistent. Corolla of 4 or 5 petals, free or united only at base. Androecium of 10 (rarely 8) stamens, free, anthers opening by terminal pores. Gynoecium a compound pistil of 4 or 5 carpels, with 4 to 5 locules, ovules numerous, placentation axile, ovary superior, stigma 5-lobed. See Figure 14-41.
Fruit   A more or less globose capsule.

Size, Distribution, and General Information   A family of about 4 genera and 45 species of north temperate and arctic distribution extending in the New World into Mexico and the West Indies.

FIGURE 14-41
Pyrola (Pyrolaceae), habit of flowering plant.

PYROLACEAE

The genera are *Chimaphila* (8) (wintergreen, pipsissewa); *Moneses; Pyrola* (shin-leaf) and *Orthilia.*

These are handsome little plants of the forest floor. In the summer, they display attractive white flowers.

Economic Importance   The family has little economic importance.

Monotropaceae: Indian Pipe Family

Field Recognition   White, yellow, brown, or red fleshy herbs; lacking chlorophyll; leaves scaly; anthers opening by longitudinal slits; CA$_{2-6}$ CO$\boxed{3-6}$A$_{6-12}$ G$\boxed{4-6}$.

Description   *Habit*   Nongreen saprophytic or parasitic herbs.
Leaves   Reduced to scales, alternate, upper ones becoming bract-like.
Inflorescences   Flowers solitary to capitate.
Flowers   Bisexual, actinomorphic. Calyx of 2 to 6 sepals. Corolla of 3 to 6 petals, free or united into a lobed corolla. Androecium of 6 to 12 stamens, free or united at base, anthers opening lengthwise by longitudinal slits. Gynoecium a compound pistil of 4 to 6 carpels, with 1 to 6 locules, ovules numerous, placentation parietal, ovary superior, stigma capitate. See Figure 14-42.
Fruit   A loculicidal capsule opening by valves.

FIGURE 14-42
Monotropa uniflora (Monotropaceae). Habit of plant in flower.

Monotropaceae

Size, Distribution, and General Information   A family of about 10 genera and 12 species of north temperate and tropical mountain distribution.

Some of the genera are *Monotropa* (5) (Indian pipe); *Sarcodes* (1) (snow plant); *Pterospora* (1) (pinedrops); and *Allotropa* (1) (sugar-stick).

These nongreen plants obtain their food through mycorrhizae from the roots of living trees. Snow plant (*Sarcodes sanguinea*) thrusts up its blood-red spike through humus in coniferous woodlands of the middle and upper elevations of the Sierra Nevada. Indian pipe (*Monotropa uniflora*) grows in eastern forests and is waxy white or tinged with pink.

Economic Importance   The family has no economic importance.

SUBCLASS IV, DILLENIIDAE; ORDER 13, PRIMULALES
Primulaceae: Primrose Family

Field Recognition   Herbs; leaves opposite, whorled, or basal; flowers 5-merous; petals united; stamens opposite the petals; seeds numerous; $CA^{\circledS}$ $CO^{\circledS}$ A^5 $\underline{G^{\circledS}}$.

Description   *Habit*   Perennial herbs, rarely annuals or subshrubs.

Leaves   Opposite, whorled, or alternate; sometimes all basal; simple, sometimes lobed.

Inflorescences   Terminal, axillary, scapose; variable from solitary to paniculate or umbellate.

Flowers   Bisexual, actinomorphic, often heterostyled. Calyx of 5 united sepals, persistent. Corolla of 5 united petals, tubular, sometimes split nearly to base, lobes usually 5. Androecium of 5 stamens, opposite the petals (that is, each stamen is directly in front of a petal lobe). Gynoecium a compound pistil of 5 carpels, with 1 locule, ovules numerous, placentation free central, ovary usually superior, style simple. See Figure 14-43.

Fruit   A capsule, variously dehiscent.

Seed   Embryo small, in fleshy or hard endosperm.

Size, Distribution, and General Information   A family of about 30 genera and 1000 species of chiefly north temperate distributioı.

Some of the genera are *Primula* (500) (primrose); *Dodecatheon* (52) (shooting star); *Cyclamen* (15); and *Lysimachia* (150) (loosestrife).

Cyclamens are native plants of the Mediterranean region, the foothills of the Alps, and Asia Minor. Some are grown for the florist trade; others are garden favorites. After pollination, the flower stalk coils in a spiral, pulling the ripe fruit close to the soil.

The largest genus is *Primula*, found largely in Europe and Asia. The flowers show heterostyly—that is, the flowers have two style lengths and two stamen positions. The long style forms have stamens deep in the tube, and the short style form has stamens high on the corolla. Many primroses are grown either in gardens or for the florist trade.

Stamens

Long style   Short style

Primulaceae

FIGURE 14-43
Flowers of *Primula* (Primulaceae); note
the heterostyly, or the two style lengths.

Several species of the yellow-flowered *Lysimachia* are attractive and easily grown
perennials for garden culture.

Economic Importance   The family is important for several ornamentals. Certain
species of *Primula* may cause contact dermatitis.

SUBCLASS V, ROSIDAE; ORDER 1, ROSALES
Hydrangeaceae: Hydrangea Family

Field Recognition   Shrubs; leaves opposite or alternate, without stipules; calyx
tube more or less fused to ovary; stamens numerous and in several series; ovary wholly
or partially inferior; $CA^{\underline{4-10}} CO^{4-10} A^{4-\infty} \overline{G}^{\underline{2-5}}$.

Description   *Habit*   Herbs, soft-wooded undershrubs, or rarely climbers.
Leaves   Opposite or alternate, simple; without stipules.
Inflorescences   Cymose or corymbose.
Flowers   Bisexual, or outer flowers sterile with large petal-like sepals. Calyx 4-
to 10-lobed or toothed, calyx tube more or less fused to the ovary. Corolla of 4 to 10
petals. Androecium of 4 to numerous stamens (in several series). Gynoecium a compound pistil of 2 to 5 united carpels, with 3 to 6 locules (or incompletely distinct),
ovules numerous, placentation axile or parietal, ovary half-inferior to inferior, styles
as many as the locules. See Figure 14-44.
Fruit   A loculicidal capsule.
Seed   Small, sometimes winged and reticulate.

Size, Distribution, and General Information   A family of about 17 genera and
170 species mostly in the Northern Hemisphere (eastern Asia and North America but
with a few in western South America).
   Some genera are *Hydrangea* (24); *Decumaria* (2) (climbing hydrangea); *Philadel-
phus* (50) (mock orange); and *Deutzia* (50).

Hydrangeaceae

FIGURE 14-44
Hydrangea quercifolia (Hydrangeaceae) inflorescence.

Economic Importance   The family is the source of many ornamental shrubs, including *Hydrangea paniculatata,* the florist's hydrangea.

SUBCLASS V, ROSIDAE; ORDER 1, ROSALES
Grossulariaceae: Gooseberry Family

Field Recognition   Shrubs or trees, often spiny; leaves simple, often deeply lobed; flowers 5-merous; calyx petaloid; ovary inferior with 2 parietal placentas; fruit a pulpy berry or a capsule CA$\overline{\text{4–5}}$CO^5 A^5 $\overline{\text{G}\,\text{2–3}}$

Description   *Habit*   Shrubs, often spiny.
Leaves   Alternate or clustered, simple; stipules absent or fused to petiole.
Inflorescences   Racemose or subsolitary.
Flowers   Bisexual or unisexual by abortion, actinomorphic. Calyx of 4 to 5 connate sepals, fused to ovary. Corolla of 5 petals mostly small or scale-like. Androecium of 5 stamens, alternate with the petals. Gynoecium a compound pistil of 2 united carpels, with 1 locule, ovules free to numerous, placentation by 2 parietal placentas, ovary inferior, styles 2, free or fused. See Figure 14-45.
Fruit   A pulpy berry crowned by persistent calyx.
Seeds   Numerous, with endosperm.

Size, Distribution, and General Information   A family of about 25 genera and 350 species of cosmopolitan distribution. Some authors segregate the genera into as many as 8 families; however, Cronquist (1981) feels that the family as recognized here provides a well defined group of reasonable size.

The genera are *Ribes* (150) (gooseberries, currants), and *Grossularia* (50), which is sometimes included in *Ribes, Itea* (20), and *Polyosma* (60).

Grossulariaceae

FIGURE 14-45
Ribes grossularia (Grossulariaceae). Flower of the common garden gooseberry.

Most edible currants and gooseberries originated in Eurasia and have been intentionally cultivated since the 1600s. Currants are nonspiny bushes whose fruits are used in jellies. Gooseberries are spiny shrubs, and the fruits are used to make pies. Certain species of *Ribes* are the alternate hosts of the white pine blister rust.

Economic Importance The family is important for gooseberries, currants, and some ornamental shrubs.

SUBCLASS V, ROSIDAE; ORDER 1, ROSALES
Crassulaceae: Stonecrop Family

Field Recognition Succulent herbs, sometimes undershrubs; leaves without stipules; flowers 4- to 5-merous; carpels the same number as the petals, scalelike gland at the base of each ovary; CA^{4-5} CO^{4-5} A^{8-10} $\underline{G}^{4-5}$.

Description *Habit* Usually succulent herbs or undershrubs, annuals or perennials.
Leaves Opposite or alternate; without stipules.
Inflorescences Usually cymose.
Flowers Bisexual, actinomorphic. Calyx of usually 4 to 5 sepals, free or united into a tube. Corolla of 4 to 5 petals, the same number as the sepals, free or variously united. Androecium of 8 to 10 stamens, as many or twice as many as the petals, or if fewer, alternate with the petals, slightly perigynous. Gynoecium of simple pistils each with 1 carpel, pistils free or united at base, each with 1 locule, ovules many or rarely few, placentation marginal, ovary superior, style short or elongate, each pistil subtended by a scalelike gland. See Figure 14-46.
Fruit A membranous or leathery follicle.
Seed Small; endosperm none or minute.

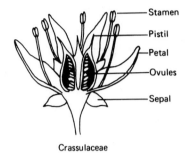

Crassulaceae

FIGURE 14-46
Diagrammatic view of a flower of the family
Crassulaceae; note the longitudinal section of two of the
carpels showing the ovules.

Size, Distribution, and General Information   A family of about 25 genera and 900 species of cosmopolitan distribution with the largest number in southern Africa. Most are xerophytic perennials.

Some of the genera are *Crassula* (250) (stonecrop, jade plant); *Sedum* (300) (orpine, stonecrop); *Sempervivum* (25) (live-forever, hen and chickens); *Cotyledon* (41); and *Kalanchoë* (120) (bryophyllum, life plant).

Members of this family are familiar rock garden plants. Most have succulent leaves and a waxy cuticle which enable the plants to withstand droughts. *Sedum telephium* was once grown in Europe as a source of a home remedy for skin wounds. *Sedum tectorum* (houseleek or thunderwort) was planted on cottage roofs to help hold the slates in place. It was also planted on thatched roofs in the belief it magically warded off lightning. Several of the bryophyllums produce plantlets from adventitious buds along the margins of their leaves. Other species of *Kalanchoë* are used in the florist trade.

Economic Importance   The Crassulaceae are most important as a source of many rock garden plants and houseplants.

SUBCLASS V, ROSIDAE; ORDER 1, ROSALES
Saxifragaceae: Saxifrage Family

Field Recognition   Perennial herbs, leaves alternate, without stipules; flowers 5-merous, perigynous; $CA^5 CO^{5(0)} A^{5 \text{ or } 10} \underline{G} \overline{(2-5)}$

Description   *Habit*   Perennial herbs.
Leaves   Alternate, without stipules.
Inflorescences   Racemose or cymose, rarely solitary.
Flowers   Bisexual, actinomorphic, perigynous or rarely epigynous. Calyx of 5 sepals. Corolla of 5 petals, alternate with the sepals or absent, often clawed. Androecium of 5 or 10 stamens, inserted with the petals, filaments free. Gynoecium a compound pistil of 2 carpels, with 1 to 3 locules, ovules numerous, placentation axile, ovary superior, free or united to the tubular receptacle, styles free. See Figure 14-47.

FIGURE 14-47
Saxifraga (Saxifragaceae). (a) Habit of flowering plant and (b) vertical section of flower.

Fruit A capsule.
Seed Small embryo surrounded by endosperm.

Size, Distribution, and General Information A family of about 40 genera and 700 species distributed mainly in cold and temperate regions. The family has been variously treated by authors because of its morphological diversification.

Some of the larger genera are *Saxifraga* (370) (saxifrage); *Heuchera* (50) (alumroot); *Astilbe* (25); *Mitella* (15) (miterwort, bishop's-cap); *Tiarella* (5) (foamflower); and *Chrysosplenium* (55) (golden saxifrage).

The name *saxifrage*, "breaker of stones," is derived from the old doctrine of signatures of the Middle Ages. The clues provided by the habit and morphology of plants suggested their medicinal uses to medieval herbalists. The pale bulbets formed in the leaf axile of *Saxifraga cernua* resembled small pebbles and hence were used to treat kidney stones.

Economic Importance   The Saxifragaceae are of little importance except for rock garden or perennial ornamentals. *Astilbe* is frequently cultivated as a garden ornamental and various species of *Saxifraga* are grown in rock gardents.

SUBCLASS V, ROSIDAE; ORDER 1, ROSALES
Rosaceae: Rose Family

Field Recognition   Herbs, shrubs, and trees; leaves with stipules; flowers actinomorphic; sepals 5; petals 5; stamens numerous; hypanthium often present; CA⁵CO⁵ A^∞ $\underline{G}^1$ or $\underline{G}^∞$ or $\overline{G}$ ⑤.

Description   *Habit*   Trees, shrubs, and herbs.
Leaves   Alternate, simple or compound, sometimes with glandular teeth; with paired stipules that are sometimes adnate to the petiole.

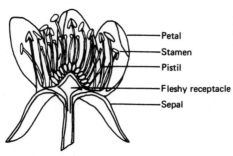

(a) *Rubus* (Rosaceae)

— Petal
— Stamen
— Pistil
— Fleshy receptacle
— Sepal

FIGURE 14-48
Vertical section of generalized flowers of (a) *Rubus* and (b) *Prunus* of family Rosaceae.

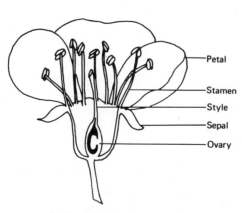

(b) *Prunus* (Rosaceae)

— Petal
— Stamen
— Style
— Sepal
— Ovary

Inflorescences   Variable, solitary flowers to racemose and cymose clusters.

Flowers   Bisexual, actinomorphic, often perigynous to some degree. Calyx of 5 sepals, united at base. Corolla of 5 petals, attached to the rim of the hypanthium or rarely absent. Androecium of numerous stamens, sometimes only 5 or 10. Gynoecium a simple pistil of 1 to numerous separate carpels or of 2 to 5 carpels united into a compound pistil, often adnate to the calyx tube, ovules usually 2 or more per carpel, ovary superior or inferior. See Figures 14-48 and 14-49.

Fruit   An achene, follicle, pome, or drupe, sometimes on a fleshy enlarged receptacle.

Seed   Usually without endosperm.

Systematics   This family is usually divided into four well marked subfamilies: (1) Spiraeoideae (fruit a follicle or capsule, *Spiraea*); (2) Maloideae (fruit a fleshy pome, ovary inferior, *Pyrus, Malus, Sorbus*); (3) Rosoideae (gynoecium of usually 10 or more pistils, fruit often dry, *Rubus, Fragaria, Potentilla, Geum, Rosa*); and (4) Prunoideae (gynoecium of a single pistil, rarely 2 to 5; fruit a drupe, *Prunus*).

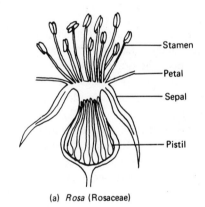

(a) *Rosa* (Rosaceae)

FIGURE 14-49
Vertical section of generalized flowers of (a) *Rosa* and (b) *Malus* of family Rosaceae.

(b) *Malus* (Rosaceae)

Size, Distribution, and General Information   A family of about 100 genera and 3000 species. Distribution cosmopolitan, but mainly north temperate.

Some important genera are *Spiraea* (100); *Rosa* (250) (rose); *Rubus* (250) (blackberry, dewberry, raspberry); *Potentilla* (500) (five-finger, cinquefoil); *Fragaria* (15) (strawberry); *Pyrus* (30) (pear); *Malus* (35) (apple); *Sorbus* (100) (mountain ash, chokeberry); *Amelanchier* (25) (serviceberry, shadbush); *Pyracantha* (10) (fire thorn); *Crataegus* (200) (hawthorn); *Prunus* (430) (plum, peach, cherry, apricot, almond); *Cotoneaster* (50); *Cydonia* (1) (quince); and *Chaenomeles* (3) (flowering quince).

The Rosaceae show great diversity in types of fruit obtained from the same general floral plan. In *Spiraea*, the separate pistils each mature into a follicle with a single seed. In *Prunus* (cherry or plum), the single pistil develops into a *drupe*, a fleshy fruit with a single stony pit containing a single seed. In *Malus* (apple) and *Pyrus* (pear), the calyx and most of the ovary wall becomes fleshy and develops into a pome. In *Fragaria* (strawberry), the receptacle develops into the familiar red, juicy, edible structure with tiny achenes embedded on the surface. *Rubus* (blackberry or raspberry) has a fleshy elongated receptacle upon which druplets are attached. In *Rosa*, the separate pistils are enclosed in a cup formed largely from the calyx. This cup, called a *hip*, enlarges and turns bright red at maturity.

Economic Importance   The Rosaceae are important in temperate regions for fruits and ornamentals. They perhaps rank third in commercial importance in the temperate zone among the families of flowering plants. The ornamentals include *Spiraea prunifolia* (bridal wreath), *S. japonica* (pink spiraea), *Kerria japonica*, *Pyracantha coccinea* (fire thorn), *Crataegus* (hawthorn), *Chaenomeles lagenaria* (flowering quince), *Rosa damascena* (damask rose), *R. multiflora* (multiflora rose), *R. fragrans* (tea rose), *Prunus caroliniana* (Carolina laurel cherry), *P. triloba* (flowering almond), *P. persica* (flowering peach), *P. serrulata* (Japanese flowering cherry), *Malus* (flowering crabs), *Cotoneaster* and *Sorbus* (which both have several ornamental species), and many more.

Fruit-producing members include *Cydonia oblonga* (quince), *Pyrus communis* (pear), *Malus* (apple), *Rubus* (blackberry and raspberry), *Fragaria* (strawberry), *Prunus spinosa* (sloe plum, which is the source of the flavoring in sloe gin), *P. amygdalus* (almond), *P. persica* (peach), *P. cerasus* (sour cherry), *P. avium* (sweet cherry), *P. domestica* (plum or prune), *Eriobotrya japonica* (loquat), and several others.

SUBCLASS V, ROSIDAE; ORDER 2, FABALES

The legumes have been traditionally treated as one large, somewhat heterogeneous family, the Leguminosae. Hutchinson (1973) and Cronquist (1981) agree that the group is perhaps best split into three separate families of the order Fabales: Mimosaceae, Caesalpiniaceae, and Fabaceae (Papilionaceae). This is the treatment used in this book, although many manuals follow the more traditional approach. In the latter case, these groups are often recognized as subfamilies.

Description of Order Fabales

Trees, shrubs, and herbs. *Leaves* simple to bipinnate, stipules present or absent. *Flowers* actinomorphic to zygomorphic. *Petals* free or some partially united. *Stamens* numerous to few, various. *Pistil* of a solitary, superior carpel. *Fruit* often but not always a legume. The order has 590 genera and 13,200 species and is cosmopolitan in distribution.

Key to Families of Order Fabales

1 Flowers actinomorphic   Mimosaceae
1 Flowers more or less to distinctly zygomorphic.
    2 The upper petal (standard) positioned within the
       adjacent lateral (wing) petals   Caesalpiniaceae
    2 The upper petal(standard) positioned outside the
       lateral (wing) petals   Fabaceae
                                                          (Papilionaceae)

Mimosaceae: Mimosa Family

Field Recognition   Trees, shrubs, or herbs; leaves often bipinnately compound; flowers actinomorphic, 5-merous; stamens 10 to many, usually extended beyond corolla, filaments often brightly colored; CA^5 CO^5 $A^{5-\infty}$ $\underline{G}^1$.

Description   *Habit*   Trees, shrubs, or herbs.
Leaves   Mostly bipinnate, rarely pinnately compound.
Inflorescences   Flowers often in tight clusters, or capitate, spicate, or racemose.
Flowers   Bisexual, actinomorphic. Calyx of 5 sepals, valvate, fused into a 5-lobed tube. Corolla of 5 petals, valvate, free or fused into a tube. Androecium of 5 to numerous stamens. Gynoecium a simple pistil of 1 carpel, with 1 locule, placentation marginal, ovary superior. See Figure 14-50.
Fruit   A legume, sometimes indehiscent.

Size, Distribution, and General Information   A family of about 40 genera and 2000 species. Mostly of tropical or subtropical distribution, with many in dry regions.
Some of the genera are *Prosopis* (40) (mesquite); *Mimosa* (450 to 500) (sensitive plant); *Acacia* (750 to 800); *Albizia* (100 to 150) (mimosa, silk tree); *Schrankia* (30) (sensitive brier); *Desmanthus* (40) (prickle weed); and *Neptunia* (11)
In Mimosaceae, which are represented mostly by woody tropical and subtropical plants, the flowers are small but grouped together into dense clusters. The stamens extend beyond the short petals and give a fluffy soft appearance to the flower cluster. Although the leaves are typically bipinnate, some species have seemingly simple leaves, which are actually phyllodes or leaflike petioles having no blade.
The mesquite (*Prosopis*) is an important small weedy tree in the arid southwestern United States. The leaves of *Mimosa pudica* (sensitive plant) close with the slightest

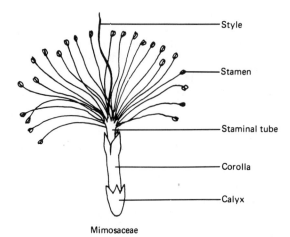

Style

Stamen

Staminal tube

Corolla

Calyx

Mimosaceae

FIGURE 14-50
Flower of Mimosaceae.

touch. Acacias are generally native to warm semiarid regions and are often grown as ornamentals or for cut flowers. *Albizia julibrissin* (mimosa tree) is widely cultivated and has become naturalized in the southeastern United States.

Economic Importance   The family is of little economic importance except for some timber species, ornamentals, and gum arabic or gum acacia from *Acacia senegal* or *A. arabica*. Mesquite wood is used in cooking meats.

Caesalpiniaceae: Caesalpinia Family

Field Recognition   Trees, shrubs, or rarely herbs; flowers more or less zygomorphic, with the large upper petal (standard) inside the two lateral petals (wings); petals 5, stamens 10; $CA^5 \ COZ^5 \ A^{10(\infty)} \ \underline{G}^1$.

**Description   *Habit*   Trees, shrubs, or rarely herbs.
Leaves   Pinnate or bipinnately compound, rarely simple or 1-foliolate; stipules mostly absent.
Inflorescences   Racemes, spikes, or rarely cymose; showy.
Flowers   Bisexual, zygomorphic, rarely subactinomorphic. Calyx of 5 sepals, the upper 2 sometimes fused. Corolla of 5 petals or fewer or absent, the upper petal inside the two lateral petals. Androecium of 10 (rarely numerous) stamens, free or fused. Gynoecium a simple pistil of 1 carpel, with 1 locule, placentation marginal, ovary superior. See Figure 14-51.
Fruit   A legume, sometimes indehiscent; often winged.

Size, Distribution, and General Information   A family of about 150 genera and 2200 species mostly of tropical or subtropical distribution.

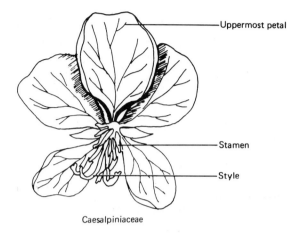

Uppermost petal

Stamen

Style

Caesalpiniaceae

FIGURE 14-51
Caesalpinaceous flower; note
that the uppermost petal is
located within the adjacent two
lateral petals.

Some of the genera are *Gleditsia* (11) (honey locust); *Cassia* (30); *Cercis* (7) (redbud, Judas tree); *Gymnocladus* (3) (Kentucky coffee tree); *Parkinsonia* (2) (palo verde); *Senna* (250); *Bauhinia* (250); and *Chamaecrista* (250).

Economic Importance   The family is important as a source of drugs, dyes, timber, and ornamentals. *Cercis canadensis* (redbud) is a favorite flowering tree in eastern North America. Judas is said to have hanged himself from a tree that we may call *Cercis siliquastrum* (Judas tree). Many species of *Senna* are cultivated for the leaves that yield the drug senna, which is the base for a laxative. *Bauhina purpurea* (orchid tree) is used as an ornamental in the warmer parts of North America. The heartwood of *Haematoxylom campechianum* (logwood) yields the dye hematoxylin.

Fabaceae or Papilionaceae: Bean or Pea Family

Field Recognition   Trees, shrubs, or herbs; leaves pinnately or palmately compound or simple; flowers papilionaceous and distinctly irregular; corolla of 5 petals forming a standard, 2 wings, and a keel (the standard is located to the outside of the 2 wing petals); stamens 10; $CA^{\circlearrowleft}COZ^5 A^{10 \text{ or } \circlearrowleft + 1 \text{ or } \circlearrowleft} \underline{G}^1$.

Description   *Habit*   Trees, shrubs, or herbs.
Leaves   Compound or 1-foliate or rarely simple.
Flowers   Bisexual, zygomorphic. Calyx of 5 sepals, more or less united in a tube. Corolla 5-merous, with a standard petal, 2 lateral wing petals, and 2 keel petals that are more or less fused by their lower margins into a keel. Androecium of 10 stamens, monadelphous or diadelphous. Gynoecium a simple pistil of 1 carpel, with 1 locule, placentation marginal, ovary superior. See Figure 14-52.

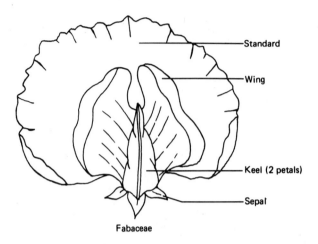

Fabaceae

FIGURE 14-52
Papilionaceous flower of the family Fabaceae; note that the standard is located outside the wing petals.

Fruit   Usually a legume, sometimes indehiscent; rarely a loment breaking into 1-seeded segments.
Seed   Usually with food reserves in cotyledons.

Size, Distribution, and General Information   A family of about 400 genera and 10,000 species, the Fabaceae occur all over the world but particularly in the warm temperate regions of both the Northern and Southern Hemispheres.

Some of the genera are *Crotalaria* (500) (rattlebox); *Lupinus* (200) (lupine); *Cytisus* (25 to 30) (Scotch broom); *Medicago* (110) (bur clover, alfalfa); *Melilotus* (25) (sweet clover); *Trifolium* (300) (clover); *Lotus* (100) (bird's-foot trefoil); *Psoralea* (130) (snakeroot, prairie turnip); *Amorpha* (20) (leadplant); *Indigofera* (500) (indigo); *Wisteria* (10); *Robinia* (20) (black locust); *Sesbania* (50); *Astragalus* (2000) (milk vetch); *Stylosanthes* (50) (pencil flower); *Arachis* (15) (peanut, groundnut); *Desmodium* (450) (beggar-lice); *Lespedeza* (100); *Vicia* (150) (vetch, broad bean); *Lathyrus* (150) (sweet pea); *Abrus* (12) (rosary pea); *Centrosema* (45) (blue pea); *Clitoria* (40) (butterfly pea); *Sophora* (50) (Japanese pagoda tree); *Baptisia* (35) (false indigo); *Glycine* (10) (soybean); *Cicer* (20) (chickpea); *Lens* (10) (lentil); *Pisum* (6) (English or garden pea); *Vigna* (80 to 100) (southern pea); *Erythrina* (100) (coral tree, coral bean); *Phaseolus* (200) (cultivated beans); and *Pueraria* (35) (kudzu).

Economic Importance   The family is of considerable importance as a source of high-protein food, oil, and forage as well as ornamentals and other uses. *Glycine max* (soybean or soya) is becoming one of the world's most important crops as a source of oil and high-protein meal. *Phaseolus vulgaris* (kidney bean), *P. lunatus* (lima beans), *P. coccineus* (scarlet runner beans), and many other cultivars of beans have been developed such as pole beans, bush beans, and half-runners. Snap or string beans are immature fruits in which the seeds have not yet ripened. *Vigna unguiculata* (cowpea) is enjoyed by people in the southern states. *Vicia faba* (the broad bean), *Pisum sativum*

(English or garden pea), and *Lens esculenta* (lentil) were used by Eurasian peoples before the New World beans were discovered and introduced into the Old World. *Cicer arietinum* (chick-pea) is grown in southern Europe, India, and elsewhere.

Alfalfa (*Medicago sativa*) is one of the world's best forage and hay crops and the various kinds of clover, *Trifolium, Melilotus,* and *Vicia,* are likewise raised to feed cattle. These same plants are good nectar producers and are sought by honeybees. Peanuts (*Arachis hypogaea*), also known as groundnuts or goobers, produce a valuable crop of edible seeds, oil, meal, and peanut butter. The yellow flower of the peanut develops above ground, but growth of the flower stalk pushes the ripening ovary into the soil where the fruits mature underground.

Indigo dye is obtained by fermenting and oxidizing the juice from the leaves of the indigo plant (*Indigofera tinctoria*). The hard, red, black-tipped seeds of *Abrus precatorius* are strung into necklaces and rosaries. The seeds are highly poisonous, and the ingestion of one seed can be fatal. The pastel-colored sweet peas (*Lathyrus odoratus*) are ornamental garden favorites. The genus *Lupinus* has contributed the cultivated lupines of the cooler areas of North America, as well as the beloved Texas bluebonnet. *Wisteria* is grown as a vine or pruned into the shape of a tree. The black locust (*Robinia pseudoacacia*) produces a cloud of pendant clusters of white flowers in the spring. Black locust wood is prized for fence posts because it is relatively resistant to decay.

SUBCLASS V, ROSIDAE; ORDER 6, MYRTALES
Lythraceae: Loosestrife Family

Field Recognition Herbs, shrubs, or trees; leaves usually opposite, entire, simple; flowers borne in racemes, panicles or cymes, actinomorphic or zygomorphic, bisexual, with a hypanthium; fruit a dry, dehiscent or indehiscent capsule; $\underline{CA^{4 \text{ or } 6} \ CO^{4 \text{ or } 6} \ A^{8 \text{ or } 12 \text{ or } \infty}} \ \underline{G \widehat{(2\text{–}6)}}$.

Description *Habit* Herbs, shrubs or trees.

Leaves Opposite, sometimes whorled or spiral, simple, entire; with small stipules or none.

Inflorescences Racemose, paniculate, or cymose.

Flowers Bisexual, actinomorphic or zygomorphic, usually 4 or 6-merous, hypanthium present, sepals appearing like lobes of hypanthium. Calyx a hollow tube. Corolla with petals crumpled in bud. Androecium with stamens inserted at different levels on the calyx tube. Gynoecium of 2–6 united carpels, 2–6 locular, ovules usually numerous, placentation axile, ovary superior, style simple, stigma usually capitate. See Figure 14-53.

Fruit Dry capsule.

Seed Without endosperm.

Size, Distribution, and General Information A small family of around 24 genera and about 500 species; widespread in tropical regions with relatively few species in temperate areas.

Lythraceae

FIGURE 14-53
Lythrum (Lythraceae). Vertical section of flower.

The family owes its name to the purple loosestrife, *Lythrum salicaria,* a plant of wetlands. Some of the larger genera include *Cuphea* (200); *Lagerstroemia* (30) (crepe myrtle); *Rotala* (50); *Lythrum* (30).

Economic Importance   The leaves of *Lawsonia inermis* are the source of the dye, henna, used largely for hair dye but also for silk, wool, and leather. Many species of *Cuphea* from South America are grown as garden or greenhouse ornamentals; *C. ignea* (cigar-flower) and *C. lanceolata,* with their red corollas, attract humming birds. *Lagerstroemia indica* is widely cultivated as an ornamental shrub in the warmer parts of the United States. Several species of *Lythrum* are grown as perennials in flower gardens.

SUBCLASS V, ROSIDAE; ORDER 6, MYRTALES
Myrtaceae: Myrtle Family

Field Recognition   Shrubs to large trees; leaves glandular-dotted; stamens numerous; ovary inferior; CA^{4-5} CO^{4-5} A^{∞} $\overline{G}^{2-3}$.

Description   *Habit*   Woody plants, mostly shrubs to large trees.
Leaves   Usually opposite, sometimes alternate, simple, leathery, evergreen, entire, characteristically glandular-dotted; without stipules.
Inflorescences   Mostly cymose, sometimes racemose, rarely solitary.
Flower   Bisexual, actinomorphic, epigynous (some perigynous). Calyx of 4 or 5 sepals, usually free, sometimes more or less united to form a cap which drops off as the flower opens. Corolla of 4–5 petals. Androecium of numerous stamens. Gynoecium of 2–3 united carpels, with one to many (often 2–5) locules, with 2-many ovules, placentation axile (rarely parietal), ovary commonly inferior, style long and simple with a capitate stigma. See Figure 14-54.

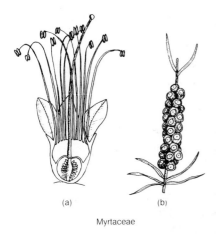

(a)   (b)

Myrtaceae

FIGURE 14-54
Callistemon (Myrtaceae). (a) Vertical section of
flower revealing the inferior ovary and numerous
stamens, and (b) fruiting branch (redrawn from
Heywood, 1978).

Fruit   A fleshy berry, rarely a drupe, or a dry capsule or nut.
Seed   With little or no endosperm.

Size Distribution, and General Information   A family of about 140 genera and
3,000 species largely distributed in subtropical and tropical regions and abundant in
Australia. Some Australian eucalyptus trees are the world's tallest angiosperms.

Systematics   The family is classified into two subfamilies: Myrtoideae with epigynous flowers and fleshy fruit; and Leptospermoideae having dry fruit and either
perigynous or epigynous flowers.
    Some of the genera are *Eucalyptus* (500); *Callistemon* (25); *Syzygium* (500); *Pimenta*
(18); *Myrtus* (100); *Melaleuca* (101); *Psidium* (140); and *Eugenia* (1000).
    Myrtles once played an important part in religious rites and ceremonies. Egyptian
women wore the classical myrtle flowers (*Myrtus communis*) along with those of the
pomegranate and the lotus on festive occasions, and in Persia, myrtles were regarded
as holy plants. To the Jew, the myrtle was a symbol of peace; among Greeks it was
sacred to Aphrodite and in Rome sacred to Venus.

Economic Importance   Economically, the most important genus is *Eucalyptus*
used for timber, ornamentals, reforestation, and the source of eucalyptus oil commonly
used as a flavoring, expectorant, and inhalant. *Psidium guajava*, the guava tree, yields
a delicious fruit. The tropical Surinam cherry is from *Eugenia uniflora*. *Syzygium
aromaticum* is the source of cloves and clove oil. Jamaican pepper, better known as
allspice or pimento is produced by a member of the Myrtaceae, *Pimenta dioica*. Another
species, *P. racemosa,* provides oil of bay rum. There are a number of particularly
beautiful ornamental shrubs in the genus *Callistemon*. The flowers of *Callistemon* have
showy stamens which are so closely crowded together they resemble bottle brushes,
the common name of the group.

SUBCLASS V, ROSIDAE; ORDER 5, MYRTALES

Onagraceae: Evening Primrose Family

Field Recognition Herbs; flowers 4-merous, rarely 2-merous; hypanthium present, and on its rim are inserted sepals, petals, and stamens; ovary inferior; $CA^4\ CO^4\ A^{4\ or\ 8}\ \overline{G}^{④}$.

Description *Habit* Herbs or rarely shrubs, sometimes aquatic.
Leaves Alternative or opposite, simple; stipules mostly absent or deciduous.
Inflorescences Spicate, racemose, or paniculate, or the flowers solitary.
Flowers Bisexual, actinomorphic. Hypanthium present. Calyx of (2)4(5) sepals, persistent or deciduous, fused to the ovary. Corolla of (2)4(5) petals, sometimes none. Androecium of 4 stamens, or twice as many as calyx lobes. Gynoecium of 1 pistil with 4 carpels, with 2 to 6 locules, ovules 1 to many, placentation axile, ovary inferior, style simple, but stigma sometimes lobed or parted. See Figure 14-55.
Fruit A capsule, nut, or berry.
Seed With little or no endosperm.

FIGURE 14-55
Oenothera biennis (Onagraceae). Vertical section of flower showing the long hypanthium and the inferior ovary.

Onagraceae

Size, Distribution, and General Information   A well-defined family of about 17 genera and 675 species of temperate and subtropical distribution.

Chief genera are *Epilobium* (200) (fireweed, willowweed); *Ludwigia* (80) (seedbox, primrose willow); *Clarkia* (36); *Oenothera* (125) (evening primrose); *Fuchsia* (90); *Gaura* (18); *Lopezia* (17); and *Circaea* (12) (enchanter's nightshade).

Named in honor of the sixteenth-century herbalist Fuchs, *Fuchsia* is a popular greenhouse or garden plant in temperate climates, and an almost endless array of cultivars have been developed. *Epilobium* quickly colonizes on burned areas in certain regions, giving it the name *fireweed*. The flowers of *Oenothera* are bright yellow or white, and sometimes turning pink or reddish. They are called *evening primroses* because their flowers characteristically open in the late afternoon and close again early the next morning.

Economic Importance   The family is of little importance. Species of several genera are cultivated as ornamentals.

SUBCLASS V, ROSIDAE; ORDER 6, MYRTALES
Melastomataceae: Melastoma Family

Field Recognition   Leaves opposite and decussate (each pair at right angles to the next), venation typically palmate and parallel; stamen filaments geniculate (elbow-shaped) with sterile appendages of various shapes; $CA^{4-5} CO^{4-5} A^{8-10} \underline{G}\ \overline{(1\text{-}14)}$ or $\overline{G}\ \overline{(1\text{-}14)}$.

Description   *Habit*   Mainly shrubs and small tress, but also a few herbs, vines, marsh plants and epiphytes.

Leaves   Opposite and decussate or rarely alternate (by abortion), main veins (3 to 9 pairs) palmate and parallel; without stipules.

Flowers   Bisexual, actinomorphic. Calyx of 4 or 5 sepals. Corolla of 4 or 5 free petals. Androecium usually of 8 to 10 stamens, filaments geniculate with sterile appendages, anthers usually dehisce by a terminal pore. Gynoecium a compound pistil of 1 to 14 carpels, with 4 or 5 locules each with two to many ovules, placentation axile, basal or parietal, ovary superior or inferior, style simple. See Figure 14-56.

Fruit   A berry or loculicidal capsule.

Seed   Small, numerous and without endosperm.

Size, Distribution, and General Information   A family of about 200 genera and 4,000 species; its distribution largely tropical and subtropical, centered in South America, but extending into the temperate zone.

Some of the genera include *Melastoma* (70), *Rhexia* (10), *Medinilla* (300), and *Miconia* (1000).

Economic Importance   The family is of no significant economic importance but there is some local use of the wood and edible fruits of some species and a few are grown as ornamentals. Several species of *Medinilla*, with their showy flowers, can

Melastomataceae

FIGURE 14-56
Melastoma (Melastomataceae).
Vertical view of a flower, note shape
of filaments.

often be found in botanical gardens where they make fine ornamentals. Several species of the genera *Bertolonia, Miconia,* and *Sonerila* are cultivated in conservatories and greenhouses for their beautiful leaves. In temperate North America, the hardy *Rhexia virginica* is often grown in gardens.

SUBCLASS V, ROSIDAE; ORDER 8, CORNALES
Cornaceae: Dogwood Family

Field Recognition   Trees and shrubs; leaves opposite or alternate, veins curved; flowers 4- to 5-merous; stamens alternate with the petals; ovary inferior; fruit a drupe or berry; CA$\underset{\smile}{4-5}$ CO $\underset{\smile}{4-5}$ A$^{4-5}$ $\overline{\text{G}}$ $^{\textcircled{2}}$.

Description   *Habit*   Trees and shrubs, or rarely perennial herbs.
Leaves   Opposite or alternate, simple, veins curved, without stipules.
Inflorescences   Cymose, corymbose, or capitate, sometimes subtended by showy, petal-like bracts; plants rarely dioecious.
Flowers   Bisexual or unisexual, actinomorphic, small. Calyx of 4 to 5 sepals, fused to ovary. Corolla of 4 to 5 petals, free, rarely absent. Androecium of 4 to 5 stamens, alternate with petals. Gynoecium a compound pistil of 2 carpels, with 1 to 4 locules, ovule solitary in each locule, placentation axile, ovary inferior, style simple. See Figure 14-57.
Fruit   A fleshy drupe or berry.
Seed   With endosperm.

Cornaceae

FIGURE 14-57
Cornus florida (Cornaceae). Inflorescence of small flowers surrounded by four large bracts.

Size, Distribution, and General Information   A family of about 11 genera and 100 species of north and south temperate and tropical mountain distribution.

Some of the genera are *Cornus* (50) (dogwood) and *Aucuba* (4) (gold-dust plant).

Dogwoods should be called "dagwoods"; in medieval times they were a source of a hardwood used for making wooden daggers. The wood is as hard as horn, hence the generic name *Cornus,* which comes from the Latin *cornu,* "horn." Several of the dogwoods have showy white bracts subtending each inflorescence.

Economic Importance   The Cornaceae are important for ornamental shrubs or small trees. *Aucuba* is grown in the warm temperate states. *Cornus florida* is widely grown in eastern North America. Western flowering dogwood (*C. nuttallii*) occurs naturally from California to British Columbia and Idaho and is used as an ornamental. Fruits of the cornelian cherry (*C. mas*) are edible.

SUBCLASS V, ROSIDAE; ORDER 11, CELASTRALES
Aquifoliaceae: Holly Family

Field Recognition   Trees or shrubs; leaves deciduous or evergreen, alternate, simple (sometimes spiny); flowers inconspicuous, greenish-white, bisexual or unisexual (plants dioecious in latter), 3-locular, style single, terminal, placentation axile; fruit a berry, usually with 4 hard pyrenes; $CA^{4(6)}$ $CO^{4(6) \, or} A^4$ $\underline{G}^{④}$. See Figure 14-58.

Size, Distribution, and General Information   A small family of 4 genera: *Ilex* (400), *Nemopanthus* (2), *Sphenostemon* (7) and *Phelline* (10); widely distributed in both temperate and tropical regions but rare in Australia and Africa.

Economic Importance   Many species of *Ilex* or hollies are grown as ornamentals; holly has long been used for religious decorating. The wood of holly is used for

(a)

(b)

(c)

Aquifoliaceae

FIGURE 14-58
Ilex (Aquifoliaceae). (a) Flowering branch, (b) pistillate flower with four staminodes, and (c) staminate flower (parts a and b redrawn from Heywood, 1978).

carvings and for inlays. The leaves of the South American *I. paraguariensis* are used to make yerba maté or Paraguay tea. Because of high caffeine content, Yerba maté basically has the same function for many South Americans as tea and coffee have in North America.

SUBCLASS V, ROSIDAE; ORDER 12, EUPHORBIALES
Euphorbiaceae: Spurge Family

Field Recognition   Herbs, shrubs, or trees; often with milky sap; leaves mostly alternate; flowers unisexual; ovary superior and usually trilocular, ovules often with a caruncle; "Euphorbia-type" flowers: $(CA^0\ CO^0\ A^1\ G^0)\ (CA^0\ CO^0\ A^0\ \underline{G}^{③})$; "non-Euphorbia"-type flowers: $(CA^{0\ or\ 5}\ CO^{0\ or\ 5}\ A^{1-∞}\ G^0)\ (CA^{0\ or\ 5}\ CO^{0\ or\ 5}\ A^0\ \underline{G}^{③})$.

Description   *Habit*   Herbs, shrubs, or trees; some xerophytic and cactus-like, often with a milky sap.

Leaves   Mostly alternate, simple or compound, often reduced or deciduous in xerophytic species; with stipules.

Inflorescences   Various, often condensed, hence giving the appearance of a single flower, a cyathium; plants monoecious or dioecious.

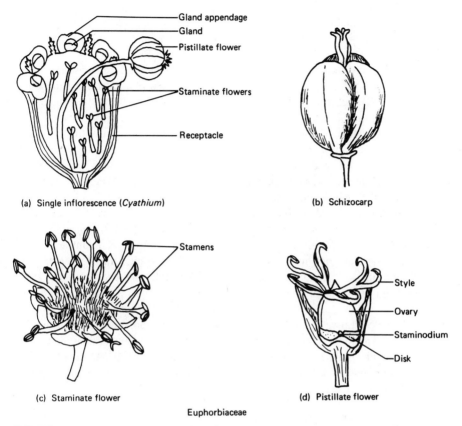

(a) Single inflorescence (*Cyathium*)

(b) Schizocarp

(c) Staminate flower

(d) Pistillate flower

Euphorbiaceae

FIGURE 14-59
Diagrammatic drawings of floral structures typical of family Euphorbiaceae. (a) "*Euphorbia*-type" inflorescence. (b) Three-lobed schizocarp. (c) "Non-*Euphorbia*"-type staminate flower. (d) "Non-*Euphorbia*"-type pistillate flower.

Flowers Unisexual, actinomorphic. Calyx of 5 sepals or none. Corolla of 5 petals or usually none. Androecium of 1 to many stamens, free or united, rudimentary ovary often present in the male flowers. Gynoecium a compound pistil of 3 united carpels, with 3 locules, ovules solitary or paired, placentation axile, ovary superior, styles free or united at base. See Figure 14-59.

Fruit A schizocarp or capsule.

Seed Often with a conspicuous caruncle.

Size, Distribution, and General Information A family of about 300 genera and 7500 species of wide distribution in tropical and temperate regions.

Some of the chief genera are *Euphorbia* (2000) (spurge, poinsettia); *Phyllanthus* (600); *Hevea* (12) (pará or Brazilian rubber tree); *Aleurites* (2) (tung oil tree); *Croton* (700) (croton oil); *Manihot* (150) (cassava, manioc, yuca, tapioca); *Acalypha* (450) (chenille plant, red hot cattail); *Ricinus* (1) (castor bean); *Hippomane* (5) (manchineel tree); *Pedilanthus* (14); *Tragia* (100) (nose-burn); *Sapium* (120) (Chinese tallow tree); and *Jatropha* (175).

Euphorbiaceae are one of the most diverse in habit, habitat, and morphology of the flowering plant families. They range from the tall tree *Hevea* of the Amazonian rain forest to small cactuslike succulents of Africa. The familiar Christmas poinsettia from Mexico was introduced into cultivation in 1828 by Mr. J. R. Poinsett, the United States minister to Mexico. The red or greenish-white leaves of poinsettia are bracts subtending the small flower clusters.

An extract from the seeds of castor bean is used as a purgative. The seeds also yield a fine machine oil. Castor beans contain a highly toxic substance called *ricin* that can cause death when small amounts are ingested. The manchineel tree (*Hippomane mancinella*) of the West Indies has a poisonous sap, and even the rainwater dripping from the tree is enough to cause dermatitis. The roots of *Manihot esculenta* (cassava) yield a starch widely used for human food in tropical countries. Many cultivars of cassava are rich in HCN (hydrocyanic acid), which must be neutralized during preparation of the roots before cooking. Croton oil, once used as a purgative, is obtained from the seeds of *Croton tiglium*.

Economic Importance   The family is of considerable importance for the following products: Brazilian rubber (*Hevea*), castor oil (*Ricinus communis*), cassava and tapioca (*Manihot*), florists' poinsettia (*Euphorbia pulcherrima*), tung oil (*Aleurites fordii*), and numerous ornamentals. Many are poisonous, causing sickness or death if ingested or dermatitis if the juice contacts the skin.

SUBCLASS V, ROSIDAE; ORDER 13, RHAMNALES
Rhamnaceae: Buckthorn Family

Field Recognition   Trees and shrubs; flowers perigynous; stamens opposite the petals; $CA^5 CO^5 A_5 \underline{G}^3$.

Description   *Habit*   Mostly trees or shrubs, often climbing, some thorny.
Leaves   Leaves simple; usually with stipules.
Inflorescences   Cymose.
Flowers   Small, bisexual or rarely unisexual, actinomorphic, sometimes apetalous. Calyx valvate of 5 sepals. Corolla of 5 small petals usually concave, often clawed at base. Androecium of stamens alternating with the sepals. Disk usually well developed. Gynoecium of 3 united carpels, free or united to receptacle, usually 2–3 locular, ovary superior, style simple or divided. See Figure 14-60.
Fruit   Dry, splitting into mericarps, or a drupe or nut.

Size, Distribution, and General Information   A family of about 55 genera and 900 species; cosmopolitan in distribution. Some of the chief genera are *Rhamnus* (150), *Ceanothus* (40), and *Zizyphus* (100).

Rhamnaceae

FIGURE 14-60
Zizyphus (Rhamnaceae). Vertical section through a flower.

Economic Importance The genus *Ceanothus,* restricted to North and Central America, has the majority of its species in the western United States. Many species of *Ceanothus* are grown for their beautiful panicles of blue, pink, or white flowers. *Ceanothus americanus* (New Jersey Tea) is widespread in the eastern United States. A delicious fruit from *Zizyphus jujuba* (jujube or Chinese date) is used to make a jellylike candy. The lotus eaters of Greek legend probably lived on the fruit of *Z. lotus.* Several dyes and medicinals are obtained from the Rhamnaceae.

SUBCLASS V, ROSIDAE; ORDER 13, RHAMNALES
Vitaceae: Grape Family

Field Recognition Woody, climbing by tendrils; inflorescences opposite the leaves; stamens opposite the petals; fruit a berry; CA$\widehat{^{4-5}}$CO$^{4-5}$ A$^{4-5}$ $\underline{G}^{②}$.

Description *Habit* Shrubs climbing by tendrils, or small trees, often with watery juice.
Leaves Alternate, simple or compound; stipules petiolar or absent.
Inflorescences Racemose, paniculate, cymose, borne opposite the leaves.
Flowers Bisexual or unisexual, actinomorphic. Calyx of 4 to 5 small sepals, united. Corolla of 4 to 5 petals, free or united at the tips. Androecium of 4 to 5 stamens, opposite the petals and arising from a disc. Gynoecium a compound pistil

Vitaceae

FIGURE 14-61
Vitis (Vitaceae). (a) Fruiting branch, (b) pistillate flower, and (c)
staminate flower.

of 2 united carpels, with 2 to 6 locules, each with 1 or 2 ovules, ovary superior, style
short, capitate. See Figure 14-61.

Fruit   Berrylike, often with watery juice.

Seed   With a straight embryo and endosperm.

Size, Distribution, and General Information   A family of about 11 genera and
700 species of tropical and warm temperate distribution.

Chief genera are *Vitis* (60 to 70) (grape); *Cissus* (300); *Ampelocissus* (95); *Parthenocissus* (15) (Virginia creeper, Boston ivy); and *Ampelopsis* (2) (pepper vine).

The wine grape (*Vitis vinifera*) is probably native to the area around the Caspian
Sea. Hieroglyphics from ancient Egypt show details of wine production. Thousands
of cultivars have been developed by hybridization and selection. These cultivars are
used for various purposes: wines, table grapes, or raisins.

Economic Importance   Vitaceae are important for the wine grapes, table grapes,
grape juice, raisins, and for several ornamentals.

SUBCLASS V, ROSIDAE; ORDER 14, LINALES

Linaceae: Flax Family

Field Recognition   Flowers 5-merous; petals distinct and often clawed; stamens
with filaments united at base; fruit a capsule; CA^5 CO^5 $A^{5 \text{ or } 10}$ $\underline{G}^{(2-5)}$.

Description *Habit* Herbs and shrubs, sometimes arborescent.
Leaves Alternate, simple, entire; stipules present or absent, sometimes gland-like.
Inflorescences Cymose.
Flowers Bisexual, actinomorphic. Calyx of (4)5 sepals, free or partially united. Corolla of (4)5 petals, free, often clawed. Androecium of 5, 10, or more stamens; if 5, alternate with the petals or sometimes alternating with small staminodes, filaments united at base. Gynoecium a compound pistil of 2 to 5 carpels, with 2 locules, ovules 2 in each locule, placentation axile, ovary superior, styles 3 to 5, free or united. See Figure 14-62.
Fruit A capsule or rarely a drupe.
Seed With fleshy endosperm and a straight embryo.

Size, Distribution, and General Information A family of about 6 genera and 220 species.

The major genus is *Linum* (230) (flax).

Flax is the stem fiber of *Linum usitatissimum* obtained by retting the softer tissues in water. Linseed oil, used in paints and varnishes, is obtained from the seeds of flax. Oil cake, which is the cake remaining after the oil is extracted, is used as cattle feed. Flax cultivation extends back at least 5000 years; linen cloth has been found in Egyptian tombs. By the 1700s, the use of flax fibers to make cloth for bed sheets became common. We continue to call them linens.

FIGURE 14-62
Linum (Linaceae). (a) Flowering branch and (b) vertical section of flower.

(b)

(a)

Linaceae

Economic Importance   The family is important for flax, linseed oil, and oil cake.

SUBCLASS V, ROSIDAE; ORDER 15, POLYGALALES

Polygalaceae: Milkwort Family

Field Recognition   Perianth greatly modified, often appearing papilionaceous; sepals often petaloid; stamens unusual, united in a split sheath beyond the middle; anthers opening by an apical pore; ovary biloculate; seeds often pilose; CA^5 COZ^{3-5} A^{3-8} $\underline{G}^{\circledcirc}$.

Description   *Habit*   Herbs, shrubs, climbers, or rarely small trees.
Leaves   Alternate, rarely opposite, simple; without stipules.
Inflorescences   Solitary, spicate, or racemose.
Flowers   Bisexual, zygomorphic. Calyx of 5 sepals, free, the 2 inner often petaloid, wing-like. Corolla of 3 to 5 petals, outer 2 free or united with the lower most, upper 2 free, or minute or scalelike. Androecium of 3 to 8 stamens, united beyond the middle, with a split sheath, sometimes fused to the petals, anthers opening by an apical pore. Gynoecium a compound pistil of 2(5) carpels, with 2(3 to 5) locules, ovules solitary in each locule, placentation axile, ovary superior, style simple. See Figure 14-63.
Fruit   Capsular or drupelike.
Seed   Often pilose.

Size, Distribution, and General Information   A family of about 12 genera and 750 species of temperate and tropical distribution.
The chief genera are *Polygala* (500) (milkwort, candy flower) and *Monnina* (150).

FIGURE 14-63
Polygala (Polygalaceae). Vertical section of flower.

Polygalaceae

Economic Importance   The family is of little economic importance. *Polygala senega* (snakeroot) is medicinal. Several species of *Polygala* are sometimes used as ornamentals.

SUBCLASS V, ROSIDAE; ORDER 16, SAPINDALES
Sapindaceae: Soapberry Family

Field Recognition   Trees or shrubs; leaves pinnately compound; flowers small; petals glandular; stamens with hairy filaments; $CA^5 CO^5 A^{10} \underline{G}^{\circledS}$.

Description   *Habit*   Trees, shrubs, or in some cases tendril-bearing vines.

Leaves   Alternate or very rarely opposite, simple or pinnately compound; stipules usually absent.

Inflorescences   Racemose, paniculate, or cymose; the plants commonly polygamo-dioecious.

Flowers   Bisexual or unisexual, actinomorphic or zygomorphic. Calyx of 5 sepals, free or united. Corolla of 5 petals, sometimes 3 or absent, equal or unequal. Androecium of (4)10(∞) stamens, inserted within a prominent receptacular disc, filaments free and often hairy. Gynoecium a compound pistil of 3 united carpels, with 1 to 4 (often 3) locules, ovules 1 to 2 or many in each locule, placentation parietal, ovary superior, style terminal. See Figure 14-64.

Fruit   A capsule, nut, berry, drupe, schizocarp, or samara.

Seed   Often arillate, with a curved embryo and no endosperm.

Size, Distribution, and General Information   A family of about 140 genera and 1500 species of mainly tropical and subtropical distribution.

Some of the genera are *Sapindus* (13) (soapberry); *Litchi* (2); *Koelreuteria* (8) (golden rain tree); *Blighia* (7) (akee, vegetable marrow); *Cardiospermum* (12) (balloon vine); and *Paullinia* (150) (guarana).

The family takes its name from the soapberry tree (*Sapindus saponaria*), which contains saponin. When saponin is moistened, it forms a lather and may be used as a soap. *Paullinia cupana* (guarana) is cultivated in Brazil. Its seeds are used like cacao to make a drink high in caffeine content. The akee tree (*Blighia sapida*), originally from tropical West Africa and grown in the West Indies, produces handsome orange or red fruits, each about 8 centimeters long. The aril is cooked and eaten, but it must be gathered at the proper time or it is poisonous. *Litchi chinensis* (lychee or litchi nut) is cultivated for its edible fruit, which is a one-seeded nut. It is a favorite of the Cantonese.

Economic Importance   The family is of some importance as the source of guarana, lychee nuts, and akee, plus some ornamentals.

(a)

Sapindaceae

(b)

(c)

FIGURE 14-64
Koelreuteria paniculata (Sapindaceae).
(a) Leaf, (b) flower, and (c) fruit.

SUBCLASS V, ROSIDAE; ORDER 16, SAPINDALES

Hippocastanaceae: Horse Chestnut or Buckeye Family

Field Recognition   Trees and shrubs; leaves opposite, palmately compound; flowers zygomorphic; $CA^{\circled{5}} COZ^{4-5} A^{5-8} \underline{G}^{\circled{3}}$.

Description   *Habit*   Trees and shrubs, with large winter buds.

Leaves   Opposite, palmately compound, leaflets serrate or entire, pinnately veined; stipules absent.

Inflorescences   In terminal panicles or racemes.

Flowers   Bisexual, zygomorphic. Calyx of 5 sepals, usually united at base. Corolla of 4 to 5 petals, free, unequal. Androecium of 5 to 8 stamens, free. Gynoecium a compound pistil of 3 united carpels, with 3 locules or by abortion 1 to 2 locules, ovules 2 in each locule, placentation axile, ovary superior, style elongated with a simple stigma. See Figure 14-65.

Fruit   A leathery capsule with 1 or more large seeds, 3-lobed or 1- or 2-lobed by abortion.

Seed   Large.

FIGURE 14-65
Aesculus hippocastanum (Hippocastanaceae). (a) Leaf, (b) flower, and (c) vertical section of flower.

Size, Distribution, and General Information   A family of 2 genera and 16 species of north temperate and South American distribution.

The two genera are *Aesculus* (13) (buckeye, horse chestnut) and *Billia* (3).

The horse chestnut (*Aesculus hippocastanum*) is widely planted in Europe and the cooler parts of North America. It is probably the most familiar species in the family. The Ohio buckeye is *A. glabra*.

Economic Importance   The family is of importance for several ornamental trees and shrubs. The seeds and apparently the foliage are poisonous.

SUBCLASS V, ROSIDAE; ORDER 16, SAPINDALES

Aceraceae: Maple Family

Field Recognition   Trees or shrubs; leaves opposite, usually simple with palmate venation; flowers actinomorphic; fruit a winged schizocarp; CA^{4-5} CO^{4-5} $A^{4 \text{ or } 8 \text{ or } 10}$ $\underline{G}^{②}$.

Description   *Habit*   Trees and shrubs.

Aceraceae

FIGURE 14-66
Acer saccharum (Aceraceae). (a) Fruit and (b) flowering branch.

Leaves   Opposite, simple, usually palmately lobed and veined, or sometimes pinnately compound.

Inflorescences   Fasciculate corymbose, racemose, or paniculate; the plants monoecious, polygamous, or dioecious.

Flowers   Bisexual or unisexual, actinomorphic. Calyx of 4 to 5 sepals. Corolla of 4 to 5 petals or none. Androecium of 4, 8, or 10 stamens, free, with a prominent receptacular disc; rudimentary ovary often present in male flowers. Gynoecium a compound pistil of 2 united carpels, with 2 locules, ovules 2 in each locule, placentation axile, ovary superior, styles 2. See Figure 14-66.

Fruit   A 2-winged schizocarp, separating when ripe.

Size, Distribution, and General Information   A family of 2 genera and 112 species of north temperate and tropical mountain distribution.

The two genera are *Acer* (110) (maple, box elder) and *Dipteronia* (2).

Few trees of eastern North America contribute so much to the autumn coloration as do the various species of maple. The maple wood or "hard maple" used in furniture is either that of sugar maple (*A. saccharum*) or black maple (*A. nigrum*). These two species also yield a water sap that is boiled to produce maple syrup.

Economic Importance   The family is important for maple wood used in furntiure and charcoal, for maple syrup, and for many ornamental trees.

SUBCLASS V, ROSIDAE; ORDER 16, SAPINDALES

Anacardiaceae: Cashew Family

Field Recognition   Trees or shrubs; flowers 5-merous; stamens inserted beneath a disc surrounding the ovary; ovary unilocular; $CA^5 \ CO^5 \ A^{10} \ \underline{G}^{③}$.

Description   *Habit*   Trees and shrubs, often with a resinous bark and a milky sap.

Leaves   Alternate, simple or compound; without stipules.

Inflorescences   Paniculate.

Flowers   Bisexual or unisexual, actinomorphic. Calyx of 5 sepals, variously divided. Corolla of (3)5(7) petals or absent, free or rarely united. Androecium usually of (5)10 stamens, arising from beneath a disc, filaments free. Gynoecium a compound pistil of (1)3(5) united carpels, with 1(2 to 5) locules, ovule solitary, placentation axile, ovary superior, styles 1 to 3. See Figure 14-67.

FIGURE 14-67
Rhus (Anacardiaceae). (a) Leaf, (b) fruiting inflorescence, and (c) bisexual flower.

(b)

(a)

(c)

Anacardiaceae

Fruit   Usually a drupe.
Seed   Embryo curved, endosperm absent.

Size, Distribution, and General Information   A family of about 60–80 genera and 600 species, mostly of tropical distribution but found in temperate areas of the Mediterranean, eastern Asia, and America.

The chief genera are *Rhus* (including *Toxicodendron*) (250) (lacquer tree, sumac, poison ivy); *Pistacia* (10) (China turpentine, pistachio nuts, mastic); *Mangifera* (40) (mango); *Anacardium* (15) (cashew nut); *Schinus* (30) (pepper tree, American mastic); and *Cotinus* (3) (smoke tree).

Economic Importance   The family is important for the cashew, pistachio, mango, resins, oils, lacquers, tannic acids, and several ornamentals. Also, it is important as a cause of contact dermatitis in humans.

The lacquer tree (*Rhus vernicifera*) of China and Japan has been milked for its poisonous latex for centuries. The viscous sap is applied by brush to various wood carvings; it turns black with oxidation, forming the common lacquer ware of the Orient. Poison ivy, poison oak, and poison sumac are well known in North America. Dermatitis in humans can be caused by touching the plants, having contact with smoke particles from burning parts of the plants, or by having contact with animals that have brushed against the plants. The leather-tanning industry uses Sicilian sumac (*Rhus coriaria*) and the red quebracho (*Schinopsis lorentzii*) of Argentina and Paraguay as sources of tannic acids.

Mangifera indica (mango) is a delightful tropical fruit. The cashew tree (*Anacardium occidentale*) of northeastern South America, Central America, and the southern West Indies bears a strange kidney-shaped fruit on a flower stalk that enlarges to form a figlike or pearlike structure. The fruit and seed coat of the cashew contain a poison; however, the seeds are edible. *Pistacia vera* of the Mediterranean is the source of pistachio nuts. The first turpentine used by artists came from the terebinth tree (*P. terebinthus*).

SUBCLASS V, ROSIDAE; ORDER 16, SAPINDALES
Rutaceae: Citrus or Rue Family

Field Recognition   Shrubs and trees with aromatic oil glands; leaves glandular punctate; outer stamens usually opposite the petals; ovary deeply lobed; CA^{4-5} $CO^{(0)4-5}$ $A^{8-10(\infty)}$ $\underline{G}^{\boxed{4-5}}$.

Description   *Habit*   Shrubs, trees, and very rarely herbs; often xerophytic and aromatic.

Leaves   Alternate or opposite, simple or compound, glandular dotted; without stipules.

Inflorescences   Cymose.

Rutaceae

FIGURE 14-68
Citrus (Rutaceae). (a) Flowering shoot and (b) vertical section
of flower.

Flowers   Bisexual or rarely unisexual, actinomorphic or rarely zygomorphic. Calyx
of 4 to 5 sepals, free or united. Corolla of 4 to 5 petals, sometimes none, mostly free.
Androecium of 8 to 10 stamens (rarely many), free or rarely united, attached to a
disc. Gynoecium a compound pistil of 4 to 5 united carpels (sometimes free at base
and united above by style), with 4 to 5 locules, ovules 1 to 2 in each locule, placentation
axile, ovary superior. See Figure 14-68.
Fruit   A capsule, hesperidium, drupe, or samara, rarely a schizocarp, or follicle.
Seed   Without endosperm.

Size, Distribution, and General Information   A family of about 150 genera and
1500 species of temperate and tropical distribution, numerous in southern Africa and
Australia.
Some of the chief genera are *Citrus* (12); *Zanthoxylum* (200) (prickly ash, toothache
tree); *Ruta* (7) (rue); *Ptelea* (3) (hop wafer tree); *Murraya* (12) (curry bush, orange
jessamine); and *Fortunella* (6) (kumquat).

Economic Importance   The family is of considerable importance as a source of
citrus fruits, curry, bitters, and several ornamentals.
Citrus produces some of the world's most important fruits, the tasty and juicy citrus
fruits which are high in vitamin C: *Citrus medica* (citron), *C. limon* (lemon), *C.
aurantiifolia* (lime), *C. sinensis* (orange), *C. paradisi* (grapefruit), and *C. reticulata*
(tangerine).

In India the leaves of *Murraya koenigii* are mixed with a little turmeric to make curry powder. Bark of *Cusparia febrifuga* from the rain forests of South America is the main flavoring in Angostura bitters used in beverages. Members of Rutaceae often have high concentration of alkaloids. Several potential anticancer drugs have recently been found in members of the family.

SUBCLASS V, ROSIDAE; ORDER 16, SAPINDALES
Zygophyllaceae: Caltrop Family

Field Recognition   Leaves usually pinnate or 2-foliolate with paired persistent stipules; flowers with a disc; stamens often with basal scales; ovary 4 to 5 locular with a terminal style; CA^{4-5} $CO^{(0)4-5}$ $A^{5,\ 10\ or\ 15}$ $\underline{G}^{⑤}$.

Description   *Habit*   Perennial herbs, shrubs, rarely trees; branches often jointed at the nodes.

Leaves   Opposite or rarely alternate, mostly pinnately compound or 2-foliolate; with paired persistent stipules, which are often spiny.

Inflorescences   Cymose or flowers solitary.

Flowers   Bisexual, actinomorphic or rarely zygomorphic. Calyx of 4 to 5 sepals, free or united at the base. Corolla of (0)4 to 5 petals, free. Androecium of 5, 10, or 15 stamens, free, often with a scale at base of each filament. Gynoecium a compound pistil of (2)5(12) carpels, with 4 to 5 locules, ovules 2 or more in each locule, placentation axile, ovary superior, style simple. See Figure 14-69.

Fruit   A capsule, schizocarp, or rarely a berry.

Seed   With or without endosperm.

FIGURE 14-69
Tribulus cistoides (Zygophyllaceae). (a) Flowering branch and (b) young fruit.

(a)   (b)

Zygophyllaceae

Size, Distribution, and General Information   A family of about 30 genera and 250 species of mainly tropical and subtropical, often arid, regions.

Some of the larger genera are *Zygophyllum* (90) (bean capers); *Guaiacum* (6) (lignum vitae wood); *Larrea* (5) (creosote bush); and *Tribulus* (20) (caltrops, puncture vine).

The Zygophyllaceae are called the *caltrop* family because the spines on the fruit of *Tribulus terrestris* are similar to the sharp iron caltrops once used on battlefields to stab the feet of men or horses.

The lignum vitae tree (*Guaiacum officinale*) produces the hardest and heaviest of commercial woods and yields the medicinal resin guaiacum, once used to treat syphilis. The wood is used for bowling balls, gears, mallets, furniture, rollers, and bearings. The creosote bush (*Larrea tridentata*) is familiar in the southwestern United States. Some species of *Zygophyllum* are used as spices: *Z. fabago* buds are used in sauces, and *Z. coccineum* is a substitute for black pepper.

Economic Importance   The family is important for lignum vitae wood, spices, and a few ornamentals.

SUBCLASS V, ROSIDAE; ORDER 17, GERANIALES
Oxalidaceae: Oxalis or Sheep Sorrel Family

Field Recognition   Leaves usually palmately compound, with a sour taste; flowers 5-merous; stamens united; styles 5; $CA^5\ CO^5\ A^{\underline{10}}\ \underline{G}^{\textcircled{5}}$.

Description   *Habit*   Perennial herbs or shrubs, often with fleshy rhizomes or tubers.

Leaves   Alternate, palmately or pinnately compound, without stipules.

Inflorescences   Solitary or subumbellate, rarely cymose, or racemose.

Flowers   Bisexual, actinomorphic. Calyx of 5 sepals. Corolla of 5 petals, short-clawed, free or slightly united at base. Androecium of 10 stamens, fused at base, sometimes 5 of the stamens are without anthers. Gynoecium a compound pistil of 5 united carpels, with 5 locules, ovules 1 or more in each locule, placentation axile, ovary superior, styles 5, free and persistent. See Figure 14-70.

Fruit   A capsule.

Seed   With a straight embryo and fleshy endosperm.

Size, Distribution, and General Information   A family of 7 or 8 genera and 900 species of mostly tropical and subtropical distribution.

Some of the genera are *Oxalis* (800) (oxalis, sour grass, sorrel); *Biophytum* (70); and *Eichleria* (2).

Indians use the tuberous roots of *Oxalis tuberosa* as food in the high Andes of South America. The roots, called *oca,* are mellowed in the sun to eliminate the calcium oxalate. Children often chew the leaves of sour grass (*Oxalis*) for the pleasant sour

Oxalidaceae

FIGURE 14-70
Oxalis (Oxalidaceae). Vertical section of a
flower.

taste. Several species of *Oxalis* are troublesome weeds, especially in greenhouses. Some are grown as ornamentals.

Economic Importance   The family is of little importance.

SUBCLASS V, ROSIDAE; ORDER 17, GERANIALES
Geraniaceae: Geranium Family

Field Recognition   Flowers 5-merous; stamens with filaments united at base; fruit with elastic dehiscent schizocarps that curl on the beak; $CA^5 CO^5 A^{5\text{-}15} \underline{G}^{\circledS}$.

Description   *Habit*   Mostly herbs, sometimes undershrubs; sometimes aromatic.
Leaves   Alternate or opposite, compound or simple, lobed or divided; with paired stipules.
Inflorescences   Cymose or umbellate, often with attractive flowers.
Flowers   Bisexual, actinomorphic or slightly zygomorphic. Calyx of 5 free sepals, persistent. Corolla of 5 petals, rarely 4, or absent. Androecium of 5 to 15 stamens, filaments united at the base. Gynoecium a compound pistil of 3 to 5 united carpels, with 3 to 5 locules, ovules 1 to 2 in each locule, placentation axile, ovary superior, styles slender and beaklike. See Figure 14-71.
Fruit   Capsular, dehiscing into 3 to 5 mericarps (usually 1 to 2 seeded), the styles usually adhering to the ovarian beak and the basal portion recurving spirally.
Seed   With a straight or folded embryo, endosperm.

Size, Distribution, and General Information   A family of about 11 genera and 700 species of wide temperate and subtropical distribution.

(a)   (b)

Geraniaceae

FIGURE 14-71
Geranium (Geraniaceae). (a) Flowering branch and (b) fruit with
persistent calyx and one carpel separating from the central axis
(latter redrawn from Heywood, 1978).

The larger genera are *Geranium* (300) (cranesbill); *Erodium* (75) (storksbill); and
Pelargonium (250) (florist geranium).

The well-known geraniums grown in pots or as bedding plants are cultivars of
several species of *Pelargonium* from South Africa. Geranium oil is distilled from *P.
odoratissimum*. *Pelargonium* has a calyx spur adnate to the pedicel; this structure is
absent in *Geranium*. Spotted geranium (*G. maculatum*) is a favorite spring wild flower
in deciduous woods of eastern North America. Several species of *Erodium* and *Geranium* are weedy. The persistent dry style on the fruit of *Erodium* twists into a
"corkscrew" and is very hygroscopic; it is sometimes used as a toy to indicate changes
in humidity.

Economic Importance   The Geraniaceae are important for the florist geranium
and geranium oil.

SUBCLASS V, ROSIDAE; ORDER 18, APIALES

Araliaceae: Aralia Family

Field Recognition   Leaves alternate, often large and compound; flowers actino-
morphic, small, mostly in umbels, fruit a berry; $CA^{4 \text{ or } 5} CO^{5(3) \text{ or } 5(3)} A^{5(3)} \overline{G}^{(5)}$.

Description   *Habit*   Herbs, shrubs, vines, and trees, some palmlike; root climbers.

Leaves   Alternate, rarely opposite or whorled, often large and compound; stipules small.

Inflorescences   Often in compound umbels.

Flowers   Bisexual or unisexual (on separate plants or occasionally male and female flowers on same plant), actinomorphic, small, typically greenish or whitish. Calyx of 4 to 5 teeth fused to ovary. Corolla of 5 or sometimes 3 free or partially fused petals. Androecium of 5 or sometimes 3 stamens, equal to the petals in number and alternate with them, attached to an ovarian disk. Gynoecium of 5 fused carpels, 5-locular, each locule with one ovule, ovary inferior. See Figure 14-72.

Fruit   A berry with 5 seed.

Seed   Embryo small, endosperm copious.

Size, Distribution, and General Information   A family of 70 genera and 700 species, chiefly tropical but also found in temperate regions; its distribution is centered in Indomalaysia and tropical America. The Araliaceae are closely related to the Umbelliferae (Apiaceae).

Araliaceae

FIGURE 14-72
Aralia spinosa (Araliaceae).
Flowering branch.

The better known genera include: *Aralia* (35); *Hedera* (15); *Fatsia* (1); *Panax* (8); *Schefflera* (150); and *Tetrapanax* (1).

Economic Importance   *Hedera helix* (English ivy) grows wild in western, central, and southern Europe. Many cultivars of English ivy are grown as house plants and as ground covers. *Hedera canariensis* (Canary Island ivy) is grown as an ornamental, but it is not as hardy as English ivy. Attractive ornamentals include *Schefflera* and *Fatsia japonica* and the bigeneric hybrid of *Fatsia* and *Hedera, Fatshedera. Acanthopanax* is often grown in botanical gardens. *Tetrapanax papyriferum* yields Chinese rice paper. The North American shrub, *Aralia spinosa* (devil's walking stick), is a fine ornamental.

Ginseng is extremely popular in China as a universal medicinal, stimulant, and aphrodisiac. The drug comes from the root of *Panax ginseng,* indigenous to China and Korea. A close American relative, *Panax quinquefolia,* is collected from the wild in North America and the roots are shipped to China. Attempts are being made to cultivate American ginseng since it has been overcollected.

SUBCLASS V, ROSIDAE; ORDER 18, APIALES
Umbelliferae or Apiaceae: Carrot or Parsley Family

Field Recognition   Aromatic herbs with hollow stems; leaves compound with sheathing bases; inflorescences umbellate; flowers 5-merous, often yellow or white; stamens 5; ovary 2-carpellate, bilocular, inferior; fruit a schizocarp; $CA^{5} CO^{5} A^{5} \overline{G}^{②}$.

Description   *Habit*   Mostly biennial or perennial herbs, rarely slightly woody, stem often stout with hollow internodes or wide, soft pith.

Leaves   Alternate, much divided, sheathing at the base.

Inflorescences   A simple or compound umbel or rarely capitate.

Flowers   Bisexual, actinomorphic. Calyx of 5 sepals, epigynous. Corolla of 5 petals, epigynous, some deciduous, mostly white or yellow. Androecium of 5 stamens, alternate with the petals. Gynoecium a compound pistil of 2 united carpels, with 2 locules, ovules solitary in each locule, placentation axile, ovary inferior, style swollen at base. See Figure 14-73.

Fruit   A dry schizocarp splitting into 2 mericarps, often ribbed.

Seed   With a small embryo in oily endosperm.

Size, Distribution, and General Information   A family of about 300 genera and 3000 species chiefly of north temperate distribution but cosmopolitan, found at high elevations in the tropics.

Some of the genera are *Hydrocotyle* (100) (pennywort); *Eryngium* (230) (snakeroot); *Sanicula* (37) (snakeroot); *Apium* (2) (celery); *Chaerophyllum* (40) (chervil); *Angelica* (80); *Daucus* (60) (carrot, Queen Anne's lace); *Conium* (4) (poison hemlock); *Cicuta* (10) (water hemlock); *Petroselinum* (5) (parsley); *Carum* (30) (caraway); *Pimpinella*

(a) Flower   (b) Schizocarp (cx) (fruit)   (c) Schizocarp (lx) (fruit)

Umbelliferae

FIGURE 14-73
Family Umbelliferae: (a) diagrammatic flower, (b) cross section of a fruit (schizocarp), and (c) vertical section of a fruit. The stylopodium is the enlarged base of the style.

(150) (anise); *Anethum* (1) (dill); *Ferula* (133) (asafoetida); *Peucedanum* (120) (parsnip); *Coriandrum* (2) (coriander); *Foeniculum* (5) (fennel); and *Pastinaca* (15) (parsnip).

Conium maculatum (poison hemlock) is the famous plant used to put to death the Greek philosoper Socrates. A native of Europe and Asia, it has spread into the New World. The North American water hemlock (*Cicuta*) is just as poisonous but not so weedy.

Known since before the time of Greece and Rome, parsnips (*Pastinaca sativa*), carrots (*Daucus carota*), parsley (*Pteroselinum hortense*), and celery (*Apium graveolens*) have been used for food, garnish, flavoring, and medicine. Seeds of Umbelliferae are of importance because of their essential oils. Of these, caraway seeds (*Carum carvi*) used in bread, rolls, and cheeses are the most important. Dill (*Anethum graveolens*) is used in flavoring dill pickles. Coriander (*Coriandrum sativum*) is added to many dishes in China and India and certain Mediterranean countries. Many species have been used for medical purposes.

Economic Importance   The Umbelliferae are important for food, flavoring, and ornamentals, and for some poisonous species.

SUBCLASS VI, ASTERIDAE; ORDER 1, GENTIANALES
Gentianaceae: Gentian Family

Field Recognition   Herbs; leaves opposite, often connate at the base, without stipules; flowers 4- or 5-merous; stamens the same number as the petals and alternate with them; ovary superior, with 2 carpels, mostly 1 locular, with 2 parietal placentas; CA$\widehat{^{4-5}}$ CO$\widehat{^{4-5}}$ A$^{4-5}$ $\underline{G}^{\textcircled{2}}$.

Description   *Habit*   Annual or perennial herbs, rarely woody.
Leaves   Opposite, simple, entire, often connate at the base or connected by a line; without stipules.

Inflorescences Cymose.

Flowers Bisexual, actinomorphic, showy. Calyx of 4 to 5(12) sepals, tubular or separate. Corolla of 4 to 5(12) united petals. Androecium of the same number of stamens as the petals, epipetalous, alternate with the corolla lobes. Gynoecium a compound pistil of 2 carpels, with 1(2) locules, ovules numerous, placentation parietal, ovary superior, style simple. See Figure 14-74.

Fruit A capsule.

Seed Small in size, with endosperm.

Size, Distribution, and General Information A family of about 75 genera and 1000 species of cosmopolitan distribution and found in a variety of habitats: arctic, alpine, saline, aquatic, tropical, and temperate.

FIGURE 14-74
Gentiana quinquefolia (Gentianaceae). (a) Flowering shoot and (b) vertical view of opened flower.

(b)

(a)

Gentianaceae

The chief genera are *Gentiana* (400) (gentian); *Sabatia* (20) (marsh pink, rose pink); *Swertia* (100) (columbo); and *Nymphoides* (20) (water snowflake).

Many species of *Gentiana* grow at high elevations in the temperate zone. The majority produce a distinctive tubular flower of an intense blue color. Since they are so showy, many are cultivated in gardens in the cold temperate zone. An extract of the roots of *G. lutea* is used for a tonic.

Nymphoides is an aquatic plant with the habit of water lilies. The flower cluster appears to develop from the top of the petiole, but actually the floating leaf grows from the inflorescence axis.

Economic Importance   The family is of importance only for showy ornamentals often grown in rock gardens.

SUBCLASS VI, ASTERIDAE; ORDER 1, GENTIANALES
Apocynaceae: Dogbane Family

Field Recognition   Sap milky; leaves opposite or whorled, stipules absent; flowers 5-merous; calyx often glandular inside; fruit usually a follicle; seed usually with a tuft of hairs; $CA^{⑤} \underline{CO^{⑤}} \underline{A^{5}} \underline{G^{\widehat{2}}}$ (Apocynaceae are likely to be confused with Asclepiadaceae. Apocynaceae lack the corona, pollinia, and translator-corpusculum of the Asclepiadaceae.)

Description   *Habit*   Trees, shrubs, perennial herbs, lianas; with milky sap.
Leaves   Opposite or whorled, rarely alternate, simple, entire; without stipules.
Inflorescences   Racemose, cymose, or solitary.
Flowers   Bisexual, actinomorphic. Calyx of (4)5 sepals, united, glandular inside. Corolla of 5 petals united into a tube. Androecium of (4)5 stamens, inserted in the tube, filaments free or rarely united. Gynoecium a compound pistil of 2 apically united carpels, with 1 or 2 locules, placentation marginal, ovary superior or half-inferior, style 1. See Figure 14-75.
Fruit   A follicle, sometimes a capsule, drupe or berry.
Seed   Flat often with a crown of hairs, embryo straight.

Size, Distribution, and General Information   A family of about 200 genera and 2000 species of mostly tropical and subtropical distribution but with a few species in the temperate zone.

Some of the genera are *Vinca* (5) (periwinkle, myrtle); *Amsonia* (25) (blue star); *Rauvolfia* (100) (Indian snakeroot); *Nerium* (3) (oleander, rosebay); *Apocynum* (7) (dogbane); *Ervatamia* (80) (crape jasmine, clavel de la India); *Allamanda* (15) (cup of gold); and *Catharanthus* (5) (periwinkle).

Economic Importance   The family is of importance for drugs and for its several ornamentals: *Amsonia, Nerium, Vinca, Allamanda, Ervatamia,* and others. Poisoning

Apocynaceae

FIGURE 14-75
Vinca major (Apocynaceae). Flowering shoot.

of humans, especially children, sometimes occurs. When pasture is poor, livestock may eat the plants.

Many species in the Apocynaceae are notorious for the poisons they contain. In Africa, poisoned arrows are made with an extract of *Acokanthera abyssinica* bark. If ingested, one leaf of *Nerium oleander* can be fatal to an adult human. The yellow oleander (*Thevetia nereifolia*) poses a similar hazard. Both are grown in subtropical areas as ornamentals. Arrow poisons have been prepared from the seeds of the African species of *Strophanthus*. Long used by native healers in India, *Rauvolfia* yields the alkaloid reserpine, which can lower blood pressure and tranquilize mental patients suffering from schizophrenia.

SUBCLASS VI, ASTERIDAE; ORDER 1, GENTIANALES
Asclepiadaceae: Milkweed Family

Field Recognition   Sap milky; leaves opposite or whorled, stipules absent; flowers 5-merous with distinctive corona, pollinia, translators, and corpuscula; fruit a follicle; seed with a tuft of silky hairs; $CA^5 \underline{CO^{\circledS}} \ \widehat{A^5 \ \underline{G^{2}}}$.

Description   *Habit*   Perennial herbs, vines, shrubs, rarely trees, with milky sap; sometimes cactuslike.

Leaves   Opposite, simple, entire, pinnately veined; without stipules.

Inflorescences   Mostly cymose, but also racemose or umbellate.

Flowers   Bisexual, actinomorphic, with an elaborate corona. Calyx of 5 sepals, with a short tube. Corolla of 5 united petals. Androecium of 5 stamens, pollen in waxy pollinia. Gynoecium a compond pistil of 2 apically united carpels, ovules numerous, ovary superior, placentation marginal, styles 2 and united at style apices, stigma 1 with 5 lobes. See Figure 14-76.

FIGURE 14-76
Diagrammatic views of Asclepiadaceae floral structures. (a) Flower. (b) Vertical section showing superior ovary. (c) Top view of the center of a flower. (d) Pollinia pair.

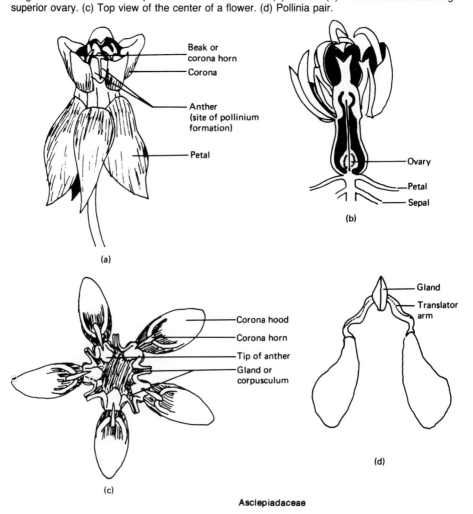

Asclepiadaceae

The stamens and carpels are united into a complex structure, the gynostegium; the carpels are free below but united into the single 5-lobed stigma. The pollinia are connected in pairs by the translators and the corpusculum (gland). A corona may be present that consists of 5 hoods, which are sometimes mistaken for petals. A beak (horn) may be associated with each hood.

Fruit   A pair of follicles, one often aborting.

Seed   Numerous, with tufts of silky hairs called a *coma*.

Size, Distribution, and General Information   A family of about 250 genera and 2000 species mainly of tropical and subtropical distribution, but with numerous species in the temperate zone.

Some of the genera are *Asclepias* (150) (milkweed); *Hoya* (150) (wax plant); *Ceropegia* (150); *Stapelia* (75) (carrion flower); *Dischidia* (80); and *Matelea* (130) (milkweed vine).

During World War II, the United States was unable to import kapok, and hair from the seeds of *Asclepias* was used as a substitute in life jackets. Monarch butterfly larvae feed on the leaves of several species of milkweed from which the larvae obtain compounds toxic to predators.

The flower tube of *Ceropegia,* lined with small hairs that point downward, forms a trap for small flies. The flies attracted by the odor cannot escape until the hairs wither. The pollinia of *Ceropegia* are attached to the flies' bodies when they escape. *Dischidia rafflesiana* has curious pitcherlike leaves. Each pitcher is about 10 centimeters deep and contains debris carried by nesting ants. If the plant is disturbed, the ants rush about defending the *Dischidia* as well as their nest.

Stapelia (carrion flower) inhabits semiarid regions of Africa. The leaves are reduced to scales, and the stems are thick and fleshy. The flowers are large with dull red or maroon color and have a carrionlike odor which attracts flies. The Asiatic genus *Hoya,* which has large clusters of highly scented waxy flowers, provides several greenhouse plants.

Economic Importance   The family is of little importance, except for some ornamentals. Some species cause livestock poisoning. In India, madar fiber is obtained from *Calotropis gigantea* and rajmahal hemp from *Marsdenia tenacissima*.

SUBCLASS VI, ASTERIDAE; ORDER 2, SOLANALES
Solanaceae; Nightshade or Potato Family

Field Recognition   Leaves alternate, stipules absent; flowers actinomorphic, 5-merous; stamens 5; ovary 2-locular, sometimes falsely divided again; ovules numerous; fruit a berry or capsule; $CA^{\circledS}\ \underline{CO^{\circledS}\ A}^5\ \underline{G}\circledZ$.

Description   *Habit*   Herbs, shrubs, or trees, or sometimes vines.

Leaves   Alternate, simple, without stipules.

Inflorescences   Cymose.

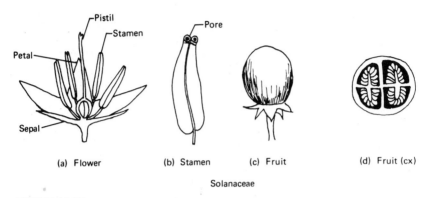

(a) Flower   (b) Stamen   (c) Fruit   (d) Fruit (cx)

Solanaceae

FIGURE 14-77
(a) Flower (vertical section), (b) stamen, (c) fruit, and (d) fruit in cross section of family
Solanaceae. Note the pores at the apex of the stamen.

Flowers   Bisexual, usually actinomorphic or weakly zygomorphic. Calyx of 5
united sepals, persistent. Corolla of 5 united petals, rotate to tubular, Androecium of
5 stamens, inserted on the corolla tube and alternate with its lobes, anthers opening
either lengthwise or by terminal pores. Gynoecium a compound pistil of 2 carpels,
sometimes divided by a false septum, with 2 locules, ovules numerous, placentation
axile, ovary superior, style terminal. See Figure 14-77.

Fruit   A berry or capsule.

Seed   With a curved or straight embryo in endosperm.

Size, Distribution, and General Information   A family of about 85 genera and
2800 species of tropical and temperate distribution. The greatest number of genera
(40) are found in Central and South America; only two or three genera are native to
Europe and Asia.

Some of the chief genera are *Solanum* (1400) (potato, nightshade, and so on);
Datura (10) (jimsonweed, Jamestown weed, angel trumpet); *Nicotiana* (21) (tobacco);
Lycium (80–90) (kaffir thorn, matrimony vine); *Atropa* (4) (belladonna); *Hyoscyamus*
(20)) (henbane); *Capsicum* (50) (pepper, chili); *Lycopersicon* (7) (tomato); *Petunia*
(40); *Schizanthus* (15) (butterfly flower); *Physalis* (100) (ground-cherry); and *Salpig-
lossis* (18).

Members of the nightshade family provide drugs and food; some are weedy, some
are poisonous, and others are handsome ornamentals. Most important is the white or
Irish potato introduced into Europe from the Andean region in the late 1500s. The
potato did well in the cooler parts of Europe and became a staple in Ireland. In 1845
and 1846 late blight struck the potato crop in Ireland. So completely dependent on
the potato were the Irish that over a million people died of famine, and over a million
migrated to North America.

Solanum melongena (eggplant) is from northern India. The Jerusalem cherry (*S.
pseudocapsicum*) is sold at Christmas in the florist trade. The fruit of Jerusalem cherry
is poisonous and is sometimes eaten by children.

Tomato (*Lycopersicon lycopersicum*), the favorite home garden vegetable in North America, was once believed to be poisonous. Tomatoes originated in the Andes and were widely cultivated throughout the Inca empire and northward. Those first seen in Europe were yellow-fruited and were called *golden apples*. Later they were known as *love apples* and supposedly had value as an aphrodisiac. By the late 1700s, tomatoes were widely grown and were introduced into northern North America by Italians and other European immigrants.

Capsicum annuum and *C. frutescens* have provided many cultivars of pepper or chili. Peppers are rich in vitamins C and A. The various cultivars provide chili powder, tabasco sauce, bell peppers, sweet and hot peppers, paprika, and pimento. (Note: Black pepper is derived from a member of the Piperaceae.)

Physalis (ground-cherry) produces an edible fruit enclosed in a bladder-like persistent calyx called the husk, hence the name husk tomatoes. *Physalis alkekengi* (Chinese lantern plant) is grown for its ornamental fruits.

Many Solanaceae contain powerful alkaloids: *Atropa belladonna* (deadly nightshade or belladonna), *Hyoscyamus niger* (henbane), *Nicotiana tabacum* (tobacco), *Datura* (jimsonweed or Jamestown weed), and *Solanum nigrum* (black nightshade). The drug atropine is obtained from belladonna. It is used as an antidote for poisoning from organic phosphate pesticides and nerve gas. Women once put belladonna juice in their eyes to enlarge the pupils to make their eyes attractive. Recently, a fad of chewing the seeds of *Datura* has often had fatal results. *Datura stramonium* is sometimes called Jamestown (jimson) weed because some British soldiers were poisoned in Jamestown in 1676 after eating cooked foliage of *D. stramonium*.

Economic Importance   The Solanaceae are of considerable importance for food, drugs, weeds, and poisonous plants.

SUBCLASS VI, ASTERIDAE; ORDER 2, SOLANALES
Convolvulaceae: Morning Glory Family

Field Recognition   Sap often somewhat milky; leaves alternate; flowers 5-merous; corolla tubular and contorted; stamens 5, epipetalous; gynoecium of 2 carpels; ovules solitary or paired and erect; $CA^5 \underline{CO^{\circledS} A^5_\cup G^{\circledcirc}}$.

Description   *Habit*   Herbs, shrubs, or trees, often a climber with milky sap.
Leaves   Alternate, simple, variously lobed or entire; without stipules.
Inflorescences   An axillary dichasium, or racemose, or paniculate, or flowers solitary.
Flowers   Bisexual, actinomorphic. Bracts often large and showy, sometimes forming an involucre. Calyx of 5 sepals, usually free, persistent. Corolla of 5 united petals, contorted. Androecium of 5 stamens, epipetalous, inserted toward base of tube and alternate with the lobes. Gynoecium a compound pistil of 2 united carpels, with 1 to 4 locules, ovules solitary or paired, erect, placentation axile, ovary superior, style terminal. See Figure 14-78.

Convolvulaceae

FIGURE 14-78
Ipomoea purpurea (Convolvulaceae). (a) Flower, (b) vertical section through flower, and (c) fruit.

Fruit   Usually a capsule.
Seed   With endosperm.

Size, Distribution, and General Information   A family of about 50 genera and 1500 species of tropical and temperate distribution.

Some of the genera are *Convolvulus* (250) (bindweed, wild morning glory); *Dichondra* (4 to 5); *Jacquemontia* (120); *Calystegia* (25); *Ipomoea* (400) (morning glory); and *Evolvulus* (100).

Some species of *Convolvulus* and *Ipomoea* are weedy. Sweet potato (*I. batatas*) is an important food crop in the southern United States and in tropical countries. Some species are grown as ornamentals: *I. purpurea* (morning glory) and *Calonyction aculeatum* (moonvine). The seeds of *I. violacea* contain *d*-lysergic acid amide and are hallucinogenic.

Economic Importance   The morning glory family is important as a source of food, for several ornamentals, for drug plants, and as weeds.

SUBCLASS VI, ASTERIDAE ORDER; 2, SOLANALES
Cuscutaceae: Dodder Family

Field Recognition   Parasites with yellowish, threadlike, leafless, twining herbaceous stems; flowers small, yellow or white, in stalked or sessile, bractless clusters; fruit a dry or fleshy capsule; $CA^{4-5 \ or} \widehat{(4-5)} CO \widehat{(4-5)} A^{\ 4-5} \underline{G}^{②}$. See Figure 14-79.

Cuscutaceae

FIGURE 14-79
Cuscuta (Cuscutaceae). (a) Habit of a plant in flower and (b) flower,
vertical section.

Size, Distribution, and General Information   Considered to be related to and
derived from the Convolvulaceae, *Cuscuta* is treated either as a subfamily of the
Convolvulaceae or as the only genus in the family Cuscutaceae. Cosmopolitan in
distribution, dodder plants of the genus *Cuscuta* comprise some 150 species.

The seeds of dodder germinate to give a leafless thread that creeps along the ground
for a short distance until a host is encountered. The stems grow free for a short length
and then wind around the host by two or three turns, penetrate the host stem by means
of miniature haustoria and continue to grow around the same or another host. Dodder
can cause damage in certain crops or among herbaceous ornamentals.

SUBCLASS VI, ASTERIDAE; ORDER 2, SOLANALES

Polemoniaceae: Phlox Family

Field Recognition   Flowers 5-merous; calyx of 5 united sepals; corolla of 5 united
petals; stamens 5, attached at various levels within the corolla; stigmas three, ovules
numerous; $CA^{\circledS} \underline{CO}^{\circledS} A^5_{\,} \underline{G}^{\circledcirc}$.

Description   *Habit*   Mostly annual to perennial herbs, rarely shrubs.
Leaves   Alternate or opposite, simple or compound; without stipules.
Inflorescences   Terminal, cymose, corymbose, or capitate, or the flowers solitary.
Flowers   Bisexual, actinomorphic, rarely slightly zygomorphic. Calyx of 5 united
sepals. Corolla of 5 united petals. Androecium of 5 stamens, epipetalous, alternate
with the lobes, free from one another, included or exserted. Gynoecium a compound
pistil of 3 united carpels, with 3 locules, ovules numerous, placentation axile, ovary
superior, style 1, stigmas 3 or rarely 2. See Figure 14-80.

Polemoniaceae

FIGURE 14-80
Phlox (Polemoniaceae). (a) Vertical section of flower and (b)
inflorescence.

FIGURE 14-81
Phacelia (Hydrophyllaceae). (a) Flowering shoot
and (b) fruit.

Hydrophyllaceae

Fruit   Usually a capsule.
Seed   With a straight embryo and endosperm.

Size, Distribution, and General Information   A family of about 18 genera and 300 species mostly in North America and the Andes of South America, a few in Northern Europe and Asia.

Some of the genera are *Polemonium* (50) (Jacob's ladder); *Phlox* (77); *Gilia* (120); *Cantua* (11) *Collomia* (15); and *Ipomopsis* (24).

Pollinators, such as long-tongued flies, bees, moths, butterflies, and hummingbirds, are attracted to the colorful corollas of the Polemoniaceae. Many of the species of this family have been adopted into flower gardens. *Phlox* is probably the most popular genus. The tall garden phloxes are largely cultivars obtained by crossing *P. carolina, P. glaberrima, P. maculata,* and *P. paniculata*. The annual *P. drummondii* from Texas is a favorite in both Europe and North America.

Economic Importance   The Polemoniaceae are important in flower gardens.

SUBCLASS VI, ASTERIDAE; ORDER 2, SOLANALES
Hydrophyllaceae: Waterleaf Family

Field Recognition   Inflorescences often helicoid cymes; flowers 5-merous; sepals united, often with appendages between; petals united; gynoecium with 1 locule; ovules numerous on 2 parietal placentas; $CA^{\circledS}\ \underset{\smile}{CO^{\circledS}}\ A^5\ \underline{G}^{\circledtwo}$.

Description   *Habit*   Annual or perennial herbs rarely shrubs, often hairy or sometimes spiny.

Leaves   Alternate or rarely opposite, sometimes basal, simple to pinnately or palmately compound.

Inflorescences   Often tending toward helicoid cymes or flowers solitary.

Flowers   Bisexual, actinomorphic. Calyx of 5 united sepals, often with appendages between the lobes. Corolla of 5 united petals, rotate. Androecium of 5 stamens, epipetalous, alternate with the lobes and often inserted toward the base of the tube. Gynoecium a compound pistil of 2 united carpels, with 1 locule, ovules often numerous, placentation of 2 parietal placentas, or rarely 2-locular with placentas on septum, ovary superior, styles 1 or 2. See Figure 14-81.

Fruit   A capsule.
Seed   With a small embryo, endosperm.

Size, Distribution, and General Information   A family of about 20 genera and 250 species widely distributed, occurring on all continents except Australia, but mainly in North America.

The chief genera are *Hydrophyllum* (10) (waterleaf); *Nemophila* (13) (baby blue-eyes); *Phacelia* (150); *Nama* (40 to 50); *Hydrolea* (20); and *Ellisia* (1) (water pod).

Economic Importance   The family is of little or no importance except for a few garden annuals and a few minor weeds.

SUBCLASS VI, ASTERIDAE; ORDER 3, LAMIALES
Boraginaceae: Borage Family

Field Recognition   Bristly herbs, stems round; leaves alternate; inflorescences of helicoid cymes; flowers 5-merous and usually actinomorphic; ovary 4-lobed, style arising from among the lobes; fruit of 4 nutlets; $CA^5 \underset{\smile}{CO}^⑤ A^5_⌣ \underline{G}^②$. (The Boraginaceae may be confused with Hydrophyllaceae, Labiatae, and Verbenaceae.)

Description   *Habit*   Herbs, shrubs, trees, or lianas.
Leaves   Usually alternate, simple, often covered by rough hairs; without stipules.
Inflorescences   Often a scorpioid (helicoid) cyme.
Flowers   Bisexual, usually actinomorphic. Calyx of 5 united sepals. Corolla of 5 united petals, funnel-form or tubular. Androecium of 5 stamens, epipetalous, alternate with the corolla lobes. Gynoecium a compound pistil of 2 united carpels, with 2 (or falsely 4) locules, ovules in pairs, placentation axile sometimes appearing basal, ovary superior, style arising from the middle of the lobes of the ovary. See Figure 14-82.
Fruit   Often deeply 4-parted into 1-seeded nutlets.
Seed   Embryo erect.

FIGURE 14-82
Diagrammatic drawing of the floral structures of Boraginaceae. (a) Symmetrical corolla lobes. (b) Deeply four-lobed ovary. (c) Gynobasic style.

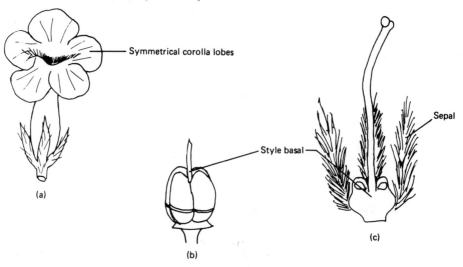

Boraginaceae

Size, Distribution, and General Information   A family of about 100 genera and 2000 species of tropical and temperate distribution but especially abundant in the Mediterranean region.

Some genera are *Tournefortia* (150); *Heliotropium* (250) (heliotrope, turnsole); *Borago* (3) (borage); *Myosotis* (50) (forget-me-not); *Lithospermum* (60) (gromwell, puccoon); *Cynoglossum* (50–60) (hound's-tongue); *Mertensia* (50) (bluebells); *Amsinckia* (50) (fiddle-neck); *Plagiobothrys* (100); and *Symphytum* (25).

A few species of *Mertensia, Myosotis, Borago, Cynoglossum,* and *Heliotropium* are cultivated in flower gardens. The geiger tree (*Cordia sebestena*) is widely planted for its handsome orange-red flowers and its edible plum-like fruits. Viper's bugloss (*Echium vulgare*) is a noxious herbaceous weed.

It is not known how the forget-me-nots (*Myosotis*) obtained their name, but one legend suggests these were the last words of a gallant gentleman who drowned while crossing a stream to collect a bouquet of these sky-blue flowers for his girl friend.

Economic Importance   The family is of no significant economic importance except for a few ornamentals. *Symphytum* is a minor forage plant.

SUBCLASS VI, ASTERIDAE; ORDER 3, LAMIALES
Verbenaceae: Vervain or Verbena Family

Field Recognition   Stems often 4-angled; leaves opposite; flowers 5-merous, zygomorphic; style single and terminal $CA^{\circledS} \underline{COZ^{\circledS}} A^{2 + 2} \underline{G}^{\circledtwo}$. (The Verbenaceae are most easily confused with the Boraginaceae, which have alternate leaves and a 4-lobed ovary, and with the Labiatae, which have opposite leaves and a style arising from the base of the ovary.)

Description   *Habit*   Herbs, shrubs, trees, and a few vines; often with square stems.

Leaves   Usually opposite, rarely alternate or whorled, simple or compound; without stipules.

Inflorescences   Racemose or cymose, sometimes with an involucre of colored bracts.

Flowers   Bisexual, zygomorphic. Calyx of (4)5(8) sepals, lobed or toothed, persistent. Corolla of 5 united petals often 2-lipped, 4 to 5 lobed. Androecium of (2)4(5) stamens, didynamous, epipetalous. Gynoecium a compound pistil usually of 2 carpels, with 2(4 or 5) locules, ovules solitary (or paired), placentation axile, ovary superior, style terminal. See Figure 14-83.

Fruit   A drupe or berry.

Size, Distribution, and General Information   A family of about 100 genera and 2600 species, mostly of tropical or subtropical distribution

Some of the genera are *Verbena* (250) (vervain); *Lantana* (150); *Clerodendrum* (400) (glory-bower); *Vitex* (250) (chaste tree); *Lippia* (200) (frogfruit); *Callicarpa* (140) (beauty-berry); *Tectona* (3) (teak); and *Avicennia* (14) (mangrove).

Style terminal

Verbenaceae ovary

FIGURE 14-83
Terminal style of family Verbenaceae.

Verbenaceae are mostly herbaceous in the temperate zone, but in the tropics many are shrubs and trees. Teak (*Tectona grandis*) is a native tree of Indomalaysia. The heartwood is relatively immune to termites and rots. The wood is remarkable also for its resistance to changes in temperature and humidity. It is especially suitable for decking and fine trim on boats, and for flooring, paneling, and furniture.

The European verbain (*Verbena officinalis*) was once regarded as a cure-all. The *Verbena* most often grown in gardens is *V. hybrida* from southern Brazil. Lantanas from tropical America are often grown as greenhouse or bedding plants. In many subtropical areas, *Lantana* has escaped and has become a weedy pest which can cause livestock poisoning. *Lippia citriodora* (lemon-scented verbena) yields oil of verbena. In temperate areas, several species of *Clerodendrum* are grown as greenhouse ornamentals including *C. paniculatum* (pagoda flower) and *C. thomsoniae* (bleeding heart). *Callicarpa americana* (beauty-berry), a woody shrub, is grown for its ornamental fruits. Another woody shrub known for its blue or white flowers is the lilac chaste tree (*Vitex agnus-castus*).

Economic Importance   The family is important for teak lumber and for many ornamental herbs and shrubs.

SUBCLASS VI, ASTERIDAE; ORDER 3, LAMIALES
Labiatae or Lamiaceae: Mint Family

Field Recognition   Herbs and shrubs with square stems; aromatic; leaves opposite; inflorescences axillary or whorled; flowers 5-merous, zygomorphic; stamens 2 or 4; ovary deeply 4-lobed, style basally attached between the 4 lobes (gynobasic); fruit of 4 nutlets; $CA^{\circledS}$ $\underline{COZ}^{\circledS}$ $A^{2\ or\ 4}$ $\underline{G}^{\circledcirc}$. (This family may be confused with the Boraginaceae, the Verbenaceae, or the Scrophulariaceae.)

Description   *Habit*   Usually herbs, sometimes shrubs or trees; stems square; with aromatic oils.
Leaves   Opposite or whorled, simple; without stipules.

(a)   (b)

Labiatae

FIGURE 14-84
Diagrammatic drawings of the floral structures of Labitae. (a) Bilabiate
corolla. (b) Vertical section showing gynobasic style (the ovary is deeply
four-lobed).

Leaves   Opposite or whorled, simple; without stipules.

Inflorescences   Axillary or whorled.

Flowers   Usually bisexual, zygomorphic. Calyx of 5 united sepals, often ribbed, persistent, often 2-lipped. Corolla of 5 united petals, 2-lipped. Androecium of 2 or 4 stamens, often 2 pairs of different lengths (didynamous), epipetalous. Gynoecium a compound pistil of 2 carpels, falsely 4-locular, placentation basal, ovary superior, style attached to base of lobes (gynobasic), stigma mostly bifid. See Figure 14-84.

Fruit   Usually a group of 4 nutlets, each with 1 seed.

Seed   With little or no endosperm.

Systematics   The Labiatae are closely allied morphologically with the Verbenaceae.

Size, Distribution, and General Information   A family of about 200 genera and 3200 species of cosmopolitan distribution but centered in the Mediterranean region.

The chief genera are *Lamium* (40 to 50) (henbit, dead nettle); *Ajuga* (40) (bugleweed); *Teucrium* (300) (germander); *Scutellaria* (200) (skullcap); *Marrubium* (40) (horehound); *Nepeta* (150) (catnip); *Prunella* (7) (self-heal); *Stachys* (200) (betony, Chinese artichoke); *Salvia* (500) (sage); *Monarda* (12) (horsemint, bee balm); *Origanum* (15 to 20) (marjoram); *Thymus* (300 to 400) (thyme); *Mentha* (25) (mint, peppermint, spearmint); *Rosmarinus* (3) (rosemary); *Coleus* (200) (Jacob's coat); *Hyptis* (400); *Ocimum* (150) (basil); *Lavandula* (28) (lavender); *Molucella* (4) (bells of Ireland); and *Glechoma* (10 to 12) (ground ivy).

Many plants from the mint family are used in cooking as herbs and spices: sage (*Salvia officinalis*), thyme (*Thymus vulgaris*), pot marjoram or oregano *(Origanum vulgare)*, sweet marjoram (*Origanum majorana*), spearmint (*Mentha spicata*), peppermint (*Mentha piperita*), basil (*Clinopodium vulgaris*), and sweet basil or tulsi (*Ocimum basilicum*).

Lavender (*Lavandula angustifolia*) and rosemary (*Rosmarinus officinalis*) have long been popular in perfumes. The essential oils are obtained by distillation of the inflorescences of these species.

The 150 species of *Coleus* have contributed countless cultivars for greenhouse or garden plantings. *Coleus* is sometimes called *Jacob's coat* because of the multicolored, variegated color patterns of the leaves.

Cats are fond of catnip (*Nepeta cataria*) and often will nibble or roll over the plants, sometimes killing the plants.

The family has many attractive ornamentals: *Salvia, Ajuga, Monarda* (horsemint), *Scutellaria* (skullcap), and *Dracocephalum* (dragonhead).

Economic Importance   The family is a source of aromatic essential oils, many ornamentals, and important culinary herbs.

SUBCLASS VI, ASTERIDAE; ORDER 5, PLANTAGINALES
Plantaginaceae: Plantago Family

Field Recognition   Herbs; leaves in a basal rosette, prominent veins are parallel; inflorescences spicate or capitate on stout or wiry scapes; flowers 4-merous; corollas membranous; stamens often exserted; $CA^{④} \underline{CO^{④} A^4} \underline{G^2}$.

Description *Habit* Herbs.

Leaves   Basal, alternate or opposite, simple, sometimes reduced, often sheathing at base.

Inflorescences   Scapose, capitate, or spicate on stout or wiry scapes.

Flowers   Usually bisexual, actinomorphic, inconspicuous. Calyx of 4 united sepals, herbaceous. Corolla of 4 united petals, scarious, 3- to 4-lobed. Androecium of 4 stamens, inserted on corolla tube. Gynoecium a compound pistil of 2 united carpels with 1 to 4 locules, ovules 1 or more in each locule, placentation axile or basal; ovary superior, style simple. See Figure 14-85.

Fruit   A capsule or bony nutlet.

Seed   With a straight embryo in fleshy endosperm.

Size, Distribution, and General Information   A family of 3 genera and 254 species of cosmopolitan distribution.

The genera are *Plantago* (250) (plantain); *Littorella* (3); and *Bougueria* (1).

Economic Importance   The family is of no significant importance, although seeds of *Plantago psyllium* are used as a laxative. A number of species of *Plantago* are troublesome weeds, especially on lawns.

Plantaginaceae

FIGURE 14-85
Plantago (Plantaginaceae). (a) Habit, (b) flower, and (c) fruit, note that the capsule is circumscissile slightly below the middle.

SUBCLASS VI, ASTERIDAE; ORDER 6, SCROPHULARIALES
Oleaceae: Olive Family

Field Recognition   Leaves opposite; flowers 4-merous; stamens 2; ovary 2-locular; seeds usually 2 per locule; $CA^{④} CO^{④} A^2 \underline{G}^{②}$.

Description   *Habit*   Shrubs and trees, sometimes climbing.
Leaves   Opposite or rarely alternate, simple or pinnately compound; stipules absent.
Inflorescences   Axillary or terminal, racemose, or paniculate.
Flowers   Usually bisexual, actinomorphic. Calyx of 4 united sepals, 4-lobed, rarely absent. Corolla of 4 united petals, 4-lobed, sometimes absent. Androecium of 2 stamens. Gynoecium a compound pistil of 2 carpels, with 2 locules, placentation axile, ovary superior, style simple, with a capitate or bifid stigma. See Figure 14-86.

Oleaceae

FIGURE 14-86
Oleaceae. (a) Flowering branch of *Chionanthus virginicus* and (b) fruit; (c)
flower of *Ligustrum sinense*.

Fruit   Berrylike, a capsule, or a drupe.
Seed   Embryo straight, endosperm may or may not be present.

Size, Distribution, and General Information   A family of about 30 genera and
600 species of cosmopolitan distribution but with the greatest diversity in temperate
and tropical Asia.

The chief genera are *Olea* (20) (olive); *Syringa* (30) (lilac); *Ligustrum* (40 to 50) (privet hedge); *Chionanthus* (125) (granny graybeard, fringe tree); *Fraxinus* (60) (ash); *Forsythia* (7) (golden bells); *Jasminum* (200) (jasmine); and *Osmanthus* (15) (tea olive, sweet olive, devilwood).

The cultivated olive is *Olea europaea,* a valuable tree of the Mediterranean region. Olives are also grown in California, Argentina, Chile, South Africa, and Australia. When freshly picked, the fruit has a bitter glycoside that renders it inedible until the glycoside is neutralized. Green olives and black olives differ in their method of commercial preparation. Ripe olives contain 20 to 30 percent oil, which is removed by pressing.

Golden bells (*Forsythia*) is a handsome yellow flowering shrub. Cultivars of *Syringa* (lilac) are fragrant flowering shrubs and are available in a range of colors from purple to white and red. Several species of *Ligustrum* are used for hedges or for foundation plantings around homes. *Osmanthus* has numerous handsome evergreen shrubs. *Osmanthus fragrans* provides the extra pleasure of a distinctive perfume in the fall. Its leaves are used to perfume tea. The wood of ash (*Fraxinus*) is valuable for being both firm and elastic.

The flowers of *Jasminum grandiflorum* are used in fine perfumes. It is cultivated along the French Riviera and the jasmine oil is obtained by enfleurage rather than distillation, since heating lowers the quality of the oil. Many of the 300 species of *Jasminum* are cultivated as ornamentals.

Economic Importance   The Oleaceae are of considerable importance as a source of olive oil, olives, ash lumber, and many ornamental shrubs.

SUBCLASS VI, ASTERIDAE; ORDER 6, SCROPHULARIALES
Scrophulariaceae: Figwort or Snapdragon Family

Field Recognition   Flowers 5-merous, zygomorphic; corolla 2-lipped; stamens 2 or 4, sometimes with a fifth staminode; ovary 2-locular, style terminal, ovules numerous; $CA^{⑤} \underline{COZ}^{⑤} A^{2 \text{ or } 4} \underline{G}^{②}$. (The Scrophulariaceae may be confused with the Labiatae, which have a gynobasic style and deeply 4-lobed ovary, or with the Solanaceae, which have actinomorphic flowers containing 5 functional stamens.)

Description   *Habit*   Mostly herbs or undershrubs, rarely trees, several climbers, and some parasitic on roots.

Leaves   Alternate, opposite or whorled, simple; without stipules.

Inflorescences   Variable.

Flowers   Bisexual, zygomorphic. Calyx of 5 united sepals. Corolla of 5 united petals, typically 2-lipped, sometimes nearly regular, limb 4- to 5-lobed or rarely 6- to 8-lobed. Androecium of 2 or 4(5) stamens, didynamous, fifth stamen sometimes a staminode inserted on the corolla. Gynoecium a compound pistil of 2 carpels, with 2 locules, ovules numerous, placentation axile, ovary superior, style terminal. See Figure 14-87.

ANGIOSPERM FAMILIES

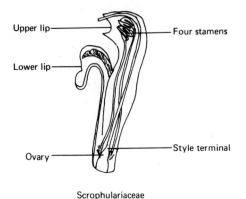

Upper lip

Lower lip

Four stamens

Style terminal

Ovary

Scrophulariaceae

FIGURE 14-87
Corolla, stamens, and pistil of family
Scrophulariaceae.

Fruit A capsule, rarely a berry.
Seed Numerous, small, with endosperm.

Size, Distribution, and General Information A family of about 190 genera and 4000 species of general distribution.

Some of the genera are *Scrophularia* (300) (figwort); *Verbascum* (300) (mullein); *Calceolaria* (300); *Linaria* (150) (toadflax, butter-and-eggs, spurred snapdragon); *Antirrhinum* (40) (snapdragon); *Chelone* (4) (turtlehead); *Penstemon* (280) (beard-tongue); *Mimulus* (100) (monkey flower); *Gratiola* (20) (hedge hyssop); *Veronica* (300) (speedwell); *Digitalis* (20) (foxglove); *Agalinis* (60) (false foxglove); *Castilleja* (150) (Indian paintbrush); *Pedicularis* (500) (lousewort); *Torenia* (50) (monkey face); and *Striga* (40) (witchweed).

Most of the species in this large family have flowers somewhat similar to the familiar cultivated snapdragons (*Antirrhinum*). Foxglove (*Digitalis purpurea*) is a source of drugs used in the treatment of heart conditions and is also appreciated for the beauty of its flowers.

Many members of this family are parasitic on the roots of other plants and can cause serious crop damage. *Striga lutea* (witchweed) is a parasitic on corn roots and has recently become established in the Carolinas. Other parasites include *Agalinis*, *Castilleja*, and *Pedicularis*.

Economic Importance The family is of little importance except for several ornamentals, root parasites, and *Digitalis*.

SUBCLASS VI, ASTERIDAE; ORDER 6, SCROPHULARIALES
Bignoniaceae: Bignonia Family

Field Recognition Usually woody vines or trees; leaves usually opposite, often compound; flowers showy and more or less zygomorphic; fruit often a woody capsule; seeds often conspicuously winged; $CA^{⑤} \underline{COZ^{⑤}} A^4 \underline{G^{②}}$.

Description   *Habit*   Mostly woody vines, trees, or rarely herbs.

Leaves   Opposite, usually pinnately or palmately compound, sometimes simple, tendrils sometimes replacing terminal leaflet; without stipules.˙

Inflorescences   Cymose.

Flowers   Bisexual, more or less zygomorphic, often showy. Calyx of 5 united sepals, campanulate, 5-toothed. Corolla of 5 united petals, the 5 lobes often forming 2 lips, the upper lip of 2 lobes. Androecium of 4 stamens, epipetalous, didynamous, alternate with corolla lobes, staminode often representing the fifth stamen. Gynoecium a compound pistil of 2 united carpels, with 2 locules, each with a placenta; or 1-locular with 2 marginal bifid placentas, ovules numerous, ovary superior, style terminal, 2-lipped.

Fruit   A capsule, often woody, or fleshy and indehiscent.

Seed   Often winged.

Size, Distribution, and General Information   A family of about 100 genera and 800 species, mostly of tropical and subtropical distribution but with a few temperate zone species.

Some of the genera are *Bignonia* (1) (cross vine); *Jacaranda* (50); *Catalpa* (11) (Indian bean, fish bait tree); *Campsis* (2) (trumpet creeper); *Crescentia* (5) (calabash tree); *Kigelia* (1) (sausage tree); and *Spathodea* (20) (African tulip tree).

Paulownia tomentosa, (empress or princess tree) provides a link between Scrophulariaceae and the Bignoniaceae.

The Indian bean (*Catalpa*) of eastern North America is one of the few members of *Bignoniaceae* to be found in the temperate zone. Catalpa "worms" (Lepidoptera larvae) feed on the leaves. The trees are sometimes planted around fish ponds, and the "worms" used for bait.

Many members of the family are woody vines or lianas, such as the temperate zone *Campsis radicans* and *Bignonia capreolata*.

Crescentia cujete of tropical America is the calabash tree. It produces a woody gourdlike berry that forms a watertight container, or calabash, after the central pulp is removed.

Economic Importance   The Bignoniaceae are important for woody ornamental vines and trees.

SUBCLASS VI, ASTERIDAE; ORDER 7, CAMPANULALES
Campanulaceae: Bluebell or Bellflower Family

Field Recognition   Largely herbaceous, rarely shrubs; leaves usually alternate, simple, without stipules; flowers showy, bisexual, actinomorphic or zygomorphic, epigynous, 5-merous; stamens epipetalous; petals predominately blue; fruit a capsule; $CA^5CO^{\circledR}$ or $\underline{COZ^5\ A^5}$ or $A^{\circledS}$ or $A^5_{\_}\ \overline{G^{\text{2 or 3 or 5}}}$ See Figure 14-88.

Campanulaceae

FIGURE 14-88
Lobelia cardinalis (Campanulaceae) inflorescence
(redrawn from Heywood, 1978).

Size, Distribution, and General Information   A family of about 70 genera and
about 2,000 species occurring in temperate, subtropic zones and on tropical mountains.
   The chief genera are *Campanula* (300) (bluebell); *Lobelia* (380); and *Centropogon*
(200).

Economic Importance   Many species, with their showy flowers, are grown as
garden ornamentals.

SUBCLASS VI, ASTERIDAE; ORDER 8, RUBIALES
Rubiaceae: Coffee or Madder Family

Field Recognition   Herbs, shrubs, and trees; leaves opposite or whorled, usually entire; flowers 4- or 5-merous; stamens as many as corolla lobes and alternate with them; ovary inferior; CA$^{4-5}$CO$^{4-5}$A$^{4-5}\overline{G}^{②}$. (Rubiaceae resemble Caprifoliaceae, and members of the two families may be confused. Among other differences, Rubiaceae have stipules, which are usually lacking in Caprifoliaceae.)

Description   *Habit*   Trees, shrubs, or rarely herbs (in North America mostly herbaceous).

Leaves   Opposite or whorled, usually entire, simple; with stipules which are often united and as large as the leaf blades so that the leaves appear whorled.

Inflorescences   Cymose, or solitary to almost capitate.

Flowers   Bisexual, actinomorphic, rarely slightly zygomorphic. Calyx of 4 to 5 sepals, fused to ovary, with (0)4 to 5 lobes. Corolla usually of 4 to 5(10) united petals, epigynous, more or less tubular, lobes ranging in number from 4 to 10. Androecium of 4 to 5(10) stamens, epipetalous (inserted in the tube or at its mouth) alternate with the corolla lobes. Gynoecium a compound pistil of (1)2 united carpels, with 2 or more locules, ovules 1 to many per locule, placentation usually axile, apical or basal, ovary inferior, style often slender, stigma capitate or variously lobed. See Figure 14-89.

Fruit   A capsule, berry, or drupe.

Seed   With a small embryo in endosperm.

Size, Distribution, and General Information   A family of about 450 genera and 6500 species, largely of tropical and subtropical distribution but some are temperate, and there are even a few arctic species.

Some of the genera are *Rubia* (60) (madder, manjit); *Hedyotis* (including *Houstonia*) (200) (bluets); *Cinchona* (40) (quinine, fever tree, Jesuit's bark); *Gardenia* (250) (cape jasmine); *Cephalanthus* (17) (buttonbush); *Coffea* (40) (coffee); *Galium* (300) (bedstraw, cleavers); *Pinckneya* (1) (fever tree); *Richardia* (10); and *Mitchella* (2) (partridgeberry, twinflower).

Coffee (*Coffea arabica*) is probably the Western world's most popular nonalcoholic beverage. It originated in Ethiopia and was introduced to the rest of the world by Arab traders. Before about 1870, the British drank much coffee; however, when disease wiped out the coffee plantations of the British Empire, they switched largely to tea. Recently, diseases and frost have caused problems in the coffee plantations of South America, and the price of coffee has increased.

Several species of *Cinchona* from the Andes yield quinine used in the prevention and treatment of malaria. *Cinchona* plantations were developed in Java by the Dutch. During World War II when Java was occupied by the Japanese, the supply of quinine to the Allied forces was cut off. Numerous plant taxonomists from the United States

Rubiaceae

FIGURE 14-89
Rubiaceae. (a) *Galium* shoot and fruit and (b) *Houstonia* shoot and flower.

were sent to the Andes to search for native *Cinchona*. Toward the end of the war, synthetic drugs were developed which have largely replaced quinine.

Houstonia caerulea (bluets) is a favorite spring wild flower. Twinflowers and two-lobed scarlet fruits of a trailing evergreen plant called partridge berry (*Mitchella repens*) are attractive.

In coastal Georgia, Florida, and South Carolina, the numerous bright pink foliaceous sepals make the beautiful fever tree (*Pinckneya bracteata*) conspicuous on the edge of swamps. The early settlers used it as a remedy for malaria.

Rubia tinctorum (madder) was formerly cultivated for its red dye (alizarin), which is now prepared artificially. Some of the bedstraws (*Galium*) have been used as sources of dyes. Some bedstraws are sweet-scented and were once used to stuff mattresses. Certain bedstraws are called *catchweed* or *cleavers* because they cling so readily to any surface. Gardenias (*Gardenia*) are evergreen shrubs that produce fragrant white flowers. *Uragoga ipecacuanha* from Brazil is the source of ipecac used in medicine.

Economic Importance The family is of significant importance for coffee and quinine as well as several ornamentals.

SUBCLASS VI, ASTERIDAE; ORDER 9, DIPSACALES
Caprifoliaceae: Honeysuckle Family

Field Recognition Shrubs, sometimes lianas; leaves opposite; flowers 4- or 5-merous, epigynous; calyx fused to ovary; gynoecium multicarpellate, ovary inferior; CA $\widehat{4-5}$ CO $\widehat{4-5}$ A $^{4-5}$ $\overline{G}$ $\widehat{\text{2 or 3 or 5 or 8}}$.

Description *Habit* Shrubs, sometimes lianas, rarely herbs.
Leaves Opposite, usually simple, without stipules or else stipules very small (except in *Sambucus*).
Inflorescences Cymose.
Flowers Bisexual, actinomorphic or zygomorphic. Calyx of 4 to 5 united sepals, fused to ovary. Corolla of 4 to 5 united petals, epigynous, sometimes 2-lipped. Androecium of 5 stamens, epipetalous, inserted on corolla tube and alternate with its lobes. Gynoecium a compound pistil of 2, 3, 5, or 8 carpels, with 2 to 5 locules, ovules 1 or more, placentation pendulous or axile, ovary inferior, style terminal, often slender. See Figure 14-90.
Fruit A berry or drupe.
Seed With endosperm.

Size, Distribution, and General Information A family of about 15 genera and 400 species mostly of north temperate and tropical mountain distribution.

Chief genera are *Viburnum* (150) (snowball); *Abelia* (30); *Diervilla* (3) (bush honeysuckle); *Symphoricarpos* (18) (snowberry, coralberry); *Sambucus* (40) (elderberry); *Lonicera* (150) (honeysuckle); *Linnaea* (1 to 3) (twinflower); *Kolkwitzia* (1) (beauty bush); and *Triosteum* (10) (horse gentian).

Children of countless generations have enjoyed the sweet nectar from the flowers of honeysuckle (*Lonicera*). Many species of *Lonicera* are used as ornamental shrubs or vines. The introduced *L. japonica* is a troublesome weed in the eastern United States.

The fruit of *Sambucus* is used to make elderberry wine or elderberry pies or preserves.

Many *Viburnum* species and cultivars are used as showy ornamental shrubs. All have white flowers; some are evergreen, others deciduous. In some cultivars, the fruits are attractive. The outer flowers of the cymose corymb of some species and cultivars of *Viburnum* are sterile and have the corolla much enlarged, in other cultivars all the

Caprifoliaceae

FIGURE 14-90
Lonicera japonica (Caprifoliaceae). (a) Flowering branch and (b) flower.

flowers are sterile. *Viburnum trilobum* (highbush cranberry) grows all across North America from New England to British Columbia, and the fruits are used in jelly.

Economic Importance   The family is important for a number of ornamental shrubs and vines.

SUBCLASS VI, ASTERIDAE; ORDER 9, DIPSACALES
Dipsacaceae: Teasel Family

Field Recognition   Herbs or rarely subshrubs; leaves opposite, without stipules; flowers 5-merous in dense cymose heads subtended by involucral bracts; fruit an achene; $CA^5 \underline{COZ^5} A^4 \overline{G}^②$. See Figure 14-91.

Size, Distribution, and General Information   A small family of 10 genera and 270 species originally distributed from Europe to eastern Asia and to central and southern Africa. In North America, *Dipsacus fullonum* (teasel) has become widely naturalized and weedy. Certain species of *Scabiosa* (80) are cultivated as ornamental flowers. The dried inflorescences of teasel are used for raising the nap on cloth or are sometimes included in dried flower arrangements.

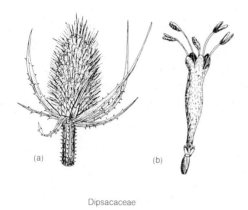

(a)   (b)

Dipsacaceae

FIGURE 14-91
Dipsacus fullonum (Dipsacaceae). (a)
Fruiting cylindric head and (b) flower.

SUBCLASS VI, ASTERIDAE; ORDER 10, ASTERALES
Compositae or Asteraceae: Sunflower or Aster Family

Field Recognition   Inflorescences of involucrate heads (capitula) of $1^{-\infty}$ florets on a common receptacle surrounded by phyllaries; pappus often present; corolla united and 5-lobed; stamens 5, forming a cylinder around the style; ovary with 2 style branches and uniloculate with a single ovule; the basic floral plan for the family is CA^x $\underset{\frown}{CO}^{\circledS}$ $A^{\widehat{5}}$ $\overline{G}^{\circledtwo}$.

Description   *Habit*   Herbs, shrubs, infrequently trees and vines. (Largely herbaceous in the temperate zone.)

Leaves   Alternate, opposite, or rarely whorled, simple but rarely truly compound, sometimes greatly reduced; without stipules.

Inflorescences   An involucrate head or capitulum with 1 to ∞ florets (flowers) on a common receptacle surrounded by an involucre of phyllaries. The heads are variously arranged.

Flowers   Bisexual or unisexual, actinomorphic or zygomorphic. Calyx epigynous, represented by the variable pappus. Corolla of 5 united petals, 5-lobed and tubular, or ligulate with 3 to 5 teeth or 2-lipped with 3-lobed upper lip and 2-lobed lower lip. Androecium of (4)5 stamens, epipetalous, with the anthers nearly always united, anthers mostly included within the corolla tube, filaments free. Gynoecium a compound pistil of 2 united carpels, with 1 locule, ovule 1, ovary inferior, style with two branches of various shapes. See Figures 14-92 and 14-93.

The florets within the heads or capitula are of five basic plans: (1) tubular (disc) florets, corolla regular, florets perfect; (2) ligulate or ray florets, zygomorphic, pistillate; (3) ligulate or ray florets, zygomorphic, sterile; (4) ligulate or ray florets, zygomorphic, perfect; and (5) tubular florets, corolla regular, florets pistillate. A head or capitulum may contain: (1) ligulate florets only; (2) tubular florets only; or (3) both ligulate and tubular florets.

Fruit   An achene (sometimes called a *cypsela*).

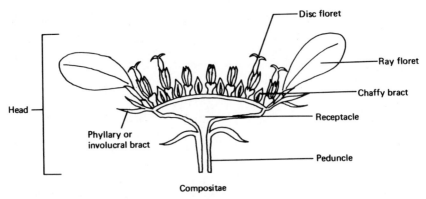

FIGURE 14-92
Diagrammatic vertical view of Compositae head.

Systematics   Although a large family, it is recognized by a number of common characters that are distinctive. The family is usually divided into 13 tribes.

1 Heliantheae (including Helenieae): Style with crown of hairs below the branches; anthers rounded at base; pappus not hairy; phyllaries not membranous at margins; receptacle naked or chaffy. A few are wind-pollinated with separate stamens and unisexual heads.

2 Astereae: All or only the central florets tubular; anthers blunt at base; stigmas flattened with marginal row of papillae and a terminal, hairy, segment.

3 Anthemideae: As in tribe Heliantheae, but with phyllaries membranous at tip and edges.

4 Arctotideae: Style thickened or with a ring of hairs below branches; anthers acute at base or with a longer or shorter point and with filaments inserted above the base.

5 Inuleae: As in tribe Astereae, with tubular florets 4- to 5-lobed; anthers tailed at base.

6 Senecioneae: *Senecio* (1500) (groundsel, ragwort).

7 Calenduleae: *Calendula* (20–30) (pot marigold); and *Dimorphotheca* (7) (cape marigold).

8 Eupatorieae: *Eupatorium* (600) (boneset, joe-pye); *Mikania* (250); and *Liatris* (40) (blazing star, gay flower).

9 Vernonieae: Florets tubular, not yellow (in ours); anthers acute, acuminate or rarely tailed; stigmas semicylindrical, long, pointed, hairy outside; stigmatic papillae inside style branches.

10 Cynareae: Florets tubular, outer florets usually sterile (i.e. disciform); anthers usually tailed; styles thickened or with a circle of hairs below stigma; receptacle usually chaffy.

11 Mutisieae: Florets tubular or sometimes with 2-lipped rays, disc florets actinomorphic or 2-lipped.

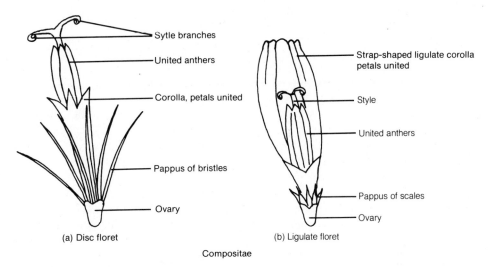

(a) Disc floret (b) Ligulate floret

Compositae

FIGURE 14-93
Diagrammatic drawings of (a) disc floret and (b) ligulate floret of the family Compositae.

12 Liabeae: Heads radiate or tubular; latex ducts absent; anthers acute or short tailed; style branches as in tribe Vernonieae.

13 Lactuceae (Cichorieae). Florets all ligulate; sap milky.

Size, Distribution, and General Information A family of about 1100 genera and 20,000 species worldwide in distribution. One of the largest families, if not the largest family, of flowering plants.

Major tribes and genera are the following:

1 Heliantheae: *Helianthus* (110) (sunflowers); *Silphium* (15) (rosinweed, compass plant); *Xanthium* (30) (cocklebur); *Ambrosia* (35 to 40) (ragweed); *Zinnia* (20); *Dahlia* (27); *Bidens* (230) (tickweed); *Cosmos* (25); *Helenium* (40) (bitterweed, sneezeweed); *Tagetes* (50) (marigold); *Rudbeckia* (25) (coneflower, black-eyed Susan); and *Gaillardia* (28) (blanketflower).

2 Astereae: *Solidago* (100) (goldenrod); *Bellis* (15) (English daisy); *Aster* (500); *Erigeron* (200) (fleabane); *Baccharis* (400) (groundsel tree); and *Chrysothamnus* (12) (rabbit bush).

3 Anthemideae: *Achillea* (200) (yarrow, milfoil); *Anthemis* (200) (dog fennel); *Chrysanthemum* (200); *Matricaria* (52) (feverfew); *Tanacetum* (50–60) (tansy); and *Artemisia* (400) (wormwood, sagebrush).

4 Arctotideae: *Arctotis* (65); and *Gazania* (40).

5 Inuleae: *Inula* (200); *Antennaria* (100) (pussytoes); and *Gnaphalium* (200) (cudweed, rabbit tobacco).

6 Senecioneae: *Senecio* (1500) (groundsel, ragwort).

7 Calenduleae: *Calendula* (20–30) (pot marigold); and *Dimorphotheca* (7) (cape marigold).

8 Eupatorieae: *Eupatorium* (600) (boneset, joe-pye); *Mikania* (250); and *Liatris* (40) (blazing star, gay flower).

9 Vernonieae: *Vernonia* (900+) (ironweed); *Elephantopus* (32) (elephant's foot); and *Stokesia* (1).

10 Cynareae: *Cynara* (14) (artichoke); *Echinops* (100) (globe thistle); *Arctium* (5) (burdock); *Carduus* (100) (thistle); *Cirsium* (150) (thistle); *Centaurea* (600) (cornflower, bachelor's button); and *Carthamus* (safflower).

11 Mutisieae: *Mutisia* (60); and *Gerbera* (70) (gerbera daisy, Transvaal daisy).

12 Liabeae: *Liabum* (90).

13 Lactuceae (Cichorieae); *Cichorium* (9) (chicory, endive); *Crepis* (200) (hawk's-beard); *Hieracium* (800) (hawkweed); *Taraxacum* (62) (dandelion); *Lactuca* (100) (lettuce); *Tragopogon* (50) (goatsbeard, salsify); and *Sonchus* (50) (sow thistle).

Economic Importance   Relative to its numbers, Compositae are not as economically important as several other families are. However, many Compositae are valuable ornamentals—e.g., *Aster, Callistephus, Chrysanthemum, Dahlia, Coreopsis, Gerbera, Helichrysum, Tagetes, Zinnia, Rudbeckia.*

Several are sources of food: *Lactuca, Cynara, Cichorium, Tragopogon, Helianthus,* and *Carthamus.*

Ragweed (*Ambrosia*) pollen is a major cause of hayfever. Some Compositae have sesquiterpene lactones that cause contact dermatitis in humans. Many Compositae are weedy.

Chrysanthemum coccineum is the source of the natural insecticide pyrethrum. The red dye safflower, obtained from *Carthamus tinctoria,* is used for coloring butter, liqueurs, candles, and rouge. Eurasian wormwood (*Artemisia absinthium*) was once used to flavor a liqueur; however, absinthe caused addiction, and its use has been declared illegal.

CLASS LILOPSIDA: MONOCOTYLEDONS

SUBCLASS I, ALISMATIDAE; ORDER 1, ALISMATALES
Alismataceae: Water Plantain or Arrowhead Family

Field Recognition   Aquatic or wetland herbs; flowers bisexual, often whorled, perianth in 2 series; sepals 3, green and sepal-like; petals 3, white; gynoecium apocarpous, usually with many free carpels; CA^3 CO^3 $A^{6-\infty}$ $\underline{G}^{6-\infty}$.

Description   *Habit*   Annual or perennial, aquatic or wetland herbs from stout rhizomes; erect or rarely with floating leaves.

Leaves   Basal, long-petioled, sheathing, blades linear-lanceolate or ovate, bases sometimes hastate or sagittate, veins parallel with the margins and converging at apex of blade.

Inflorescences   Flowers often whorled or in racemes or panicles.

Flowers   Bisexual or rarely polygamous, actinomorphic. Calyx of 3 green sepals. Corolla of 3 petals, white, larger than sepals, deciduous or rarely absent. Androecium of (3)6–∞ stamens, free. Gynoecium of 6 or more simple pistils each having 1 carpel, with 1 locule, ovary superior, style persistent, receptacle flat to globose. See Figure 14-94.

Fruit   A spiral or ring of achenes.

Seed   With a curved embryo.

Size, Distribution, and General Information   A family of about 12 genera and 75 species of cosmopolitan distribution.

The chief genera are *Alisma* (5) (water plaintain); *Echinodorus* (25) (burhead); and *Sagittaria* (20) (wapata, arrowhead, swamp potato).

In North America, the Indians once dug the rhizomes of *Sagittaria* for food, hence the name *swamp potato*. A Eurasian species (*S. sagittifolia*) is occasionally cultivated.

FIGURE 14-94
Sagittaria latifolia (Alismataceae). (a) Habit of plant in flower, (b) staminate flower, and (c) pistillate flower.

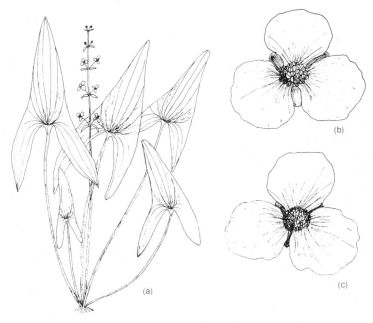

Alismataceae

Economic Importance   The family is of little importance to humans, but many species are important wildlife food plants.

SUBCLASS I, ALISMATIDAE; ORDER 2, HYDROCHARITALES
Hydrocharitaceae: Frog's-bit Family

Field Recognition   Aquatic herbs of fresh water and marine habitats; leaves simple, usually submerged and ribbonlike, sometimes floating or partly emergent; flowers bisexual or unisexual (male and female on different plants); perianth CA^3 CO^3 $A^{2-\infty}$ $\overline{G}$ (3-6).

FIGURE 14-95
Egeria (Elodea) densa (Hydrocharitaceae). Flowering shoot with pistillate flower. *Egeria* is a dioecious, submerged aquatic.

Hydrocharitaceae

Description   *Habit*   Annual or perennial aquatic herbs with either a creeping rhizome with leaves in two vertical rows, or an erect main shoot with roots at the base and spirally arranged or whorled leaves.

Leaves   Simple, submerged, or sometimes floating or emergent, linear to orbicular, with or without a petiole.

Inflorescences   Axillary, enclosed at first in spathe of usually 2 or more fused leaves.

Flowers   Bisexual or unisexual, usually regular. Perianth of 3 distinct, green sepals and 3 white or colored petals. Androecium of 2 or 3 to numerous stamens in one or more series. Gynoecium a compound pistil of (2) 3–6 (20) united carpels, 1-locular, numerous ovules, placentation parietal, ovary inferior, styles as many as the carpels. See Figure 14-95.

Fruits   Variable, dehiscent or indehiscent.

Seed   Embryo straight, without endosperm.

Size, Distribution, and General Information   A small family of about 15 genera and almost 100 species; cosmopolitan in distribution but mainly tropical.

Some of the genera include: *Egeria* (*Elodea*) (15); *Hydrocharis* (6); *Vallisneria* (8); *Hydrilla* (1); *Halophila* (4); and *Thalassia* (1).

Thalassia and *Halophila* are marine angiosperms that grow in tropical to subtropical seas. *Hydrilla verticillata*, a submerged freshwater aquatic, has been introduced into North America where it has become a serious weed in lakes and ponds. The family is noteworthy for interesting and unusual pollination mechanisms, e.g., free floating male flowers in *Elodea* and *Vallisneria*, threadlike pollen grains carried by ocean currents in *Halophila*, and explosive release of pollen by the anthers of *Hydrilla*, etc.

Economic Importance   The family is the source of some marvelous ornamentals for aquaria and numerous aquatic weeds.

SUBCLASS I, ALISMATIDAE; ORDER 3, NAJADALES
Potamogetonaceae: Pondweed Family

Field Recognition   Aquatic herbs often submerged or with both floating and submerged leaves; flowers with perianth of 4 segments, rudimentary, or none; stamens 1 to 4; gynoecium of 1 to 4 separate carpels, 1-loculed, with 1 seed per ovary; $CA^{0 \text{ or } 4} CO^0 A^{1-4} \underline{G}^{1-4}$.

Description   *Habit*   Aquatic, freshwater herbs, with creeping rhizomes, stems mostly submerged.

Leaves   Submerged or floating, sheathing, alternate or opposite.

Inflorescences   Axillary spikes, peduncle surrounded by a sheath at the base.

Flowers   Bisexual. Perianth of 4 free, rudimentary, short-clawed segments, or none. Androecium of 1–4 stamens, inserted at or on the claws of the perianth segments. Gynoecium of 4 simple pistils, each having 1 carpel and 1 locule, ovary superior, stigmas sessile or on short styles. See Figure 14-96.

Potamogetonaceae

FIGURE 14-96
Potamogeton pulcher (Potamogetonaceae). Habit
of plant in flower, note the upper floating leaves
and the lower submerged leaves.

Fruit   Sessile, free, 1-seeded, indehiscent, drupe-like when fresh.
Seed   With no endosperm.

Size, Distribution, and General Information   A family of 2 genera and about
100 species of cosmopolitan distribution.
The two genera are *Potamogeton* (100) (pondweed) and *Groenlandia* (1).

The sago pondweed (*Potamogeton pectinatus*) fruits in autumn during the fall migration of waterfowl and provides much food for ducks. Some species are troublesome weeds in ponds and lakes.

Economic Importance   The family is of little importance.

SUBCLASS I, ALISMATIDAE; ORDER 3, NAJADALES
Zosteraceae: Eel Grass Family

Field Recognition   Grasslike, submerged herbs of marine habitats; stems creeping rhizomes; $(CA^0 \, CO^0 \, A^1 \, G^0)$ $(CA^0 \, CO^0 \, A^0 \, G^{②})$.

Description   *Habit*   Submerged marine aquatics.
Leaves   Linear and grasslike, bases sheathing.
Inflorescences   Flattened spadix, enclosed at flowering by the spathe.
Flowers   Unisexual, dioecious, or monoecious. Male flower of one stamen. Female flower of 2 united carpels, ovule solitary, 1 locular, style short, stigmas 2, long.
Fruit   Ovoid or ellipsoidal, pericarp thin, dry, and crescent shaped, exocarp soft, endocarp fibrous.
Seed   Without endosperm.

Size, Distribution, and General Information   A family of 3 genera and 18 species distributed along temperate coastlines of the northern and southern hemispheres. Pollination in the Zosteraceae is interesting. For example, in *Zostera* (12 species), the long threadlike pollen has the same specific gravity as sea water, and when discharged it floats freely at various depths and drifts about until trapped by the long stigmas. Other genera in the family are *Heterozostera* (1) and *Phyllospadix* (5).

Economic Importance   The beds of eel grasses support various plants and animals that in turn supply food for many species of birds and fish. *Zostera marina,* common eel-grass, is an important food for waterfowl.

SUBCLASS II, ARECIDAE; ORDER 1, ARECALES
Palmae or Arecaceae: Palm Family

Field Recognition   Woody shrubs or trees; leaves large, fan-shaped or pinnately compound, with sheathing bases; inflorescence paniculate, large, spathes often present; flowers small; $CA^3 \, CO^3 \, A^6 \, \underline{G}^{3 \text{ or } ③}$ or $CA^3 \, CO^3 \, A^6 \, G^0$ and $CA^3 \, CO^3 \, A^0 \, \underline{G}^{3 \text{ or } ③}$.

Description   *Habit*   Trees or shrubs, sometimes climbing, stem stout to slender, short to over 30 meters tall, trees usually unbranched.
Leaves   Blades palmate, pinnate, or simple, often very large, petiole sheathing at base, leaves usually in a terminal cluster.

(a)

(b)

Palmae

FIGURE 14-97
Sabal (Palmae). (a) Inflorescence and (b) flower.

Inflorescences Large, paniculate, among or below the leaves, subtended by one or more spathes, plants monoecious or dioecious or flowers bisexual.

Flowers Unisexual or bisexual, actinomorphic. Calyx of 3 sepals, small, separate or united. Corolla of 3 petals, small, separate or united. Androecium of usually 6 stamens, in 2 series. Gynoecium usually a compound pistil having 3 united carpels, with 1 to 3 locules, ovule solitary, ovary superior, rudimentary in staminate flowers. See Figure 14-97.

Fruit Berries or drupes, exocarp fleshy or leathery.

Seed Endosperm relatively large, sometimes milky, embryo small.

Size, Distribution, and General Information A family of about 200 genera and 3000 species of wide tropical and subtropical distribution, a few in warm temperate regions. The palms form a characteristic feature of tropical vegetation.

Some of the genera are *Areca* (54) (betel nut); *Cocos* (1) (coconut palm); *Lodoicea* (1) (double coconut, coco-de-mer); *Phoenix* (17) (date palm); *Phytelephas* (15) (ivory-nut palm or vegetable ivory); *Elaeis* (2) (oil palm); *Calamus* (300+) (rattan, rattan cane); *Sabal* (25) (palmetto, cabbage palm, cabbage tree); *Serenoa* (1) (saw palmetto); *Washingtonia* (2) (fan palm); *Copernicia* (30) (wax palm); *Metroxylon* (15) (sago palm); *Coccothrinax* (50) (Biscayne palm); and *Roystonea* (17) (royal palm).

The date palm (*Phoenix dactylifera*) has been cultivated for at least 5000 years. Each pistillate tree can yield as much as 50 kilograms of dates each year. The date palm is dioecious, and pollen from staminate trees must be hand-transferred to the pistillate trees to insure pollination of cultivated dates. Other species of *Phoenix* are tapped for a sweet sap which can be made into palm sugar, or jaggery, or fermented to make palm "wine." Various species of the genus *Metroxylon*, native to India and Malaysia, yield starch or sago made from the pith of the stems.

Areca catechu is cultivated in tropical Asia for its seeds called *betel nuts*. The seed is cut into slices and rolled up with a little slaked lime in a leaf of betel pepper (*Piper betle*). When chewed, it turns the saliva bright red; it stimulates the digestive organs and is used by millions of people.

Oil palm (*Elaeis guineensis*), native to West Africa, yields a valuable oil that is both edible and useful as a lubricant. Increasing numbers of oil palm plantations are being planted in tropical countries, causing some commercial competition for soybean growers.

Coconuts (*Cocos nucifera*) are widely grown in tropical areas, especially near the sea. The young fruit contains a pint or more of a sweetish fluid. The kernels are eaten raw or cooked; oil is extracted by boiling or pressure. The coconut has literally hundreds of uses in areas where it is grown. *Lodoicea maldivica* (the double coconut or coco-de-mer) is one of the largest fruits known and reputedly takes 10 years to ripen. The terminal buds of a number of species of palms are used for food and are called *hearts of palm*. Each time a heart of palm is obtained, a palm tree must be killed. Cabbage palm (*Sabal palmetto*) was once much used in this fashion by Seminole Indians in Florida.

Economic Importance   The palm family is of considerable importance in tropical and subtropical regions, where it is used for food, shelter, clothing, copra, coconuts, oils, dates, rattan, ivory nuts, and wax. In addition, the palm family is important everywhere because the products of tropical palms enter temperate-zone commerce.

SUBCLASS, ARECIDAE; ORDER 3, PANDANALES
Pandanaceae: Screwpine Family

Field Recognition   Mostly seacoast or marshy plants, stems tall, usually supported by aerial roots, often branched; leaves 3-ranked, but appearing spiral, long and narrow; flowers unisexual in a racemose spadix, plants dioecious; ($CA^0 \; CO^0 \; A^{1-\infty} \; G^0$) ($CA^0 \; CO^0 \; A^0 \; \underline{G}^{\infty(1-few)}$).

Descriptions   *Habit*   Plants with tall stems bearing leaf scars, branched, usually supported by aerial roots, some are lianas.

Leaves   Located near the young stem tips, 3-ranked, but stems twisted to give a spiral arrangement to the leaves, parallel-veined, long and narrow with open sheath, margins toothed, often sharply bent down near the middle.

Pandanaceae

FIGURE 14-98
Pandanus (Pandanaceae). Habit
showing aerial roots at base of
trunk.

Inflorescences   Typically, a racemose spadix subtended by a spathe which is sometimes colored.

Flowers   Unisexual, borne on separate plants. Calyx and corolla absent. Androecium of male flowers with numerous racemose or umbellate, free or fused stamens. Gynoecium of female flower typically of numerous carpels arranged in a ring, locules one to numerous, ovules 1 to many per locule, ovary superior, stigmas sessile. See Figure 14-98.

Fruit   Berry or multilocular drupe.

Seeds   Small; endosperm fleshy; embryo minute.

Size, Distribution, and General Information   The Pandanaceae consists of 3 genera and about 800 species, distributed in the Old World tropics and subtropics. The genera are *Pandanus* (600) (screw pines); *Freycinetia* (180); and *Sararanga* (2).

Economic Importance   The fruits of many species are edible and said to taste like apples. The leaves are often used as thatching material to cover roofs and for basket-weaving. Many species are grown as tropical foliage plants because of their interesting form and habit.

SUBCLASS II, ARECIDAE; ORDER 4, ARALES
Araceae: Arum, Philodendron, or Aroid Family

Field Recognition   North American species are herbaceous; plants often of wet habitats; inflorescence a spadix enveloped or subtended by a single spathe; flowers small or minute; $CA^0 \ CO^0 \ A^{6 \ or \ less} \ \underline{G}^{2 \ or \ 3}$.

Description   *Habit*   Variable, herbs with aerial stems, tubers, or rhizomes; climbing shrubs, epiphytes; or marsh plants. Sap often contains raphides (calcium oxalate crystals).

Leaves   Variable, solitary or few, mostly basal (in ours), or alternate (in tropical species); entire to variously arranged, often hastate or sagittate, with a sheath at the base of the petiole.

Inflorescences   A spadix usually subtended by a spathe.

Flowers   Bisexual or unisexual, small, often bad-smelling and attracting carrion flies. Perianth absent or small and scalelike of 4 to 6 parts. Androecium of 6 or fewer stamens, opposite the perianth segments, staminodes sometimes present. Gynoecium a compound pistil (1)2 to 3(9) united carpels, with 1 to several locules, placentation parietal, axile, basal or apical, ovary superior or immersed in the spadix, style various, sometimes greatly reduced. See Figure 14-99.

Fruit   A berry, often many clustered closely together on the spadix and resembling a multiple fruit. Fruit sometimes leathery and rupturing, with 1 to many seeds.

Seed   With or without endosperm.

Size, Distribution, and General Information   A family of about 110 genera and 1800 species, primarily of tropical and subtropical distribution but with about 8 percent of its species in temperate regions.

Some of the genera are *Arum* (15) (arrowroot); *Anthurium* (500); *Arisaema* (100 +) (jack-in-the-pulpit, Indian turnip); *Peltandra* (4) (arrow arum); *Symplocarpus* (1) (eastern skunk cabbage); *Orontium* (1) (golden club, never-wet); *Acorus* (2) (sweet flag); *Philodendron* (255); *Pistia* (1) (water lettuce); *Lysichiton* (2) (western skunk cabbage);

Araceae

FIGURE 14-99
Vertical section of an inflorescence from the family Araceae. The flowers are clustered into a grouping called a *spadix* and subtended by a bract called a *spathe.* (Note: The spathe is cut away to show the spadix.)

Zantedeschia (8 to 9) (florist's calla lily); *Pothos* (75); *Dieffenbachia* (30) (dumb cane); *Caladium* (15); *Monstera* (50); *Algaonema* (21) (Chinese evergreen); *Colocasia* (8) (taro); and *Alocasia* (70) (elephant ear).

In rich, moist woods of eastern North America, *Arisaema* is often called *jack-in-the-pulpit* or *Indian turnip*. It has an upright spadix as "jack" and a spathe as the "pulpit." The rhizomes of *Arisaema* may be eaten if boiled and dried to eliminate the oxalates. In Southeast Asia and the Pacific Islands, taro (*Colocasia esculenta*) is cultivated for its rhizome which when boiled loses its poisonous nature and forms valuable starchy food. It is the *poi* of Hawaiian culture.

The western skunk cabbage (*Lysichiton americanum*) and the eastern skunk cabbage (*Symplocarpus foetidus*) are unusual wild flowers of cold, wet places. The fetid odor of the flower attracts flies in large numbers. Never-wet or golden club (*Orontium aquaticum*) is a lovely wild flower of aquatic habitats in the coastal plain of the Eastern states. The golden yellow spadix does not have an obvious spathe.

Dumb cane (*Dieffenbachia*), often grown as a foliage plant, gets its name from the prompt irritation and swelling on the tongue and mouth that develops when a piece of leaf is chewed. *Monstera deliciosa,* with giant slotted leaves, is grown as a popular foliage plant. The ripened fruits are delicious when chilled and served as a dessert. Many species of *Philodendron* are grown as houseplants.

Many cultivars of *Caladium,* often called fancy-leaved caladiums, are grown as greenhouse and bedding plants. The white spathe of *Caladium* is hidden in the foliage and usually overlooked because of the attractive, brightly colored leaves. *Anthurium* cultivars have large, often bright red, spathes with a slender spadix. The calla lily of florists is *Zantedeschia aethiopica.*

The aroid family includes the free-floating aquatic water lettuce (*Pistia stratiotes*). It is sometimes used in aquaria, has escaped cultivation, and may be a weed in the warmer parts of the United States.

Economic Importance   The aroid family is of considerable importance as a source of ornamentals and a starchy food (taro).

SUBCLASS II, ARECIDAE; ORDER 4, ARALES
Lemnaceae: Duckweed Family

Field Recognition   Small or minute (larger plants only a few mm in diameter), floating or submerged aquatics; flowering rare; reproducing vegetatively; ($CA^0 CO^0 A^1 G^0$) ($CA^0 CO^0 A^0 \underline{G}^1$).

Description   *Habit*   Small to minute, free-floating or submerged freshwater aquatics; roots simple and threadlike or lacking; plant body leafless, consisting of an undifferentiated thallus body or frond (thalluses) of different shapes; vegetative reproduction by buds is common.

Inflorescences   Consists of 1 female and 2 male flowers, naked or surrounded by a spathe.

Lemnaceae

FIGURE 14-100
Spirodela polyrrhiza (Lemnaceae). Thalli with long adventitious roots.

Flowers   Unisexual. Androecium of male flowers with 1 stamen. Gynoecium of female flowers of 1 carpel, 1 locular, with 1–4 ovules, ovary superior, style short. See Figure 14-100.

Fruit   Utricle, 1–4 seeded.

Seeds   Smooth or ribbed; embryo straight, endosperm fleshy or lacking.

Size, Description, and General Information   A family of 6 genera and about 29 species; cosmopolitan in distribution, in freshwater habitats. Some of the genera include *Lemna* (9) (duckweed); *Spirodela* (4); *Wolffiella* (5) (bog mat); and *Wolffia* (7) (water meal). Many of the species are tiny. *Wolffia arrhiza* is the smallest known flowering plant; individuals are barely visible to the naked eye and masses of the plants are often mistaken for green algae on the surface of the water.

Economic Importance   Said to be a source of food for water fowl and fish. Sometimes cultivated as aquarium plants.

SUBCLASS III, COMMELINIDAE; ORDER 1, COMMELINALES
Xyridaceae: Yellow-eyed-grass Family

Field Recognition   Herbaceous, tufted, wetland plants; leaves sheathing; flowers bisexual, slightly irregular, arranged in densely bracteate spikes or heads, each flower in axil of overlapping bract; calyx zygomorphic, sepals 3, the 2 lateral sepals small, the inner sepal enclosing the corolla; androecium of 3 epipetalous stamens; fruit a capsule with numerous seeds; $CAZ^3\ CO^3\ A^{3\ \text{staminodes}\ +3\ \text{or}\ 3}\ \underline{G}^\circledS$. See Figure 14-101.

Xyridaceae

FIGURE 14-101
Xyris (Xyridaceae). (a) Habit of plant and (b) vertical section of flower.

Size, Distribution, and General Information A small, economically unimportant family of 4 genera, *Xyris* with 200 species, and the smaller genera *Achlyphila, Abolboda* and *Orectanthe* with about 20 species altogether; tropical and subtropical in distribution.

SUBCLASS III, COMMELINIDAE; ORDER 1, COMMELINALES
Commelinaceae: Spiderwort Family

Field Recognition Herbs with succulent stems; leaves with a closed basal sheath; sepals 3, green; petals 3, often blue; filaments usually hairy; ovary superior, style simple: $CA^3 \ CO^3 \ A^6 \ \underline{G}^③$.

Description *Habit* Herbaceous annuals or perennials; stems jointed.
Leaves Sheathing at the base, alternate, parallel-veined, entire.
Inflorescences Axillary clusters or terminal cymes or panicles.
Flowers Bisexual, usually actinomorphic (zygomorphic in *Commelina*). Calyx of 3 sepals, green, free. Corolla of 3 petals, equal or unequal, usually ephemeral, rarely

(b)

(a)

Commelinaceae

FIGURE 14-102
Tradescantia (Commelinaceae). (a) Flowering shoot and (b) flower.

united. Androecium of 6 stamens, sometimes 3 plus 3 staminodes or reduced to 1 or 2 fertile stamens, filaments often hairy. Gynoecium a compound pistil of 3 united carpels, with 3 locules, ovules few to solitary, placentation axile, ovary superior, style terminal and simple. See Figure 14-102.

Fruit   A capsule.
Seed   With endosperm.

Size, Distribution, and General Information   A family of about 50 genera and 700 species of mostly tropical and subtropical distribution, but also in warm temperate regions.

Some of the chief genera are *Commelina* (150–200) (dayflower); *Aneilema* (100); *Tradescantia* (60) (spiderwort); *Rhoeo* (1) (Moses-in-the-bulrushes); and *Zebrina* (4 to 5) (wandering Jew).

Tradescantia is sometimes called *spiderwort* because of the soft, stringy mucilaginous material can be pulled from the broken ends of the stem. The material will harden into a cobweb-like thread after exposure to the air. *Commelina* has two large petals and a third quite small petal. The flowers are in tight clusters; each day one flower opens then closes during the day. The next day, a new flower will open—hence the name day flower.

Zebrina pendula (wandering Jew) is a favorite, easily grown houseplant. *Rhoeo spathacea* produces clusters of flowers located between a pair of large bracts almost hidden in some rather stiff leaves. This suggests the common name Moses-in-the-bulrushes.

Economic Importance   The family is of little importance except for several ornamentals.

SUBCLASS III, COMMELINIDAE; ORDER 2, ERIOCAULALES
Eriocaulaceae: Pipe-wort Family

Field Recognition   Annual or perennial herbs of wetlands; leaves often grasslike in appearance; flowers unisexual, inconspicuous, arranged in involucrate heads similar to those in the Compositae, heads solitary (or in umbels); perianth not clearly differentiated; fruit a membranous capsule; CA^{2-3} CO^{0-3} A^{2-6} $\underline{G}^{(2-3)}$. See Figure 14-103.

FIGURE 14-103
Eriocaulon compressum (Eriocaulaceae). (a) Habit, (b) pistillate flower, and (c) staminate flower.

(b)

(c)

(a)

Eriocaulaceae

Size, Distribution, and General Information   A family of 13 genera and 1200 species; mainly tropical and subtropical, centered in the New World, extending northward into eastern North America.

The chief genera are *Eriocaulon* (400) (pipewort); *Syngonanthus* (200); *Paepalanthus* (500); and *Lachnocaulon* (10) (ladies-hat-pins).

Economic Importance   Of little importance other than that the scapes and heads are often used for dried floral arrangements.

SUBCLASS III, COMMELINIDAE; ORDER 4, JUNCALES
Juncaceae: Rush Family

Field Recognition   Tufted herbs; leaves sometimes reduced to a basal sheath; perianth in 2 series with 6 segments; stamens 6; fruit a capsule; $CA^3 \ CO^3 \ A^6 \ \underline{G}^③$.

Description   *Habit*   Perennial or annual tufted herbs, rarely shrublike, stems usually leafy only at the base.

Leaves   Basal, cylindrical to flat, linear or filiform, sheathing basally or reduced to only a sheath.

Inflorescences   Flowers in cymes grouped in a panicle, corymb, or head, or flowers solitary.

Flowers   Usually bisexual, actinomorphic, small. Perianth segments 6, in 2 series, scalelike, greenish or brownish. Androecium of (3)6 stamens, opposite the perianth segments. Gynoecium a compound pistil of 3 united carpels, 1-locular or with 3 locules, ovules 3 to numerous, placentation parietal, ovary superior, styles 3. See Figure 14-104.

Fruit   A capsule.

Seed   With endosperm and a straight embryo.

FIGURE 14-104
Juncus (Juncaceae). Vertical section of flower.

Juncaceae

Size, Distribution, and General Information   A family of about 8 genera and 300 species of temperate, arctic, or tropical mountain distribution, in moist, cool places.

The chief genera are *Juncus* (300) (rush); and *Luzula* (80) (wood rush).

The tussocks of rushes often provide stepping-stones for crossing a wet meadow, as well as hiding places for many kinds of birds and mammals. In some countries, rushes are woven into mats, baskets, or chair seats. The pith has been used for candlewicks.

Economic Importance   The Juncaceae are of little importance.

SUBCLASS III, COMMELINIDAE; ORDER 5, CYPERALES
Cyperaceae: Sedge Family

Field Recognition   Herbs, stems often triangular, solid; leaves 3-ranked, sheaths closed; ligule absent; flowers subtended by a single bract, lodicule absent; perianth represented by bristles, scales or absent; $CA^0 \, CO^0 \, A^{1-3} \, \underline{G} \, \textcircled{2 \text{ or } 3}$ or $CA^0 \, CO^0 \, A^{1-3} G^0$ and $CA^0 \, CO^0 \, A^0 \, \underline{G} \, \textcircled{2 \text{ or } 3}$. (The Cyperaceae are easily confused with the Gramineae, but are readily distinguished by the combination of characters listed above.)

Description   *Habit*   Perennial or annual herbs, often of damp or marshy habitats, with solid, usually triangular stems.

Leaves   Three-ranked, with a closed sheath, the ligule absent, often in a basal tuft of crowded on the lower part of stem, blades narrow and grass-like.

Inflorescences   Spicate, racemose, paniculate, or umbellate; a spikelet is often the basic unit (spikelet unlike that of family Gramineae); spikelets usually solitary within a bract; bracts distichously or spirally arranged; plants monoecious or dioecious; inflorescence often subtended by one or more bracts.

Flowers   Bisexual or unisexual, inconspicuous. Perianth represented by bristles or scales, often absent. Androecium of 1 to 3(6) stamens. Gynoecium a compound pistil of 2 or 3 united carpels, with 1 locule, ovule solitary, ovary superior, (in *Carex*, enclosed in a unique saclike structure, the *perigynium*) with 2 or 3 style branches. See Figures 14-105 and 14-106.

Fruit   A triangular or lens-shaped achene or nutlet.

Systematics   Tribes of Cyperaceae and representative genera: Rhynchosporeae (*Rhynchospora*); Scirpeae (*Scirpus*); Cypereae (*Cyperus*); Hypolytreae (*Hypolytrum*); Sclerieae (*Scleria*); Cryptangieae (*Cryptangium*); and Cariceae (*Carex*).

Size, Distribution, and General Information   A family of about 70 genera and 4000 species of worldwide distribution, especially in temperate and cold regions.

Some of the chief genera are *Cyperus* (600) (sedge); *Eriophorum* (20) (cotton grass); *Scirpus* (250) (bulrush, tule); *Eleocharis* (200) (spike rush); *Fimbristylis* (200); *Rhynchospora* (250) (beak rush); *Scleria* (200) (nut rush); *Carex* (1100) (carex, sedge); and *Dichromena* (60) (whitetop sedge).

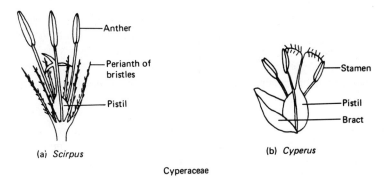

FIGURE 14-105
Vertical views of flowers of (a) *Scirpus* and (b) *Cyperus* (Cyperaceae). The
perianth is replaced by bristles or is absent in *Cyperus.*

Perhaps as early as 2400 B.C., Egyptians made a paper (papyrus) from *Cyperus papyrus,* a plant of marshy or riverside habitats. The stems were split into thin strips which were pressed together while still wet. *Cyperus papyrus* is often grown as an ornamental.

Nut grass (*Cyperus rotundus*) is a serious weed that is extremely difficult to control in lawns and cultivated fields. The closely related *C. esculentus* (chufa or Zulu nuts) produces an edible tuber. Chufas are sometimes planted as a wildlife food plant. *Cyperus alternifolius* (umbrella plant) is often grown as an ornamental. *Eleocharis dulcis* is Chinese water chestnut.

FIGURE 14-106
Vertical views of pistillate floral structures of *Carex* (Cyperaceae). The
drawing to the right has the perigynium partially removed.

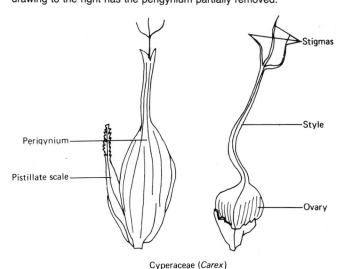

Cyperaceae (*Carex*)

The name *bulrush* is applied to the plants of the genus *Scirpus* which are found in wetlands or aquatic habitats. The fruits and rhizomes are eaten by waterfowl and muskrats. At Lake Titicaca in the high Andes, Indians build fishing canoes from *S. totora*. Cotton grass (*Eriophorum*) inhabits poorly drained areas in cold zones of both the Northern and Southern Hemispheres. *Carex* is a large genus of much taxonomic complexity.

Economic Importance   The Cyperaceae are of no significant importance. A few are grown as ornamentals and some are noxious weeds. Some sedge hay is produced for fodder in cold, wet regions, but it is inferior to grass hay.

SUBCLASS III, COMMELINIDAE; ORDER 5, CYPERALES
Gramineae or Poaceae: Grass Family

Field Recognition   Stems round, internodes usually hollow; leaves 2-ranked, sheaths open or sometimes closed, ligule usually present; bracts of glumes, lemma and palea; perianth of 0–3 lodicules; stamens usually 3; fruit a grain or caryopsis; $CA^0 CO^0 A^3$ $\underline{G^{(2 \text{ or } 3)}}$. (The Gramineae may be confused with the Cyperaceae and Juncaceae. The grasses have round stems, the sedges have triangular stems, and the rushes have many-seeded capsules and round stems.)

Description   *Habit*   Annual or perennial herbs, rarely shrubs or trees; stems (culms) erect, ascending, prostrate, or creeping; culms round, usually hollow at the internodes, solid at nodes, a few are solid throughout.

Leaves   Two-ranked, alternate, parallel-veined, consisting of sheath, ligule, and blade; sheath encircling the culm.

Inflorescences   Composed of units called *spikelets,* variously arranged in spikes, racemes, or panicles; each spikelet has one or more florets, florets arranged on an axis (rachilla), 2 glumes subtend each spikelet.

Flowers   Bisexual or sometimes unisexual. Each floret has 2 bracts; the outer (lemma) and the inner (palea). Perianth reduced to 2 or 3 lodicules located just above the palea, or sometimes absent. Androecium of (1)3(6) stamens. Gynoecium a compound pistil of 2 or 3 united carpels, with 1 locule, ovary superior, (1)2(3) styles, stigmas usually featherlike. See Figure 14-107 and 14-108.

Fruit   A caryopsis (grain), rarely a nut, berry, or a utricle.

Seed   With starchy endosperm.

Systematics   The classification of the family Gramineae has been intensively studied in recent years. The treatment presented here (Gould and Shaw, 1983) differs substantially from that of Hitchcock (1950). The changes largely reflect new information from cytogenetics and comparative plant anatomy.

Size, Distribution, and General Information   A family of about 500 genera and 8,000 species forming one of the larger families of flowering plants; widely dispersed

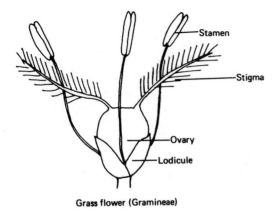

Grass flower (Gramineae)

FIGURE 14-107
Vertical view of a grass flower (family
Gramineae). The lodicules are
homologous with the perianth.

FIGURE 14-108
Grass spikelet (family Gramineae). A typical grass spikelet is subtended by the first and second
glumes (bracts) and contains one or more florets, each subtended by an outer lemma (bract)
and an inner palea (bract).

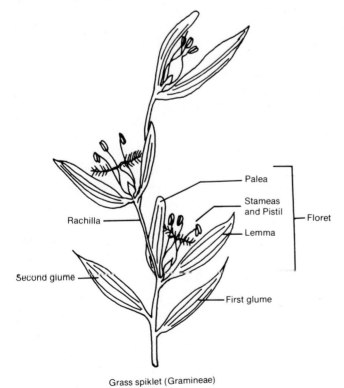

Grass spiklet (Gramineae)

in all regions of the world wherever vascular plants can survive, often dominating the aspect of the vegetation.

Some of the genera are:

Subfamily Festucoideae: Tribe 1. Festuceae: *Bromus* (50) (bromegrass); *Festuca* (80) (fescue); *Lolium* (12) (ryegrass); *Poa* (300) (bluegrass); and *Dactylis* (5) (orchard grass). Tribe 2. Aveneae: *Avena* (70) (oats); *Phalaris* (20) (canary grass); *Ammophila* (2) (beach grass); *Agrostis* (150 to 200) (bent grass); and *Phleum* (15) (timothy). Tribe 3. Triticeae: *Triticum* (20) (wheat); *Agropyron* (100 to 150) (wheatgrass); *Secale* (5) (rye); *Elymus* (70) (wild rye); and *Hordeum* (20) (barley). Tribe 4. Meliceae: *Melica* (70) (melic grass); and *Glyceria* (40) (manna grass). Tribe 5. Stipeae: *Stipa* (250) (needlegrass); and *Oryzopsis* (50), (rice grass). Tribe 6. Brachyelytreae: *Brachyelytrum* (4). Tribe 7. Diarrheneae: *Diarrhena* (1). Tribe 8. Nardeae: *Nardus* (1). Tribe 9. Monermeae: *Monerma* (1).

Subfamily Panicoideae: Tribe 10. Paniceae: *Panicum* (400) (millet, panic grass); *Digitaria* (380) (crabgrass); *Paspalum* (200) (Dallas grass, Bahia grass); *Echinochloa* (30) (barnyard grass, jungle rice); and *Setaria* (140) (foxtail, Italian millet). Tribe 11. Andropogoneae: *Andropogon* (113) (bluestem, broom sedge); *Saccharum* (5) (sugarcane); *Schizachyrium* (50) (little bluestem); *Sorghum* (60) (milo, sorghum, Johnson grass, Sudan grass); and *Zea* (1) (corn, maize).

Subfamily Eragrostoideae: Tribe 12. Eragrosteae: *Eragrostis* (300) (love grass); *Muhlenbergia* (100) (muhly grass, bull grass); and *Sporobolus* (150) (dropseed, smut grass). Tribe 13. Chlorideae: *Eleusine* (9) (goose grass); *Cynodon* (10) (Bermuda grass); *Bouteloua* (40) (side oats grama, grama grass): *Buchlöe* (1) (buffalo grass); and *Spartina* (16) (cord grass). Tribe 14. Zoysieae: *Zoysia* (10). Tribe 15. Aeluropodeae: *Distichlis* (13) (salt grass). Tribe 16. Unioleae: *Uniola* (2) (sea oats). Tribe 17. Pappophoreae: *Pappophorum* (7) (pappus grass). Tribe 18. Orcuttieae: *Orcuttia* (4). Tribe 19. Aristideae: *Aristida* (330) (wire grass, three-awn grass).

Subfamily Bambusoideae: Tribe 20. Bambuseae: *Arundinaria* (150) (giant cane, switch cane). Tribe 21. Phareae: *Pharus* (7 to 8).

Subfamily Oryzoideae: Tribe 22. Oryzeae: *Oryza* (25) (rice); *Zizania* (3) (wild rice).

Subfamily Arundinoideae: Tribe 23. Arundineae: *Phragmites* (3) (common reed). Tribe 24. Danthonieae: *Danthonia* (10) (poverty oat grass). Tribe 25. Centotheceae: *Chasmanthium* (5).

Economic Importance   The grass family is of greater importance than any other family of flowering plants, as indicated by the following: (1) food crops for human consumption—rice, wheat, corn, barley, millet, rye, oats, milo, and cane sugar; (2) forage and grain for domesticated animals; (3) range forage (in North America—big bluestem, little bluestem, Indian grass, switch grass, side oats grama, blue grama, and buffalo grass); (4) industrial uses—ethyl alcohol, starch, and so on; (5) shelter—bamboo, thatch; (6) soil conservation; (7) turf—Bermuda grass, St. Augustine grass, centipede grass, bluegrasses, bent grasses, fescues, ryegrass; (8) ornamentals; and (9) wildlife food.

SUBCLASS III, COMMELINIDAE; ORDER 7, TYPHALES
Typhaceae: Cattail Family

Field Recognition   Large perennial herbs, of fresh to slightly brackish marshes and shores; leaves 2-ranked, blades linear, thick and spongy; inflorescence a dense cylindrical spike divided into a staminate and a pistillate part; (perianth$^\infty$ A$^{2-5\ \text{or}\ 2-5}$ G^0) (perianth$^\infty$ A^0 $\underline{G}^1$).

Description   *Habit*   Rhizomatous, erect perennials.

Leaves   Linear, erect, blades thick and spongy, sheathing.

Inflorescences   Dense cylindrical spikes, often divided into two parts, the upper male part usually yellowish, the lower female part brownish.

Flowers   Unisexual. Perianth segments of numerous slender threads or elongated spoonlike scales. Androecium of 2–5 stamens, free or with fused filaments. Gynoecium a single carpel, 1-locular, 1 seeded, ovary superior, style long. See Figure 14-109.

FIGURE 14-109
Typha latifolia (Typhaceae). (a) Inflorescence with staminate flowers above, pistillate flowers below. (b) Pistillate flower and (c) staminate flower.

(a)

(b)

(c)

Typhaceae

Fruit   Achene on stipe with long hairs.
Seed   Embryo long and narrow; endosperm mealy.

Size, Distribution, and General Information   A small family of 1 genus, *Typha*, with 10 or more species; cosmopolitan in distribution.

Economic Importance   The inflorescences are used in dried floral arrangements and the leaves are used as weaving material. Cattails are occasionally grown as ornamentals. Rhizomes and leaf bases are eaten by humans and other mammals.

SUBCLASS IV, ZINGIBERIDAE; ORDER 1, BROMELIALES
Bromeliaceae: Pineapple Family

Field Recognition   Usually epiphytic with stiff leaves that are often brightly colored toward the base; highly colored 3-merous flowers subtended by brightly colored bracts; $CA^3 \ CO^3 \ A^6 \ \overline{G}^{③}$ or $\underline{G}^{③}$.

Description   *Habit*   Mostly short-stemmed epiphytes.
Leaves   Mostly basal and rosette forming, usually stiff and often spiny, often brightly colored toward the base.
Inflorescences   Flowers in a terminal head, spike, or panicle, often with highly colored bracts.
Flowers   Bisexual or rarely unisexual, actinomorphic, hypogynous to epigynous. Perianth in 2 series, outer whorl of 3 calyxlike parts and inner of 3 corollalike segments. Androecium of 6 stamens, mostly inserted at the base of the perianth, free or partially fused to them. Gynoecium a compound pistil of 3 united carpels, 3-locular, placentation axile, ovary superior or inferior. See Figure 14-110.
Fruit   A berry, capsule, or multiple.
Seed   With a small embryo in mealy endosperm.

Size, Distribution, and General Information   A family of about 45 genera and 2000 species mostly of tropical America and the West Indies. One species occurs in west tropical Africa.

The chief genera are *Navia* (60); *Pitcairnia* (250); *Puya* (140); *Tillandsia* (400); *Bromelia* (40); and *Ananas* (5).

The pineapple (*Ananas comosus*) was long cultivated by American Indians. It was introduced to the Old World by Spanish and Portuguese travelers. Seedless cultivars were developed by the Europeans and reintroduced into tropical America. The bracts, ovaries, pedicels, and stalk develop and fuse into one sweet, juicy mass.

Most members of the family grow as epiphytes on trees in the tropical forests in the New World. A few occur in dry areas and some terrestrial species in the Andes have flower stalks 10 to 12 feet tall. *Tillandsia usneoides* (Spanish moss) is a familiar epiphyte hanging in gray masses from trees and telephone wires in the warmer parts of the southeastern states.

Bromeliaceae

FIGURE 14-110
Billbergia (Bromeliaceae). (a) Habit of plant in flower and (b) vertical section of flower.

Economic Importance   The family is of importance for the pineapple. Several species are sources of cordage and fiber for fabrics. Many are grown in greenhouses or out-of-doors in tropical areas as ornamentals.

SUBCLASS V, LILIIDAE; ORDER 1, LILIALES
Pontederiaceae: Pickerel-weed Family

Field Recognition   Annuals or perennials; submerged, free-floating or rooted emergent aquatics; stems of rhizomes or stolons, or erect and unbranched; leaves opposite or whorled, bases sheathing; inflorescences racemose or paniculate, subtended by a spathe-like sheath; flowers bisexual; fruit a capsule or nutlet; seed with straight embryo and copious endosperm; CA^3 CO^3 A^6 $\underline{G}^{③}$. See Figure 14–111.

Size, Discription, and General Information   A small family of water plants with about 9 genera and 30 species; distribution is pantropical extending into the temperate zone.

(a)

(b)

Pontederiaceae

FIGURE 14-111
Pontederiaceae. (a) *Eichhornia crassipes,* habit of plant in flower, note the inflated petioles which provide buoyancy to this free-floating species, and (b) *Pontederia cordata* flower.

Economic Importance   *Eichhornia crassipes* (the water hyacinth) and *Pontederia cordata* (pickerel weed) are sometimes utilized as ornamentals in aquatic situations. The free floating *Eichhornia crassipes* cloggs waterways, covers lakes, ponds and marshes, and is a serious aquatic weed in some parts of the world.

SUBCLASS V, LILIIDAE; ORDER 1, LILIALES
Liliaceae (including Amaryllidaceae): Lily Family

Field Recognition   Herbaceous perennials; flowers often showy, actinomorphic; sepals 3, petaloid; petals 3; stamens 6, anthers opening by lengthwise slits; ovary superior or inferior; fruit a capsule or berry; CA^3 CO^3 A^6 $\underline{G}^③$ or $\overline{G}^③$.

Description *Habit* Mostly perennial herbs, from rhizomes, corms, or bulbs; stems erect or climbing, leafy or scapose.

Leaves   Alternate, simple, linear, with parallel venation, leaves sometimes few and basal, appearing before or after the flowers.

Inflorescences   Racemose, axillary, umbellate, or solitary.

Flowers   Bisexual, usually actinomorphic. Calyx of 3 sepals, nearly always petaloid. Corolla of 3 petals. Androecium of (3)6(12) stamens, filaments free or variously united, anthers opening by a slit lengthwise. Gynoecium a compound pistil of 3 united carpels, with 3 locules, ovules numerous, placentation axile or rarely 1-locular with parietal placenta, ovary superior or inferior. See Figure 14-112.

Fruit   A capsule or a fleshy berry.

Seed   With endosperm, embryo straight or curved.

Systematics   Cronquist (1981) considers separation of the Amaryllidaceae and Liliaceae on the basis of ovary position to be unreasonable. Hutchinson (1973) admits that the character of superior versus inferior ovary has been overemphasized in the monocotyledons, although he treats the families separately. The treatment here follows that of Cronquist with the two families combined. Some genera traditionally included in the Liliaceae are removed to other families: e.g. *Smilax* (Smilacaceae), *Aloe* (Aloeaceae), and so on.

Size, Distribution, and General Information   A family of about 280 genera and 4000 species of worldwide distribution.

Some of the genera are: *Lilium* (80) (lily); *Uvularia* (4) (bellwort); *Hemerocallis* (20) (day lily); *Colchicum* (65) (autumn crocus); *Gloriosa* (5) (gloriosa lily); *Tulipa*

FIGURE 14-112
Vertical sections of diagrammatic Liliaceae flowers. (a) *Lilium* with a superior ovary. (b) *Narcissus* with an inferior ovary and a corona. *Narcissus* is placed in Amaryllidaceae by some authors.

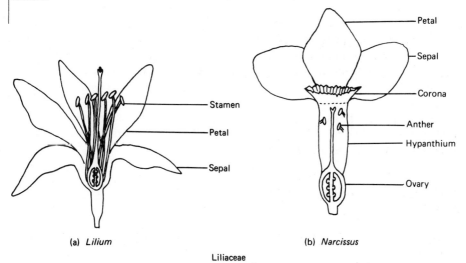

(a) *Lilium*   (b) *Narcissus*

Liliaceae

(100) (tulip); *Hyacinthus* (30) (hyacinth); *Convallaria* (1) (lily of the valley); *Smilacina* (25) (false Solomon's-seal); *Asparagus* (300); *Amaryllis* (1); *Hippeastrum* (75) (amaryllis); *Crinum* (100 to 110) (swamp lily); *Hymenocallis* (50) (spider lily); *Allium* (450) (onion, chive, garlic, leek, shallot); *Narcissus* (60) (jonquil, daffodil); *Zephyranthes* (35 to 40) (rain lilies); *Lycoris* (10) (surprise lily); *Hypoxis* (100) (yellow star grass); *Erythronium* (25) (fawn lily); *Ornithogalum* (150) (star-of-Bethlehem); *Scilla* (80) (squill); *Trillium* (30) (wake-robin); and *Polygonatum* (50) (Solomon's-seal).

Many species and cultivars of *Lilium* are cultivated: *L. candidum* (Madonna lily); *L. longiflorum* (Easter or white trumpet lily); *L. tigrinum* (tiger lily); *L. auratum* (golden-banded lily); and *L. superbum* (Turk's-cap lily), and so on.

The autumn crocus (*Colchicum autumnale*) produces a poisonous alkaloid, colchicine, which is used in plant breeding to produce polyploids. Colchicine interferes with cell division, resulting in cells with an abnormal double number of chromosomes.

In the large genus *Asparagus*, the leaves are reduced to scales. The young stems of *A. officinalis* provide a delicious vegetable. The asparagus fern (*A. setaceus*) is used in the florist's trade. Sprengeri (*A. densiflorus*) is an ideal plant for pots or hanging baskets.

There are some 450 species of *Allium*, many of which are used either as ornamentals or in cooking. They are famous for their characteristically pungent odor. Best known are *A. cepa* (onion); *A. sativum* (garlic); *A. ascalonicum* (shallot); *A. porrum* (leek); *A. schoenoprasum* (chive); and *A. vineale* (wild onion), which is sometimes a problem to the dairy industry, because cows grazing on *A. vineale* produce garlic-flavored milk. In many species, some or all of the flowers are replaced by bulbils.

Holland is known for its cultivated hyacinths (*Hyacinthus orientalis*), originally from Greece and Asia Minor, and tulips (*Tulipa gesneriana*), introduced from Turkey. *Narcissus* (daffodil, jonquil) are universal spring favorites. Most of the species were natives to southern Europe. Narcissus was a youth in Greek mythology who is said to have changed into a flower by sitting motionless (the root of the word is related to *narcotic*) while pining away for love of his own reflection in a pond.

A number of Liliaceae produce poisonous bulbs: star-of-Bethlehem (*Ornithogalum umbellatum*); lily of the valley (*Convallaria majalis*); squill (*Scilla*); and red squill (*Urginea scilla*). Red squill was once used as an effective rat poison. *Zigadenus*, death camas, is very well known to sheep raisers throughout the West since it is especially poisonous to sheep.

Economic Importance The Liliaceae are important for the large number of genera used in ornamental horticulture. *Asparagus* and *Allium* are important vegetable crops. Several drugs or poisons are obtained from the family.

SUBCLASS V, LILIIDAE; ORDER 1, LILIALES
Iridaceae: Iris Family

Field Recognition Herbs with equitant leaves; sepals 3, petaloid; petals 3; stamens 3; ovary inferior; CA^3 CO^3 A^3 $\overline{G}^{\circledcirc}$.

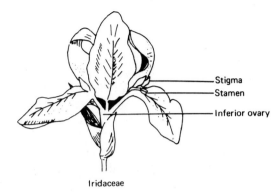

Stigma
Stamen
Inferior ovary

Iridaceae

FIGURE 14-113
Iris (Iridaceae) flower; note the
three-petaloid style branches with
the stigma located beneath (the
labeled style branch is raised). In
turn, the stamens are beneath the
style branches.

Description   *Habit*   Herbaceous, from rhizomes, bulbs, or corms; stems solitary or several, or plants scapose.

Leaves   Mostly basal, often crowded at the base of the stem, mostly linear or broadly linear, flattened at the sides, sheathing at the base, and equitant (folded and overlapping).

Inflorescences   Racemose or paniculate, or solitary.

Flowers   Bisexual, actinomorphic or zygomorphic, showy. Calyx of 3 sepals, petaloid. Corolla of 3 petals often similar to the sepals. Perianth united below into a tube. Androecium of 3 stamens, opposite the sepals. Gynoecium a compound pistil of 3 united carpels, with 3 locules, ovules usually numerous, placentation axile of 1-locular with 3 parietal placentas, ovary inferior, rarely superior, style 3-lobed, sometimes petaloid. See Figure 14-113.

Fruit   A capsule dehiscent by valves.

Seed   With a small embryo in hard endosperm.

Size, Distribution, and General Information   A family of about 80 genera and 1500 species of tropical and temperate distribution with the chief centers of distribution in South Africa and tropical America.

Some of the genera are *Iris* (200) (flag, fleur-de-lis); *Crocus* (75); *Sisyrinchium* (60) (blue-eyed grass); *Tritonia* (55) (montbretia); *Gladiolus* (150); *Freesia* (20); *Belamcanda* (2) (blackberry lily); *Ixia* (45); and *Tigridia* (12) (tiger flower).

The dried styles of *Crocus sativus* are used to make saffron, which was once used as a dye but is now used chiefly in Spanish and Iranian cooking to give color to cooked rice. Around 100,000 styles are required to produce 1 kilogram of saffron. Spring-flowering crocuses (*C. vernus*) herald the arrival of spring with their clumps of brightly colored flowers.

There are countless cultivars of *Iris* and *Gladiolus* available in the horticultural trade. *Iris germanica* yields orrisroot, which is used in perfume and in dentifrices.

Economic Importance   Most of the genera in the Iridaceae contain species that are used or could be used as ornamentals.

SUBCLASS V, LILIIDAE; ORDER 1, LILIALES

Agavaceae: Agave Family

Field Recognition Robust, often woody, sometimes treelike shrubs or trees, occasionally climbing, sometimes succulent, rhizomatous; leaves basal or crowded at base of stem, stiff, often fleshy and sharp pointed; inflorescences racemose or paniculate; flowers actinomorphic (or slightly zygomorphic); fruit usually a capsule; seed with straight embryo and hard endosperm; $CA^3 \ CO^3 \ \overline{A}^{3+3} \ \underline{\overline{G}}^{\circledR}$. See Figure 14-114.

Size, Distribution, General Information A family of about 18 genera and 600 species; mainly of arid tropical and subtropical regions. The largest genera are *Agave* (300); *Dracaena* (80); *Sansevieria* (50); *Yucca* (35) and *Cordyline* (15).

Economic Importance Several species of *Yucca* make splendid ornamentals. Often cultivated as tropical foliage plants, species of *Cordyline* are in great demand

FIGURE 14-114
Agave (Agavaceae). (a) Habit of plant in flower and (b) flower.

(b)

(a)

Agavaceae

as indoor plants. Many of the 80 species of *Dracaena* from the Old World tropics are used as beautiful foliage plants. Species of *Sansevieria* (Mother-in-law tongues) are sturdy house plants. A fiber, called bowstring hemp, is obtained from *Sansevieria*. A better known fibre is sisal hemp, obtained from the leaves of *Agave sisalana,* and used in making bailing twine and cordage. Many Agaves are cultivated as ornamentals. Several species yield the drink pulque, which when distilled is called mezcal (mescal), and the well-known tequila from *A. tequilana*.

SUBCLASS V, LILIIDAE; ORDER 1, LILIALES
Smilacaceae: Smilax or Sarsaparilla Family

Field Recognition   Mostly woody (or herbaceous) vines climbing by stipular tendrils or erect herbs, stems sometimes prickly; leaves alternate, reticulately veined; inflorescences axillary racemes, spikes or umbels; flowers unisexual, (in *Smilax* borne on separate plants), actinomorphic; fruit a berry containing 1–3 seeds; seeds with a small embryo and hard endosperm; $(CA^3 \ CO^3 \ A^{3+3} \ G^0) \ (CA^3 \ CO^3 \ A^0 \ G^{®})$. See Figure 14-115.

Size, Distribution, and General Information   A mainly tropical or subtropical family of 12 genera and around 350 species; the largest genus, *Smilax,* with about 300 species.

Economic Importance   The drug sarsaparilla, used for treating rheumatism, is obtained from *Smilax*. In the southeastern United States, some evergreen species of *Smilax* are cut for decorative greenery.

FIGURE 14-115
Smilax bona-nox (Smilacaceae) in fruit.

Smilacaceae

SUBCLASS V, LILIIDAE; ORDER 2, ORCHIDALES
Orchidaceae: Orchid Family

Field Recognition   Herbaceous perennials; leaves 2-ranked; flowers 3-merous, zygomorphic; petals 2-lateral and one a labellum or lip; pollinia often produced; ovary inferior: $CA^3 \; COZ^{2 \; +1} \; A^{1-2} \; \overline{G}^{\circledcirc}$.

Description   *Habit*   Perennial herbs, terrestrial, epiphytic or saprophytic, with rhizomes, tuberous roots, or rootstock; stem leafy or scapose, often with pseudobulbs and aerial roots.

Leaves   Usually opposite, simple, sometimes reduced to scales, often fleshy, sheathing basally.

Inflorescences   Spicate, racemose, paniculate, or solitary.

Flowers   Usually bisexual, zygomorphic, showy and colorful or small and inconspicuous. Calyx of 3 sepals, green or colored. Corolla of 2 lateral petals and a middle petal called the labellum that is often larger and different in shape from the lateral petals. Androecium of 1 or 2 stamens, joined to the style in a unique structure, the column, anther 1, pollen often in waxy pollinia. Gynoecium a compound pistil of 3 carpels, with 1 locule and placentation parietal, or rarely 3-locular, placentation axile, ovary inferior, stigmas 3, the lateral 2 often fertile and the other sterile forming a beak or rostellum. See Figures 14-116 and 14-117.

Fruit   A capsule.

Seed   Small, numerous, without endosperm.

Embryo   Not differentiated.

Size, Distribution, and General Information   A family of about 1000 genera and 15–20,000 species; one of the largest families of flowering plants, of worldwide distribution but most abundant in tropical areas and rare in arctic regions.

Some of the genera are *Orchis* (35) (showy orchid); *Cypripedium* (50) (lady's slipper, moccasin flower); *Goodyera* (40) (rattlesnake plantain); *Spiranthes* (25) (ladies' tresses); *Ophrys* (30) (bee orchid); *Habenaria* (600) (fringe orchid); *Vanilla* (90); *Epidendrum* (400) (greenfly orchid); *Cattleya* (60) (florist's orchid); *Cymbidium* (40); *Odontoglossum* (200); *Liparis* (250) (twayblades); *Corallorhiza* (15) (coralroot); *Vanda* (60); *Calopogon* (4) (grass pink); *Phalaenopsis* (35); *Dendrobium* (1500); *Malaxis* (300) (adder's mouth); *Tipularia* (4) (cranefly orchid).

Probably no other family contains so great a variety of flowers. The beauty, the strange shapes, and the longevity of many orchid flowers, together with the comparative ease with which they can be cultivated, have made them favorites of horticulturists. Hybrids of *Cypripedium, Cymbidium, Cattleya,* and *Odontoglossum* are generally used, but among the most popular for corsages are cultivars of *Cattleya.*

Many orchids show great specialization in pollination relationships with insects and often depend solely on particular insects for pollination. Among the most bizarre is the bee orchid (*Ophrys insectifera*) of southern Europe, the flower of which provides a combination of appearance and odor that attracts male wasps. The male wasps attempt to copulate with the orchid flower, and in doing so, effect pollination.

Median sepal

Petal
Fertile anther
Staminode
Lip cavity

Lip or labellum

Lateral sepal points

Staminode
Stigma
Anther
Column

Ovary

(a)

(b)

Cypripedium (Orchidaceae)

FIGURE 14-116
Cypripedium (Orchidaceae). (a) Flower and (b) vertical view of reproductive features.

Some orchids, such as coralroot (*Corallorhiza*), are saprophytic and obtain food from decaying organic matter. Many species of orchids are epiphytic. Lady's slipper (*Cypripedium*) is among the loveliest of all our wild flowers.

The flavoring vanilla is obtained from the pods of certain species in the genus *Vanilla*. Europeans learned of vanilla from the Aztecs of Mexico. The vanilla fruits, known as beans, are fermented and cured in order to produce the familiar flavoring.

FIGURE 14-117
Cattleya (Orchidaceae) flower.

Petal

Sepal

Lip

Cattleya (Orchidaceae)

Economic Importance   The orchid family is of importance primarily for the ornamentals used in the florist trade.

SELECTED REFERENCES

Bailey, L. H. (compiler): *Hortus Third,* revised by the staff of Liberty Hyde Bailey Hortorium, Macmillan, Riverside, N.J., 1976.

Baillon, H.: *Histoire des plantes,* 13 vols. Hachette, Paris, 1867–1895.

Baumgardt, J. P.: *How to Identify Flowering Plant Families,* Timber Press, Portland, OR, 1982. [Highly opinionated, but nevertheless useful.]

Cronquist, A.: *An Integrated System of Classification of Flowering Plants,* Columbia, New York, 1981.

Gould, F. W. and R. B. Shaw: *Grass Systematics* 2nd ed., Texas A & M University Press, College Station, 1983.

Graf, A. B.: *Exotica, 3,* Roehrs Co., East Rutherford, N.J., 1963.

Graf, A. B.: *Exotica,* series 4 international, 2 vols., 11th ed., Roehrs Co., East Rutherford, N.J. 1982.

Heywood, V. H. (ed.): *Flowering Plants of the World,* Mayflower Books, New York, 1978.

Hickey, M. and C. King: *100 Families of Flowering Plants,* Cambridge University Press, Cambridge, 1981.

Hitchcock, A. S.: *Manual of Grasses of the United States,* 2d ed., revised by A. Chase, U.S. Department of Agriculture Miscellaneous Publication, no. 200, 1950.

Holmes, S.: *Outline of Plant Classification,* Longman, London, 1983.

Howes, F. N.: *A Dictionary of Useful and Everyday Plants and Their Common Names,* Cambridge University Press, Cambridge, 1975.

Hutchinson, J.: *Evolution and Phylogeny of Flowering Plants,* Academic, New York, 1969.

Hutchinson, J.: *The Familes of Flowering Plants,* 3rd. ed., Clarendon Press, Oxford, 1973.

Langer, R. H. M. and G. D. Hill: *Agricultural Plants,* Cambridge University Press, Cambridge, 1982.

Lawrence, G. H. M.: *Taxonomy of Vascular Plants,* Macmillan, New York, 1951.

Smith, J. P.: *Vascular Plant Families,* Mad River Press, Humboldt, CA, 1977.

Taylor, N. (ed.): *Taylor's Encyclopedia of Gardening,* 4th ed., Houghton Mifflin Company, Boston, 1976.

Thonner, F.: *Thonner's Analytical Key to the Families of Flowering Plants.* Leiden University Press, The Hague, 1981. [Translated and revised by R. Geesink, et al.]

Uphof, J. C. Th.: *Dictionary of Economic Plants,* 2nd ed., J. Cramer, Lehre, 1968.

Von Reis, S.: *Drugs and Foods from Little-Known Plants,* Harvard University Press, Cambridge, 1973.

Willis, J. C.: *A Dictionary of the Flowering Plants and Ferns,* 8th ed., revised by H. K. A. Shaw, University Press, Cambridge, England, 1973.

Wit, H. C. D. de: *Plants of the World,* 3 vol., E. P. Dutton, New York, 1966.

APPENDIX ONE

GLOSSARY OF GREEK AND LATIN WORDS

SOME COMMON SPECIFIC EPITHETS AND THEIR MEANINGS

Specific epithets may be formed from nouns, adjectives, present participles, etc., and are often combined with prefixes and suffixes. When an adjective is used as the specific epithet, it must agree with the generic name in gender. For more complete listings and for feminine and neuter endings, either Featherly (1954) or Stearn (1973) should be consulted.

acanthus   thorn (Gk)*
acaulis   stemless (L)*
acerifolius   maple-leaved (L/L)*
acicularis   needlelike (L)
aestivalis   summer (L)
affinis   related (L)
agrestis   related to fields, in the country (L)
alatus   winged (L)
albiflorus   white-flowered (L/L)
albus   white (L)
alleghениensis   of the Alleghenies
alpinus   alpine (L)
alternifolius   alternate-leaved (L)
altus   tall (L)
americanus   of America
amoenus   charming, pleasant (L)
amphibius   amphibious (Gk)

amplexicaulis   clasping the stem, embracing the stem (L/L)
angularis   angular (L)
angustifolius   narrow-leaved (L/L)
annuus   annual (L)
apetalus   without petals (Gk)
apiculatus   pointed at the tip (L)
aquaticus   aquatic (L)
aquifolius   with pointed leaves (L/L)
arborescens   treelike, becoming treelike (L)
arenarius   of sand (L)
aristatus   awned (L)
aromaticus   aromatic (Gk)
articulatus   with joints (L)
arvensis   of cultivated fields (L)
ascendens   ascending (L)
asper   rough (L)

*L = Latin; Gk = Greek; Gk → L = Greek root but taken into Medieval Latin and treated as Latin; L/L = both roots for a compound word are Latin; Gk/Gk = both roots for a compound word are Greek.

aureus   golden (L)
auriculatus   eared (L)
australis   southern (L)
autumnalis   of autumn (L)
axillaris   growing in an axil (L)

baccatus   berrylike, pearllike (L)
barbatus   barbed or bearded (L)
bellus   beautiful (L)
bicolor   two-colored (L/L)
bidens   with two teeth (L/L)
biennis   biennial (L)
biflorus   two-flowered (L/L)
borealis   northern (L but derived from Gk mythology)
bracteosus   bearing bracts (L)
brevicaulis   short-stemmed (L/L)
brevis   short (L)
bulbosus   bulbous (L)

caeruleus   blue (L)
caespitosus   tufted (L)
calcareus   chalky, limy (L)
campanulatus   bell-shaped (L)
campestris   growing in fields (L)
canadensis   of Canada
candidus   white (L)
canescens   grayish, becoming gray (L)
capillaris   hairlike (L)
capitatus   growing in heads (L)
capreolatus   twining, tendril-producing (L)
cardinalis   cardinal-red (L)
carneus   flesh-colored (L)
carolinianus   of the Carolinas
caudatus   tailed (L)
caulescens   becoming a stem (Gk → L)
cernuus   drooping, nodding (L)
chinensis   of China
chrysanthus   golden-flowered (Gk/Gk)
ciliatus   ciliate, like an eyelash (L)
cinnamomeus   cinnamon-brown (L)
clavatus   club-shaped (L)
coccineus   scarlet (L)
communis   growing in common (L)
commutatus   changing (L)
concolor   uniform in color (L/L)
confertus   crowded (L)
conglomeratus   crowded (L)

contortus   twisted (L/L)
convolvulus   twining (L/L)
cordatus   heart-shaped (L)
coriaceus   leathery (L)
corniculatus   horned, with a little horn (L)
coronatus   crowned (L)
corymbosus   corymblike (Gk)
crenatus   scalloped (L)
crispus   curled (L)
cristatus   crested (L)
cruciformis   cross-shaped (L/L)
cuneifolius   wedge-shaped leaves (L/L)
cyaneus   blue (Gk)
cymosus   bearing cymes (Gk)

dactyloides   finger-shaped (Gk)
debilis   weak, disabled (L)
deciduus   deciduous (L)
decumbens   reclining (L)
decurrens   extending down (L)
deltoides   triangular (L)
densus   thick (L)
dentatus   toothed (L)
depauperatus   stunted (L)
didymus   in pairs (Gk)
diffusus   loosely branching (L)
digitatus   finger-shaped (L)
discolor   of two colors (Gk/L → L)
dissectus   deeply cut (Gk/L → L)
distichus   two-ranked (Gk/Gk)
diurnus   relating to the day (Gk/L → L)
divaricatus   spreading out (Gk/L → L)
divergens   wide-spreading, turning (Gk/L → L)
dulcis   sweet (L)
dumosus   bushy habit (L)

echinatus   spiny (Gk)
edulis   edible (L)
effusus   loose-spreading (L)
elatus   tall (L)
elegans   elegant (L)
ellipticus   elliptical (Gk)
elongatus   long (L)
emarginatus   with a notch at apex (L)
erectus   upright (L)
ericoides   heathlike (Gk/L)
erythrocarpus   red-fruited (Gk/Gk)

esculentus   edible (L)

falcatus   sickle-shaped (L)
farinosus   mealy (L)
fasciculatus   clustered, bundled (L)
ferrugineus   rusty-colored (L/L)
fertilis   fertile (L)
fibrosus   fibrous (L)
filamentosus   filamentous (L)
filiformis   threadlike (L/L)
fimbriatus   fringed (L)
fistulosus   hollow, cylindrical (L)
flabelliformis   fan-shaped (L/L)
flaccidus   soft, flabby (L)
flavens   yellowish (L)
flexuosus   flexible (L)
floribundus   free-flowering (L)
floridanus   flowering or of Florida (L)
foetidus   having a bad odor (L)
foliosus   leafy (L)
fragilis   fragile (L)
fragrans   fragrant (L)
frondosus   full of leaves (L)
fruticosus   shrubby (L)
fulvus   brownish-yellow (L)
fusiformis   spindle-shaped (L/L)

geminatus   twin (L)
gibbosus   swollen on one side, humped (L)
giganteus   very large (Gk → L)
glabellus   smooth (L)
glabratus   smooth (L)
glandulosus   glandular (L)
glaucescens   waxy (Gk)
globosus   shaped like a globe (L)
glomeratus   dense clusters (L)
glutinosus   gluey or sticky (L)
gramineus   grassy (L)
graminifolius   with grasslike leaves (L/L)
grandiflorus   with large flowers (L/L)
grandifolius   with large leaves (L/L)

hastatus   spear-shaped (L)
herbaceus   not woody (L)
heterophyllus   with leaves of several shapes (Gk/Gk)
hirsutus   hairy (L)
hispidus   bristly (L)

humifusus   sprawling (L)
humilis   dwarf (L)
hybridus   hybrid (L)
hyemalis   of winter (L)

ilicifolius   holly-leaved (L/L)
imbricatus   overlapping, shingled (L)
induratus   hardened (L)
inequalis   unequal (L)
inflatus   inflated (L)
inodorus   without odor (L)
integrifolius   with entire leaves (L/L)

junceus   rushlike (L)

kewensis   relating to Kew Gardens

labiatus   with a lip (L)
laciniatus   cut, torn (Gk → L)
lactatus   milky (L)
laevigatus   smooth (L)
laevis   smooth (L)
lanceolatus   lance-shaped (L)
lancifolius   leaves lance-shaped (L/L)
lanosus   wooly (L)
latiflorus   broad-flowered (L/L)
laxiflorus   loose-flowered (L/L)
laxus   loose (L)
lenticularis   like a lens, like a lentil (L)
lepidotus   with small scales (Gk)
leucanthus   white-flowered (Gk/Gk)
lignosus   like wood (L)
ligularis   strap-shaped (L)
limosus   of muddy places (L)
linearifolius   with long, slender leaves (L/L)
litoralis   of the seashore (L)
lobatus   lobed (L)
longiflorus   long-flowered (L/L)
longifolius   long-leaved (L/L)
lucidus   shining (L)
ludovicianus   of Louisiana
lunulatus   crescent-shaped (L)
luteus   yellow, mud-colored (L)
lyratus   lyre-shaped (Gk → L)

macrophyllus   large-leaved (Gk/Gk)
maculatus   spotted (L)
major   larger (L)

marginalis   marginal (L)
marilandicus   of Maryland
maritimus   growing near the sea (L)
maximus   the largest, greatest (L)
medius   medium (L)
microcarpus   small-fruited (Gk/Gk)
microphyllus   small-leaved (Gk/Gk)
miliaceus   millet-like (L)
millefolius   many-leaved (L/L)
minimus   smallest (L)
minor   smaller (L)
mirabilis   wonderful (L)
mollis   soft (L)
montanus   of mountains (L)
monticola   growing in the mountains (L)
multicaulis   with many stems (L/L)
multiflorus   many-flowered (L/L)
muricatus   roughened by hard points
   (L)
mutabilis   variable (L)

nanus   dwarf (Gk)
natans   floating (L)
neglectus   neglected (L)
nemoralis   growing in woods (L)
nervosus   nerved (L)
niger   black (L)
nitens   shining (L)
niveus   snow-white (L)
nobilis   noble, or well known (L)
noctiflorus   night-flowering (L/L)
nodosus   with nodes (L)
notatus   marked (L)
novae-angliae   of New England
noveboracensis   of New York
nudatus   nude (L)
nudicaulis   naked-stemmed (L/L)
nudiflorus   naked-flowered (L/L)
nutans   nodding (L)
nyctagineus   night-flowering (L)

obtusifolius   with blunt leaves (L/L)
occidentalis   western (L)
odoratissimus   very fragrant (L)
odoratus   with an odor (L)
officinalis   a formally recognized medicinal
   (L)
oleraceus   from a vegetable garden (L)
orientalis   eastern (L)

pallens   pale (L)
palmatus   palmate (L)
paludosus   marshy (L)
paniculatus   in panicles (L)
papyrifer   paper-bearing (L)
parviflorus   small-flowered (L/L)
parvifolius   small-leaved (L/L)
patens   spreading (L)
pauciflorus   few-flowered (L/L)
pedatus   palmately divided (L)
pedicularis   with a stalk (L)
peduncularis   with peduncles (L)
peltatus   shield-shaped (Gk)
pendulus   hanging down (L)
perennis   perennial (L)
petiolaris   relating to the petiole (L)
plumosus   feathery (L)
praealtus   very tall (L/L)
praecox   precocious, premature (L/L)
pratensis   growing in meadows (L)
procumbens   prostrate (L)
pubens   downy (L)
pubescens   with soft hairs, becoming
   downy (L)
pulchellus   beautiful (L)
pumilus   dwarf, small (L)
punctatus   marked with dots (L)
puniceus   reddish-purple (L)
purpureus   purple (L)
pusillus   insignificant or very small (L)

quadrangularis   four-angled (L/L)
quadrifolius   with four leaves (L/L)
quercifolius   oak-leaved (L/L)
quinquefolius   with five leaves (L/L)

racemosus   in racemes (L)
radiatus   with rays, spreading from center
   (L)
radicans   rooting (L)
ramosus   branched (L)
recurvus   curved back (L/L)
regalis   royal (L)
repens   creeping (L)
reptans   crawling (L)
resinosus   resinous (L)
reticulatus   netlike (L)
revolutus   rolled backward or inward (L)
rigidus   stiff (L)

riparius   growing along a river (L)
roseus   rose-colored (L)
rotundifolius   round-leaved (L/L)
rubens   red (L)
ruderalis   growing among rubbish (L)
rugosus   wrinkled (L)
rupestris   growing on rocks (L)

saccharoides   sweet (Gk)
sagittifolius   arrow-leaved (L/L)
salicifolius   willow-leaved (L/L)
sativus   cultivated (L)
saxicola   dweller among rocks (L/L)
scaber   rough (L)
scandens   climbing (L)
scoparius   broomlike, like a bundle of
   twigs (L)
secundus   on the side (L)
semperflorens   ever-blooming (L/L)
sempervirens   evergreen (L/L)
sensibilis   sensible (L)
septentrionalis   northern (L/L)
sericeus   silky (Gk)
sessiliflorus   flowers without stems
   (L/L)
sessilifolius   leaves without petioles (L/L)
sessilis   apparently stemless (L)
setosus   bristly (L)
silvaticus   pertaining to woods (L)
simplex   unbranched (L)
sinensis   of China
speciosus   beautiful (L)
spectabilis   spectacular, visible (L)
spicatus   with spikes (L)
spinosus   with spines (L)
splendens   splendid (L)
squarrosus   spreading at tip, rough because
   of spreading bracts (L)
stamineus   with prominent stamens (L)
stellatus   starlike (L)
stolonifer   with stolons (L)
stramineus   straw-colored (L)
strictus   stiff, upright, drawn together (L)
strigosus   with stiff bristles, with a few stiff
   bristles (L)

subulatus   awl-shaped (L/L)
suffruticosus   shrubby (L/L)
sylvaticus   of forests (L)
sylvestris   growing in woods (L)

tenellus   slender (L)
tenuiflorus   slender flowers (L/L)
tenuifolius   slender-leaved (L/L)
tenuis   slender, thin (L)
teres   round in cross section (L)
ternatus   arranged in threes (L)
terrestris   growing in dry ground (L)
tinctorius   used for dyeing (L)
tomentosus   felty (L)
tortuosus   twisted, winding (L)
tricanthus   three-spined (L/Gk)
tridens   with three teeth (L/L)
trifoliatus   three-leaved (L/L)
tuberosus   with tubers (L)

umbellatus   with umbels (L)
uniflorus   one-flowered (L/L)
urens   stinging (L)
utricularis   bladder-shaped, leather-bag-
   shaped (L)

vacillans   swaying, wavering (L)
variabilis   variable, mottled (L)
velutinus   velvety (L)
venosus   with veins (L)
vernalis   spring flowering (L)
versicolor   variously colored (L/L)
verticillatus   whorled (L)
villosus   with soft hairs (L)
violaceus   violet (L)
virgatus   twiggy (L)
virginianus   of Virginia
viridis   green (L)
viscosus   sticky (L)
vulgaris   common (L)

xanthinus   yellow (Gk)
xanthorrhizus   yellow-rooted (Gk/Gk)

zebrinus   zebra-striped

SOME COMMON GREEK AND LATIN PREFIXES

A prefix is added to the beginning of a word in order to modify its meaning. For more complete lists refer to Featherly (1954) or Stearn (1983).

a-, ab-:   away from (L)

a-, an-:   without (Gk)

actino-:   starlike (Gk)

amphi-:   of two kinds (Gk)

andro-:   male (Gk)

angusti-:   narrow (L)

bi-:   two (L)

brevi-:   short (L)

chloro-:   green (Gk)

chori-:   separate (Gk)

chryso-:   golden (Gk)

co-, col-, com-:   together (L)

cyath-:   cuplike (Gk)

di-:   two, separate, apart (Gk)

e-, ef-, ex-:   lacking (L)

endo-:   within (Gk)

epi: upon (Gk)

erythro-:   reddish (Gk)

fili-:   thread-like (L)

fimbri-:   fringed (L)

flavi-:   yellowish (L)

grandi-:   large (L)

gymno-:   naked (Gk)

gyno-:   female (Gk)

hirsuti-:   hairy (L)

laevi-:   smooth (L)

lanci-:   lance-shaped (L)

lati-:   broad (L)

laxi-:   loose (L)

leio-:   smooth (Gk)

lepido-:   scaly (Gk)

leuco-:   white (Gk)

macro-:   large (Gk)

mega-:   very large (Gk)

melano-:   black (Gk)

micro-:   small (Gk)

mono-:   one, single (Gk)

multi-:   many (L)

nudi-:   naked (L)

octo-:   eight (Gk)

odonto-:   toothed (Gk)

pauci-:   few (L)

peri-:   around (Gk)

phyllo-:   relating to a leaf (Gk)

pleio-:   many (Gk)

poly-:   many (Gk)

pseudo-:   false (Gk)

ptero-:   winged (Gk)

quadr-:   four (L)

rhizo-:   relating to a root (Gk)

schiz-:   split, divided (Gk)

semper-:   always (L)

sessili-:   sessile (L)

tenui-:   slender (L)

tri-:   three (L)

tetra-:   four (Gk)

uni-:   one (L)

viridi-:   green (L)

xantho-:   yellow (Gk)

xero-:   dry (Gk)

xylo-:   woody (Gk)

zygo-:   fused, a yoke (Gk)

COMMON BOTANICAL LATIN ABBREVIATIONS

These abbreviations are often used in systematic botany.

aff.   *affinis,* "related to"

ca.   *circa,* "around, about"

comb. nov.   *combinatio nova,* "new combination"

cv.   *cultivarietas,* "cultivar"

det.   *determinavit,* "identified by"

exs.   *exsiccatus,* "dried [herbarium] specimen"

f.   *filius,* "son" (after a personal noun)

f.   *forma,* "form" (before an epithet)

hab.   *habitat,* place where a plant grows

herb.   *herbarium,* "herbarium"

hort.   *hortorum,* "from gardens"

s.l.   *sensu lato,* "in a broad sense"

s. str.   *sensu stricto,* "in a narrow sense"

s.n.   *sine numero,* "without a [collection] number"

sp.   *species,* "species" (singular)

spp.   *species,* "species" (plural)

subsp.   *subspecies,* "subspecies"

var.   *varietas,* "variety"

sp. nov.   *species nova,* "new species"

REFERENCES FOR APPENDIX 1

Borror, D. J.: *Dictionary of Word Roots and Combining Forms,* Mayfield Publishing Company, Palo Alto, Calif., 1960. (A handy, inexpensive paperback book.)

Featherly, H. I.: *Taxonomic Terminology of the Higher Plants,* The Iowa State College Press, Ames, 1954.

Radford, L. S.: "Botanical Names," in A. E. Radford et al., *Vascular Plant Systematics,* Harper & Row, New York, 1974, pp. 57–71.

Stearn, W. T.: *Botanical Latin,* 3rd ed., David and Charles, Newton Abbot, England, 1983.

TWO

SELECTED LITERATURE FOR THE IDENTIFICATION OF VASCULAR PLANTS IN NORTH AMERICA NORTH OF MEXICO

There are three major types of identification aids: floras, manuals, and guides. A *flora* provides an inventory of the plants of an area and is often restricted to the vascular plants. Floras may contain keys and descriptions. A *manual* always has keys for identification and may contain all the vascular plants of a given area or may treat limited groups, such as the grasses of the United States or the aquatic plants of the southeastern states. In practice, the distinctions between a flora and a manual are not sharp, and the two terms are often used interchangeably. A *guide* is a brief treatment of plants in a particular area and consists of keys and a list of taxa. There is no complete flora, manual, or guide of native plants for North America north of Mexico, although many exist for restricted parts of the area.

Selected references for plant identification are listed here. No attempt was made to include all manuals and floras that might be of historical importance. References are provided for special groups such as aquatics, cacti, ferns, grasses, legumes, orchids, poisonous plants, weeds, and woody plants. A section on selected references helpful for identifying cultivated or exotic plants is included. In addition, a section is provided for popular wild flower treatments.

MANUALS, FLORAS, AND GUIDES

Abrams, L.: *An Illustrated Flora of the Pacific States,* 4 vols., vol. 4 by R. Ferris, Stanford University Press, Stanford, Calif., 1923–1960.

Anderson, J. P. See Welsh, S. L.

Bare, J. E.: *Wildflowers and Weeds of Kansas,* Regents Press of Kansas, Lawrence, 1979.

Barkley, T. M.: *A Manual of the Flowering Plants of Kansas,* Kansas State University Endowment Association, Manhattan, 1968.

Batson, W. T.: *Genera of Eastern Plants,* 3d ed., rev., University of South Carolina Press, Columbia, 1984 (Pocket-size.)

———: *Genera of the Western Plants,* State Print Co., Columbia, S. C., 1982.

Braun, E. L: *The Vascular Flora of Ohio.* Vol. I., *The Monocotyledoneae,* Ohio State University Press, Columbus, 1967.

Budd, A. C.: *"Budd's Flora of the Canadian Prairie Provinces,"* Rev. by J. Looman and K. F. Best. Canada Department of Agriculture Publication, no. 1662, 1979.

Clovis, J. F., et al.: *Common Vascular Plants of the Mid-Appalachian Region,* Book Exchange, Morgantown, W.Va., 1972.

Correll, D. S., and M. C. Johnston: *Manual of the Vascular Plants of Texas,* Texas Research Foundation, Renner, Tex., 1970.

Cronquist, A., et al.: *Intermountain Flora; Vascular Plants of the Intermountain West, U.S.A.,* Hafner, New York, 1972– . (Projected six volumes.)

Davis, R. J.: *Flora of Idaho,* Brown, Dubuque, Iowa, 1952.

Deam, C. C.: *Flora of Indiana,* Indiana Department of Conservation, Indianapolis, 1940.

Fassett, N. C.: *Spring Flora of Wisconsin,* 4th ed., University of Wisconsin Press, Madison, 1976.

Fernald, M. L. See Gray, A.

Frodin, D. G.: *Guide to Standard Floras of the World,* Cambridge University Press, Cambridge, 1984.

Gilkey, H. M., and L. R. J. Dennis: *Handbook of Northwestern Plants,* Oregon State University Bookstore, Corvallis, 1967.

Gleason, H. A.: *New Britton and Brown Illustrated Flora of the Northeastern United States and Adjacent Canada,* 3 vols., New York Botanical Garden, New York, 1952. (Illustrations; excellent keys.)

———and A. Cronquist: *Manual of the Vascular Plants of the Northeastern United States and Adjacent Canada,* Van Nostrand, Princeton, N.J., 1963. (Keys are excellent; one of the standard floras of northeastern North America.)

Goodman, G. J.: *Spring Flora of Central Oklahoma,* University of Oklahoma Duplicating Service, Norman, 1958.

Gray, A.: *Manual of Botany,* 8th ed., M. L. Fernald (ed.), American Book, New York, 1950. (One of the standard floras for the northeastern United States and adjacent Canada; the family keys, although workable, are technical and difficult for the beginner.)

Great Plains Flora Association: *Atlas of the Flora of the Great Plains,* Iowa State University Press, Ames, 1977.

Harrington, H. D.: *Manual of the Plants of Colorado,* Sage, Denver, Colo., 1954.

Harvill, A. M.: *Spring Flora of Virginia,* McClain, Parsons, W. Va., 1970.

Hitchcock, C. L., et al.: *Vascular Plants of the Pacific Northwest,* parts 1–5, University of Washington Press, Seattle, 1955–1969. (Excellent family keys.)

——— and A. Cronquist: *Flora of the Pacific Northwest: an Illustrated Manual,* University of Washington Press, Seattle, 1973.

Hultén, E.: *Flora of the Aleutian Islands,* 2d ed., J. Cramer, Weinheim, West Germany, 1960.

———: *Flora of Alaska and Neighboring Territories; A Manual of the Vascular Plants,* Stanford University Press, Stanford, Calif., 1968.

Jepson, W. L.: *A Manual of the Flowering Plants of California,* University of California Press, Berkeley, 1925.

Jones, F. B.: *Flora of the Texas Coastal Bend,* Welder Wildlife Foundation, Sinton, Tex., 1975.

Jones, G. N.: *Flora of Illinois,* 3d ed., University of Notre Dame Press, Notre Dame, Ind., 1963.

Kartesz, J. T., and R. Kartesz: *Synonymized Checklist of the Vascular Flora of the United States, Canada and Greenland,* University of North Carolina Press, Chapel Hill, 1980.

Kearney, T. H., and R. H. Peebles, *Arizona Flora*, 2d ed., University of California Press, Berkeley, 1960.

Kuijt, J.: *A Flora of Waterton Lakes National Park*, University of Alberta Press, Edmonton, Alta., Canada, 1982.

Lakela, O.: *A Flora of Northeastern Minnesota*, University of Minnesota Press, Minneapolis, 1965.

Lloyd, R., and R. S. Mitchell: *A Flora of the White Mountains, California and Nevada*, University of California Press, Berkeley, 1973.

Long, R. W., and O. Lakela: *A Flora of Tropical Florida*, University of Miami Press, Coral Gables, Fla., 1971. (For southern Florida.)

Marie-Victorin, F.: *Flore Laurentienne (Québec)*, 2d ed., Presses de l'Université de Montréal, Montréal, 1964. (In French.)

Martin, W. C., and C. R. Hutchins: *A Flora of New Mexico*, 2 vols., J. Cramer, Vaduz, 1980.

Mason, G.: *Guide to the Plants of the Wallowa Mountains of Northeast Oregon*, Museum of Natural History, University of Oregon, Eugene, 1975.

McDougall, W. B.: *Seed Plants of Northern Arizona*, Museum of Northern Arizona, Flagstaff, 1973.

Mohlenbrock, R. H.: *Flowering Plants: Flowering Rush to Rushes*, Southern Illinois University Press, Carbondale, 1970.

———: *Flowering Plants: Lilies to Orchids*, Southern Illinois University Press, Carbondale, 1970.

———: *Guide to the Vascular Flora of Illinois*, Southern Illinois University Press, Carbondale, 1975.

———: *Sedges*, Southern Illinois University Press, Carbondale, 1976.

———: *Flowering Plants: Hollies to Loasas*, Southern Illinois University Press, Carbondale, 1978.

———: *Flowering Plants: Willows to Mustards*, Southern Illinois University Press, Carbondale, 1980.

———: *Flowering Plants: Magnolias to Pitcher Plants*, Southern Illinois University Press, Carbondale, 1981.

———: *Flowering Plants: Basswoods to Spurges*, Southern Illinois University Press, Carbondale, 1982.

——— and J. W. Voight: *A Flora of Southern Illinois*, Southern Illinois University Press, Carbondale, 1959.

Morley, T.: *Spring Flora of Minnesota*, University of Minnesota Press, Minneapolis, 1969.

Moss, E. H.: *Flora of Alberta*, 2nd ed., University of Toronto Press, Toronto, 1983.

Munz, P. A., in collaboration with D. D. Keck: *A California Flora*, University of California Press, Berkeley, 1959, supplement 1968, combined edition 1973. (Lists major community types; selected illustrations; the standard flora for California.)

———: *A Flora of Southern California*, University of California Press, Berkeley, 1974.

National List of Scientific Plant Names, 2 vols., Soil Conservation Service Tech. Pub. 159, 1982.

Pease, A. S.: *A Flora of Northern New Hampshire*, New England Botanical Club, Cambridge, Mass., 1964.

Peck, M. E.: *A Manual of the Higher Plants of Oregon*, 2d ed., Binford and Mort, Portland, Ore. 1961.

Perry, F., and R. Hay: *A Field Guide to Tropical and Subtropical Plants*, Van Nostrand Reinhold, New York, 1982.

Pohl, R. W.: *Keys to Iowa Vascular Plants*, Kendall-Hunt, Dubuque, 1975.

Polunin, N.: *Circumpolar Arctic Flora*, Clarendon, Oxford, 1959.

Porsild, A. E.: *"Illustrated Flora of the Canadian Arctic Archipelago,"* 2nd ed., National Museum of Canada Bull. no. 146, 1973.

———, and W. J. Cody: *Vascular Plants of Continental Northwest Territories, Canada*, National Museum of Natural Science, National Museums of Canada, Ottawa, 1980.

Porter, C. L.: *A Flora of Wyoming*, University of Wyoming Agricultural Experiment Station Bulletin nos. 402, 404, 418, and 434, 1962–65.

Radford, A. E., H. E. Ahles, and C. R. Bell: *Manual of the Vascular Flora of the Carolinas*, University of North Carolina Press, Chapel Hill, 1968. (Useful in southeastern United States; family keys difficult; selected illustrations.)

Roland, A. E., and E. C. Smith: "Flora of Nova Scotia," *Proc. N. S. Inst. Sci.*, **26:**3–238, 277–743, 1962–1969.

Rydberg, P. A.: *Flora of the Rocky Mountains and Adjacent Plains*, 2d ed., published by the author, New York, 1922. (Facsimile, Hafner, New York, 1954; many of the names are now obsolete.)

———: *Flora of the Prairies and Plains of Central North America*, New York Botanical Garden, New York, 1932. (Many of the names are now obsolete.)

Scoggan, H. J.: *Flora of Manitoba*, National Museum of Canada Bulletin, no. 140, 1957.

———: *The Flora of Canada*, National Museum of Natural Science Publications in Botany, no. 7, 1978–1979. (Treats ferns, conifers, and flowering plants, keys.)

Seymour, F. C.: *The Flora of New England*, 2nd ed., Moldenke, Plainfield, N. J., 1982.

Shetler, S. G., and L. E. Skog: *A Provisional Checklist of Species for Flora North America*, Missouri Botanical Garden, St. Louis, 1978.

Shinners, L. H.: *Shinners' Spring Flora of the Dallas-Fort Worth Area, Texas*, 2d ed., W. H. Mahler (ed.), Prestige Press, Ft. Worth, 1972.

Shreve, F., and I. L. Wiggins: *Vegetation and Flora of the Sonoran Desert*, 2 vols., Stanford University Press, Stanford, Calif., 1964.

Small, J. K.: *Manual of the Southeastern Flora*, published by the author, 1933. (Facsimile, Hafner, New York, 1972. Many of the names are obsolete; good illustrations of each genus.)

Smith, E. B.: *An Atlas and Annotated List of the Vascular Plants of Arkansas*, Student Union Bookstore, University of Arkansas, Fayetteville, 1978.

Stevens, O. A.: *Handbook of North Dakota Plants*, North Dakota Agricultural College, Fargo, 1963.

Steyermark, J. A.: *Flora of Missouri*, The Iowa State University Press, Ames, 1963. (Well illustrated and has excellent keys.)

Strausbaugh, P. D., and E. L. Core: *Flora of West Virginia*, introduction and parts I-IV, West Virginia University, Morgantown, 1952–1964. (Parts I and II revised in 1970, 1971.)

Taylor, R. L.: *Vascular Plants of British Columbia*, University of British Columbia Press, Vancouver, 1977.

Taylor, R. L., and B. MacBryde: *Vascular Plants of British Columbia*, University of British Columbia Press, Vancouver, 1977. (An inventory printed from computer-stored information.)

Thomas, J. H.: *Flora of the Santa Cruz Mountains of California, A Manual of Vascular Plants*, Stanford University Press, Stanford, Calif., 1961.

Tidestrom, I., and T. R. Kittel: *A Flora of Arizona and New Mexico*, 2 vols., Catholic University of America Press, Washington, D.C., 1941.

Van Bruggen, T.: *The Vascular Plants of South Dakota*, Iowa State University Press, Ames, 1976.

Voss, E. G.: *Michigan Flora*, part 1, *Gymnosperms and Monocots*, Cranbrook Institute of Science Bulletin, No. 55, 1972.

Waterfall, U. T.: *Keys to the Flora of Oklahoma*, 5th ed., published by the author, Oklahoma State University Bookstore, Stillwater, 1972.

Weber, W. A.: *Rocky Mountain Flora: A Field Guide for the Identification of the Ferns, Conifers, and Flowering Plants*, Colorado Associate University Press, Boulder, 1976.

Welsh, S. L.: *Anderson's Flora of Alaska and Adjacent Parts of Canada*, Brigham Young University Press, Provo, Utah, 1974.

———, and G. Moore: *Utah Plants; Tracheophyta*, 3rd ed., Brigham Young University Press, Provo, 1973.

Wiggins, I. L., and J. H. Thomas: *A Flora of the Alaskan Arctic Slope*, Arctic Institute of North America Special Publication, no. 4, 1962.

Wooten, E. O., and P. C. Standley: *Flora of New Mexico*, Contributions from the United States National Herbarium, no. 19, 1915. (Some of the nomenclature is now obsolete.)

Wunderlin, R. P.: *Guide to the Vascular Plants of Central Florida*, University Presses of Florida, Gainesville, 1982.

AQUATIC PLANTS

Beal, E. O.: *A Manual of Marsh and Aquatic Vascular Plants of North Carolina; with Habitat Data*, North Carolina Agricultural Experiment Station Technical Bulletin, no. 247, 1977.

Carlton, J. M.: *A Guide to Common Florida Salt Marsh and Mangrove Vegetation*, Florida Marine Research Publications, no. 6, 1975.

Cook, C. D. K., et al.: *Water Plants of the World*, Junk, The Hague, 1974.

Correll, D. S., and H. B. Correll: *Aquatic and Wetland Plants of Southwestern United States*, E.P.A., U.S. Government Printing Office, Washington, D.C., 1972. (Facsimile edition, Stanford Unversity Press, Stanford, Calif., 1975; keys, descriptions, excellent illustrations.)

Eleuterius, L. N.: *An Illustrated Guide to Tidal Marsh Plants of Mississippi and Adjacent States*, Mississippi-Alabama Sea Grant Consortium, Ocean Springs, Miss., 1981.

Eyles, D. E., and J. L. Robertson: *A Guide and Key to the Aquatic Plants of the Southeastern United States*, U.S. Bureau of Sport Fisheries and Wildlife Circular, no. 158, 1963. (A reprint of U.S. Public Health Bulletin, no. 286, 1944; easily used by the nonprofessional.)

Fassett, N. C.: *A Manual of Aquatic Plants*, University of Wisconsin Press, Madison, 1957. (With revised appendix by E. C. Ogden.)

Godfrey, R. K., and J. W. Wooten, *Aquatic and Wetland Plants of Southeastern United States: Monocotyledons*, University of Georgia Press, Athens, 1979.

———, and ———, *Aquatic and Wetland Plants of Southeastern United States: Dicotyledons*, University of Georgia Press, Athens, 1981.

Hotchkiss, N.: *Common Marsh and Floating-leaved Plants of the United States and Canada*, Dover, New York, 1972. (Reprint of U.S. Bureau of Sport Fisheries and Wildlife Resources Publication, nos. 44 and 93. Illustrated.)

Mason, H. L.: *A Flora of the Marshes of California*, University of California Press, Berkeley, 1957. (Illustrations; excellent illustrated glossary.)

Matsumara, Y., and H. D. Harrington: *The True Aquatic Vascular Plants of Colorado*, Colorado Agricultural Experiment Station Technical Bulletin, no. 57, 1955.

Muenscher, W. C.: *Aquatic Plants of the United States*, Comstock, Ithaca, New York, 1944. (An excellent manual covering the entire United States.)

Ogden, E. C., et al.: *Field Guide to the Aquatic Plants of Lake George New York,* New York State Museum, Bulletin No. 426, 1976.

Prescott, G. W.: *How to Know the Aquatic Plants,* Brown, Dubuque, Iowa, 1969. (Keys; line drawings.)

Steward, A. N., L. J. Dennis, and H. M. Gilkey: *Aquatic Plants of the Pacific Northwest with Vegetative Keys,* 2d ed., Oregon State University Press, Corvallis, 1963.

Winterringer, G. S., and A. C. Lopinot: *Aquatic Plants of Illinois,* Illinois State Museum Popular Science Series, no. 6, 1977.

CACTI

Benson, L.: *The Cacti of Arizona,* 3d ed., University of Arizona Press, Tucson, 1969.

————: *The Native Cacti of California,* Stanford University Press, Stanford, Calif., 1969. (Designed for use by professionals and amateurs.)

————: *The Cacti of the United States and Canada,* Stanford University Press, Stanford, Calif., 1982.

Britton, N. L., and J. N. Rose: *The Cactaceae: Descriptions and Illustrations of Plants of the Cactus Family,* 4 vols., Carnegie Institution of Washington Publication, no. 248, 1919–1923. (Keys, descriptions, illustrations.)

Dawson, E. Y.: *How to Know the Cacti,* Brown, Dubuque, Iowa, 1963. (Includes descriptions, keys, line drawings, black-and-white photographs.)

————: *The Cacti of California,* University of California Press, Berkeley, 1966. (A popular illustrated guide to the native cacti of the state.)

Weniger, D.: *Cacti of the Southwest,* University of Texas Press, Austin, 1969.

————: *Cacti of Texas and Neighboring States,* University of Texas Press, Austin, 1984.

CULTIVATED PLANTS AND ORNAMENTALS

Bailey, L. H.: *The Standard Cyclopedia of Horticulture,* 3 vols., Macmillan, New York, 1928. (First published in 1900 as *Cyclopedia of American Horticulture,* it remains an excellent source of information on horticultural plants, including some help with identification.)

————: *Manual of Cultivated Plants,* rev. ed., Macmillan, New York, 1949. (A manual for identification of plants cultivated in the United States; the keys are generally unsatisfactory.)

————, compiler: *Hortus Third,* revised by the staff of Liberty Hyde Bailey Hortorium, Macmillan, Riverside, N.J., 1976. (A concise dictionary of plants cultivated in the United States and Canada; indispensable to those working with cultivated plants.)

Bean, W. J.: *Trees and Shrubs Hardy in the British Isles,* 8th ed. rev., 4 vols., St. Martin's, New York, 1981.

Chittenden, F. J. (ed.): *Dictionary of Gardening,* 2nd ed., 4 vols., Clarendon, Oxford, 1974.

Everett, T. H.: *The New York Botanical Garden Illustrated Encyclopedia of Horticulture,* 10 vols., Garland Publishing, New York, 1980–82.

Graf, A. B.: *Exotic Plant Manual,* 5th ed., Roehrs, East Rutherford, N. J., 1978.

————: *Tropica,* 2nd ed., Roehrs, East Rutherford, N. J., 1981.

————: *Exotica, Series 4; Pictorial Cyclopedia of Exotic Plants, From Tropical and Near-tropic Regions,* 11th ed., 2 vols., Roehrs, East Rutherford, N. J., 1982.

Halfacre, R. G., and A. R. Shawcroft: *Carolina Landscape Plants,* 2d ed., Sparks Press, Raleigh, N.C., 1975. (Line drawings, horticultural notes.)

Helmer, M. J. C.: *Pictorial Library of Landscape Plants,* 2nd ed., Merchants Publishing Company, Kalamazoo, Mich., 1979.

Hillier, H. G.: *Hillier's Manual of Trees and Shrubs,* 5th ed., Van Nostrand Reinhold, New York, 1981.

Kunkel, G.: *Flowering Trees and Subtropical Gardens,* Junk, The Hague, 1978.

Ouden, P. D., and B. K. Boom: *Manual of Cultivated Conifers; Hardy in the Cold- and Warm-Temperatue Zone,* Martinus Nijhoff, The Hague, Netherlands, 1965. (Technical, black-and-white photos, descriptions.)

Perry, F. (ed.): *Simon & Schuster's Complete Guide to Plants and Flowers,* Simon and Schuster, New York, 1974. (Horticultural information, color photos.)

Rehder, A.: *Manual of Cultivated Trees and Shrubs Hardy in North America,* 2d ed., Macmillan, New York, 1940. (Keys to taxa are included.)

————: *Bibliography of Cultivated Trees and Shrubs Hardy in the Cooler Temperate Regions of the Northern Hemisphere,* Arnold Arboretum of Harvard University, Jamaica Plain, Mass., 1949. (Provides references to the sources of scientific names.)

Reisch, K. W., P. C. Kozel, and G. A. Weinstein: *Woody Ornamentals for the Midwest (Deciduous),* Kendall/Hunt, Dubuque, Iowa, 1975. (Descriptions, line drawings.)

Spangler, R. L., and J. Ripperda: *Landscape Plants for Central and Northeastern United States,* Burgess Pub. Co., Minneapolis, 1977.

Uphof, J. C. Th.: *Dictionary of Economic Plants,* 2d ed., Stechert-Hafner, New York, 1968..

Whitcomb, C. E.: *Know It and Grow It: A Guide to the Identification and Use of Landscape Plants in the Southern States,* published by the author, Tulsa, Okla., 1976.

————: *Know It and Grow it II: a Guide to the Identification and Use of Landscape Plants,* Lacebark Pub., Stillwater, Okla., 1983.

Wigginton, B. E.: *Trees and Shrubs for the Southeast,* University of Georgia Press; Athens, 1963. (Black-and-white photos.)

Wilson, E. H., and A. Rehder: *A Monograph of Azaleas,* University Press, Cambridge, England, 1921.

Wyman, D.: *Trees for American Gardens,* Macmillan, New York, 1959, (Black-and-white photos, descriptions.)

————: *Shrubs and Vines for American Gardens,* rev. ed., Macmillan, New York, 1969. (Black-and-white photos, descriptions.)

————: *Wyman's Gardening Encyclopedia,* rev. ed., Macmillan, New York, 1977. (An encyclopedia format with horticultural information.)

PTERIDOPHYTES

Billington, C.: *Ferns of Michigan,* Cranbrook Institute of Science Bulletin, no. 32, 1952.

Brown, C. A., and D. S. Correll: *Ferns and Fern Allies of Louisiana,* Louisiana State University Press, Baton Rouge, 1942.

Chrysler, M. A., and J. L. Edwards: *The Ferns of New Jersey,* Rutgers University Press, New Brunswick, N.J., 1947.

Cobb, B.: *A Field Guide to the Ferns,* Houghton Mifflin, Boston, 1956. (Peterson Field Guide Series.)

Cody, W. J.: *Ferns of the Ottawa District,* Canada Department of Agriculture Publication 974, 1978.

Correll, D. S.: *Ferns and Fern Allies of Texas,* Contributions from the Texas Research Foundation, vol. 2, 1956.

Cranfill, R.: *Ferns and Fern Allies of Kentucky,* Kentucky Nature Preserves Commission, Frankfort, 1980.

Grillos, S. J.: *Ferns and Fern Allies of California,* University of California Press, Berkeley, 1966.

Harrington, H. D., and L. W. Durrell: *Colorado Ferns and Fern Allies,* Colorado Agricultural Research Foundation, Fort Collins, 1950.

Key, J. S.: *Field Guide to Missouri Ferns,* Missouri Department of Conservation, Jefferson City, 1982.

Lakela, O., and R. W. Long: *Ferns of Florida,* Banyan Books, Miami, 1976.

Massey, A. B.: *The Ferns and Fern Allies of Virginia,* 2d ed., Virginia Polytechnic Institute Agriculture Extension Service Bulletin, no. 256, 1958.

McVaugh, R., and J. H. Pyron: *Ferns of Georgia,* University of Georgia Press, Athens, 1951.

Mickel, J. T.: *How to Know the Ferns and Fern Allies,* Wm. C. Brown Co., Dubuque, Iowa, 1979.

Mohlenbrock, R. H.: *Ferns,* Southern Illinois University Press, Carbondale, 1967.

Peck, J. H.: *Ferns and Fern Allies of the Driftless Area of Illinois, Iowa, Minnesota, and Wisconsin.* Milwaukee Public Museum, Milwaukee, 1982.

Petrik-ott, A. J.: *The Pteridophytes of Kansas, Nebraska, South Dakota, USA,* Nova Hedwiga: Beihefte, no. 61, 1979.

Small, J. K.: *Ferns of the Southeastern States,* Science Press, Lancaster, Pa., 1938. (Many of the names used are now obsolete.)

Taylor, T. M. C.: *Pacific Northwest Ferns and Their Allies,* University of Toronto Press, Toronto, 1970.

Taylor, W. C.: *Arkansas Ferns and Fern Allies,* Milwaukee Public Museum, Milwaukee, 1984.

Thieret, J. W.: *Louisiana Ferns and Fern Allies,* Lafayette Natural History Museum, University of Southwestern Louisiana, Lafayette, 1980.

Tryon, R. M., et al.: *The Ferns and Fern Allies of Wisconsin,* 2d ed., University of Wisconsin Press, Madison, 1953.

———: *Ferns of Minnesota,* 2nd ed., University of Minnesota Press, Minneapolis, 1980.

———, and A. F. Tryon: *Ferns and Allied Plants,* Springer-Verlag, New York, 1982.

Wherry, E. T.: *The Fern Guide, Northeastern and Midland United States and Adjacent Canada,* Doubleday, Garden City, N.Y., 1961, (Keys, descriptions, line drawings.)

———: *The Southern Fern Guide,* Doubleday, Garden City, N.Y., 1964. (Line drawings, descriptions.)

GRASSES

Allen, C. M.: *Grasses of Louisiana,* University of Southwestern Louisiana, Lafayette, 1980.

Barnard, C. M., and L. D. Potter: *New Mexico Grasses; a Vegetative Key,* University of New Mexico Press, Albuquerque, 1984.

Blomquist, H. L.: *The Grasses of North Carolina,* Duke University Press, Durham, 1948. (Excellent illustrations, a vegetative key, photographs.)

Deam, C. C.: *Grasses of Indiana,* Indiana Department of Conservation Publication, no. 82, 1929. (Illustrated.)

Dore, W. G., and J. McNeil: *Grasses of Ontario,* Canada Department of Agriculture Research Branch Monograph 26, 1980.

Gould, F. W.: *Grasses of Southwestern United States,* University of Arizona, Tucson, 1951.
———: *Grass Systematics,* McGraw-Hill, New York, 1968. (A textbook on all aspects of grasses including a revised system of classification.)
———: *The Grasses of Texas,* Texas A&M University Press, College Station, 1975.
———and T. D. Box: *Grasses of the Texas Coastal Bend,* Texas A&M University Press, College Station, 1965.
Gould, F. W.: *Common Texas Grasses,* Texas A&M University Press, College Station, 1978.
Harrington, H. D.: *How to Identify Grasses and Grasslike Plants,* Swallow, Chicago, Ill., 1977.
Hitchcock, A. S.: *Manual of Grasses of the United States,* 2d ed., revised by A. Chase, U.S. Department of Agriculture Miscellaneous Publication, no. 200, 1950. (A basic illustrated reference to the grasses; classification system is now out of date. Reprinted by Dover Publication, New York.)
Looman, J.: *Prairie Grasses, Identified and Described by Vegetative Characters,* Agriculture Canada Publication 1413, 1982.
Mohlenbrock, R. H.: *Grasses: Bromus to Paspalum,* Southern Illinois University Press, Carbondale, 1972.
———: *Grasses: Panicum to Danthonia,* Southern Illinois University Press, Carbondale, 1973.
Pohl, R. W.: "The Grasses of Iowa," *Iowa State J. Sci.* **40:**341–566, 1966.
———: *How to Know the Grasses,* 3rd ed., W. C. Brown Co., Dubuque, Iowa, 1978.

LEGUMES

Fassett, N. C.: *The Leguminous Plants of Wisconsin,* University of Wisconsin Press, Madison, 1939.
Gambill, W. G.: "The Leguminosae of Illinois," *Ill. Biol. Monogr.,* **22**(4):1–117, 1953.
Isley, D.: "The Leguminosae of the North-Central States," *Iowa State J. Sci.,* **25:**439–482, 1951; **30:**33–118, 1955; **32:**355–393, 1958; **37:**103–162, 1962.
———: "Leguminosae of the United States: I. Subfamily Mimosoideae; II. Subfamily Caesalpinoideae," *Mem. N.Y. Bot. Gard.,* **25**(1):1–152, 1973; **25:**(2):1–228, 1975.
———: "Leguminosae of the United States: III. Subfamily Papilionoidae, Tribes Sophoreae, Podalyrieae, Loteae," *Mem. N. Y. Bot. Gard.* **25**(3):1–264, 1981.
Lasseigne, A.: *Louisiana Legumes,* University of Southwestern Louisana, Lafayette, 1973.
Mahler, W. F.: "Manual of the Legumes of Tennessee," *J. Tenn. Acad. Sci.,* **45:**65–96, 1970.
Turner, B. L.: *The Legumes of Texas,* University of Texas Press, Austin, 1959.
Wilbur, R. L.: *Leguminous Plants of North Carolina,* North Carolina Agricultural Experiment Station Technical Bulletin, no. 151, 1963. (Illustrations, keys, and descriptions.)

ORCHIDS

Case, F. W.: *Orchids of the Western Great Lakes Region,* Cranbrook Institute of Science Bulletin, no. 48, 1964. (Keys, descriptions, black-and-white and color photographs.)
Correll, D. S.: *Native Orchids of North America North of Mexico,* Chronica Botanica Company, Waltham, Mass., 1950.
Luer, C. A.: *The Native Orchids of Florida,* New York Botanical Garden, Bronx, 1972. (High-quality, excellent reproduction of color pohotgraphs.)
———: *The Native Orchids of the United States and Canada Excluding Florida,* New York Botanical Garden, Bronx, 1975. (Excellent, high-quality color reproduction.)

Williams, J. G., and A. E. Williams: *Field Guide to Orchids of North America,* Universe Books, New York, 1983.

POISONOUS PLANTS

Hardin, J. W., and J. M. Arena: *Human Poisoning from Native and Cultivated Plants,* 2d rev. ed., Duke University Press, Durham, N.C., 1974.

Kingsbury, J. M.: *Poisonous Plants of the United States and Canada,* Prentice-Hall, Englewood Cliffs, N.J., 1964. (Contains well-documented information.)

Lampe, K. F., and M. A. McCann: *AMA Handbook of Poisonous and Injurious Plants,* American Medical Association, Chicago, Ill., 1985.

Stephens, H. A.: *Poisonous Plants of the Central United States,* Regents Press of Kansas, Lawrence, 1980.

WEEDS*

Barkley, T. M.: *Field Guide to the Common Weeds of Kansas,* University Press of Kansas, Lawrence, 1983.

Delorit, R. J.: *An Illustrated Taxonomy Manual of Weed Seeds,* Agronomy Publications, River Falls, Wis., 1970. (Photographs of seeds.)

Dennis, L. J.: *Gilkey's Weeds of the Pacific Northwest,* Oregon State University, Corvallis, 1980.

Frankton, C.: *Weeds of Canada,* rev. ed., Canada Department of Agriculture Publication, no. 948, 1977.

Montgomery, F. H.: *Weeds of Northern United States and Canada,* Warne, New York, 1964.

Muenscher, W. C.: *Weeds,* 2d ed., Macmillan, New York, 1955.

Mulligan, G. A.: *Common Weeds of Canada: Les mauvaises herbes communes du Canada,* McClelland and Stewart, Toronto, 1976.

Nebraska Weeds, Nebraska Department of Agriculture, Lincoln, 1975. (An excellent color picture book.)

Parker, K. F.: *An Illustrated Guide to Arizona Weeds,* University of Arizona Press, Tucson, 1972.

Reed, C. F.: *Selected Weeds of the United States,* U.S. Department of Agriculture, Agriculture Handbook, no. 366, 1970. (Illustrated; useful for the layperson.)

Wax, L. M., et al. (eds.): *Weeds of the North Central States,* North Central Regional Publication, no. 281, 1981.

Wilkinson, R. E., and H. E. Jaques: *How to Know the Weeds,* 3rd ed., W. C. Brown Company, Dubuque, Iowa, 1979.

EDIBLE WILD PLANTS

Elias, T. S., and P. A. Dykeman: *Field Guide to North American Edible Wild Plants,* Van Nostrand Reinhold, New York, 1982.

Fernald, M. L., and A. C. Kinsey: *Edible Wild Plants of Eastern North America,* rev. ed. by R. C. Rollins, Harper & Row, New York, 1958. (The standard book for edible wild plants.)

---

*Most states have illustrated publications identifying local weeds. These are available from county agents of the Cooperative Extension Service.

Knap, A. H.: *Wild Harvest,* Arco Publishing Company, Inc., New York, 1975. (Field guide, recipes.)

Kunkel, G.: *Plants for Human Consumption: An Annotated Checklist of the Edible Phanerogams and Ferns,* Koeltz, Koenigstein, Germany, 1984.

Peterson, L.: *A Field Guide to Edible Wild Plants of Eastern and Central North America,* Houghton-Mifflin, Boston, 1978. (Peterson Field Guide Series.)

Szczawinski, A. F.: *Wild Green Vegetables of Canada,* National Museum of Natural Sciences, Ottawa, 1980.

———, and N. J. Turner: *Edible Garden Weeds of Canada,* National Museum of Natural Sciences, Ottawa, 1978.

Turner, N. J., and A. F. Szczawinski: *Wild Coffee and Tea Substitutes of Canada,* National Museum of Natural Sciences, National Museums of Canada, Ottawa, 1978.

———, and A. F. Szczawinski: *Edible Wild Fruits and Nuts of Canada,* National Museum of Natural Sciences, Ottawa, 1979.

Weatherbee, E. E., and J. G. Bruce: *Edible Wild Plants: A Guide to Collecting and Cooking,* 2nd ed. published by the authors, Ann Arbor, 1982.

POPULAR WILD FLOWER BOOKS

Armstrong, M. N.: *Field Book of Western Wild Flowers,* Putnam, New York, 1915. (A popular field guide.)

Ahmadjian, V.: *Flowering Plants of Massachusetts,* University of Massachusetts Press, Amherst, 1979.

Ajilvsgi, G.: *Wild Flowers of the Big Thicket, East Texas and Western Louisiana,* Texas A&M University Press, College Station, 1979.

———: *Wild Flowers of Texas,* Shearer, Bryan, Texas, 1984.

Batson, W. I.: *Wild Flowers in South Carolina,* The University of South Carolina Press, Columbia, 1964. (Color photos.)

Bell, C. R., and B. J. Taylor: *Florida Wild Flowers and Roadside Plants,* Laurel Hill Press, Chapel Hill, N. C., 1982.

Brown, C. A.: *Wildflowers of Louisiana and Adjoining States,* Louisiana State University Press, Baton Rouge, 1972. (Color photos.)

Budd, A. C.: *Wild Plants of the Canadian Prairies,* Canada Department of Agriculture Publication, no. 983, 1957. (Keys, descriptions, line drawings.)

Campbell, C. C., W. F. Hutson, and A. J. Sharp: *Great Smoky Mountains Wildflowers,* 3d ed., University of Tennessee Press, Knoxville, 1970. (Color photos.)

Clark, L. J., and T. G. Trelawny: *Wild Flowers of the Pacific Northwest from Alaska to Northern California,* Gray's Publishing Ltd., Sidney, B. C., Canada, 1976. (Color photos.)

Clark, W. L.: *Lewis Clark's Field Guide to Wild Flowers of Forest and Woodland in the Pacific Northwest,* University of Washington Press, Seattle, 1984.

Craighead, J. J., F. C. Craighead, and R. J. Davis: *A Field Guide to Rocky Mountain Wildflowers,* Houghton Mifflin, Boston, 1963. (Keys, descriptions, line drawings, and color photographs. Peterson Field Guide Series.)

Dean, B. E., A. Mason, and J. L. Thomas: *Wild Flowers of Alabama and Adjoining States,* University of Alabama Press, Tuscaloosa, 1973. (Color photos.)

Denison, E.: *Missouri Wildflowers,* 3rd ed., Missouri Dept. of Conservation, Jefferson City, 1978.

Duncan, W. H., and L. E. Foote: *Wildflowers of the Southeastern United States,* University of Georgia Press, Athens, 1975. (Descriptions, color photos.)

Edsall, M. S.: *Roadside Plants and Flowers*, University of Wisconsin Press, Madison, 1984.

Eisendrath, E. R.: *Missouri Wildflowers of the St. Louis Area*, Missouri Botanical Garden, St. Louis, 1978.

Ferguson, M., and R. M. Saunders: *Wildflowers*, Van Nostrand, New York, 1976.

Fleming, G., P. Genelle, and R. W. Long: *Wild Flowers of Florida*, Banyan Books, Miami, 1976.

Foxx, T. S., and D. Hoard: *Flowers of the Southwestern Forests and Woodlands*, Los Alamos Historical Society, Los Alamos, N.M., 1984.

Grimm, W. C.: *Recognizing Wild Plants*, Stackpole, Harrisburg, Pa., 1968. (Keys, descriptions, line drawings.)

Gupton, O. W., and F. C. Swope: *Wildflowers of the Shenandoah Valley and Blue Ridge Mountains*, University Press of Virginia, Charlottesville, 1979.

——, and ——: *Wildflowers of Tidewater Virginia*, University Press of Virginia, Charlottesville, 1980.

Haskin, L. L., and L. G. Haskin: *Wild Flowers of the Pacific Coast*, Binford and Mort, Portland, Ore., 1967. (Descriptions, black-and-white and color photos.)

Heller, C.: *Wild Flowers of Alaska*, Graphic Arts Center, Portland, Ore., 1966. (Descriptions, color photos.)

Hinds, H. R., and W. A. Hathaway: *Wildflowers of Cape Cod*, Chatham Press, Chatham, Mass., 1968.

Horn, E. L.: *The Sierra Nevada*, Touchstone Press, Beaverton, Ore., 1976. (Wildflowers in the Sierra Nevada Mountains.)

House, H. D.: *Wild Flowers*, Macmillan, New York, 1961. (Northeastern United States; black-and-white and color photos.)

Hylander, C. J., and E. F. Johnston: *Macmillan Wild Flower Book*, Macmillan, New York, 1954. (Eastern United States, watercolors.)

Jaeger, E. C.: *Desert Wild Flowers*, rev. ed., Stanford University Press, Stanford, Calif., 1969. (Desert plants arranged by family, many illustrations.)

Jaques, H. E.: *Plant Families: How to Know Them*, 2d ed., Brown, Dubuque, Iowa, 1949. (Keys, descriptions, line drawings.)

Justice, W. S., and C. R. Bell: *Wild Flowers of North Carolina*, University of North Carolina Press, Chapel Hill, 1968. (Descriptions, color photos.)

Klein, I. H.: *Wild Flowers of Ohio and Adjacent States*, Cleveland Museum of Natural History, Press of Case Western Reserve University, Cleveland, 1970.

Klimas, J. E., and J. A. Cunningham: *Wildflowers of Eastern North America*, Knopf, New York, 1974. (Color photos.)

Lemmon, R. S., and C. Johnson: *Wildflowers of North America*, Hanover House, Doubleday, Garden City, N.Y., 1961. (Descriptions, color photos.)

Lommasson, R. C.: *Nebraska Wildflowers*, University of Nebraska Press, Lincoln, 1973. (Color photos.)

Martin, W. C., and C. R. Hutchins: *Spring Wildflowers of New Mexico*, University of New Mexico Press, Albuquerque, 1984.

Monserud, W., and G. B. Ownbey: *Common Wild Flowers of Minnesota*, The University of Minnesota Press, Minneapolis, 1971. (Line drawings.)

Montgomery, F. H.: *Plants from Sea to Sea*, Ryerson Press, Toronto, 1966. (Canada.)

Munz, P. A.: *California Spring Wildflowers*, University of California Press, Berkeley, 1961. (Descriptions, line drawings, color photos.)

——: *California Desert Wildflowers*, University of California Press, Berkeley, 1962. (Descriptions, line drawings, color photos.)

————: *California Mountain Wildflowers,* University of California Press, Berkeley, 1963. (Descriptions, line drawings, color photos.)

————: *Shore Wildflowers of California, Oregon and Washington,* University of California Press, Berkeley, 1964. (Descriptions, line drawings, color photos.)

Nelson, R. A.: *Handbook of Rocky Mountain Plants,* 3rd ed., Skyland Pub., Estes Park, Col., 1979.

Niehaus, T. F. and C. L. Ripper: *A Field Guide to Pacific States Wildflowers.* Houghton Mifflin, Boston, 1976. (Peterson Field Guide Series.)

————: *A Field Guide to Southwestern and Texas Wildflowers,* Houghton Mifflin, Boston, 1984. (Peterson Field Guide Series.)

Perry, F., and R. Hay: *A Field Guide to Tropical and Subtropical Plants,* Van Nostrand Reinhold, New York, 1982.

Niering, W. A., and N. C. Olmstead: *The Audubon Society Field Guide to North American Wildflowers, Eastern Region,* Knopf, New York, 1979.

Orr, R. T., and M. C. Orr: *Wild Flowers of Western America,* Knopf, New York, 1974. (Descriptions, color photos.)

Owensby, C. E.: *Kansas Prairie Wildflowers,* Iowa State University Press, Ames, 1980.

Page, N. M., and R. E. Weaver: *Wild Plants in the City,* Quadrangle, New York Times Book Company, New York, 1975. (Interesting color photos.)

Peterson, R. T., and M. McKenny: *A Field Guide to Wildflowers of Northeastern and North-central North America,* Houghton Mifflin, Boston, 1968. (Descriptions, line drawings, color photos; Peterson Field Guide Series.)

Petry, L. C., and M. G. Norman: *A Beachcomber's Botany,* Chatham Conservancy Foundation, Chatham, Mass., 1968. (Plants grouped by habitat, black-and-white drawings.)

Porsild, A. E.: *Rocky Mountain Wild Flowers,* National Museums of Canada, Ottawa, 1974.

Rickett, H. W. *The New Field Book of American Wild Flowers,* Putnam, New York, 1963. (Keys, descriptions, line drawings, and color photos.)

————: *Wild Flowers of the United States,* 6 vols., McGraw-Hill, New York, 1966–1975. (A series of volumes with color photographs and descriptions of selected wild flowers; undoubtedly the best of the wild flower photograph books; not suitable for use in the field because of size of the volumes.)

Smith, A. I.: *A Guide to Wildflowers of the Mid-South,* Memphis State University, Memphis, 1979.

Smith, H. V.: *Michigan Wildflowers,* rev. ed., Cranbrook Institute Science Bulletin, no. 42, 1966. (Color photos.)

Spellenberg, R.: *The Audubon Society Field Guide to North American Wildflowers, Western Region,* Knopf, New York, 1979.

Stevens, W. C.: *Kansas Wild Flowers,* 2d ed., University of Kansas Press, Lawrence, 1961. (Color photos.)

Stupka, A.: *Wildflowers in Color,* Harper & Row, New York, 1965. (Southern Appalachians; color photos.)

Taylor, R. J., and G. W. Douglas: *Mountain Wild Flowers of the Pacific Northwest,* Binford and Mort, Portland, Ore., 1975.

Thompson, E. R.: *Wildflower Portraits,* University of Oklahoma Press, Norman, 1964. (Central United States, especially Texas; watercolors.)

Vance, F. R.: *Wildflowers Across the Prairies,* Western Producer Prairie Books, Saskatoon, Sask., 1977.

————, J. R. Jowsey, and J. S. McLean: *Wildflowers of the Northern Great Plains,* 2nd ed., University of Minnesota Press, Minneapolis, 1984.

Verhoek, S.: *How to Know the Spring Flowers,* 2nd ed., W. C. Brown, Dubuque, Iowa, 1982.

Walshe, S.: *Plants of Quetico and the Ontario Shield,* University of Toronto Press, Toronto, 1980.

Welsh, S. L.: *Flowers of the Canyon Country,* rev. ed., Brigham Young University Press, Provo, Utah, 1977.

Wharton, M. E., and R. W. Barbour: *A Guide to the Wildflowers and Ferns of Kentucky,* University Press of Kentucky, Lexington, 1971.

Wills, M. M., and H. S. Irwin: *Roadside Flowers of Texas,* University of Texas Press, Austin, 1961. (Keys, notes, descriptions, watercolor drawings.)

Woodward, C. H., and H. W. Rickett: *Common Wildflowers of the Northwestern United States,* Barron's, Woodbury, New York, 1979.

Zichmanis, Z., and J. Hodgins: *Flowers of the Wild; Ontario and the Great Lakes Region,* Oxford University Press, Toronto, 1984. (The drawings and plates are of exceptional quality.)

WOODY PLANTS

Baerg, H. J.: *How to Know the Western Trees,* 2d ed., Brown, Dubuque, Iowa, 1973.

Barnes, B. V., and W. H. Wagner, Jr.: *Michigan Trees,* University of Michigan Press, Ann Arbor, 1981.

Batson, W. T.: *Landscape Plants for the Southeast,* University of South Carolina Press, Columbia, 1984.

Benson, L. D., and R. A. Darrow: *Trees and Shrubs of the Southwestern Deserts,* 3rd ed. rev., University of Arizona Press, Tucson, 1981.

Blackburn, B. C.: *Trees and Shrubs in Eastern North America,* Oxford University Press, New York, 1952. (Keys to native and horticultural species, excludes conifers.)

Blackwell, W. H.: *Guide to the Woody Plants of the Tri-State Area, Southwestern Ohio, Southern Indiana, and Northern Kentucky,* Kendall-Hunt, Dubuque, Iowa, 1976.

Braun, E. L.: *The Woody Plants of Ohio,* Ohio State University Press, Columbus, 1961. (Good line drawings, maps, useful keys.)

Brockman, C. F.: *Trees of North America,* Golden Press, New York, 1968. (An inexpensive and popular field guide to the common trees north of Mexico; colored drawings, distribution maps.)

Brown, R. G., and M. L. Brown: *Woody Plants of Maryland,* Student Supply Store, University of Maryland, College Park, 1972. (Illustrated.)

Clark, R. C.: "The Woody Plants of Alabama," *Ann. Mo. Bot. Gard.,* **58:**99–242, 1971. (Keys, notes, and distribution maps.)

Coker, W. C., and H. R. Totten: *Trees of the Southeastern States,* 3d ed., University of North Carolina Press, Chapel Hill, 1945. (Comments, illustrations, keys, descriptions.)

Core, E. L., and N. P. Ammons: *Woody Plants in Winter; A Manual of Common Trees and Shrubs in Winter in the Northeastern United States and Southeastern Canada,* Boxwood Press, Pittsburgh, 1958. (Keys, line drawings.)

Deam, C. C., and T. E. Shaw: *Trees of Indiana,* 3d rev. ed., Indiana Department of Conservation Publication, no. 13a, 1953.

Duncan, W. H.: *Woody Vines of the Southeastern States,* University of Georgia Press, Athens, 1975. (Distribution maps, keys.)

Ferris, R. S.: *Native Shrubs of the San Francisco Bay Region,* University of California Press, Berkeley, 1968. (A popular illustrated guide useful in much of northern California.)

Grimm, W. C.: *The Book of Trees,* 2d ed., Stackpole, Harrisburg, Pa., 1962.(Keys, black-and-white illustrations.)

————: *Recognizing Native Shrubs*, Stackpole, Harrisburg, Pa., (Keys, line drawings.)

Gupton, O. W., and F. C. Swope: *Trees and Shrubs of Virginia*, University Press of Virginia, Charlottesville, 1981.

Harlow, W. M.: *Trees of the Eastern and Central United States and Canada*, corrected ed., Dover Publications, New York, 1957. (Keys, descriptions, black-and-white photos.)

————: *Fruit Key and Twig Key to Trees and Shrubs*, Dover Publications, New York, 1959. (Keys, illustrations.)

Harrar, E. S., and J. G. Harrar: *Guide to Southern Trees*, 2d ed., Dover Publications, New York, 1962. (Illustrated.)

Hosie, R. C.: *Native Trees of Canada*, 8th ed., Fitzhenry & Whiteside, Don Mills, Ontario, 1979.

Jepson, W. L.: *The Trees of California*, 2d ed., Sather Gate Bookshop, Berkeley, 1923.

Kurz, H., and R. K. Godfrey: *Trees of Northern Florida*, University of Florida Press, Gainesville, 1962, (Illustrations, keys.)

Little, E. L.: *Checklist of United States Trees (Native and Naturalized)*, U.S.D.A. Agriculture Handbook, no. 541, 1979.

————: *The Audubon Society Field Guide to North American Trees*, 2 vols., Knopf, New York, 1980. (v. 1, Eastern region; v. 2, Western region.)

————and B. H. Honkala: *Trees and Shrubs of the United States—A Bibliography for Identification*, U.S. Department of Agriculture Miscellaneous Publication, no. 1336, 1976. (A bibliography for identification.)

McMinn, H. E.: *An Illustrated Manual of California Shrubs*, University of California Press, Berkeley, 1964. (Line drawings.)

————and E. Maino: *An Illustrated Manual of Pacific Coast Trees*, 2d ed., University of California Press, Berkeley, 1937. (A manual of Pacific Coast trees, both native and introduced.)

Meijer, W.: *Tree Flora of Kentucky*, Thomas Hunt Morgan School Biological Sciences, University of Kentucky, Lexington, 1971. (Keys.)

Muenscher, W. C.: *Keys to Woody Plants*, 6th ed., Comstock, Ithaca, N.Y., 1950.

Otis, C. H.: *Michigan Trees*, 9th ed., The Regents, Ann Arbor, Mich., 1931.

Petrides, G. A.: *A Field Guide to Trees and Shrubs*, 2d ed., Houghton Mifflin, Boston, 1972. (Peterson Field Guide Series.)

Preston, R. J.: *North American Trees*, 3d ed., Iowa State University Press, Ames, 1976.

Randall, W. R.: *Manual of Oregon Trees and Shrubs*, Oregon State University Bookstore, Corvallis, 1958. (Revised by R. F. Keniston, 1968.)

Raven, P. H.: *Native Shrubs of Southern California*, University of California Press, Berkeley, 1966. (Keys, illustrations.)

Rosendahl, C. O.: *Trees and Shrubs of the Upper Mid-west*, University of Minnesota Press, Minneapolis, 1955.

Sargent, C. S.: *Manual of the Trees of North America,*2d corrected ed., 2 vols., Dover, New York, reprinted 1965. (Technical descriptions, line drawings.)

Stephens, H. A.: *Trees, Shrubs, and Woody Vines in Kansas*, University Press of Kansas, Lawrence, 1969.

————: *Woody Plants of the North Central States*, University Press of Kansas, Lawrence, 1973. (Contains excellent illustrations, descriptions, distribution maps.)

Sudword, G. B.: *Forest Trees of the Pacific Slope*, Dover, New York, 1967. (Reprint of 1908 edition; illustrations, descriptions, no keys.)

Symonds, G. W. D.: *The Tree Identification Book*, Barrows, New York, 1958.

————: *The Shrub Identification Book,* Barrows, New York, 1963. (Photographs of leaves, flowers, twigs, and so on.)

Trelease, W.: *Winter Botany,* 3d ed., Dover, New York, 1967. (Reprint of 1931 edition; keys to trees in the winter condition.)

Treshow, M., S. L. Welsh, and G. Moore: *Guide to the Woody Plants of the Mountain States,* Brigham Young University Press, Provo, Utah, 1970. (Includes both summer and winter key to genera.)

Van der Linden, P. J., and D. R. Farrar: *Forest and Shade Trees of Iowa,* Iowa State University Press, Ames, 1984.

Viereck, L. A., and E. L. Little: *Alaska Trees and Shrubs,* U.S. Department of Agriculture, Agriculture Handbook, no. 410, 1972. (Illustrations, maps.)

————and————: *Guide to Alaska Trees,* U.S. Department of Agriculture, Agriculture Handbook, no. 472, 1974.

Vines, R. A.: *Trees, Shrubs and Woody Vines of the Southwest,* University of Texas Press, Austin, 1960.

————: *Trees of East Texas,* University of Texas Press, Austin, 1977.

————: *Trees of North Texas,* University of Texas Press, Austin, 1982.

————: *Trees of Central Texas,* University of Texas Press, Austin, 1984.

Wharton, M. E., and R. W. Barbour: *Trees and Shrubs of Kentucky,* University Press of Kentucky, Lexington, 1973.

Thomas, J. H., and D. R. Parnell: *Native Shrubs of the Sierra Nevada,* University of California Press, Berkeley, 1974. (An illustrated guide.)

SELECTED PERIODICALS OF INTEREST TO PLANT TAXONOMISTS IN NORTH AMERICA

Much research and many taxonomic revisions are published in periodicals. Scientific publications are frequently published by a learned society, such as the American Society of Plant Taxonomists, or by herbaria or botanical gardens, such as the Field Museum or Missouri Botanical Garden. Some of the more important periodicals containing systematic research on plants from North America are listed below.

Aliso. Journal of the Rancho Santa Ana Botanic Garden. 1948–
American Fern Journal. American Fern Society. 1910–
American Journal of Botany. Botanical Society of America. 1914–
American Midland Naturalist. 1909–
Brittonia. New York Botanical Garden. 1931–
California. University. University of California Publications in Botany. 1902–
Canadian Journal of Botany. 1951–
Castanea. Southern Appalachian Botanical Club. 1936–
Cladistics. 1985–
Evolution. Society of the Study of Evolution. 1947–
Field Museum of Natural History, Chicago. Fieldiana: Botany. 1895–
Harvard University. Arnold Arboretum. Journal of the Arnold Arboretum. 1920–
Harvard University. Gray Herbarium. Contributions. 1891–
Madroño. California Botanical Society. 1916–
New York. Botanical Garden. Memoirs. 1900–
Rhodora. New England Botanical Club. 1899–
St. Louis. Missouri Botanical Garden. Annals. 1914–

Sida. 1962–

Systematic Botany. American Society of Plant Taxonomists. 1976–

Taxon. International Association for Plant Taxonomy. 1951–

Torrey Botanical Club. Bulletin. 1870–

Torrey Botanical Club. Memoirs. 1889–

U.S. National Herbarium. Contributions. 1891–

A LIST OF THE CLASSES, SUBCLASSES, ORDERS, AND FAMILIES OF THE ANGIOSPERMS ACCORDING TO THE CRONQUIST SYSTEM OF CLASSIFICATION*

Division MAGNOLIOPHYTA

Class MAGNOLIOPSIDA (Dicots)

Subclass I. Magnoliidae
  Order 1. Magnoliales
    Family 1. Winteraceae
      2. Degeneriaceae
      3. Himantandraceae
      4. Eupomatiaceae
      5. Austrobaileyaceae
      6. Magnoliaceae
      7. Lactoridaceae
      8. Annonaceae
      9. Myristicaceae
      10. Canellaceae
  Order 2. Laurales
    Family 1. Amborellaceae
      2. Trimeniaceae
      3. Monimiaceae
      4. Gomortegaceae
      5. Calycanthaceae
      6. Idiospermaceae
      7. Lauraceae
      8. Hernandiaceae
  Order 3. Piperales
    Family 1. Chloranthaceae
      2. Saururaceae
      3. Piperaceae
  Order 4. Aristolochiales
    Family 1. Aristolochiaceae
  Order 5. Illiciales
    Family 1. Illiciaceae
      2. Schisandraceae
  Order 6. Nymphaeales
    Family 1. Nelumbonaceae
      2. Nymphaeaceae
      3. Barclayaceae
      4. Cabombaceae
      5. Ceratophyllaceae
  Order 7. Ranunculales
    Family 1. Ranunculaceae
      2. Circaeasteraceae
      3. Berberidaceae
      4. Sargentodoxaceae
      5. Lardizabalaceae
      6. Menispermaceae

*This treatment has been very kindly furnished by Dr. Arthur Cronquist and is used with his permission. Modifications in the list have been added from Cronquist's *An Integrated System of Classification of Flowering Plants,* Columbia University Press, 1981.

7. Coriariaceae
8. Sabiaceae
Order 8. Papaverales
Family 1. Papaveraceae
    2. Fumariaceae

Subclass II. Hamamelidae
Order 1. Trochodendrales
Family 1. Tetracentraceae
    2. Trochodendraceae
Order 2. Hamamelidales
Family 1. Cercidiphyllaceae
    2. Eupteliaceae
    3. Platanaceae
    4. Hamamelidaceae
    5. Myrothamnaceae
Order 3. Daphniphyllales
Family 1. Daphniphyllaceae
Order 4. Didymelales
Family 1. Didymelaceae
Order 5. Eucommiales
Family 1. Eucommiaceae
Order 6. Urticales
Family 1. Barbeyaceae
    2. Ulmaceae
    3. Cannabaceae
    4. Moraceae
    5. Cecropiaceae
    6. Urticaceae
Order 7. Leitneriales
Family 1. Leitneriaceae
Order 8. Juglandales
Family 1. Rhoipteleaceae
    2. Juglandaceae
Order 9. Myricales
Family 1. Myricaceae
Order 10. Fagales
Family 1. Balanopaceae
    2. Fagaceae
    3. Betulaceae
Order 11. Casuarinales
Family 1. Casuarinaceae

Subclass III. Caryophyllidae
Order 1. Caryophyllales
Family 1. Phytolaccaceae
    2. Achatocarpaceae
    3. Nyctaginaceae
    4. Aizoaceae

5. Didiereaceae
6. Cactaceae
7. Chenopodiaceae
8. Amaranthaceae
9. Portulacaceae
10. Basellaceae
11. Molluginaceae
12. Caryophyllaceae
Order 2. Polygonales
Family 1. Polygonaceae
Order 3. Plumbaginales
Family 1. Plumbaginaceae

Subclass IV. Dilleniidae
Order 1. Dilleniales
Family 1. Dilleniaceae
    2. Paeoniaceae
Order 2. Theales
Family 1. Ochnaceae
    2. Sphaerosepalaceae
    3. Sarcolaenaceae
    4. Dipterocarpaceae
    5. Caryocaraceae
    6. Theaceae
    7. Actinidiaceae
    8. Scytopetalaceae
    9. Pentaphylacaceae
    10. Tetrameristaceae
    11. Pellicieraceae
    12. Oncothecaceae
    13. Marcgraviaceae
    14. Quiinaceae
    15. Elatinaceae
    16. Paracryphiaceae
    17. Medusagynaceae
    18. Clusiaceae (Guttiferae)
Order 3. Malvales
Family 1. Elaeocarpaceae
    2. Tiliaceae
    3. Sterculiaceae
    4. Bombacaceae
    5. Malvaceae
Order 4. Lecythiadales
Family 1. Lecythidaceae
Order 5. Nepenthales
Family 1. Sarraceniaceae
    2. Nepenthaceae
    3. Droseraceae
Order 6. Violales

Family 1. Flacourtiaceae
2. Peridiscaceae
3. Bixaceae
4. Cistaceae
5. Huaceae
6. Lacistemataceae
7. Scyphostegiaceae
8. Stachyuraceae
9. Violaceae
10. Tamaricaceae
11. Frankeniaceae
12. Dioncophyllaceae
13. Ancistrocladaceae
14. Turneraceae
15. Malesherbiaceae
16. Passifloraceae
17. Achariaceae
18. Caricaceae
19. Fouquieriaceae
20. Hoplestigmataceae
21. Cucurbitaceae
22. Datisaceae
23. Begoniaceae
24. Loasaceae
Order 7. Salicales
Family 1. Salicaceae
Order 8. Capparales
Family 1. Tovariaceae
2. Capparaceae
3. Brassicaceae (Cruciferae)
4. Moringaceae
5. Resedaceae
Order 9. Batales
Family 1. Gyrostemonaceae
2. Bataceae
Order 10. Ericales
Family 1. Cyrillaceae
2. Clethraceae
3. Grubbiaceae
4. Empetraceae
5. Epacridaceae
6. Ericaceae
7. Pyrolaceae
8. Monotropaceae
Order 11. Diapensiales
Family 1. Diapensiaceae
Order 12. Ebenales
Family 1. Sapotaceae
2. Ebenaceae

3. Styracaceae
4. Lissocarpaceae
5. Symplocaceae
Order 13. Primulales
Family 1. Theophrastaceae
2. Myrsinaceae
3. Primulaceae

Subclass V. Rosidae
Order 1. Rosales
Family 1. Brunelliaceae
2. Connaraceae
3. Eucryphiaceae
4. Cunoniaceae
5. Davidsoniaceae
6. Dialypetalanthaceae
7. Pittosporaceae
8. Byblidaceae
9. Hydrangeaceae
10. Columelliaceae
11. Grossulariaceae
12. Greyiaceae
13. Bruniaceae
14. Anisophylleaceae
15. Alseuosmiaceae
16. Crassulaceae
17. Cephalotaceae
18. Saxifragaceae
19. Rosaceae
20. Neuradaceae
21. Crossosomataceae
22. Chrysobalanaceae
23. Surianaceae
24. Rhabdodendraceae
Order 2. Fabales
Family 1. Mimosaceae
2. Caesalpiniaceae
3. Fabaceae
Order 3. Proteales
Family 1. Elaeagnaceae
2. Proteaceae
Order 4. Podostemales
Family 1. Podostemaceae
Order 5. Haloragales
Family 1. Haloragaceae
2. Gunneraceae
Order 6. Myrtales
Family 1. Sonneratiaceae
2. Lythraceae

    3. Penaeaceae
    4. Crypteroniaceae
    5. Thymelaeaceae
    6. Trapaceae
    7. Myrtaceae
    8. Punicaceae
    9. Onagraceae
    10. Oliniaceae
    11. Melastomataceae
    12. Combretaceae
Order 7. Rhizophorales
  Family 1. Rhizophoraceae
Order 8. Cornales
  Family 1. Alangiaceae
    2. Nyssaceae
    3. Cornaceae
    4. Garryaceae
Order 9. Santalales
  Family 1. Medusandraceae
    2. Dipentodontaceae
    3. Olacaceae
    4. Opiliaceae
    5. Santalaceae
    6. Misodendraceae
    7. Loranthaceae
    8. Viscaceae
    9. Eremolepidaceae
    10. Balanophoraceae
Order 10. Rafflesiales
  Family 1. Hydnoraceae
    2. Mitrastemonaceae
    3. Rafflesiaceae
Order 11. Celastrales
  Family 1. Geissolomataceae
    2. Celastraceae
    3. Hippocrateaceae
    4. Stackhousiaceae
    5. Salvadoraceae
    6. Aquifoliaceae
    7. Icacinaceae
    8. Aextoxicaceae
    9. Cardiopteridaceae
    10. Corynocarpaceae
    11. Dichapetalaceae
Order 12. Euphorbiales
  Family 1. Buxaceae
    2. Simmondsiaceae
    3. Pandaceae
    4. Euphorbiaceae

Order 13. Rhamnales
  Family 1. Rhamnaceae
    2. Leeaceae
    3. Vitaceae
Order 14. Linales
  Family 1. Erythroxylaceae
    2. Humiriaceae
    3. Ixonanthaceae
    4. Hugoniaceae
    5. Linaceae
Order 15. Polygalales
  Family 1. Malpighiaceae
    2. Vochysiaceae
    3. Trigoniaceae
    4. Tremandraceae
    5. Polygalaceae
    6. Xanthophyllaceae
    7. Krameriaceae
Order 16. Sapindales
  Family 1. Staphyleaceae
    2. Melianthaceae
    3. Bretschneideraceae
    4. Akaniaceae
    5. Sapindaceae
    6. Hippocastanaceae
    7. Aceraceae
    8. Burseraceae
    9. Anacardiaceae
    10. Julianiaceae
    11. Simaroubaceae
    12. Cneoraceae
    13. Meliaceae
    14. Rutaceae
    15. Zygophyllaceae
Order 17. Geraniales
  Family 1. Oxalidaceae
    2. Geraniaceae
    3. Limnanthaceae
    4. Tropaeolaceae
    5. Balsaminaceae
Order 18. Apiales
  Family 1. Araliaceae
    2. Apiaceae (Umbelliferae)

Subclass VI. Asteridae
  Order 1. Gentianales
    Family 1. Loganiaceae
      2. Retziaceae
      3. Gentianaceae

4. Saccifoliaceae
5. Apocynaceae
6. Asclepiadaceae

Order 2. Solanales
Family 1. Duckeodendraceae
2. Nolanaceae
3. Solanaceae
4. Convolvulaceae
5. Cuscutaceae
6. Menyanthaceae
7. Polemoniaceae
8. Hydrophyllaceae

Order 3. Lamiales
Family 1. Lennoaceae
2. Boraginaceae
3. Verbenaceae
4. Lamiaceae (Labiatae)

Order 4. Callitrichales
Family 1. Hippuridaceae
2. Callitrichaceae
3. Hydrostachyaceae

Order 5. Plantaginales
Family 1. Plantaginaceae

Order 6. Scrophulariales
Family 1. Buddlejaceae
2. Oleaceae
3. Scrophulariaceae
4. Globulariaceae
5. Myoporaceae
6. Orobanchaceae
7. Gesneriaceae
8. Acanthaceae
9. Pedaliaceae
10. Bignoniaceae
11. Mendonciaceae
12. Lentibulariaceae

Order 7. Campanulales
Family 1. Pentaphragmataceae
2. Sphenocleaceae
3. Campanulaceae
4. Stylidiaceae
5. Donatiaceae
6. Brunoniaceae
7. Goodeniaceae

Order 8. Rubiales
Family 1. Rubiaceae
2. Theligonaceae

Order 9. Dipsacales
Family 1. Caprifoliaceae

2. Adoxaceae
3. Valerianaceae
4. Dipsacaceae

Order 10. Calycerales
Family 1. Calyceraceae

Order 11. Asterales
Family 1. Asteraceae (Compositae)

Class LILIOPSIDA (Monocots)

Subclass I. Alismatidae
Order 1. Alismatales
Family 1. Butomaceae
2. Limnocharitaceae
3. Alismataceae

Order 2. Hydrocharitales
Family 1. Hydrocharitaceae

Order 3. Najadales
Family 1. Aponogetonaceae
2. Scheuchzeriaceae
3. Juncaginaceae
4. Potamogetonaceae
5. Ruppiaceae
6. Najadaceae
7. Zannichelliaceae
8. Posidoniaceae
9. Cymodoceaceae
10. Zosteraceae

Order 4. Triuridales
Family 1. Petrosaviaceae
2. Triuridaceae

Subclass II. Arecidae
Order 1. Arecales
Family 1. Arecaceae (Palmae)

Order 2. Cyclanthales
Family 1. Cyclanthaceae

Order 3. Pandanales
Family 1. Pandanaceae

Order 4. Arales
Family 1. Araceae
2. Lemnaceae

Subclass III. Commelinidae
Order 1. Commelinales
Family 1. Rapateaceae
2. Xyridaceae
3. Mayacaceae
4. Commelinaceae

Order 2. Eriocaulales
  Family 1. Eriocaulaceae
Order 3. Restionales
  Family 1. Flagellariaceae
        2. Joinvilleaceae
        3. Restionaceae
        4. Centrolepidaceae
Order 4. Juncales
  Family 1. Juncaceae
        2. Thurniaceae
Order 5. Cyperales
  Family 1. Cyperaceae
        2. Poaceae (Gramineae)
Order 6. Hydatellales
  Family 1. Hydatellaceae
Order 7. Typhales
  Family 1. Sparganiaceae
        2. Typhaceae

Subclass IV. Zingiberidae
Order 1. Bromeliales
  Family 1. Bromeliaceae
Order 2. Zingiberales
  Family 1. Strelitziaceae
        2. Heliconiaceae
        3. Musaceae
        4. Lowiaceae

        5. Zingiberaceae
        6. Costaceae
        7. Cannaceae
        8. Marantaceae

Subclass V. Liliidae
Order 1. Liliales
  Family 1. Philydraceae
        2. Pontederiaceae
        3. Haemodoraceae
        4. Cyanastraceae
        5. Liliaceae
        6. Iridaceae
        7. Velloziaceae
        8. Aloeaceae
        9. Agavaceae
       10. Xanthorrhoeaceae
       11. Hanguanaceae
       12. Taccaceae
       13. Stemonaceae
       14. Smilacaceae
       15. Dioscoreaceae
Order 2. Orchidales
  Family 1. Geosiridaceae
        2. Burmanniaceae
        3. Corsiaceae
        4. Orchidaceae

APPENDIX FOUR

THORNE'S SYNOPSIS OF THE CLASS ANGIOSPERMAE (ANNONOPSIDA)*

Subclass: Dicotyledoneae (Annonidae)

Superorder: Annoniflorae
Order: Annonales
Suborder: Winterineae
Family: Winteraceae
Suborder: Illiciineae
Family: Illiciaceae
Family: Schisandraceae
Suborder: Annonineae
Family: Magnoliaceae
Family: Degeneriaceae
Family: Himantandraceae
Family: Austrobaileyaceae
Family: Eupomatiaceae
Family: Annonaceae
Family: Myristicaceae
Family: Canellaceae
Suborder: Aristolochiineae
Family: Aristolochiaceae
Suborder: Laurineae
Family: Amborellaceae
Family: Trimeniaceae

Family: Chloranthaceae
Family: Lactoridaceae
Family: Monimiaceae
Family: Gomortegaceae
Family: Calycanthaceae
Family: Lauraceae
Family: Hernandiaceae
Suborder: Piperineae
Family: Saururaceae
Family: Piperaceae
Order: Nelumbonales
Family: Nelumbonaceae
Family: Ceratophyllaceae
Order: Paeoniales
Family: Paeoniaceae
Family: Glaucidiaceae
Order: Berberidales
Suborder: Berberidineae
Family: Lardizabalaceae
Family: Sargentodoxaceae
Family: Menispermaceae
Family: Nandinaceae
Family: Berberidaceae

*From Nordic J. Bot. 3:102–111, 1983 and personal communications; for more detailed inclusions, see original paper.

483

Family: Ranunculaceae
Family: Circaeasteraceae
Suborder: Papaverineae
Family: Papaveraceae
Superorder: Nymphaeiflorae
  Order: Nymphaeales
      Family: Cabombaceae
      Family: Nymphaeaceae
Superorder: Rafflesiiflorae
  Order: Rafflesiales
      Family: Rafflesiaceae
      Family: Hydnoraceae
Superorder: Theiflorae
  Order: Theales
    Suborder: Dilleniineae
      Family: Dilleniaceae
    Suborder: Theineae
      Family: Actinidiaceae
      Family: Paracryphiaceae
      Family: Stachyuraceae
      Family: Theaceae
      Family: Symplocaceae
      Family: Caryocaraceae
      Family: Oncothecaceae
      Family: Aquifoliaceae
      Family: Phellinaceae
      Family: Icacinaceae
      Family: Sphenostemonaceae
      Family: Cardiopteridaceae
      Family: Marcgraviaceae
    Suborder: Clethrineae
      Family: Pentaphylacaceae
      Family: Clethraceae
      Family: Cyrillaceae
    Suborder: Sarraceniineae
      Family: Sarraceniaceae
    Suborder: Scytopetalineae
      Family: Ochnaceae
      Family: Quiinaceae
      Family: Scytopetalaceae
      Family: Sphaerosepalaceae
      Family: Medusagynaceae
      Family: Strasburgeriaceae
      Family: Ancistrocladaceae
      Family: Dioncophyllaceae
    Suborder: Nepenthineae
      Family: Nepenthaceae
    Suborder: Hypericineae

Family: Clusiaceae (incl.
      Hypericaceae)
Family: Elatinaceae
Suborder: Lecythidineae
Family: Lecythidaceae
Order: Ericales
Family: Ericaceae
Family: Epacridaceae
Family: Empetraceae
Order: Fouquieriales
Family: Fouquieriaceae
Order: Ebenales
Suborder: Ebenineae (Sapotineae)
Family: Ebanaceae
Family: Lissocarpaceae
Family: Sapotaceae
Suborder: Styracineae
Family: Styracaceae
Order: Primulales
Suborder: Primulineae
Family: Myrsinaceae
Family: Primulaceae
Suborder: Plumbaginineae
Family: Plumbaginaceae
Order: Polygonales
Family: Polygonaceae
Superorder: Chenopodiiflorae
      (Centrospermae)
Order: Chenopodiales
Suborder: Chenopodiineae
Family: Phytolaccaceae
Family: Barbeuiaceae
Family: Achatocarpaceae
Family: Stegnospermataceae
Family: Aizoaceae
Family: Caryophyllaceae
Family: Halophytaceae
Family: Nyctaginaceae
Family: Chenopodiaceae
Family: Amaranthaceae
Suborder: Portulacineae
Family: Portulacaceae
Family: Basellaceae
Family: Didiereaceae
Family: Cactaceae
Superorder: Geraniiflorae
Order: Geraniales
Suborder: Linineae

Family: Houmiriaceae
Family: Ctenolophonaceae
Family: Linaceae
Family: Erythroxylaceae
Family: Zygophyllaceae
Suborder: Geraniineae
Family: Oxalidaceae
Family: Geraniaceae
Family: Vivianiaceae
Family: Ledocarpaceae
Family: Balsaminaceae
Family: Tropaeolaceae
Family: Limnanthaceae
Suborder: Polygalineae
Family: Malpighiaceae
Family: Polygalaceae
Family: Krameriaceae
Family: Trigoniaceae
Family: Vochysiaceae
Superorder: Celastriflorae
Order: Celastrales
Family: Celastraceae
Family: Lophopyxidaceae
Family: Stackhousiaceae
Superorder: Santaliflorae
Order: Santalales
Family: Olacaceae
Family: Medusandraceae
Family: Santalaceae
Family: Eremolepidaceae
Family: Misodendraceae
Family: Loranthaceae
Family: Viscaceae
Order: Balanophorales
Family: Balanophoraceae
Family: Cynomoriaceae
Superorder: Violiflorae
Order: Violales
Suborder: Violineae
Family: Flacourtiaceae
Family: Dipentodontaceae
Family: Peridiscaceae
Family: Scyphostegiaceae
Family: Violaceae
Family: Passifloraceae
Family: Turneraceae
Family: Malesherbiaceae
Family: Achariaceae

Family: Caricaceae
Suborder: Salicineae
Family: Salicaceae
Suborder: Tamaricineae
Family: Tamaricaceae
Family: Frankeniaceae
Suborder: Cucurbitineae
Family: Cucurbitaceae
Suborder: Begoniineae
Family: Begoniaceae
Family: Datiscaceae
Order: Capparales
Family: Resedaceae
Family: Capparaceae
Family: Brassicaceae
Superorder: Malviflorae
Order: Malvales
Family: Sterculiaceae
Family: Huaceae
Family: Elaeocarpaceae
Family: Plagiopteraceae
Family: Tiliaceae
Family: Dipterocarpaceae
Family: Sarcolaenaceae
Family: Bixaceae
Family: Cochlospermaceae
Family: Cistaceae
Family: Bombacaceae
Family: Malvaceae
Order: Urticales
Family: Ulmaceae
Family: Urticaceae
Family: Cannabaceae
Order: Rhamnales
Family: Rhamnaceae
Family: Elaeagnaceae
Order: Euphorbiales
Family: Euphorbiaceae
Family: Pandaceae
Family: Simmondsiaceae
Family: Aextoxicaceae
Family: Dichapetalaceae
Family: Thymelaeaceae
Superorder: Rutiflorae
Order: Rutales
Suborder: Rutineae
Family: Rutaceae
Family: Cneoraceae

Family: Simaroubaceae
Family: Tepuianthaceae
Family: Ptaeroxylaceae
Family: Meliaceae
Family: Burseraceae
Family: Anacardiaceae
Family: Leitneriaceae
Suborder: Juglandineae
Family: Rhoipteleaceae
Family: Juglandaceae
Suborder: Myricineae
Family: Myricaceae
Suborder: Coriariineae
Family: Coriariaceae
Suborder: Sapindineae
Family: Sapindaceae
Family: Gyrostemonaceae
Family: Bataceae
Family: Sabiaceae
Family: Melianthaceae
Family: Akaniaceae
Family: Aceraceae
Family: Hippocastanaceae
Family: Bretschneideraceae
Family: Moringaceae
Suborder: Fabineae
Family: Surianaceae
Family: Connaraceae
Family: Fabaceae
Superorder: Proteiflorae
Order: Proteales
Family: Proteaceae
Superorder: Hamamelidiflorae
Order: Hamamelidales
Suborder: Trochodendrineae
Family: Trochodendraceae
Family: Tetracentraceae
Family: Eupteleaceae
Family: Cercidiphyllaceae
Suborder: Eucommineae
Family: Eucommiaceae
Suborder: Hamamelidineae
Family: Hamamelidaceae
Family: Platanaceae
Order: Casuarinales
Family: Casuarinaceae
Order: Fagales
Family: Fagaceae
Family: Betulaceae

Superorder: Rosiflorae
Order: Rosales
Suborder: Rosineae
Family: Rosaceae
Family: Chrysobalanaceae
Family: Crossosomataceae
Suborder: Saxifragineae
Family: Crassulaceae
Family: Cephalotaceae
Family: Saxifragaceae
Family: Parnassiaceae
Family: Stylidiaceae
Family: Droseraceae
Family: Greyiaceae
Family: Podostemaceae
Family: Diapensiaceae
Suborder: Cunoniineae
Family: Cunoniaceae
Family: Baueraceae
Family: Davidsoniaceae
Family: Brunelliaceae
Family: Eucryphiaceae
Family: Staphyleaceae
Family: Corynocarpaceae
Order: Pittosporales
Suborder: Buxineae
Family: Buxaceae
Family: Didymelaceae
Family: Daphniphyllaceae
Family: Balanopaceae
Suborder: Pittosporineae
Family: Pittosporaceae
Family: Byblidaceae
Family: Tremandraceae
Suborder: Brunineae
Family: Roridulaceae
Family: Bruniaceae
Family: Geissolomataceae
Family: Grubbiaceae
Family: Myrothamnaceae
Family: Hydrostachyaceae
Superorder: Loasiflorae
Order: Loasales
Family: Loasaceae
Superorder: Myrtiflorae
Order: Myrtales
Suborder: Lythrineae
Family: Lythraceae
Family: Rhynchocalycaceae

Family: Penaeaceae
Family: Trapaceae
Family: Oliniaceae
Family: Alzateaceae
Family: Crypteroniaceae
Family: Melastomataceae
Family: Combretaceae
Suborder: Onagrineae
Family: Onagraceae
Suborder: Myrtineae
Family: Myrtaceae
Superorder: Gentianiflorae
Order: Oleales
Family: Salvadoraceae
Family: Oleaceae
Order: Gentianales
Family: Loganiaceae
Family: Buddlejaceae
Family: Rubiaceae
Family: Dialypetalanthaceae
Family: Apocynaceae (incl.
    Asclepiadaceae)
Family: Gentianaceae
Family: Menyanthaceae
Order: Bignoniales
Family: Bignoniaceae
Family: Pedaliaceae
Family: Martyniaceae
Family: Myoporaceae
Family: Scrophulariaceae
Family: Plantaginaceae
Family: Lentibulariaceae
Family: Acanthaceae
Family: Gesneriaceae
Order: Lamiales
Family: Verbenaceae
Family: Lamiaceae
Family: Callitrichaceae
Superorder: Solaniflorae
Order: Solanales
Suborder: Boraginineae
Family: Hydrophyllaceae
Family: Hoplestigmataceae
Family: Boraginaceae
Family: Lennoaceae
Suborder: Solanineae
Family: Solanaceae
Family: Convolvulaceae
Suborder: Polemoniineae

Family: Polemoniaceae
Order: Campanulales
Family: Pentaphragmataceae
Family: Campanulaceae
Family: Goodeniaceae
Superorder: Corniflorae
Order: Cornales
Suborder: Rhizophorineae
Family: Rhizophoraceae
Suborder: Vitineae
Family: Vitaceae
Suborder: Haloragineae
Family: Haloragaceae
Family: Gunneraceae
Family: Hippuridaceae
Suborder: Cornineae
Family: Nyssaceae
Family: Cornaceae
Family: Alangiaceae
Family: Garryaceae
Family: Aucubaceae
Order: Araliales
Family: Helwingiaceae
Family: Torricelliaceae
Family: Araliaceae (incl. Apiaceae)
Order: Dipsacales
Family: Caprifoliaceae
Family: Adoxaceae
Family: Valerianaceae
Family: Dipsacaceae
Family: Calyceraceae
Superorder: Asteriflorae
Order: Asterales
Family: Asteraceae
Subclass: Monocotyledoneae (Liliidae)
Superorder: Liliiflorae
Order: Liliales
Suborder: Liliineae
Family: Liliaceae
Suborder: Dioscoreineae
Family: Alstroemerioceae
Family: Philesiaceae
Family: Smilacaceae
Family: Stemonaceae
Family: Dioscoreaceae
Family: Trichopodaceae
Family: Taccaceae
Suborder: Iridineae
Family: Iridaceae

Family: Burmanniaceae
Suborder: Orchidineae
Family: Orchidaceae
Superorder: Triuridiflorae
Order: Triuridales
Family: Triuridaceae
Superorder: Alismatiflorae
Order: Alismatales
Family: Butomaceae
Family: Alismataceae
Family: Hydrocharitaceae
Order: Zosterales
Suborder: Aponogetonineae
Family: Aponogetonaceae
Suborder: Potamogetonineae
Family: Juncaginaceae
Family: Potamogetonaceae
Family: Posidoniaceae
Family: Zannichelliaceae
Family: Cymodoceaceae
Suborder: Zosterineae
Family: Zosteraceae
Order: Najadales
Family: Najadaceae
Superorder: Ariflorae
Order: Arales
Family: Araceae
Family: Lemnaceae
Superorder: Cyclanthiflorae
Order: Cyclanthales
Family: Cyclanthaceae
Superorder: Pandaniflorae
Order: Pandanales
Family: Pandanaceae
Superorder: Areciflorae
Order: Arecales
Family: Arecaceae
Superorder: Typhiflorae
Order: Typhales
Family: Typhaceae

Superorder: Commeliniflorae
Order: Commelinales
Suborder: Bromeliineae
Family: Bromeliaceae
Family: Rapateaceae
Family: Xyridaceae
Suborder: Velloziineae
Family: Velloziaceae
Suborder: Pontederiineae
Family: Pontederiaceae
Family: Philydraceae
Family: Haemodoraceae
Suborder: Juncineae
Family: Juncaceae
Family: Cyperaceae
Suborder: Commelinineae
Family: Commelinaceae
Family: Mayacaceae
Suborder: Eriocaulineae
Family: Eriocaulaceae
Suborder: Flagellariineae
Family: Flagellariaceae
Family: Restionaceae
Family: Centrolepidaceae
Suborder: Poineae
Family: Poaceae
Order: Zingiberales
Suborder: Musineae
Family: Musaceae
Family: Strelitziaceae
Family: Heliconiaceae
Family: Lowiaceae
Suborder: Zingiberineae
Family: Zingiberaceae
Family: Costaceae
Family: Cannaceae
Family: Marantaceae

INDEX TO TAXA

SUBJECT INDEX

Page numbers in *italic* indicate illustrations